The DETECTIVE STORY

from Sherlock Holmes to Hemlock Jones, a panorama of great detective mysteries

Saul Schwartz

National Textbook Company
a division of *NTC Publishing Group* • Lincolnwood, Illinois USA

The author wishes to express his gratitude to William Brittain, Frederic Dannay, and John Ball for their encouraging letters regarding this project, and to Lillian Schwartz for her valuable assistance and encouragement.

"A Study in Scarlet," "The Final Problem," and "The Adventure of the Empty House" by Sir Arthur Conan Doyle. Reprinted by permission of the Estate of Sir Arthur Conan Doyle.

"The Telltale Bottle," "My Queer Dean," and "The President's Half-Disme" by Ellery Queen, reprinted by permission of the author and Scott Meredith Literary Agency, Inc., 580 Fifth Avenue, New York, N.Y. 10036.

"The Problem of Cell 13" by Jacques Futrelle, from *Best "Thinking Machine" Detective Stories*, courtesy of Dover Publications, Inc. New York, N.Y.

"The Invisible Man" by G. K. Chesterton, reprinted by permission of Dodd, Mead & Company, Inc. from *The Innocence of Father Brown* by G. K. Chesterton. Copyright 1910, 1911, by The Curtis Publishing Company. Copyright 1911 by Dodd, Mead & Company. Copyright renewed 1938 by Oliver Chesterton.

"The Mystery of Hunter's Lodge" from *Poirot Investigates* by Agatha Christie © 1924 by Dodd, Mead & Company, Inc. Copyright renewed 1952 by Agatha Christie Mallowan.

"The Adventurous Exploit of the Cave of Ali Baba" from *Lord Peter: A Collection of All the Lord Peter Wimsey Stories* by Dorothy Sayers (Harper & Row, Publishers, Inc. 1972).

"Mr. Strang Performs an Experiment" by William Brittain copyright © 1967 by Davis Publications. First published in *Ellery Queen's Mystery Magazine*.

"Locked Doors" from *Miss Pinkerton* by Mary Roberts Rinehart. Copyright 1932 by Mary Roberts Rinehart. Copyright © 1960 by Stanley M. Rinehart Jr., Frederick R. Rinehart and Alan G. Rinehart. Reprinted by permission of Holt, Rinehart and Winston, Publishers.

"Tape-Measure Murder" ("Village Murders") from *Three Blind Mice and Other Stories* by Agatha Christie © 1941 by Agatha Christie. Copyright renewed 1969 by Agatha Christie Mallowan. Reprinted by permission of Dodd, Mead & Company, Inc.

"You Bet Your Life" by Stuart Palmer, reprinted by permission of the author's Estate and the agents for the Estate, Scott Meredith Literary Agency, Inc., 580 Fifth Avenue, New York, N.Y. 10036.

"Mom and the Haunted Mink" by James Yaffe, reprinted by permission of Brandt & Brandt, New York, N.Y.

In the Heat of the Night by John Ball (excerpts), reprinted by permission of the author.

"The World Series Murders" by Rex Stout, reprinted by permission of the author.

"The Day the Children Vanished" by Hugh Pentecost. First published in *This Week Magazine* copyright © 1958 by Hugh Pentecost. Reprinted by permission of Brandt & Brandt.

1989 Printing

Introduction

Detective stories appeal to most people. To satisfy such a vast audience, an unending parade of anthologies has been published throughout the years.

Why then another: *this one?*

Because when you start reading, you'll immediately notice something different. In addition to the stories, themselves, there is presented perhaps the most intriguing narrative of all, *the history of the origins and development of the detective story,* itself.

To put it another way: *The Detective Story* deals with *history* as well as *mystery.*

Such histories have appeared previously but, despite the popularity of the genre, they have been few and far between. These histories discuss and analyze the famous tales of the literature, but do not include them. *The Detective Story* does both, and in this collection, history is as captivating as the mysteries, themselves.

The background material in this book reads like a series of detective stories and presents an almost mirror image of the ingredients that make detective tales so popular, suspense, mystery, and surprise endings. Also, this history is populated by a cast of literary personalities whose lives are as fascinating as those of the fictional sleuths they created.

For example, did you know that Edgar Allan Poe and Sir Arthur Conan Doyle became jealous of their protagonists, Dupin and Holmes, and began yearning for real-life cases of their own to solve? Later, Poe's involvement with the Mary Rogers disappearance and Doyle's with the Edalje affair became intriguing episodes in their careers which came to rival their fictional plots. And what about the secret of Ellery Queen who remained unknown for the first five years of his career? Eventually, Ellery made his debut but when he did so, he only complicated the mystery *for he was wearing a mask.*

But what about the tales themselves for, without them, there wouldn't be a history?

The stories in this book have not been randomly selected; each has contributed to the genre's evolution. Included are the fabulous firsts: the first detective story ever, the first secret code yarn, and the first historical detective story. As for fictional sleuths, you'll meet the first of the teacher-detectives, Augustus S.F.X. Van Dusen a.k.a. The Thinking Machine, the first black investigator, Virgil Tibbs, and the first Jewish mother sleuth, Mom, the Mayvin, who was done so well, there's been no need of another.

What's also different within these pages is the attempt made to sharpen literary sensibilities. Each chapter contains questions and projects designed to help you set up your own critical standards. And not only for detective literature *but for other forms of fiction.*

You may ask, "How, other forms?"

Well, the detective story bears the same relationship to the rest of fiction that *the sonnet* does to poetry. The sonnet is a stylized poem with rigid rules imposed upon its practitioners. Poets mastering this form acquire very sharp skills which make it easier for them to work with other and less rigid forms of poetry.

Similarly, the detective story is a form of fiction with equally strict and limiting rules. These rules are expounded upon in this book. Once you become aware of them, you discover you have absorbed elements which are contained in the entire art of storytelling. Thus, your newly-acquired sensitivity makes you a more sophisticated patron of detective stories—and, of fiction, in general.

As your knowledge of detective literature deepens, you may find yourself wanting to contribute to an ongoing debate which has taken place among mystery fans over the years in relation to the following questions:

1) Why, the genre's immense popularity?
2) Can the detective story be considered an important branch of literature?

If you, after completing your reading, find yourself involved in some such brouhaha, don't be surprised. It only means our efforts have been successful and that you're probably well on your way to becoming a mystery aficionado in your own right.

If so, welcome to the fold!

Saul Schwartz,
Member, *Mystery Writers of America*

Contents

1. *Whodunit?*   1
   Stories by Edgar Allan Poe
    "The Murders in the Rue Morgue"   2
    "The Purloined Letter"   29
    "The Gold Bug"   47

2. *A Tale of Two Doctors*   77
   Stories by Sir Arthur Conan Doyle
    A Study in Scarlet (excerpts)   81
    "The Final Problem"   95
    "The Adventure of the Empty House"   109

3. *The American Sherlock Holmes*   137
   Stories by Ellery Queen
    "The Telltale Bottle"   141
    "My Queer Dean!"   158
    "The Adventure of the President's Half Disme"   166

4. *The Others*   187
   "The Problem of Cell 13" by Jacques Futrelle   189
   "The Invisible Man" by G. K. Chesterton   217
   "The Mystery of Hunter's Lodge" by Agatha Christie   231
   "The Adventurous Exploit of the Cave of Ali Baba" by
    Dorothy Sayers   241
   "Mr. Strang Performs an Experiment" by William Brittain   264

5. *There Were Female Sleuths Before
Women's Liberation*   279
   "Locked Doors" by Mary Roberts Rinehart   281
   "Village Murders" by Agatha Christie   316
   "You Bet Your Life" by Stuart Palmer   326
   "Mom and the Haunted Mink" by James Yaffe   340

6. *Variations*   355
   In the Heat of the Night (excerpts) by John Ball   359
   "The World Series Murder" by Rex Stout   376
   "The Day the Children Vanished" by Hugh Pentecost   407
   "The Stolen Cigar Case" by Bret Harte   429

   An Epilogue   437
   Notes   438
   Bibliography   441

EDGAR ALLAN POE
Reproduced from the Brady-Handy Collection, the Library of Congress.

1.

Whodunit?

It All Began with Poe

An American writer, Edgar Allan Poe, created the world's first detective story.

Before Poe, there had been puzzle stories, suspense and murder tales, and adventure and horror narratives—but, clearly, as one critic put it, ". . . there could be no detective stories until there were detectives."[1] This new form of police activity began to evolve at the beginning of the nineteenth century.

The early 1800s witnessed the growth of criminal investigation departments in the police systems of the great cities of the world. In Paris, the *Sûreté* came into being; its individual investigators, working without uniforms, were called *agents*. The name given to the operatives of the Criminal Investigation Department of the London Metropolitan Police was, at first, the Bow Street Runners; later, the name of the department was changed to *Scotland Yard*. In Italy, plain-clothes policemen were organized into bureaus labeled *La Publica Sicurrezza;* as the population of the world's urban centers increased, more and more of these bureaus appeared.

The first detective story was written shortly afterwards. The publication of Poe's "The Murders in the Rue Morgue" in April 1841 was a milestone in literary history. It marked the birth, not only of detective fiction, but also of Monsieur C. Auguste Dupin, the first detective hero. Later, Dupin was to become the prototype for a long line of fictional sleuths that continue to be created to this very day. As you read the historic tale that follows, you will become aware of plot ingredients encountered time and again in books, television, motion pictures, and on the stage. Keep in mind that their appearance in Poe's story was an historic first. Here they are:

1) An unusual detective of high intelligence who employs methods of deductive logic.
2) An assistant of lesser intelligence.
3) A member of the police force who is never as effective as our master sleuth.
4) A varied assortment of misleading clues.
5) A gathering of suspects by the detective at the plot's climax to hear the clarifying explanation.[2]

The story that follows will transport you magically into the nineteenth century. Perhaps, if you try, you may be able to solve the mystery before Dupin does.

(*EDITOR'S NOTE:* This story opens with a short essay on the philosophy of analysis. Poe's discourse is brilliant, but it does tend to postpone the beginning of his story-line and so we have eliminated it here. The tale you are about to read begins with the fifth paragraph of the original.)

The Murders in the Rue Morgue

Residing in Paris during the spring and part of the summer of 18———, I there became acquainted with a Monsieur C. Auguste Dupin. This young gentleman was of an excellent, indeed of an illustrious family, but, by a variety of untoward events, had been reduced to such poverty that the energy of his character succumbed beneath it, and he ceased to bestir himself in the world, or to care for the retrieval of his fortunes. By courtesy of his creditors, there still remained in his possession a small remnant of his patrimony; and, upon the income arising from this, he managed, by means of a rigorous economy, to procure the necessities of life, without troubling himself about its superfluities. Books, indeed, were his sole luxuries, and in Paris these are easily obtained.

Our first meeting was at an obscure library in the Rue Montmartre, where the accident of our both being in search of the same very rare and very remarkable volume, brought us into closer communion. We saw each other again and again. I was deeply interested in the little family history which he detailed to me with all that candor which a Frenchman indulges whenever mere self is the theme. I was astonished, too, at the vast extent of his reading; and, above all, I felt my soul enkindled within me by the wild fervor, and the vivid freshness of his imagination. Seeking in Paris the objects I then sought, I felt that the society of such a man would be to me a treasure beyond price; and this feeling I frankly confided to him. It was at length arranged that we should live together during my stay in the city; and as my worldly circumstances were somewhat less embarrassed than his own, I was permitted to be at the expense of renting, and furnishing in a style which suited the rather fantastic gloom of our common temper, a time-eaten and grotesque mansion, long deserted through superstitions into which we did not inquire, and tottering to its fall in a retired and desolate portion of the Faubourg St. Germain.*

Had the routine of our life at this place been known to the world, we should have been regarded as madmen—although, perhaps, as madmen of a harmless nature. Our seclusion was perfect. We admitted no visitors. Indeed the locality of our retirement had been carefully kept a secret from my own former associates; and it had been many years since Dupin had ceased to know or be known in Paris. We existed within ourselves alone.

It was a freak of fancy in my friend (for what else shall I call it?) to be enamored of the night for her own sake; and into this *bizarrerie*,† as into all his others, I quietly fell; giving myself up to his wild whims with a perfect *abandon*. The sable divinity would not herself dwell with us always; but we could counterfeit her presence. At the first dawn of the morning we closed all the massy shutters of our old building; lighted a couple of tapers which, strongly perfumed, threw out only the ghastliest and feeblest of rays. By the aid of these we then busied our souls in dreams—reading, writing, or conversing, until warned by the clock of the advent of true Darkness. Then we sallied forth into the streets, arm in arm, continuing the topics of the day, or roaming far and wide until a late hour, seeking, amid the wild lights and shadows of the populous city, that infinity of mental excitement which quiet observation can afford.

At such times I could not help remarking and admiring (although from his rich ideality I had been prepared to expect it) a peculiar analytic ability in Dupin. He seemed, too, to take an eager delight in its exercise—if not exactly in its display—and did not hesitate to confess the pleasure thus derived. He boasted to me, with a low chuckling laugh, that most men, in

---

*An ancient, once aristocratic section of Paris
†Strange or unusual conduct (French)

respect to himself, wore windows in their bosoms, and was wont to follow up such assertions by direct and very startling proofs of his intimate knowledge of my own. His manner at these moments was frigid and abstract; his eyes were vacant in expression; while his voice, usually a rich tenor, rose into a treble which would have sounded petulant but for the deliberateness and entire distinctness of the enunciation. Observing him in these moods, I often dwelt meditatively upon the old philosophy of the Bi-Part Soul, and amused myself with the fancy of a double Dupin—the creative and the resolvent.

Let it not be supposed, from what I have just said, that I am detailing any mystery, or penning any romance. What I have described in the Frenchman was merely the result of an excited, or perhaps of a diseased, intelligence. But of the character of his remarks at the periods in question an example will best convey the idea.

We were strolling one night down a long dirty street, in the vicinity of the Palais Royal. Being both, apparently, occupied with thought, neither of us had spoken a syllable for fifteen minutes at least. All at once Dupin broke forth with these words:

"He is a very little fellow, that's true, and would do better for the *Théâtre des Variétés.*"*

"There can be no doubt of that," I replied, unwittingly, and not at first observing (so much had I been absorbed in reflection) the extraordinary manner in which the speaker had chimed in with my meditations. In an instant afterward I recollected myself, and my astonishment was profound.

"Dupin," said I, gravely, "this is beyond my comprehension. I do not hesitate to say that I am amazed, and can scarcely credit my senses. How was it possible you should know I was thinking of—?" Here I paused, to ascertain beyond a doubt whether he really knew of whom I thought.

"—of Chantilly," said he, "why do you pause? You were remarking to yourself that his diminutive figure unfitted him for tragedy."

This was precisely what had formed the subject of my reflections. Chantilly was a *quondam*† cobbler of the Rue St. Denis, who, becoming stage-mad, had attempted the *rôle* of Xerxes, in Crébillon's tragedy so called, and been notoriously *Pasquinaded*‡ for his pains.

"Tell me, for Heaven's sake," I exclaimed, "the method—if there is—by which you have been enabled to fathom my soul in this matter." In fact, I was even more startled than I would have been willing to express.

"It was the fruiterer," replied my friend, "who brought you to the conclusion that the mender of soles was not of sufficient height for Xerxes *et id genus omne.*"§

"The fruiterer!—you astonish me—I know no fruiterer whomsoever."

---

*Theater featuring vaudeville (French)
†Former (derived from Latin)
‡Ridiculed in public (derived from Latin)
§A quotation from the Roman poet, Horace—"and all persons of that kind"

"The man who ran up against you as we entered the street—it may have been fifteen minutes ago."

I now remembered that, in fact, a fruiterer, carrying upon his head a large basket of apples, had nearly thrown me down, by accident, as we passed from the Rue C——into the thoroughfare where we stood; but what this had to do with Chantilly I could not possibly understand.

There was not a particle of *charlatânerie** about Dupin. "I will explain," he said, "and that you may comprehend all clearly, we will first retrace the course of your meditations, from the moment in which I spoke to you until that of the *rencontre*† with the fruiterer in question. The larger links of the chain run thus—Chantilly, Orion, Dr. Nichols, Epicurus, Stereotomy, the street stones, the fruiterer."

There are few persons who have not, at some period of their lives, amused themselves in retracing the steps by which particular conclusions of their own minds have been attained. The occupation is often full of interest; and he who attempts it for the first time is astonished by the apparently illimitable distance and incoherence between the starting-point and the goal. What, then, must have been my amazement, when I heard the Frenchman speak what he had just spoken, and when I could not help acknowledging that he had spoken the truth. He continued:

"We had been talking of horses, if I remember aright, just before leaving the Rue C——. This was the last subject we discussed. As we crossed into this street, a fruiterer, with a large basket upon his head, brushing quickly past us, thrust you upon a pile of paving-stones collected at a spot where the causeway is undergoing repair. You stepped upon one of the loose fragments, slipped, slightly strained your ankle, appeared vexed or sulky, muttered a few words, turned to look at the pile, and then proceeded in silence. I was not particularly attentive to what you did; but observation has become with me, of late, a species of necessity.

"You kept your eyes upon the ground—glancing, with a petulant expression, at the holes and ruts in the pavement (so that I saw you were still thinking of the stones), until we reached the little alley called Lamartine, which has been paved, by way of experiment, with the overlapping and riveted blocks. Here your countenance brightened up, and, perceiving your lips move, I could not doubt that you murmured the word 'stereotomy,'‡ a term very affectedly applied to this species of pavement. I knew that you could not say to yourself 'stereotomy' without being brought to think of atomies, and thus of the theories of Epicurus; and since, when we discussed this subject not very long ago, I mentioned to you how singularly, yet with how little notice, the vague guesses of that noble Greek had met with

---

*Insincerity, dishonesty (French)
†Encounter (French)
‡The skill of stone-cutting

confirmation in the late nebular cosmogony,* I felt that you could not avoid casting your eyes upward to the great *nebula* in Orion, and I certainly expected that you would do so. You did look up; and I was now assured that I had correctly followed your steps. But in that bitter *tirade* upon Chantilly, which appeared in yesterday's *'Musée,'* the satirist, making some disgraceful allusions to the cobbler's change of name upon assuming the buskin,† quoted a Latin line about which we have often conversed. I mean the line

Perdidit antiquum litera prima sonum.‡

I had told you that this was in reference to Orion, formerly written Urion; and, from certain pungencies connected with this explanation, I was aware that you could not have forgotten it. It was clear, therefore, that you would not fail to combine the two ideas of Orion and Chantilly. That you did combine them I saw by the character of the smile which passed over your lips. You thought of the poor cobbler's immolation. So far, you had been stopping in your gait; but now I saw you draw yourself up to your full height. I was then sure that you reflected upon the diminutive figure of Chantilly. At this point I interrupted your meditations to remark that as, in fact, he *was* a very little fellow—that Chantilly—he would do better at the *Théâtre des Variétés.*"

Not long after this, we were looking over an evening edition of the *Gazette des Tribunaux,* when the following paragraphs arrested our attention.

"EXTRAORDINARY MURDERS.—This morning, about three o'clock, the inhabitants of the Quartier St. Roch were roused from sleep by a succession of terrific shrieks, issuing, apparently, from the fourth story of a house in the Rue Morgue, known to be in the sole occupancy of one Madame L'Espanaye, and her daughter, Mademoiselle Camille L'Espanaye. After some delay, occasioned by a fruitless attempt to procure admission in the usual manner, the gateway was broken in with a crowbar, and eight or ten of the neighbors entered, accompanied by two *gendarmes.*§ By this time the cries had ceased; but, as the party rushed up the first flight of stairs, two or more rough voices, in angry contention, were distinguished, and seemed to proceed from the upper part of the house. As the second landing was reached, these sounds, also, had ceased, and every thing remained perfectly quiet. The party spread themselves, and hurried from room to room. Upon arriving at a large back chamber in the fourth story (the door of which, being found locked, with the key inside, was forced open), a spectacle presented

---

*An hypothesis as to how the universe came into being
†Half boot with low heel (worn by actors appearing in Greek tragedy)
‡"The first letter of the alphabet destroyed primitive illiteracy." (Latin)
§French policemen

itself which struck every one present not less with horror than with astonishment.

"The apartment was in the wildest disorder—the furniture broken and thrown about in all directions. There was only one bedstead; and from this the bed had been removed, and thrown into the middle of the floor. On a chair lay a razor, besmeared with blood. On the hearth were two or three long and thick tresses of gray human hair, also dabbled with blood, and seeming to have been pulled out by the roots. Upon the floor were found four Napoleons, an ear-ring of topaz, three large silver spoons, three smaller of *métal d'Alger,* * and two bags, containing nearly four thousand francs in gold. The drawers of a bureau, which stood in one corner, were open, and had been, apparently, rifled, although many articles still remained in them. A small iron safe was discovered under the *bed* (not under the bedstead). It was open, with the key still in the door. It had no contents beyond a few old letters, and other papers of little consequence.

"Of Madame L'Espanaye no traces were here seen; but an unusual quantity of soot being observed in the fireplace, a search was made in the chimney, and (horrible to relate!) the corpse of the daughter, head downward, was dragged therefrom; it having been thus forced up the narrow aperture for a considerable distance. The body was quite warm. Upon examining it, many excoriations† were perceived, no doubt occasioned by the violence with which it had been thrust up and disengaged. Upon the face were many severe scratches, and, upon the throat, dark bruises, and deep indentations of finger nails, as if the deceased had been throttled to death.

"After a thorough investigation of every portion of the house without farther discovery, the party made its way into a small paved yard in the rear of the building, where lay the corpse of the old lady, with her throat so entirely cut that, upon an attempt to raise her, the head fell off. The body, as well as the head, was fearfully mutilated—the former so much so as scarcely to retain any semblance of humanity.

"To this horrible mystery there is not as yet, we believe, the slightest clue."

The next day's paper had these additional particulars:

"*The Tragedy in the Rue Morgue.*—Many individuals have been examined in relation to this most extraordinary and frightful affair," [the word '*affaire*' has not yet, in France, that levity of import which it conveys with us] "but nothing whatever has transpired to throw light upon it. We give below all the material testimony elicited.

"*Pauline Dubourg,* laundress, deposes that she has known both the deceased for three years, having washed for them during that period. The old lady and her daughter seemed on good terms—very affectionate toward each other. They were excellent pay. Could not speak in regard to their mode or means of living. Believe that Madame L. told fortunes for a living. Was reputed to have money put by. Never met any person in the house

---

*An alloy having the appearance of silver. French for "metal of Algeria"
†Bruises, scratches

when she called for the clothes or took them home. Was sure that they had no servant in employ. There appeared to be no furniture in any part of the building except in the fourth story.

"*Pierre Moreau,* tobacconist, deposes that he has been in the habit of selling small quantities of tobacco and snuff to Madame L'Espanaye for nearly four years. Was born in the neighborhood, and has always resided there. The deceased and her daughter had occupied the house in which the corpses were found, for more than six years. It was formerly occupied by a jeweler, who under-let the upper rooms to various persons. The house was the property of Madame L. She became dissatisfied with the abuse of the premises by her tenant, and moved into them herself, refusing to let any portion. The old lady was childish. Witness had seen the daughter some five or six times during the six years. The two lived an exceedingly retired life—were reputed to have money. Had heard it said among the neighbors that Madame L. told fortunes—did not believe it. Had never seen any person enter the door except the old lady and her daughter, a porter once or twice, and a physician some eight or ten times.

"Many other persons, neighbors, gave evidence to the same effect. No one was spoken of as frequenting the house. It was not known whether there were any living connections of Madame L. and her daughter. The shutters of the front windows were seldom opened. Those in the rear were always closed, with the exception of the large back room, fourth story. The house was a good house—not very old.

"*Isidore Musèt, gendarme,* deposes that he was called to the house about three o'clock in the morning, and found some twenty or thirty persons at the gateway, endeavoring to gain admittance. Forced it open, at length, with a bayonet—not with a crowbar. Had but little difficulty in getting it open, on account of its being a double or folding gate, and bolted neither at bottom nor top. The shrieks were continued until the gate was forced—and then suddenly ceased. They seemed to be screams of some person (or persons) in great agony—were loud and drawn out, not short and quick. Witness led the way up stairs. Upon reaching the first landing, heard two voices in loud and angry contention—the one a gruff voice, the other much shriller—a very strange voice. Could distinguish some words of the former, which was that of a Frenchman. Was positive that it was not a woman's voice. Could distinguish the words '*Sacré*'* and '*diable.*'† The shrill voice was that of a foreigner. Could not be sure whether it was the voice of a man or of a woman. Could not make out what was said, but believed the language to be Spanish. The state of the room and of the bodies was described by this witness as we described them yesterday.

"*Henri Duval,* a neighbor, and by trade a silver-smith, deposes that he was one of the party who first entered the house. Corroborates the testimony of Musèt in general. As soon as they forced an entrance, they reclosed

---

*An oath, such as "Cursed!" or "Confounded!" (French)

†Another oath, meaning "Devil!" (French)

the door, to keep out the crowd, which collected very fast, notwithstanding the lateness of the hour. The shrill voice, this witness thinks, was that of an Italian. Was certain it was not French. Could not be sure that it was a man's voice. It might have been a woman's. Was not acquainted with the Italian language. Could not distinguish the words, but was convinced by the intonation that the speaker was an Italian. Knew Madame L. and her daughter. Had conversed with both frequently. Was sure that the shrill voice was not that of either of the deceased.

"———*Odenheimer, restaurateur.** —This witness volunteered his testimony. Not speaking French, was examined through an interpreter. Is a native of Amsterdam. Was passing the house at the time of the shrieks. They lasted for several minutes—probably ten. They were long and loud—very awful and distressing. Was one of those who entered the building. Corroborated the previous evidence in every respect but one. Was sure that the shrill voice was that of a man—of a Frenchman. Could not distinguish the words uttered. They were loud and quick—unequal—spoken apparently in fear as well as in anger. The voice was harsh—not so much shrill as harsh. Could not call it a shrill voice. The gruff voice said repeatedly, *'sacré,' 'diable,'* and once *'mon Dieu.'†*

"*Jules Mignaud,* banker, of the firm of Mignaud et Fils, Rue Deloraine. Is the elder Mignaud. Madame L'Espanaye had some property. Had opened an account with his banking house in the spring of the year ——— (eight years previously). Made frequent deposits in small sums. Had checked for nothing until the third day before her death, when she took out in person the sum of 4000 francs. This sum was paid in gold, and a clerk sent home with the money.

"*Adolphe Le Bon,* clerk of Mignaud et Fils, deposes that on the day in question, about noon, he accompanied Madame L'Espanaye to her residence with the 4000 francs, put up in two bags. Upon the door being opened, Mademoiselle L. appeared and took from his hands one of the bags, while the old lady relieved him of the other. He then bowed and departed. Did not see any person in the street at the time. It is a by-street—very lonely.

"*William Bird,* tailor, deposes that he was one of the party who entered the house. Is an Englishman. Has lived in Paris two years. Was one of the first to ascend the stairs. Heard the voices in contention. The gruff voice was that of a Frenchman. Could make out several words, but cannot now remember all. Heard distinctly *'sacré'* and *'mon Dieu.'* There was a sound at the moment as if of several persons struggling—a scraping and scuffling sound. The shrill voice was very loud—louder than the gruff one. Is sure that it was not the voice of an Englishman. Appeared to be that of a German. Might have been a woman's voice. Does not understand German.

"Four of the above-named witnesses, being recalled, deposed that the door of the chamber in which was found the body of Mademoiselle L. was

---

*Restaurant owner (French)

†My God! (French)

locked on the inside when the party reached it. Every thing was perfectly silent—no groans or noises of any kind. Upon forcing the door no person was seen. The windows, both of the back and front room, were down and firmly fastened from within. A door between the two rooms was closed but not locked. The door leading from the front room into the passage was locked, with the key on the inside. A small room in the front of the house, on the fourth story, at the head of the passage, was open, the door being ajar. This room was crowded with old beds, boxes, and so forth. These were carefully removed and searched. There was not an inch of any portion of the house which was not carefully searched. Sweeps were sent up and down the chimneys. The house was a four-story one, with garrets (*mansardes*).* A trap-door on the roof was nailed down very securely—did not appear to have been opened for years. The time elapsing between the hearing of the voices in contention and the breaking open of the room door was variously stated by the witnesses. Some made it as short as three minutes—some as long as five. The door was opened with difficulty.

"*Alfonzo Garcio,* undertaker, deposes that he resides in the Rue Morgue. Is a native of Spain. Was one of the party who entered the house. Did not proceed up stairs. Is nervous, and was apprehensive of the consequences of agitation. Heard the voices in contention. The gruff voice was that of a Frenchman. Could not distinguish what was said. The shrill voice was that of an Englishman—is sure of this. Does not understand the English language, but judges by the intonation.

"*Alberto Montani,* confectioner,† deposes that he was among the first to ascend the stairs. Heard the voices in question. The gruff voice was that of a Frenchman. Distinguished several words. The speaker appeared to be expostulating. Could not make out the words of the shrill voice. Spoke quick and unevenly. Thinks it the voice of a Russian. Corroborates the general testimony. Is an Italian. Never conversed with a native of Russia.

"Several witnesses, recalled, here testified that the chimneys of all the rooms on the fourth story were too narrow to admit the passage of a human being. By 'sweeps' were meant cylindrical sweeping-brushes, such as are employed by those who clean chimneys. These brushes were passed up and down every flue in the house. There is no back passage by which any one could have descended while the party proceeded up stairs. The body of Mademoiselle L'Espanaye was so firmly wedged in the chimney that it could not be got down until four or five of the party united their strength.

"*Paul Dumas,* physician, deposes that he was called to view the bodies about daybreak. They were both then lying on the sacking of the bedstead in the chamber where Mademoiselle L. was found. The corpse of the young lady was much bruised and excoriated. The fact that it had been thrust up the chimney would sufficiently account for these appearances. The throat was greatly chafed. There were several deep scratches just below the chin,

---

*Attics (French)
†Maker of candies or sweets (French)

together with a series of livid spots which were evidently the impression of fingers. The face was fearfully discolored, and the eyeballs protruded. The tongue had been partially bitten through. A large bruise was discovered upon the pit of the stomach, produced, apparently, by the pressure of a knee. In the opinion of M. Dumas, Mademoiselle L'Espanaye had been throttled to death by some person or persons unknown. The corpse of the mother was horribly mutilated. All the bones of the right leg and arm were more or less shattered. The left *tibia* much splintered, as well as all the ribs of the left side. Whole body dreadfully bruised and discolored. It was not possible to say how the injuries had been inflicted. A heavy club of wood, or a broad bar of iron—a chair—any large, heavy, and obtuse weapon would have produced such results, if wielded by the hands of a very powerful man. No woman could have inflicted the blows with any weapon. The head of the deceased, when seen by witness, was entirely separated from the body, and was also greatly shattered. The throat had evidently been cut with some very sharp instrument—probably with a razor.

"*Alexandre Etienne,* surgeon, was called with M. Dumas to view the bodies. Corroborated the testimony, and the opinions of M. Dumas.

"Nothing further of importance was elicited, although several other persons were examined. A murder so mysterious, and so perplexing in all its particulars, was never before committed in Paris—if indeed a murder has been committed at all. The police are entirely at fault—an unusual occurrence in affairs of this nature. There is not, however, the shadow of a clew apparent."

The evening edition of the paper stated that the greatest excitement still continued in the Quartier St. Roch—that the premises in question had been carefully re-searched, and fresh examinations of witnesses instituted, but all to no purpose. A postscript, however, mentioned that Adolphe Le Bon had been arrested and imprisoned—although nothing appeared to criminate him beyond the facts already detailed.

Dupin seemed singularly interested in the progress of this affair—at least so I judged from his manner, for he made no comments. It was only after the announcement that Le Bon had been imprisoned, that he asked me my opinion respecting the murders.

I could merely agree with all Paris in considering them an insoluble mystery. I saw no means by which it would be possible to trace the murderer.

"We must not judge of the means," said Dupin, "by this shell of an examination. The Parisian police, so much extolled for *acumen,* are cunning, but no more. There is no method in their proceedings, beyond the method of the moment. They make a vast parade of measures; but, not unfrequently, these are so ill-adapted to the objects proposed, as to put us in mind of Monsieur Jourdain's* calling for his *robe-de-chambre—pour*

---

*The principal character in Molière's "The Would-Be Gentleman," noted for his snobbishness *mieux entendre la musique.** The results attained by them are not unfrequently surprising, but, for the most part, are brought about by simple diligence and activity. When these qualities are unavailing, their schemes fail. Vidocq, for example, was a good guesser, and a persevering man. But, without educated thought, he erred continually by the very intensity of his investigations. He impaired his vision by holding the object too close. He might see, perhaps, one or two points with unusual clearness, but in so doing he, necessarily, lost sight of the matter as a whole. Thus there is such a thing as being too profound. Truth is not always in a well. In fact, as regards the more important knowledge, I do believe that she is invariably superficial. The depth lies in the valleys where we seek her, and not upon the mountain-tops where she is found. The modes and sources of this kind of error are well typified in the contemplation of the heavenly bodies. To look at a star by glances—to view it in a sidelong way, by turning toward it the exterior portions of the *retina* (more susceptible of feeble impressions of light than the interior), is to behold the star distinctly—is to have the best appreciation of its lustre—a lustre which grows dim just in proportion as we turn our vision *fully* upon it. A greater number of rays actually fall upon the eye in the latter case, but in the former, there is the more refined capacity for comprehension. By undue profundity we perplex and enfeeble thought; and it is possible to make even Venus herself vanish from the firmament by a scrutiny too sustained, too concentrated, or too direct.

"As for these murders, let us enter into some examinations for ourselves, before we make up an opinion respecting them. An inquiry will afford us amusement," [I thought this an odd term, so applied, but said nothing] "and besides, Le Bon once rendered me a service for which I am not ungrateful. We will go and see the premises with our own eyes. I know G——, the Prefect of Police, and shall have no difficulty in obtaining the necessary permission."

The permission was obtained, and we proceeded at once to the Rue Morgue. This is one of those miserable thoroughfares which intervene between the Rue Richelieu and the Rue St. Roch. It was late in the afternoon when we reached it, as this quarter is at a great distance from that in which we resided. The house was readily found; for there were still many persons gazing up at the closed shutters, with an objectless curiosity, from the opposite side of the way. It was an ordinary Parisian house, with a gateway, on one side of which was a glazed watch-box, with a sliding panel in the window, indicating a *loge de concierge.*† Before going in we walked up the street, turned down an alley, and then, again turning, passed in the rear of the building—Dupin, meanwhile, examining the whole neighborhood, as well as the house, with a minuteness of attention for which I could see no possible object.

---

*Calling for his "dressing gown so as to hear the music better"

†A *concierge* (French) is a doorkeeper or manager. The *loge de concierge* is his or her room or apartment. French tenants do not have keys to the front doors of apartment houses.

Retracing our steps we came again to the front of the dwelling, rang, and, having shown our credentials, were admitted by the agents in charge. We went upstairs—into the chamber where the body of Mademoiselle L'Espanaye had been found, and where both the deceased still lay. The disorders of the room had, as usual, been suffered to exist. I saw nothing beyond what had been stated in the *Gazette des Tribunaux*. Dupin scrutinized every thing—not excepting the bodies of the victims. We then went into the other rooms, and into the yard; a *gendarme* accompanying us throughout. The examination occupied us until dark, when we took our departure. On our way home my companion stepped in for a moment at the office of one of the daily papers.

I have said that the whims of my friend were manifold, and that *Je les ménageais:** —for this phrase there is no English equivalent. It was his humor, now, to decline all conversation on the subject of the murder, until about noon the next day. He then asked me, suddenly, if I had observed any thing *peculiar* at the scene of the atrocity.

There was something in his manner of emphasizing the word *"peculiar,"* which caused me to shudder, without knowing why.

"No, nothing *peculiar,*" I said; "nothing more, at least, than we both saw stated in the paper."

"The *Gazette,*" he replied, "has not entered, I fear, into the unusual horror of the thing. But dismiss the idle opinions of this print. It appears to me that this mystery is considered insoluble, for the very reason which should cause it to be regarded as easy of solution—I mean for the *outré*† character of its features. The police are confounded by the seeming absence of motive—not for the murder itself—but for the atrocity of the murder. They are puzzled, too, by the seeming impossibility of reconciling the voices heard in contention, with the facts that no one was discovered upstairs but the assassinated Mademoiselle L'Espanaye, and that there were no means of egress without the notice of the party ascending. The wild disorder of the room; the corpse thrust, with the head downward, up the chimney; the frightful mutilation of the body of the old lady; these considerations, with those just mentioned, and others which I need not mention, have sufficed to paralyze the powers, by putting completely at fault the boasted *acumen,* of the government agents. They have fallen into the gross but common error of confounding the unusual with the abstruse. But it is by these deviations from the plane of the ordinary, that reason feels its way, if at all, in its search for the true. In investigations such as we are now pursuing, it should not be so much asked 'what has occurred,' as 'what has occurred that has never occurred before.' In fact, the facility with which I shall arrive, or have arrived, at the solution of this mystery, is in the direct ratio of its apparent insolubility in the eyes of the police."

I stared at the speaker in mute astonishment.

---

*"I could diplomatically handle them." (French)
†Unusual, odd (French)

"I am now awaiting," continued he, looking toward the door of our apartment—"I am now awaiting a person who, although perhaps not the perpetrator of these butcheries, must have been in some measure implicated in their perpetration. Of the worst portion of the crimes committed, it is probable that he is innocent. I hope that I am right in this supposition; for upon it I build my expectation of reading the entire riddle. I look for the man here—in this room—every moment. It is true that he may not arrive; but the probability is that he will. Should he come, it will be necessary to detain him. Here are pistols; and we both know how to use them when occasion demands their use."

I took the pistols, scarcely knowing what I did, or believing what I heard, while Dupin went on, very much as if in a soliloquy. I have already spoken of his abstract manner at such times. His discourse was addressed to myself; but his voice, although by no means loud, had that intonation which is commonly employed in speaking to some one at a great distance. His eyes, vacant in expression, regarded only the wall.

"That the voices heard in contention," he said, "by the party upon the stairs, were not the voices of the women themselves, was fully proved by the evidence. This relieves us of all doubt upon the question whether the old lady could have first destroyed the daughter, and afterward have committed suicide. I speak of this point chiefly for the sake of method; for the strength of Madame L'Espanaye would have been utterly unequal to the task of thrusting her daughter's corpse up the chimney as it was found; and the nature of the wounds upon her own person entirely precludes the idea of self-destruction. Murder, then, has been committed by some third party; and the voices of this third party were those heard in contention. Let me now advert—not to the whole testimony respecting these voices—but to what was *peculiar* in that testimony. Did you observe any thing peculiar about it?"

I remarked that, while all the witnesses agreed in supposing the gruff voice to be that of a Frenchman, there was much disagreement in regard to the shrill, or, as one individual termed it, the harsh voice.

"That was the evidence itself," said Dupin, "but it was not the peculiarity of the evidence. You have observed nothing distinctive. Yet there *was* something to be observed. The witnesses, as you remark, agreed about the gruff voice; they were here unanimous. But in regard to the shrill voice, the peculiarity is—not that they disagreed—but that, while an Italian, an Englishman, a Spaniard, a Hollander, and a Frenchman attempted to describe it, each one spoke of it as that *of a foreigner*. Each is sure that it was not the voice of one of his own countrymen. Each likens it—not to the voice of an individual of any nation with whose language he is conversant—but the converse. The Frenchman supposes it the voice of a Spaniard, and 'might have distinguished some words *had he been acquainted with the Spanish.*' The Dutchman maintains it to have been that of a Frenchman; but we find it stated that '*not understanding French this witness was examined through an interpreter.*' The Englishman thinks it the voice of a German, and '*does not understand German,*' The Spaniard 'is sure' that it was that of an Englishman, but 'judges by the intonation' altogether, *'as he has no knowledge of the English.'* The Italian believes it the voice of a Russian, but *'has never conversed with a native of Russia.'* A second Frenchman differs, moreover, with the first, and is positive that the voice was that of an Italian; but *not being cognizant of that tongue,* is like the Spaniard, 'convinced by the intonation.' Now, how strangely unusual must that voice have really been, about which such testimony as this *could* have been elicited!—in whose *tones,* even denizens of the five great divisions of Europe could recognize nothing familiar! You will say that it might have been the voice of an Asiatic—of an African. Neither Asiatics nor Africans abound in Paris; but, without denying the inference, I will now merely call your attention to three points. The voice is termed by one witness 'harsh rather than shrill.' It is represented by two others to have been 'quick and *unequal.'* No words—no sounds resembling words—were by any witness mentioned as distinguishable.

"I know not," continued Dupin, "what impression I may have made, so far, upon your own understanding; but I do not hesitate to say that legitimate deductions even from this portion of the testimony—the portion respecting the gruff and shrill voices—are in themselves sufficient to engender a suspicion which should give direction to all farther progress in the investigation of the mystery. I said 'legitimate deductions'; but my meaning is not thus fully expressed. I designed to imply that the deductions are the *sole* proper ones, and that the suspicion arises *inevitably* from them as a single result. What the suspicion is, however, I will not say just yet. I merely wish you to bear in mind that, with myself, it was sufficiently forcible to give a definite form—a certain tendency—to my inquiries in the chamber.

"Let us now transport ourselves, in fancy, to this chamber. What shall we first seek here? The means of egress employed by the murderers. It is not too much to say that neither of us believes in praeternatural events. Madame and Mademoiselle L'Espanaye were not destroyed by spirits. The doers of the deed were material, and escaped materially. Then how? Fortunately there is but one mode of reasoning upon the point, and that mode *must* lead us to a definite decision. Let us examine, each by each, the possible means of egress. It is clear that the assassins were in the room where Mademoiselle L'Espanaye was found, or at least in the room adjoining, when the party ascended the stairs. It is, then, only from these two apartments that we have to seek issues. The police have laid bare the floors, the ceiling, and the masonry of the walls, in every direction. No *secret* issues could have escaped their vigilance. But, not trusting to *their* eyes, I examined with my own. There were, then, *no* secret issues. Both doors leading from the rooms into the passage were securely locked, with the keys inside. Let us turn to the chimneys. These, although of ordinary width for some eight or ten feet above the hearths, will not admit, throughout their extent, the body of a large cat. The impossibility of egress, by means already stated, being thus absolute, we are reduced to the windows. Through those of the front room no one could have escaped without notice from the crowd in the street. The murderers *must* have passed, then, through those of the back room. Now, brought to this conclusion in so unequivocal a manner as we are, it is not our part, as reasoners, to reject it on account of apparent impossibilities. It is only left for us to prove that these apparent 'impossibilities' are, in reality, not such.

"There are two windows in the chamber. One of them is unobstructed by furniture, and is wholly visible. The lower portion of the other is hidden from view by the head of the unwieldy bedstead which is thrust close up against it. The former was found securely fastened from within. It resisted the utmost force of those who endeavored to raise it. A large gimlet-hole had been pierced in its frame to the left, and a very stout nail was found fitted therein, nearly to the head. Upon examining the other window, a similar nail was seen similarly fitted in it; and a vigorous attempt to raise this sash failed also. The police were now entirely satisfied that egress had not been in these directions. And, *therefore,* it was thought a matter of supererogation to withdraw the nails and open the windows.

"My own examination was somewhat more particular, and was so for the reason I have just given—because here it was, I knew, that all apparent impossibilities *must* be proved to be not such in reality.

"I proceeded to think thus—*a posteriori.** The murderers *did* escape from one of these windows. This being so, they could not have re-fastened the sashes from the inside, as they were found fastened;—the consideration which put a stop, through its obviousness, to the scrutiny of the police in this quarter. Yet the sashes *were* fastened. They *must,* then, have the power of fastening themselves. There was no escape from this conclusion. I stepped to the unobstructed casement, withdrew the nail with some difficulty, and attempted to raise the sash. It resisted all my efforts, as I had anticipated. A concealed spring must, I now knew, exist; and this corroboration of my idea convinced me that my premises, at least, were correct, however mysterious still appeared the circumstances attending the nails. A careful search soon brought to light the hidden spring. I pressed it, and, satisfied with the discovery, forbore to upraise the sash.

"I now replaced the nail and regarded it attentively. A person passing out through this window might have reclosed it, and the spring would have caught—but the nail could not have been replaced. The conclusion was plain, and again narrowed in the field of my investigations. The assassins *must* have escaped through the other window. Supposing, then, the springs upon each sash to be the same, as was probable, there must be found a difference between the nails, or at least between the modes of their fixture. Getting upon the sacking of the bedstead, I looked over the head-board minutely at the second casement. Passing my hand down behind the board, I readily discovered and pressed the spring, which was, as I had supposed, identical in character with its neighbor. I now looked at the nail. It was as

---

*A term in logic referring to reasoning from effects to causes. Literally means, "From the latter." (Latin)

stout as the other, and apparently fitted in the same manner—driven in nearly up to the head.

"You will say that I was puzzled; but, if you think so, you must have misunderstood the nature of the inductions. To use a sporting phrase, I had not been once 'at fault.' The scent had never for an instant been lost. There was no flaw in any link of the chain. I had traced the secret to its ultimate result,—and that result was *the nail*. It had, I say, in every respect, the appearance of its fellow in the other window; but this fact was an absolute nullity (conclusive as it might seem to be) when compared with the consideration that here, at this point, terminated the clew. 'There *must* be something wrong,' I said, 'about the nail.' I touched it; and the head, with about a quarter of an inch of the shank, came off in my fingers. The rest of the shank was in the gimlet-hole, where it had been broken off. The fracture was an old one (for its edges were incrusted with rust), and had apparently been accomplished by the blow of a hammer, which had partially imbedded, in the top of the bottom sash, the head portion of the nail. I now carefully replaced this head portion in the indentation whence I had taken it, and the resemblance to a perfect nail was complete—the fissure was invisible. Pressing the spring, I gently raised the sash for a few inches; the head went up with it, remaining firm in its bed. I closed the window, and the semblance of the whole nail was again perfect.

"This riddle, so far, was now unriddled. The assassin had escaped through the window which looked upon the bed. Dropping of its own accord upon his exit (or perhaps purposely closed), it had become fastened by the spring; and it was the retention of this spring which had been mistaken by the police for that of the nail,—farther inquiry being thus considered unnecessary.

"The next question is that of the mode of descent. Upon this point I had been satisfied in my walk with you around the building. About five feet and a half from the casement in question there runs a lightning-rod. From this rod it would have been impossible for any one to reach the window itself, to say nothing of entering it. I observed, however, that the shutters of the fourth story were of the peculiar kind called by Parisian carpenters *ferrades* —a kind rarely employed at the present day, but frequently seen upon very old mansions at Lyons and Bordeaux. They are in the form of an ordinary door (a single, not a folding door), except that the lower half is latticed or worked in open trellis—thus affording an excellent hold for the hands. In the present instance these shutters are fully three feet and a half broad. When we saw them from the rear of the house, they were both about half open—that is to say they stood off at right angles from the wall. It is probable that the police, as well as myself, examined the back of the tenement; but, if so, in looking at these *ferrades* in the line of their breadth (as they must have done), they did not perceive this great breadth itself, or, at all events, failed to take it into due consideration. In fact, having once satisfied themselves that no egress could have been made in this quarter, they would naturally bestow here a very cursory examination. It was clear to me, however, that the shutter belonging to the window at the head of the bed, would, if swung fully back to the wall, reach to within two feet of the lightning-rod. It was also evident that, by exertion of a very unusual degree of activity and courage, an entrance into the window, from the rod, might have been thus effected. By reaching to the distance of two feet and a half (we now suppose the shutter open to its whole extent) a robber might have taken a firm grasp upon the trelliswork. Letting go, then, his hold upon the rod, placing his feet securely against the wall, and springing boldly from it, he might have swung the shutter so as to close it, and, if we imagine the window open at the time, might even have swung himself into the room.

"I wish you to bear especially in mind that I have spoken of a *very* unusual degree of activity as requisite to success in so hazardous and so difficult a feat. It is my design to show you first, that the thing might possibly have been accomplished:—but, secondly and *chiefly,* I wish to impress upon your understanding the *very extraordinary*—the almost praeternatural character of that agility which could have accomplished it.

"You will say, no doubt, using the language of the law, that 'to make out my case,' I should rather undervalue than insist upon a full estimation of the activity required in this matter. This may be the practice in law, but it is not the usage of reason. My ultimate object is only the truth. My immediate purpose is to lead you to place in juxtaposition, that *very unusual* activity of which I have just spoken, with that *very peculiar* shrill (or harsh) and *unequal* voice, about whose nationality no two persons could be found to agree, and in whose utterance no syllabification could be detected."

At these words a vague and half-formed conception of the meaning of Dupin flitted over my mind. I seemed to be upon the verge of comprehension, without power to comprehend—as men, at times, find themselves upon the brink of remembrance, without being able, in the end, to remember. My friend went on with his discourse.

"You will see," he said, "that I have shifted the question from the mode of egress to that of ingress. It was my design to convey the idea that both were effected in the same manner, at the same point. Let us now revert to the interior of the room. Let us survey the appearances here. The drawers of the bureau, it is said, had been rifled, although many articles of apparel still remained within them. The conclusion here is absurd. It is a mere guess—a very silly one—and no more. How are we to know that the articles found in the drawers were not all these drawers had originally contained? Madame L'Espanaye and her daughter lived an exceedingly retired life— saw no company—seldom went out—had little use for numerous changes of habiliment.* Those found were at least of as good quality as any likely to be possessed by these ladies. If a thief had taken any, why did he not take the best—why did he not take all? In a word, why did he abandon four thousand francs in gold to encumber himself with a bundle of linen? The gold *was* abandoned. Nearly the whole sum mentioned by Monsieur Mignaud, the banker, was discovered, in bags, upon the floor. I wish you therefore, to discard from your thoughts the blundering idea of *motive,* engendered in the brains of the police by that portion of the evidence which

---

*Clothing, attire (French)

speaks of money delivered at the door of the house. Coincidences ten times as remarkable as this (the delivery of the money, and murder committed within three days upon the party receiving it), happen to all of us every hour of our lives, without attracting even momentary notice. Coincidences, in general, are great stumbling-blocks in the way of that class of thinkers who have been educated to know nothing of the theory of probabilities—that theory to which the most glorious objects of human research are indebted for the most glorious of illustration. In the present instance, had the gold been gone, the fact of its delivery three days before would have formed something more than a coincidence. It would have been corroborative of this idea of motive. But, under the real circumstances of the case, if we are to suppose gold the motive of this outrage, we must also imagine the perpetrator so vacillating an idiot as to have abandoned his gold and his motive together.

"Keeping now steadily in mind the points to which I have drawn your attention—that peculiar voice, that unusual agility, and that startling absence of motive in a murder so singularly atrocious as this—let us glance at the butchery itself. Here is a woman strangled to death by manual strength, and thrust up a chimney head downward. Ordinary assassins employ no such mode of murder as this. Least of all, do they thus dispose of the murdered. In the manner of thrusting the corpse up the chimney, you will admit that there was something *excessively outré*—something altogether irreconcilable with our common notions of human action, even when we suppose the actors the most depraved of men. Think, too, how great must have been that strength which could have thrust the body *up* such an aperture so forcibly that the united vigor of several persons was found barely sufficient to drag it *down*!

"Turn, now, to other indications of the employment of a vigor most marvellous. On the hearth were thick tresses—very thick tresses—of gray human hair. These had been torn out by the roots. You are aware of the great force necessary in tearing thus from the head even twenty or thirty hairs together. You saw the locks in question as well as myself. Their roots (a hideous sight!) were clotted with fragments of the flesh of the scalp—sure token of the prodigious power which had been exerted in uprooting perhaps half a million of hairs at a time. The throat of the old lady was not merely cut, but the head absolutely severed from the body: the instrument was a mere razor. I wish you also to look at the *brutal* ferocity of these deeds. Of the bruises upon the body of Madame L'Espanaye I do not speak. Monsieur Dumas, and his worthy coadjutor Monsieur Etienne, have pronounced that they were inflicted by some obtuse instrument; and so far these gentlemen are very correct. The obtuse instrument was clearly the stone pavement in the yard, upon which the victim had fallen from the window which looked in upon the bed. This idea, however simple it may now seem, escaped the police for the same reason that the breadth of the shutters escaped them—because, by the affair of the nails, their perceptions had been hermetically sealed against the possibility of the windows having ever been opened at all.

"If now, in addition to all these things, you have properly reflected upon the odd disorder of the chamber, we have gone so far as to combine the ideas of an agility astounding, a strength superhuman, a ferocity brutal, a butchery without motive, a *grotesquerie* in horror absolutely alien from humanity, and a voice foreign in tone to the ears of men of many nations, and devoid of all distinct or intelligible syllabification. What result, then, has ensued? What impression have I made upon your fancy?"

I felt a creeping of the flesh as Dupin asked me the question. "A madman," I said, "has done this deed—some raving maniac, escaped from a neighboring *Maison de Santé.*"*

"In some respects," he replied, "your idea is not irrelevant. But the voices of madmen, even in their wildest paroxysms, are never found to tally with that peculiar voice heard upon the stairs. Madmen are of some nation, and their language, however incoherent in its words, has always the coherence of syllabification. Besides, the hair of a madman is not such as I now hold in my hand. I disentangled this little tuft from the rigidly clutched fingers of Madame L'Espanaye. Tell me what you can make of it."

"Dupin!" I said, completely unnerved; "this hair is most unusual—this is no *human* hair."

"I have not asserted that it is," said he; "but, before we decide this point, I wish you to glance at the little sketch I have here traced upon this paper. It is a *facsimile* drawing of what has been described in one portion of the testimony as 'dark bruises and deep indentations of finger nails' upon the throat of Mademoiselle L'Espanaye, and in another (by Messrs. Dumas and Etienne) as a 'series of livid spots, evidently the impression of fingers.'

"You will perceive," continued my friend, spreading out the paper upon the table before us, "that this drawing gives the idea of a firm and fixed hold. There is no *slipping* apparent. Each finger has retained—possibly until the death of the victim—the fearful grasp by which it originally imbedded itself. Attempt, now, to place all your fingers, at the same time, in the respective impressions as you see them."

I made the attempt in vain.

"We are possibly not giving this matter a fair trial," he said. "The paper is spread out upon a plane surface; but the human throat is cylindrical. Here is a billet of wood, the circumference of which is about that of the throat. Wrap the drawing around it, and try the experiment again."

I did so; but the difficulty was even more obvious than before. "This," I said, "is the mark of no human hand."

"Read now," replied Dupin, "this passage from Cuvier."

It was a minute anatomical and generally descriptive account of the large fulvous Ourang-Outang of the East Indian Islands. The gigantic stature, the prodigious strength and activity, the wild ferocity, and the imitative propensities of these mammalia are sufficiently well known to all. I understood the full horrors of the murder at once.

"The description of the digits," said I, as I made an end of the reading,

---

*A mental hospital (French)

"is in exact accordance with this drawing. I see that no animal but an Ourang-Outang, of the species here mentioned, could have impressed the indentations as you have traced them. This tuft of tawny hair, too, is identical in character with that of the beast of Cuvier. But I cannot possibly comprehend the particulars of this frightful mystery. Besides, there were *two* voices heard in contention, and one of them was unquestionably the voice of a Frenchman."

"True; and you will remember an expression attributed almost unanimously, by the evidence, to this voice,—the expression '*mon Dieu!*' This, under the circumstances, has been justly characterized by one of the witnesses (Montani, the confectioner) as an expression of remonstrance or expostulation. Upon these two words, therefore, I have mainly built my hopes of a full solution of the riddle. A Frenchman was cognizant of the murder. It is possible—indeed it is far more than probable—that he was innocent of all participation in the bloody transactions which took place. The Ourang-Outang may have escaped from him. He may have traced it to the chamber; but, under the agitating circumstances which ensued, he could never have recaptured it. It is still at large. I will not pursue these guesses— for I have no right to call them more—since the shades of reflection upon which they are based are scarcely of sufficient depth to be appreciable by my own intellect, and since I could not pretend to make them intelligible to the understanding of another. We will call them guesses, then, and speak of them as such. If the Frenchman in question is indeed, as I suppose, innocent of this atrocity, this advertisement, which I left last night, upon our return home, at the office of *Le Monde* (a paper devoted to the shipping interest, and much sought by sailors), will bring him to our residence."

He handed me a paper, and I read thus:

"CAUGHT—*In the Bois de Boulogne, early in the morning of the* —— *inst.* (the morning of the murder), *a very large, tawny Ourang-Outang of the Bornese species. The owner (who is ascertained to be a sailor, belonging to a Maltese vessel) may have the animal again, upon identifying it satisfactorily, and paying a few charges arising from its capture and keeping. Call at No.* —— *Rue*——, *Faubourg St. Germain—au troisième.*"

"How was it possible," I asked, "that you should know the man to be a sailor, and belonging to a Maltese vessel?"

"I do *not* know it," said Dupin. "I am not *sure* of it. Here, however, is a small piece of ribbon, which from its form, and from its greasy appearance, has evidently been used in tying the hair in one of those long *queues** of which sailors are so fond. Moreover, this knot is one which few besides sailors can tie, and is peculiar to the Maltese. I picked the ribbon up at the foot of the lightning-rod. It could not have belonged to either of the deceased. Now if, after all, I am wrong in my induction from this ribbon, that the Frenchman was a sailor belonging to a Maltese vessel, still I can

---

*A pigtail (French)

have done no harm in saying what I did in the advertisement. If I am in error, he will merely suppose that I have been misled by some circumstance into which he will not take the trouble to inquire. But if I am right, a great point is gained. Cognizant although innocent of the murder, the Frenchman will naturally hesitate about replying to the advertisement—about demanding the Ourang-Outang. He will reason thus:—'I am innocent; I am poor; my Ourang-Outang is of great value—to one in my circumstance a fortune of itself—why should I lose it through idle apprehensions of danger? Here it is, within my grasp. It was found in the Bois de Boulogne—at a vast distance from the scene of that butchery. How can it ever be suspected that a brute beast should have done the deed? The police are at fault—they have failed to procure the slightest clew. Should they even trace the animal, it would be impossible to prove me cognizant of the murder, or to implicate me in guilt on account of that cognizance. Above all, *I am known*. The advertiser designates me as the possessor of the beast. I am not sure to what limit his knowledge may extend. Should I avoid claiming a property of so great value, which it is known that I possess, I will render the animal at least, liable to suspicion. It is not my policy to attract attention either to myself or to the beast. I will answer the advertisement, get the Ourang-Outang, and keep it close until this matter has blown over.' "

At this moment we heard a step upon the stairs.

"Be ready," said Dupin, "with your pistols, but neither use them nor show them until at a signal from myself."

The front door of the house had been left open, and the visitor had entered, without ringing, and advanced several steps upon the staircase. Now, however, he seemed to hesitate. Presently we heard him descending. Dupin was moving quickly to the door, when we again heard him coming up. He did not turn back a second time, but stepped up with decision, and rapped at the door of our chamber.

"Come in," said Dupin, in a cheerful and hearty tone.

A man entered. He was a sailor, evidently,—a tall, stout, and muscular-looking person, with a certain dare-devil expression of countenance, not altogether unprepossessing. His face, greatly sunburnt, was more than half hidden by whisker and *mustachio*. He had with him a huge oaken cudgel, but appeared to be otherwise unarmed. He bowed awkwardly, and bade us "good evening," in French accents, which, although somewhat Neufchâtelish,* were still sufficiently indicative of a Parisian origin.

"Sit down, my friend," said Dupin. "I suppose you have called about the Ourang-Outang. Upon my word, I almost envy you the possession of him; a remarkably fine, and no doubt a very valuable animal. How old do you suppose him to be?"

The sailor drew a long breath, with the air of a man relieved of some intolerable burden, and then replied, in an assured tone:

---

*From Neufchâtel in France

"I have no way of telling—but he can't be more than four or five years old. Have you got him here?"

"Oh, no; we had no conveniences for keeping him here. He is at a livery stable in the Rue Dubourg, just by. You can get him in the morning. Of course you are prepared to identify the property?"

"To be sure I am, sir."

"I shall be sorry to part with him," said Dupin.

"I don't mean that you should be at all this trouble for nothing, sir," said the man. "Couldn't expect it. Am very willing to pay a reward for the finding of the animal—that is to say, any thing in reason."

"Well," replied my friend, "that is all very fair, to be sure. Let me think!—what should I have? Oh! I will tell you. My reward shall be this. You shall give me all the information in your power about these murders in the Rue Morgue."

Dupin said the last words in a very low tone, and very quietly. Just as quietly, too, he walked toward the door, locked it, and put the key in his pocket. He then drew a pistol from his bosom and placed it, without the least flurry, upon the table.

The sailor's face flushed up as if he were struggling with suffocation. He started to his feet and grasped his cudgel; but the next moment he fell back into his seat, trembling violently, and with the countenance of death itself. He spoke not a word. I pitied him from the bottom of my heart.

"My friend," said Dupin, in a kind tone, "you are alarming yourself unnecessarily—you are indeed. We mean you no harm whatever. I pledge you the honor of a gentleman, and of a Frenchman, that we intend you no injury. I perfectly well know that you are innocent of the atrocities in the Rue Morgue. It will not do, however, to deny that you are in some measure implicated in them. From what I have already said, you must know that I have had means of information about this matter—means of which you could never have dreamed. Now the thing stands thus. You have done nothing which you could have avoided—nothing, certainly, which renders you culpable. You were not even guilty of robbery, when you might have robbed with impunity. You have nothing to conceal. You have no reason for concealment. On the other hand, you are bound by every principle of honor to confess all you know. An innocent man is now imprisoned, charged with that crime of which you can point out the perpetrator."

The sailor had recovered his presence of mind, in a great measure, while Dupin uttered these words; but his original boldness of bearing was all gone.

"So help me God!" said he, after a brief pause, "I *will* tell you all I know about this affair;—but I do not expect you to believe one half I say—I would be a fool indeed if I did. Still, I *am* innocent, and I will make a clean breast if I die for it."

What he stated was, in substance, this. He had lately made a voyage to the Indian Archipelago. A party, of which he formed one, landed at Borneo, and passed into the interior on an excursion of pleasure. Himself and a companion had captured the Ourang-Outang. This companion dying, the animal fell into his own exclusive possession. After great trouble, occasioned by the intractable ferocity of his captive during the home voyage, he at length succeeded in lodging it safely at his own residence in Paris, where, not to attract toward himself the unpleasant curiosity of his neighbors, he kept it carefully secluded, until such time as it should recover from a wound in the foot, received from a splinter on board ship. His ultimate design was to sell it.

Returning home from some sailors' frolic on the night, or rather in the morning, of the murder, he found the beast occupying his own bedroom, into which it had broken from a closet adjoining, where it had been, as was thought, securely confined. Razor in hand, and fully lathered, it was sitting before a looking-glass, attempting the operation of shaving, in which it had no doubt previously watched its master through the keyhole of the closet. Terrified at the sight of so dangerous a weapon in the possession of an animal so ferocious, and so well able to use it, the man, for some moments, was at a loss what to do. He had been accustomed, however, to quiet the creature, even in its fiercest moods, by the use of a whip, and to this he now resorted. Upon sight of it, the Ourang-Outang sprang at once through the door of the chamber, down the stairs, and thence, through a window, unfortunately open, into the street.

The Frenchman followed in despair; the ape, razor still in hand, occasionally stopping to look back and gesticulate at his pursuer, until the latter had nearly come up with it. It then again made off. In this manner the chase continued for a long time. The streets were profoundly quiet, as it was nearly three o'clock in the morning. In passing down an alley in the rear of the Rue Morgue, the fugitive's attention was arrested by a light gleaming from the open window of Madame L'Espanaye's chamber, in the fourth story of her house. Rushing to the building, it perceived the lightning-rod, clambered up with inconceivable agility, grasped the shutter, which was thrown fully back against the wall, and, by its means, swung itself directly upon the headboard of the bed. The whole feat did not occupy a minute. The shutter was kicked open again by the Ourang-Outang as it entered the room.

The sailor, in the meantime, was both rejoiced and perplexed. He had strong hopes of now recapturing the brute, as it could scarcely escape from the trap into which it had ventured, except by the rod, where it might be intercepted as it came down. On the other hand, there was much cause for anxiety as to what it might do in the house. This latter reflection urged the man still to follow the fugitive. A lightning-rod is ascended without difficulty, especially by a sailor; but, when he had arrived as high as the window, which lay far to his left, his career was stopped; the most that he could accomplish was to reach over so as to obtain a glimpse of the interior of the room. At this glimpse he nearly fell from his hold through excess of horror. Now it was that those hideous shrieks arose upon the night, which had startled from slumber the inmates of the Rue Morgue. Madame L'Espanaye and her daughter, habited in their night clothes, had apparently been occupied in arranging some papers in the iron chest already mentioned, which had been wheeled into the middle of the room. It was open, and its contents lay beside it on the floor. The victims must have been sitting with their backs toward the window; and, from the time elapsing between the ingress of the beast and the screams, it seems probable that it was not immediately perceived. The flapping-to of the shutter would naturally have been attributed to the wind.

As the sailor looked in, the gigantic animal had seized Madame L'Espanaye by the hair (which was loose, as she had been combing it), and was flourishing the razor about her face, in imitation of the motions of a barber. The daughter lay prostrate and motionless; she had swooned. The screams and struggles of the old lady (during which the hair was torn from her head) had the effect of changing the probably pacific purposes of the Ourang-Outang into those of wrath. With one determined sweep of its muscular arm it nearly severed her head from her body. The sight of blood inflamed its anger into phrensy.* Gnashing its teeth, and flashing fire from its eyes, it flew upon the body of the girl, and imbedded its fearful talons in her throat, retaining its grasp until she expired. Its wandering and wild glances fell at this moment upon the head of the bed, over which the face of its master, rigid with horror, was just discernible. The fury of the beast, who no doubt bore still in mind the dreaded whip, was instantly converted into fear. Conscious of having deserved punishment, it seemed desirous of concealing its bloody deeds, and skipped about the chamber in an agony of nervous agitation; throwing down and breaking the furniture as it moved, and dragging the bed from the bedstead. In conclusion, it seized first the corpse of the daughter, and thrust it up the chimney, as it was found; then that of the old lady, which it immediately hurled through the window headlong.

As the ape approached the casement with its mutilated burden, the sailor shrank aghast to the rod, and, rather gliding than clambering down it, hurried at once home—dreading the consequences of the butchery, and gladly abandoning, in his terror, all solicitude about the fate of the Ourang-Outang. The words heard by the party upon the staircase were the Frenchman's exclamations of horror and affright, commingled with the fiendish jabberings of the brute.

I have scarcely any thing to add. The Ourang-Outang must have escaped from the chamber, by the rod, just before the breaking of the door. It must have closed the window as it passed through it. It was subsequently caught by the owner himself, who obtained for it a very large sum at the *Jardin des Plantes.*† Le Bon was instantly released, upon our narration of the circumstances (with some comments from Dupin) at the *bureau* of the Prefect of Police. This functionary, however well disposed to my friend, could not altogether conceal his chagrin at the turn which affairs had taken, and was fain to indulge in a sarcasm or two about the propriety of every person minding his own business.

"Let him talk," said Dupin, who had not thought it necessary to reply. "Let him discourse; it will ease his conscience. I am satisfied with having defeated him in his own castle. Nevertheless, that he failed in the solution

---

*An earlier spelling of "frenzy"
†The Museum of Natural History which includes a zoo (French)

of this mystery, is by no means that matter for wonder which he supposes it; for, in truth, our friend the Prefect is somewhat too cunning to be profound. In his wisdom is no *stamen*. It is all head and no body, like the pictures of the Goddess Laverna—or, at best, all head and shoulders, like a codfish. But he is a good creature after all. I like him especially for one master stroke of cant, by which he has attained his reputation for ingenuity. I mean the way he has *'de nier ce qui est, et d'expliquer ce qui n'est pas.'* "*

Aubrey Beardsley's drawing for "The Murders in the Rue Morgue," from the Henry W. and Albert A. Berg Collection of the New York Public Library (Astor, Lenox and Tilden Foundations).

---

*From Rousseau's *Nouvelle Héloise*— "Of denying what is and explaining what isn't." (French)

ACTIVITIES

1)   Without looking back, write the five plot ingredients of the detective story that were listed for you in the introduction to "The Murders in the Rue Morgue." Then provide a concrete example for each element from the story itself.

2)   The first scene of this story has become world-famous. The anonymous narrator (the "I" of the tale) is given a remarkable demonstration of his new roommate's analytical talents; it is as if he wears ". . . a window in his bosom" with Dupin able to "see" his innermost thoughts. Can you give a step-by-step description of how Dupin "deduced" that his friend was thinking about Chantilly, the actor?

3)   List the clues that enabled Dupin to focus on such an unlikely murder culprit as an orang-utang.

4)   Dupin and the narrator became friends because they were alike in some ways and different in others. How were they alike? How were they different? Would you say the old adage "Opposites attract" applies here?

RESEARCH ACTIVITIES

1)   Early nineteenth century authors had a disturbing literary technique of wandering from their original story-line and interspersing short essays about everything "under the sun." Poe's story opened with a discussion of the characteristics of the analytical mind, then made the argumentative statement that chess-playing does not contribute to the enhancement of analytic ability. Organize a committee (and make sure that it contains chess players) who will look up this introduction in some other source and then summarize it for the class. Some, particularly the chess players, may want to disagree with Poe's contentions; others may feel like defending them. At any rate, a lively discussion may ensue from your committee's enterprising efforts.

2)   In "The Murders in the Rue Morgue," Dupin makes allusions to Epicurus and Orion, two famous names of Greek mythology. Have some class members look up these names in your school library and then report to the others. How do these two names fit into Dupin's analysis of the narrator's thoughts?

Poe Competes With Dupin

All told, Poe wrote three Dupin stories.

After "The Murders in the Rue Morgue" came "The Mystery of Marie Rogêt," to be followed by "The Purloined Letter." The second proved to be the least popular, the reason being that it was an attempt by Poe to solve an actual murder case.

As you become better acquainted with detective story authors, you will become aware of an interesting facet of their personalities. At some time during their writing careers, they seem to become jealous of their detective heroes and begin yearning for a real-life mystery that they can solve themselves. Poe started feeling this way—and so later did Sir Arthur Conan Doyle. In a letter written to Dr. J. E. Snodgrass in June 1842, Poe described the origins of his second Dupin adventure:

> The story is based upon that of the real murder of Mary Cecilia Rogers, which created so vast an excitement some months ago in New York. I have handled the design in a very singular and entirely novel manner. A young grisette,* one Marie Rogêt, has been murdered under precisely similar circumstances with Mary Rogers. Thus, under pretence of showing how Dupin (the hero of the Rue Morgue) unravelled the mystery of Marie's assassination, I, in fact, enter into a very rigorous examination of the *real* tragedy in New York. *No point* is omitted. I examine, each by each, the opinion and arguments of our press on the subject, and show (I think satisfactorily) that this subject has never *yet* been *approached*. The press has been entirely on the wrong scent. In fact, I really believe, not only that I have demonstrated the falsity of the idea that the girl was the victim of a gang, but have indicated the *assassin*. My main object, however . . . is the analysis of the principles of investigation in cases of like character. Dupin reasons the matter throughout.[3]

Thus, "The Mystery of Marie Rogêt" became more of a documentary case study of Poe's investigation of Mary Rogers' murder, rather than a story providing suspense and entertainment. The public reacted badly to it and we feel you would, too. We have omitted it here. But what Poe meant by his principles of investigation is worthy of presentation because his ideas were to have great influence on future detective writers. Here are his basic concepts:

1) If the appearance of a case suggests apparent unsolvability because of complex and contradictory evidence, the ease with which the solution may be uncovered is in direct ratio to its apparent image. In other words, the true solution may be disarmingly simple.
2) The famous detection technique of inference that "when you have eliminated all the impossibilities then, whatever remains, however improbable, must be the truth."[4]

In "The Murders in the Rue Morgue," Poe illustrated the first concept by having his police search for complex explanations with Dupin finally

---

*A French working girl or salesgirl

unveiling a brilliant but simple solution. An example of the second concept was Dupin's deducing that only an animal like an orang-utang could have committed the murders and then persistently following that path of "improbable truth."

These principles will be even more brilliantly illustrated in our next Poe tale, "The Purloined Letter." As you read, you'll once again be matching wits with C. Auguste Dupin.

The Purloined Letter

Nil sapientiae odiosius acumine nimio.—*Seneca**

At Paris, just after dark one gusty evening in the autumn of 18———, I was enjoying the twofold luxury of meditation and a meerschaum, in company with my friend, C. Auguste Dupin, in his little back library, or book-closet, *au troisième*, No. 33 *Rue Dunôt, Faubourg St. Germain.* For one hour at least we had maintained a profound silence; while each, to any casual observer, might have seemed intently and exclusively occupied with the curling eddies of smoke that oppressed the atmosphere of the chamber. For myself, however, I was mentally discussing certain topics which had formed matter for conversation between us at an earlier period of the evening; I mean the affair of the Rue Morgue, and the mystery attending the murder of Marie Rogêt. I looked upon it, therefore, as something of a coincidence, when the door of our apartment was thrown open and admitted our old acquaintance, Monsieur G———, the Prefect of the Parisian police.

We gave him a hearty welcome; for there was nearly half as much of the entertaining as of the contemptible about the man, and we had not seen him for several years. We had been sitting in the dark, and Dupin now arose for the purpose of lighting a lamp, but sat down again, without doing so, upon G.'s saying that he had called to consult us, or rather to ask the opinion of my friend, about some official business which had occasioned a great deal of trouble.

"If it is any point requiring reflection," observed Dupin, as he forbore to enkindle the wick, "we shall examine it to better purpose in the dark."

"That is another of your odd notions," said the Prefect, who had the fashion of calling everything "odd" that was beyond his comprehension, and thus lived amid an absolute legion of "oddities."

"Very true," said Dupin, as he supplied his visitor with a pipe, and rolled toward him a comfortable chair.

---

*"Nothing is more hateful to wisdom than too little keenness of insight." (Latin)

"And what is the difficulty now?" I asked. "Nothing more in the assassination way I hope?"

"Oh, no; nothing of that nature. The fact is, the business is *very* simple indeed, and I make no doubt that we can manage it sufficiently well ourselves; but then I thought Dupin would like to hear the details of it, because it is so excessively *odd.*"

"Simple and odd," said Dupin.

"Why, yes; and not exactly that either. The fact is, we have all been a good deal puzzled because the affair *is* so simple, and yet baffles us altogether."

"Perhaps it is the very simplicity of the thing which puts you at fault," said my friend.

"What nonsense you *do* talk!" replied the Prefect, laughing heartily.

"Perhaps the mystery is a little *too* plain," said Dupin.

"Oh, good heavens! who ever heard of such an idea?"

"A little *too* self-evident."

"Ha! ha! ha!—ha! ha! ha!—ho! ho! ho!" roared our visitor, profoundly amused, "oh, Dupin, you will be the death of me yet!"

"And what, after all, *is* the matter on hand?" I asked.

"Why, I will tell you," replied the Prefect, as he gave a long, steady, and contemplative puff, and settled himself in his chair. "I will tell you in a few words; but, before I begin, let me caution you that this is an affair demanding the greatest secrecy, and that I should most probably lose the position I now hold, were it known that I confided it to any one."

"Proceed," said I.

"Or not," said Dupin.

"Well, then; I have received personal information, from a very high quarter, that a certain document of the last importance has been purloined from the royal apartments. The individual who purloined it is known; this beyond a doubt; he was seen to take it. It is known, also, that it still remains in his possession."

"How is this known?" asked Dupin.

"It is clearly inferred," replied the Prefect, "from the nature of the document, and from the non-appearance of certain results which would at once arise from its passing *out* of the robber's possession—that is to say, from his employing it as he must design in the end to employ it."

"Be a little more explicit," I said

"Well, I may venture so far as to say that the paper gives its holder a certain power in a certain quarter where such power is immensely valuable." The Prefect was fond of the cant of diplomacy.

"Still I do not quite understand," said Dupin.

"No? Well; the disclosure of the document to a third person, who shall be nameless, would bring in question the honor of a personage of most exalted station; and this fact gives the holder of the document an ascendancy over the illustrious personage whose honor and peace are so jeopardized."

"But this ascendancy," I interposed, "would depend upon the robber's knowledge of the loser's knowledge of the robber. Who would dare—"

"The thief," said G., "is the Minister D——, who dares all things, those unbecoming as well as those becoming a man. The method of the theft was not less ingenious than bold. The document in question—a letter, to be frank—had been received by the personage robbed while alone in the royal *boudoir*. During its perusal she was suddenly interrupted by the entrance of the other exalted personage from whom especially it was her wish to conceal it. After a hurried and vain endeavor to thrust it in a drawer, she was forced to place it, open it was, upon a table. The address, however, was uppermost, and, the contents thus unexposed, the letter escaped notice. At this juncture enters the Minister D——. His lynx eye immediately perceives the paper, recognizes the handwriting of the address, observes the confusion of the personage addressed, and fathoms her secret. After some business transactions, hurried through in his ordinary manner, he produces a letter somewhat similar to the one in question, opens it, pretends to read it, and then places it in close juxtaposition to the other. Again he converses, for some fifteen minutes, upon the public affairs. At length, in taking leave, he takes also from the table the letter to which he had no claim. Its rightful owner saw, but, of course, dared not call attention to the act, in the presence of the third personage who stood at her elbow. The minister decamped; leaving his own letter—one of no importance—upon the table."

"Here, then," said Dupin to me, "you have precisely what you demand to make the ascendancy complete—the robber's knowledge of the loser's knowledge of the robber."

"Yes," replied the Prefect; "and the power thus attained has, for some months past, been wielded, for political purposes, to a very dangerous extent. The personage robbed is more thoroughly convinced, every day, of the necessity of reclaiming her letter. But this, of course, cannot be done openly. In fine, driven to despair, she has committed the matter to me."

"Than whom," said Dupin, amid a perfect whirlwind of smoke, "no more sagacious agent could, I suppose, be desired, or even imagined."

"You flatter me," replied the Prefect; "but it is possible that some such opinion may have been entertained."

"It is clear," said I, "as you observe, that the letter is still in the possession of the minister; since it is this possession, and not any employment of the letter, which bestows the power. With the employment the power departs."

"True," said G.; "and upon this conviction I proceeded. My first care was to make thorough search of the minister's hotel; and here my chief embarrassment lay in the necessity of searching without his knowledge. Beyond all things, I have been warned of the danger which would result from giving him reason to suspect our design."

"But," said I, "you are quite *au fait** in these investigations. The Parisian police have done this thing often before."

---

*Well-informed (French)

"Oh, yes; and for this reason I did not despair. The habits of the minister gave me, too, a great advantage. He is frequently absent from home all night. His servants are by no means numerous. They sleep at a distance from their master's apartment, and, being chiefly Neapolitans,* are readily made drunk. I have keys, as you know, with which I can open any chamber or cabinet in Paris. For three months a night has not passed, during the greater part of which I have not been engaged, personally, in ransacking the D——— Hotel. My honor is interested, and, to mention a great secret, the reward is enormous. So I did not abandon the search until I had become fully satisfied that the thief is a more astute man than myself. I fancy that I have investigated every nook and corner of the premises in which it is possible that the paper can be concealed."

"But is it not possible," I suggested, "that although the letter may be in possession of the minister, as it unquestionably is, he may have concealed it elsewhere than upon his own premises?"

"This is barely possible," said Dupin. "The present peculiar condition of affairs at court, and especially of those intrigues in which D——— is known to be involved, would render the instant availability of the document—its susceptibility of being produced at a moment's notice—a point of nearly equal importance with its possession."

"Its susceptibility of being produced?" said I.

"That is to say, of being *destroyed,*" said Dupin.

"True," I observed; "the paper is clearly then upon the premises. As for its being upon the person of the minister, we may consider that as out of the question."

"Entirely," said the Prefect. "He has been twice waylaid, as if by foot-pads, and his person rigidly searched under my own inspection."

"You might have spared yourself this trouble," said Dupin. "D———, I presume, is not altogether a fool, and, if not, must have anticipated these waylayings, as a matter of course."

"Not *altogether* a fool," said G., "but then he is a poet, which I take to be only one remove from a fool."

"True," said Dupin, after a long and thoughtful whiff from his meerschaum, "although I have been guilty of certain doggerel myself."

"Suppose you detail," said I, "the particulars of your search."

"Why, the fact is, we took our time, and we searched *everywhere.* I have had long experience in these affairs. I took the entire building, room by room; devoting the nights of a whole week to each. We examined, first, the furniture of each apartment. We opened every possible drawer; and I presume you know that, to a properly trained police-agent, such a thing as a 'secret' drawer is impossible. Any man is a dolt who permits a 'secret' drawer to escape him in a search of this kind. The thing is *so* plain. There is a certain amount of bulk—of space—to be accounted for in every cabinet. Then we have accurate rules. The fiftieth part of a line could not escape us.

---

*Italians from Naples

After the cabinets we took the chairs. The cushions we probed with the fine long needles you have seen me employ. From the tables we removed the tops."

"Why so?"

"Sometimes the top of a table, or other similarly arranged piece of furniture, is removed by the person wishing to conceal an article; then the leg is excavated, the article deposited within the cavity, and the top replaced. The bottoms and tops of bedposts are employed in the same way."

"But could not the cavity be detected by sounding?" I asked.

"By no means, if, when the article is deposited, a sufficient wadding of cotton be placed around it. Besides, in our case, we were obliged to proceed without noise."

"But you could not have removed—you could not have taken to pieces *all* articles of furniture in which it would have been possible to make a deposit in the manner you mention. A letter may be compressed into a thin spiral roll, not differing much in shape or bulk from a large knitting-needle, and in this form it might be inserted into the rung of a chair, for example. You did not take to pieces all the chairs?"

"Certainly not; but we did better—we examined the rungs of every chair in the hotel, and, indeed, the jointings of every description of furniture, by the aid of a most powerful microscope. Had there been any traces of recent disturbance we should not have failed to detect it instantly. A single grain of gimlet-dust, for example, would have been as obvious as an apple. Any disorder in the gluing—any unusual gaping in the joints—would have sufficed to insure detection."

"I presume you looked to the mirrors, between the boards and the plates, and you probed the beds and the bedclothes, as well as the curtains and carpets."

"That of course; and when we had absolutely completed every particle of the furniture in this way, then we examined the house itself. We divided its entire surface into compartments, which we numbered, so that none might be missed; then we scrutinized each individual square inch throughout the premises, including the two houses immediately adjoining, with the microscope, as before."

"The two houses adjoining!" I exclaimed; "you must have had a great deal of trouble."

"We had; but the reward offered is prodigious."

"You include the *grounds* about the houses?"

"All the grounds are paved with brick. They gave us comparatively little trouble. We examined the moss between the bricks, and found it undisturbed."

"You looked among D———'s papers, of course, and into the books of the library?"

"Certainly; we opened every package and parcel; we not only opened every book, but we turned over every leaf in each volume, not contenting ourselves with a mere shake, according to the fashion of some of our police officers. We also measured the thickness of every book-*cover,* with the most accurate admeasurement, and applied to each the most jealous scrutiny of the microscope. Had any of the bindings been recently meddled with, it would have been utterly impossible that the fact should have escaped observation. Some five or six volumes, just from the hands of the binder, we carefully probed, longitudinally, with the needles."

"You explored the floors beneath the carpets?"

"Beyond doubt. We removed every carpet, and examined the boards with the microscope."

"And the paper on the walls?"

"Yes."

"You looked into the cellars?"

"We did."

"Then," I said, "you have been making a miscalculation, and the letter is *not* upon the premises, as you suppose."

"I fear you are right there," said the Prefect. "And now, Dupin, what would you advise me to do?"

"To make a thorough research of the premises."

"That is absolutely needless," replied G———. "I am not more sure that I breathe than I am that the letter is not at the hotel."

"I have no better advice to give you," said Dupin. "You have, of course, an accurate description of the letter?"

"Oh, yes!"—And here the Prefect, producing a memorandum-book, proceeded to read aloud a minute account of the internal, and especially of the external, appearance of the missing document. Soon after finishing the perusal of this description, he took his departure, more entirely depressed in spirits than I had ever known the good gentleman before.

In about a month afterward he paid us another visit, and found us occupied very nearly as before. He took a pipe and a chair and entered into some ordinary conversation. At length I said:

"Well, but G., what of the purloined letter? I presume you have at last made up your mind that there is no such thing as overreaching the minister?"

"Confound him, say I—yes; I made the re-examination, however, as Dupin suggested—but it was all labor lost, as I knew it would be."

"How much was the reward offered, did you say?" asked Dupin.

"Why, a very great deal—a *very* liberal reward—I don't like to say how much, precisely, but one thing I *will* say, that I wouldn't mind giving my individual check for fifty thousand francs to any one who could obtain me that letter. The fact is, it is becoming of more and more importance every day; and the reward has been lately doubled. If it were trebled, however, I could do no more than I have done."

"Why, yes," said Dupin, drawlingly, between the whiffs of his meerschaum, "I really—think, G., you have not exerted yourself—to the utmost in this matter. You might—do a little more, I think, eh?"

"How?—in what way?"

"Why—puff, puff—you might—puff, puff—employ counsel in the matter, eh?—puff, puff, puff. Do you remember the story they tell of Abernethy?"

"No; hang Abernethy!"

"To be sure! hang him and welcome. But, once upon a time, a certain rich miser conceived the design of sponging upon this Abernethy for a medical opinion. Getting up, for this purpose, an ordinary conversation in a private company, he insinuated his case to the physician, as that of an imaginary individual."

" 'We will suppose,' said the miser, 'that his symptoms are such and such; now, doctor, what would *you* have directed him to take?' "

" 'Take!' said Abernethy, 'why, take *advice,* to be sure.' "

"But," said the Prefect, a little discomposed, "*I* am *perfectly* willing to take advice, and to pay for it. I would *really* give fifty thousand francs to any one who would aid me in the matter."

"In that case," replied Dupin, opening a drawer, and producing a check-book, "you may as well fill me up a check for the amount mentioned. When you have signed it, I will hand you the letter."

I was astounded. The Prefect appeared absolutely thunderstricken. For some minutes he remained speechless and motionless, looking incredulously at my friend with open mouth, and eyes that seemed starting from their sockets; then apparently recovering himself in some measure, he seized a pen, and after several pauses and vacant stares, finally filled up and signed a check for fifty thousand francs, and handed it across the table to Dupin. The latter examined it carefully and deposited it in his pocket-book; then, unlocking an *escritoire,** took thence a letter and gave it to the Prefect. This functionary grasped it in a perfect agony of joy, opened it with a trembling hand, cast a rapid glance at its contents, and then, scrambling and struggling to the door, rushed at length unceremoniously from the room and from the house, without having uttered a syllable since Dupin had requested him to fill up the check.

When he had gone, my friend entered into some explanations.

"The Parisian police," he said, "are exceedingly able in their way. They are persevering, ingenious, cunning, and thoroughly versed in the knowledge which their duties seem chiefly to demand. Thus, when G——— detailed to us his mode of searching the premises at the Hotel D———, I felt entire confidence in his having made a satisfactory investigation—so far as his labors extended."

"So far as his labors extended?" said I.

"Yes," said Dupin. "The measures adopted were not only the best of their kind, but carried out to absolute perfection. Had the letter been deposited within the range of their search, these fellows would, beyond a question, have found it."

I merely laughed—but he seemed quite serious in all that he said.

"The measures, then," he continued, "were good in their kind, and well executed; their defect lay in their being inapplicable to the case and to the man. A certain set of highly ingenious resources are, with the Prefect, a sort

---

*A writing desk, sometimes called a secretary, with drawers and pigeon-holes

of Procrustean bed,* to which he forcibly adapts his designs. But he perpetually errs by being too deep or too shallow for the matter in hand; and many a school-boy is a better reasoner than he. I knew one about eight years of age, whose success at guessing in the game of 'even and odd' attracted universal admiration. This game is simple, and is played with marbles. One player holds in his hand a number of these toys, and demands of another whether that number is even or odd. If the guess is right, the guesser wins one; if wrong, he loses one. The boy to whom I allude won all the marbles of the school. Of course he had some principle of guessing; and this lay in mere observation and admeasurement of the astuteness of his opponents. For example, an arrant simpleton is his opponent, and, holding up his closed hand, asks, 'Are they even or odd?' Our school-boy replies, 'Odd,' and loses; but upon the second trial he wins, for he then says to himself: 'The simpleton had them even upon the first trial, and his amount of cunning is just sufficient to make him have them odd upon the second; I will therefore guess odd';—he guesses odd, and wins. Now, with a simpleton a degree above the first, he would have reasoned thus: 'This fellow finds that in the first instance I guessed odd, and, in the second, he will propose to himself, upon the first impulse, a simple variation from even to odd, as did the first simpleton; but then a second thought will suggest that this is too simple a variation, and finally he will decide upon putting it even as before. I will therefore guess even';—he guesses even, and wins. Now this mode of reasoning in the school-boy, whom his fellows termed 'lucky,'—what, in its last analysis, is it?"

"It is merely," I said, "an identification of the reasoner's intellect with that of his opponent."

"It is," said Dupin; "and, upon inquiring of the boy by what means he effected the *thorough* identification in which his success consisted, I received answer as follows: 'When I wish to find out how wise, or how stupid, or how good, or how wicked is any one, or what are his thoughts at the moment, I fashion the expression of my face, as accurately as possible, in accordance with the expression of his, and then wait to see what thoughts or sentiments arise in my mind or heart, as if to match or correspond with the expression.' This response of the school-boy lies at the bottom of all the spurious profundity which has been attributed to a Rochefoucault, to La Bougive, to Machiavelli, and to Campanella."†

"And the identification," I said, "of the reasoner's intellect with that of his opponent, depends, if I understand you aright, upon the accuracy with which the opponent's intellect is admeasured."

"For its practical value it depends upon this," replied Dupin; "and the

---

*Procrustus, a character in Greek mythology, was a highwayman who tied his victims to an iron bed and cut off their feet or stretched them if they didn't fit on the bed. Used here as a figure of speech to state that the prefect is tailoring the facts to fit his theories.

†Rochefoucault and La Bougive were 17th-century French writers. Machiavelli was an Italian statesman of the 16th century, and Campanella was a 17th century Italian philosopher.

Prefect and his cohort fail so frequently, first, by default of this identification, and, secondly, by ill-admeasurement, or rather through non-admeasurement, of the intellect with which they are engaged. They consider only their *own* ideas of ingenuity; and, in searching for any thing hidden, advert only to the modes in which *they* would have hidden it. They are right in this much—that their own ingenuity is a faithful representative of that of *the mass;* but when the cunning of the individual felon is diverse in character from their own, the felon foils them, of course. This always happens when it is above their own, and very usually when it is below. They have no variation of principle in their investigations; at best, when urged by some unusual emergency—by some extraordinary reward—they extend or exaggerate their old modes of *practice,* without touching their principles. What, for example, in this case of D——, has been done to vary the principle of action? What is all this boring, and probing, and sounding, and scrutinizing with the microscope, and dividing the surface of the building into registered square inches—what is it all but an exaggeration *of the application* of the one principle or set of principles of search, which are based upon the one set of notions regarding human ingenuity, to which the Prefect, in the long routine of his duty, has been accustomed? Do you not see he has taken it for granted that *all* men proceed to conceal a letter, not exactly in a gimlet-hole bored in a chair-leg, but, at least, in *some* out-of-the-way hole or corner suggested by the same tenor of thought which would urge a man to secrete a letter in a gimlet-hole bored in a chair-leg? And do you not see also, that such *recherchés* nooks for concealment are adapted only for ordinary occasions, and would be adopted only by ordinary intellects; for, in all cases of concealment, a disposal of the article concealed—a disposal of it in this *recherché* manner,—is, in the very first instance, presumable and presumed; and thus its discovery depends, not at all upon the acumen, but altogether upon the mere care, patience, and determination of the seekers; and where the case is of importance—or, what amounts to the same thing in the political eyes, when the reward is of magnitude,—the qualities in question have *never* been known to fail. You will now understand what I meant in suggesting that, had the purloined letter been hidden anywhere within the limits of the Prefect's examination—in other words, had the principle of its concealment been comprehended within the principles of the Prefect—its discovery would have been a matter altogether beyond question. This functionary, however, has been thoroughly mystified; and the remote source of his defeat lies in the supposition that the Minister is a fool, because he has acquired renown as a poet. All fools are poets; this the Prefect *feels;* and he is merely guilty of a *non distributio medii** in thence inferring that all poets are fools."

"But is this really the poet?" I asked. "There are two brothers, I know; and both have attained reputation in letters. The Minister I believe has

---

*A philosophical Latin term used in logical argumentation meaning, "There is no distribution of the half."

written learnedly on the Differential Calculus. He is a mathematician, and no poet."

"You are mistaken; I know him well; he is both. As poet *and* mathematician, he would reason well; as mere mathematician, he could not have reasoned at all, and thus would have been at the mercy of the Prefect."

"You surprise me," I said, "by these opinions, which have been contradicted by the voice of the world. You do not mean to set at naught the well-digested idea of centuries. The mathematical reason has long been regarded as *the* reason *par excellence.*"

" '*Il y a à parier,*' " replied Dupin, quoting from Chamfort, " '*que toute idée publique, toute convention reçue, est une sottise, car elle a convenue au plus grand nombre.*'*.The mathematicians, I grant you, have done their best to promulgate the popular error to which you allude, and which is none the less an error for its promulgation as truth. With an art worthy a better cause, for example, they have insinuated the term 'analysis' into application to algebra. The French are the originators of this particular deception; but if a term is of any importance—if words derive any value from applicability—then 'analysis' conveys 'algebra' about as much as, in Latin, '*ambitus*' implies 'ambition,' '*religio*' 'religion,' or '*homines honesti*' a set of '*honorable* men.' "†

"You have a quarrel on hand, I see," said I, "with some of the algebraists of Paris; but proceed."

"I dispute the availability, and thus the value, of that reason which is cultivated in any especial form other than the abstractly logical. I dispute, in particular, the reason educed by mathematical study. The mathematics are the science of form and quantity; mathematical reasoning is merely logic applied to observation upon form and quantity. The great error lies in supposing that even the truths of what is called *pure* algebra are abstract or general truths. And this error is so egregious that I am confounded at the universality with which it has been received. Mathematical axioms are *not* axioms of general truth. What is true of *relation*—of form and quantity—is often grossly false in regard to morals, for example. In this latter science it is very usually *un*true that the aggregated parts are equal to the whole. In chemistry also the axiom fails. In the consideration of motive it fails; for two motives, each of a given value, have not, necessarily, a value when united, equal to the sum of their values apart. There are numerous other mathematical truths which are only truths within the limits of *relation*. But the mathematician argues from his *finite truths,* through habit, as if they were of an absolutely general applicability—as the world indeed imagines them to be. Bryant, in his very learned 'Mythology,' mentions an analogous source of error, when he says that 'although the pagan fables are not believed, yet we

---

*"One can bet that every public idea and every accepted convention is a stupidity because it serves the greatest number."

†These are all Latin words: *ambitus* means "a going around," *religio,* "reverence for the gods," and *homines honesti,* "men of distinction."

forget ourselves continually, and make inferences from them as existing realities.' With the algebraists, however, who are pagans themselves, the 'pagan fables' *are* believed, and the inferences are made, not so much through lapse of memory as through an unaccountable addling of the brains. In short, I never yet encountered the mere mathematician who would be trusted out of equal roots, or one who did not clandestinely hold it as a point of his faith that $x^2 + px$ was absolutely and unconditionally equal to q. Say to one of these gentlemen, by way of experiment, if you please, that you believe occasions may occur where $x^2 + px$ is *not* altogether equal to q, and, having made him understand what you mean, get out of his reach as speedily as convenient, for, beyond doubt, he will endeavor to knock you down.

"I mean to say," continued Dupin, while I merely laughed at his last observations, "that if the Minister had been no more than a mathematician, the Prefect would have been under no necessity of giving me this check. I knew him, however, as both mathematician and poet, and my measures were adapted to his capacity, with reference to the circumstances by which he was surrounded. I knew him as a courtier, too, and as a bold *intrigant.** Such a man, I considered, could not fail to be aware of the ordinary policial modes of action. He could not have failed to anticipate—and events have proved that he did not fail to anticipate—the waylayings to which he was subjected. He must have foreseen, I reflected, the secret investigations of his premises. His frequent absences from home at night, which were hailed by the Prefect as certain aids to his success, I regarded only as *ruses,* to afford opportunity for thorough search to the police, and thus the sooner to impress them with the conviction to which G———, in fact, did finally arrive—the conviction that the letter was not upon the premises. I felt, also, that the whole train of thoughts, which I was at some pains in detailing to you just now, concerning the invariable principle of policial action in searches for articles concealed—I felt that this whole train of thought would necessarily pass through the mind of the Minister. It would imperatively lead him to despise all the ordinary *nooks* of concealment. *He* could not, I reflected, be so weak as not to see that the most intricate and remo.e recess of his hotel would be as open as his commonest closets to the eyes, to the probes, to the gimlets, and to the microscopes of the Prefect. I saw, in fine, that he would be driven, as a matter of course, to *simplicity,* if not deliberately induced to it as a matter of choice. You will remember, perhaps, how desperately the Prefect laughed when I suggested, upon our first interview, that it was just possible this mystery troubled him so much on account of its being so *very* self-evident."

"Yes," said I, "I remember his merriment well. I really thought he would have fallen into convulsions."

"The material world," continued Dupin, "abounds with very strict analogies to the immaterial; and thus some color of truth has been given to the

---

*A person who engages in intrigue or intrigues (French)

rhetorical dogma, that metaphor, or simile, may be made to strengthen an argument as well as to embellish a description. The principle of the *vis inertiae,* * for example, seems to be identical in physics and metaphysics. It is not more true in the former, that a large body is with more difficulty set in motion than a smaller one, and that its subsequent *momentum* is commensurate with this difficulty, than it is, in the latter, that intellects of the vaster capacity, while more forcible, more constant, and more eventful in their movements than those of inferior grade, are yet the less readily moved, and more embarrassed, and full of hesitation in the first few steps of their progress. Again: have you ever noticed which of the street signs, over the shop doors, are the most attractive of attention?"

"I have never given the matter a thought," I said.

"There is a game of puzzles," he resumed, "which is played upon a map. One party playing requires another to find a given word—the name of town, river, state, or empire—any word, in short, upon the motley and perplexed surface of the chart. A novice in the game generally seeks to embarrass his opponents by giving them the most minutely lettered names; but the adept selects such words as stretch, in large characters, from one end of the chart to the other. These, like the over-largely lettered signs and placards of the street, escape observation by dint of being excessively obvious; and here the physical oversight is precisely analogous with the moral inapprehension by which the intellect suffers to pass unnoticed those considerations which are too obtrusively and too palpably self-evident. But this is a point, it appears, somewhat above or beneath the understanding of the Prefect. He never once thought it probable, or possible, that the Minister had deposited the letter immediately beneath the nose of the whole world, by way of best preventing any portion of that world from perceiving it.

"But the more I reflected upon the daring, dashing, and discriminating ingenuity of D———; upon the fact that the document must always have been *at hand,* if he intended to use it to good purpose; and upon the decisive evidence, obtained by the Prefect, that it was not hidden within the limits of that dignitary's ordinary search—the more satisfied I became that, to conceal this letter, the minister had resorted to the comprehensive and sagacious expedient of not attempting to conceal it at all.

"Full of these ideas, I prepared myself with a pair of green spectacles, and called one fine morning, quite by accident, at the Ministerial hotel. I found D——— at home, yawning, lounging, and dawdling, as usual, and pretending to be in the last extremity of *ennui.*† He is, perhaps, the most really energetic human being now alive—but that is only when nobody sees him.

"To be even with him, I complained of my weak eyes, and lamented the necessity of the spectacles, under cover of which I cautiously and thorough-

---

*Latin for Newton's first law of motion, which states that a body at rest or in motion will continue in that state unless acted upon by an outside force

†Weariness or boredom (French)

ly surveyed the whole apartment, while seemingly intent only upon the conversation of my host.

"I paid especial attention to a large writing-table near which he sat, and upon which lay confusedly, some miscellaneous letters and other papers, with one or two musical instruments and a few books. Here, however, after a long and very deliberate scrutiny, I saw nothing to excite particular suspicion. "At length my eyes, in going the circuit of the room, fell upon a trumpery filigree* card-rack of pasteboard, that hung dangling by a dirty blue ribbon, from a little brass knob just beneath the middle of the mantelpiece. In this rack, which had three or four compartments, were five or six visiting cards and a solitary letter. This last was much soiled and crumpled. It was torn nearly in two, across the middle—as if a design, in the first instance, to tear it entirely up as worthless, had been altered, or stayed, in the second. It had a large black seal, bearing the D——— cipher *very* conspicuously, and was addressed, in a diminutive female hand, to D———, the Minister, himself. It was thrust carelessly, and even, as it seemed, contemptuously, into one of the uppermost divisions of the rack.

"No sooner had I glanced at this letter than I concluded it to be that of which I was in search. To be sure, it was, to all appearance, radically different from the one of which the Prefect had read us so minute a description. Here the seal was large and black, with the D——— cipher; there it was small and red, with the ducal arms of the S——— family. Here, the address, to the Minister, was diminutive and feminine; there the superscription, to a certain royal personage, was markedly bold and decided; the size alone formed a point of correspondence. But, then, the *radicalness* of these differences, which was excessive; the dirt; the soiled and torn condition of the paper, so inconsistent with the *true* methodical habits of D———, and so suggestive of a design to delude the beholder into an idea of the worthlessness of the document;—these things, together with the hyperobtrusive situation of this document, full in the view of every visitor, and thus exactly in accordance with the conclusions to which I had previously arrived; these things, I say, were strongly corroborative of suspicion, in one who came with the intention to suspect.

"I protracted my visit as long as possible, and, while I maintained a most animated discussion with the Minister, upon a topic which I knew well had never failed to interest and excite him, I kept my attention really riveted upon the letter. In this examination, I committed to memory its external appearance and arrangement in the rack; and also fell, at length, upon a discovery which set at rest whatever trivial doubt I might have entertained. In scrutinizing the edges of the paper, I observed them to be more *chafed* than seemed necessary. They presented the *broken* appearance which is manifested when a stiff paper, having been once folded and pressed with a folder, is refolded in a reversed direction, in the same creases or edges which had formed the original fold. This discovery was sufficient. It was clear to

---

*A *trumpery* is something that is deceptively showy while a *filigree* is an ornamental design. Thus the card rack was made to look as if it were delicate jewelwork.

me that the letter had been turned, as a glove, inside out, re-directed and re-sealed. I bade the Minister good-morning, and took my departure at once, leaving a gold snuff-box upon the table.

"The next morning I called for the snuff-box, when we resumed, quite eagerly, the conversation of the preceding day. While thus engaged, however, a loud report, as if of a pistol, was heard immediately beneath the windows of the hotel, and was succeeded by a series of fearful screams, and the shoutings of a terrified mob. D—— rushed to a casement, threw it open, and looked out. In the meantime I stepped to the card-rack, took the letter, put it in my pocket, and replaced it by a *facsimile*, (so far as regards externals) which I had carefully prepared at my lodgings—imitating the D—— cipher, very readily, by means of a seal formed of bread.

"The disturbance in the street had been occasioned by the frantic behavior of a man with a musket. He had fired it among a crowd of women and children. It proved, however, to have been without ball, and the fellow was suffered to go his way as a lunatic or a drunkard. When he had gone, D—— came from the window, whither I had followed him immediately upon securing the object in view. Soon afterward I bade him farewell. The pretended lunatic was a man in my own pay."

"But what purpose had you," I asked, "in replacing the letter by a *facsimile*? Would it not have been better, at the first visit, to have seized it openly, and departed?"

"D——," replied Dupin, "is a desperate man, and a man of nerve. His hotel, too, is not without attendants devoted to his interests. Had I made the wild attempt you suggest, I might never have left the Ministerial presence alive. The good people of Paris might have heard of me no more. But I had an object apart from these considerations. You know my political prepossessions. In this matter, I act as a partisan of the lady concerned. For eighteen months the Minister has had her in his power. She has now him in hers—since, being unaware that the letter is not in his possession, he will proceed with his exactions as if it was. Thus will he inevitably commit himself, at once, to his political destruction. His downfall, too, will not be more precipitate than awkward. It is all very well to talk about the *facilis descensus Averni*,* but in all kinds of climbing, as Catalani said of singing, it is far more easy to get up than to come down. In the present instance I have no sympathy—at least no pity—for him who descends. He is that *monstrum horrendum*,† an unprincipled man of genius. I confess, however, that I should like very well to know the precise character of his thoughts, when, being defied by her whom the Prefect terms 'a certain personage,' he is reduced to opening the letter which I left for him in the card-rack."

"How? Did you put any thing particular in it?"

"Why—it did not seem altogether right to leave the interior blank—that would have been insulting. D——, at Vienna once, did me an evil turn,

---

*From the Roman poet, Virgil: "The way down to Hell is easy." (Latin)
†"Dreadful monster" (Latin)

which I told him, quite good-humoredly, that I should remember. So, as I knew he would feel some curiosity in regard to the identity of the person who had outwitted him, I thought it a pity not to give him a clew. He is well acquainted with my MS., and I just copied into the middle of the blank sheet the words—

"'——— ————Un dessein si funeste,
S'il n'est digne d'Atrée, est digne de Thyeste.'*

They are to be found in Crébillon's 'Atrée.' "

ACTIVITIES

1) Let us repeat Poe's second concept of his *principles of investigation,* ". . . [W]hen you have eliminated all the impossibilities then, whatever remains, however improbable, must be the truth. . ."

Write a paragraph or two illustrating how Dupin utilizes the above concept in his recovery of the purloined letter. Do your writing without looking back to the story for help. Then check yourself to see how much of your reading you remembered and understood.

2) Why were Dupin and Prefect G——— certain that the purloined letter had to be somewhere in Minister D———'s apartment?

3) Poe describes a particular kind of behavior by having his narrator speak of ". . . an identification of the reasoner's intellect with that of his opponent." What exactly did the narrator mean by this? Be sure you provide specific examples of this trait from the story itself.

RESEARCH ACTIVITIES

1) The French police or *Sûreté* figure prominently in the preceding stories. Write a research paper on the origins and history of this agency. Perhaps some of the papers could be read in class.

2) After what we said about "The Mystery of Marie Rogêt," some of you may find yourself curious about it. If so, the curious ones should organize themselves into a committee whose job it would be to research Poe's second Dupin story and report back to the class. In their report, committee members might consider the following questions:

A) Does "Marie Rogêt" compare favorably or unfavorably with the other Dupin stories and why?

---

*In Greek mythology, Atrée (Atreus) and Thyeste (Thyestes) were brothers who hated each other. In English slang, Dupin's French means, "What's sauce for the goose is sauce for the gander."

B) Give the history of the original Mary Rogers murder case. Do you think Poe was correct in his deductions?

Yes, Poe Dunit. But Who Was This Edgar Allan Poe?

"Poe invented the detective story in order that he might not go mad," wrote Joseph Wood Crutch, a literary critic.[5]

He is "a ghost haunting America," stated Philip Van Doren Stern, a biographer.[6]

As you may "deduce" from these comments, the life of Edgar Allan Poe (1809–1849) was a tragic one. In a sense, he was born into tragedy, for his actor father, a reckless ne'er-do-well and an alcoholic, deserted the family while his son was still an infant. Shortly afterwards, Poe's actress mother, Elizabeth Arnold Hopkins, became ill during an engagement in Richmond and died.

An orphan now, Poe was taken into the home of a wealthy merchant, John Allan, and given his name. As the child grew up in pre-Civil War Richmond, he was given every reason to believe that he would someday become his foster-father's heir. At the age of seventeen, he began to suspect otherwise.

John Allan sent him to the University of Virginia but then started treating him in miserly fashion, giving him barely enough money to live on. To acquire additional funds, Edgar took to gambling. Instead of making money, he lost. To recoup, he began drinking but soon found that alcohol had a deleterious effect on him. Hostility flared between Edgar and his foster-father, particularly when John Allan, hearing of his son's debts and escapades, removed him from the university. The tension between them deepened until finally, Edgar left home.

He joined the Army and spent four years there but, after an honorable discharge, found himself again without funds; again, John Allan refused to help him. But his foster-father did use his influence to obtain an appointment for Poe at West Point. The military discipline there was too much for him. He consistently "cut" parades, classes, and chapel until finally he was charged with neglect of duty, court-martialled, and summarily dismissed. When John Allan died in the year 1834, his will completely ignored his adopted son.

Poe was on his own now.

Having previously published a pamphlet of poetry, the young man decided he would try earning his living as a professional writer. He obtained a job as an assistant editor in Richmond. There he lived alone, made desperately unhappy by a deep depression that drove him again and again to drink and to thoughts of suicide. His state of unhappiness seemed to end when, in the year 1835, he decided to marry Virginia Clemm, then thirteen years old. The young wife and her mother joined Poe in Richmond where they set up housekeeping in a boarding house on his meager salary of fifteen dollars a week.

His job didn't last long. Other temporary positions followed. Next, the family moved to Philadelphia, where he had obtained a post with *Graham's Magazine.* It was in this periodical that "The Murders in the Rue Morgue" first appeared. For probably the first time that he could remember, happiness had entered the life of Edgar Allan Poe.

It left abruptly in January of 1842.

Virginia ruptured a blood vessel and it appeared that she would die. Poe wrote of this period, "... I became insane with long intervals of horrible insanity. During these fits of absolute unconsciousness I drank, God only knows how often or how much."[7]

Yet, during this time of terrible torment, he managed somehow to turn out some of his finest tales, including "The Mystery of Marie Roget" and "The Gold Bug".

His writings brought him some fame—but he remained as poor as ever. He moved to New York, became editor and publisher of a new newspaper, *The Broadway Journal,* but the Poe jinx would not go away; the paper was forced into bankruptcy and he was back where he had started. In the summer of 1846, he moved his dying wife and himself into a cottage at Fordham; there, he, too, became ill and now he could not hold any kind of job.

Virginia Clemm Poe died on January 30, 1847. Her death introduced the most tragic period of Poe's life. Amidst bouts of drinking, drug-taking, and several suicide attempts, he still continued his writing, consistently turning out more stories, essays, and poems. Two years passed in this fashion.

In September 1849, he took a boat from Richmond to Baltimore with New York as his ultimate destination. He had intended to settle some business affairs and to prepare for a new marriage to an old childhood sweetheart, but the wedding was never to take place.

On a Baltimore city street, Poe was found one day, unconscious, dirty, and very near death. He was taken to Washington College Hospital where, for four days, he struggled to remain alive. On the morning of October 7, 1849, he passed away.

Poe's nightmarish life may well explain the eerie quality of his tales of horror. But the detective stories dealt with reason and logic and their writing was probably a very therapeutic experience for him—even though the activity did not succeed in ridding him of his anguish. We can regret the unhappiness of his life but we can never regret the creation of the literary material itself. Whatever his motivations for bringing them into being, the fiction and poetry of Edgar Allan Poe have provided untold excitement and entertainment to countless readers for over a hundred years. And now you, too, are sharing in the experience ...

A RESEARCH ACTIVITY

Have several class members look up an essay by Edgar Allan Poe entitled "Review of 'Twice Told Tales,' " where he explains his theory for the writing of a short story. Poe called it the formula of "the single effect."

These students can then explain the "single effect" theory to the rest of the class. Perhaps this will lead to a general discussion using the Poe stories of this chapter as examples.

XZ4 *#5Z W4V*(4 YOQ4&45Q4R YO 54V&4Q $&YQYOU

"Uh, oh! You goofed, Mr. Editor. Forgot to proofread your own textbook."

Sorry. The book *was* proofread, and the above *is* legitimate writing.

But it is the kind of writing that is used when one wishes to conceal communication from everyone except the receiver of the message. Intelligence agencies, police, and diplomats use it all the time. The name used for this secret language is *cryptography.*

The above cryptogram or cipher is based upon a simple substitution principle. We simply represented the original letters of the heading by other letters, figures, and symbols. Here is the cipher alphabet that we created and used:

a—*	e—4	i—y	m—(	q—8	u—g	y—%
b—w	f—m	j—¢	n—o	r—&	v—@	z—t
c—v	g—u	k—a	o—z	s—5	w—$	
d—r	h—p	l—#	p—x	t—q	x—2	

Now go ahead and decipher our message. (On a separate sheet of paper, of course.)

Look at the footnote below* to see if you've worked it out correctly.

So, you see, not only did we proofread carefully but we checked and doublechecked the writing of our secret message. Had we not done so, you would not have had a proper cryptogram to decipher.

Yes, Poe was very much interested in cryptography. In 1841, he published a series of articles on the subject in *Graham's Magazine* in which he

---

*"Poe also became interested in secret writing."

traced secret writing back to the days of Ancient Sparta and possibly even before. He stated that it is fairly easy "... to invent a method of secret writing which (baffles) investigation,"[8] but he also asserted that "... human ingenuity cannot concoct a cipher which human ingenuity cannot solve."[9]

Imaginative author that he was, Poe then set about dramatizing this assertion in a short story entitled "The Gold Bug." Here, the main character, William Legrand, is confronted with an extremely complicated cryptogram. We'll show it to you beforehand:

"53‡‡†305))6*;4826)4‡.)4‡);806*;48†8¶60))85;1‡(;:‡*8†83(88)5*†;46
(;88*96*?;8)*‡(;485);5*†2:*‡(;4956*2 (5*—4) 8¶8*;4069285);)6†8)4‡‡;1
(‡9;48081;8:8‡1;48†85;4)485†528806*81(‡9;48; (88;4(‡?34;48)
4‡;161;:188;‡?;"

Remember, you solved our cryptogram because we gave you the key. Legrand worked without such a key. This may seem impossible to you but Poe, through Legrand, will prove to you it can be done. "The Gold Bug" became one of his most popular stories. As you read it, keep a copy of the above secret message by your side and work along with the protagonist as he unravels its contents.

Not only will you have fun but you'll find yourself learning something about cryptography—*and the English language.*

The Gold Bug

What ho! this fellow is dancing mad!
He hath been bitten by the Tarantula.

—All in the Wrong

Many years ago, I contracted an intimacy with a Mr. William Legrand. He was of an ancient Huguenot family, and had once been wealthy; but a series of misfortunes had reduced him to want. To avoid the mortification consequent upon his disasters, he left New Orleans, the city of his forefathers, and took up his residence at Sullivan's Island, near Charleston, South Carolina.

This island is a very singular one. It consists of little else than the sea sand, and is about three miles long. Its breadth at no point exceeds a quarter of a mile. It is separated from the mainland by a scarcely perceptible creek, oozing its way through a wilderness of reeds and slime, a favorite resort of the marsh-hen. The vegetation, as might be supposed, is scant, or at least dwarfish. No trees of any magnitude are to be seen. Near the western extremity, where Fort Moultrie stands, and where are some miserable frame buildings, tenanted, during summer, by the fugitives from Charleston dust and fever, may be found, indeed, the bristly palmetto; but the whole island, with the exception of this western point, and a line of hard, white beach on the sea-coast, is covered with a dense undergrowth of the sweet myrtle so much prized by the horticulturists of England. The shrub here often attains the height of fifteen or twenty feet, and forms an almost impenetrable coppice, burthening the air with its fragrance.

In the inmost recesses of this coppice, not far from the eastern or more remote end of the island, Legrand had built himself a small hut, which he occupied when I first, by mere accident, made his acquaintance. This soon ripened into friendship—for there was much in the recluse to excite interest and esteem. I found him well educated, with unusual powers of mind, but infected with misanthropy, and subject to perverse moods of alternate enthusiasm and melancholy. He had with him many books, but rarely employed them. His chief amusements were gunning and fishing, or sauntering along the beach and through the myrtles, in quest of shells or entomological specimens—his collection of the latter might have been envied by a Swammerdamm. In these excursions he was usually accompanied by an old Negro, called Jupiter, who had been manumitted before the reverses of the family, but who could be induced, neither by threats nor by promises, to abandon what he considered his right of attendance upon the footsteps of his young "Massa Will." It is not improbable that the relatives of Legrand, conceiving him to be somewhat unsettled in intellect, had contrived to instil this obstinacy into Jupiter, with a view to the supervision and guardianship of the wanderer.

The winters in the latitude of Sullivan's Island are seldom very severe, and in the fall of the year it is a rare event indeed when a fire is considered necessary. About the middle of October, 18——, there occurred, however, a day of remarkable chilliness. Just before sunset I scrambled my way through the evergreens to the hut of my friend, whom I had not visited for several weeks—my residence being, at that time, in Charleston, a distance of nine miles from the island, while the facilities of passage and re-passage were very far behind those of the present day. Upon reaching the hut I rapped, as was my custom, and getting no reply, sought for the key where I knew it was secreted, unlocked the door, and went in. A fine fire was blazing upon the hearth. It was a novelty, and by no means an ungrateful one. I threw off an overcoat, took an arm-chair by the crackling logs, and awaited patiently the arrival of my hosts.

Soon after dark they arrived, and gave me a most cordial welcome. Jupiter, grinning from ear to ear, bustled about to prepare some marsh-hens for supper. Legrand was in one of his fits—how else shall I term them?—of enthusiasm. He had found an unknown bivalve, forming a new genus, and, more than this, he had hunted down and secured, with Jupiter's assistance, a *scarabaeus** which he believed to be totally new, but in respect to which he wished to have my opinion on the morrow.

"And why not to-night?" I asked, rubbing my hands over the blaze, and wishing the whole tribe of *scarabaei* at the devil.

"Ah, if I had only known you were here!" said Legrand, "but it's so long since I saw you; and how could I foresee that you would pay me a visit this very night of all others? As I was coming home I met Lieutenant G——, from the fort, and, very foolishly, I lent him the bug; so it will be impossible for you to see it until the morning. Stay here to-night, and I will send Jup down for it at sunrise. It is the loveliest thing in creation!"

"What?—sunrise?"

"Nonsense! no!—the bug. It is of a brilliant gold color—about the size of a large hickory-nut—with two jet black spots near one extremity of the back, and another, somewhat longer, at the other. The *antennae* are—"

"They ain't *no* tin in him, Massa Will, I keep a tellin' on you," here interrupted Jupiter;† "the bug is a gold bug, solid, every bit of him, inside and all, 'cept his wing—never feel so heavy a bug in my life."

"Well, suppose it is, Jup," replied Legrand, somewhat more earnestly, it seemed to me, than the case demanded; "is that any reason for your letting the birds burn? The color"—here he turned to me—"is really almost enough to warrant Jupiter's idea. You never saw a more brilliant metallic lustre than the scales emit—but of this you cannot judge till to-morrow. In the meantime I can give you some idea of the shape." Saying this, he seated himself at a small table, on which were a pen and ink, but no paper. He looked for some in a drawer, but found none.

"Never mind," he said at length, "this will answer"; and he drew from his waistcoat pocket a scrap of what I took to be very dirty foolscap, and made upon it a rough drawing with the pen. While he did this, I retained my seat by the fire, for I was still chilly. When the design was complete, he handed it to me without rising. As I received it, a loud growl was heard, succeeded by a scratching at the door. Jupiter opened it, and a large Newfoundland, belonging to Legrand, rushed in, leaped upon my shoulders, and loaded me with caresses; for I had shown him much attention during previous visits. When his gambols were over, I looked at the paper, and, to speak the truth, found myself not a little puzzled at what my friend had depicted.

"Well!" I said, after contemplating it for some minutes, "this *is* a strange *scarabaeus,* I must confess; new to me; never saw any thing like it before—unless it was a skull, or a death's-head, which it more nearly resembles than any thing else that has come under *my* observation."

"A death's-head!" echoed Legrand. "Oh—yes—well, it has something of that appearance upon paper, no doubt. The two upper black spots look like

---

*A large black beetle, revered in ancient Egypt and depicted in charms (Latin)

†Throughout this story, Jupiter's dialogue has been edited from the original version, for the convenience of the contemporary reader.

eyes, eh? and the longer one at the bottom like a mouth—and then the shape of the whole is oval."

"Perhaps so," said I; "but, Legrand, I fear you are no artist. I must wait until I see the beetle itself, if I am to form any idea of its personal appearance."

"Well, I don't know," said he, a little nettled, "I draw tolerably—*should* do it at least—have had good masters, and flatter myself that I am not quite a blockhead."

"But, my dear fellow, you are joking then," said I, "this is a very passable *skull*—indeed, I may say that it is a very *excellent* skull, according to the vulgar notions about such specimens of physiology—and your *scarabaeus* must be the queerest *scarabaeus* in the world if it resembles it. Why, we may get up a very thrilling bit of superstition upon this hint. I presume you will call the bug *scarabaeus caput hominis,* or something of that kind—there are many similar titles in the Natural Histories. But where are the *antennae* you spoke of?"

"The *antennae!*" said Legrand, who seemed to be getting unaccountably warm upon the subject; "I am sure you must see the *antennae.* I made them as distinct as they are in the original insect, and I presume that is sufficient."

"Well, well," I said, "perhaps you have—still I don't see them"; and I handed him the paper without additional remark, not wishing to ruffle his temper; but I was much surprised at the turn affairs had taken; his ill humor puzzled me—and, as for the drawing of the beetle, there were positively *no antennae* visible, and the whole *did* bear a very close resemblance to the ordinary cuts of a death's-head.

He received the paper very peevishly, and was about to crumple it, apparently to throw it in the fire, when a casual glance at the design seemed suddenly to rivet his attention. In an instant his face grew violently red—in another as excessively pale. For some minutes he continued to scrutinize the drawing minutely where he sat. At length he arose, took a candle from the table, and proceeded to seat himself upon a sea-chest in the farthest corner of the room. Here again he made an anxious examination of the paper; turning it in all directions. He said nothing, however, and his conduct greatly astonished me; yet I thought it prudent not to exacerbate the growing moodiness of his temper by any comment. Presently he took from his coat-pocket a wallet, placed the paper carefully in it, and deposited both in a writing-desk, which he locked. He now grew more composed in his demeanor; but his original air of enthusiasm had quite disappeared. Yet he seemed not so much sulky as abstracted. As the evening wore away he became more and more absorbed in revery, from which no sallies of mine could arouse him. It had been my intention to pass the night at the hut, as I had frequently done before, but, seeing my host in this mood, I deemed it proper to take leave. He did not press me to remain, but, as I departed, he shook my hand with even more than his usual cordiality.

It was about a month after this (and during the interval I had seen nothing of Legrand) when I received a visit, at Charleston, from his man, Jupiter. I had never seen the good old Negro look so dispirited, and I feared that some serious disaster had befallen my friend.

"Well, Jup," said I, "what is the matter now?—how is your master?"

"Why, to speak the truth, massa, him not so very well as might be."

"Not well! I am truly sorry to hear it. What does he complain of?"

"There! that's it!—him never 'plain of nothin'—but him very sick for all that."

"*Very* sick, Jupiter!—why didn't you say so at once? Is he confined to bed?"

"No, that he ain't!—he ain't 'fin'd nowhere—that's just where the shoe pinch—my mind is got to be very heavy 'bout poor Massa Will."

"Jupiter, I should like to understand what it is you are talking about. You say your master is sick. Hasn't he told you what ails him?"

"Why, massa, 'tain't worth while for to get mad about the matter—Massa Will say nothin' at all ain't the matter with him—but then what makes him go about lookin' this here way, with his head down and his shoulders up, and as white as a ghost? And then he keeps a syphon all the time—"

"Keeps a what, Jupiter?"

"Keeps a syphon with the figures on the slate—the queerest figures I ever did see. Ise gettin' to be scared, I tell you. Have for to keep mighty tight eye 'pon his maneuvers. The other day he give me slip 'fore sun up and was gone the whole of the blessed day. I had a big stick ready cut for to give him deuced good beatin' when he did come—but Ise such a fool that I hadn't the heart after all—he looked so very poorly."

"Eh?—what?—ah yes!—upon the whole I think you had better not be too severe with the poor fellow—don't flog him, Jupiter—he can't very well stand it—but can you form no idea of what has occasioned this illness, or rather this change of conduct? Has any thing unpleasant happened since I saw you?"

"No, massa, they ain't been nothin' unpleasant *since* then—'twas 'fore then I'm 'fraid—was the very day you was there."

"How? what do you mean?"

"Why, massa, I mean the bug—there now."

"The what?"

"The bug—I'm very certain that Massa Will been bit somewhere 'bout the head by that gold bug."

"And what cause have you, Jupiter, for such a supposition?"

"Claws enough, massa, and mouth, too. I never did see such a deuced bug—he kick and bite every thing what come near him. Massa Will catch him first, but had for to let him go again mighty quick, I tell you—then was the time he must ha' got the bite. I didn't like the look of the bug mouth, myself, nohow, so I wouldn't take hold of him with my finger, but I catch him with a piece of paper that I found. I wrap him up in the paper and stuff a piece of it in his mouth—that was the way."

"And you think, then, that your master was really bitten by the beetle, and that the bite made him sick?"

"I don't think nothin' about it—I knows it. What make him dream 'bout the gold bug so much, if 'tain't 'cause he bit by the gold bug? Ise heard 'bout them gold bugs 'fore this."

"But how do you know he dreams about gold?"

"How I know? why, 'cause he talks about it in his sleep—that's how I knows."

"Well, Jup, perhaps you are right; but to what fortunate circumstance am I to attribute the honor of a visit from you today?"

"What's the matter, massa?"

"Did you bring any message from Mr. Legrand?"

"No, massa, I bring this here 'pistle"; and here Jupiter handed me a note which ran thus:

"MY DEAR———

"Why have I not seen you for so long a time? I hope you have not been so foolish as to take offence at any little *brusquerie** of mine; but no, that is improbable.

"Since I saw you I have had great cause for anxiety. I have something to tell you, yet scarcely know how to tell it, or whether I should tell it at all.

"I have not been quite well for some days past; and poor old Jup annoys me, almost beyond endurance, by his well-meant attentions. Would you believe it?—he had prepared a huge stick, the other day, with which to chastise me for giving him the slip, and spending the day, *solus,*† among the hills on the main land. I verily believe that my ill looks alone saved me a flogging.

"I have made no addition to my cabinet since we met.

"If you can, in any way, make it convenient, come over with Jupiter. *Do* come. I wish to see you *to-night,* upon business of importance. I assure you that it is of the *highest* importance.

"Ever yours,
"WILLIAM LEGRAND"

There was something in the tone of this note which gave me great uneasiness. Its whole style differed materially from that of Legrand. What could he be dreaming of? What new crotchet possessed his excitable brain? What "business of the highest importance" could *he* possibly have to transact? Jupiter's account of him boded no good. I dreaded lest the continued pressure of misfortune had, at length, fairly unsettled the reason of my friend. Without a moment's hesitation, therefore, I prepared to accompany the Negro.

Upon reaching the wharf, I noticed a scythe and three spades, all apparently new, lying in the botton of the boat in which we were to embark.

"What is the meaning of all this, Jup?" I inquired.

"This scythe, massa, and spade."

"Very true; but what are they doing here?"

"This the scythe and the spade that Massa Will insisted 'pon my buying

---

*Brusque or abrupt behavior (French)
†Alone (Latin)

for him in the town, and the devil's own lot of money I had to give for 'em."

"But what, in the name of all that is mysterious, is your 'Massa Will' going to do with scythes and spades?"

"That's more than *I* know, and devil take me if I don't believe 'tis more than he know too. But it's all come of the bug."

Finding that no satisfaction was to be obtained of Jupiter, whose whole intellect seemed to be absorbed by "the bug," I now stepped into the boat, and made sail. With a fair and strong breeze we soon ran into the little cove to the northward of Fort Moultrie, and a walk of some two miles brought us to the hut. It was about three in the afternoon when we arrived. Legrand had been waiting us in eager expectation. He grasped my hand with a nervous *empressement** which alarmed me and strengthened the suspicions already entertained. His countenance was pale even to ghastliness, and his deep-set eyes glared with unnatural luster. After some inquiries respecting his health, I asked him, not knowing what better to say, if he had yet obtained the *scarabaeus* from Lieutenant G——.

"Oh, yes," he replied, coloring violently, "I got it from him the next morning. Nothing should tempt me to part with that *scarabaeus.* Do you know what Jupiter is quite right about it?"

"In what way?" I asked, with a sad foreboding at heart.

"In supposing it to be a bug of *real gold.*" He said this with an air of profound seriousness, and I felt inexpressibly shocked.

"This bug is to make my fortune," he continued, with a triumphant smile; "to reinstate me in my family possessions. Is it any wonder, then, that I prize it? Since Fortune has thought fit to bestow it upon me, I have only to use it properly, and I shall arrive at the gold of which it is the index. Jupiter, bring me that *scarabaeus!*"

"What! the bug, massa? I'd rather not go for trouble that bug; you must get him for your own self." Hereupon Legrand arose, with a grave and stately air, and brought me the beetle from a glass case in which it was enclosed. It was a beautiful *scarabaeus,* and, at that time, unknown to naturalists—of course a great prize in a scientific point of view. There were two round black spots near one extremity of the back, and a long one near the other. The scales were exceedingly hard and glossy, with all the appearance of burnished gold. The weight of the insect was very remarkable, and, taking all things into consideration, I could hardly blame Jupiter for his opinion respecting it; but what to make of Legrand's concordance with that opinion, I could not, for the life of me, tell.

"I sent for you," said he, in a grandiloquent tone, when I had completed my examination of the beetle, "I sent for you that I might have your counsel and assistance in furthering the views of Fate and of the bug—"

"My dear Legrand," I cried, interrupting him, "you are certainly unwell, and had better use some little precautions. You shall go to bed, and I will remain with you a few days, until you get over this. You are feverish and—"

---

*display of cordiality (French)

"Feel my pulse," said he.

I felt it, and, to say the truth, found not the slightest indication of fever.

"But you may be ill and yet have no fever. Allow me this once to prescribe for you. In the first place go to bed. In the next—"

"You are mistaken," he interposed, "I am as well as I can expect to be under the excitement which I suffer. If you really wish me well, you will relieve this excitement."

"And how is this to be done?"

"Very easily. Jupiter and myself are going upon an expedition into the hills, upon the mainland, and, in this expedition, we shall need the aid of some person in whom we can confide. You are the only one we can trust. Whether we succeed or fail, the excitement which you now perceive in me will be equally allayed."

"I am anxious to oblige you in any way," I replied; "but do you mean to say that this infernal beetle has any connection with your expedition into the hills?"

"It has."

"Then, Legrand, I can become a party to no such absurd proceeding."

"I am sorry—very sorry—for we shall have to try it by ourselves."

"Try it by yourselves! The man is surely mad!—but stay!—how long do you propose to be absent?"

"Probably all night. We shall start immediately, and be back, at all events, by sunrise."

"And will you promise me, upon your honor, that when this freak of yours is over, and the bug business (good God!) settled to your satisfaction, you will then return home and follow my advice implicitly, as that of your physician?"

"Yes; I promise; and now let us be off, for we have no time to lose."

With a heavy heart I accompanied my friend. We started about four o'clock—Legrand, Jupiter, the dog, and myself. Jupiter had with him the scythe and spades—the whole of which he insisted upon carrying—more through fear, it seemed to me, of trusting either of the implements within reach of his master, than from any excess of industry or complaisance. His demeanor was dogged in the extreme, and "that deuced bug" were the sole words which escaped his lips during the journey. For my own part, I had charge of a couple of dark lanterns, while Legrand contented himself with the *scarabaeus,* which he carried attached to the end of a bit of whip-cord; twirling it to and fro, with the air of a conjuror, as he went. When I observed this last, plain evidence of my friend's aberration of mind, I could scarcely refrain from tears. I thought it best, however, to humor his fancy, at least for the present, or until I could adopt some more energetic measures with a chance of success. In the meantime, I endeavored, but all in vain, to sound him in regard to the object of the expedition. Having succeeded in inducing me to accompany him, he seemed unwilling to hold conversation upon any topic of minor importance, and to all my questions vouchsafed no other reply than "we shall see!"

We crossed the creek at the head of the island by means of a skiff, and, ascending the high grounds on the shore of the main land, proceeded in a northwesterly direction, through a tract of country excessively wild and desolate, where no trace of a human footstep was to be seen. Legrand led the way with decision; pausing only for an instant, here and there, to consult what appeared to be certain landmarks of his own contrivance upon a former occasion.

In this manner we journeyed for about two hours, and the sun was just setting when we entered a region infinitely more dreary than any yet seen. It was a species of table-land, near the summit of an almost inaccessible hill, densely wooded from base to pinnacle, and interspersed with huge crags that appeared to lie loosely upon the soil, and in many cases were prevented from precipitating themselves into the valleys below, merely by the support of the trees against which they reclined. Deep ravines, in various directions, gave an air of still sterner solemnity to the scene.

The natural platform to which we had clambered was thickly overgrown with brambles, through which we soon discovered that it would have been impossible to force our way but for the scythe; and Jupiter, by direction of his master, proceeded to clear for us a path to the foot of an enormously tall tulip-tree, which stood, with some eight or ten oaks, upon the level, and far surpassed them all, and all other trees which I had then ever seen, in the beauty of its foliage and form, in the wide spread of its branches, and in the general majesty of its appearance. When we reached this tree, Legrand turned to Jupiter, and asked him if he thought he could climb it. The old man seemed a little staggered by the question, and for some moments made no reply. At length he approached the huge trunk, walked slowly around it, and examined it with minute attention. When he had completed his scrutiny, he merely said:

"Yes, massa, Jup climb any tree he ever see in his life."

"Then up with you as soon as possible, for it will soon be too dark to see what we are about?"

"How far mus' go up, massa?" inquired Jupiter.

"Get up the main trunk first, and then I will tell you which way to go—and here—stop! take this beetle with you."

"The bug, Massa Will!—the gold-bug!" cried the Negro, drawing back in dismay—"what for must tote the bug way up the tree?—d—n if I do!"

"If you are afraid, Jup, a great big Negro like you, to take hold of a harmless little dead beetle, why you can carry it up by this string—but, if you do not take it up with you in some way, I shall be under the necessity of breaking your head with this shovel."

"What's the matter now, massa?" said Jup, evidently shamed into compliance; "always want for to raise fuss with old Jupiter. Was only funnin' anyhow. *Me* 'fraid of the bug! what I care for the bug?" Here he took cautiously hold of the extreme end of the string, and, maintaining the insect as far from his person as circumstances would permit, prepared to ascend the tree.

In youth, the tulip-tree, or *Liriodendron Tulipiferum,* the most magnificent of American foresters, has a trunk peculiarly smooth, and often rises to a great height without lateral branches; but, in its riper age, the bark becomes gnarled and uneven, while many short limbs make their appearance on the stem. Thus the difficulty of ascension, in the present case, lay more in semblance than in reality. Embracing the huge cylinder, as closely as possible, with his arms and knees, seizing with his hands some projections, and resting his naked toes upon others, Jupiter, after one or two narrow escapes from falling, at length wriggled himself into the first great fork, and seemed to consider the whole business as virtually accomplished. The *risk* of the achievement was, in fact, now over, although the climber was some sixty or seventy feet from the ground.

"Which way mus' go now, Massa Will?" he asked.

"Keep up the largest branch—the one on this side," said Legrand. The Negro obeyed him promptly, and apparently with but little trouble; ascending higher and higher, until no glimpse of his squat figure could be obtained through the dense foliage which enveloped it. Presently his voice was heard in a sort of halloo.

"How much further to go?"

"How high up are you?" asked Legrand.

"Ever so far," replied the Negro; "can see the sky through the top of the tree."

"Never mind the sky, but attend to what I say. Look down the trunk and count the limbs below you on this side. How many limbs have you passed?"

"One, two, three, four, five—I done passed five big limbs, massa, 'pon this side."

"Then go one limb higher."

In a few minutes the voice was heard again, announcing that the seventh limb was attained.

"Now, Jup," cried Legrand, evidently much excited, "I want you to work your way out upon that limb as far as you can. If you see any thing strange let me know."

By this time what little doubt I might have entertained of my poor friend's insanity was put finally at rest. I had no alternative but to conclude him stricken with lunacy, and I became seriously anxious about getting him home. While I was pondering upon what was best to be done, Jupiter's voice was again heard.

"Most 'fraid for to venture 'pon this limb very far—'tis dead limb pretty much all the way."

"Did you say it was a *dead* limb, Jupiter?" cried Legrand in a quavering voice.

"Yes, massa, him dead as the door-nail—done up for certain—done departed this here life."

"What in the name of heaven shall I do?" asked Legrand, seemingly in the greatest distress.

"Do!" said I, glad of an opportunity to interpose a word, "why, come home and go to bed. Come now!—that's a fine fellow. It's getting late, and, besides, you remember your promise."

"Jupiter," cried he, without heeding me in the least, "do you hear me?"

"Yes, massa, hear you ever so plain."

"Try the wood well, then, with your knife, and see if you think it *very* rotten."

"Him rotten, massa, sure 'nough," replied the Negro in a few moments, "but not so very rotten as might be. Might venture out little way 'pon this limb by myself, that's true."

"By yourself!—what do you mean?"

"Why, I mean the bug. 'Tis *very* heavy bug. S'pose I drop him down, first, and then the limb won't break with just the weight of one black man."

"You infernal scoundrel!" cried Legrand, apparently much relieved, "what do you mean by telling me such nonsense as that? As sure as you drop that beetle I'll break your neck. Look here, Jupiter, do you hear me?"

"Yes, massa, needn't holler at poor Jup that style."

"Well! now listen!—if you will venture out on the limb as far as you think safe, and not let go the beetle, I'll make you a present of a silver dollar as soon as you get down."

"I'm goin', Massa Will—indeed I is," replied the Negro very promptly— "most out to the end now."

"Out to the end!" here fairly screamed Legrand; "do you say you are out to the end of that limb?"

"Soon be on the end, massa—o-o-o-o-oh! Lor-gol-amercy! what *is* this here 'pon the tree?"

"Well!" cried Legrand, highly delighted, "what is it?"

"Why tain't nothin' but a skull—somebody been left his head up the tree, and the crows gobbled every bit of the meat off."

"A skull, you say!—very well,—how is it fastened to the limb?—what holds it on?"

"Sure 'nough, massa; must look. Why this very curious circumstance, 'pon my word—there's a great big nail in the skull, what fastens it on to the tree."

"Well now, Jupiter, do exactly as I tell you—do you hear?"

"Yes, massa."

"Pay attention, then—find the left eye of the skull."

"Ho! ho! that's good! why they ain't no eye left at all."

"Curse your stupidity! do you know your right hand from your left?"

"Yes, I knows that—know all about that—'tis my left hand what I chops wood with."

"To be sure! you are left-handed; and your left eye is on the same side as your left hand. Now, I suppose, you can find the left eye of the skull, or the place where the left eye has been. Have you found it?"

Here was a long pause. At length the Negro asked:

"Is the left eye of the skull 'pon the same side as the left hand of the skull too?—'cause the skull ain't got not a bit of a hand at all—never mind! I got the left eye now—here's the left eye! what must do with it?"

"Let the beetle drop through it, as far as the string will reach—but be careful and not let go your hold of the string."

"All that done, Massa Will; mighty easy thing for to put the bug through the hole—look out for him there below!"

During this colloquy no portion of Jupiter's person could be seen; but the beetle, which he had suffered to descend, was now visible at the end of the string, and glistened, like a globe of burnished gold, in the last rays of the setting sun, some of which still faintly illumined the eminence upon which we stood. The *scarabaeus* hung quite clear of any branches, and, if allowed to fall, would have fallen at our feet. Legrand immediately took the scythe, and cleared with it a circular space, three or four yards in diameter, just beneath the insect, and, having accomplished this, ordered Jupiter to let go the string and come down from the tree.

Driving a peg, with great nicety, into the ground, at the precise spot where the beetle fell, my friend now produced from his pocket a tape measure. Fastening one end of this at that point of the trunk of the tree which was nearest the peg, he unrolled it till it reached the peg and thence further unrolled it, in the direction already established by the two points of the tree and the peg, for the distance of fifty feet—Jupiter clearing away the brambles with the scythe. At the spot thus attained a second peg was driven, and about this, as a centre, a rude circle, about four feet in diameter, described. Taking now a spade himself, and giving one to Jupiter and one to me, Legrand begged us to set about digging as quickly as possible.

To speak the truth, I had no especial relish for such amusement at any time, and, at that particular moment, would most willingly have declined it; for the night was coming on, and I felt much fatigued with the exercise already taken; but I saw no mode of escape, and was fearful of disturbing my poor friend's equanimity by a refusal. Could I have depended, indeed, upon Jupiter's aid, I would have had no hesitation in attempting to get the lunatic home by force; but I was too well assured of the old Negro's disposition, to hope that he would assist me, under any circumstances, in a personal contest with his master. I made no doubt that the latter had been infected with some of the innumerable Southern superstitions about money buried, and that his phantasy had received confirmation by the finding of the *scarabaeus,* or, perhaps, by Jupiter's obstinacy in maintaining it to be "a bug of real gold." A mind disposed to lunacy would readily be led away by such suggestions—especially if chiming in with favorite preconceived ideas—and then I called to mind the poor fellow's speech about the beetle's being "the index of his fortune." Upon the whole, I was sadly vexed and puzzled, but, at length, I concluded to make a virtue of necessity—to dig with a good will, and thus the sooner to convince the visionary, by ocular demonstration, of the fallacy of the opinions he entertained.

The lanterns having been lit, we all fell to work with a zeal worthy a more rational cause; and, as the glare fell upon our persons and implements, I could not help thinking how picturesque a group we composed, and how strange and suspicious our labors must have appeared to any interloper who, by chance, might have stumbled upon our whereabouts.

We dug very steadily for two hours. Little was said; and our chief embarrassment lay in the yelpings of the dog, who took exceeding interest in our proceedings. He, at length, became so obstreperous that we grew fearful of his giving the alarm to some stragglers in the vicinity,—or, rather, this was the apprehension of Legrand;—for myself, I should have rejoiced at any interruption which might have enabled me to get the wanderer home. The noise was, at length, very effectually silenced by Jupiter, who, getting out of the hole with a dogged air of deliberation, tied the brute's mouth up with one of his suspenders, and then returned, with a grave chuckle, to his task.

When the time mentioned had expired, we had reached a depth of five feet, and yet no signs of any treasure became manifest. A general pause ensued, and I began to hope that the farce was at an end. Legrand, however, although evidently much disconcerted, wiped his brow thoughtfully and recommenced. We had excavated the entire circle of four feet diameter, and now we slightly enlarged the limit, and went to the farther depth of two feet. Still nothing appeared. The gold-seeker, whom I sincerely pitied, at length clambered from the pit, with the bitterest disappointment imprinted upon every feature, and proceeded, slowly and reluctantly, to put on his coat, which he had thrown off at the beginning of his labor. In the meantime I made no remark. Jupiter, at a signal from his master, began to gather up his tools. This done, and the dog having been unmuzzled, we turned in profound silence toward home.

We had taken, perhaps, a dozen steps in this direction, when, with a loud oath, Legrand strode up to Jupiter, and seized him by the collar. The astonished Negro opened his eyes and mouth to the fullest extent, let fall the spades, and fell upon his knees.

"You scoundrel!" said Legrand, hissing out the syllables from between his clenched teeth—"you infernal black villain!—speak, I tell you!—answer me this instant, without prevarication!—which—which is your left eye?"

"Oh, my golly, Massa Will! ain't this here my left eye for certain?" roared the terrified Jupiter, placing his hand upon his *right* organ of vision, and holding it there with a desperate pertinacity, as if in immediate dread of his master's attempt at a gouge.

"I thought so!—I knew it! hurrah!" vociferated Legrand, letting the Negro go and executing a series of curvets and caracols, much to the astonishment of his valet, who, arising from his knees, looked, mutely, from his master to myself, and then from myself to his master.

"Come! we must go back," said the latter, "the game's not up yet"; and he again led the way to the tulip-tree.

"Jupiter," said he, when we reached its foot, "come here! was the skull nailed to the limb with the face outward, or with the face to the limb?"

"The face was out, massa, so that the crows could get at the eyes good, without any trouble."

"Well, then, was it this eye or that through which you dropped the beetle?"—here Legrand touched each of Jupiter's eyes.

" 'Twas this eye,—massa—the left eye—just as you tell me," and here it was his right eye that the Negro indicated.

"That will do—we must try it again."

Here my friend, about whose madness I now saw, or fancied that I saw, certain indications of method, removed the peg which marked the spot where the beetle fell, to a spot about three inches to the westward of its former position. Taking, now, the tape measure from the nearest point of the trunk to the peg, as before, and continuing the extension in a straight line to the distance of fifty feet, a spot was indicated, removed, by several yards, from the point at which we had been digging.

Around the new position a circle, somewhat larger than in the former instance, was now described, and we again set to work with the spade. I was dreadfully weary, but, scarcely understanding what had occasioned the change in my thoughts, I felt no longer any great aversion from the labor imposed. I had become most unaccountably interested—nay, even excited. Perhaps there was something, amid all the extravagant demeanor of Legrand—some air of forethought, or of deliberation, which impressed me. I dug eagerly, and now and then caught myself actually looking, with something that very much resembled expectation, for the fancied treasure, the vision of which had demented my unfortunate companion. At a period when such vagaries of thought most fully possessed me, and when we had been at work perhaps an hour and a half, we were again interrupted by the violent howlings of the dog. His uneasiness, in the first instance, had been, evidently, but the result of playfulness or caprice, but he now assumed a bitter and serious tone. Upon Jupiter's again attempting to muzzle him, he made furious resistance, and, leaping into the hole, tore up the mould frantically with his claws. In a few seconds he had uncovered a mass of human bones, forming two complete skeletons, intermingled with several buttons of metal, and what appeared to be the dust of decayed woollen. One or two strokes of a spade upturned the blade of a large Spanish knife, and, as we dug farther, three or four loose pieces of gold and silver coins came to light.

At sight of these the joy of Jupiter could scarcely be restrained, but the countenance of his master wore an air of extreme disappointment. He urged us, however, to continue our exertions, and the words were hardly uttered when I stumbled and fell forward, having caught the toe of my boot in a large ring of iron that lay half buried in the loose earth.

We now worked in earnest, and never did I pass ten minutes of more intense excitement. During this interval we had fairly unearthed an oblong chest of wood, which, from its perfect preservation and wonderful hardness, had plainly been subjected to some mineralizing process—perhaps that of the bichloride of mercury. This box was three feet and a half long, three feet broad, and two and a half feet deep. It was firmly secured by bands of wrought iron, riveted, and forming a kind of open trellis-work over the whole. On each side of the chest, near the top, were three rings of iron—six in all—by means of which a firm hold could be obtained by six persons. Our utmost united endeavors served only to disturb the coffer very slightly in its bed. We at once saw the impossibility of removing so great a weight. Luckily, the sole fastenings of the lid consisted of two sliding bolts. These we drew back—trembling and panting with anxiety. In an instant, a treasure of incalculable value lay gleaming before us. As the rays of the lanterns fell within the pit, there flashed upward a glow and a glare, from a confused heap of gold and of jewels, that absolutely dazzled our eyes.

I shall not pretend to describe the feelings with which I gazed. Amazement was, of course, predominant. Legrand appeared exhausted with excitement, and spoke very few words. Jupiter's countenance wore, for some minutes, as deadly a pallor as it is possible, in the nature of things, for any Negro's visage to assume. He seemed stupefied—thunderstricken. Presently he fell upon his knees in the pit, and burying his naked arms up to the elbows in gold, let them there remain, as if enjoying the luxury of a bath. At length, with a deep sigh, he exclaimed, as if in a soliloquy:

"And this all come of the gold-bug! the pretty gold-bug! the poor little gold-bug, what I bossed in that savage kind of style! Ain't you ashamed of yourself, Jupiter?—answer me that!"

It became necessary, at last, that I should arouse both master and valet to the expediency of removing the treasure. It was growing late, and it behooved us to make exertion, that we might get every thing housed before daylight. It was difficult to say what should be done, and much time was spent in deliberation—so confused were the ideas of all. We, finally, lightened the box by removing two thirds of its contents, when we were enabled, with some trouble, to raise it from the hole. The articles taken out were deposited among the brambles, and the dog left to guard them, with strict orders from Jupiter neither, upon any pretence, to stir from the spot, nor to open his mouth until our return. We then hurriedly made for home with the chest; reaching the hut in safety, but after excessive toil, at one o'clock in the morning. Worn out as we were, it was not in human nature to do more immediately. We rested until two, and had supper; starting for the hills immediately afterward, armed with three stout sacks, which, by good luck, were upon the premises. A little before four we arrived at the pit, divided the remainder of the booty, as equally as might be, among us, and, leaving the holes unfilled, again set out for the hut, at which, for the second time, we deposited our golden burthens, just as the first faint streaks of the dawn gleamed from over the tree-tops in the east.

We were now thoroughly broken down; but the intense excitement of the time denied us repose. After an unquiet slumber of some three or four hours' duration, we arose, as if by preconcert, to make examination of our treasure.

The chest had been full to the brim, and we spent the whole day, and the greater part of the next night, in a scrutiny of its contents. There had been nothing like order or arrangement. Every thing had been heaped in promiscuously. Having assorted all with care, we found ourselves possessed of even vaster wealth than we had at first supposed. In coin there was rather more than four hundred and fifty thousand dollars—estimating the value of the pieces, as accurately as we could, by the tables of the period. There was not a particle of silver. All was gold of antique date and of great variety—French, Spanish, and German money, with a few English guineas, and some counters, of which we had never seen specimens before. There were several very large and heavy coins, so worn that we could make nothing of their inscriptions. There was no American money. The value of the jewels we found more difficulty in estimating. There were diamonds—some of them exceedingly large and fine—a hundred and ten in all, and not one of them small; eighteen rubies of remarkable brilliancy;—three hundred and ten emeralds, all very beautiful; and twenty-one sapphires, with an opal. These stones had all been broken from their settings and thrown loose in the chest. The settings themselves, which we picked out from among the other gold, appeared to have been beaten up with hammers, as if to prevent identification. Besides all this, there was a vast quantity of solid gold ornaments: nearly two hundred massive finger- and ear-rings; rich chains—thirty of these, if I remember; eighty-three very large and heavy crucifixes; five gold censers of great value; a prodigious golden punch-bowl, ornamented with richly chased vine-leaves and Bacchanalian figures; with two sword-handles exquisitely embossed, and many other smaller articles which I cannot recollect. The weight of these valuables exceeded three hundred and fifty pounds avoirdupois; and in this estimate I have not included one hundred and ninety-seven superb gold watches; three of the number being worth each five hundred dollars, if one. Many of them were very old, and as timekeepers valueless; the works having suffered, more or less, from corrosion—but all were richly jewelled and in cases of great worth. We estimated the entire contents of the chest, that night, at a million and a half of dollars; and upon the subsequent disposal of the trinkets and jewels (a few being retained for our own use), it was found that we had greatly undervalued the treasure.

When, at length, we had concluded our examination, and the intense excitement of the time had, in some measure, subsided, Legrand, who saw that I was dying with impatience for a solution of this most extraordinary riddle, entered into a full detail of all the circumstances connected with it.

"You remember," said he, "the night when I handed you the rough sketch I had made of the *scarabaeus.* You recollect also, that I became quite vexed at you for insisting that my drawing resembled a death's-head. When you first made this assertion I thought you were jesting; but afterward I called to mind the peculiar spots on the back of the insect, and admitted to myself that your remark had some little foundation in fact. Still, the sneer at my graphic powers irritated me—for I am considered a good artist—and therefore, when you handed me the scrap of parchment, I was about to crumple it up and throw it angrily into the fire."

"The scrap of paper, you mean," said I.

"No; it had much of the appearance of paper, and at first I supposed it to be such, but when I came to draw upon it, I discovered it at once to be a piece of very thin parchment. It was quite dirty, you remember. Well, as I was in the very act of crumpling it up, my glance fell upon the sketch at which you had been looking, and you may imagine my astonishment when I perceived, in fact, the figure of a death's-head just where, it seemed to me, I had made the drawing of the beetle. For a moment I was too much amazed to think with accuracy. I knew that my design was very different in detail from this—although there was a certain similarity in general outline. Presently I took a candle, and seating myself at the other end of the room, proceeded to scrutinize the parchment more closely. Upon turning it over, I saw my own sketch upon the reverse, just as I had made it. My first idea, now, was mere surprise at the really remarkable similarity of outline—at the singular coincidence involved in the fact that, unknown to me, there should have been a skull upon the other side of the parchment, immediately beneath my figure of the *scarabaeus,* and that this skull, not only in outline, but in size, should so closely resemble my drawing. I say the singularity of this coincidence absolutely stupefied me for a time. This is the usual effect of such coincidences. The mind struggles to establish a connection—a sequence of cause and effect—and, being unable to do so, suffers a species of temporary paralysis. But, when I recovered from this stupor, there dawned upon me gradually a conviction which startled me even far more than the coincidence. I began distinctly, positively, to remember that there had been *no* drawing upon the parchment when I made my sketch of the *scarabaeus.* I became perfectly certain of this; for I recollected turning up first one side and then the other, in search of the cleanest spot. Had the skull been then there, of course I could not have failed to notice it. Here was indeed a mystery which I felt it impossible to explain; but, even at that early moment, there seemed to glimmer, faintly, within the most remote and secret chambers of my intellect, a glow-worm-like conception of that truth which last night's adventure brought to so magnificent a demonstration. I arose at once, and putting the parchment securely away, dismissed all further reflection until I should be alone.

"When you had gone, and when Jupiter was fast asleep, I betook myself to a more methodical investigation of the affair. In the first place I considered the manner in which the parchment had come into my possession. The spot where we discovered the *scarabaeus* was on the coast of the mainland, about a mile eastward of the island, and but a short distance above high-water mark. Upon my taking hold of it, it gave me a sharp bite, which caused me to let it drop. Jupiter, with his accustomed caution, before seizing the insect, which had flown toward him, looked about him for a leaf, or something of that nature, by which to take hold of it. It was at this moment that his eyes, and mine also, fell upon the scrap of parchment, which I then supposed to be paper. It was lying half buried in the sand, a corner sticking up. Near the spot where we found it, I observed the remnants of the hull of what appeared to have been a ship's long-boat. The wreck seemed to have been there for a very great while; for the resemblance to boat timbers could scarcely be traced.

"Well, Jupiter picked up the parchment, wrapped the beetle in it, and gave it to me. Soon afterward we turned to go home, and on the way met Lieutenant G———. I showed him the insect, and he begged me to let him take it to the fort. Upon my consenting, he thrust it forthwith into his waistcoat pocket, without the parchment in which it had been wrapped, and which I had continued to hold in my hand during his inspection. Perhaps he dreaded my changing my mind, and thought it best to make sure of the prize at once—you know how enthusiastic he is on all subjects connected with Natural History. At the same time, without being conscious of it, I must have deposited the parchment in my own pocket.

"You remember that when I went to the table, for the purpose of making a sketch of the beetle, I found no paper where it was usually kept. I looked in the drawer, and found none there. I searched my pockets, hoping to find an old letter, when my hand fell upon the parchment. I thus detail the precise mode in which it came into my possession; for the circumstances impressed me with peculiar force.

"No doubt you will think me fanciful—but I had already established a kind of *connection.* I had put together two links of a great chain. There was a boat lying upon the sea-coast, and not far from the boat was a parchment—*not a paper*—with a skull depicted upon it. You will, of course, ask 'where is the connection?' I reply that the skull, or death's-head is the well-known emblem of the pirate. The flag of the death's-head is hoisted in all engagements.

"I have said that the scrap was parchment, and not paper. Parchment is durable—almost imperishable. Matters of little moment are rarely consigned to parchment; since, for the mere ordinary purposes of drawing or writing, it is not nearly so well adapted as paper. This reflection suggested some meaning—some relevancy—in the death's-head. I did not fail to observe, also, the *form* of the parchment. Although one of its corners had been, by some accident, destroyed, it could be seen that the original form was oblong. It was just such a slip, indeed, as might have been chosen for a memorandum—for a record of something to be long remembered and carefully preserved."

"But," I interposed, "you say that the skull was *not* upon the parchment when you made the drawing of the beetle. How then do you trace any connection between the boat and the skull—since this latter, according to your own admission, must have been designed (God only knows how or by whom) at some period subsequent to your sketching the *scarabaeus?*"

"Ah, hereupon turns the whole mystery; although the secret, at this point, I had comparatively little difficulty in solving. My steps were sure, and could afford a single result. I reasoned, for example, thus: When I drew the *scarabaeus,* there was no skull apparent upon the parchment. When I had completed the drawing I gave it to you, and observed you narrowly until you returned it. *You,* therefore, did not design the skull, and no one else was present to do it. Then it was not done by human agency. And nevertheless it was done.

"At this stage of my reflections I endeavored to remember, and *did* remember, with entire distinctness, every incident which occurred about the period in question. The weather was chilly (oh, rare and happy accident!), and a fire was blazing upon the hearth. I was heated with exercise and sat near the table. You, however, had drawn a chair close to the chimney. Just as I placed the parchment in your hand, and as you were in the act of inspecting it, Wolf, the Newfoundland, entered, and leaped upon your shoulders. With your left hand you caressed him and kept him off, while your right, holding the parchment, was permitted to fall listlessly between your knees, and in close proximity to the fire. At one moment I thought the blaze had caught it, and was about to caution you, but, before I could speak, you had withdrawn it, and were engaged in its examination. When I considered all these particulars, I doubted not for a moment that *heat* had been the agent in bringing to light, upon the parchment, the skull which I saw designed upon it. You are well aware that chemical preparations exist, and have existed time out of mind, by means of which it is possible to write upon either paper or vellum, so that the characters shall become visible only when subjected to the action of fire. Zaffre, digested in *aqua regia*,* and diluted with four times its weight of water, is sometimes employed; a green tint results. The regulus of cobalt, dissolved in spirit of nitre, gives a red. These colors disappear at longer or shorter intervals after the material written upon cools, but again become apparent upon the re-application of heat.

"I now scrutinized the death's-head with care. Its outer edges—the edges of the drawing nearest the edge of the vellum—were far more *distinct* than the others. It was clear that the action of the caloric had been imperfect or unequal. I immediately kindled a fire, and subjected every portion of the parchment to a glowing heat. At first, the only effect was the strengthening of the faint lines in the skull; but, upon persevering in the experiment, there became visible, at the corner of the slip, diagonally opposite to the spot in which the death's-head was delineated, the figure of what I at first supposed to be a goat. A closer scrutiny, however, satisfied me that it was intended for a kid."

"Ha! ha!" said I, "to be sure I have no right to laugh at you—a million and a half of money is too serious a matter for mirth—but you are not about to establish a third link in your chain—you will not find any especial connection between your pirates and a goat—pirates, you know, have nothing to do with goats; they appertain to the farming interest."

"But I have just said that the figure was *not* that of a goat."

"Well, a kid then—pretty much the same thing."

"Pretty much, but not altogether," said Legrand. "You may have heard of one *Captain* Kidd. I at once looked upon the figure of the animal as a kind of punning or hieroglyphical signature. I say signature; because its position upon the vellum suggested this idea. The death's-head at the corner diagonally opposite, had, in the same manner, the air of a stamp, or seal. But I was sorely put out by the absence of all else—of the body to my imagined instrument—of the text for my context."

"I presume you expected to find a letter between the stamp and the signature."

"Something of that kind. The fact is, I felt irresistibly impressed with a presentiment of some vast good fortune impending. I can scarcely say why. Perhaps, after all, it was rather a desire than an actual belief;—but do you know that Jupiter's silly words, about the bug being of solid gold, had a remarkable effect upon my fancy? And then the series of accidents and coincidences—these were so *very* extraordinary. Do you observe how mere an accident it was that these events should have occurred upon the *sole* day of all the year in which it has been, or may be sufficiently cool for fire, and

---

Royal water is a mixture of certain acids (nitric and muriatic) which is used to melt metals, such as gold or platinum.

that without the fire, or without the intervention of the dog at the precise moment in which he appeared, I should never have become aware of the death's-head, and so never the possessor of the treasure?"

"But proceed—I am all impatience."

"Well; you have heard, of course, the many stories current—the thousand vague rumors afloat about money buried, somewhere upon the Atlantic coast, by Kidd and his associates. These rumors must have had some foundation in fact. And that the rumors have existed so long and so continuous, could have resulted, it appeared to me, only from the circumstance of the buried treasure still *remaining* entombed. Had Kidd concealed his plunder for a time, and afterward reclaimed it, the rumors would scarcely have reached us in their present unvarying form. You will observe that the stories told are all about money-seekers, not about money-finders. Had the pirate recovered his money, there the affair would have dropped. It seemed to me that some accident—say the loss of a memorandum indicating its locality— had deprived him of the means of recovering it, and that this accident had become known to his followers, who otherwise might never have heard that treasure had been concealed at all, and who, busying themselves in vain, because unguided, attempts to regain it, had given first birth, and then universal currency, to the reports which are now so common. Have you ever heard of any important treasure being unearthed along the coast?"

"Never."

"But that Kidd's accumulations were immense, is well known. I took it for granted, therefore, that the earth still held them; and you will scarcely be surprised when I tell you that I felt a hope, nearly amounting to certainty, that the parchment so strangely found involved a lost record of the place of deposit."

"But how did you proceed?"

"I held the vellum again to the fire, after increasing the heat, but nothing appeared. I now thought it possible that the coating of dirt might have something to do with the failure: so I carefully rinsed the parchment by pouring warm water over it, and, having done this, I placed it in a tin pan, with the skull downward, and put the pan upon a furnace of lighted charcoal. In a few minutes, the pan having become thoroughly heated, I removed the slip, and, to my inexpressible joy, found it spotted, in several places, with what appeared to be figures arranged in lines. Again I placed it in the pan, and suffered it to remain another minute. Upon taking it off, the whole was just as you see it now."

Here Legrand, having re-heated the parchment, submitted it to my inspection. The following characters were rudely traced, in a red tint, between the death's-head and the goat:

"53‡‡†305))6*;4826)4‡.)4‡);806*;48†8¶60))85;1‡(;:‡*8†83(88)5*†;46
(;88*96*?;8)*‡(;485);5*†2:*‡(;4956*2(5*—4)8¶8*;4069285);)6†8)
4‡‡;1(‡9;48081;8:8‡1;48†85;4)485†528806*81(‡9;48;(88;4(‡?34;48)
4‡;161;:188; ‡?;"

"But," said I, returning him the slip, "I am as much in the dark as ever. Were all the jewels of Golconda* awaiting me upon my solution of this enigma, I am quite sure that I should be unable to earn them."

"And yet," said Legrand, "the solution is by no means so difficult as you might be led to imagine from the first hasty inspection of the characters. These characters, as any one might readily guess, form a cipher—that is to say, they convey a meaning; but then from what is known of Kidd, I could not suppose him capable of constructing any of the more abstruse cryptographs. I made up my mind, at once, that this was of a simple species—such, however, as would appear, to the crude intellect of the sailor, absolutely insoluble without the key."

"And you really solved it?"

"Readily; I have solved others of an abstruseness ten thousand times greater. Circumstances, and a certain bias of mind, have led me to take interest in such riddles, and it may well be doubted whether human ingenuity can construct an enigma of the kind which human ingenuity may not, by proper application, resolve. In fact, having once established connected and legible characters, I scarcely gave a thought to the mere difficulty of developing their import.

"In the present case—indeed in all cases of secret writing—the first question regards the *language* of the cipher; for the principles of solution, so far, especially, as the more simple ciphers are concerned, depend upon, and are varied by, the genius of the particular idiom. In general, there is no alternative but experiment (directed by probabilities) of every tongue known to him who attempts the solution, until the true one be attained. But, with the cipher now before us all difficulty was removed by the signature. The pun upon the word 'Kidd' is appreciable in no other language than the English. But for this consideration I should have begun my attempts with the Spanish and French, as the tongues in which a secret of this kind would most naturally have been written by a pirate of the Spanish main. As it was, I assumed the cryptograph to be English.

"You observe there are no divisions between the words. Had there been divisions the task would have been comparatively easy. In such cases I should have commenced with a collation and analysis of the shorter words, and, had a word of a single letter occurred, as is most likely (*a* or *I*, for example), I should have considered the solution as assured. But there being no division, my first step was to ascertain the predominant letters, as well as the least frequent. Counting all, I constructed a table thus:

Of the character 8 there are 33.

;	"	26.
4	"	19.
‡)	"	16.
*	"	13.

---

*A ruined city in India, once a diamond-trading center

$$
\begin{array}{ccc}
5 & \text{``} & 12. \\
6 & \text{``} & 11. \\
\dagger 1 & \text{``} & 8. \\
0 & \text{``} & 6. \\
92 & \text{``} & 5. \\
:3 & \text{``} & 4. \\
? & \text{``} & 3. \\
\P & \text{``} & 2. \\
\text{—.} & \text{``} & 1. \\
\end{array}
$$

"Now, in English, the letter which most frequently occurs is *e*. Afterward, the succession runs thus: *a/o/i/d/h/n/r/s/t/u/y/c/f/g/l/m/w/b/k/ p/q/x/z*. *E* predominates so remarkably, that an individual sentence of any length is rarely seen in which it is not the prevailing character.

"Here, then, we have, in the very beginning, the groundwork for something more than a mere guess. The general use which may be made of the table is obvious—but, in this particular cipher, we shall only very partially require its aid. As our predominant character is 8, we will commence by assuming it as the *e* of the natural alphabet. To verify the supposition, let us observe if the 8 be seen often in couples—for *e* is doubled with great frequency in English—in such words, for example, as 'meet,' 'fleet,' 'speed,' 'seen,' 'been,' 'agree,' etc. In the present instance we see it doubled no less than five times, although the cryptograph is brief.

"Let us assume 8, then, as *e*. Now, of all *words* in the language, 'the' is most usual; let us see, therefore, whether there are not repetitions of any three characters, in the same order of colocation, the last of them being 8. If we discover repetitions of such letters, so arranged, they will most probably represent the word 'the.' Upon inspection, we find no less than seven such arrangements, the characters being ;48. We may, therefore, assume that ; represents *t*, 4 represents *h*, and 8 represents *e*—the last being now well confirmed. Thus a great step has been taken.

"But, having established a single word, we are enabled to establish a vastly important point; that is to say, several commencements and terminations of other words. Let us refer, for example, to the last instance but one, in which the combination, ;48 occurs—not far from the end of the cipher. We know that the ; immediately ensuing is the commencement of a word, and, of the six characters succeeding this 'the,' we are cognizant of no less than five. Let us set these characters down, thus, by the letters we know them to represent, leaving a space for the unknown—

t eeth.

"Here we are enabled, at once, to discard the '*th*,' as forming no portion of the word commencing with the first *t;* since, by experiment of the entire alphabet for a letter adapted to the vacancy, we perceive that no word can be formed of which this *th* can be a part. We are thus narrowed into

t ee,

and, going through the alphabet, if necessary, as before, we arrive at the word 'tree,' as the sole possible reading. We thus gain another letter, *r,* represented by (, with the words 'the tree' in juxtaposition.

"Looking beyond these words, for a short distance, we again see the combination ;48, and employ it by way of *termination* to what immediately precedes. We have thus this arrangement:

the tree ;4(‡?34 the,

or, substituting the natural letters, where known, it reads thus:

the tree thr‡?3h the.

"Now, if, in place of the unknown characters, we leave blank spaces, or substitute dots, we read thus:

the tree thr...h the,

when the word *'through'* makes itself evident at once. But this discovery gives us three new letters, *o, u,* and *g,* represented by ‡, ?, and 3.

"Looking now, narrowly, through the cipher for combinations of known characters, we find, not very far from the beginning, this arrangement,

83(88, or †egree,

which, plainly, is the conclusion of the word 'degree,' and gives us another letter, *d,* represented by †.

"Four letters beyond the word 'degree,' we perceive the combination

;46(;88.

"Translating the known characters, and representing the unknown by dots, as before, we read thus:

th.rtee,

an arrangement immediately suggestive of the word 'thirteen,' and again furnishing us with two new characters, *i* and *n,* represented by 6 and *.

"Referring, now, to the beginning of the cryptograph, we find the combination,

53‡‡†

"Translating as before, we obtain

good,

which assures us that the first letter is *A,* and that the first two words are 'A good.'

"It is now time that we arrange our key, as far as discovered, in a tabular form, to avoid confusion. It will stand thus:

5	represents	a
†	"	d
8	"	e
3	"	g
4	"	h
6	"	i
*	"	n
‡	"	o
(	"	r
;	"	t
?	"	u

"We have, therefore, no less than eleven of the most important letters represented, and it will be unnecessary to proceed with the details of the solution. I have said enough to convince you that ciphers of this nature are readily soluble, and to give you some insight into the *rationale* of their development. But be assured that the specimen before us appertains to the very simplest species of cryptograph. It now only remains to give you the full translation of the characters upon the parchment, as unriddled. Here it is:

" *'A good glass in the bishop's hostel in the devil's seat forty-one degrees and thirteen minutes northeast and by north main branch seventh limb east side shoot from the left eye of the death's-head a bee-line from the tree through the shot fifty feet out.'* "

"But," said I, "the enigma seems still in as bad a condition as ever. How is it possible to extort a meaning from all this jargon about 'devil's seat,' 'death's-heads,' and 'bishop's hostels'?"

"I confess," replied Legrand, "that the matter still wears a serious aspect, when regarded with a casual glance. My first endeavor was to divide the sentence into the natural division intended by the cryptographist."

"You mean, to punctuate it?"

"Something of that kind."

"But how was it possible to effect this?"

"I reflected that it had been a *point* with the writer to run his words together without division, so as to increase the difficulty of solution. Now, a not over-acute man, in pursuing such an object, would be nearly certain to overdo the matter. When, in the course of his composition, he arrived at a break in his subject which would naturally require a pause, or a point, he would be exceedingly apt to run his characters, at this place, more than usually close together. If you will observe the MS., in the present instance, you will easily detect five such cases of unusual crowding. Acting upon this hint, I made the division thus:

" *'A good glass in the bishop's hostel in the devil's seat—forty-one degrees and thirteen minutes—northeast and by north—main branch seventh limb east side—shoot from the left eye of the death's-head—a bee-line from the tree through the shot fifty feet out.'* "

"Even this division," said I, "leaves me still in the dark."

"It left me also in the dark," replied Legrand, "for a few days; during which I made diligent inquiry, in the neighborhood of Sullivan's Island, for any building which went by the name of the 'Bishop's Hotel'; for, of course, I dropped the obsolete word 'hostel.' Gaining no information on the subject, I was on the point of extending my sphere of search, and proceeding in a more systematic manner, when, one morning, it entered into my head, quite suddenly, that this 'Bishop's Hostel' might have some reference to an old family, of the name of Bessop, which, time out of mind, had held possession of an ancient manor-house, about four miles to the northward of the island. I accordingly went over to the plantation, and re-instituted my inquiries among the older Negroes of the place. At length one of the most aged of the women said that she had heard of such a place as *Bessop's Castle,* and thought that she could guide me to it, but that it was not a castle, nor a tavern, but a high rock.

"I offered to pay her well for her trouble, and, after some demur, she consented to accompany me to the spot. We found it without much difficulty, when, dismissing her, I proceeded to examine the place. The 'castle' consisted of an irregular assemblage of cliffs and rocks—one of the latter being quite remarkable for its height as well as for its insulated and artificial appearance. I clambered to its apex, and then felt much at a loss as to what should be next done.

"While I was busied in reflection, my eyes fell upon a narrow ledge in the eastern face of the rock, perhaps a yard below the summit upon which I stood. This ledge projected about eighteen inches, and was not more than a foot wide, while a niche in the cliff just above it gave it a rude resemblance to one of the hollow-backed chairs used by our ancestors. I made no doubt that here was the 'devil's seat' alluded to in the MS., and now I seemed to grasp the full secret of the riddle.

"The 'good glass,' I knew, could have reference to nothing but a telescope; for the word 'glass' is rarely employed in any other sense by seamen. Now here, I at once saw, was a telescope to be used, and a definite point of view, *admitting no variation,* from which to use it. Nor did I hesitate to believe that the phrases, 'forty-one degrees and thirteen minutes,' and 'northeast and by north,' were intended as directions for the levelling of the glass. Greatly excited by these discoveries, I hurried home, procured a telescope, and returned to the rock.

"I let myself down to the ledge, and found that it was impossible to retain a seat upon it except in one particular position. This fact confirmed my preconceived idea. I proceeded to use the glass. Of course, the 'forty-one degrees and thirteen minutes' could allude to nothing but elevation above the visible horizon, since the horizontal direction was clearly indicated by the words, 'northeast and by north.' This latter direction I at once established by means of a pocket-compass; then, pointing the glass as nearly at an angle of forty-one degrees of elevation as I could do it by guess, I moved it cautiously up or down, until my attention was arrested by a circular rift or opening in the foliage of a large tree that overtopped its fellows in the distance. In the centre of this rift I perceived a white spot, but could not, at first, distinguish what it was. Adjusting the focus of the telescope, I again looked, and now made it out to be a human skull.

"Upon this discovery I was so sanguine as to consider the enigma solved; for the phrase 'main branch, seventh limb, east side,' could refer only to the position of the skull upon the tree, while 'shoot from the left eye of the death's-head' admitted, also, of but one interpretation, in regard to a search for buried treasure. I perceived that the design was to drop a bullet from the left eye of the skull, and that a bee-line, or, in other words, a straight line, drawn from the nearest point of the trunk through 'the shot' (or the spot where the bullet fell), and thence extended to a distance of fifty feet, would indicate a definite point—and beneath this point I thought it at least *possible* that a deposit of value lay concealed."

"All this," I said, "is exceedingly clear, and, although ingenious, still simple and explicit. When you left the 'Bishop's Hotel,' what then?"

"Why, having carefully taken the bearings of the tree, I turned homeward. The instant that I left 'the devil's seat,' however, the circular rift vanished; nor could I get a glimpse of it afterward, turn as I would. What seems to me· the chief ingenuity in this whole business, is the fact (for repeated experiment has convinced me it *is* a fact) that the circular opening in question is visible from no other attainable point of view than that afforded by the narrow ledge upon the face of the rock.

"In this expedition to the 'Bishop's Hotel' I had been attended by Jupiter, who had, no doubt, observed, for some weeks past, the abstraction of my demeanor, and took especial care not to leave me alone. But, on the next day, getting up very early, I contrived to give him the slip, and went into the hills in search of the tree. After much toil I found it. When I came home at night my valet proposed to give me a flogging. With the rest of the adventure I believe you are as well acquainted as myself."

"I suppose," said I, "you missed the spot, in the first attempt at digging, through Jupiter's stupidity in letting the bug fall through the right instead of through the left eye of the skull."

"Precisely. This mistake made a difference of about two inches and a half in the 'shot'—that is to say, in the position of the peg nearest the tree; and had the treasure been *beneath* the 'shot,' the error would have been of little moment; but 'the shot,' together with the nearest point of the tree, were merely two points for the establishment of a line of direction; of course the error, however trivial in the beginning, increased as we proceeded with the line, and by the time we had gone fifty feet threw us quite off the scent. But for my deep-seated impressions that treasure was here somewhere actually buried, we might have had all our labor in vain."

"But your grandiloquence, and your conduct in swinging the beetle—how excessively odd! I was sure you were mad. And why did you insist upon letting fall the bug, instead of a bullet, from the skull?"

"Why, to be frank, I felt somewhat annoyed by your evident suspicions touching my sanity, and so resolved to punish you quietly, in my own way, by a little bit of sober mystification. For this reason I swung the beetle, and for this reason I let it fall from the tree. An observation of yours about its great weight suggested the latter idea."

"Yes, I perceive; and now there is only one point which puzzles me. What are we to make of the skeletons found in the hole?"

"That is a question I am no more able to answer than yourself. There seems, however, only one plausible way of accounting for them—and yet it is dreadful to believe in such atrocity as my suggestion would imply. It is clear that Kidd—if Kidd indeed secreted this treasure, which I doubt not—it is clear that he must have had assistance in the labor. But this labor concluded, he may have thought it expedient to remove all participants in his secret. Perhaps a couple of blows with a mattock* were sufficient, while his coadjutors were busy in the pit; perhaps it required a dozen—who shall tell?"

ACTIVITIES

1) In his essay, "A Few Words on Secret Writing," Poe stated that "analytic" ability was necessary for the deciphering of cryptograms. Do you possess this "analytic" type of mind? The following is a very simple cipher involving the substitution principle. Using some of the techniques you've learned from William Legrand, try your hand at unravelling the following secret message. (Answers to this and the following cryptograms will be found at the end of the chapter.)

UIF EFUFDUJWF BSSFTUFE UIF DSJNJOBM BOE CSPVHIU IJN UP UIF QPMJDF TUBUJPO

2) Without the invention of writing, we could not have had cryptography. The basis for all writing is, of course, some kind of alphabet. Our alphabet also operates on the substitution principle, each letter or symbol representing a sound; thus, it is known as a *phonetic,* or *sound,* alphabet. When you create substitution ciphers in cryptography, you are merely substituting new symbols for the phonetic symbols of our alphabet.

---

*A digging tool that combines the qualities of an ax and a pick

The purpose of cryptography was not always the concealment of messages. Because written messages had to be delivered, ways had to be found to send them faster and over longer distances. Sometimes carrying the message on means of transportation like horses, camels, boats, and trains was just not fast enough. About 200 years ago, therefore, a system of visual signalling came into being, involving a code with a new alphabet. It was called *the semaphore system* and it enabled man to send messages as fast and far as the eye could see. Semaphores helped speed the sending of messages—but distance was still an obstructing factor.

Then, in 1844, came Samuel Morse with his telegraph. With the advent of electricity, it became possible to send messages at the speed of an electric current: 186,000 miles per second. To use his telegraph, Morse had to invent a new kind of substitution alphabet based upon the idea of turning an electric current on and off. He came up with an idea involving dots and dashes. A short flow of current heard on his telegraph sounder made two clicks—this was written as a *dot*. A current three times as long—more clicks—represented a *dash*. Thus, he created a new dot and dash alphabet that became known as the Morse Code.

Here it is:

A	•—	M	——	Y	—•——
B	—•••	N	—•	Z	——••
C	—•—•	O	———	1	•————
D	—••	P	•——•	2	••———
E	•	Q	——•—	3	•••——
F	••—•	R	•—•	4	••••—
G	——•	S	•••	5	•••••
H	••••	T	—	6	—••••
I	••	U	••—	7	——•••
J	•———	V	•••—	8	———••
K	—•—	W	•——	9	————•
L	•—••	X	—••—	0	—————

(International Morse Code)

A)   Encoding is the process of turning a readable or clear message into a code. *Decoding* is the opposite procedure, the solving or breaking of a code. Try encoding the following "clears" into Morse Code.

1) The life of Poe was a tragic one.
2) Doyle made the detective story popular.
3) Dupin was the first fictional detective.
4) Shorthand is another form of substitution cipher.
5) My Boy Scout troop uses the semaphore system.

B) A *cryptographer* is one who encodes while the *cryptanalyst* specializes in decoding. By decoding the following Morse Code messages, you'll get some idea of what the cryptanalyst's job is like.

1) ·— —··· ·—· ·— ···· ·— —— / ·—·· ·· —· —·· —·· ··· ·—·· —· / ·—·· ·· —·· · —·· / — ———
/ ·—· · ·— —·· / ·—·· ——· · ·—· / ··· — ——— ·—· ·· · ···· /

2) — ——— —·· ·— —·· / — ···· · / ·—· · ·— ·—·· — · ·· —·· · / ··· — ——— ·—· ——·
/ ·· ··· / ·—·· · ·—· —·· —·· / ·—·· ——— ·—· —·· ·· ·—·· —· ·—· /

3) ··· ·— —— ·— · ·—· / —— ——— ·—· ···· · / ·—· ——— —· / ·—— · ·— ·—·· — ···· /
·— —· —·· / ·—·· ·— —— · /

4) ···· · / —··· ·· · ·—·· —·· / ·· — / ·——— ————· ————·· ·——— /

5) ·—— ···· ·— — / ···· ·— — — ···· / —·· ——— —·· / ·—· ·—· ——— ··· —· —— ···· — /

3) Now that you're familiar with substitution ciphers, how about creating a substitution system of your own. When you're finished, write a message with your cipher which others can try to decode. If someone breaks your code, that person should be able to explain the system you devised. If not, then be prepared to do the explaining yourself.

A Literary Treasure Hunt

Edgar Allan Poe wrote many other tales—mystery, fantasy, and horror. If there are those of you who want to continue your reading of Poe, why not organize yourselves into a literary "scouting party" whose function it would be to read this material and make recommendations to others. In this way, you may induce your classmates to follow in your footsteps.

Here are some more Poe titles:

"The Telltale Heart"
"The Pit and the Pendulum"
"The Man of the Crowd"
"The Masque of the Red Death"
"The Fall of the House of Usher"
"The Black Cat"
"The Oval Portrait"
"The Premature Burial"

"MS Found in a Bottle"
"The Cask of Amontillado"

Answers to Activities (Pages 73–4)

1)   The detective arrested the criminal and brought him to the police station.

2A)   1) – .... . / .–.. .. .–.. . / .––– .––. / .––.. .––– . / .––– .– ... / .. / – .–.. .– .––– .. .––. / .–––
                      –. . /

        2) –... .––– .–––– .––. . / .–– .–– .– .––. . / .– .–... . / .––. .– . .– .–––. .––. .– .– .––.. . / .––. ... .– .––– .––. .––. .–.. / .–... .–––. .–.. .–... ... .–.. .––. .–.. /

        3) –... .–.. .–.. .–.. .– .. / .–––. .–... .–... / – .–... . / .–... .. .–... .. .– .– / .–... .. .–... .– .– .–... .–.. .–... .–.. / .–... .– . . .–.. .–... .– .– .–... . / .–... . /

        4) ... .––– .–... .– . .–.. .–... .– .– .–... / .. .... / .–... .. .––. .–––. . .–.. .... / .–... .––– .––– .–.. .– .– / .––– .... .––– . / .–– .– .... .– .– .–... .–.. .– . .–... .–.. .––. .–... / .–––. .–... . . .–... .–.. . .–.. . .–.. /

        5) –– .––– / .––. .–... .––– .–.. .... / .–... .– . .–... / – / .– .––. .– .–... .–... .––– / .––. .––– ... .–.. / – .–... . .
                      / .... .– .–– .–... .–––. .... .– .–... .–... / .... .––– .–.. .–.. .–... .– . . . / – .–... /

2B)   1) Abraham Lincoln liked to read Poe's stories.
        2) Today, the detective story is very popular.
        3) Samuel Morse won wealth and fame.
        4) He died in 1871.
        5) "What hath God wrought."

2.

A Tale of Two Doctors

Poe Invented It but Doyle Made the Detective Story Popular

American readers of the nineteenth century never really appreciated the "serious" work of Edgar Allan Poe—but they did like his detective stories. Poe, however, channeled his energies toward what he considered his "worthier" writing and so there were never too many of the stories involving true detection. After his death, other American authors did not pursue the new literary form and it appeared as if the "tale of ratiocination," as Poe had called it, would die soon after its birth.

But Poe's stories were reprinted in France and England and there, during the years 1860 to 1870, three writers did carry on the new tradition. They were Emile Gaboriau, Wilkie Collins, and Charles Dickens; though their books were well received, they did not yet elicit the voracious demand for the detective story that was to develop toward the end of the century. That demand was to be created, not by a professional writer, but by an English physician who started to write because of a lack of patients and too much time on his hands. As a matter of fact, it would be more accurate to say the demand was created by *two doctors.*

Their names were Arthur Conan Doyle and Joseph Bell.

They met at the Royal Infirmary of the University of Edinburgh in the year 1876. Doyle was a struggling medical student and his favorite instructor was Dr. Bell, the infirmary's consulting surgeon, who had a talent for diagnosis that was legendary. Seemingly at a glance, Bell could tell not only what a patient's ailment was, but also his trade or profession and even what part of the country or world he came from.

Bell liked Doyle and made him his outpatient clerk. Doyle's job was to obtain information from patients about their complaints before he ushered them into the student-filled lecture hall, where the patients were interviewed by Dr. Bell. Conan Doyle never failed to be astounded by Bell's accurate observations and analyses; most of the time they involved facts that were not communicated to Bell by the patients but that nonetheless coincided with the information already obtained by his outpatient clerk.

An example of Bell's uncanny ability took place on a day when Doyle interviewed a man with swollen limbs. Finished, he sent the patient into the lecture chamber.

Bell began his examination with a statement, not a question. "Well, my man, you've served in the Army, I see."

"Aye, sir," came the patient's reply. (Remember, Bell had not seen any of Doyle's notes.)

"Not long discharged?"

"No, sir."

"A Highland (Scottish) regiment?"

"Aye, sir."

"And you were stationed in Barbados?"

The patient nodded while Doyle and the other students watched in amazement. Then, their instructor explained his "deductions."

"You see, gentlemen, the man is respectful, yet he did not remove his hat. In the Army, they did not. But he has not been long discharged or he would have learned civilian ways. His speech tells us he is a Scot. His air of authority marks him as an officer, but other factors point to the noncommissioned rather than the regular officer—a sergeant or corporal, I should think. As to Barbados—that was simple, gentlemen. He complains of elephantiasis, a disease found in the West Indies, never in Britain."[1]

Later, after Doyle and Bell had become close friends, the teacher had the following remarks to make about diagnosis:

"Observation, my boy, is the basis of an intelligent diagnosis, and a diagnosis is, after all, a medical deduction based upon physical symptoms. One observes with the senses—the eyes, the ears, the fingertips, yes, even

SIR ARTHUR CONAN DOYLE
Reproduced with permission of the Henry E.
Huntington Library and Art Gallery.

"We were clear of the town and hastening down a country road." A Sidney Piaget illustration from the Sherlock Holmes tales, reproduced with permission of the Henry E. Huntington Library and Art Gallery.

the nose. Unfortunately, most people never learn to use their senses properly."[2]

Doyle never forgot Dr. Bell—nor his words.

Seven years later, on a gloomy day in autumn, his memories returned to him in full force.

He was A. Conan Doyle, M.D., now and he had put out his shingle in Southsea, a suburb of Portsmouth on the southern seacoast of England. He had been in private practice for about four years but patients had been few and far between, and this had given the struggling young physician a chance to do some writing. He had even sold a few short stories but his earnings from medicine and writing were extremely meager, barely enough to support himself and his new bride. He had even tried writing a novel but this project had been rejected by all publishers.

So he sat at his second-hand desk that day and pondered unhappily.

Gradually, the idea came to him and he grasped at it desperately. As a change of pace from his medical and economic problems, he had begun doing what Poe had done—working out solutions to stories of crime and murder that appeared in the newspapers. Also, he had read Poe's detective stories and been intrigued by Dupin. However, he felt that the American author had not really created a flesh-and-blood character. The image of Dr. Bell began to haunt him: Bell, thin and lean with a hawk-like nose and penetrating eyes, Bell, with his uncanny gift for observation and deduction.

His fantasy enthused him. Why not write a detective story like Poe's, a novel perhaps because it would sell for more money, and model his detective hero upon the personality of his old professor? The narrative itself could be a composite of all the newspaper crime stories he had attempted to solve.

Despondency forgotten, he took up pen and paper and eagerly set to work. What he created was the most fabulous character in the history of detective fiction—in all of literature, perhaps. The character's name was Sherlock Holmes and so real did he seem in Doyle's portrayal that millions of readers have come to believe that he had really existed.

In a few weeks, Arthur Conan Doyle had completed the first of the Sherlock Holmes stories. He called the work *A Study in Scarlet* and submitted it to the publishing houses, where it made the rounds for many months. Finally, it was published—and for the paltry sum of twenty-five pounds. At first, there were few sales—and then, the book caught on. An American magazine publisher asked for another Holmes tale. After the appearance of *The Sign of the Four,* the second in the series, readers "fell in love" with Sherlock Holmes and the detective story.

They demanded more of him.

And so will you when you read two chapters from that historic first novel.

Our setting is nineteenth-century London, with its foggy, gas-lit streets and shadowy hansom cabs rattling through the night. As Sherlock Holmes would say, "The game's afoot."

Read on . . .

A Study in Scarlet

Part 1

BEING A REPRINT FROM THE REMINISCENCES OF JOHN H. WATSON, M.D., LATE OF THE ARMY MEDICAL DEPARTMENT

Chapter 1

MR. SHERLOCK HOLMES

In the year 1878 I took my degree of Doctor of Medicine of the University of London, and proceeded to Netley to go through the course prescribed for surgeons in the Army. Having completed my studies there, I was duly attached to the Fifth Northumberland Fusiliers as assistant surgeon. The regiment was stationed in India at the time, and before I could join it, the second Afghan war had broken out. On landing at Bombay, I learned that my corps had advanced through the passes, and was already deep in the enemy's country. I followed, however, with many other officers who were in the same situation as myself, and succeeded in reaching Candahar in safety, where I found my regiment, and at once entered upon my new duties.

The campaign brought honours and promotion to many, but for me it had nothing but misfortune and disaster. I was removed from my brigade and attached to the Berkshires, with whom I served at the fatal battle of Maiwand. There I was struck on the shoulder by a Jezail bullet, which shattered the bone and grazed the subclavian artery. I should have fallen into the hands of the murderous Ghazis had it not been for the devotion and courage shown by Murray, my orderly, who threw me across a pack-horse, and succeeded in bringing me safely to the British lines.

Worn with pain, and weak from the prolonged hardships which I had undergone, I was removed, with a great train of wounded sufferers, to the base hospital at Peshawar. Here I rallied, and had already improved so far as to be able to walk about the wards, and even to bask a little upon the veranda, when I was struck down by enteric fever, that curse of our Indian possessions. For months my life was despaired of, and when at last I came to myself and became convalescent, I was so weak and emaciated that a medical board determined that not a day should be lost in sending me back to England. I was despatched, accordingly, in the troopship *Orontes,* and landed a month later on Portsmouth jetty, with my health irretrievably ruined, but with permission from a paternal government to spend the next nine months in attempting to improve it.

I had neither kith nor kin in England, and was therefore as free as air—or as free as an income of eleven shillings and sixpence a day will permit a man to be. Under such circumstances I naturally gravitated to London, that great cesspool into which all the loungers and idlers of the Empire are irresistibly drained. There I stayed for some time at a private hotel in the Strand, leading a comfortless, meaningless existence, and spending such money as I had, considerably more freely than I ought. So alarming did the state of my finances become, that I soon realized that I must either leave the metropolis and rusticate somewhere in the country, or that I must make a complete alteration in my style of living. Choosing the latter alternative, I began by making up my mind to leave the hotel, and take up my quarters in some less pretentious and less expensive domicile.

On the very day that I had come to this conclusion, I was standing at the Criterion Bar, when someone tapped me on the shoulder, and turning round I recognized young Stamford, who had been a dresser under me at Bart's. The sight of a friendly face in the great wilderness of London is a pleasant thing indeed to a lonely man. In old days Stamford had never been a particular crony of mine, but now I hailed him with enthusiasm, and he, in his turn, appeared to be delighted to see me. In the exuberance of my joy, I asked him to lunch with me at the Holborn, and we started off together in a hansom.

"Whatever have you been doing with yourself, Watson?" he asked in undisguised wonder, as we rattled through the crowded London streets. "You are as thin as a lath and as brown as a nut."

I gave him a short sketch of my adventures, and had hardly concluded it by the time that we reached our destination.

"Poor devil!" he said, commiseratingly, after he had listened to my misfortunes. "What are you up to now?"

"Looking for lodgings," I answered. "Trying to solve the problem as to whether it is possible to get comfortable rooms at a reasonable price."

"That's a strange thing," remarked my companion; "you are the second man to-day that has used that expression to me."

"And who was the first?" I asked.

"A fellow who is working at the chemical laboratory up at the hospital. He was bemoaning himself this morning because he could not get someone to go halves with him in some nice rooms which he had found, and which were too much for his purse."

"By Jove!" I cried; "if he really wants someone to share the rooms and the expense, I am the very man for him. I should prefer having a partner to being alone."

Young Stamford looked rather strangely at me over his wineglass. "You don't know Sherlock Holmes yet," he said; "perhaps you would not care for him as a constant companion."

"Why, what is there against him?"

"Oh, I didn't say there was anything against him. He is a little queer in his ideas—an enthusiast in some branches of science. As far as I know he is a decent fellow enough."

"A medical student, I suppose?" said I.

"No—I have no idea what he intends to go in for. I believe he is well up in anatomy, and he is a first-class chemist; but, as far as I know, he has never taken out any systematic medical classes. His studies are very desultory and eccentric, but he has amassed a lot of out-of-the-way knowledge which would astonish his professors."

"Did you never ask him what he was going in for?" I asked.

"No; he is not a man that it is easy to draw out, though he can be communicative enough when the fancy seizes him."

"I should like to meet him," I said. "If I am to lodge with anyone, I should prefer a man of studious and quiet habits. I am not strong enough yet to stand much noise or excitement. I had enough of both in Afghanistan to last me for the remainder of my natural existence. How could I meet this friend of yours?"

"He is sure to be at the laboratory," returned my companion. "He either avoids the place for weeks, or else he works there from morning till night. If you like, we will drive round together after luncheon."

"Certainly," I answered, and the conversation drifted away into other channels.

As we made our way to the hospital after leaving the Holborn, Stamford gave me a few more particulars about the gentleman whom I proposed to take as a fellow-lodger.

"You mustn't blame me if you don't get on with him," he said; "I know nothing more of him than I have learned from meeting him occasionally in the laboratory. You proposed this arrangement, so you must not hold me responsible."

"If we don't get on it will be easy to part company," I answered. "It seems to me, Stamford," I added, looking hard at my companion, "that you have some reason for washing your hands of the matter. Is this fellow's temper so formidable, or what is it? Don't be mealymouthed about it."

"It is not easy to express the inexpressible," he answered with a laugh. "Holmes is a little too scientific for my tastes—it approaches to cold-bloodedness. I could imagine his giving a friend a little pinch of the latest vegetable alkaloid, not out of malevolence, you understand, but simply out of a spirit of inquiry in order to have an accurate idea of the effects. To do him justice, I think that he would take it himself with the same readiness. He appears to have a passion for definite and exact knowledge."

"Very right too."

"Yes, but it may be pushed to excess. When it comes to beating the subjects in the dissecting-rooms with a stick, it is certainly taking rather a bizarre shape."

"Beating the subjects!"

"Yes, to verify how far bruises may be produced after death. I saw him at it with my own eyes."

"And yet you say he is not a medical student?"

"No. Heaven knows what the objects of his studies are. But here we are, and you must form your own impressions about him." As he spoke, we turned down a narrow lane and passed through a small side-door, which opened into a wing of the great hospital. It was familiar ground to me, and I needed no guiding as we ascended the bleak stone staircase and made our way down the long corridor with its vista of whitewashed wall and dun-coloured doors. Near the farther end a low arched passage branched away from it and led to the chemical laboratory.

This was a lofty chamber, lined and littered with countless bottles. Broad, low tables were scattered about, which bristled with retorts, test-tubes, and little Bunsen lamps, with their blue flickering flames. There was only one student in the room, who was bending over a distant table absorbed in his work. At the sound of our steps he glanced round and sprang to his feet with a cry of pleasure. "I've found it! I've found it," he shouted to my companion, running towards us with a test-tube in his hand. "I have found a re-agent which is precipitated by haemoglobin, and by nothing else." Had he discovered a gold mine, greater delight could not have shone upon his features.

"Dr. Watson, Mr. Sherlock Holmes," said Stamford, introducing us.

"How are you?" he said cordially, gripping my hand with a strength for which I should hardly have given him credit. "You have been in Afghanistan, I perceive."

"How on earth did you know that?" I asked in astonishment.

"Never mind," said he, chuckling to himself. "The question now is about haemoglobin. No doubt you see the significance of this discovery of mine?"

"It is interesting, chemically, no doubt," I answered, "but practically—"

"Why, man, it is the most practical medico-legal discovery for years. Don't you see that it gives us an infallible test for blood stains? Come over here now!" He seized me by the coat-sleeve in his eagerness, and drew me over to the table at which he had been working. "Let us have some fresh blood," he said, digging a long bodkin into his finger, and drawing off the resulting drop of blood in a chemical pipette. "Now, I add this small quantity of blood to a litre of water. You perceive that the resulting mixture has the appearance of pure water. The proportion of blood cannot be more than one in a million. I have no doubt, however, that we shall be able to obtain the characteristic reaction." As he spoke, he threw into the vessel a few white crystals, and then added some drops of a transparent fluid. In an instant the contents assumed a dull mahogany colour, and a brownish dust was precipitated to the bottom of the glass jar.

"Ha! ha!" he cried, clapping his hands, and looking as delighted as a child with a new toy. "What do you think of that?"

"It seems to be a very delicate test," I remarked.

"Beautiful! beautiful! The old guaiacum test was very clumsy and uncertain. So is the microscopic examination for blood corpuscles. The latter is valueless if the stains are a few hours old. Now, this appears to act as well whether the blood is old or new. Had this test been invented, there are hundreds of men now walking the earth who would long ago have paid the penalty of their crimes."

"Indeed!" I murmured.

"Criminal cases are continually hinging upon that one point. A man is suspected of a crime months perhaps after it has been committed. His linen or clothes are examined and brownish stains discovered upon them. Are they blood stains, or mud stains, or rust stains, or fruit stains, or what are they? That is a question which has puzzled many an expert, and why? Because there was no reliable test. Now we have the Sherlock Holmes's test, and there will no longer be any difficulty."

His eyes fairly glittered as he spoke, and he put his hand over his heart and bowed as if to some applauding crowd conjured up by his imagination.

"You are to be congratulated," I remarked, considerably surprised at his enthusiasm.

"There was the case of Von Bischoff at Frankfort last year. He would certainly have been hung had this test been in existence. Then there was Mason of Bradford, and the notorious Muller, and Lefevre of Montpellier, and Samson of New Orleans. I could name a score of cases in which it would have been decisive."

"You seem to be a walking calendar of crime," said Stamford with a laugh. "You might start a paper on those lines. Call it the 'Police News of the Past.' "

"Very interesting reading it might be made, too," remarked Sherlock Holmes, sticking a small piece of plaster over the prick on his finger. "I have to be careful," he continued, turning to me with a smile, "for I dabble with poisons a good deal." He held out his hand as he spoke, and I noticed that it was all mottled over with similar pieces of plaster, and discoloured with strong acids.

"We came here on business," said Stamford, sitting down on a high three-legged stool, and pushing another one in my direction with his foot. "My friend here wants to take diggings; and as you were complaining that you could get no one to go halves with you, I thought that I had better bring you together."

Sherlock Holmes seemed delighted at the idea of sharing his rooms with me. "I have my eye on a suite in Baker Street," he said, "which would suit us down to the ground. You don't mind the smell of strong tobacco, I hope?"

"I always smoke 'ship's' myself," I answered.

"That's good enough. I generally have chemicals about, and occasionally do experiments. Would that annoy you?"

"By no means."

"Let me see—what are my other shortcomings? I get in the dumps at times, and don't open my mouth for days on end. You must not think I am sulky when I do that. Just let me alone, and I'll soon be right. What have you to confess now? It's just as well for two fellows to know the worst of one another before they begin to live together."

I laughed at this cross-examination. "I keep a bull pup," I said, "and I object to rows because my nerves are shaken, and I get up at all sorts of ungodly hours, and I am extremely lazy. I have another set of vices when I'm well, but those are the principal ones at present."

"Do you include violin playing in your category of rows?" he asked, anxiously.

"It depends on the player," I answered. "A well-played violin is a treat for the gods—a badly played one——"

"Oh, that's all right," he cried, with a merry laugh. "I think we may consider the thing as settled—that is, if the rooms are agreeable to you."

"When shall we see them?"

"Call for me here at noon to-morrow, and we'll go together and settle everything," he answered.

"All right—noon exactly," said I, shaking his hand.

We left him working among his chemicals, and we walked together towards my hotel.

"By the way," I asked suddenly, stopping and turning upon Stamford, "how the deuce did he know that I had come from Afghanistan?"

My companion smiled an enigmatical smile. "That's just his little peculiarity," he said. "A good many people have wanted to know how he finds things out."

"Oh! a mystery is it?" I cried, rubbing my hands. "This is very piquant. I am much obliged to you for bringing us together. 'The proper study of mankind is man,' you know."

"You must study him, then," Stamford said, as he bade me good-bye. "You'll find him a knotty problem, though. I'll wager he learns more about you than you about him. Good-bye."

"Good-bye," I answered, and strolled on to my hotel, considerably interested in my new acquaintance.

Chapter 2

THE SCIENCE OF DEDUCTION

We met next day as he had arranged, and inspected the rooms at No. 221B, Baker Street, of which he had spoken at our meeting. They consisted of a couple of comfortable bedrooms and a single large airy sitting-room, cheerfully furnished, and illuminated by two broad windows. So desirable in every way were the apartments, and so moderate did the terms seem when divided between us, that the bargain was concluded upon the spot, and we at once entered into possession. That very evening I moved my things round from the hotel, and on the following morning Sherlock Holmes followed me with several boxes and portmanteaus. For a day or two we were busily employed in unpacking and laying out our property to the best advantage. That done, we gradually began to settle down and to accommodate ourselves to our new surroundings.

Holmes was certainly not a difficult man to live with. He was quiet in his ways, and his habits were regular. It was rare for him to be up after ten at night, and he had invariably breakfasted and gone out before I rose in the morning. Sometimes he spent his day at the chemical laboratory, sometimes in the dissecting-rooms, and occasionally in long walks, which appeared to take him into the lowest portions of the city. Nothing could exceed his energy when the working fit was upon him; but now and again a reaction would seize him, and for days on end he would lie upon the sofa in the sitting-room, hardly uttering a word or moving a muscle from morning to night. On these occasions I have noticed such a dreamy, vacant expression in his eyes, that I might have suspected him of being addicted to the use of some narcotic, had not the temperance and cleanliness of his whole life forbidden such a notion.

As the weeks went by, my interest in him and my curiosity as to his aims in life gradually deepened and increased. His very person and appearance were such as to strike the attention of the most casual observer. In height he was rather over six feet, and so excessively lean that he seemed to be considerably taller. His eyes were sharp and piercing, save during those intervals of torpor to which I have alluded; and his thin, hawk-like nose gave his whole expression an air of alertness and decision. His chin, too, had the prominence and squareness which mark the man of determination. His hands were invariably blotted with ink and stained with chemicals, yet he was possessed of extraordinary delicacy of touch, as I frequently had occasion to observe when I watched him manipulating his fragile philosophical instruments.

The reader may set me down as a hopeless busybody, when I confess how much this man stimulated my curiosity, and how often I endeavoured to break through the reticence which he showed on all that concerned himself. Before pronouncing judgment, however, be it remembered how objectless was my life, and how little there was to engage my attention. My health forbade me from venturing out unless the weather was exceptionally genial, and I had no friends who would call upon me and break the monotony of my daily existence. Under these circumstances, I eagerly hailed the little mystery which hung around my companion, and spent much of my time in endeavouring to unravel it.

He was not studying medicine. He had himself, in reply to a question, confirmed Stamford's opinion upon that point. Neither did he appear to have pursued any course of reading which might fit him for a degree in science or any other recognized portal which would give him an entrance into the learned world. Yet his zeal for certain studies was remarkable, and within eccentric limits his knowledge was so extraordinarily ample and minute that his observations have fairly astounded me. Surely no man would work so hard or attain such precise information unless he had some definite end in view. Desultory readers are seldom remarkable for the exactness of their learning. No man burdens his mind with small matters unless he has some very good reason for doing so.

His ignorance was as remarkable as his knowledge. Of contemporary literature, philosophy and politics he appeared to know next to nothing. Upon my quoting Thomas Carlyle, he inquired in the naïvest way who he might be and what he had done. My surprise reached a climax, however, when I found incidentally that he was ignorant of the Copernican Theory and of the composition of the Solar System. That any civilized human being in this nineteenth century should not be aware that the earth travelled round the sun appeared to me to be such an extraordinary fact that I could hardly realize it.

"You appear to be astonished," he said, smiling at my expression of surprise. "Now that I do know it I shall do my best to forget it."

"To forget it!"

"You see," he explained, "I consider that a man's brain originally is like a little empty attic, and you have to stock it with such furniture as you choose. A fool takes in all the lumber of every sort that he comes across, so that the knowledge which might be useful to him gets crowded out, or at best is jumbled up with a lot of other things, so that he has a difficulty in laying his hands upon it. Now the skillful workman is very careful indeed as to what he takes into his brain-attic. He will have nothing but the tools which may help him in doing his work, but of these he has a large assortment, and all in the most perfect order. It is a mistake to think that that little room has elastic walls and can distend to any extent. Depend upon it there comes a time when for every addition of knowledge you forget something that you knew before. It is of the highest importance, therefore, not to have useless facts elbowing out the useful ones."

"But the Solar System!" I protested.

"What the deuce is it to me?" he interrupted impatiently: "you say that we go round the sun. If we went round the moon it would not make a pennyworth of difference to me or to my work."

I was on the point of asking him what that work might be, but something in his manner showed me that the question would be an unwelcome one. I pondered over our short conversation, however, and endeavoured to draw my deductions from it. He said that he would acquire no knowledge which did not bear upon his object. Therefore all the knowledge which he possessed was such as would be useful to him. I enumerated in my own mind all the various points upon which he had shown me that he was exceptionally well informed. I even took a pencil and jotted them down. I could not help smiling at the document when I had completed it. It ran in this way:

Sherlock Holmes—his limits

1. Knowledge of Literature.—Nil.
2. Knowledge of Philosophy.—Nil.
3. Knowledge of Astronomy.—Nil.

4. Knowledge of Politics.—Feeble.
5. Knowledge of Botany.—Variable.
    Well up in belladonna, opium, and poisons generally. Knows nothing of practical gardening.
6. Knowledge of Geology.—Practical, but limited.
    Tells at a glance different soils from each other. After walks has shown me splashes upon his trousers, and told me by their colour and consistence in what part of London he had received them.
7. Knowledge of Chemistry.—Profound.
8. Knowledge of Anatomy.—Accurate, but unsystematic.
9. Knowledge of Sensational Literature.—Immense.
    He appears to know every detail of every horror perpetrated in the century.
10. Plays the violin well.
11. Is an expert singlestick player, boxer, and swordsman.
12. Has a good practical knowledge of British law.

When I had got so far in my list I threw it into the fire in despair. "If I can only find what the fellow is driving at by reconciling all these accomplishments, and discovering a calling which needs them all," I said to myself, "I may as well give up the attempt at once."

I see that I have alluded above to his powers upon the violin. These were very remarkable, but as eccentric as all his other accomplishments. That he could play pieces, and difficult pieces, I knew well, because at my request he has played me some of Mendelssohn's *Lieder,* and other favourites. When left to himself, however, he would seldom produce any music or attempt any recognized air. Leaning back in his armchair of an evening, he would close his eyes and scrape carelessly at the fiddle which was thrown across his knee. Sometimes the chords were sonorous and melancholy. Occasionally they were fantastic and cheerful. Clearly they reflected the thoughts which possessed him, but whether the music aided those thoughts, or whether the playing was simply the result of a whim or fancy, was more than I could determine. I might have rebelled against these exasperating solos had it not been that he usually terminated them by playing in quick succession a whole series of my favourite airs as a slight compensation for the trial upon my patience.

During the first week or so we had no callers, and I had begun to think that my companion was as friendless a man as I was myself. Presently, however, I found that he had many acquaintances, and those in the most different classes of society. There was one little sallow, rat-faced, dark-eyed fellow, who was introduced to me as Mr. Lestrade, and who came three or four times in a single week. One morning a young girl called, fashionably dressed, and stayed for half an hour or more. The same afternoon brought a gray-headed, seedy visitor, looking like a Jew peddler, who appeared to me to be much excited, and who was closely followed by a slipshod elderly woman. On another occasion an old white-haired gentleman had an interview with my companion; and on another, a railway porter in his velveteen uniform. When any of these nondescript individuals put in an appearance, Sherlock Holmes used to beg for the use of the sitting-room, and I would retire to my bedroom. He always apologized to me for putting me to this inconvenience. "I have to use this room as a place of business," he said, "and these people are my clients." Again I had an opportunity of asking him a point-blank question, and again my delicacy prevented me from forcing another man to confide in me. I imagined at the time that he had some strong reason for not alluding to it, but he soon dispelled the idea by coming round to the subject of his own accord.

It was upon the 4th of March, as I have good reason to remember, that I rose somewhat earlier than usual, and found that Sherlock Holmes had not yet finished his breakfast. The landlady had become so accustomed to my late habits that my place had not been laid nor my coffee prepared. With the unreasonable petulance of mankind I rang the bell and gave a curt intimation that I was ready. Then I picked up a magazine from the table and attempted to while away the time with it, while my companion munched silently at his toast. One of the articles had a pencil mark at the heading, and I naturally began to run my eye through it.

Its somewhat ambitious title was "The Book of Life," and it attempted to show how much an observant man might learn by an accurate and systematic examination of all that came in his way. It struck me as being a remarkable mixture of shrewdness and of absurdity. The reasoning was close and intense, but the deductions appeared to me to be far fetched and exaggerated. The writer claimed by a momentary expression, a twitch of a muscle or a glance of an eye, to fathom a man's inmost thoughts. Deceit, according to him, was an impossibility in the case of one trained to observation and analysis. His conclusions were as infallible as so many propositions of Euclid. So startling would his results appear to the uninitiated that until they learned the processes by which he had arrived at them they might well consider him as a necromancer.*

"From a drop of water," said the writer, "a logician could infer the possibility of an Atlantic or a Niagara without having seen or heard of one or the other. So all life is a great chain, the nature of which is known whenever we are shown a single link of it. Like all other arts, the Science of Deduction and Analysis is one which can only be acquired by long and patient study, nor is life long enough to allow any mortal to attain the highest possible perfection in it. Before turning to those moral and mental aspects of the matter which present the greatest difficulties, let the inquirer begin by mastering more elementary problems. Let him, on meeting a fellow-mortal, learn at a glance to distinguish the history of the man, and the trade or profession to which he belongs. Puerile as such an exercise may seem, it sharpens the faculties of observation, and teaches one where to look

---

*fortune-teller

and what to look for. By a man's finger-nails, by his coat-sleeve, by his boots, by his trouser-knees, by the callosities of his forefinger and thumb, by his expression, by his shirt-cuffs—by each of these things a man's calling is plainly revealed. That all united should fail to enlighten the competent inquirer in any case is almost inconceivable."

"What ineffable twaddle!" I cried, slapping the magazine down on the table; "I never read such rubbish in my life."

"What is it?" asked Sherlock Holmes.

"Why, this article," I said, pointing at it with my eggspoon as I sat down to my breakfast. "I see that you have read it since you have marked it. I don't deny that it is smartly written. It irritates me, though. It is evidently the theory of some armchair lounger who evolves all these neat little paradoxes in the seclusion of his own study. It is not practical. I should like to see him clapped down in a third-class carriage on the Underground, and asked to give the trades of all his fellow-travellers. I would lay a thousand to one against him."

"You would lose your money," Holmes remarked calmly. "As for the article, I wrote it myself."

"You!"

"Yes; I have a turn both for observation and for deduction. The theories which I have expressed there, and which appear to you to be so chimerical, are really extremely practical—so practical that I depend upon them for my bread and cheese."

"And how?" I asked involuntarily.

"Well, I have a trade of my own. I suppose I am the only one in the world. I'm a consulting detective, if you can understand what that is. Here in London we have lots of government detectives and lots of private ones. When these fellows are at fault, they come to me, and I manage to put them on the right scent. They lay all the evidence before me, and I am generally able, by the help of my knowledge of the history of crime, to set them straight. There is a strong family resemblance about misdeeds, and if you have all the details of a thousand at your finger ends, it is odd if you can't unravel the thousand and first. Lestrade is a well-known detective. He got himself into a fog recently over a forgery case, and that was what brought him here."

"And these other people?"

"They are mostly sent on by private inquiry agencies. They are all people who are in trouble about something and want a little enlightening. I listen to their story, they listen to my comments, and then I pocket my fee."

"But do you mean to say," I said, "that without leaving your room you can unravel some knot which other men can make nothing of, although they have seen every detail for themselves?"

"Quite so. I have a kind of intuition that way. Now and again a case turns up which is a little more complex. Then I have to bustle about and see things with my own eyes. You see I have a lot of special knowledge which I apply to the problem, and which facilitates matters wonderfully. Those rules of deduction laid down in that article which aroused your scorn are invaluable to me in practical work. Observation with me is second nature. You appeared to be surprised when I told you, on our first meeting, that you had come from Afghanistan."

"You were told, no doubt."

"Nothing of the sort. I *knew* you came from Afghanistan. From long habit the train of thoughts ran so swiftly through my mind that I arrived at the conclusion without being conscious of intermediate steps. There were such steps, however. The train of reasoning ran, 'Here is a gentleman of a medical type, but with the air of a military man. Clearly an army doctor, then. He has just come from the tropics, for his face is dark, and that is not the natural tint of his skin, for his wrists are fair. He has undergone hardship and sickness, as his haggard face says clearly. His left arm has been injured. He holds it in a stiff and unnatural manner. Where in the tropics could an English army doctor have seen much hardship and got his arm wounded? Clearly in Afghanistan.' The whole train of thought did not occupy a second. I then remarked that you came from Afghanistan, and you were astonished."

"It is simple enough as you explain it," I said, smiling. "You remind me of Edgar Allan Poe's Dupin. I had no idea that such individuals did exist outside of stories."

Sherlock Holmes rose and lit his pipe. "No doubt you think that you are complimenting me in comparing me to Dupin," he observed. "Now, in my opinion, Dupin was a very inferior fellow. That trick of his of breaking in on his friends' thoughts with an apropos remark after a quarter of an hour's silence is really very showy and superficial. He had some analytical genius, no doubt; but he was by no means such a phenomenon as Poe appeared to imagine."

"Have you read Gaboriau's works?" I asked. "Does Lecoq come up to your idea of a detective?"

Sherlock Holmes sniffed sardonically. "Lecoq was a miserable bungler," he said, in an angry voice; "he had only one thing to recommend him, and that was his energy. That book made me positively ill. The question was how to identify an unknown prisoner. I could have done it in twenty-four hours. Lecoq took six months or so. It might be made a textbook for detectives to teach them what to avoid."

I felt rather indignant at having two characters whom I had admired treated in this cavalier style. I walked over to the window and stood looking out into the busy street. "This fellow may be very clever," I said to myself, "but he is certainly very conceited."

"There are no crimes and no criminals in these days," he said, querulously. "What is the use of having brains in our profession? I know well that I have it in me to make my name famous. No man lives or has ever lived who has brought the same amount of study and of natural talent to the detection of crime which I have done. And what is the result? There is no crime to detect, or, at most, some bungling villainy with a motive so transparent that even a Scotland Yard official can see through it."

I was still annoyed at his bumptious style of conversation. I thought it best to change the topic.

"I wonder what that fellow is looking for?" I asked, pointing to a stalwart, plainly dressed individual who was walking slowly down the other side of the street, looking anxiously at the numbers. He had a large blue envelope in his hand, and was evidently the bearer of a message.

"You mean the retired sergeant of Marines," said Sherlock Holmes.

"Brag and bounce!" thought I to myself. "He knows that I cannot verify his guess."

The thought had hardly passed through my mind when the man whom we were watching caught sight of the number on our door, and ran rapidly across the roadway. We heard a loud knock, a deep voice below, and heavy steps ascending the stair.

"For Mr. Sherlock Holmes," he said, stepping into the room and handing my friend the letter.

Here was an opportunity of taking the conceit out of him. He little thought of this when he made that random shot. "May I ask, my lad," I said, in the blandest voice, "what your trade may be?"

"Commissionaire, sir," he said gruffly. "Uniform away for repairs."

"And you were?" I asked, with a slightly malicious glance at my companion.

"A sergeant, sir, Royal Marine Light Infantry, sir. No answer? Right, sir."

He clicked his heels together, raised his hand in salute, and was gone.

ACTIVITIES

1) A) Compare Poe's characterization of C. Auguste Dupin with Doyle's portrait of Sherlock Holmes. How are they alike? How are they different? Do you agree with Doyle's contention that Dupin was not really a flesh-and-blood character? Which fictional sleuth do you like better and why?

B) Compare the narrator or "I" of "The Murders in the Rue Morgue" with Dr. John H. Watson of *A Study in Scarlet.* How are they alike? How are they different? Which of these assistants do you like better and why?

2) Doyle's characterization of Sherlock Holmes fascinated his readers; this was mainly due to the fact that his creator endowed him with eccentricities as well as deductive talents. List Holmes's eccentricities. Why would these behaviorisms fascinate a reading public? Would they be considered eccentric today? Explain. (Hopefully you will be intrigued with Holmes to the point of reading the entire novel.)

RESEARCH ACTIVITY

The setting for the above story is London. Here, we briefly meet Inspector Lestrade of the world-famous Scotland Yard (now called New Scotland

Yard). Write a research paper on the origins and history of this noted police agency, as you did for the Sûreté.

Conan Doyle Gives Birth to Sherlock Holmes— and Then Kills Him.

Though an American creation, the detective story had never become very popular in the United States or Great Britain. Then came Sherlock Holmes and Americans and Englishmen began to take notice. A clamor arose from both sides of the Atlantic for more Holmes stories. Conan Doyle not only breathed new life into Poe's brainchild but he also aroused the interest of other writers; they began realizing it might be fun to write "a tale of ratiocination."

More Holmes yarns came from Conan Doyle's pen; these short stories were later incorporated into an anthology entitled *The Adventures of Sherlock Holmes*. But, Like Poe, Conan Doyle also became interested in other types of writing. He composed two historical novels, *Micah Clark* and *The White Company*; though they were not as well received as the Sherlock Holmes tales, they did attract the attention of such well-known literary figures as Oscar Wilde and H. G. Wells. Conan Doyle's writing assignments increased to the point that he finally abandoned his medical practice altogether.

In addition to writing historical fiction, Doyle started writing drama and science-fiction. But his publishers demanded more and more Holmes stories. Pulled in two directions, Conan Doyle found himself becoming tired of Holmes.

"I feel like a man who has consumed too much *pâté de foie gras,*" he told his family. "The very mention of Sherlock Holmes is beginning to nauseate me."[3]

A solution to his growing dilemma came to him. He had given life to Sherlock Holmes and he could just as easily destroy him. How? By having him die at the end of one of his adventures.

And Conan Doyle did exactly that. He wrote what he intended to be his concluding Sherlock Holmes tale. Entitled "The Final Problem" it was presented to his readers in December 1893. With a sigh of relief, Doyle turned to what he now considered his important writing.

He had not reckoned, however, with the power of the character he had created. Holmes simply would not allow himself to be killed that easily.

But—we're getting ahead of ourselves. Following is the famous "final" adventure. At the end of it, Holmes dies—

Or—*does he?*

If this seems confusing, to find out what really happened, you will have to read the story . . .

The Final Problem

It is with a heavy heart that I take up my pen to write these the last words in which I shall ever record the singular gifts by which my friend Mr. Sherlock Holmes was distinguished. In an incoherent and, as I deeply feel, an entirely inadequate fashion, I have endeavoured to give some account of my strange experiences in his company from the chance which first brought us together at the period of the "Study in Scarlet," up to the time of his interference in the matter of the "Naval Treaty"—an interference which had the unquestionable effect of preventing a serious international complication. It was my intention to have stopped there, and to have said nothing of that event which has created a void in my life which the lapse of two years has done little to fill. My hand has been forced, however, by the recent letters in which Colonel James Moriarty defends the memory of his brother, and I have no choice but to lay the facts before the public exactly as they occurred. I alone know the absolute truth of the matter, and I am satisfied that the time has come when no good purpose is to be served by its suppression. As far as I know, there have been only three accounts in the public press: that in the *Journal de Genève* on May 6th, 1891, the Reuter's dispatch in the English papers on May 7th, and finally the recent letters to which I have alluded. Of these the first and second were extremely condensed, while the last is, as I shall now show, an absolute perversion of the facts. It lies with me to tell for the first time what really took place between Professor Moriarty and Mr. Sherlock Holmes.

It may be remembered that after my marriage, and my subsequent start in private practice, the very intimate relations which had existed between Holmes and myself became to some extent modified. He still came to me from time to time when he desired a companion in his investigations, but these occasions grew more and more seldom, until I find that in the year 1890 there were only three cases of which I retain any record. During the winter of that year and the early spring of 1891, I saw in the papers that he had been engaged by the French government upon a matter of supreme importance, and I received two notes from Holmes, dated from Narbonne and from Nîmes, from which I gathered that his stay in France was likely to be a long one. It was with some surprise, therefore, that I saw him walk into my consulting-room upon the evening of April 24th. It struck me that he was looking even paler and thinner than usual.

"Yes, I have been using myself up rather too freely," he remarked, in answer to my look rather than to my words; "I have been a little pressed of late. Have you any objection to my closing your shutters?"

The only light in the room came from the lamp upon the table at which I had been reading. Holmes edged his way round the wall, and, flinging the shutters together, he bolted them securely.

"You are afraid of something?" I asked.

"Well, I am."

"Of what?"

"Of air-guns."

"My dear Holmes, what do you mean?"

"I think that you know me well enough, Watson, to understand that I am by no means a nervous man. At the same time, it is stupidity rather than courage to refuse to recognize danger when it is close upon you. Might I trouble you for a match?" He drew in the smoke of his cigarette as if the soothing influence was grateful to him.

"I must apologize for calling so late," said he, "and I must further beg you to be so unconventional as to allow me to leave your house presently by scrambling over your back garden wall."

"But what does it all mean?" I asked.

He held out his hand, and I saw in the light of the lamp that two of his knuckles were burst and bleeding.

"It's not an airy nothing, you see," said he, smiling. "On the contrary, it is solid enough for a man to break his hand over. Is Mrs. Watson in?"

"She is away upon a visit."

"Indeed! You are alone?"

"Quite."

"Then it makes it the easier for me to propose that you should come away with me for a week to the Continent."

"Where?"

"Oh, anywhere. It's all the same to me."

There was something very strange in all this. It was not Holmes's nature to take an aimless holiday, and something about his pale, worn face told me that his nerves were at their highest tension. He saw the question in my eyes, and, putting his finger-tips together and his elbows upon his knees, he explained the situation.

"You have probably never heard of Professor Moriarty?" said he.

"Never."

"Ay, there's the genius and the wonder of the thing!" he cried. "The man pervades London, and no one has heard of him. That's what puts him on a pinnacle in the records of crime. I tell you Watson, in all seriousness, that if I could beat that man, if I could free society of him, I should feel that my own career had reached its summit, and I should be prepared to turn to some more placid line in life. Between ourselves, the recent cases in which I have been of assistance to the royal family of Scandinavia, and to the French republic, have left me in such a position that I could continue to live in the quiet fashion which is most congenial to me, and to concentrate my attention upon my chemical researches. But I could not rest, Watson, I could not sit quiet in my chair, if I thought that such a man as Professor Moriarty were walking the streets of London unchallenged."

"What has he done, then?"

"His career has been an extraordinary one. He is a man of good birth and excellent education, endowed by nature with a phenomenal mathematical faculty. At the age of twenty-one he wrote a treatise upon the binomial theorem, which has had a European vogue. On the strength of it he won the mathematical chair at one of our smaller universities, and had, to all appearances, a most brilliant career before him. But the man had hereditary tendencies of the most diabolical kind. A criminal strain ran in his blood, which, instead of being modified, was increased and rendered infinitely more dangerous by his extraordinary mental powers. Dark rumours gathered round him in the university town, and eventually he was compelled to resign his chair and to come down to London, where he set up as an army coach. So much is known to the world, but what I am telling you now is what I have myself discovered.

"As you are aware, Watson, there is no one who knows the higher criminal world of London so well as I do. For years past I have continually been conscious of some power behind the malefactor, some deep organizing power which forever stands in the way of the law, and throws its shield over the wrong-doer. Again and again in cases of the most varying sorts—forgery cases, robberies, murders—I have felt the presence of this force, and I have deduced its action in many of those undiscovered crimes in which I have not been personally consulted. For years I have endeavoured to break through the veil which shrouded it, and at last the time came when I seized my thread and followed it, until it led me, after a thousand cunning windings, to ex-Professor Moriarty, of mathematical celebrity.

"He is the Napoleon of crime, Watson. He is the organizer of half that is evil and of nearly all that is undetected in this great city. He is a genius, a philosopher, an abstract thinker. He has a brain of the first order. He sits motionless, like a spider in the centre of its web, but that web has a thousand radiations, and he knows well every quiver of each of them. He does little himself. He only plans. But his agents are numerous and splendidly organized. Is there a crime to be done, a paper to be abstracted, we will say, a house to be rifled, a man to be removed—the word is passed to the professor, the matter is organized and carried out. The agent may be caught. In that case money is found for his bail or his defence. But the central power which uses the agent is never caught—never so much as suspected. This was the organization which I deduced, Watson, and which I devoted my whole energy to exposing and breaking up.

"But the professor was fenced round with safeguards so cunningly devised that, do what I would, it seemed impossible to get evidence which would convict in a court of law. You know my powers, my dear Watson, and yet at the end of three months I was forced to confess that I had at last met an antagonist who was my intellectual equal. My horror at his crimes was lost in my admiration at his skill. But at last he made a trip—only a little, little trip—but it was more than he could afford, when I was so close upon him. I had my chance, and, starting from that point, I have woven my net round him until now it is all ready to close. In three days—that is to say, on Monday next—matters will be ripe, and the professor, with all the principal members of his gang, will be in the hands of the police. Then will come the greatest criminal trial of the century, the clearing up of over forty mysteries, and the rope for all of them; but if we move at all prematurely, you understand, they may slip out of our hands even at the last moment.

"Now, if I could have done this without the knowledge of Professor Moriarty, all would have been well. But he was too wily for that. He saw every step which I took to draw my toils round him. Again and again he strove to break away, but I as often headed him off. I tell you, my friend, that if a detailed account of that silent contest could be written, it would take its place as the most brilliant bit of thrust-and-parry work in the history of detection. Never have I risen to such a height, and never have I been so hard pressed by an opponent. He cut deep, and yet I just undercut him. This morning the last steps were taken, and three days only were wanted to complete the business. I was sitting in my room thinking the matter over when the door opened and Professor Moriarty stood before me.

"My nerves are fairly proof, Watson, but I must confess to a start when I saw the very man who had been so much in my thoughts standing there on my threshold. His appearance was quite familiar to me. He is extremely tall and thin, his forehead domes out in a white curve, and his two eyes are deeply sunken in his head. He is a clean-shaven, pale, and ascetic-looking, retaining something of the professor in his features. His shoulders are rounded from much study, and his face protrudes forward and is forever slowly oscillating from side to side in a curiously reptilian fashion. He peered at me with great curiosity in his puckered eyes.

" 'You have less frontal development than I should have expected,' said he at last. 'It is a dangerous habit to finger loaded firearms in the pocket of one's dressing-gown.'

"The fact is that upon his entrance I had instantly recognized the extreme personal danger in which I lay. The only conceivable escape for him lay in silencing my tongue. In an instant I had slipped the revolver from the drawer into my pocket and was covering him through the cloth. At his remark I drew the weapon out and laid it cocked upon the table. He still smiled and blinked, but there was something about his eyes which made me feel very glad that I had it there.

" 'You evidently don't know me,' said he.

" 'On the contrary,' I answered, 'I think it is fairly evident that I do. Pray take a chair. I can spare you five minutes if you have anything to say.'

" 'All that I have to say has already crossed your mind,' said he.

" 'Then possibly my answer has crossed yours,' I replied.

" 'You stand fast?'

" 'Absolutely.'

"He clapped his hand into his pocket, and I raised the pistol from the table. But he merely drew out a memorandum-book in which he had scribbled some dates.

" 'You crossed my path on the fourth of January,' said he. 'On the twenty-third you incommoded me; by the middle of February I was seriously inconvenienced by you; at the end of March I was absolutely hampered in my plans; and now, at the close of April, I find myself placed in such a position through your continual persecution that I am in positive danger of losing my liberty. The situation is becoming an impossible one.'

" 'Have you any suggestion to make?' I asked.

" 'You must drop it, Mr. Holmes,' said he, swaying his face about. 'You really must, you know.'

" 'After Monday,' said I.

" 'Tut, tut!' said he. 'I am quite sure that a man of your intelligence will see that there can be but one outcome to this affair. It is necessary that you should withdraw. You have worked things in such a fashion that we have only one resource left. It has been an intellectual treat to me to see the way in which you have grappled with this affair, and I say, unaffectedly, that it would be a grief to me to be forced to take any extreme measure. You smile, sir, but I assure you that it really would.'

" 'Danger is part of my trade,' I remarked.

" 'This is not danger,' said he. 'It is inevitable destruction. You stand in the way not merely of an individual but of a mighty organization, the full extent of which you, with all your cleverness, have been unable to realize. You must stand clear, Mr. Holmes, or be trodden under foot.'

" 'I am afraid,' said I, rising, 'that in the pleasure of this conversation I am neglecting business of importance which awaits me elsewhere.'

"He rose also and looked at me in silence, shaking his head sadly.

" 'Well, well,' said he at last. 'It seems a pity, but I have done what I could. I know every move of your game. You can do nothing before Monday. It has been a duel between you and me, Mr. Holmes. You hope to place me in the dock. I tell you that I will never stand in the dock. You hope to beat me. I tell you that you will never beat me. If you are clever enough to bring destruction upon me, rest assured that I shall do as much to you.'

" 'You have paid me several compliments, Mr. Moriarty,' said I. 'Let me pay you one in return when I say that if I were assured of the former eventuality I would, in the interests of the public, cheerfully accept the latter.'

" 'I can promise you the one, but not the other,' he snarled, and so turned his rounded back upon me and went peering and blinking out of the room.

"That was my singular interview with Professor Moriarty. I confess that it left an unpleasant effect upon my mind. His soft, precise fashion of speech leaves a conviction of sincerity which a mere bully could not produce. Of course, you will say: 'Why not take police precautions against him?' The reason is that I am well convinced that it is from his agents the blow would fall. I have the best of proofs that it would be so."

"You have already been assaulted?"

"My dear Watson, Professor Moriarty is not a man who lets the grass grow under his feet. I went out about midday to transact some business in Oxford Street. As I passed the corner which leads from Bentinck Street on to the Welbeck Street crossing a two-horse van furiously driven whizzed round and was on me like a flash. I sprang for the foot-path and saved myself by the fraction of a second. The van dashed round by Marylebone Lane and was gone in an instant. I kept to the pavement after that, Watson, but as I walked down Vere Street a brick came down from the roof of one of the houses and was shattered to fragments at my feet. I called the police and had the place examined. There were slates and bricks piled up on the roof preparatory to some repairs, and they would have me believe that the wind had toppled over one of these. Of course I knew better, but I could prove nothing. I took a cab after that and reached my brother's rooms in Pall Mall, where I spent the day. Now I have come round to you, and on my way I was attacked by a rough with a bludgeon. I knocked him down, and the police have him in custody; but I can tell you with the most absolute confidence that no possible connection will ever be traced between the gentleman upon whose front teeth I have barked my knuckles and the retiring mathematical coach, who is, I daresay, working out problems upon a black-board ten miles away. You will not wonder, Watson, that my first act on entering your rooms was to close your shutters, and that I have been compelled to ask your permission to leave the house by some less conspicuous exit than the front door."

I had often admired my friend's courage, but never more than now, as he sat quietly checking off a series of incidents which must have combined to make up a day of horror.

"You will spend the night here?" I said.

"No, my friend, you might find me a dangerous guest. I have my plans laid, and all will be well. Matters have gone so far now that they can move without my help as far as the arrest goes, though my presence is necessary for a conviction. It is obvious, therefore, that I cannot do better than get away for the few days which remain before the police are at liberty to act. It would be a great pleasure to me, therefore, if you could come on to the Continent with me."

"The practice is quiet," said I, "and I have an accommodating neighbour. I should be glad to come."

"And to start to-morrow morning?"

"If necessary."

"Oh, yes, it is most necessary. Then these are your instructions, and I beg, my dear Watson, that you will obey them to the letter, for you are now playing a double-handed game with me against the cleverest rogue and the most powerful syndicate of criminals in Europe. Now listen! You will dispatch whatever luggage you intend to take by a trusty messenger unaddressed to Victoria to-night. In the morning you will send for a hansom, desiring your man to take neither the first nor the second which may present itself. Into this hansom you will jump, and you will drive to the Strand end of the Lowther Arcade, handing the address to the cabman upon a slip of paper, with a request that he will not throw it away. Have your fare ready, and the instant that your cab stops, dash through the Arcade, timing yourself to reach the other side at a quarter-past nine. You will find a small brougham waiting close to the curb, driven by a fellow with a heavy black cloak tipped at the collar with red. Into this you will step, and you will reach Victoria in time for the Continental express."

"Where shall I meet you?"

"At the station. The second first-class carriage from the front will be reserved for us."

"The carriage is our rendezvous, then?"

"Yes."

It was in vain that I asked Holmes to remain for the evening. It was evident to me that he thought he might bring trouble to the roof he was under, and that that was the motive which impelled him to go. With a few hurried words as to our plans for the morrow he rose and came out with me into the garden, clambering over the wall which leads into Mortimer Street, and immediately whistling for a hansom, in which I heard him drive away.

In the morning I obeyed Holmes's injunctions to the letter. A hansom was procured with such precautions as would prevent its being one which was placed ready for us, and I drove immediately after breakfast to the Lowther Arcade, through which I hurried at the top of my speed. A brougham was waiting with a very massive driver wrapped in a dark cloak, who, the instant that I had stepped in, whipped up the horse and rattled off to Victoria Station. On my alighting there he turned the carriage, and dashed away again without so much as a look in my direction.

So far all had gone admirably. My luggage was waiting for me, and I had no difficulty in finding the carriage which Holmes had indicated, the less so as it was the only one in the train which was marked "Engaged." My only source of anxiety now was the non-appearance of Holmes. The station clock marked only seven minutes from the time when we were due to start. In vain I searched among the groups of travellers and leave-takers for the lithe figure of my friend. There was no sign of him. I spent a few minutes in assisting a venerable Italian priest, who was endeavouring to make a porter understand, in his broken English, that his luggage was to be booked through to Paris. Then, having taken another look round, I returned to my carriage, where I found that the porter, in spite of the ticket, had given me my decrepit Italian friend as a travelling companion. It was useless for me to explain to him that his presence was an intrusion, for my Italian was even more limited than his English, so I shrugged my shoulders resignedly, and continued to look out anxiously for my friend. A chill of fear had come over me, as I thought that his absence might mean that some blow had fallen during the night. Already the doors had all been shut and the whistle blown, when——

"My dear Watson," said a voice, "you have not even condescended to say good-morning."

I turned in uncontrollable astonishment. The aged ecclesiastic had turned his face towards me. For an instant the wrinkles were smoothed away, the nose drew away from the chin, the lower lip ceased to protrude and the mouth to mumble, the dull eyes regained their fire, the drooping figure expanded. The next the whole frame collapsed again, and Holmes had gone as quickly as he had come.

"Good heavens!" I cried, "how you startled me!"

"Every precaution is still necessary," he whispered. "I have reason to think that they are hot upon our trail. Ah, there is Moriarty himself."

The train had already begun to move as Holmes spoke. Glancing back, I saw a tall man pushing his way furiously through the crowd, and waving his hand as if he desired to have the train stopped. It was too late, however, for we were rapidly gathering momentum, and an instant later had shot clear of the station.

"With all our precautions, you see that we have cut it rather fine," said Holmes, laughing. He rose, and throwing off the black cassock and hat which had formed his disguise, he packed them away in a hand-bag.

"Have you seen the morning paper, Watson?"

"No."

"You haven't seen about Baker Street, then?"

"Baker Street?"

"They set fire to our rooms last night. No great harm was done."

"Good heavens, Holmes, this is intolerable!"

"They must have lost my track completely after their bludgeonman was arrested. Otherwise they could not have imagined that I had returned to my rooms. They have evidently taken the precaution of watching you, however, and that is what has brought Moriarty to Victoria. You could not have made any slip in coming?"

"I did exactly what you advised."

"Did you find your brougham?"

"Yes, it was waiting."

"Did you recognize your coachman?"

"No."

"It was my brother Mycroft. It is an advantage to get about in such a case without taking a mercenary into your confidence. But we must plan what we are to do about Moriarty now."

"As this is an express, and as the boat runs in connection with it, I should think we have shaken him off very effectively."

"My dear Watson, you evidently did not realize my meaning when I said that this man may be taken as being quite on the same intellectual plane as myself. You do not imagine that if I were the pursuer I should allow myself to be baffled by so slight an obstacle. Why, then, should you think so meanly of him?"

"What will he do?"

"What I should do."

"What would you do, then?"

"Engage a special."

"But it must be late."

"By no means. This train stops at Canterbury; and there is always at least a quarter of an hour's delay at the boat. He will catch us there."

"One would think that we were the criminals. Let us have him arrested on his arrival."

"It would be to ruin the work of three months. We should get the big fish, but the smaller would dart right and left out of the net. On Monday we should have them all. No, an arrest is inadmissible."

"What then?"

"We shall get out at Canterbury."

"And then?"

"Well, then we must make a cross-country journey to Newhaven, and so over to Dieppe. Moriarty will again do what I should do. He will get on to Paris, mark down our luggage, and wait for two days at the depot. In the meantime we shall treat ourselves to a couple of carpet-bags, encourage the manufacturers of the countries through which we travel, and make our way at our leisure into Switzerland, *via* Luxembourg and Basle."

At Canterbury, therefore, we alighted, only to find that we should have to wait an hour before we could get a train to Newhaven.

I was still looking rather ruefully after the rapidly disappearing luggage-van which contained my wardrobe, when Holmes pulled my sleeve and pointed up the line.

"Already, you see," said he.

Far away, from among the Kentish woods there rose a thin spray of smoke. A minute later a carriage and engine could be seen flying along the open curve which leads to the station. We had hardly time to take our place behind a pile of luggage when it passed with a rattle and a roar, beating a blast of hot air into our faces.

"There he goes," said Holmes, as we watched the carriage swing and rock over the points. "There are limits, you see, to our friend's intelligence. It would have been a *coup-de-maître** had he deduced what I would deduce and acted accordingly."

"And what would he have done had he overtaken us?"

"There cannot be the least doubt that he would have made a murderous attack upon me. It is, however, a game at which two may play. The question now is whether we should take a premature lunch here, or run our chance of starving before we reach the buffet at Newhaven."

We made our way to Brussels that night and spent two days there, moving on upon the third day as far as Strasbourg. On the Monday morning Holmes had telegraphed to the London police, and in the evening we found a reply waiting for us at our hotel. Holmes tore it open, and then with a bitter curse hurled it into the grate.

"I might have known it!" he groaned. "He has escaped!"

"Moriarty?"

"They have secured the whole gang with the exception of him. He has given them the slip. Of course, when I had left the country there was no one to cope with him. But I did think that I had put the game in their hands. I think that you had better return to England, Watson."

"Why?"

"Because you will find me a dangerous companion now. This man's occupation is gone. He is lost if he returns to London. If I read his character right he will devote his whole energies to revenging himself upon me. He said as much in our short interview, and I fancy that he meant it. I should certainly recommend you to return to your practice."

It was hardly an appeal to be successful with one who was an old cam-

---

*Master stroke (French)

paigner as well as an old friend. We sat in the Strasbourg *salle-à-manger**
arguing the question for half an hour, but the same night we had resumed
our journey and were well on our way to Geneva.

For a charming week we wandered up the valley of the Rhone, and then,
branching off at Leuk, we made our way over the Gemmi Pass, still deep
in snow, and so, by way of Interlaken, to Meiringen. It was a lovely trip,
the dainty green of the spring below, the virgin white of the winter above;
but it was clear to me that never for one instant did Holmes forget the
shadow which lay across him. In the homely Alpine villages or in the lonely
mountain passes, I could still tell by his quick glancing eyes and his sharp
scrutiny of every face that passed us, that he was well convinced that, walk
where we would, we could not walk ourselves clear of the danger which was
dogging our footsteps.

Once, I remember, as we passed over the Gemmi, and walked along the
border of the melancholy Daubensee, a large rock which had been dislodged
from the ridge upon our right clattered down and roared into the lake
behind us. In an instant Holmes had raced up on to the ridge, and standing
upon a lofty pinnacle, craned his neck in every direction. It was in vain that
our guide assured him that a fall of stones was a common chance in the
springtime at that spot. He said nothing, but he smiled at me with the air
of a man who sees the fulfilment of that which he had expected.

And yet for all his watchfulness he was never depressed. On the contrary,
I can never recollect having seen him in such exuberant spirits. Again and
again he recurred to the fact that if he could be assured that society was
freed from Professor Moriarty he would cheerfully bring his own career to
a conclusion.

"I think that I may go so far as to say, Watson, that I have not lived wholly
in vain," he remarked. "If my record were closed to-night I could still
survey it with equanimity. The air of London is the sweeter for my presence.
In over a thousand cases I am not aware that I have ever used my powers
upon the wrong side. Of late I have been tempted to look into the problems
furnished by nature rather than those more superficial ones for which our
artificial state of society is responsible. Your memoirs will draw to an end,
Watson, upon the day that I crown my career by the capture or extinction
of the most dangerous and capable criminal in Europe."

I shall be brief, and yet exact, in the little which remains for me to tell.
It is not a subject on which I would willingly dwell, and yet I am conscious
that a duty devolves upon me to omit no detail.

It was on the third of May that we reached the little village of Meiringen,
where we put up at the Englischer Hof, then kept by Peter Steiler the elder.
Our landlord was an intelligent man and spoke excellent English, having
served for three years as waiter at the Grosvenor Hotel in London. At his
advice, on the afternoon of the fourth we set off together, with the intention

---

*Dining room (French)

of crossing the hills and spending the night at the hamlet of Rosenlaui. We had strict injunctions, however, on no account to pass the falls of Reichenbach, which are about halfway up the hills, without making a small detour to see them.

It is, indeed, a fearful place. The torrent, swollen by the melting snow, plunges into a tremendous abyss, from which the spray rolls up like the smoke from a burning house. The shaft into which the river hurls itself is an immense chasm, lined by glistening coal-black rock, and narrowing into a creaming, boiling pit of incalculable depth, which brims over and shoots the stream onward over its jagged lip. The long sweep of green water roaring forever down, and the thick flickering curtain of spray hissing forever upward, turn a man giddy with their constant whirl and clamour. We stood near the edge peering down at the gleam of the breaking water far below us against the black rocks, and listening to the half-human shout which came booming up with the spray out of the abyss.

The path has been cut halfway round the fall to afford a complete view, but it ends abruptly, and the traveller has to return as he came. We had turned to do so, when we saw a Swiss lad come running along it with a letter in his hand. It bore the mark of the hotel which we had just left and was addressed to me by the landlord. It appeared that within a very few minutes of our leaving, an English lady had arrived who was in the last stage of consumption. She had wintered at Davos Platz and was journeying now to join her friends at Lucerne, when a sudden hemorrhage had overtaken her. It was thought that she could hardly live a few hours, but it would be a great consolation to her to see an English doctor, and, if I would only return, etc. The good Steiler assured me in a postscript that he would himself look upon my compliance as a very great favour, since the lady absolutely refused to see a Swiss physician, and he could not but feel that he was incurring a great responsibility.

The appeal was one which could not be ignored. It was impossible to refuse the request of a fellow-countrywoman dying in a strange land. Yet I had my scruples about leaving Holmes. It was finally agreed, however, that he should retain the young Swiss messenger with him as guide and companion while I returned to Meiringen. My friend would stay some little time at the fall, he said, and would then walk slowly over the hill to Rosenlaui, where I was to rejoin him in the evening. As I turned away I saw Holmes, with his back against a rock and his arms folded, gazing down at the rush of the waters. It was the last that I was ever destined to see of him in this world.

When I was near the bottom of the descent I looked back. It was impossible, from that position, to see the fall, but I could see the curving path which winds over the shoulder of the hills and leads to it. Along this a man was, I remember, walking very rapidly.

I could see his black figure clearly outlined against the green behind him. I noted him, and the energy with which he walked, but he passed from my mind again as I hurried on upon my errand.

It may have been a little over an hour before I reached Meiringen. Old Steiler was standing at the porch of his hotel.

"Well," said I, as I came hurrying up, "I trust that she is no worse?"

A look of surprise passed over his face, and at the first quiver of his eyebrows my heart turned to lead in my breast.

"You did not write this?" I said, pulling the letter from my pocket. "There is no sick Englishwoman in the hotel?"

"Certainly not!" he cried. "But it has the hotel mark upon it! Ha, it must have been written by that tall Englishman who came in after you had gone. He said——"

But I waited for none of the landlord's explanation. In a tingle of fear I was already running down the village street, and making for the path which I had so lately descended. It had taken me an hour to come down. For all my efforts two more had passed before I found myself at the fall of Reichenbach once more. There was Holmes's Alpine-stock still leaning against the rock by which I had left him. But there was no sign of him, and it was in vain that I shouted. My only answer was my own voice reverberating in a rolling echo from the cliffs around me.

It was the sight of that Alpine-stock which turned me cold and sick. He had not gone to Rosenlaui, then. He had remained on that three-foot path, with sheer wall on one side and sheer drop on the other, until his enemy had overtaken him. The young Swiss had gone too. He had probably been in the pay of Moriarty and had left the two men together. And then what had happened? Who was to tell us what had happened then?

I stood for a minute or two to collect myself, for I was dazed with the horror of the thing. Then I began to think of Holmes's own methods and to try to practice them in reading this tragedy. It was, alas, only too easy to do. During our conversation we had not gone to the end of the path, and the Alpine-stock marked the place where we had stood. The blackish soil is kept forever soft by the incessant drift of spray, and a bird would leave its tread upon it. Two lines of footmarks were clearly marked along the farther end of the path, both leading away from me. There were none returning. A few yards from the end the soil was all ploughed up into a patch of mud, and the brambles and ferns which fringed the chasm were torn and bedraggled. I lay upon my face and peered over with the spray spouting up all around me. It had darkened since I left, and now I could only see here and there the glistening of moisture upon the black walls, and far away down at the end of the shaft the gleam of the broken water. I shouted; but only that same half-human cry of the fall was borne back to my ears.

But it was destined that I should, after all, have a last word of greeting from my friend and comrade. I have said that his Alpine-stock had been left leaning against a rock which jutted on to the path. From the top of this bowlder the gleam of something bright caught my eye, and raising my hand I found that it came from the silver cigarette-case which he used to carry. As I took it up a small square of paper upon which it had lain fluttered down on to the ground. Unfolding it, I found that it consisted of three pages torn from his notebook and addressed to me. It was characteristic of the man that the direction was as precise, and the writing as firm and clear, as though it had been written in his study.

MY DEAR WATSON [it said]:

I write these few lines through the courtesy of Mr. Moriarty, who awaits my convenience for the final discussion of those questions which lie between us. He has been giving me a sketch of the methods by which he avoided the English police and kept himself informed of our movements. They certainly confirm the very high opinion which I had formed of his abilities. I am pleased to think that I shall be able to free society from any further effects of his presence, though I fear that it is at a cost which will give pain to my friends, and especially, my dear Watson, to you. I have already explained to you, however, that my career had in any case reached its crisis, and that no possible conclusion to it could be more congenial to me than this. Indeed, if I may make a full confession to you, I was quite convinced that the letter from Meiringen was a hoax, and I allowed you to depart on the errand under the persuasion that some development of this sort would follow. Tell Inspector Patterson that the papers which he needs to convict the gang are in pigeonhole M., done up in a blue envelope and inscribed "Moriarty." I made every disposition of my property before leaving England and handed it to my brother Mycroft. Pray give my greetings to Mrs. Watson, and believe me to be, my dear fellow,

Very sincerely yours,
SHERLOCK HOLMES.

A few words may suffice to tell the little that remains. An examination by experts leaves little doubt that a personal contest between the two men ended, as it could hardly fail to end in such a situation, in their reeling over, locked in each other's arms. Any attempt at recovering the bodies was absolutely hopeless, and there, deep down in that dreadful cauldron of swirling water and seething foam, will lie for all time the most dangerous criminal and the foremost champion of the law of their generation. The Swiss youth was never found again, and there can be no doubt that he was one of the numerous agents whom Moriarty kept in his employ. As to the gang, it will be within the memory of the public how completely the evidence which Holmes had accumulated exposed their organization, and how heavily the hand of the dead man weighed upon them. Of their terrible chief few details came out during the proceedings, and if I have now been compelled to make a clear statement of his career, it is due to those injudicious champions who have endeavoured to clear his memory by attacks upon him whom I shall ever regard as the best and the wisest man whom I have ever known.

ACTIVITIES

1) The pivotal character in any story or play is the *protagonist*. Webster's dictionary defines a protagonist as ". . . one who takes the lead in any movement or cause." Anyone obstructing the protagonist, his adversary or opponent, is called the *antagonist*.

Why do you suppose that Professor James Moriarty has always been considered a truly worthy antagonist for Sherlock Holmes? Consider Moriarty's actions as well as Holmes's description of him.

2) Many times an author will give his readers clues about events that will occur later in his tale. This literary technique is known as *foreshadowing*. Can you point out specific instances where Conan Doyle foreshadowed his tragic climax? Why do you think an author uses this technique?

3) In the next section, you will learn how the fans of Sherlock Holmes were affected by his unexpected "death." Before reading it, you might find it interesting to take a poll regarding the class's feelings about the event.

You will probably discover that some students were affected, others not. Discuss the reasons for this difference in reaction.

Holmes Refuses to Die

After the publication of "The Final Problem," Arthur Conan Doyle discovered that he had completely underestimated his readers' reactions. They responded as if a real person, a beloved national hero, had passed away.

At first, the Holmes fans were plunged into grief. Then, they furiously struck back at the man responsible for the tragedy—Conan Doyle. Letters poured in from all over the world to his agent and publisher, letters so insulting and abusive that those two gentlemen hesitated in showing them to the author. One woman addressed Conan Doyle as "You brute!" Others denounced him as a "murderer." In London, young city men appeared at their offices with black crepe bands tied around their hats in mourning while other people wept openly.

Conan Doyle remained callous to it all by immersing himself in his other writing. Notwithstanding Holmes's death, his publishers insisted upon tempting him with high prices for more Holmes stories.

He relented once—in 1901. In that year, he visited Dartmoor in Devon, England, and became fascinated by the lonely, rock-strewn moor there and the ancient legends surrounding it, particularly one about a giant animal. It gave him an idea for a detective story, a perfect puzzle for his old friend Holmes. But Holmes was dead; so Conan Doyle wrote it as an earlier unpublished case written by Dr. Watson before the time-period of "The

Final Problem." Entitled *The Hound of the Baskervilles,* it turned out to be one of the finest of the Holmes adventures.

Again, Conan Doyle had made a mistake.

The clamor for more Holmes tales was renewed with additional vigor. Try as he might, Conan Doyle could not remove the eccentric sleuth from his consciousness. Even after he had been knighted in 1902 for a polemical pamphlet defending England's participation in the Boer War, he found himself addressed not as Sir Arthur Conan Doyle—but as *Sir Sherlock Holmes.*

In 1903, ten years after Holmes' death, Doyle gave in to the pressures from publisher and public. He signed a contract for a new series of adventures to be entitled *The Return of Sherlock Holmes;* in the first story of that book he tackled the problem of bringing a dead man back to life. That famous story, "The Adventure of the Empty House," is our next reading selection.

Before starting it, put yourself in the author's shoes. You're back in the year 1903 faced with the literary problem of resurrecting Sherlock Holmes.

How would you do it?

Then compare your handling of the problem with how Doyle solved it.

The Adventure of the Empty House

It was in the spring of the year 1894 that all London was interested, and the fashionable world dismayed, by the murder of the Honourable Ronald Adair under most unusual and inexplicable circumstances. The public has already learned those particulars of the crime which came out in the police investigation, but a good deal was suppressed upon that occasion, since the case for the prosecution was so overwhelmingly strong that it was not necessary to bring forward all the facts. Only now, at the end of nearly ten years, am I allowed to supply those missing links which make up the whole of that remarkable chain. The crime was of interest in itself, but that interest was as nothing to me compared to the inconceivable sequel, which afforded me the greatest shock and surprise of any event in my adventurous life. Even now, after this long interval, I find myself thrilling as I think of it, and feeling once more that sudden flood of joy, amazement, and incredulity which utterly submerged my mind. Let me say to that public, which has shown some interest in those glimpses which I have occasionally given them of the thoughts and actions of a very remarkable man, that they are not to blame me if I have not shared my knowledge with them, for I should have considered it my first duty to do so, had I not been barred by a positive prohibition from his own lips, which was only withdrawn upon the third of last month.

It can be imagined that my close intimacy with Sherlock Holmes had interested me deeply in crime, and that after his disappearance I never failed to read with care the various problems which came before the public. And I even attempted, more than once, for my own private satisfaction, to employ his methods in their solution, though with indifferent success. There was none, however, which appealed to me like this tragedy of Ronald Adair. As I read the evidence at the inquest, which led up to a verdict of willful murder against some person or persons unknown, I realized more clearly than I had ever done the loss which the community had sustained by the death of Sherlock Holmes. There were points about this strange business which would, I was sure, have specially appealed to him, and the efforts of the police would have been supplemented, or more probably anticipated, by the trained observation and the alert mind of the first criminal agent in Europe. All day, as I drove upon my round, I turned over the case in my mind and found no explanation which appeared to me to be adequate. At the risk of telling a twice-told tale, I will recapitulate the facts as they were known to the public at the conclusion of the inquest.

The Honourable Ronald Adair was second son of the Earl of Maynooth, at that time governor of one of the Australian colonies. Adair's mother had returned from Australia to undergo the operation for cataract, and she, her son Ronald, and her daughter Hilda were living together at 427 Park Lane. The youth moved in the best society—had, so far as was known, no enemies and no particular vices. He had been engaged to Miss Edith Woodley, of Carstairs, but the engagement had been broken off by mutual consent some months before, and there was no sign that it had left any very profound feeling behind it. For the rest of the man's life moved in a narrow and conventional circle, for his habits were quiet and his nature unemotional. Yet it was upon this easy-going young aristocrat that death came, in most strange and unexpected form, between the hours of ten and eleven-twenty on the night of March 30, 1894.

Ronald Adair was fond of cards—playing continually but never for such stakes as would hurt him. He was a member of the Baldwin, the Cavendish, and the Bagatelle card clubs. It was shown that, after dinner on the day of his death, he had played a rubber of whist at the latter club. He had also played there in the afternoon. The evidence of those who had played with him—Mr. Murray, Sir John Hardy, and Colonel Moran—showed that the game was whist, and that there was a fairly equal fall of the cards. Adair might have lost five pounds, but not more. His fortune was a considerable one, and such a loss could not in any way affect him. He had played nearly every day at one club or other, but he was a cautious player, and usually rose a winner. It came out in evidence that, in partnership with Colonel Moran, he had actually won as much as four hundred and twenty pounds in a sitting, some weeks before, from Godfrey Milner and Lord Balmoral. So much for his recent history as it came out at the inquest.

On the evening of the crime, he returned from the club exactly at ten. His mother and sister were out spending the evening with a relation. The servant deposed that she heard him enter the front room on the second floor, generally used as his sitting-room. She had lit a fire there, and as it smoked she had opened the window. No sound was heard from the room until eleven-twenty, the hour of the return of Lady Maynooth and her daughter. Desiring to say good-night, she attempted to enter her son's room. The door was locked on the inside, and no answer could be got to their cries and knocking. Help was obtained, and the door forced. The unfortunate young man was found lying near the table. His head had been horribly mutilated by an expanding revolver bullet, but no weapon of any sort was to be found in the room. On the table lay two banknotes for ten pounds each and seventeen pounds ten in silver and gold, the money arranged in little piles of varying amount. There were some figures also upon a sheet of paper, with the names of some club friends opposite to them, from which it was conjectured that before his death he was endeavouring to make out his losses or winnings at cards.

A minute examination of the circumstances served only to make the case more complex. In the first place, no reason could be given why the young man should have fastened the door upon the inside. There was the possibility that the murderer had done this, and had afterwards escaped by the window. The drop was at least twenty feet, however, and a bed of crocuses in full bloom lay beneath. Neither the flowers nor the earth showed any sign of having been disturbed, nor were there any marks upon the narrow strip of grass which separated the house from the road. Apparently, therefore, it was the young man himself who had fastened the door. But how did he come by his death? No one could have climbed up to the window without leaving traces. Suppose a man had fired through the window, he would indeed be a remarkable shot who could with a revolver inflict so deadly a wound. Again, Park Lane is a frequented thoroughfare; there is a cab stand within a hundred yards of the house. No one had heard a shot. And yet there was a dead man, and there the revolver bullet, which had mushroomed out, as soft-nosed bullets will, and so inflicted a wound which must have caused instantaneous death. Such were the circumstances of the Park Lane Mystery, which were further complicated by entire absence of motive, since, as I have said, young Adair was not known to have any enemy, and no attempt had been made to remove the money or valuables in the room.

All day I turned these facts over in my mind, endeavouring to hit upon some theory which could reconcile them all, and to find that line of least resistance which my poor friend had declared to be the starting-point of every investigation. I confess that I made little progress. In the evening I strolled across the Park, and found myself about six o'clock at the Oxford Street end of Park Lane. A group of loafers upon the pavements, all staring up at a particular window, directed me to the house which I had come to see. A tall, thin man with coloured glasses, whom I strongly suspected of being a plain-clothes detective, was pointing out some theory of his own, while the others crowded round to listen to what he said. I got as near him as I could, but his observations seemed to me to be absurd, so I withdrew again in some disgust. As I did so I struck against an elderly, deformed man, who had been behind me, and I knocked down several books which he was carrying. I remember that as I picked them up, I observed the title of one of them, *The Origin of Tree Worship,* and it struck me that the fellow must be some poor bibliophile, who, either as a trade or as a hobby, was a collector of obscure volumes. I endeavoured to apologize for the accident, but it was evident that these books which I had so unfortunately maltreated were very precious objects in the eyes of their owner. With a snarl of contempt he turned upon his heel, and I saw his curved back and white side-whiskers disappear among the throng.

My observations of No. 427 Park Lane did little to clear up the problem in which I was interested. The house was separated from the street by a low wall and railing, the whole not more than five feet high. It was perfectly easy, therefore, for anyone to get into the garden, but the window was entirely inaccessible, since there was no waterpipe or anything which could help the most active man to climb it. More puzzled than ever, I retraced my steps to Kensington. I had not been in my study five minutes when the maid entered to say that a person desired to see me. To my astonishment it was none other than my strange old book collector, his sharp, wizened face peering out from a frame of white hair, and his precious volumes, a dozen of them at least, wedged under his right arm.

"You're surprised to see me, sir," said he, in a strange, croaking voice.

I acknowledged that I was.

"Well, I've a conscience, sir, and when I chanced to see you go into this house, as I came hobbling after you, I thought to myself, I'll just step in and see that kind gentleman, and tell him that if I was a bit gruff in my manner there was not any harm meant, and that I am much obliged to him for picking up my books."

"You make too much of a trifle," said I. "May I ask how you knew who I was?"

"Well, sir, if it isn't too great a liberty, I am a neighbour of yours, for you'll find my little bookshop at the corner of Church Street, and very happy to see you, I am sure. Maybe you collect yourself, sir. Here's *British Birds,* and *Catullus,* and *The Holy War*—a bargain, every one of them. With five volumes you could just fill that gap on that second shelf. It looks untidy, does it not, sir?"

I moved my head to look at the cabinet behind me. When I turned again, Sherlock Holmes was standing smiling at me across my study table. I rose to my feet, stared at him for some seconds in utter amazement, and then it appears that I must have fainted for the first and the last time in my life. Certainly a gray mist swirled before my eyes, and when it cleared I found my collar-ends undone and the tingling aftertaste of brandy upon my lips. Holmes was bending over my chair, his flask in his hand.

"My dear Watson," said the well-remembered voice, "I owe you a thousand apologies. I had no idea that you would be so affected."

I gripped him by the arms.

"Holmes!" I cried. "Is it really you? Can it indeed be that you are alive? Is it possible that you succeeded in climbing out of that awful abyss?"

"Wait a moment," said he. "Are you sure that you are really fit to discuss things? I have given you a serious shock by my unnecessarily dramatic reappearance."

"I am all right, but indeed, Holmes, I can hardly believe my eyes. Good heavens! to think that you—you of all men—should be standing in my study." Again I gripped him by the sleeve, and felt the thin, sinewy arm beneath it. "Well, you're not a spirit, anyhow," said I. "My dear chap, I'm overjoyed to see you. Sit down, and tell me how you came alive out of that dreadful chasm."

He sat opposite to me, and lit a cigarette in his old, nonchalant manner. He was dressed in the seedy frockcoat of the book merchant, but the rest of that individual lay in a pile of white hair and old books upon the table. Holmes looked even thinner and keener than of old, but there was a dead-white tinge in his aquiline face which told me that his life recently had not been a healthy one.

"I am glad to stretch myself, Watson," said he. "It is no joke when a tall man has to take a foot off his stature for several hours on end. Now, my dear fellow, in the matter of these explanations, we have, if I may ask for your coöperation, a hard and dangerous night's work in front of us. Perhaps it would be better if I gave you an account of the whole situation when that work is finished."

"I am full of curiosity. I should much prefer to hear now."

"You'll come with me to-night?"

"When you like and where you like."

"This is, indeed, like the old days. We shall have time for a mouthful of dinner before we need go. Well, then, about that chasm. I had no serious difficulty in getting out of it, for the very simple reason that I never was in it."

"You never were in it?"

"No, Watson, I never was in it. My note to you was absolutely genuine. I had little doubt that I had come to the end of my career when I perceived the somewhat sinister figure of the late Professor Moriarty standing upon the narrow pathway which led to safety. I read an inexorable purpose in his gray eyes. I exchanged some remarks with him, therefore, and obtained his courteous permission to write the short note which you afterwards received. I left it with my cigarette-box and my stick, and I walked along the pathway, Moriarty still at my heels. When I reached the end I stood at bay. He drew no weapon, but he rushed at me and threw his long arms around me. He knew that his own game was up, and was only anxious to revenge himself upon me. We tottered together upon the brink of the fall. I have some knowledge, however, of baritsu, or the Japanese system of wrestling, which has more than once been very useful to me. I slipped through his grip, and he with a horrible scream kicked madly for a few seconds, and clawed the air with both his hands. But for all his efforts he could not get his balance, and over he went. With my face over the brink, I saw him fall for a long way. Then he struck a rock, bounded off, and splashed into the water."

I listened with amazement to this explanation, which Holmes delivered between the puffs of his cigarette.

"But the tracks!" I cried. "I saw, with my own eyes, that two went down the path and none returned."

"It came about in this way. The instant that the Professor had disappeared, it struck me what a really extraordinary lucky chance Fate had placed in my way. I knew that Moriarty was not the only man who had sworn my death. There were at least three others whose desire for vengeance upon me would only be increased by the death of their leader. They were all most dangerous men. One or other would certainly get me. On the other hand, if all the world was convinced that I was dead they would take liberties, these men, they would soon lay themselves open, and sooner or later I could destroy them. Then it would be time for me to announce that I was still in the land of the living. So rapidly does the brain act that I believe I had thought this all out before Professor Moriarty had reached the bottom of the Reichenbach Fall.

"I stood up and examined the rocky wall behind me. In your picturesque account of the matter, which I read with great interest some months later, you assert that the wall was sheer. That was not literally true. A few small footholds presented themselves, and there was some indication of a ledge. The cliff is so high that to climb it all was an obvious impossibility, and it was equally impossible to make my way along the wet path without leaving some tracks. I might, it is true, have reversed my boots, as I have done on similar occasions, but the sight of three sets of tracks in one direction would certainly have suggested a deception. On the whole, then, it was best that I should risk the climb. It was not a pleasant business, Watson. The fall roared beneath me. I am not a fanciful person, but I give you my word that I seemed to hear Moriarty's voice screaming at me out of the abyss. A mistake would have been fatal. More than once, as tufts of grass came out in my hand or my foot slipped in the wet notches of the rock, I thought that I was gone. But I struggled upward, and at last I reached a ledge several feet deep and covered with soft green moss, where I could lie unseen, in the most perfect comfort. There I was stretched, when you, my dear Watson, and all your following were investigating in the most sympathetic and inefficient manner the circumstances of my death.

"At last, when you had all formed your inevitable and totally erroneous conclusions, you departed for the hotel, and I was left alone. I had imagined that I had reached the end of my adventures, but a very unexpected occurrence showed me that there were surprises still in store for me. A huge rock, falling from above, boomed past me, struck the path, and bounded over into the chasm. For an instant I thought that it was an accident, but a moment later, looking up, I saw a man's head against the darkening sky, and another stone struck the very ledge upon which I was stretched, within a foot of my head. Of course, the meaning of this was obvious. Moriarty had not been alone. A confederate—and even that one glance had told me how dangerous a man that confederate—had kept guard while the Professor had attacked me. From a distance, unseen by me, he had been a witness of his friend's death and of my escape. He had waited, and then making his way round to the top of the cliff, he had endeavoured to succeed where his comrade had failed.

"I did not take long to think about it, Watson. Again I saw that grim face look over the cliff, and I knew that it was the precursor of another stone. I scrambled down on to the path. I don't think I could have done it in cold blood. It was a hundred times more difficult than getting up. But I had no time to think of the danger, for another stone sang past me as I hung by my hands from the edge of the ledge. Halfway down I slipped, but, by the blessing of God, I landed, torn and bleeding, upon the path. I took to my heels, did ten miles over the mountains in the darkness, and a week later I found myself in Florence, with the certainty that no one in the world knew what had become of me.

"I had only one confidant—my brother Mycroft. I owe you many apologies, my dear Watson, but it was all-important that it should be thought I was dead, and it is quite certain that you would not have written so convincing an account of my unhappy end had you not yourself thought that it was true. Several times during the last three years I have taken up my pen to write to you, but always I feared lest your affectionate regard for me should tempt you to some indiscretion which would betray my secret. For that reason I turned away from you this evening when you upset my books, for I was in danger at the time, and any show of surprise and emotion upon your part might have drawn attention to my identity and led to the most deplorable and irreparable results. As to Mycroft, I had to confide in him in order to obtain the money which I needed. The course of events in London did not run so well as I had hoped, for the trial of the Moriarty gang left two of its most dangerous members, my own most vindictive enemies, at liberty. I travelled for two years in Tibet, therefore, and amused myself by visiting Lhassa, and spending some days with the head lama. You may have read of the remarkable explorations of a Norwegian named Sigerson, but I am sure that it never occurred to you that you were receiving news of your friend. I then passed through Persia, looked in at Mecca, and paid a short but interesting visit to the Khalifa at Khartoum, the results of which I have communicated to the Foreign Office. Returning to France, I spent some months in a research into the coal-tar derivatives, which I conducted in a laboratory at Montpellier, in the south of France. Having concluded this to my satisfaction and learning that only one of my enemies was now left in London, I was about to return when my movements were hastened by the news of this very remarkable Park Lane Mystery, which not only appealed to me by its own merits, but which seemed to offer some most peculiar personal opportunities. I came over at once to London, called in my own person at Baker Street, threw Mrs. Hudson into violent hysterics, and found that Mycroft had preserved my rooms and my papers exactly as they had always been. So it was, my dear Watson, that at two o'clock to-day I found myself in my old armchair in my own old room, and only wishing that I could have seen my old friend Watson in the other chair which he has so often adorned."

Such was the remarkable narrative to which I listened on that April evening—a narrative which would have been utterly incredible to me had it not been confirmed by the actual sight of the tall, spare figure and the keen, eager face, which I had never thought to see again. In some manner he had learned of my own sad bereavement, and his sympathy was shown in his manner rather than in his words. "Work is the best antidote to sorrow, my dear Watson," said he; "and I have a piece of work for us both to-night which, if we can bring it to a successful conclusion, will in itself justify a man's life on this planet." In vain I begged him to tell me more. "You will hear and see enough before morning," he answered. "We have three years of the past to discuss. Let that suffice until half-past nine, when we start upon the notable adventure of the empty house."

It was indeed like old times when, at that hour, I found myself seated beside him in a hansom, my revolver in my pocket, and the thrill of adventure in my heart. Holmes was cold and stern and silent. As the gleam of the streetlamps flashed upon his austere features, I saw that his brows were drawn down in thought and his thin lips compressed. I knew not what wild beast we were about to hunt down in the dark jungle of criminal London, but I was well assured, from the bearing of this master huntsman, that the adventure was a most grave one—while the sardonic smile which occasionally broke through his ascetic gloom boded little good for the object of our quest.

I had imagined that we were bound for Baker Street, but Holmes stopped the cab at the corner of Cavendish Square. I observed that as he stepped out he gave a most searching glance to right and left, and at every subsequent street corner he took the utmost pains to assure that he was not followed. Our route was certainly a singular one. Holmes's knowledge of the byways of London was extraordinary, and on this occasion he passed rapidly and with an assured step through a network of mews and stables, the very existence of which I had never known. We emerged at last into a small road, lined with old, gloomy houses, which led us into Manchester Street, and so to Blandford Street. Here he turned swiftly down a narrow passage, passed through a wooden gate into a deserted yard, and then opened with a key the back door of a house. We entered together, and he closed it behind us.

The place was pitch dark, but it was evident to me that it was an empty house. Our feet creaked and crackled over the bare planking, and my outstretched hand touched a wall from which the paper was hanging in ribbons. Holmes's cold, thin fingers closed round my wrist and led me forward down a long hall, until I dimly saw the murky fanlight over the door. Here Holmes turned suddenly to the right, and we found ourselves in a large, square, empty room, heavily shadowed in the corners, but faintly lit in the centre from the lights of the street beyond. There was no lamp near, and the window was thick with dust, so that we could only just discern each other's figures within. My companion put his hand upon my shoulder and his lips close to my ear.

"Do you know where we are?" he whispered.

"Surely that is Baker Street," I answered, staring through the dim window.

"Exactly. We are in Camden House, which stands opposite to our own old quarters."

"But why are we here?"

"Because it commands so excellent a view of that picturesque pile. Might I trouble you, my dear Watson, to draw a little nearer to the window, taking every precaution not to show yourself, and then to look up at our old rooms—the starting-point of so many of your little fairy-tales? We will see if my three years of absence have entirely taken away my power to surprise you."

I crept forward and looked across at the familiar window. As my eyes fell upon it, I gave a gasp and a cry of amazement. The blind was down, and a strong light was burning in the room. The shadow of a man who was seated in a chair within was thrown in hard, black outline upon the luminous screen of the window. There was no mistaking the poise of the head, the squareness of the shoulders, the sharpness of the features. The face was turned half-round, and the effect was that of one of those black silhouettes which our grandparents loved to frame. It was a perfect reproduction of Holmes. So amazed was I that I threw out my hand to make sure that the man himself was standing beside me. He was quivering with silent laughter.

"Well?" said he.

"Good heavens!" I cried. "It is marvellous."

"I trust that age doth not wither nor custom stale my infinite variety," said he, and I recognized in his voice the joy and pride which the artist takes in his own creation. "It really is rather like me, is it not?"

"I should be prepared to swear that it was you."

"The credit of the execution is due to Monsieur Oscar Meunier, of Grenoble, who spent some days in doing the moulding. It is a bust in wax. The rest I arranged myself during my visit to Baker Street this afternoon."

"But why?"

"Because, my dear Watson, I had the strongest possible reason for wishing certain people to think that I was there when I was really elsewhere."

"And you thought the rooms were watched?"

"I *knew* that they were watched."

"By whom?"

"By my old enemies, Watson. By the charming society whose leader lies in the Reichenbach Fall. You must remember that they knew, and only they knew, that I was still alive. Sooner or later they believed that I should come back to my rooms. They watched them continuously, and this morning they saw me arrive."

"How do you know?"

"Because I recognized their sentinel when I glanced out of my window. He is a harmless enough fellow, Parker by name, a garroter by trade, and a remarkable performer upon the jew's-harp. I cared nothing for him. But I cared a great deal for the much more formidable person who was behind him, the bosom friend of Moriarty, the man who dropped the rocks over the cliff, the most cunning and dangerous criminal in London. That is the man who is after me to-night, Watson, and that is the man who is quite unaware that we are after *him.*"

My friend's plans were gradually revealing themselves. From this convenient retreat, the watchers were being watched and the trackers tracked. That angular shadow up yonder was the bait, and we were the hunters. In silence we stood together in the darkness and watched the hurrying figures who passed and repassed in front of us. Holmes was silent and motionless; but I could tell that he was keenly alert, and that his eyes were fixed intently upon the stream of passers-by. It was a bleak and boisterous night, and the wind whistled shrilly down the long street. Many people were moving to and fro, most of them muffled in their coats and cravats. Once or twice it seemed to me that I had seen the same figure before, and I especially noticed two men who appeared to be sheltering themselves from the wind in the doorway of a house some distance up the street. I tried to draw my companion's attention to them; but he gave a little ejaculation of impatience, and continued to stare into the street. More than once he fidgeted with his feet and tapped rapidly with his fingers upon the wall. It was evident to me that he was becoming uneasy, and that his plans were not working out altogether as he had hoped. At last, as midnight approached and the street gradually cleared, he paced up and down the room in uncontrollable agitation. I was about to make some remark to him, when I raised my eyes to the lighted window, and again experienced almost as great a surprise as before. I clutched Holmes's arm, and pointed upward.

"The shadow has moved!" I cried.

It was indeed no longer the profile, but the back, which was turned towards us.

Three years had certainly not smoothed the asperities of his temper or his impatience with a less active intelligence than his own.

"Of course it has moved," said he. "Am I such a farcical bungler, Watson, that I should erect an obvious dummy, and expect that some of the sharpest men in Europe would be deceived by it? We have been in this room two hours, and Mrs. Hudson has made some change in that figure eight times, or once in every quarter of an hour. She works it from the front, so that her shadow may never be seen. Ah!" He drew in his breath with a shrill, excited intake. In the dim light I saw his head thrown forward, his whole attitude rigid with attention. Outside the street was absolutely deserted. Those two men might still be crouching in the doorway, but I could no longer see them. All was still and dark, save only that brilliant yellow screen in front of us with the black figure outlined upon its centre. Again in the utter silence I heard that thin, sibilant note which spoke of intense suppressed excitement. An instant later he pulled me back into the blackest corner of the room and I felt his warning hand upon my lips. The fingers which clutched me were quivering. Never had I known my friend more moved, and yet the dark street still stretched lonely and motionless before us.

But suddenly I was aware of that which his keener senses had already distinguished. A low, stealthy sound came to my ear, not from the direction of Baker Street, but from the back of the very house in which we lay concealed. A door opened and shut. An instant later steps crept down the passage—steps which were meant to be silent, but which reverberated harshly through the empty house. Holmes crouched back against the wall, and I did the same, my hand closing upon the handle of my revolver. Peering through the gloom, I saw the vague outline of a man, a shade blacker than the blackness of the open door. He stood for an instant, and then he crept forward, crouching, menacing, into the room. He was within three yards of us, this sinister figure, and I had braced myself to meet his spring, before I realized that he had no idea of our presence. He passed close beside us, stole over to the window, and very softly and noiselessly raised it for half a foot. As he sank to the level of this opening, the light of the street, no longer dimmed by the dusty glass, fell full upon his face. The man seemed to be beside himself with excitement. His two eyes shone like stars, and his features were working convulsively. He was an elderly man, with a thin, projecting nose, a high, bald forehead, and a huge grizzled moustache. An opera hat was pushed to the back of his head, and an evening dress shirt-front gleamed out through his open overcoat. His face was gaunt and swarthy, scored with deep, savage lines. In his hand he carried what appeared to be a stick, but as he laid it down upon the floor it gave a metallic clang. Then from the pocket of his overcoat he drew a bulky object, and he busied himself in some task which ended with a loud, sharp click, as if a spring or bolt had fallen into its place. Still kneeling upon the floor he bent forward and threw all his weight and strength upon some lever, with the result that there came a long, whirling, grinding noise, ending once more in a powerful click. He straightened himself then, and I saw that what he held in his hand was a sort of gun, with a curiously misshapen butt. He opened it at the breech, put something in, and snapped the breech-lock. Then, crouching down, he rested the end of the barrel upon the ledge of the open window, and I saw his long moustache droop over the stock and his eye gleam as it peered along the sights. I heard a little sigh of satisfaction as he cuddled the butt into his shoulder, and saw that amazing target, the black man on the yellow ground, standing clear at the end of his foresight. For an instant he was rigid and motionless. Then his finger tightened on the trigger. There was a strange, loud whiz and a long, silvery tinkle of broken glass. At that instant Holmes sprang like a tiger on to the marksman's back, and hurled him flat upon his face. He was up again in a moment, and with convulsive strength he seized Holmes by the throat, but I struck him on the head with the butt of my revolver, and he dropped again upon the floor. I fell upon him, and as I held him my comrade blew a shrill call upon a whistle. There was the clatter of running feet upon the pavement, and two policemen in uniform, with one plainclothes detective, rushed through the front entrance and into the room.

"That you, Lestrade?" said Holmes.

"Yes, Mr. Holmes. I took the job myself. It's good to see you back in London, sir."

"I think you want a little unofficial help. Three undetected murders in one year won't do, Lestrade. But you handled the Molesey Mystery with less than your usual—that's to say, you handled it fairly well."

We had all risen to our feet, our prisoner breathing hard, with a stalwart constable on each side of him. Already a few loiterers had begun to collect in the street. Holmes stepped up to the window, closed it, and dropped the blinds. Lestrade had produced two candles, and the policemen had uncovered their lanterns. I was able at last to have a good look at our prisoner.

It was a tremendously virile and yet sinister face which was turned towards us. With the brow of a philosopher above and the jaw of a sensualist below, the man must have started with great capacities for good or for evil. But one could not look upon his cruel blue eyes, with their drooping, cynical lids, or upon the fierce, aggressive nose and the threatening, deep-lined brow, without reading Nature's plainest danger-signals. He took no heed of any of us, but his eyes were fixed upon Holmes's face with an expression in which hatred and amazement were equally blended. "You fiend!" he kept on muttering. "You clever, clever fiend!"

"Ah, Colonel!" said Holmes, arranging his rumpled collar. " 'Journeys end in lovers' meetings,' as the old play says. I don't think I have had the pleasure of seeing you since you favoured me with those attentions as I lay on the ledge above the Reichenbach Fall."

The colonel still stared at my friend like a man in a trance. "You cunning, cunning fiend!" was all that he could say.

"I have not introduced you yet," said Holmes. "This, gentlemen, is Colonel Sebastian Moran, once of Her Majesty's Indian Army, and the best heavy-game shot that our Eastern Empire has ever produced. I believe I am correct, Colonel, in saying that your bag of tigers still remains unrivalled?"

The fierce old man said nothing, but still glared at my companion. With his savage eyes and bristling moustache he was wonderfully like a tiger himself.

"I wonder that my very simple stratagem could deceive so old a *shikari*,"* said Holmes. "It must be very familiar to you. Have you not tethered a young kid under a tree, lain above it with your rifle, and waited for the bait to bring up your tiger? This empty house is my tree, and you are my tiger. You have possibly had other guns in reserve in case there should be several tigers, or in the unlikely supposition of your own aim failing you. These," he pointed around, "are my other guns. The parallel is exact."

Colonel Moran sprang forward with a snarl of rage, but the constables dragged him back. The fury upon his face was terrible to look at.

"I confess that you had one small surprise for me," said Holmes. "I did not anticipate that you would yourself make use of this empty house and this convenient front window. I had imagined you as operating from the street, where my friend Lestrade and his merry men were awaiting you. With that exception, all has gone as I expected."

Colonel Moran turned to the official detective.

"You may or may not have just cause for arresting me," said he, "but at

*Big-game hunter in India

least there can be no reason why I should submit to the gibes of this person. If I am in the hands of the law, let things be done in a legal way."

"Well, that's reasonable enough," said Lestrade. "Nothing further you have to say, Mr. Holmes, before we go?"

Holmes had picked up the powerful air-gun from the floor, and was examining its mechanism.

"An admirable and unique weapon," said he, "noiseless and of tremendous power: I knew Von Herder, the blind German mechanic, who constructed it to the order of the late Professor Moriarty. For years I have been aware of its existence, though I have never before had the opportunity of handling it. I commend it very specially to your attention, Lestrade, and also the bullets which fit it."

"You can trust us to look after that, Mr. Holmes," said Lestrade, as the whole party moved towards the door. "Anything further to say?"

"Only to ask what charge you intend to prefer?"

"What charge, sir? Why, of course, the attempted murder of Mr. Sherlock Holmes."

"Not so, Lestrade. I do not propose to appear in the matter at all. To you, and to you only, belongs the credit of the remarkable arrest which you have effected. Yes, Lestrade, I congratulate you! With your usual happy mixture of cunning and audacity, you have got him."

"Got him! Got whom, Mr. Holmes?"

"The man that the whole force has been seeking in vain—Colonel Sebastian Moran, who shot the Honourable Ronald Adair with an expanding bullet from an air-gun through the open window of the second-floor front of No. 427 Park Lane, upon the thirtieth of last month. That's the charge, Lestrade. And now, Watson, if you can endure the draught from a broken window, I think that half an hour in my study over a cigar may afford you some profitable amusement."

Our old chambers had been left unchanged through the supervision of Mycroft Holmes and the immediate care of Mrs. Hudson. As I entered I saw, it is true, an unwonted tidiness, but the old landmarks were all in their place. There were the chemical corner and the acid-stained, deal-topped table. There upon a shelf was the row of formidable scrapbooks and books of reference which many of our fellow-citizens would have been so glad to burn. The diagrams, the violin-case, and the pipe-rack—even the Persian slipper which contained the tobacco—all met my eyes as I glanced round me. There were two occupants of the room—one, Mrs. Hudson, who beamed upon us both as we entered—the other, the strange dummy which had played so important a part in the evening's adventures. It was a wax-coloured model of my friend, so admirably done that it was a perfect facsimile. It stood on a small pedestal table with an old dressing-gown of Holmes's so draped round it that the illusion from the street was absolutely perfect.

"I hope you observed all precautions, Mrs. Hudson?" said Holmes.

"I went to it on my knees, sir, just as you told me."

"Excellent. You carried the thing out very well. Did you observe where the bullet went?"

"Yes, sir. I'm afraid it has spoilt your beautiful bust, for it passed right through the head and flattened itself on the wall. I picked it up from the carpet. Here it is!"

Holmes held it out to me. "A soft revolver bullet, as you perceive, Watson. There's genius in that, for who would expect to find such a thing fired from an air-gun? All right, Mrs. Hudson. I am much obliged for your assistance. And now, Watson, let me see you in your old seat once more, for there are several points which I should like to discuss with you."

He had thrown off the seedy frockcoat, and now he was the Holmes of old in the mouse-coloured dressing-gown which he took from his effigy.

"The old *shikari's* nerves have not lost their steadiness, nor his eyes their keenness," said he, with a laugh, as he inspected the shattered forehead of his bust.

"Plumb in the middle of the back of the head and smack through the brain. He was the best shot in India, and I expect that there are few better in London. Have you heard the name?"

"No, I have not."

"Well, well, such is fame! But then, if I remember right, you had not heard the name of Professor James Moriarty, who had one of the great brains of the century. Just give me down my index of biographies from the shelf."

He turned over the pages lazily, leaning back in his chair and blowing great clouds from his cigar.

"My collection of M's is a fine one," said he. "Moriarty himself is enough to make any letter illustrious, and here is Morgan the poisoner, and Merridew of abominable memory, and Mathews, who knocked out my left canine in the waiting-room at Charing Cross, and, finally, here is our friend of to-night."

He handed over the book, and I read:

Moran, Sebastian, Colonel. Unemployed. Formerly 1st Bangalore Pioneers. Born London, 1840. Son of Sir Augustus Moran, C.B., once British Minister to Persia. Educated Eton and Oxford. Served in Jowaki Campaign, Afghan Campaign, Charasiab (despatches), Sherpur, and Cabul. Author of *Heavy Game of the Western Himalayas* (1881); *Three Months in the Jungle* (1884). Address: Conduit Street. Clubs: The Anglo-Indian, the Tankerville, the Bagatelle Card Club.

On the margin was written, in Holmes's precise hand:

The second most dangerous man in London.

"This is astonishing," said I, as I handed back the volume. "The man's career is that of an honourable soldier."

"It is true," Holmes answered. "Up to a certain point he did well. He was always a man of iron nerve, and the story is still told in India how he crawled down a drain after a wounded man-eating tiger. There are some trees, Watson, which grow to a certain height, and then suddenly develop some unsightly eccentricity. You will see it often in humans. I have a theory that the individual represents in his development the whole procession of his ancestors, and that such a sudden turn to good or evil stands for some strong influence which came into the line of his pedigree. The person becomes, as it were, the epitome of the history of his own family."

"It is surely rather fanciful."

"Well, I don't insist upon it. Whatever the cause, Colonel Moran began to go wrong. Without any open scandal, he still made India too hot to hold him. He retired, came to London, and again acquired an evil name. It was at this time that he was sought out by Professor Moriarty, to whom for a time he was chief of the staff. Moriarty supplied him liberally with money, and used him only in one or two very high-class jobs, which no ordinary criminal could have undertaken. You may have some recollection of the death of Mrs. Stewart, of Lauder, in 1887. Not? Well, I am sure Moran was at the bottom of it, but nothing could be proved. So cleverly was the colonel concealed that, even when the Moriarty gang was broken up, we could not incriminate him. You remember at that date, when I called upon you in your rooms, how I put up the shutters for fear of air-guns? No doubt you thought me fanciful. I knew exactly what I was doing, for I knew of the existence of this remarkable gun, and I knew also that one of the best shots in the world would be behind it. When we were in Switzerland he followed us with Moriarty, and it was undoubtedly he who gave me that evil five minutes on the Reichenbach ledge.

"You may think that I read the papers with some attention during my sojourn in France, on the look-out for any chance of laying him by the heels. So long as he was free in London, my life would really not have been worth living. Night and day the shadow would have been over me, and sooner or later his chance must have come. What could I do? I could not shoot him at sight, or I should myself be in the dock. There was no use appealing to a magistrate. They cannot interfere on the strength of what would appear to them to be a wild suspicion. So I could do nothing. But I watched the criminal news, knowing that sooner or later I should get him. Then came the death of this Ronald Adair. My chance had come at last. Knowing what I did, was it not certain that Colonel Moran had done it? He had played cards with the lad, he had followed him home from the club, he had shot him through the open window. There was not a doubt of it. The bullets alone are enough to put his head in a noose. I came over at once. I was seen by the sentinel, who would, I knew, direct the colonel's attention to my presence. He could not fail to connect my sudden return with his crime, and to be terribly alarmed. I was sure that he would make an attempt to get me out of the way *at once,* and would bring round his murderous weapon for that purpose. I left him an excellent mark in the window, and, having warned the police that they might be needed—by the way, Watson, you spotted their presence in that doorway with unerring accuracy—I took up what seemed to me to be a judicious post for observation, never dreaming that he would choose the same spot for his attack. Now, my dear Watson, does anything remain for me to explain?"

"Yes," said I. "You have not made it clear what was Colonel Moran's motive in murdering the Honourable Ronald Adair?"

"Ah! my dear Watson, there we come into those realms of conjecture, where the most logical mind may be at fault. Each may form his own hypothesis upon the present evidence, and yours is as likely to be correct as mine."

"You have formed one, then?"

"I think that it is not difficult to explain the facts. It came out in evidence that Colonel Moran and young Adair had, between them, won a considerable amount of money. Now, Moran undoubtedly played foul—of that I have long been aware. I believe that on the day of the murder Adair had discovered that Moran was cheating. Very likely he had spoken to him privately, and had threatened to expose him unless he voluntarily resigned his membership of the club, and promised not to play cards again. It is unlikely that a youngster like Adair would at once make a hideous scandal by exposing a well-known man so much older than himself. Probably he acted as I suggest. The exclusion from his clubs would mean ruin to Moran, who lived by his ill-gotten card-gains. He therefore murdered Adair, who at the time was endeavouring to work out how much money he should himself return, since he could not profit by his partner's foul play. He locked the door lest the ladies should surprise him and insist upon knowing what he was doing with these names and coins. Will it pass?"

"I have no doubt that you have hit upon the truth."

"It will be verified or disproved at the trial. Meanwhile, come what may, Colonel Moran will trouble us no more. The famous air-gun of Von Herder will embellish the Scotland Yard Museum, and once again Mr. Sherlock Holmes is free to devote his life to examining those interesting little problems which the complex life of London so plentifully presents."

ACTIVITIES

1)   What do you think of the way Doyle brought Holmes back again? Was the resurrection plausible or did you find flaws in it? Explain.

2)   Before reading the story, did you come up with a method for "returning Holmes from the dead"? If so, what was your way and how does it compare with Conan Doyle's?

3)   What was there about nineteenth-century readers that made them react as they did to the death of a fictional hero? Do you think the reading public of today would react in the same way? Explain your response by comparing it to your own class poll.

Conan Doyle Competes with Holmes

As you may remember, Edgar Allan Poe attempted to solve a real-life murder mystery using the deductive style of his fictional detective, Dupin.

Sir Arthur Conan Doyle followed right along in Poe's footsteps by involving himself in several actual crime cases. Like those of Holmes, his efforts proved successful; he was instrumental in freeing two convicted men from criminal charges of which they were totally innocent.

The most notorious of these cases was the one concerning George Edalje; its reverberations shook most of England. After Sir Arthur entered the case, the entire world was to hear of it. As you read about these events, you may be reminded of the old adage, "truth is stranger than fiction," for, if anything, this real case is even more bizarre than any of the Holmes adventures.

George Edalje was the son of the Reverend S. Edalje, a vicar of the Anglican parish of Great Wyrley. But the Reverend Edalje was also a Parsee.* The vicar's wife, however, was an Englishwoman. Their son, the half-caste George, was a young man of the finest character, a talented student who had won the highest honors in his law studies. But there was racism in nineteenth-century England even as we find it in many parts of the world today. As Conan Doyle stated later on, "How the vicar came to be a Parsee, or how the Parsee came to be the vicar, I have no idea ... [T]hough the vicar was an amiable and devoted man, the appearance of a coloured clergyman with a half-caste son in a rude, unrefined parish was bound to cause some regrettable situation."[4]

That it did.

The family became a target for a rash of "poison pen" letters and other forms of neighborhood prejudice and malice. Shortly afterwards, an epidemic of deliberate and vicious horse-maiming took place in the surrounding countryside and these incidents continued incessantly with the police unable to apprehend the criminal.

George Edalje was arrested for the crime. The principal evidence against him was contained in the anonymous letters that had been plaguing his family. In some of these missives, the writer had hinted at a knowledge of crimes involving horses.

George was accused of writing the letters!

As incredibly far-fetched and weak as this evidence was, it did enable the police to secure a conviction. In the year 1903, George was tried, found guilty, and sentenced to seven years' imprisonment.

Three years later, Conan Doyle became acquainted with these thus-far obscure facts. "I realized I was in the presence of an appalling tragedy," he said, "and that I was called upon to do what I could to set it right."[5]

Immediately, he instigated an exhaustive investigation that included research, a visit with the Edalje family, and a thorough inspection of the area where the various horse-cripplings had taken place. In the year 1907, he

---

*Parsees, originally from Persia, are lighter-skinned than Indians, who are not black.

began the publication of a series of newspaper articles analyzing what had occurred up to then.

Doyle showed how unlikely it was for a person of George's character and personality to have committed such actions. According to people who had watched him grow up, George had never shown any of the traits of cruelty attributed to him in his indictment. Instead, the young man had become a skilled and devoted lawyer who, at the early age of 27, had written a fine book on the subject of railroad law. He did not smoke or drink and he had very bad eyesight, which made it impossible for him to recognize anyone at a distance of six yards. The proposition that George could have reached fields containing horses a good distance away from his home, at night with tracks, fences, and hedges in the way, was too absurd for Sir Arthur's logical mind. The criminal had to be a man who could see far better than the virtually blind Edalje.

Doyle did more than just prove the impossibility of George's involvement; he began pointing the finger at the real criminal. While investigating the Edalje affair, Sir Arthur had received several letters threatening his life if he did not stop. The handwriting seemed the same as that which had appeared in the "poison-pen" letters. After further investigation, Doyle got hold of the writing of a man who lived in Wyrley. In his autobiography, Doyle called this man, "X"; he was able to obtain from "X's" belongings a peculiar knife or horse lancet.[6] The author-sleuth interviewed an acquaintance of the new suspect, who informed him that he had seen the tool in "X's" possession and that the man had boasted of performing the mutilations with it.

Additional investigation revealed that "X" had been trained in the slaughter-yard and was used to butchering livestock. Also, the man had a record of committing destructive acts and of writing anonymous letters. A handwriting expert was sure that "X's" handwriting and that found in the "poison-pen" letters were one and the same.

Clearly, racial prejudice and police bungling had sent an innocent man to jail. Conan Doyle succeeded in having the case reopened. Edalje was finally freed and the new suspect arrested.

One thing marred Sir Arthur's "cracking of" the case; the innocent victim never received any compensation or expression of regret from the authorities who had unjustly convicted him.

". . . [A] blot upon the record of English Justice," an angry, yet happy Conan Doyle commented.[7] At that moment, Sherlock Holmes would have been very proud of his talented creator.

RESEARCH ACTIVITY

If you enjoyed reading about Conan Doyle and the Edalje affair, you may be interested in researching another real-life case in which the author-sleuth was involved. Your school library probably has information about it; it was called *the Oscar Slater case.* After you have uncovered these facts, probably the rest of your class will enjoy receiving an oral or written report.

Like Poe, Doyle, Too, Became Interested in Secret Writing

Late in his career, Sir Arthur Conan Doyle stated the following: "Not only is Poe the originator of the detective story; all treasure-hunting, crypto-gram-solving yarns trace back to his 'Gold Bug'."[8]

He had created the fabulous Sherlock Holmes and had made Poe's detective genre world-famous but he himself had never written a cryptography story. Bringing Holmes back to life gave him the opportunity.

He made up his mind that one tale of *The Return of Sherlock Holmes* would be a yarn involving secret writing. The idea for the particular cipher he would use came to him one day on an automobile trip to the Hill House Hotel in Norfolk, then kept by a family named Cubitt. The small son of the proprietor had a "cute" habit of writing his signature like a line of dancing men. Sparked by these figures, Doyle began working on his "Gold Bug" tale in the Green Room of the hotel.

Needless to say, when the chambermaid came to clean the room, she found the floor strewn with all kinds of dancing sketches. Doyle entitled his story, "The Dancing Men," and we recommend that you read and enjoy this story in your school library.

RESEARCH ACTIVITY

There may be those among you who would like to delve further into the subject of cryptography. If so, may we suggest that you browse through your school library for other material. Two very excellent texts dealing with codes are *Cryptography* by Lawrence Dwight Smith and *Secret Writing* by James Raymond Wolfe. If the library does not have these books, we are sure that you will find others that will prove just as useful. You are certain to run across a number of fascinating substitution and transposition codes—so why not "funnel them" into your classroom for others to enjoy?

The Glorious "Put-On"

One of the difficulties of creative writing is that of fashioning a character who will seem real and believable to a reader. One might say, in the case of Sir Arthur Conan Doyle, that he exceeded any writer's wildest hopes. As you know, Sherlock Holmes became so real to his fans that many were ready to "tar and feather" his creator when Conan Doyle killed him off.

Some of you might argue that those readers who thought Holmes a living person were naive and gullible. Just imagine, you might say, not knowing a real from an imaginary person!

We would have to agree with you.

But you would have to agree with us that those gullible ones also possessed imagination, and imagination is what any art form is all about. Think of all the enjoyment you have received from reading novels, short stories, and poems, from viewing stage, movie, and TV plays, from looking at paintings and photographs, and from listening to all kinds of music—from classical to folk-rock. You could not have experienced this enjoyment had you lacked the capacity to imagine. And the artists who did the creating not only needed imagination as one of their resources but had to possess the skill to use it deftly and precisely—even as a surgeon uses a scalpel.

True, uncontrolled imagination can lead to all kinds of psychological problems, neuroses and even psychoses. At the very least, it produces the gullibility and naiveté of the nineteenth-century reader mentioned above. But when people learn how to channel imagination in the manner of creative artists or sophisticated appreciators of art, then mankind has another powerful instrument at its disposal to bring knowledge and pleasure unto itself.

In fact, we would like to tell you about a marvelous game of imagination involving Sherlock Holmes, played by a group of sophisticated readers. These people, some of them world-famous scholars, writers, scientists, and politicians, know full well that Holmes never existed. But because they loved the character so much, *they decided to make believe that he had.* They began to treat Holmes as if he had been an important historical figure.

For example, a railway locomotive running out of the Baker Street Station was named in his honor. In 1951, at the Festival of Britain, people flocked to a life-sized "reconstruction" of Holmes's sitting room at 221B Baker Street. Today, this reconstruction can be found in a restaurant on Northumberland Street appropriately named "The Sherlock Holmes."

More amazing was the tremendous amount of published material that began to appear about Holmes, written by some of these sophisticated readers and game players. Using the Holmes short stories and novels as source material, they derived fun and satisfaction from constructing biographies, not only of Holmes and Watson, but also of Mrs. Hudson, Professor James Moriarty, Colonel Sebastian Moran, and the other marvelous figments of Doyle's imagination. The most famous of these biographies were *The Private Life of Sherlock Holmes* by Vincent Starrett and *Profile by Gaslight* by Edgar W. Smith. These books could not have been better written or exhibited finer scholarship than if they had been biographies of flesh-and-blood people.

Another aspect of this glorious "put-on" were the clubs and societies that began to form world-wide in honor of Sherlock Holmes. Two of these became famous and issued periodicals and magazines of their own. The

American society, called the Baker Street Irregulars, was founded by Author Christopher Morley in 1934; its membership list included some of the famous names in American literature and government. It issued a quarterly periodical known as *The Baker Street Journal,* which printed all kinds of Holmes material, including poems, puzzles, and debates about various aspects of Holmes's life. The British organization, The Sherlock Holmes Society of London, was established at about the same time and it published a magazine entitled *The Sherlock Holmes Journal;* its membership roster constituted a Who's Who of English public life.

Famous people are not the only ones who can gain admittance to these clubs. Each of you can also join. However, you would have to pass a comprehensive examination proving that you are well acquainted with what club-members call the Sacred Writings, the entire body of Sherlock Holmes fiction.

If the idea of becoming a member of these societies appeals to you, allow us to present here a copy of the Constitution of the Baker Street Irregulars. Reading it is not a solemn task!

CONSTITUTION AND BUY-LAWS OF THE BAKER STREET IRREGULARS

ARTICLE I

The name of this society shall be *The Baker Street Irregulars.*

ARTICLE II

Its purpose shall be the study of The Sacred Writings.

ARTICLE III

All persons shall be eligible for membership who pass an examination in the Sacred Writings set by officers of the society, and who are considered suitable.

ARTICLE IV

The officers shall be: a Gasogene,* a Tantalus,† and a Commissionaire.‡

The duties of the Gasogene shall be those commonly performed by a President.

---

*An apparatus for making soda water (for cocktails)
†Stand or rack with decanters of wines and liquors secured by a lock.
‡A porter or messenger.

The duties of the Tantalus shall be those commonly performed by a Secretary.

The duties of the Commissionaire shall be to telephone down for ice, White Rock, and whatever else may be required and available; to conduct all negotiations with waiters; and to assess the members pro rata for the costs of same.

BUY-LAWS

(1) An annual meeting shall be held on January 6th, or thereabouts, at which the Conanical toasts shall be drunk; after which the members shall drink at will.

(2) The current round shall be bought by a member who fails to identify, by title of story and context, any quotation from the Sacred Writings submitted by any other member.

Qualification A—If two or more members fail so to identify, a round shall be bought by each of those so failing.

Qualification B—If the submitter of the quotation, upon challenge, fails to identify it correctly, he shall buy the round.

(3) Special meetings may be called at any time or place by any one of three members, two of whom shall constitute a quorum.

Qualification A—If said two are of opposite sexes, they shall use care in selecting the place of meeting, to avoid misinterpretation (or interpretation either, for that matter.)

Qualification B—If such two persons of opposite sexes be clients of the Personal Column of the Saturday Review of Literature, the foregoing does not apply; such persons being presumed to let their consciences be their guide.

(4) All other business shall be left for the monthly meeting.

(5) There shall be no monthly meeting.[9]

ACTIVITIES

The Baker Street Irregulars have branches or "scions" in many different American cities. If you too have become Sherlock Holmes fans, you may want to organize one of these "scions" right in your own school or town. By writing to the parent organization at 33 Riverside Drive, New York, N.Y. 10023, you will obtain further information on how to proceed.

1) If you do organize such a club, one of the first things you can do is write your own Constitution. By all means, write it with tongue-in-cheek, just like the original. Also it might be fun to make up your own qualifying examination based upon some or all of the Sacred Writings.

2) After the club's formation, you may want to emulate some of the parent organization's activities. For instance, you can publish a journal or periodical along the lines of *The Baker Street Journal* or *The Sherlock Holmes Journal*. True, printing is expensive but there is no reason why you cannot cut down your costs by mimeographing or dittoing your publication. Possibly you can get the job done right at your school, utilizing existing facilities.

Such a magazine can elicit all kinds of creative writing assignments from club-members and other students. For instance, those who like to write poetry can exercise their talents, even as the parent organization's members do, by writing various kinds of verse about the Holmesian characters.
Such as:

A) A Parody is a poem (or prose work) that imitates the patterns of another work in an amusing manner. A parody is written to evoke laughter, and cleverness and poetic talent are required to construct one. The Holmesian characters are natural targets for this kind of humor and The Baker Street Irregulars have made good use of the parody in the construction of what they call their club "anthem". The following appeared in *The Baker Street Journal* and is a parody of Rudyard Kipling's *Road to Mandalay*. It is sung at gatherings of the society.

"The Road to Baker Street"
by Harvey Officer
(with apologies to Rudyard Kipling)

1)　In a restaurant in Holborn, where young Stamford ate his lunch,
　　He revealed to Doctor Watson news that proved a lucky hunch,
　　For he "did immortal service," whence his memory is bright,
　　Introducing to the Doctor whom we honour here tonight.
　　　　On the road to Baker Street,
　　　　Where Lestrade and Gregson meet,
　　Where the art of crime detection found its scientific feet.
　　　　On the road to Baker Street,
　　　　Where we sit at Sherlock's feet,
　　And we read again the Canon* with the stories all complete.

2)　Now his eyes were sharp and piercing and his nose was long and thin,
　　And his hands were stained with acids, square and prominent his
　　　　chin,
　　His tobacco in a slipper, in a scuttle his cigars,
　　With a gasogene and tantalus not found in modern bars.

---

*All the Sherlock Holmes stories

We begin in Baker Street,
On a day of wind and sleet,
When the "tall, ascetic" figure once again we gladly meet,
For "the game's afoot," he cries,
From his bed must Watson rise,
And they rattle in a hansom for adventurous surprise.

3) But when crime was on vacation and the thugs were lying low,
In his armchair Sherlock fiddled, scraping chords with careless bow,
Chords sonorous, chords fantastic, how he did it no one sees,
For you cannot play such music with your fiddle on your knees.

Had we been in Baker Street,
Would those chords have sounded sweet?
And would we with Doctor Watson have been patient and discreet?
Ah, the years how fast they fleet,
Since those days in Baker Street,
Let us hope that even Mendelssohn from him would be a treat.

4) Ship me off to Piccadili, to a London bobby's beat,
Where a hansom cab would take me to the shrine in Baker Street,
For the bells of London call me, and it's there that I would be,
Sitting in with Doctor Watson on a night-long story spree.

O ye sons of Baker Street,
As we sit at Sherlock's feet,
Be ye sure the land that knew him shall not ever know defeat,
For the men of England's fleet
Once again their foes will beat.
Nor shall foreign armies ever tread the stones of Baker Street.[10]

Try writing an anthem for your school or class "scion." Like what you have read, it can be a parody of any poem or song that appeals to you. Utilize the following rules when you write this kind of verse:

a) The poem or song you choose should be well known, that is, its rhythm should be familiar so that your readers will immediately make the connection between the parody and its model.

b) Imitate the meter, rhyme arrangement, and stanza form of the original as closely as you can. If you wander too far from the style of your model, the less clever your work will sound.

B) One of the oldest forms of poetry is the *limerick,* a type of verse that lends itself well to humor. The limerick is one of the oldest forms of poetry, and down through the ages many people have tried writing it. In 1956, The Sherlock Holmes Society of London held a limerick contest which garnered responses from all over the British Isles and other countries as well. Following are two of the award-winning contributions to what the Journal called its *Sherlimerock competition:*

a)   Based upon "The Final Problem":

The Master remained hale and hearty
Till he wrestled with James Moriarty.
   There are those who will foster
   The idea an imposter
Returned from the Reichenbach party.

                                  —Nathan L. Bengis

b)   Based upon *The Hound of the Baskervilles:*

Mr. Stapleton (born Roger Baskerville),
Preserved in his hideous task of ill;
   Till Holmes came to the Moor,
   Played the Man on the Tor,
And from each Hound plucked the mask of ill.

                          —Roger Lancelyn Green[11]

Have your class participate in a Sherlimerock, individually or jointly. The best ones can, of course, be printed in your class periodical.

Limericks follow a definite form but are easy to write. Here is the way it is done:

Each of the five lines has the following specific meter—

da DUM—da da DUM—da da DUM,	(a)
da DUM—da da DUM—da da DUM	(a)
da da DUM—da da DUM	(b)
da da DUM—da da DUM,	(b)
da da DUM—da da DUM—da da DUM.	(a)

The letters at the ends of the above lines indicate the stanza's rhyme scheme. The three long lines share one rhyme while the two short lines rhyme with each other.

C)   After Sir Arthur Conan Doyle's death, other authors attempted to write Sherlock Holmes stories. Among them was Sir Arthur's son, Adrian Conan Doyle who, in collaboration with John Dickson Carr, published an anthology called *The Exploits of Sherlock Holmes.* Critics have generally agreed that these tales are competent but do not match the level of the originals.

An untold number of stage, radio, TV, and motion picture dramatizations have also been written around the character of Sherlock Holmes. Many actors have portrayed Holmes but the two most remembered for their performances have been William Gillette and Basil Rathbone.

If you like writing short stories or plays, try your hand at some original

Sherlock Holmes yarns. *And what better place to see your words in print than your own class journal . . .*

Conan Doyle's Legacy

After the publication of *The Return of Sherlock Holmes* in 1903, additional Holmes stories continued to appear—until three years before Conan Doyle's death. The former doctor had become a prolific writer, his output approaching fifty books, including historical novels, science-fiction works, and adventure stories, as well as detective tales. This does not include the contributions he made to the field of nonfiction—several history books, many journalistic articles, and a host of essays about spiritualism, a subject in which he and Lady Doyle became interested late in life.

Doyle still kept in touch with his old professor, Dr. Joseph Bell. After Sherlock Holmes became a household name, Bell became creatively inspired and suggested some plots to his old student. Unfortunately, Doyle did not use them because they were "not very practical," he said.[12] Whether Dr. Bell's ego was damaged by this rebuff was not recorded. It shouldn't have been. Bell, the inspiration and model for Holmes, had made enough of a contribution to world literature.

In his Preface to *The Case Book of Sherlock Holmes,* Conan Doyle wrote the following:

> One likes to think there is some fantastic limbo for the children of imagination . . . where [Sir Walter] Scott's heroes may strut, [Charles] Dickens' delightful Cockneys still raise a laugh, and [William] Thackeray's worldlings continue to carry on their reprehensible careers. Perhaps in some humble corner of such a Valhalla, Sherlock and his Watson may for a time find such a place, while some astute sleuth with some even less astute comrade may fill the stage which they have vacated.[13]

In the year 1930, Sir Arthur Conan Doyle, a human being, died. But Sherlock Holmes and Dr. Watson, because they were creatures of a genius's imagination, live on in the hearts of those who love them. Which probably now includes some of you. As for "some more astute sleuth" and "a less-astute comrade," many such were to follow in their footsteps, as you will discover in the chapters to come.

The Sacred Writings

Perhaps you are not satisfied with being a member of a school or class Holmes club. You would rather join the parent organizations, The Baker Street Irregulars or The Sherlock Holmes Society.

If so, you had better begin making your Sacred Preparations for a compre-

hensive examination in the Sacred Writings. For these serious students—
and those others who would simply like to read more Holmes tales—we are
presenting the titles of the rest of the Canon.

To the serious readers, happy studying. To those who are merely brow-
sing, happy reading. To both groups, we guarantee an enjoyable literary
experience.

Novels

The Sign of the Four
The Hound of the Baskervilles
The Valley of Fear

Anthologies

The Adventures of Sherlock Holmes
Memoirs of Sherlock Holmes
The Return of Sherlock Holmes
The Case Book of Sherlock Holmes
His Last Bow

3.

The American Sherlock Holmes

A Pattern Is Set

By the turn of the century, the Dupin-Narrator, Holmes-Watson relationship had begun to stimulate the imaginations of many European and American writers. They were eager to work in the new literary form, and England and America experienced a veritable deluge of detective stories.

Many, of course, were rank imitations of Poe and Doyle and soon disappeared. But the more creative writers developed the new form further by making unique contributions to it.

In England, for example, Arthur Morrison originated the character of Martin Hewitt, a lawyer-turned-detective, and his Watson was one Brett, a journalist. In contrast to Sherlock Holmes, Hewitt was anything but eccentric. Instead he was a commonplace individual who ended up surprising everyone by his brilliant deductions.

R. Austin Freeman gave birth to Dr. John Thorndyke, the first of the "scientific" detectives, and this fictional character received the honor of having his methods put into use by real police. Unlike his predecessors, Thorndyke had not one, but two, associates, Jervis and Polton.

Another twist was contributed by G. K. Chesterton, whose detective hero was a mild, cherubic Catholic priest named Father Brown. Unlike Dupin and Holmes, the good Father was not above placing great reliance upon hunches and an everyday knowledge of human psychology. His part-time assistant was Flambeau, an ex-criminal whom the priest-sleuth had been instrumental in reforming.

Meanwhile in America, Jacques Futrelle was fashioning an even more eccentric sleuth than Sherlock Holmes. Futrelle labeled him The Thinking Machine but his complete name was Augustus S. F. X. Van Dusen, Ph.D., L.L.D., M.D., and M.D.S. and he was employed by a big-city university; his companion-in-detection was a reporter named Hutchison Hatch. Futrelle used humor for the first time in the detective story, thus leading away from the pompous tone of some earlier stories.

Also from America came a woman mystery writer in the person of Mary Roberts Rinehart; loyal to her sex, she was not averse to using women in her detective roles. One of her famous characters was a professional nurse known as Miss Pinkerton.

Another American contribution was S. S. Van Dine's Philo Vance, mystery fiction's first "intellectual" detective. Vance, very cultured, knew "everything there was to know about everything"; today we would call him a snob but when he first appeared, he captured readers' attention and enjoyed a temporary popularity.

Not to be outdone by America, England was blessed with its own female mystery author, a very talented and productive woman named Agatha Christie. She created two particularly memorable sleuths, Hercule Poirot, a male Belgian investigator, and Miss Marple, a sweet-faced elderly spinster.

And there were others, many, many others.

As the twentieth century moved on, fictional sleuths and assistants were fashioned of every conceivable size, nationality, race, and religion possible. They bore such assorted names as Charlie Chan, Sam Spade, Hildegarde Withers, Lord Peter Wimsey, Uncle Abner, Nero Wolfe, Perry Mason, Mr. Strang, etc. Each was a unique character and garnered his or her own disciples from what was fast becoming a mystery-addicted reading public. But not one of them seemed to capture the imagination in the unsurpassed manner of Sherlock Holmes.

It seemed as if Conan Doyle's creation was destined to remain in a class by himself.

And then, in the year 1929, Ellery Queen came along.

The Adventure of the Unknown Author

In 1929, the stockmarket crashed and the Great Depression began in the United States.

Despite its economic problems, the nation continued to buy and read detective stories. Even as Edgar Allan Poe had written detective tales "to keep from going mad," American readers immersed themselves in the plot complications of detective fiction as an escape from the everyday problems caused by a system that had apparently stopped working. The depression did not seem to affect the business of turning out better written and more puzzling detective fiction.

For in that first depression year, *McClure's Magazine* and the Frederick Stokes Publishing Company jointly sponsored a detective story contest with a top-prize award of $7,500. Many manuscripts were submitted and the winner turned out to be a novel entitled *The Roman Hat Mystery*. (Later, McClure's went out of business and the prize was rescinded but the Stokes Company liked the work and published it anyway.) After it came off the presses, detective story readers discovered that two new wrinkles had been added to what had now become an established literary form.

First, just before the novel's dénouement or climax, the author had stopped the progress of his tale, informed his readers directly that they now possessed the same clues as the detective-hero, and challenged them to beat his sleuth to the solution. Thus, readers were invited to "play detective" themselves before continuing with the rest of the narrative.

Second, the names of the fictional sleuth and the author were one and the same—Ellery Queen. Yet, the novel itself was written without the use of the first person "I." In addition, the occupation of the fictional Ellery Queen was the same as that of his creator; he, too, was a detective story writer.

Readers began to ask, "What's it all about?"

But the publishers maintained secrecy about the new author. Needless to say, the public's curiosity was aroused.

In 1930, a second Ellery Queen book, *The French Powder Mystery,* appeared. Readers liked it; in fact, as one critic, Anthony Boucher put it, "... Ellery Queen is the logical successor to Sherlock Holmes."[1] People wanted to meet the author who used the same name as his protagonist. Unfortunately, his publishers could not or would not produce him in the flesh. The Ellery Queen novels contained ingenious solutions to intriguing mysteries, but it appeared as though no one had the solution to the mystery of the new writer's identity.

The public began to clamor, "Who is Ellery Queen?"

In the meantime, more Queen tales appeared, including *The Chinese Orange Mystery* and an anthology of short stories called *The Adventures of Ellery Queen.*

And, in 1932, when Ellery Queen finally stepped forward to meet his readers, lo and behold, *he wore a mask.* Evidently, author Queen intended to continue spinning out the web of his real-life mystery.

The Fictional Ellery

One part fun mixed with an equal proportion of frustration ...

This seemed to be the basic recipe for the steady diet provided by the new detective story writer to an ever-increasing readership during those early 1930s. For the first five years of his career, author Queen succeeded in remaining relatively unknown, and his fans were understandably frustrated. After all, their reason for wanting to meet him was that the fictional Ellery had provided them with so much fun.

Time for you to share in that enjoyment.

We're sure that once you meet the fictional Ellery, history will repeat itself and you, too, will demand to know more about his creator.

Like other fictional sleuths, Ellery, too, had a "Watson," his father, Inspector Richard Queen of the New York Police Department. Here is how the author must have first imagined them; in the foreword to that prize-winning novel, *The Roman Hat Mystery,* a fictional narrator known only as J. J. Mc. described them thusly:

> "I have always found it extremely difficult to explain to strangers the peculiar affinity which bound Richard to Ellery Queen ... they are persons of by no means uncomplicated natures. Richard Queen, sprucely middle-aged after thirty-two years' service in the city police, earned his Inspector's chevrons not so much through diligence as by an extraordinary grasp of the technique of criminal investigation. ...

> "Queen, with his habitual shyness toward newspaper eulogy was the first to scoff at ... the efforts of imaginative journalists to make a legend of him ... I cannot emphasize too strongly the fact that he was heavily dependent upon his son's wit for success in many of his professional achievements.

> "This is not a matter of public knowledge ... but the intuitive sense, the gift of imagination, belonged to Ellery Queen, the fiction-writer. The two might have been twins, impotent by themselves, but vigorous when applied one to another. Richard Queen, far from resenting the bond which made his success so spectacularly possible ... took pains to make (his proud fatherhood) plain to his friends. ..."[2]

Now that you have been properly introduced, let's view the fictional Ellery and his father in action ...

The Adventure of the Telltale Bottle

"Now regarding this folksy fable, this almost-myth, this canard upon history," continued Ellery, "what are the facts? The facts, my dear Nikki, are these:

"It was *not* a good harvest. Oh, they had twenty acres planted to seed corn, but may I remind you that the corn had been pilfered from the Cape Indians? And had it not been for Tisquantum——"

"Tis-who?" asked Inspector Queen feebly.

"—corruptly known as Squanto—there would have been no harvest that year at all. For it took the last of the more-or-less noble Patuxet to teach our bewildered forefathers how to plant it properly."

"Well, you can't deny they decreed *some* sort of holiday," flashed Nikki, "so that they might 'rejoyce' together!"

"I have no desire to distort the facts," replied Ellery with dignity. "To the contrary. They had excellent reason to 'rejoyce'—some of them were still alive. And tell me: Who actually participated in that first American festival?"

"Why, the Pilgrims," said Inspector Queen uneasily.

"And I suppose you'll tell me that as they stuffed themselves with all the traditional goodies other revered forefathers came running out of the woods with arrows through their hats?"

"I remember a picture like that in my grade-school history book—yes," said Nikki defiantly.

"The *fact* is," grinned Ellery, "they were on such good terms with the Indians during that fall of 1621 that the most enthusiastic celebrants at the feast were Massasoit of the Wampanoag and ninety of his braves!—all very hungry, too. And tell me this: What was the menu on that historic occasion?"

"Turkey!"

"Cranberry sauce!"

"Pumpkin pie!"

"And—so forth," concluded the Inspector. He was at home that day receiving Madame La Grippe and he had been—until Ellery unleashed his eloquence—the most ungracious host in New York. But now he was neglecting Madame beautifully.

"I accept merely the and-so-forths," said Ellery indulgently. "If they had 'Turkies' at that feast, there is no mention of them in the record. Yes, there were plenty of cranberries in the bogs—but it is more than doubtful that the Pilgrim ladies knew what to do with them. And we can definitely assert that the pastry possibilities of the Narraganset *askútasquash* were not yet dreamed of by the pale green females who had crept off the *Mayflower.*"

"Listen to him," said the Inspector comfortably.

"I suppose," said Nikki, grinding her teeth, "I suppose they just sat there and munched on that old corn."

"By no means. The menu was regal, considering their customary diet of wormy meal. They gorged themselves on eels——"

"*Eels!*"

"And clams, venison, water-fowl, and so on. For dessert—wild plums and dried berries; and—let's face it—wild grape wine throughout," said Ellery, looking sad. "And—oh, yes. How long did this first thanksgiving celebration last?"

"Thanksgiving day? How long would a day *be*? A day!"

"Three days. And why do we celebrate Thanksgiving in the month of November?"

"Because—because——"

"Because the Pilgrims celebrated it in the month of October," concluded Ellery. "And there you have it, Nikki—the whole sordid record of historical misrepresentation, simply another example of our national vainglory. I say, if we must celebrate Thanksgiving, let us give thanks to the red man, whose land we took away. I say—let us have facts!"

"And *I* say," cried Nikki, "that you're a factual showoff, a—a darned old talking encyclopedia, Ellery Queen, and I don't care what your precious 'facts' are because all I wanted to do was take Thanksgiving baskets of turkeys and cranberries and stuff to those people down on the East side that I take baskets to every year because they're too poor to have decent Thanksgiving dinners tomorrow, and especially this year with prices sky-high and so many refugee children here who ought to learn the American traditions and who's to teach them if . . . And, anyway, one of them *is* an Indian—way back—so there!"

"Why, Nikki," mourned Ellery, joining Nikki on the floor, where she was now hugging the carpet, in tears, "why didn't you tell me one of them is an Indian? That makes all the difference—don't you see?" He sprang erect, glowing fiercely with the spirit of Thanksgiving. "Turkeys! Cranberries! Pumpkin pies! To Mr. Sisquencchi's!"

The affair of the Telltale Bottle was a very special sort of nastiness culminating in that nastiest of nastiness, murder; but it is doubtful if, even had Ellery been a lineal descendant of Mother Shipton, who would have called the bountiful excursion off or in any other wise tarnished that silvery day.

For Mr. Sisquencchi of the market around the corner made several glittering suggestions regarding the baskets; there was a lambency about Miss Porter which brightened with the afternoon; and even Manhattan shone, getting into a snowy party dress as Ellery's ancient Duesenberg padded patiently about the East side.

Ellery lugged baskets and assorted packages through medieval hallways and up donjon* staircases until his arms protested; but this was a revolt of the flesh only—the spirit grew fresher as they knocked on the doors of

---

*dungeon-like

O'Keefes, Del Florios, Cohens, Wilsons, Olsens, Williamses, Pomerantzes, and Johnsons and heard the cries of various Pats, Sammies, Antonios, Olgas, Clarences, and Petunias.

"But where's the Indian?" he demanded, as they sat in the car while Nikki checked over her list. The sun was setting, and several thousand ragamuffins were crawling over the Duesenberg, but it was still a remarkable day.

"Check," said Nikki, "Orchard Street. That's the Indian, Ellery. I mean—oh, she's not an *Indian,* just has some Indian blood way back, Iroquois, I think. She's the last."

"Well, I won't quibble," frowned Ellery, easing old Duesey through the youth of America. "Although I *do* wish——"

"Oh, shut up. Mother Carey's the darlingest old lady—scrubs floors for a living."

"Mother Carey's!"

But at the Orchard Street tenement, under a canopy of ermine-trimmed fire escapes, a janitor was all they found of Ellery's Indian.

"The old hag don't live here no more."

"Oh, dear," said Nikki. "Where's she moved to?"

"She lammed outa here with all her junk in a rush the other day—search me." The janitor spat, just missing Nikki's shoe.

"Any idea where the old lady works?" asked Ellery, just missing the janitor's shoe.

The janitor hastily withdrew his foot. "I think she cleans up some Frog chow joint near Canal Street regular."

"I remember!" cried Nikki. "Fouchet's, Ellery. She's worked there for years. Let's go right over there—maybe they know her new address."

"Fouchet's!" said Ellery gaily; and so infected was he by the enchantment of the fairy-tale afternoon that for once his inner voice failed him.

Fouchet's Restaurant was just off Canal Street, a few blocks from Police Headquarters—squeezed between a button factory and ship chandler's. Cars with Brooklyn accents whished by its plate glass front, and it looked rather frightened by it all. Inside they found round tables covered with checkered oilcloths, a wine bar, walls decorated with prewar French travel posters, a sharp and saucy odour, and a cashier named Clothilde.

Clothilde had a large bosom, a large cameo on it, a large black-velvet ribbon in her hair, and when she opened her mouth to say: "The old woman who clean up?" Nikki saw that she also had a large gold tooth. "Ask Monsieur Fouchet. 'E will be right back." She examined Nikki with very sharp black eyes.

"If the Pilgrims could eat eels," Ellery was mumbling, over a menu, "Why not? *Escargots!* Nikki, let's have dinner here!"

"Well," said Nikki doubtfully. "I suppose . . . as long as we have to wait for Mr. Fouchet, anyway. . . ." A waiter with a long, dreary face led them to a table, and Ellery and the waiter conferred warmly over the menu, but Nikki was not paying attention—she was too busy exchanging brief feminine glances with Clothilde. It was agreed: the ladies did not care for each other. Thereafter, Clothilde wore an oddly watchful expression, and Nikki looked uneasy.

"Ellery ..." said Nikki.

"—only the very best," Ellery was saying baronially. "Now where the devil did that waiter go? I haven't got to the wine. Pierre!"

"*Un moment, Monsieur,*" came the voice of the waiter with the long, dreary face.

"You know, Nikki, less than five per cent of all the wine produced in the world can be called really fine wine——"

"Ellery, I don't like this place," said Nikki.

"The rest is *pour la soif**——"

"Let's ... not eat here after all, Ellery. Let's just find out about Mother Carey and——"

Ellery looked astonished. "Why, Nikki, I thought you loved French food. Consequently, we'll order the rarest, most exquisitely balanced, most perfectly fermented wine. Pierre! Where the deuce has he gone? A Sauterne with body, bouquet, breeding ..."

"Oh!" squeaked Nikki, then she looked guilty. It was only Pierre breathing down her neck.

"After all, it's a special occasion. Ah, there you are. *La carte des vins!*† No, never mind, I know what I want. Pierre," said Ellery magnificently, "a bottle of ... *Chateau d'Yquem!*"

The dreary look on the waiter's face rather remarkably vanished.

"But, monsieur," he murmured, "*Chateau d'Yquem* ... ? That is an expensive wine. We do not carry so fine a wine in our cellar."

And still, as Pierre said this, he contrived to give the impression that something of extraordinary importance had just occurred. Nikki glanced anxiously at Ellery to see if he had caught that strange overtone; but Ellery was merely looking crushed.

"Carried away by the spirit of Thanksgiving Eve. Very stupid of me, Pierre. Of course. Give us the best you have—which," Ellery added as Pierre walked rapidly away, "will probably turn out to be *vin ordinaire.*" And Ellery laughed.

Something is horribly wrong, thought Nikki, and she wondered how long it would take Ellery to become himself again.

It happened immediately after the *pêches flambeaux* and the *demitasse.* Or, rather, two things happened. One involved the waiter. The other involved Clothilde.

The waiter seemed confused: Upon handing Ellery *l'addition,*‡ he simultaneously whisked a fresh napkin into Ellery's lap! This astounding *non sequitor* brought Mr. Queen to his slumbering senses. But he made no remark, merely felt the napkin and, finding something hard and flat

---

*For the thirst (French)
†Wine list (French)
‡Check or bill (French)

concealed in its folds, he extracted it without looking at it and slipped it into his pocket.

As for the cashier, she too seemed confused. In payment of *l'addition,* Ellery tossed a twenty-dollar bill on the desk. Clothilde made change, chattering pleasantly all the while about *Monsieur* and *Mad'moiselle* and 'ow did they like the dinner?—and she made change very badly. She was ten dollars short.

Ellery had just pointed out this deplorable unfamiliarity with the American coinage system when a stout little whirlwind arrived, scattering French before him like leaves.

*"Mais Monsieur Fouchet, je fais une méprise . . ."**

"Bête à manger du foin†—silence!" And M. Fouchet fell upon Ellery, almost weeping. *"Monsieur,* this 'as never 'appen before. I give you my assurance——"

For a chilled moment Nikki thought Ellery was going to produce what lay in his pocket for M. Fouchet's inspection. But Ellery merely smiled and accepted the missing ten-dollar bill graciously and asked for Mother Carey's address. M. Fouchet threw up his hands and ran to the rear of the restaurant and ran back to press an oil-stained scrawl upon them, chattering in French at Ellery, at Nikki, at his cashier; and then they were on the street and making for the Duesenberg in a great show of postprandial content . . . for through the plate glass M. Fouchet, and Clothilde, and—yes—Pierre of the long face were watching them closely.

"Ellery, what . . . ?"

"Not now, Nikki. Get into the car."

Nikki kept glancing nervously at the three Gallic faces as Ellery tried to start the Duesenberg. "Huh?"

"I said it won't start, blast it. Battery." Ellery jumped out into the snow and began tugging at the basket. "Grab those other things and get out, Nikki."

"But——"

"Cab!" A taxicab parked a few yards beyond Fouchet's shot forward. "Driver, get this basket and stuff in there beside you, will you? Nikki, hop to it. Get into the cab!"

"You're leaving the *car?*"

"We can pick it up later. What are you waiting for, driver?"

The driver looked weary. "Ain't you startin' your Thanksgivin' celebratin' a little premature?" he asked. "I ain't no fortune-teller. Where do I go?"

"Oh. That slip Fouchet gave me. Nikki, where . . . ? Here! 214-B Henry Street, cab. The East Side."

The cab slid away. "Wanna draw me diagrams?" muttered the driver.

"Now, Nikki. Let's have a look at Pierre's little gift."

It was a stiff white-paper packet. Ellery unfolded it.

---

*Mr. Fouchet, I've made a mistake." (French)

†You're just as dumb as an ox! (French colloquialism)

It contained a large quantity of a powdery substance—a white crystalline powder.

"Looks like snow," giggled Nikki. "What is it?"

"That's what it is."

"*Snow?*"

"Cocaine."

"That's the hell of this town," the cab-driver was remarking. "Anything can happen. I remember once——"

"Apparently, Nikki," said Ellery with a frown, "I gave Pierre some password or other. By accident."

"He thought you're an addict! That means Fouchet is——"

"A depot for the distribution of narcotics. I wonder what I said that made Pierre ... *The wine!*"

"I don't follow you," complained the driver.

Ellery glared. The driver looked hurt and honked at an elderly Chinese in a black straw hat.

"*Chateau d'Yquem,* Nikki. That was the password! Pearls in a swinery ... of course, of course."

"I *knew* something was wrong the minute we walked in there, Ellery."

"Mmm. We'll drop this truck at Mrs. Carey's, then we'll shoot back uptown and get Dad working on this Fouchet nastiness."

"Watch the Inspector snap out of that cold," laughed Nikki; then she stopped laughing. "Ellery ... do you suppose all this has anything to do with Mother Carey?"

"Oh, nonsense, Nikki."

It was a bad day for the master.

For when they got to 214-B Henry Street and knocked on the door of Apartment 3-A and a voice as shaky as the stairs called out, "who's there?" and Nikki identified herself ... something happened. There were certain sounds. Strange rumbly, sliding sounds. The door was not opened at once.

Nikki bit her lip, glancing timidly at Ellery. Ellery was frowning.

"She don't act any too anxious to snag this turk-bird," said the cab-driver, who had carried up the pumpkin pie and the bottle of California wine which had been one of Mr. Sisquencchis' inspirations, while Nikki took odds and ends and Ellery the noble basket. "My old lady'd be tickled to death——"

"I'd rather it were you," said Ellery violently. "When she opens the door, dump the pie and wine inside, then wait for us in the cab——"

But at that instant the door opened, and a chubby little old woman with knobby forearms and flushed cheeks stood there, looking not even remotely like an Indian.

"Miss Porter!"

"Mother Carey."

It was a poor little room with an odour. Not the odour of poverty; the room was savagely clean. Ellery barely listened to the chirrupings of the two women: he was too busy using his eyes and his nose. He seemed to have forgotten Massasoit and the Wampanoag.

When they were back in the cab, he said abruptly: "Nikki, do you happen to recall Mother Carey's old apartment?"

"The one on Orchard Street? Yes—why?"

"How many rooms did she have there?"

"Two. A bedroom and a kitchen. Why?"

Ellery asked casually: "Did she always live alone?"

"I think so."

"Then why has she suddenly—so very suddenly, according to that Orchard Street janitor—moved to a *three*-room flat?"

"You mean the Henry Street place has——?"

"Three rooms—from the doors. Now why should a poor old scrubwoman living alone suddenly need an *extra* room?"

"Cinch," said the cab-driver. "She's takin' in boarders."

"Yes," murmured Ellery, without umbrage. "Yes, I suppose that might account for the odour of cheap cigar smoke."

"Cigar smoke!"

"Maybe she's runnin' a horse parlour," suggested the driver.

"Look, friend," said Nikki angrily, "how about letting us take the wheel and you coming back here?"

"Keep your bra on, lady."

"The fact is," mused Ellery, "before she opened her door she moved furniture away from it. Those sounds? She'd barricaded that door, Nikki."

"Yes," said Nikki in a small voice. "And that doesn't sound like a boarder, does it?"

"It sounds," said Ellery, "like a hideout." He leaned forward just as the driver opened his mouth. "And don't bother," he said. "Nikki, it's somebody who can't go out—or doesn't dare to. . . . I'm beginning to think there's a connection between the cigar smoker your Mrs. Carey's hiding, and the packet of drugs Pierre slipped me at Fouchet's by mistake."

"Oh, no, Ellery," moaned Nikki.

Ellery took her hand. "It's a rotten way to wind up a heavenly day, honey, but we have no choice. I'll have Dad give orders to arrest Pierre to-night the minute we get home, and let's hope . . . Hang the Pilgrims!"

"That's subversive propaganda, brother," said the driver.

Ellery shut the communicating window, violently.

Inspector Queen sniffled: "She's in it, all right."

"Mother Carey?" wailed Nikki.

"Three years ago," nodded the Inspector, drawing his bathrobe closer about him, "Fouchet's was mixed up in a drug-peddling case. And a Mrs. Carey was connected with it."

Nikki began to cry.

"Connected how, Dad?"

"One of Fouchet's waiters was the passer——"

"Pierre?"

"No. Pierre was working there at that time—or at least a waiter of that name was—but the guilty waiter was an old man named Carey ... whose wife was a scrubwoman."

"Lo the poor Indian," said Ellery, and he sat down with his pipe. After a moment, he said: "Where's Carey now, Dad?"

"In the clink doing a tenner. We found a couple of hundred dollars' worth of snow in the old geezer's bedroom—they lived on Mulberry then. Carey claimed he was framed—but they all do."

"And Fouchet?" murmured Ellery, puffing.

"Came out okay. Apparently he hadn't known. It was Carey all by himself."

"Strange. It's still going on."

The Inspector looked startled, and Ellery shrugged.

Nikki cried: "Mr. Carey was *framed*!"

"Could be," muttered the old gentleman. "Might have been this Pierre all the time—felt the heat on and gave us a quick decoy. Nikki hand me the phone."

"I knew it, I knew it!"

"And while you're on the phone, Dad," said Ellery mildly, "you might ask why Headquarters hasn't picked up Carey."

"Picked him up? I told, Ellery, he's in stir. Hello?"

"Oh, no, he's not," said Ellery. "He's hiding out in Apartment 3-A at 214-B Henry Street."

"The cigar smoke," breathed Nikki. "The barricade. The extra room!"

"Velie!" snarled the Inspector. "Has a con named Frank Carey broken out of stir?"

Sergeant Velie, bewildered by this clairvoyance stammered; "Yeah. Inspector, a few days ago, ain't been picked up yet, we're tryin' to locate his wife but she's moved and——But you been home sick!"

"She's moved," sighed the Inspector. "Well, well, she's probably moved to China." Then he roared: "She's hiding him out! But never mind—you take those Number Fourteens of yours right down to Fouchet's Restaurant just off Canal and arrest a waiter named Pierre! And if he isn't there, don't take two weeks finding out where he lives. I want that man to-night!"

"But Carey——"

"I'll take care of Carey myself. Go on—don't waste a second!" The old man hung up, fuming. "Where's my pants, dad blast the——?"

"Dad!" Ellery grabbed him. "You're not going out *now*. You're still sick."

"I'm picking up Carey personally," said his father gently. "Do you think you're man enough to stop me?"

The old scrubwoman sat at her kitchen table stolidly, and this time the Iroquois showed.

There was no one else in the Henry Street flat.

"We know your husband was here, Mrs. Carey," said Inspector Queen. "He got word to you when he broke out of jail, you moved, and you've been hiding him here. Where's he gone to now?"

The old lady said nothing.

"Mother Carey, please," said Nikki. "We want to help you."

"We believe your husband was innocent of that drug-passing charge, Mrs. Carey," said Ellery quietly.

The bluish lips tightened. The basket, the turkey, the pumpkin pie, the bottle of wine, the packages were still on the table.

"I think, Dad," said Ellery, "Mrs. Carey wants a bit more evidence of official good faith. Mother, suppose I tell you I not only believe your husband was framed three years ago, but that the one who framed him was——"

"That Pierre," said Mother Carey in a hard voice. "He was the one. He was the brains. He used to be 'friendly' with Frank."

"The one—but not the brains."

"What d'ye mean, Ellery?" demanded Inspector Queen.

"Isn't Pierre working alone?" asked Nikki.

"If he is, would he have handed me—a total stranger—a packet of dope worth several hundred dollars . . . without a single word about payment?" asked Ellery dryly.

Mother Carey was staring up at him.

"*Those were Pierre's instructions,*" said the Inspector slowly.

"Exactly. So there's someone behind Pierre who's using him as the passer, payment being arranged for by some other means——"

"Probably in advance!" The Inspector leaned forward. "Well, Mrs. Carey, won't you talk now? Where is Frank?"

"Tell the Inspector, Mother," begged Nikki. "The truth!"

Mother Carey looked uncertain. But then she said, "We told the truth three years ago," and folded her lacerated hands.

There is a strength in the oppressed which yields to nothing.

"Let it go," sighed the Inspector. "Come on, son—we'll go over to Fouchet's and have a little chin with Mr. Pierre, find out who his bossman is——"

And it was then that Mother Carey said, in a frightened quick voice: "No!" and put her hand to her mouth, appalled.

"Carey's gone to Fouchet's," said Ellery slowly. "Of course, Mrs. Carey would have a key—she probably opens the restaurant. Carey's gone over with some desperate idea that he can dig up some evidence that will clear him. That's it, Mother, isn't it?"

But Inspector Queen was already out in the unsavoury hall.

Sergeant Velie was standing miserably in the entrance to Fouchet's when the squad car raced up.

"Now Inspector, don't get mad——"

The Inspector said benignly: "You let Pierre get away."

"Oh, no!" said Sergeant Velie. "Pierre's in there, Inspector. Only he's dead."

"*Dead!*"

"Dead of what, Sergeant?" asked Ellery swiftly.

"Of a carvin' knife in the chest, that's of what, Maestro. We came right over here like you said, Inspector, only some knife artist beat us to it." The Sergeant relaxed. It was all right. The Old Man was smiling.

"Frank Carey did it, of course?"

The Sergeant stopped relaxing. "Heck, no, Inspector. Carey didn't do it."

"Velie——!"

"Well, he didn't! When we rolled up we spot Carey right here at the front door. Place is closed for the night—just a night-light. He's got a key. We watch him unlock the door, go in, and wham! he damn' near falls over this Pierre. So the feeble-minded old cluck bends down and takes the knife out of Pierre's chest and stands there in a trance lookin' at it. He's been standin' like that ever since."

"Without the knife, I hope," said the Inspector nastily; and they went in.

And found an old man among the detectives in the posture of a question-mark leaning against an oilcloth-covered table under a poster advertising Provençal, with his toothless mouth ajar and his watery old eyes fixed on the extinct *garçon*. The extinct *garçon* was still in his monkey-suit; his right palm was upturned, as if appealing for mercy, or the usual *pourboire.**

"Carey," said Inspector Queen.

Old man Carey did not seem to hear. He was fascinated by Ellery; Ellery was on one knee, peering at Pierre's eyes.

"Carey, who killed this Frenchman?"

Carey did not reply.

"Plain case of busted gut," remarked Sergeant Velie.

"You can hardly blame him!" cried Nikki. "Framed for dope-peddling three years ago, convicted, jailed for it—and now he thinks he's being framed for murder!"

"I wish we could get something out of him," said the Inspector thoughtfully. "It's a cinch Pierre stayed after closing time because he had a date with somebody."

"His boss!" said Nikki.

"Whoever he's been passing the snow for, Nikki."

"Dad." Ellery was on his feet looking down at the long dreary face that now seemed longer and drearier. "Do you recall if Pierre was ticketed as a drug addict three years ago?"

"I don't think he was." The Inspector looked surprised.

"Look at his eyes."

"Say!"

"Far gone, too. If Pierre wasn't an addict at the time of Carey's arrest, he'd taken to the habit in the past three years. And that explains why he was murdered to-night."

"He got dangerous," said the Inspector grimly. "With Carey loose and Pierre pulling that boner with you to-night, the boss knew the whole Fouchet investigation would be reopened."

Ellery nodded. "Felt he couldn't trust Pierre any longer. Weakened by

---

*Tip (French)

drugs, the fellow would talk as soon as the police pulled him in, and this mysterious character knew it."

"Yeah," said the Sergeant sagely. "Put the heat on a smecker and he squirts like whipped cream."

But Ellery wasn't listening. He had sat down at one of the silent tables and was staring over at the wine-bar.

Mr. Fouchet flew in in a strong tweed overcoat, showing a dent in his Homburg where it should not have been.

"Selling of the dope—again! This *Pierre* ... !" hissed M. Fouchet, and he glared down at his late waiter with quite remarkable venom.

"Know anything about this job, Fouchet?" asked the Inspector courteously.

"Nothing, *Monsieur l'inspecteur*. I give you my word, no thing. Pierre stay late to-night. He says to me he will fix up the tables for to-morrow. He stays and—pfft! *il se fait tuer!*"* M. Fouchet's fat lips began to dance. "Now the bank will give me no more credit." He sank into a chair.

"Oh? You're not in good shape financially, Fouchet?"

"I serve *escargots* near Canal Street. It should be pretzels! The bank, I owe 'im five thousand dollars."

"And that's the way it goes," said the Inspector sympathetically. "All right, Mr. Fouchet, go home. Where's that cashier?"

A detective pushed Clothilde forward. Clothilde had been weeping into her make-up. But not now. Now she glared down at Pierre quite as M. Fouchet had glared. Pierre glared back.

"Clothilde?" muttered Ellery, suddenly coming out of deep reverie.

"Velie turned up something," whispered the Inspector.

"She's in it. She's got something to do with it," Nikki said excitedly to Ellery. "I knew it!"

"Clothilde," said the Inspector, "how much do you make in this restaurant?"

"Forty-five dollar a week."

Sergeant Velie drawled: "How much dough you got in the bank, mademazelle?"

Clothilde glanced at the behemoth very quickly indeed. Then she began to sniffle, shaking in several places. "I have no money in the bank. Oh, may be a few dollars——"

"This is your bank book, isn't it, Clothilde?" asked the Inspector.

Clothilde stopped sniffling just as quickly as she had begun. "Where do you get that? Give it to me!"

"Uh-uh-uh," said the Sergeant, embracing her. "Say ...!"

She flung his arm off. "That is my bank book!"

"And it shows," murmured the Inspector, "deposits totalling more than seventeen thousand dollars, Clothilde. Rich Uncle?"

---

*He gets killed! (French)

"*Voleurs*!* That is my money! I save!"

"She's got a new savings system, Inspector," explained the Sergeant. "Out of forty-five bucks per week, she manages to sock away, some weeks, sixty, some weeks eighty-five.... It's wonderful. How do you do it, Cloey?

Nikki glanced at Ellery, startled. He nodded gloomily.

"*Fils de lapin! Jongleur! Chienloup!*"† Clothilde was screaming. "All right! Some time I short-change the customer. I am cashier, *non?* But—nothing else!" She jabbed her elbow into Sergeant Velie's stomach. "And take your 'and off me!"

"I got my duty, mademazelle," said the Sergeant, but he looked a little guilty. Inspector Queen said something to him in an undertone, and the Sergeant reddened, and Clothilde came at him claws first, and detectives jumped in, and in the midst of it Ellery got up from the table and drew his father aside and said: "Come on back to Mother Carey's."

"What for, Ellery? I'm not through here——"

"I want to wash this thing up. To-morrow's Thanksgiving, poor Nikki is out on her feet——"

"*Ellery,*" said Nikki.

He nodded, still gloomily.

The sight of his wife turned old man Carey into a human being again, and he clung to her and blubbered that he had done nothing and they were trying to frame him for the second time, only this time it was the hot seat they were steering him into. And Mrs. Carey kept nodding and picking lint off his jacket collar. And Nikki tried to look invisible.

"Where's Velie?" grumbled the Inspector. He seemed irritated by Carey's blubbering and the fact that Ellery had insisted on sending all the detectives home, as if this were a piece of business too delicate for the boys' sensibilities.

"I've sent Velie on an errand," Ellery replied, and then he said: "Mr. and Mrs. Carey, would you go into that room there and shut the door?" Mother Carey took her husband by the hand without a word. And when the door had closed behind them, Ellery said abruptly: "Dad, I asked you to arrest Pierre to-night. You phoned Velie to hurry right over to Fouchet's. Velie obeyed—and found the waiter stabbed to death."

"So?"

"Police Headquarters is on Centre Street. Fouchet's is just off Canal. A few blocks apart."

"Hey?"

"Didn't it strike you as extraordinary," murmured Ellery, "that Pierre should have been murdered *so quickly*? Before Velie could negotiate those few blocks?"

---

*Thieves! Robbers! (French)
†Son of a rabbit! Trickster! Wolfhound! (French)

"You mean this boss dope peddler struck so fast to keep his man from being arrested? We went through all that before, son."

"Hm," said Ellery. "But what did Pierre's killer have to know in order to strike so quickly to-night? Two things: That Pierre had slipped me a packet of dope by mistake this evening; and that I was intending to have Pierre pulled in *to-night.*"

"But Ellery," said Nikki with a frown, "nobody knew about either of those things except you, me, and the Inspector ..."

"Interesting?"

"I don't get it," growled his father. "The killer knew Pierre was going to be picked up even before Velie reached Fouchet's. He must have, because he beat Velie to it. But if only the three of us knew——"

"Exactly—then how did the killer find out?"

"I give up," said the Inspector promptly. He had discovered many years before that this was, after all, the best way.

But Nikki was young. "Someone overheard you talking it over with me and the Inspector?"

"Well, let's see, Nikki. We discussed it with Dad in our apartment when we got back from Mrs. Carey's. ..."

"But nobody could have overheard *there,*" said the Inspector.

"Then Ellery, you and I must have been overheard before we got to the apartment."

"Good enough, Nikki. And the only place you and I discussed the case— the only place we *could* have discussed it ..."

"Ellery!"

"We opened the packet in the cab on our way over to Henry Street here," nodded Ellery, "and we discussed its contents quite openly—in the cab. In fact," he added dryly, "if you'll recall, Nikki, our conversational cab-driver joined our discussion with enthusiasm."

"*The cab-driver, by Joe,*" said Inspector Queen softly.

"Whom we had picked up just outside Fouchet's, Dad, where he was parked. It fits."

"The same cab-driver," Ellery went on glumly, "who took us back up-town from here, Nikki—remember? And it was on that uptown trip that I told you I was going to have Dad arrest Pierre to-night. ... Yes, the cab-driver, and only the cab-driver—the only outsider who could have over-heard the two statements which would make the boss dope-peddler kill his pusher quickly to prevent an arrest, a police grilling, and an almost certain revelation of the boss's identity."

"Works a cab," muttered the Inspector. "Cute dodge. Parks outside his headquarters. Probably hacks his customers to Fouchet's and collects beforehand. Let Pierre pass the white stuff afterwards. Probably carted them away." He looked up, beaming. "Great work, son! I'll nail that hack so blasted fast——"

"You'll nail whom, Dad?" asked Ellery, still glum.

"The cab-driver!"

"*But who is the cab-driver?*"

Ellery is not proud of this incident.

"You're asking *me?*" howled his father.

Nikki was biting her lovely nails. "Ellery, I didn't even *notice*——"

"Ha, ha," said Ellery. "That's what I was afraid of."

"Do you mean to say," said Inspector Queen in a terrible voice, "that *my son* didn't read a hack police-identity card?"

"Er . . ."

"It's the LAW!"

"It's Thanksgiving Eve, Dad," muttered Ellery. "Squanto—the Pilgrims —the Iroquois heritage of Mother Carey——"

"Stop drivelling! Can't you give me a description?"

"Er . . ."

"No description," whispered his father. It was really the end of all things.

"Inspector, *nobody* looks at a cab-driver," said Nikki brightly. "You know. A cab-driver? He—he's just *there.*"

"The invisible man," said Ellery hopefully. "Chesterton?"

"Oh, so you do remember his name!"

"No, no, Dad——"

"I'd know his voice," said Nikki. "If I ever heard it again."

"We'd have to catch him first, and if we caught him we'd hardly need his voice!"

"Maybe he'll come cruising back around Fouchet's."

The Inspector ejaculated one laughing bark.

"Fine thing. Know who did it—and might's well not know. Listen to me, you detective. You're going over to the Hack Licence Bureau with me, and you're going to look over the photo of every last cab jockey in——"

"Wait. Wait!"

Ellery flung himself at Mother Carey's vacated chair. He sat on the bias, chin propped on the heel of his hand, knitting his brows, unknitting them, knitting them again until Nikki thought there was something wrong with his eyes. Then he shifted and repeated the process in the opposite direction. His father watched him with great suspicion. This was not Ellery to-night; it was someone else. All these gyrations . . .

Ellery leaped to his feet, kicking the chair over. "I've got it! We've got him!"

"How? What?"

"Nikki." Ellery's tone was mysterious, dramatic—let's face it, thought the old gentleman: corny. "Remember when we lugged the stuff from the cab up to Mother Carey's kitchen here? The cab-driver helped us up— *carried this bottle of wine.*"

"Huh?" gaped the Inspector. Then he cried: "No, no, Nikki, don't touch it!" And he chortled over the bottle of California wine. *"Prints."* That's it, son—that's my boy! We'll just take this little old bottle of grape back to Headquarters, bring out the fingerprints, compare the prints on it with the file sets at the Hack Bureau——"

"Oh, yeah?" said the cab-driver.

He was standing in the open doorway, there was a dirty handkerchief tied around his face below the eyes and his cap was pulled low, and he was pointing a Police Positive midway between father and son.

"I thought you were up to somethin' when you all came back here from Fouchet's," he sneered. "And then leavin' this door open so I could hear the whole thing. You—the old guy. Hand me that bottle of wine."

"You're not very bright," said Ellery wearily. "All right, Sergeant, shoot it out of his hand."

And Ellery embraced his father and his secretary and fell to Mother Carey's spotless floor with them as Sergeant Velie stepped into the doorway behind the cab-driver and very carefully shot the gun out of the invisible man's hand.

"Happy Thanksgivin', sucker," said the Sergeant.

ACTIVITIES

1)   Author Queen's contribution to the relationship between "an unusual detective of high intelligence" and "an assistant of lesser intelligence" was the introduction of a father and son team. Compare the Ellery and Richard Queen relationship to the one between Holmes and Watson. How is it alike? How is it different? Use the foreword to *The Roman Hat Mystery* (page 138) to help you formulate your answer.

2)   In *A Study in Scarlet,* Sherlock Holmes stated, "I consider that a man's brain originally is like a little empty attic, and you have to stock it with such furniture as you choose. A fool takes in all the lumber of every sort that he comes across. . . ."

Would Ellery Queen agree with Sherlock Holmes? Explain and substantiate with references from the story.

3)   One notable absence from the Poe and Doyle detective tales was the element of romance. In "The Telltale Bottle," we meet Nikki Porter, the fictional Ellery's secretary, and there is a strong hint of more than just an employer-employee relationship between them.

Does the introduction of the romantic element contribute to the telling of a detective story or does it detract? Would the Sherlock Holmes narratives, today considered classics of the genre, have benefited from the inclusion of a Nikki Porter character?

As If One Mask Were Not Enough . . .

And now back to author Queen.

As stated before, he made his first public appearance in a mask. The event, in good mystery story tradition, was a surprise—and took place in the following way.

By the early 1930s, the detective story had become so firmly a part of

American literature that the Graduate School of Journalism of New York's Columbia University decided to hold a symposium on the subject to which it invited a score of noted mystery writers. It also sent an invitation to the mysterious Queen but it did so half-heartedly, anticipating that the unknown author would not really make an appearance.

Everyone at the event was surprised when Queen did show up.

Despite his mask, Ellery Queen proved charming, intelligent, and extremely knowledgeable about the history and development of detective fiction. After his departure, the man personally remained as much of a mystery as before. However, he did tantalize his audience further by promising them more personal appearances.

He kept his promise.

As further Ellery Queen material appeared, like *The Siamese Twin Mystery, The American Gun Mystery,* and others, a masked author would appear at department stores and publishers' parties to autograph the new books. The public's curiosity was intensified. Good mystery writer that he was, Queen did not hand them the solution *yet*; he merely added a new complication to the real-life plot.

For suddenly, another masked writer of detective stories appeared on the literary scene.

His name was Barnaby Ross and his detective novels were entitled *The Tragedy of X, The Tragedy of Y,* and *The Tragedy of Z.* Containing well-constructed plots and a fascinating sleuth in the person of one Drury Lane, an old Shakespearean actor, these works and their protagonist were well-received. No doubt influenced by Ellery's style, the new author also autographed his books wearing a mask.

Ellery's publishers hit upon a great publicity idea.

Why not, they reasoned, have these two masked writers appear on lecture platforms and at radio stations throughout the country as competing crime experts challenging each other's skills as detectives? Each would present a knotty mystery plot for the other to unravel. And each, of course, would try to "top" the other's deductive ability.

The lecture tour was organized—and proved a great success. The masked men seemed evenly-matched. Each concocted involved plots designed to stump the other; both proved very difficult to stump. Needless to say while all this was going on, Ellery Queen and Barnaby Ross books sold like "hot cakes"—*and the public still didn't know their identities.*

Yes, another glorious "put-on!"

Except this one took place at the beginning of a fictional sleuth's career—not, as happened with Sherlock Holmes, at the end. The Holmes "put-on" still continues; the Ellery Queen one came to an end.

A slight mystery remains as to how Ellery was finally unmasked.

One story has it that publisher Frederick Stokes, feeling sorry for his

Queen readers and speaking in an unguarded moment, gave the whole thing away at a party. Another version accuses Columbia Pictures of revealing the secret in Hollywood when it purchased a Queen novel for a movie.

Our guess is that Ellery himself decided to terminate the clever charade because, good plot-constructor that he was, only he could possibly know when the time would be ripe for a suitable climax. When the moment of revelation did come, it turned out just like his fictional dénouements—full of surprises.

Such as:

Surprise 1—Ellery Queen and Barnaby Ross turned out to be one and the same author. *The Roman Hat Mystery* and *The Tragedy of X* were created by the same fertile imagination though one featured Ellery Queen and the other, Drury Lane.

Surprise 2—Ellery Queen was really the *nom de plume* or pen name for two writers working together as a collaborative team. Their real names—Frederic Dannay and Manfred B. Lee.

No wonder Ellery Queen and Barnaby Ross had worked so well together as "rivals" on their lecture tour. Their "competitiveness" had been simply another example of the fine teamwork exhibited by collaborators who work well together. A more candid billing for that tour might have been "Another Friendly Hoax by Dannay and Lee."[3]

"So," you're probably muttering, "you've cleared up the mystery of Ellery Queen for us. But who are Frederic Dannay and Manfred B. Lee?" Possibly a way of making your curiosity more intense might be to "throw" another Queen tale at you.

Let's try it. But first, a necessary briefing.

All of you have probably learned about *spoonerisms* in your English classes. If not, or if you don't remember them, let's briefly review them here. The word comes from the name of an English clergyman of the last century, the Reverend William A. Spooner. He had the embarrassing habit of switching the initial sounds of the first syllables of two or more words. For example, from his lips, "conquering kings" would emerge as "kinquering congs" and "the Duke and Duchess" became "The Duck and Doochess." Today, we honor the dear old Reverend by calling such slips of the tongue *spoonerisms.*

Well, Ellery Queen (or Dannay and Lee, if you prefer) used this tidbit of language history in a fascinating detective story. He called it "My Queer Dean!" and we will leave it to your imagination and reading ability to find out why.

My Queer Dean!

The queerness of Matthew Arnold Hope, beloved teacher of Ellery's Harvard youth and lately dean of liberal arts in a New York university, is legendary.

The story is told, for instance, of baffled students taking Dr. Hope's Shakespeare course for the first time. "History advises us that Richard II died peacefully at Pontefract, probably of pneumonia," Dr. Hope scolds. "But what does Shakespeare say, Act V, Scene V? That Exton struck him down," and here the famous authority on Elizabethan literature will pause for emphasis, "with a blushing crow!"

Imaginative sophomores have been known to suffer nightmares as a result of this remark. Older heads nod intelligently, of course, knowing that Dr. Hope meant merely to say—in fact, thought he was saying—"a crushing blow."

The good dean's unconscious spoonerisms, like the sayings of Miss Parker and Mr. Goldwyn, are reverently preserved by aficionados, among whom Ellery counts himself a charter member. It is Ellery who has saved for posterity that deathless pronouncement of Dr. Hope's to a freshman class in English composition: "All those who persist in befouling their theme papers with cant and other low expressions not in good usage are warned for the last time: Refine your style or be exiled from this course with the rest of the vanished Bulgarians!"

But perhaps Dean Hope's greatest exploit began recently in the faculty lunchroom. Ellery arrived at the dean's invitation to find him waiting impatiently at one of the big round tables with three members of the English Department.

"Dr. Agnes Lovell, Professor Oswald Gorman, Mr. Morgan Naseby," the dean said rapidly. "Sit down, Ellery. Mr. Queen will have the cute frocktail and the horned beef cash—only safe edibles on the menu today, my boy— well, go fetch, young man! Are you dreaming that you're back in class?" The waiter, a harried-looking freshman, fled. Then Dr. Hope said solemnly, "My friends, prepare for a surprise."

Dr. Lovell, a very large woman in a tight suit said roguishly: "Wait, Matthew! Let me guess. Romance?"

"And who'd marry—in Macaulay's imperishable phrase—a living concordance?"* said Professor Gorman in a voice like an abandoned winch. He was a tall freckled man with strawberry eyebrows and a quarrelsome jaw. "A real surprise, Dr. Hope, would be a departmental salary rise."

"A consummation devoutly et cetera," said Mr. Naseby, immediately blushing. He was a stout young man, with an eager manner, evidently a junior in the department.

---

*An alphabetical index of the principal words of a book.

"May I have your attention?" Dean Hope looked about cautiously. "Suppose I tell you," he said in a trembling voice, "that by tonight I may have it within my power to deliver the death blow—I repeat, the death blow!—to the cockypop that Francis Bacon wrote Shakespeare's plays?"

There were two gasps, a snort, and one inquiring hum.

"Matthew!" squealed Dr. Lovell. "You'd be famous!"

"Immortal, Dean Hope," said Mr. Naseby adoringly.

"Deluded," said Professor Gorman, the snorter. "The Baconian benightedness, like the Marlowe mania, has no known specific."

"Ah, but even a fanatic," cried the dean, "would have to yield before the nature of this evidence."

"Sounds exciting, Doc," murmured Ellery. "What is it?"

"A man called at my office this morning, Ellery. He produced credentials identifying him as a London rare book dealer, Alfred Mimms. He has in his possession, he said a copy of the 1613 edition of *The Essaies of Sir Francis Bacon Knight the kings solliciter generall,* an item ordinarily bringing four or five hundred dollars. He claims that this copy, however, is unique, *being inscribed on the title page in Bacon's own hand to Will Shakespeare.*"

Amid the cries, Ellery asked: "Inscribed how?"

"In an encomium,* " quavered Dean Hope, "an encomium to Shakespeare expressing Bacon's admiration and praise for—and I quote—*'the most excellent plaies of your sweet wit and hand'!*"

"Take that!" whispered Mr. Naseby to an invisible Baconian.

"That does it," breathed Dr. Lovell.

"That would do it," said Professor Gorman, "if."

"Did you actually see the book, Doc?" asked Ellery.

"He showed me a photostat of the title page. He'll have the original for my inspection tonight, in my office."

"And Mimms's asking price is—?"

"Ten thousand dollars."

"Proof positive that it's a forgery," said Professor Gorman rustily. "It's far too little."

"Oswald," hissed Dr. Lovell, "you creak, do you know that?"

"No, Gorman is right," said Dr. Hope. "An absurd price if the inscription is genuine, as I pointed out to Mimms. However, he had an explanation. He is acting, he said, at the instructions of the book's owner, a tax-poor British nobleman whose identity he will reveal tonight if I purchase the book. The owner, who has just found it in a castle room boarded up and forgotten for two centuries, prefers an American buyer in a confidential sale—for tax reasons, Mimms hinted. But, as a cultivated man, the owner wishes a scholar to have it rather than some ignorant Croesus. Hence the relatively low price."

"Lovely," glowed Mr. Naseby. "And so typically British."

"Isn't it," said Professor Gorman. "Terms cash, no doubt? On the line? Tonight?"

---

*A formal expression of high praise.

"Well, yes." The old dean took a bulging envelope from his breast pocket and eyed it ruefully. Then, with a sigh, he tucked it back. "Very nearly my life's savings ... But I'm not altogether senile," Dr. Hope grinned. "I'm asking you to be present, Ellery—with Inspector Queen. I shall be working at my desk on administrative things into the evening. Mimms is due at eight o'clock."

"We'll be here at seven-thirty," promised Ellery. "By the way, Doc, that's a lot of money to be carrying around in your pocket. Have you confided this business to anyone else?"

"No, no."

"Don't. And may I suggest that you wait behind a locked door? Don't admit Mimms—or anyone else you don't trust—until we get here. I'm afraid, Doc, I share the professor's skepticism."

"Oh, so do I," murmured the dean. "The odds on this being a swindle are, I should think, several thousand to one. But one can't help saying to oneself ... suppose it's not?"

It was nearly half-past seven when the Queens entered the Arts Building. Some windows on the upper floors were lit up where a few evening classes were in session, and the dean's office was bright. Otherwise the building was dark.

The first thing Ellery saw as they stepped out of the self-service elevator onto the dark third floor was the door of Dean Hope's anteroom ... wide open.

They found the old scholar crumpled on the floor just inside the doorway. His white hairs dripped red.

"Crook came early," howled Inspector Queen. "Look at the dean's wrist-watch. Ellery—smashed in his fall at 7:15."

"I warned him not to unlock his door," wailed Ellery. Then he bellowed, "He's breathing! Call an ambulance!"

He had carried the dean's frail body to a couch in the inner office and was gently wetting the blue lips from a paper cup when the Inspector turned from the telephone.

The eyes fluttered open. "Ellery ..."

"Doc, what happened?"

"Book ... taken ..." The voice trailed off in a mutter.

"Book taken?" repeated the Inspector incredulously. "That means Mimms not only came early, but Dr. Hope found the book was genuine! Is the money on him, son?"

Ellery searched the dean's pockets, the office, the anteroom. "It's gone."

"Then he did buy it. Then somebody came along, cracked him on the skull, and lifted the book."

"Doc!" Ellery bent over the old man again. "Doc, who struck you? Did you see?"

"Yes ... Gorman ..." Then the battered head rolled to one side and Dr. Hope lost consciousness.

"Gorman? Who's Gorman, Ellery?"

"Professor Oswald Gorman," Ellery said through his teeth, "one of the English faculty at the lunch today. *Get him.*"

When Inspector Queen returned to the dean's office guiding the agitated elbow of Professor Gorman, he found Ellery waiting behind the dean's flower vase as if it were a bough from Birnam Wood.

The couch was empty.

"What did the ambulance doctor say, Ellery?"

"Concussion. How bad they don't know yet." Ellery rose, fixing Professor Gorman with a Macduffian glance.

"And where did you find this pedagogical louse, Dad?"

"Upstairs on the seventh floor, teaching a Bible class."

"The title of my course, Inspector Queen," said the Professor furiously, "is *The Influence of the Bible on English Literature.*"

"Trying to establish an alibi, eh?"

"Well, son," said his father in a troubled voice, "the professor's more than just tried. He's done it."

"Established an alibi?" Ellery cried.

"It's a two-hour seminar, from six to eight. He's alibied for every second from 6 P.M. on by the dozen people taking the course—including a minister, a priest and a rabbi. What's more," mused the Inspector, "even assuming the 7:15 on the dean's broken watch was a plant, Professor Gorman can account for every minute of his day since your lunch broke up. Ellery, something is rotten in New York County."

"I beg your pardon," said a British voice from the anteroom. "I was to meet Dr. Hope here at eight o'clock."

Ellery whirled. Then he swooped down upon the owner of the voice, a pale skinny man in a bowler hat carrying a package under one arm.

"Don't tell me you're Alfred Mimms and you're just bringing the Bacon!"

"Yes, but I'll—I'll come back," stammered the visitor, trying to hold on to his package. But it was Ellery who won the tug of war, and as he tore the wrappings away the pale man turned to run.

And there was Inspector Queen in the doorway with his pistol showing. "Alfred Mimms, is it?" said the Inspector genially. "Last time, if memory serves, it was Lord Chalmerston. Remember, Dink, when you were sent up for selling a phony First Folio to that Oyster Bay millionaire? Ellery, this is Dink Chalmers of Flatbush, one of the cleverest confidence men in the rare book game." Then the Inspector's geniality faded. "But, son, this leaves us in more of a mess than before."

"No, dad," said Ellery. "This clears the mess up."

From Inspector Queen's expression, it did nothing of the kind.

"Because what did Doc Hope reply when I asked him what happened?" Ellery said. "He replied, 'Book taken.' Well, obviously, the book wasn't taken. The book was never here. Therefore he didn't mean to say 'book taken.' Professor, you're a communicant of the Matthew Arnold Hope Cult of Spoonerisms: What must the dean have meant to say?"

" 'Took ... Bacon'!" said Professor Gorman.

"Which makes no sense, either, unless we recall, Dad, that his voice trailed off. As if he meant to add a word, but failed. Which word? The word 'money'—'took Bacon *money.*' Because while the Bacon book wasn't here to be taken, the ten thousand dollars Doc Hope was toting around all day to pay for it was.

"And who took the Bacon money? The one who knocked on the dean's door just after seven o'clock and asked to be let in. The one who, when Dr. Hope unlocked the door—indicating the knocker was someone he knew and trusted—promptly clobbered the old man and made off with his life's savings."

"But when you asked who hit him," protested the Inspector, "he answered 'Gorman'."

"Which he couldn't have meant, either, since the professor has an alibi of granite. Therefore—"

"Another spoonerism!" exclaimed Professor Gorman.

"I'm afraid so. And since the only spoonerism possible from the name 'Gorman' is 'Morgan,' hunt up Mr. Morgan Naseby of the underpaid English department, Dad, and you'll have Doc's assailant and his ten grand back, too."

Later, at Bellevue Hospital, an indestructible Elizabethan scholar squeezed the younger Queen's hand feebly. Conversation was forbidden, but the good pedagogue and spoonerist extraordinary did manage to whisper, "My queer Dean ..."

ACTIVITIES

1) *Spoonerisms* abound in the preceding story; they are even an integral part of the plot. They occur many times in speeches and on radio and television. Can you remember any that you may have heard? If not, make up some of your own, put them into appropriate sentences, and then share these with your classmates. They in turn can attempt to figure out what you originally meant to say.

2) Another source of humor in language is the *pun.* A pun is a play on words; that is, a word is used in such a way as to suggest two possible meanings. Examples of these are the following:

a) "Our teacher must have had a dramatic experience. Her leg is in a cast."

b) A sign in a plant nursery reads: "We sell every blooming thing."

Shifting between the meaning of a word and its sound is another way of utilizing the pun. Here's how these work:

a) A butcher's sign might declare he would like to "meat" you.

b) In Shakespeare's *Romeo and Juliet,* dying Mercutio says to his friend Romeo, "Ask for me tomorrow, and you shall find me a grave man."

Make up some puns of your own and try them out on your class. Don't be surprised by the reaction you get; it will probably be *a large groan.* But don't let that groan fool you. It is the best tribute a pun can possibly get, the universal tribute that all puns have elicited since time immemorial.

3) *Malapropisms* are another form of intentional or unintentional misuse of words. Malapropisms can be created deliberately—for humorous effect—but, most of the time, they occur because of a speaker's or writer's unfamiliarity with words. They are caused by confusing a difficult word with a simpler one because of a similarity in sounds:

"with *incredulous* bravery" for "with *incredible* bravery"
"a *congenial* disease" for "a *congenital* disease"
"to give a *facetious* name" for "to give a *fictitious* name"
"*allegories* on the banks of the Nile" for "*alligators* on the banks of the Nile"

Like spoonerism, the word *malapropism* is derived from a person's name, Mrs. Malaprop, a character in Richard Sheridan's *The Rivals.* As you can guess, Mrs. Malaprop was very adept at creating guess-what's. Don't become another Mrs. Malaprop—unless you do it intentionally.

Speaking of intentional malapropisms, take an opportunity for you and your classmates to create some of your own. Your dictionaries and thesauruses can be of great help here.

Manny and Danny

Now—back to the authors of the Ellery Queen stories . . . We know that Edgar Allan Poe and Sir Arthur Conan Doyle both possessed *individually* great creative minds. Now, with the collaborative team of Frederic Dannay and Manfred B. Lee, we encounter something fascinatingly different: two separate imaginations working so well together that it would appear they sprang from a single intelligence. A reporter of the time put it very well when he said of Dannay and Lee after an interview: "It's like talking to one man."[4]

Perhaps they were twins, you might say, who had learned to adjust to each other's ways through intimate association.

They were not.

But they were related—first cousins—born nine months apart to two Brooklyn sisters in the year 1905. Raised together in a modest neighbor-

Manfred B. Lee   Frederic Dannay

hood, they became childhood friends and remained friends into adulthood. They became known then as Manny and Danny and early acquired a reputation for honesty and industriousness. Manny worked after school as a Western Union messenger, Danny as a soda-fountain clerk. They both graduated together from Brooklyn's Boys' High School.

At this point in their lives, their paths diverged. Fred Dannay decided that he had had enough of school and went to work, while Cousin Manny chose to continue with his education. Dannay learned the skill of bookkeeping and used it to progress in a series of jobs, while Lee supported himself at New York University by leading a five-piece jazz band. By the time Manny earned his bachelor's degree, Cousin Fred had worked his way up to the position of copywriter and art-director for a New York advertising agency. Not to be outdone, Manny, the college graduate, acquired a job writing publicity and advertising for the eastern office of a movie company. Both found themselves working at offices located a few blocks from each other. Naturally, they began frequenting the same restaurant for lunch.

There it was one noon in the fall of 1928 that they saw the newspaper announcement of the McClure-Stokes detective story competition. Before lunch was over, they had decided to enter the contest.

The career of "Ellery Queen" had begun.

Research Activity

How had the two become interested in the detective genre?

Fred Dannay later wrote about his "addiction" but Cousin Manny remained silent on the subject. If the detective story is becoming a "habit" with you, too, why not read Mr. Dannay's article, "Who Shall Ever Forget?" and compare experiences. This essay can most likely be found in your school or local library.

After reading it, by all means share its contents with your class.

"Masters" of the Modern Detective Story

By the time the forties rolled around, Frederic Dannay and Manfred B. Lee were being acknowledged as the "masters" of the modern detective story. Their fictional detective, Ellery Queen, now shared a pinnacle of literary sleuthdom previously occupied by Sherlock Holmes alone. Actually, Ellery's capture of public imagination with an even more remarkable feat than Holmes's. One must remember that "Inspector Queen's little boy," as Ellery referred to himself, had all kinds of fictional competitors (see pages 137–38), while Dr. Watson's roommate had monopolized the field in his day.

Manny and Danny had long ago given up their jobs. By 1943, Ellery Queen was earning for them the considerable sum of $100,000 a year; he had by then expanded his fictional operations from the media of the novel and short story to those of radio and motion pictures. A radio program, *The Adventures of Ellery Queen,* written by Dannay and Lee, remained on the air for nine years and made detective drama popular on the young medium. Several motion pictures, inspired by the novels, made their appearance and were well-received; the noted actors, Hugh Marlowe and Ralph Bellamy, added to their accomplishments by playing the role of Ellery Queen at different times. During the last years of the decade, television came into its own, and Manny and Danny widened their horizons by writing for the new medium. By the year 1950, *TV Guide* had given the Ellery Queen program its national award for the best mystery show on television.[5]

And now, enough of author Queen and back to the fictional Ellery.

Twice in his fabulous career, Ellery Queen found himself matching wits, not with nefarious criminals or murderers, but with two of the most noted presidents of the United States, George Washington and Abraham Lincoln. Yes, these two chief executives were involved in a pair of baffling mysteries that took all of Ellery's celebrated deductive ingenuity to solve.

We are going to present one of these cases here. Ellery Queen, a creature of the twentieth century, is our *protagonist.* His *antagonist* is the eighteenth-century father of our country, George Washington. As a matter of fact, the following tale is a first of its kind, the first of what might be called *the historical detective story.*

What *is* an historical detective story?

Read on and find out . . .

The Adventure of the President's Half Disme

Those few curious men who have chosen to turn off the humdrum highway to hunt for their pleasure along the back trails expect—indeed, they look confidently forward to—many strange encounters; and it is the dull stalk which does not turn up at least a hippogriff. But it remained for Ellery Queen to experience the ultimate excitement. On one of his prowls he collided with a President of the United States.

This would have been joy enough if it had occurred as you might imagine: by chance, on a dark night, in some back street of Washington, D.C., with Secret Service men closing in on the delighted Mr. Queen to question his motives by way of his pockets while a large black bullet-proof limousine rushed up to spirit the President away. But mere imagination fails in this instance. What is required is the power of fancy, for the truth is fantastic. Ellery's encounter with the President of the United States took place, not on a dark night, but in the unromantic light of several days (although the night played its role, too). Nor was it by chance: the meeting was arranged by a farmer's daughter. And it was not in Washington, D.C., for this President presided over the affairs of the nation from a different city altogether. Not that the meeting took place in that city, either; it did not take place in a city at all, but on a farm some miles south of Philadelphia. Oddest of all, there was no limousine to spirit the Chief Executive away, for while the President was a man of great wealth, he was still too poor to possess an automobile, and what is more, not all the resources of his Government—indeed, not all the riches of the world—could have provided one for him.

There are even more curious facets to this jewel of paradox. This was an encounter in the purest sense, and yet, physically, it did not occur at all. The President in question was dead. And while there are those who would not blink at a rubbing of shoulders or a clasping of hands even though one of the parties was in his grave, and to such persons the thought might occur that the meeting took place on a psychic plane—alas, Ellery Queen is not of their company. He does not believe in ghosts, consequently he never encounters them. So he did not collide with the President's shade, either.

And yet their meeting was as palpable as, say, the meeting between two chess masters, one in London and the other in New York, who never leave their respective armchairs and still play a game to a decision. It is even more wonderful than that, for while the chess players merely annihilate space, Ellery and the father of his country annihilated time—a century and a half of it.

In fine, this is the story of how Ellery Queen matched wits with George Washington.

Those who are finicky about their fashions complain that the arms of coincidence are too long; but in this case the Designer might say that He cut to measure. Or, to put it another way, an event often brews its own mood. Whatever the cause, the fact is The Adventure of the President's Half Disme, which was to concern itself with the events surrounding President Washington's fifty-ninth birthday, actually first engrossed Ellery on February the nineteenth and culminated three days later.

Ellery was in his study that morning of the nineteenth of February, wrestling with several reluctant victims of violence, none of them quite flesh and blood, since his novel was still in the planning stage. So he was annoyed when Nikki came in with a card.

"James Ezekiel Patch," growled the great man; he was never in his best humour during the planning stage. "I don't know any James Ezekiel Patch, Nikki. Toss the fellow out and get back to transcribing those notes on Possible Motives——"

"Why Ellery," said Nikki. "This isn't like you at all."

"What isn't like me?"

"To renege on an appointment."

"Appointment? Does this Patch character claim——"

"He doesn't merely claim it. He proves it."

"Someone's balmy," snarled Mr. Queen; and he strode into the living room to contend with James Ezekiel Patch. This, he perceived as soon as James Ezekiel Patch rose from the Queen fireside chair, was likely to be a heroic project. Mr. Patch, notwithstanding his mild, even studious eyes, seemed to rise indefinitely; he was a large, a very large, man.

"Now what's all this, what's all this?" demanded Ellery fiercely; for after all Nikki was there.

"That's what I'd like to know," said the large man amiably. "What did you want with me, Mr. Queen?"

"What did I want with you! What did you want with me?"

"I find this very strange, Mr. Queen."

"Now see here, Mr. Patch, I happen to be extremely busy this morning——"

"So am I." Mr. Patch's large thick neck was reddening and his tone was no longer amiable. Ellery took a cautious step backward as his visitor lumbered forward to thrust a slip of yellow paper under his nose. "Did you send me this wire, or didn't you?"

Ellery considered it tactically expedient to take the telegram, although for strategic reasons he did so with a bellicose scowl.

IMPERATIVE YOU CALL AT MY HOME TO-MORROW
FEBRUARY NINETEEN PROMPTLY TEN A.M. SIGNED
ELLERY QUEEN

"Well, sir?" thundered Mr. Patch. "Do you have something on Washington for me, or don't you?"

"Washington?" said Ellery absently, studying the telegram.

"*George* Washington, Mr. Queen! I'm Patch the antiquarian. I *collect* Washington. I'm an *authority* on Washington. I have a large fortune and I spend it all on Washington! I'd never have wasted my time this morning if your name hadn't been signed to this wire! This is my busiest week of the year. I have engagements to speak on Washington——"

"Desist, Mr. Patch," said Ellery. "This is either a practical joke, or——"

"The Baroness Tchek," announced Nikki clearly. "With another telegram." And then she added: "And Professor John Cecil Shaw, ditto."

The three telegrams were identical.

"Of course I didn't send them," said Ellery thoughtfully, regarding his three visitors. Baroness Tchek was a short, powerful woman, resembling a dumpling with grey hair; an angry dumpling. Professor Shaw was lank and long-jawed, wearing a sack suit which hung in some places and failed in its purpose by inches at the extremities. Along with Mr. Patch, they constituted as deliciously queer a trio as had ever congregated in the Queen apartment. Their host suddenly determined not to let go of them. "On the other hand someone obviously did, using my name . . ."

"Then there's nothing more to be said," snapped the Baroness, snapping her bag for emphasis.

"I should think there's a great deal more to be said," began Professor Shaw in a troubled way. "Wasting people's time this way——"

"It's not going to waste any more of *my* time," growled the large Mr. Patch. "Washington's Birthday only three days off——!"

"Exactly," smiled Ellery. "Won't you sit down? There's more in this than meets the eye . . . Baroness Tchek, if I'm not mistaken, you're the one who brought that fabulous collection of rare coins into the United States just before Hitler invaded Czechoslovakia? You're in the rare-coin business in New York now?"

"Unfortunately," said the Baroness coldly, "one must eat."

"And you, sir? I seem to know you."

"Rare books," said the Professor in the same troubled way.

"Of course. John Cecil Shaw, the rare-book collector. We've met at Mim's and other places. I abandon my first theory. There's a pattern here, distinctly unhumorous. An antiquarian, a coin-dealer, and a collector of rare books—Nikki? Whom have you out there this time?"

"If this one collects anything," muttered Nikki into her employer's ear, "I'll bet it has two legs and hair on its chest. A darned pretty girl——"

"Named Martha Clarke," said a cool voice; and Ellery turned to find himself regarding one of the most satisfying sights in the world.

"Ah, I take it, Miss Clarke, you also received one of these wires signed with my name?"

"Oh, no," said the pretty girl. "I'm the one who sent them."

There was something about the comely Miss Clarke which inspired, if not confidence, at least an openness of mind. Perhaps it was the self-possessed manner in which she sat all of them, including Ellery, down in Ellery's living-room while she waited on the hearth-rug, like a conductor on the podium, for them to settle in their chairs. And it was the measure of Miss Clarke's assurance that none of them was indignant, only curious.

"I'll make it snappy," said Martha Clarke briskly. "I did what I did the way I did it because, first, I had to make sure I could see Mr. Patch, Baroness Tchek, and Professor Shaw to-day. Second, because I may need a detective before I'm through ... Third," she added, almost absently, "because I'm pretty desperate.

"My name is Martha Clarke. My father Tobias is a farmer. Our farm lies just south of Philadelphia; it was built by a Clarke in 1761, and it's been in our family ever since. I won't go gooey on you. We're broke and there's a mortgage. Unless Papa and I can raise six thousand dollars in the next couple of weeks we lose the old homestead."

Professor Shaw looked vague. But the Baroness said: "Deplorable, Miss Clarke. Now if I'm to run my auction this afternoon——"

And James Ezekiel Patch grumbled: "If it's money you want, young woman——"

"Certainly it's money I want. But I have something to sell."

"Ah!" said the Baroness.

"Oh?" said the Professor.

"Hm," said the antiquarian.

Mr. Queen said nothing, and Miss Porter jealously chewed the end of her pencil.

"The other day while I was cleaning out the attic, I found an old book."

"Well, now," said Professor Shaw indulgently. "An old book, eh?"

"It's called *The Diary of Simeon Clarke*. Simeon Clarke was Papa's great-great-great-something or other. His *Diary* was privately printed in 1792 in Philadelphia, Professor, by a second cousin of his, Jonathan, who was in the printing business there."

"Jonathan Clarke. *The Diary of Simeon Clarke*," mumbled the cadaverous book-collector. "I don't believe I know either, Miss Clarke. Have you ...?"

Martha Clarke carefully unclasped a large Manila envelope and drew forth a single yellowed sheet of badly printed paper. "The title page was loose, so I brought it along."

Professor Shaw silently examined Miss Clarke's exhibit, and Ellery got up to squint at it. "Of course," said the Professor after a long scrutiny, in which he held the sheet up to the light, peered apparently at individual characters, and performed other mysterious rites, "mere age doesn't connote rarity, nor does rarity of itself constitute value. And while this page looks genuine for the purported period and is rare enough to be unknown to me, still ..."

"Suppose I told you," said Miss Martha Clarke, "that the chief purpose of the *Diary*—which I have at home—is to tell the story of how George Washington visited Simeon Clarke's farm in the winter of 1791——"

"Clarke's farm? 1791?" exclaimed James Ezekiel Patch. "Preposterous. There's no record of——"

"And of what George Washington buried there," the farmer's daughter concluded.

By executive order, the Queen telephone was taken off its hook, the door was bolted, the shades were drawn, and the long interrogation began. By the middle of the afternoon, the unknown chapter in the life of the Father of His country was fairly sketched.

Early on an icy grey February morning in 1791, Farmer Clarke had looked up from the fence he was mending to observe a splendid cortège galloping down on him from the direction of the City of Philadelphia. Outriders thundered in the van, followed by a considerable company of gentlemen on horseback and several great coaches-and-six driven by live-ried Negroes. To Simeon Clarke's astonishment, the entire equipage stopped before his farmhouse. He began to run. He could hear the creak of springs and the snorting of sleek and sweating horses. Gentlemen and lackeys were leaping to the frozen ground and, by the time Simeon had reached the farmhouse, all were elbowing about the first coach, a magnificent affair bearing a coat of arms. Craning, the farmer saw within the coach a very large, great-nosed gentleman clad in a black velvet suit and a black cloak faced with gold; there was a cocked hat on his wigged head and a great sword in a white leather scabbard at his side. This personage was on one knee, leaning with an expression of considerable anxiety over a chubby lady of middle age, swathed in furs, who was half-sitting, half-lying on the upholstered seat, her eyes closed and her cheeks waxen under the rouge. Another gentleman, soberly attired, was stooping over the lady, his fingers on one pale wrist.

"I fear," he was saying with great gravity to the kneeling man, "that it would be imprudent to proceed another yard in this weather, Your Excellency. Lady Washington requires physicking and a warm bed immediately."

Lady Washington! Then the large, richly dressed gentleman was the President! Simeon Clarke pushed excitedly through the throng.

"Your Mightiness! Sir!" he cried. "I am Simeon Clarke. This is my farm. We have warm beds, Sarah and I!"

The President considered Simeon briefly. "I thank you, Farmer Clarke. No, no, Dr. Craik. I shall assist Lady Washington myself."

And George Washington carried Martha Washington into the little Pennsylvania farmhouse of Simeon and Sarah Clarke. An aide informed the Clarkes that President Washington had been on his way to Virginia to celebrate his fifty-ninth birthday in the privacy of Mount Vernon.

Instead, he passed his birthday on the Clarke farm, for the physician insisted that the President's lady could not be moved, even back to the nearby Capital, without risking complications. On His Excellency's order, the entire incident was kept secret. "It would give needless alarm to the people," he said. But he did not leave Martha's bedside for three days and three nights.

Presumably during those seventy-two hours, while his lady recovered from her indisposition, the President devoted some thought to his hosts, for on the fourth morning he sent black Christopher, his body-servant, to summon the Clarkes. They found George Washington by the kitchen fire, shaven and powdered and in immaculate dress, his stern features composed.

"I am told, Farmer Clarke, that you and your good wife refuse reimbursement for the livestock you have slaughtered in the accommodation of our large company."

"You're my President, Sir," said Simeon. "I wouldn't take money."

"We—we wouldn't take money, Your Worship," stammered Sarah.

"Nevertheless, Lady Washington and I would acknowledge your hospitality in some kind. If you give me leave, I shall plant with my own hands a grove of oak saplings behind your house. And beneath one of the saplings I propose to bury two of my personal possessions." Washington's eyes twinkled ever so slightly. "It is my birthday—I feel a venturesome spirit. Come, Farmer Clarke and Mistress Clarke, would you like that?"

"What—what were they?" choked James Ezekiel Patch, the Washington collector. He was pale.

Martha Clarke replied: "The sword at Washington's side, in its white leather scabbard, and a silver coin the President carried in a secret pocket."

"Silver *coin?*" breathed Baroness Tchek, the rare-coin dealer. "What kind of coin, Miss Clarke?"

"The *Diary* calls it 'a half disme,' with an *s,*" replied Martha Clarke, frowning. "I guess that's the way they spelled dime in those days. The book's full of queer spellings."

"A United States of America half disme?" asked the Baroness in a very odd way.

"That's what it says, Baroness."

"And this was in 1791?"

"Yes."

The Baroness snorted, beginning to rise. "I thought your story was too impossibly romantic, young woman. The United States Mint didn't begin to strike off half dismes until 1792!"

"Half dismes or any other U.S. coinage, I believe," said Ellery. "How come, Miss Clarke?"

"It was an experimental coin," said Miss Clarke coolly. "The *Diary* isn't clear as to whether it was the Mint which struck it off, or some private agency—maybe Washington himself didn't tell Simeon—but the President did say to Simeon that the half disme in his pocket had been coined from silver he himself had furnished and had been presented to him as a keepsake."

"There's a half disme with a story like that behind it in the possession of The American Numismatic Society," muttered the Baroness, "but it's definitely called one of the earliest coins struck off by the Mint. It's possible,

I suppose, that in 1791, the preceding year, some specimen coins may have been struck off——"

"Possible my foot," said Miss Clarke. "It's so. The *Diary* says so. I imagine President Washington was pretty interested in the coins to be issued by the new country he was head of."

"Miss Clarke, I—I want that half disme. I mean—I'd like to buy it from you," said the Baroness.

"And I," said Mr. Patch carefully, "would like to ah . . . purchase Washington's sword."

"The *Diary*," moaned Professor Shaw. "I'll buy *The Diary of Simeon Clarke* from you, Miss Clarke!"

"I'll be happy to sell it to you, Professor Shaw—as I said, I found it in the attic, and I have it locked up in a highboy in the parlour at home. But as for the other two things . . ." Martha Clarke paused, and Ellery looked delighted. He thought he knew what was coming. "I'll sell you the sword, Mr. Patch, and you the half disme, Baroness Tchek, provided"—and now Miss Clarke turned her clear eyes on Ellery—"provided you, Mr. Queen, will be kind enough to find them."

And there was the farmhouse in the frosty Pennsylvania morning, set in the barren winter acres, and looking as bleak as only a little Revolutionary house with a mortgage on its head can look in the month of February.

"There's an apple orchard over there," said Nikki as they got out of Ellery's car. "But where's the grove of oaks? I don't see any!" And then she added sweetly: "Do you, Ellery?"

Ellery's lips tightened. They tightened further when his solo on the front-door knocker brought no response.

"Let's go around," he said briefly; and Nikki preceded him with cheerful step.

Behind the house there was a barn; and beyond the barn there was comfort, at least for Ellery. For beyond the barn there were twelve ugly holes in the earth, and beside each hole lay either a freshly felled oak tree and its stump, or an ancient stump by itself, freshly uprooted. On one of the stumps sat an old man in earth-stained blue jeans, smoking a corncob pugnaciously.

"Tobias Clarke?" asked Ellery.

"Yump."

"I'm Ellery Queen. This is Miss Porter. Your daughter visited me in New York yesterday——"

"Know all about it."

"May I ask where Martha is?"

"Station. Meetin' them there other folks." Tobias Clarke spat and looked away—at the holes. "Don't know what ye're all comin' down here for. Wasn't nothin' under them oaks. Dug 'em all up t'other day. Trees that were standin' and the stumps of the ones that'd fallen years back. Look at them holes. Hired hand and me dug down most to China. Washin'ton's Grove, always been called. Now look at it. Firewood—for someone else, I guess."

There was iron bitterness in his tone. "We're losin' this farm, Mister, unless . . ." And Tobias Clarke stopped. "Well, maybe we won't," he said. "There's always that there book Martha found."

"Professor Shaw, the rare-book collector, offered your daughter two thousand dollars for it if he's satisfied with it, Mr. Clarke," said Nikki.

"So she told me last night when she got back from New York," said Tobias Clarke. "Two thousand—and we need six." He grinned, and he spat again.

"Well," said Nikki sadly to Ellery, "that's that." She hoped Ellery would immediately get into the car and drive back to New York—immediately.

But Ellery showed no disposition to be sensible. "Perhaps, Mr. Clarke, some trees died in the course of time and just disappeared, stumps, roots, and all. Martha"—Martha!—"said the *Diary* doesn't mention the exact number Washington planted here."

"Look at them holes. Twelve of 'em, ain't there? In a triangle. Man plants trees in a triangle, he plants trees in a triangle. Ye don't see no place between holes big enough for another tree, do ye? Anyways, there was the same distance between all the trees. No, sir, Mister, twelve was all there was ever; and I looked under all twelve."

"What's the extra tree doing in the centre of the triangle? You haven't uprooted that one, Mr. Clarke."

Tobias Clarke spat once more. "Don't know much about trees, do ye? That's a cherry saplin' I set in myself six years ago. Ain't got nothin' to do with George Washington."

Nikki tittered.

"If you'd sift the earth in those holes——"

"I sifted it. Look, Mister, either somebody dug that stuff up a hundred years ago or the whole yarn's a Saturday night whopper. Which it most likely is. There's Martha now with them other folks." And Tobias Clarke added, spitting for the fourth time: "Don't let me be keepin' ye."

"It reveals Washington rather er . . . out of character," said James Ezekiel Patch that evening. They were sitting about the fire in the parlour, as heavy with gloom as with Miss Clarke's dinner; and that, at least in Miss Porter's view, was heavy indeed. Baroness Tchek wore the expression of one who is trapped in a cave; there was no further train until morning, and she had not yet resigned herself to a night in a farmhouse bed. The better part of the day had been spent poring over *The Diary of Simeon Clarke,* searching for a clue to the buried Washingtonia. But there was no clue; the pertinent passage referred merely to "a Triangle of Oake Trees behinde the red Barn, which His Excellency the President did plant with his own Hands, as he had promis'd me, and then did burie his Sworde and the Half Disme for his Pleasure in a Case of copper beneathe one of the Oakes, the which, he said (the Case), had been fashion'd by Mr. Revere of Boston who is experimenting with this Mettle in his Furnasses."

"How out of character, Mr. Patch?" asked Ellery. He had been staring into the fire for a long time, scarcely listening.

"Washington wasn't given to romanticism," said the large man dryly. "No folderol about him. I don't know of anything in his life which prepares us for such a yarn as this. I'm beginning to think——"

"But Professor Shaw himself says the *Diary* is no forgery!" cried Martha Clarke.

"Oh, the book's authentic enough." Professor Shaw seemed unhappy. "But it may simply be a literary hoax, Miss Clarke. The woods are full of them. I'm afraid that unless the story is confirmed by the discovery of that copper case with its contents ..."

"Oh, dear," said Nikki impulsively; and for a moment she was sorry for Martha Clarke, she really was.

But Ellery said: "I believe it. Pennsylvania farmers in 1791 weren't given to literary hoaxes, Professor Shaw. As for Washington, Mr. Patch—no man can be so rigidly consistent. And with his wife just recovering from an illness—on his own birthday ..." And Ellery fell silent again.

Almost immediately he leaped from his chair. "Mr. Clarke!"

Tobias stirred from his dark corner. "What?"

"Did you ever hear your father, or grandfather—anyone in your family— talk of *another barn behind the house?*"

Martha stared at him. Then she cried: "Papa, that's it! It was a different barn, in a different place, and the original Washington's Grove was cut down, or died——"

"Nope," said Tobias Clarke. "Never was but this one barn. Still got some of its original timbers. Ye can see the date burned into the cross-tree— 1761."

Nikki was up early. A steady *hack-hack-hack* borne on the frosty air woke her. She peered out of her back window, the coverlet up to her nose, to see Mr. Ellery Queen against the dawn, like a pioneer, wielding an axe powerfully.

Nikki dressed quickly, shivering, flung her mink-dyed muskrat over her shoulders, and ran downstairs, out of the house, and around it past the barn.

"Ellery! What do you think you're doing? It's practically the middle of the night!"

"Chopping," said Ellery, chopping.

"There's *mountains* of firewood stacked against the barn," said Nikki. "Really, Ellery, I think this is carrying a flirtation too far." Ellery did not reply. "And, anyway, there's something—something gruesome and inde- cent about chopping up trees George Washington planted. It's vandalism."

"Just a thought," panted Ellery, pausing for a moment. "A hundred and fifty-odd years is a long time, Nikki. Lots of queer things could happen, even to a tree, in that time. For instance——"

"The copper case," breathed Nikki, visibly. "The roots grew *around* it. It's *in* one of these stumps!"

"Now you're functioning," said Ellery, and he raised the axe again.

He was still at it two hours later, when Martha Clarke announced break- fast.

At 11:30 a.m. Nikki returned from driving the Professor, the Baroness, and James Ezekiel Patch to the railroad station. She found Mr. Queen seated before the fire in the kitchen in his undershirt, while Martha Clarke caressed his naked right arm.

"Oh!" said Nikki faintly. "I *beg* your pardon."

"Where are you going, Nikki?" said Ellery irritably. "Come in. Martha's rubbing liniment into my biceps."

"He's not very accustomed to chopping wood, is he?" asked Martha Clarke in a cheerful voice.

"Reduced those foul 'oakes' to splinters," groaned Ellery. "Martha, ouch!"

"I should think you'd be satisfied *now*," said Nikki coldly. "I suggest we imitate Patch, Shaw, and the Baroness, Ellery—there's a 3:05. We can't impose on Miss Clarke's hospitality forever."

To Nikki's horror, Martha Clarke chose this moment to burst into tears.

"Martha!"

Nikki felt like leaping upon her and shaking the cool look back into her perfidious eyes.

"Here—here, now, Martha." That's right, thought Nikki contemptuously. Embrace her in front of me! "It's those three rats. Running out that way! Don't worry—I'll find that sword and half disme for you yet."

"You'll never find them," sobbed Martha, wetting Ellery's undershirt. "Because they're not here. They *never* were here. When you s-stop to think of it ... *burying* that coin, his sword ... if the story were true, he'd have given them to Simeon and Sarah ..."

"Not necessarily, not necessarily," said Ellery with a hateful haste. "The old boy had a sense of history, Martha. They all did in those days. They knew they were men of destiny and that the eyes of posterity were upon them. Burying 'em is *just* what Washington would have done!"

"Do you really th-think so?"

Oh ... *pfui.*

"But even if he did bury them," Martha sniffled, "it doesn't stand to reason Simeon and Sarah would have let them *stay* buried. They'd have dug that copper box up like rabbits the minute G-George turned his back."

"Two simple countryfolk?" cried Ellery. "Salt of the earth? The new American earth? Disregard the wishes of His Mightiness, George Washington, First President of the United States? Are you out of your mind? And anyway, what would Simeon do with a dress-sword?"

Beat it into a ploughshare, thought Nikki spitefully—*that's* what he'd do.

"And that half disme. How much could it have been worth in 1791? Martha, they're here under your farm somewhere. You wait and see——"

"I wish I could b-believe it ... Ellery."

"Shucks, child. Now stop crying——"

From the door Miss Porter said stiffly: "You might put your shirt back on, Superman, before you catch pneumonia."

Mr. Queen prowled about the Clarke acres for the remainder of that day, his nose at a low altitude. He spent some time in the barn. He devoted at least twenty minutes to each of the twelve holes in the earth. He reinspected the oaken wreckage of his axework like a palaeontologist examining an ancient petrifaction for the impression of a dinosaur foot. He measured off the distance between the holes; and, for a moment, a faint tremor of emotion shook him. George Washington had been a surveyor in his youth; here was evidence that his passion for exactitude had not wearied with the years. As far as Ellery could make out, the twelve oaks had been set into the earth at exactly equal distances, in an equilateral triangle.

It was at this point that Ellery had seated himself upon the seat of a cultivator behind the barn, wondering at his suddenly accelerated circulation. Little memories were knocking at the door. And as he opened to admit them, it was as if he were admitting a personality. It was, of course, at this time that the sense of personal conflict first obtruded. He had merely to shut his eyes in order to materialize a tall, large-featured man carefully pacing off the distances between twelve points—pacing them off in a sort of objective challenge to the unborn future. George Washington ...

The man Washington had from the beginning possessed an affinity for numbers. It had remained with him all his life. To count things, not so much for the sake of the things, perhaps, as for the counting, had been of the utmost importance to him. As a boy in Mr. William's school in Westmorland, he excelled in arithmetic, long division, subtraction, weights and measures—to calculate cords of wood and pecks of peas, pints and gallons and avoirdupois—young George delighted in these as other boys delighted in horseplay. As a man, he merely directed his passion into the channel of his possessions. Through his possessions he apparently satisfied his curious need for enumeration. He was not content simply to keep accounts of the acreage he owned, its yield, his slaves, his pounds and pence. Ellery recalled the extraordinary case of Washington and the seed. He once calculated the number of seeds in a pound troy weight of red clover. Not appeased by the statistics on red clover, Washington then went to work on a pound of timothy seed. His conclusions were: 71,000 and 298,000. His appetite unsatisfied, he thereupon fell upon the problem of New River grass. Here he tackled a calculation worthy of his prowess: his mathematical labours produced the great, pacifying figure of 844,800.

This man was so obsessed with numbers, Ellery thought, staring at the ruins of Washington's Grove, that he counted the windows in each house of his Mount Vernon estate and the number of "Paynes" in each window of each house, and then triumphantly recorded the exact number of each in his own handwriting.

It was like a hunger, requiring periodic appeasement. In 1747, as a boy of fifteen, George Washington drew "A Plan of Major Law: Washington's Turnip Field as Survey'd by me." In 1786, at the age of fifty-four, General Washington, the most famous man in the world, occupied himself with determining the exact elevation of his piazza above the Potomac's high-water mark. No doubt he experienced a warmer satisfaction thereafter for knowing that when he sat upon his piazza looking down upon the river he was sitting exactly 124 feet 10½ inches above it.

And in 1791, as President of the United States, Ellery mused, he was striding about right here, setting saplings into the ground, twelve of them in an equilateral triangle, and beneath one of them he buried a copper case containing his sword and the half disme coined from his own silver. Beneath one of them . . . But it was not beneath one of them. Or had it been? And had long ago been dug up by a Clarke? But the story had apparently died with Simeon and Sarah. On the other hand . . .

Ellery found himself irrationally reluctant to conclude the obvious. George Washington's lifelong absorption with figures kept intruding. Twelve trees, equidistant, in an equilateral triangle.

"What is it?" he kept asking himself, almost angrily. "Why isn't it satisfying me?"

And then, in the gathering dusk, a very odd explanation insinuated itself. *Because it wouldn't have satisfied him!*

That's silly, Ellery said to himself abruptly. It has all the earmarks of a satisfying experience. There is no more satisfying figure in all geometry than an equilateral triangle. It is closed, symmetrical, definite, a whole and balanced and finished thing.

But it wouldn't have satisfied George Washington . . . for all its symmetry and perfection.

Then perhaps there is a symmetry and perfection beyond the cold beauty of figures?

At this point, Ellery began to question his own postulates . . . lost in the dark and to his time . . .

They found him at ten-thirty, crouched on the cultivator seat, numb and staring.

He permitted himself to be led into the house, he suffered Nikki to subject him to the indignity of having his shoes and socks stripped off and his frozen feet rubbed to life, he ate Martha Clarke's dinner—all with a detachment and indifference which alarmed the girls and even made old Tobias look uneasy.

"If it's going to have this effect on him," began Martha, and then she said: "Ellery, give it up. Forget it." But she had to shake him before he heard her.

He shook his head. "They're there."

"Where?" cried the girls simultaneously.

"In Washington's Grove."

"Ye found 'em?" croaked Tobias Clarke, half-rising.

"No."

The Clarkes and Nikki exchanged glances.

"Then how can you be so certain they're buried there, Ellery?" asked Nikki gently.

Ellery looked bewildered. "Darned if I know *how* I know," he said, and he even laughed a little. "Maybe George Washington told me." Then he stopped laughing and went into the firelit parlour and—pointedly—slid the doors shut.

At ten minutes past midnight Martha Clarke gave up the contest.

"Isn't he ever going to come out of there?" she said, yawning.

"You never can tell what Ellery will do," replied Nikki.

"Well, I can't keep my eyes open another minute."

"Funny," said Nikki. "I'm not in the least bit sleepy."

"You city girls."

"You country girls."

They laughed. Then they stopped laughing, and for a moment there was no sound in the kitchen but the patient sentry-walk of the grandfather clock and the snores of Tobias assaulting the ceiling from above.

"Well," said Martha. Then she said: "I just *can't*. Are you staying up, Nikki?"

"For a little while. You go to bed, Martha."

"Yes. Well. Good night."

"Good night, Martha."

At the door Martha turned suddenly: "Did he say *George Washington told him?*"

"Yes."

Martha went rather quickly up the stairs.

Nikki waited fifteen minutes. Then she tiptoed to the foot of the stairs and listened. She heard Tobias snuffling and snorting as he turned over in his bed, and an uneasy moan from the direction of Martha's bedroom, as if she were dreaming an unwholesome dream. Nikki set her jaw grimly and went to the parlour doors and slid them open.

Ellery was on his knees before the fire. His elbows were resting on the floor. His face was propped in his hands. In this attitude his posterior was considerably higher than his head.

"Ellery!"

"Huh?"

"Ellery, what on earth——?"

"Nikki. I thought you'd gone to bed long ago." In the firelight his face was haggard.

"But what have you been *doing?* You looked exhausted?"

"I am. I've been wrestling with a man who could bend a horseshoe with his naked hands. A very strong man. In more ways than one."

"What are you talking about? Who?"

"George Washington. Go to bed, Nikki."

"George ... Washington?"

"Go to bed."

"... *Wrestling* with him?"

"Trying to break through his defenses. Get into his mind. It's not an easy mind to get into. He's been dead such a long time—that makes the difference. The dead are stubborn, Nikki. Aren't you going to bed?"

Nikki backed out shivering.

The house *was* icy.

It was even icier when an inhuman bellow accompanied by a thunder that shook the Revolutionary walls of her bedroom brought Nikki out of bed with a yelping leap.

But it was only Ellery.

He was somewhere up the hall, in the first glacial light of dawn, hammering on Martha Clarke's door.

"Martha. *Martha!* Wake up, damn you, and tell me where I can find a book in this damned house! A biography of Washington—a history of the United States—an almanac ... *anything!*"

The parlour fire had long since given up the ghost. Nikki and Martha in wrappers, and Tobias Clarke in an ancient bathrobe over his marbled long underwear, stood around shivering and bewildered as a dishevelled, daemonic Ellery leafed eagerly through a 1921 edition of *The Farmer's Fact Book and Complete Compendium*.

"Here it is!" The words shot out of his mouth like bullets, leaving puffs of smoke.

"What is it, Ellery?"

"What on earth are you looking for?"

"He's loony, I tell ye!"

Ellery turned with a look of ineffable peace, closing the book.

"That's it," he said. "That's it."

"What's it?"

"Vermont. The State of Vermont."

"Vermont ... ?"

"Ver*mont?*"

"Vermont. What in the crawlin' creepers's Vermont got to do with——"

"Vermont," said Ellery with a tired smile, "did not enter the Union until March fourth, 1791. So that proves it, don't you see?"

"Proves *what?*" shrieked Nikki.

"Where George Washington buried his sword and half disme."

"Because," said Ellery in the rapidly lightening dawn behind the barn, "Vermont was the fourteenth State to do so. The *fourteenth*. Tobias, would you get me an axe, please?"

"An axe," mumbled Tobias. He shuffled away, shaking his head.

"Come on, Ellery, I'm d-dying of c-cold!" chattered Nikki, dancing up and down before the cultivator.

"Ellery," said Martha Clarke piteously, "I don't understand *any* of this."

"It's very simple, Martha—oh, thank you, Tobias—as simple," said Ellery, "as simple arithmetic. Numbers, my dears—numbers tell this remarkable story. Numbers and their influence on our first President who was, above all things, a number-man. That was my key. I merely had to discover the lock to fit it into. Vermont was the lock. And the door's open."

Nikki seated herself on the cultivator. You had to give Ellery his head in a situation like this; you couldn't drive him for beans. Well, she thought grudgingly, seeing how pale and how tired-looking he was after a night's wrestling with George Washington, he's earned it.

"The number was wrong," said Ellery solemnly, leaning on Tobias's axe. "Twelve trees. Washington apparently planted twelve trees—Simeon Clarke's *Diary* never did mention the number twelve, but the evidence seemed unquestionable—there were twelve oaks in an equilateral triangle, each one an equal distance from its neighbour.

"And yet . . . I felt that *twelve* oaks couldn't be, perfect as the triangle was. Not if they were planted by George Washington. Not on February the twenty-second, New Style, in the year of our Lord 1791.

"Because on February the twenty-second, 1791—in fact, until March the fourth, when Vermont entered the Union to swell its original number by one—there was *another* number in the United States so important, so revered, so much a part of the common speech and the common living—and dying—that it was more than a number; it was a solemn and sacred thing; almost not a number at all. It overshadowed other numbers like the still-unborn Paul Bunyan. It was memorialized on the New American flag in the number of its stars and the number of its stripes. It was a number of which George Washington was the standard-bearer!—the head and only recently the strong right arm of the new Republic which had been born out of the blood and muscle of its integers. It was a number which was in the hearts and minds and mouths of all Americans.

"No. If George Washington, who was not merely the living symbol of all this but carried with him that extraordinary compulsion toward numbers which characterized his whole temperament besides, had wished to plant a number of oak trees to commemorate a birthday visit in the year 1791 . . . he would have, he could have, selected only one number out of all the mathematical trillions at his command—*the number thirteen.*"

The sun was looking over the edge of Pennsylvania at Washington's Grove.

"George Washington planted thirteen trees here that day, and under one of them he buried Paul Revere's copper case. Twelve of the trees he arranged in an equilateral triangle, and we know that the historic treasure was not under any of the twelve. Therefore he must have buried the case under the thirteenth—a thirteenth oak sapling which grew to oakhood and, some time during the past century and a half, withered and died and vanished, vanished so utterly that it left no trace, not even its roots.

"Where would Washington have planted that thirteenth oak? Because beneath the spot where it once stood—there lies the copper case containing his sword and the first coin to be struck off in the new United States."

And Ellery glanced tenderly at the cherry sapling which Tobias Clarke had set into the earth in the middle of Washington's Grove six years before.

"Washington the surveyor, the geometer, the man whose mind cried out for integral symmetries? Obviously, in only one place: *In the centre of the triangle.* Any other place would be unthinkable."

And Ellery hefted Tobias's axe and strode toward the six-year-old tree. He raised the axe.

But suddenly he lowered it, and turned, and said in a rather startled way: "See here! Isn't to-day ... ?"

"Washington's Birthday," said Nikki.

Ellery grinned and began to chop down the cherry tree.

ACTIVITIES

1) How would you define an *historical detective story?* You have read and studied historical fiction before. If you know what *historical fiction* is, then you should be able to come up with a good definition here.

2) At one point in the story, Ellery states that he has been "wrestling with George Washington." What exactly does he mean by this? Could Ellery have solved the mystery without a knowledge of American history?

3) Some of you have trouble with spelling; your teachers have consistently stressed "correct" spelling.

What have you learned about the spelling of American English words from this story? What exactly do your teachers mean by "correct" spelling?

4) Besides American history, in what other subjects must Frederic Dannay and Manfred B. Lee have been proficient in order to write this particular E.Q. yarn? What are the qualifications for becoming a good creative writer? A good detective story writer?

RESEARCH ACTIVITIES

1) Ready for another bout with mystery and history?

We wager that your teacher will gladly award you an extra-credit grade if you decide to look up and read Ellery Queen's second historical detective story. It is entitled "The Adventures of Abraham Lincoln's Clue" and is as equally intriguing as the tale that you have just finished.

Incidentally, Edgar Allan Poe also figures prominently in that story. Why? Well, Lincoln was one of Poe's most ardent fans.

2) Speaking of Abraham Lincoln, did you know that he was once purported to have solved a murder mystery? You can find out more about

it by searching for an old nineteenth-century historical novel called *The Graysons* by Edward Eggleston. Chapter 22 deals with a murder case solved by a young prairie lawyer, Lincoln himself. The chapter can be read independently of the novel.

Eggleston utilized an old legend about Lincoln that may or may not be true. Your history teacher may have more information about the chapter's authenticity.

Ellery Queen—Scholar, Editor, and Teacher

It may be hard to believe but, during the 1930s, detective short stories were difficult to market. Most book publishers favored novels; occasionally, an anthology of short stories was printed but these were few and far between.

There were some crime pulp magazines to which the short story writer could sell, such as *Street and Smith's Detective Story, Black Mask,* and *Detective Fiction Weekly.* But these were, in the main, periodicals restricted to one category of story—the tough, hard-boiled tale of action then being popularized by Dashiell Hammett, Raymond Chandler, and Cornell Woolrich. The magazine market provided virtually no outlet for other forms of detective stories, such as the story analyzing motivation, the detective story with social commentary, the yarn starring the female sleuth, the sports-detective narrative, and others.

Thus, in 1933, Fred Dannay and Manny Lee, both already considered top mystery novelists, found the pulp magazines all but closed to their kind of short story. They decided to start their own magazine. Unfortunately, their publication, entitled *Mystery League,* collapsed after four months because of financial problems.

At this point—in order to preserve the form—they made up their minds to become collectors of mystery and detective short stories. They ended up with what turned out to be the world's finest collection of all types of crime fiction, a collection that today is housed in the Library of the University of Texas. They then went on to put together a scholarly bibliography on the subject, which they called *The Detective Short Story.* This work is considered the most authoritative of its kind in the field of detective literature.

But the failure of their magazine venture continued to rankle.

Then, one day, they met Lawrence E. Spivack, a well-known magazine publisher. Spivack became intrigued by their format for a new type of mystery magazine, and he decided to back them financially. In 1941, the first issue of *Ellery Queen's Mystery Magazine* appeared. This time, their periodical not only caught on but became so popular that it continues to be published to this very day.

Through this successful publication, Ellery Queen began to exert a

The cover of the first issue of *Ellery Queen's Mystery Magazine* (EQMM) which appeared during Fall of 1941.

marked influence upon America's detective story writers. *Ellery Queen's Mystery Magazine* (EQMM) has, throughout the years, probably published every important mystery author in our time who ever wrote short stories. It has also attracted a large number of serious writers who became intrigued by detective fiction. During the years of EQMM's existence, a host of Pulitzer and Nobel prizewinners have appeared in its pages, among them such illustrious names as Arthur Miller, William Faulkner, John Steinbeck, MacKinley Kantor, and others. (What a contrast to those early days when Edgar Allan Poe and Arthur Conan Doyle had wanted to "escape" from detective fiction!)

But, most important of all, EQMM encouraged new and unpublished writers to submit their offerings, too. Today, an entire new generation of popular detective story writers can say that they are EQMM alumni; a number had their first stories published in the magazine. Among this group are such noted modern names as Lillian de la Torre, Edward Hoch, Jack Finney, James Yaffe, William Brittain, and many others.

Frederic Dannay and Manfred B. Lee were more than just good editors; they became encouraging and sensitive teachers as well. When the occasion demanded it (and there were many such occasions), that is, when a story by a newcomer showed promise but was not entirely ready for publication, they worked individually with the aspiring writer until that individual's talents were fully realized and his story ready to appear in print. (This was especially true of Frederic Dannay who devoted a great deal of his time to magazine activities.)

Poe "had given birth" to the genre and Doyle had nurtured "the struggling infant" until it could stand on "its own two feet." But it was Ellery Queen, in the role of imaginative author, meticulous scholar, able editor, and creative teacher, who guided the "adolescent" literary form into respectable maturity.

Truly, to re-direct a question of Frederic Dannay's: "Who shall ever forget?"[6]

Death Finally Separates the Team: Dannay Carries on

The 1960s, with the Viet Nam War, riots in the cities, political assassinations, and campus strikes, was considered a decade of violence. Frederic Dannay and Manfred B. Lee refused to be swayed by the times. They continued to write, but force remained an inconsequential factor in their books. If violence had to become part of a story (as it invariably does in the detective genre), it was always overshadowed by the brilliant deductive feats of Mr. Ellery Queen.

In point of fact, Dannay and Lee detested violence. Neither of them ever owned a gun or went hunting. During the late sixties, Manny Lee even declared his property in Roxbury, Connecticut, a game preserve with hunting absolutely forbidden.

By the time the seventies arrived, Dannay and Lee had sold over 100,000,000 copies of their books. The collaborative team responsible for Ellery Queen seemed destined to remain inseparable.

Unfortunately, it was not to remain this way.

As he became older, Manfred B. Lee suffered from heart disease and diabetes. On April 4, 1971, he became ill at his Roxbury home and was taken by ambulance to a hospital in Waterbury. Lee died en route.[7]

Heartbroken by the death of his long-time collaborator, cousin, and friend, Frederic Dannay decided to carry on the Ellery Queen enterprises by himself. After forty-two years of collaboration and many more of personal friendship, Dannay probably knows well how Lee would respond to a given literary problem. In a sense, Manny Lee is still "spiritually" with him.

At any rate, books by Ellery Queen and the monthly issues of *Ellery Queen's Mystery Magazine* continue to roll off the presses.

And their quality remains as high as ever.

Only an Appetizer

As with the previous chapters, the three short stories were presented herein for the purpose of whetting your literary appetite. If you have become a confirmed Queen fan by now, you are in luck. Ellery Queen is one of the most prolific of all mystery story writers, and there are many, many more novels and short stories on the Queen bill of fare.

Here is a list of what is available:

Novels

The Roman Hat Mystery	*The Murderer Is a Fox*
The French Powder Mystery	*Ten Days' Wonder*
The Dutch Shoe Mystery	*Cat of Many Tails*
The Greek Coffin Mystery	*Double, Double*
The Egyptian Cross Mystery	*The Origin of Evil*
The American Gun Mystery	*The King Is Dead*
The Siamese Twin Mystery	*The Scarlet Letters*
The Chinese Orange Mystery	*The Glass Village*
The Spanish Cape Mystery	*Inspector Queen's Own Case*
Halfway House	*The Finishing Stroke*
The Door Between	*The Player on the Other Side*
The Devil to Pay	*And on the Eighth Day*
The Four of Hearts	*The Fourth Side of the Triangle*
The Dragon's Teeth	*A Study in Terror*
Calamity Town	*Face to Face*
There Was an Old Woman	*The House of Brass*
	The Lamp of God

Short Story Anthologies

The Adventures of Ellery Queen	*Q.B.I.: Queen's Bureau of Investigation*
The New Adventures of Ellery Queen	*Queens Full*
Calendar of Crime	*Q.E.D.: Queen's Experiments in Detection*

4.

The Others

Introduction

Though Edgar Allan Poe, Sir Arthur Conan Doyle, and Ellery Queen had blazed an historic trail into a new area of imagination, many other authors stepped forward in the early twentieth century to help cultivate that terrain by contributing their own unique character and plot innovations.

Mostly, "the others" came from England and the United States. The fictional characters they created were, like Dupin, Holmes, and Queen, either amateurs who made their living in different occupational areas, or else private detectives consulted by official police investigators or by private clients in distress. In order for these new sleuths to gain a reader following all their own, their author-creators had to develop them as distinct personalities utterly independent of old fictional heroes and adventures. There might be a similarity to the elements introduced by Poe, namely, "an unusual detective of high intelligence . . ." and "an assistant of lesser intelli-

187

gence," but the characterizations had to be fresh and different and the cases that they were called upon to solve original as well as baffling.

Thanks to Conan Doyle's Sherlock Holmes, an entire reading world had become interested in detective literature. But that interest never became non-selective; the public remained remarkably able to distinguish between the talented creators and the imitative "hacks." The imitators were summarily rejected; the innovators were granted the same recognition and praise as had been lavished upon "the masters."

Who were these "others"?

What were their character and plot innovations?

We cannot introduce you to all of them; there are simply too many. All we can do is enable you to meet some of that select company who had accepted the challenge thrown to them by the pioneers. Perhaps they will inspire you to seek out "the other 'others'" on your own.

Jacques Futrelle—and The Thinking Machine

October 30, 1905, occurred on a Monday.

On that morning, in the pages of *The Boston American,* a Hearst newspaper, appeared the first episode of a six-part story entitled "The Problem of Cell 13." With the chapter there appeared an invitation to enter a contest.

The tale began with the protagonist, a brilliant but eccentric professor, wagering that he could escape from the impenetrable confines of a penitentiary's death-cell; the newspaper's readers were offered $100 in prizes if they could come up with a resolution to the dilemma as brilliant as the one to be provided by the author.

The story's premise was fascinating; day after day, the paper's devotees read on while entries to the contest poured in. However, the narrative proved so suspenseful in itself that the contest became a mere background prop. Everyone awaited only one resolution—*the author's.*

When the sixth and final episode appeared on Sunday, November 5, only perfunctory interest was displayed toward the names of the contest winners. The readers had become interested in only one name—the story's writer, Jacques Futrelle.

He turned out to be a member of the *Boston American's* editorial staff. Never had that gentleman's editorials generated the kind of public interest drawn by his initial detective story. Today, "The Problem of Cell 13" is considered a classic. In 1905, it appeared that America had produced a Conan Doyle of its own.

It was not to be.

In 1912, Jacques Futrelle died at the early age of thirty-seven. He and his wife, May, had been passengers on the *Titanic,* a luxury ocean liner that, as you probably know, sank on its maiden voyage after striking an iceberg. A tragic ending to a promising career ...

Futrelle was born in Pike County, Georgia, in 1875 of French-Huguenot parentage. He became a newspaperman and then a theatrical manager. Before his death, he managed to write a fair amount of fiction, most of which appeared in the pages of newspapers.

The eccentric professor of "The Problem of Cell 13" became known as "The Thinking Machine." His real name was as remarkable as his personality: Augustus S. F. X. Van Dusen, followed by a string of impressive degrees. His interest could never be captured by an ordinary puzzle; for him, his creator had always to construct a supposedly unsolvable plot situation.

And Jacques Futrelle became known as the master of the "impossible."

Before his death, more Thinking Machine stories appeared, but Futrelle's first remains the best-remembered. One of the reasons for its fame lies in the fact that it's a classic example of the "locked room" story.[1]

What is a "locked room" story?

You have already read one—Poe's "The Murders in the Rue Morgue." Remember the sealed room where the murders took place and the problem posed as to how the killer escaped? Well, that is the kind of situation that occurs in this story.

The Problem of Cell 13

I

Practically all those letters remaining in the alphabet after Augustus S. F. X. Van Dusen was named were afterward acquired by that gentleman in the course of a brilliant scientific career, and, being honorably acquired, were tacked on to the other end. His name, therefore, taken with all that belonged to it, was a wonderfully imposing structure. He was a Ph.D., an LL.D., an F.R.S., an M.D., and an M.D.S. He was also some other things—just what he himself couldn't say—through recognition of his ability by various foreign educational and scientific institutions.

In appearance he was no less striking than in nomenclature. He was slender with the droop of the student in his thin shoulders and the pallor of a close, sedentary life on his clean-shaven face. His eyes wore a perpetual, forbidding squint—of a man who studies little things—and when they could be seen at all through his thick spectacles, were mere slits of watery blue. But above his eyes was his most striking feature. This was a tall, broad brow, almost abnormal in height and width, crowned by a heavy shock of bushy, yellow hair. All these things conspired to give him a peculiar, almost grotesque, personality.

Professor Van Dusen was remotely German. For generations his ancestors had been noted in the sciences; he was the logical result, the master mind. First and above all he was a logician. At least thirty-five years of the half-century or so of his existence had been devoted exclusively to proving that two and two always equal four, except in unusual cases, where they equal three or five, as the case may be. He stood broadly on the general proposition that all things that start must go somewhere, and was able to bring the concentrated mental force of his forefathers to bear on a given problem. Incidentally it may be remarked that Professor Van Dusen wore a No. 8 hat.

The world at large had heard vaguely of Professor Van Dusen as The Thinking Machine. It was a newspaper catch-phrase applied to him at the time of a remarkable exhibition at chess; he had demonstrated then that a stranger to the game might, by the force of inevitable logic, defeat a champion who had devoted a lifetime to its study. The Thinking Machine! Perhaps that more nearly described him than all his honorary initials, for he spent week after week, month after month, in the seclusion of his small laboratory from which had gone forth thoughts that staggered scientific associates and deeply stirred the world at large.

It was only occasionally that The Thinking Machine had visitors, and these were usually men who, themselves high in the sciences, dropped in to argue a point and perhaps convince themselves. Two of these men, Dr. Charles Ransome and Alfred Fielding, called one evening to discuss some theory which is not of consequence here.

"Such a thing is impossible," declared Dr. Ransome emphatically, in the course of the conversation.

"Nothing is impossible," declared The Thinking Machine with equal emphasis. He always spoke petulantly. "The mind is master of all things. When science fully recognizes that fact a great advance will have been made."

"How about the airship?" asked Dr. Ransome.

"That's not impossible at all," asserted The Thinking Machine. "It will be invented some time. I'd do it myself, but I'm busy."

Dr. Ransome laughed tolerantly.

"I've heard you say such things before," he said. "But they mean nothing. Mind may be master of matter, but it hasn't yet found a way to apply itself. There are some things that can't be *thought* out of existence, or rather which would not yield to any amount of thinking."

"What, for instance?" demanded The Thinking Machine.

Dr. Ransome was thoughtful for a moment as he smoked. "Well, say prison walls," he replied. "No man can *think* himself out of a cell. If he could, there would be no prisoners."

"A man can so apply his brain and ingenuity that he can leave a cell, which is the same thing," snapped The Thinking Machine.

Dr. Ransome was slightly amused.

"Let's suppose a case," he said, after a moment. "Take a cell where prisoners under sentence of death are confined—men who are desperate and, maddened by fear, would take any chance to escape—suppose you were locked in such a cell. Could you escape?"

"Certainly," declared The Thinking Machine.

"Of course," said Mr. Fielding, who entered the conversation for the first time, "you might wreck the cell with an explosive—but inside, a prisoner, you couldn't have that."

"There would be nothing of that kind," said The Thinking Machine. "You might treat me precisely as you treated prisoners under sentence of death, and I would leave the cell."

"Not unless you entered it with tools prepared to get out," said Dr. Ransome.

The Thinking Machine was visibly annoyed and his blue eyes snapped.

"Lock me in any cell in any prison anywhere at any time, wearing only what is necessary, and I'll escape in a week," he declared, sharply.

Dr. Ransome sat up straight in the chair, interested. Mr. Fielding lighted a new cigar.

"You mean you could actually *think* yourself out?" asked Dr. Ransome.

"I would get out," was the response.

"Are you serious?"

"Certainly I am serious."

Dr. Ransome and Mr. Fielding were silent for a long time.

"Would you be willing to try it?" asked Mr. Fielding, finally.

"Certainly," said Professor Van Dusen, and there was a trace of irony in his voice. "I have done more asinine things than that to convince other men of less important truths."

The tone was offensive and there was an undercurrent strongly resembling anger on both sides. Of course it was an absurd thing, but Professor Van Dusen reiterated his willingness to undertake the escape and it was decided upon.

"To begin now," added Dr. Ransome.

"I'd prefer that it begin tomorrow," said The Thinking Machine, "because—"

"No, now," said Mr. Fielding, flatly. "You are arrested, figuratively, of course, without any warning locked in a cell with no chance to communicate with friends, and left there with identically the same care and attention that would be given to a man under sentence of death. Are you willing?"

"All right, now, then," said The Thinking Machine, and he arose.

"Say, the death-cell in Chisholm Prison."

"The death-cell in Chisholm Prison."

"And what will you wear?"

"As little as possible," said The Thinking Machine. "Shoes, stockings, trousers and a shirt."

"You will permit yourself to be searched, of course?"

"I am to be treated precisely as all prisoners are treated," said The Thinking Machine. "No more attention and no less."

There were some preliminaries to be arranged in the matter of obtaining permission for the test, but all three were influential men and everything was done satisfactorily by telephone, albeit the prison commissioners, to whom the experiment was explained on purely scientific grounds, were sadly bewildered. Professor Van Dusen would be the most distinguished prisoner they had ever entertained.

When The Thinking Machine had donned those things which he was to wear during his incarceration he called the little old woman who was his housekeeper, cook and maidservant all in one.

"Martha," he said, "it is now twenty-seven minutes past nine o'clock. I am going away. One week from to-night, at half-past nine, these gentlemen and one, possibly two, others will take supper with me here. Remember Dr. Ransome is very fond of artichokes."

The three men were driven to Chisholm Prison, where the warden was awaiting them, having been informed of the matter by telephone. He understood merely that the eminent Professor Van Dusen was to be his prisoner, if he could keep him, for one week; that he had committed no crime, but that he was to be treated as all other prisoners were treated.

"Search him," instructed Dr. Ransome.

The Thinking Machine was searched. Nothing was found on him; the pockets of the trousers were empty; the white, stiff-bosomed shirt had no pocket. The shoes and stockings were removed, examined, then replaced. As he watched all these preliminaries—the rigid search and noted the pitiful, childlike physical weakness of the man, the colorless face, and the thin, white hands—Dr. Ransome almost regretted his part in the affair.

"Are you sure you want to do this?" he asked.

"Would you be convinced if I did not?" inquired The Thinking Machine in turn.

"No."

"All right. I'll do it."

What sympathy Dr. Ransome had was dissipated by the tone. It nettled him, and he resolved to see the experiment to the end; it would be a stinging reproof to egotism.

"It will be impossible for him to communicate with any one outside?" he asked.

"Absolutely impossible," replied the warden. "He will not be permitted writing materials of any sort."

"And your jailers, would they deliver a message from him?"

"Not one word, directly or indirectly," said the warden. "You may rest assured of that. They will report anything he might say or turn over to me anything he might give them."

"That seems entirely satisfactory," said Mr. Fielding, who was frankly interested in the problem.

"Of course, in the event he fails," said Dr. Ransome, "and asks for his liberty, you understand you are to set him free?"

"I understand," replied the warden.

The Thinking Machine stood listening, but had nothing to say until this was all ended, then:

"I should like to make three small requests. You may grant them or not, as you wish."

"No special favors, now," warned Mr. Fielding.

"I am asking none," was the stiff response. "I would like to have some tooth powder—buy it yourself to see that it is tooth powder—and I should like to have one five-dollar and two ten-dollar bills."

Dr. Ransome, Mr. Fielding and the warden exchanged astonished glances. They were not surprised at the request for tooth powder, but were at the request for money.

"Is there any man with whom our friend would come in contact that he could bribe with twenty-five dollars?" asked Dr. Ransome of the warden.

"Not for twenty-five hundred dollars," was the positive reply.

"Well, let him have them," said Mr. Fielding. "I think they are harmless enough."

"And what is the third request?" asked Dr. Ransome.

"I should like to have my shoes polished."

Again the astonished glances were exchanged. This last request was the height of absurdity, so they agreed to it. These things all being attended to, The Thinking Machine was led back into the prison from which he had undertaken to escape.

"Here is Cell 13," said the warden, stopping three doors down the steel corridor. "This is where we keep condemned murderers. No one can leave it without my permission; and no one in it can communicate with the outside. I'll stake my reputation on that. It's only three doors back of my office and I can readily hear any unusual noise."

"Will this cell do, gentlemen?" asked The Thinking Machine. There was a touch of irony in his voice.

"Admirably," was the reply.

The heavy steel door was thrown open, there was a great scurrying and scampering of tiny feet, and The Thinking Machine passed into the gloom of the cell. Then the door was closed and double locked by the warden.

"What is that noise in there?" asked Dr. Ransome, through the bars.

"Rats—dozens of them," replied The Thinking Machine, tersely.

The three men, with final good nights, were turning away when The Thinking Machine called:

"What time is it exactly, warden?"

"Eleven seventeen," replied the warden.

"Thanks. I will join you gentlemen in your office at half-past eight o'clock one week from to-night," said The Thinking Machine.

"And if you do not?"

"There is no 'if' about it."

II

Chisholm Prison was a great, spreading structure of granite, four stories in all, which stood in the center of acres of open space. It was surrounded by a wall of solid masonry eighteen feet high, and so smoothly finished inside and out as to offer no foothold to a climber, no matter how expert. Atop of this fence, as a further precaution, was a five-foot fence of steel rods, each terminating in a keen point. This fence in itself marked an absolute deadline between freedom and imprisonment, for, even if a man escaped from his cell, it would seem impossible for him to pass the wall.

The yard, which on all sides of the prison building was twenty-five feet wide, that being the distance from the building to the wall, was by day an exercise ground for those prisoners to whom was granted the boon of occasional semiliberty. But that was not for those in Cell 13.

At all times of the day there were armed guards in the yard, four of them, one patrolling each side of the prison building.

By night the yard was almost as brilliantly lighted as by day. On each of the four sides was a great arc light which rose above the prison wall and gave to the guards a clear sight. The lights, too, brightly illuminated the spiked top of the wall. The wires which fed the arc lights ran up the side of the prison building on insulators and from the top story led out to the poles supporting the arc lights.

All these things were seen and comprehended by The Thinking Machine, who was only enabled to see out his closely barred cell window by standing on his bed. This was on the morning following his incarceration. He gathered, too, that the river lay over there beyond the wall somewhere, because he heard faintly the pulsation of a motor boat and high up in the air saw a river bird. From that same direction came the shouts of boys at play and the occasional crack of a batted ball. He knew then that between the prison wall and the river was an open space, a playground.

Chisholm Prison was regarded as absolutely safe. No man had ever escaped from it. The Thinking Machine, from his perch on the bed, seeing what he saw, could readily understand why. The walls of the cell, though built he judged twenty years before, were perfectly solid, and the window bars of new iron had not a shadow of rust on them. The window itself, even with the bars out, would be a difficult mode of egress because it was small.

Yet, seeing these things, The Thinking Machine was not discouraged. Instead, he thoughtfully squinted at the great arc light—there was bright sunlight now—and traced with his eyes the wire which led from it to the building. That electric wire, he reasoned, must come down the side of the building not a great distance from his cell. That might be worth knowing.

Cell 13 was on the same floor with the offices of the prison—that is, not in the basement, nor yet upstairs. There were only four steps up to the office floor, therefore the level of the floor must be only three or four feet above the ground. He couldn't see the ground directly beneath his window, but he could see it further out toward the wall. It would be an easy drop from the window. Well and good.

Then The Thinking Machine fell to remembering how he had come to the cell. First, there was the outside guard's booth, a part of the wall. There were two heavily barred gates there, both of steel. At this gate was one man always on guard. He admitted persons to the prison after much clanking of keys and locks, and let them out when ordered to do so. The warden's office was in the prison building, and in order to reach that official from the prison yard one had to pass a gate of solid steel with only a peep-hole in it. Then coming from that inner office to Cell 13, where he was now, one must pass a heavy wooden door and two steel doors into the corridors of the prison; and always there was the double-locked door to Cell 13 to reckon with.

There were then, The Thinking Machine recalled, seven doors to be overcome before one could pass from Cell 13 into the outer world, a free man. But against this was the fact that he was rarely interrupted. A jailer appeared at his cell door at six in the morning with a breakfast of prison fare; he would come again at noon, and again at six in the afternoon. At nine o'clock at night would come the inspection tour. That would be all.

"It's admirably arranged, this prison system," was the mental tribute paid by The Thinking Machine. "I'll have to study it a little when I get out. I had no idea there was such great care exercised in the prisons."

There was nothing, positively nothing, in his cell, except his iron bed, so firmly put together that no man could tear it to pieces save with sledges or a file. He had neither of these. There was not even a chair, or a small table, or a bit of tin or crockery. Nothing! The jailer stood by when he ate, then took away the wooden spoon and bowl which he had used.

One by one these things sank into the brain of The Thinking Machine. When the last possibility had been considered he began an examination of his cell. From the roof, down the walls on all sides, he examined the stones and the cement between them. He stamped over the floor carefully time after time, but it was cement, perfectly solid. After the examination he sat on the edge of the iron bed and was lost in thought for a long time. For Professor Augustus S. F. X. Van Dusen, The Thinking Machine, had something to think about.

He was disturbed by a rat, which ran across his foot, then scampered away into a dark corner of the cell, frightened at its own daring. After a while The Thinking Machine, squinting steadily into the darkness of the corner where the rat had gone, was able to make out in the gloom many little beady eyes staring at him. He counted six pair, and there were perhaps others; he didn't see very well.

Then The Thinking Machine, from his seat on the bed, noticed for the first time the bottom of his cell door. There was an opening there of two inches between the steel bar and the floor. Still looking steadily at this opening, The Thinking Machine backed suddenly into the corner where he had seen the beady eyes. There was a great scampering of tiny feet, several squeaks of frightened rodents, and then silence.

None of the rats had gone out the door, yet there were none in the cell. Therefore there must be another way out of the cell, however small. The Thinking Machine, on hands and knees, started a search for this spot, feeling in the darkness with his long, slender fingers.

At last his search was rewarded. He came upon a small opening in the floor, level with the cement. It was perfectly round and somewhat larger than a silver dollar. This was the way the rats had gone. He put his fingers deep into the opening; it seemed to be a disused drainage pipe and was dry and dusty.

Having satisfied himself on this point, he sat on the bed again for an hour, then made another inspection of his surroundings through the small cell window. One of the outside guards stood directly opposite, beside the wall, and happened to be looking at the window of Cell 13 when the head of The Thinking Machine appeared. But the scientist didn't notice the guard.

Noon came and the jailer appeared with the prison dinner of repulsively plain food. At home The Thinking Machine merely ate to live; here he took what was offered without comment. Occasionally he spoke to the jailer who stood outside the door watching him.

"Any improvements made here in the last few years?" he asked.

"Nothing particularly," replied the jailer. "New wall was built four years ago."

"Anything done to the prison proper?"

"Painted the woodwork outside, and I believe about seven years ago a new system of plumbing was put in."

"Ah!" said the prisoner. "How far is the river over there?"

"About three hundred feet. The boys have a baseball ground between the wall and the river."

The Thinking Machine had nothing further to say just then, but when the jailer was ready to go he asked for some water.

"I get very thirsty here," he explained. "Would it be possible for you to leave a little water in a bowl for me?"

"I'll ask the warden," replied the jailer, and he went away.

Half an hour later he returned with water in a small earthen bowl.

"The warden says you may keep this bowl," he informed the prisoner. "But you must show it to me when I ask for it. If it is broken, it will be the last."

"Thank you," said The Thinking Machine. "I shan't break it."

The jailer went on about his duties. For just the fraction of a second it seemed that The Thinking Machine wanted to ask a question, but he didn't.

Two hours later this same jailer, in passing the door of Cell No. 13, heard a noise inside and stopped. The Thinking Machine was down on his hands and knees in a corner of the cell, and from that same corner came several frightened squeaks. The jailer looked on interestedly.

"Ah, I've got you," he heard the prisoner say.

"Got what?" he asked, sharply.

"One of these rats," was the reply. "See?" And between the scientist's long fingers the jailer saw a small gray rat struggling. The prisoner brought it over to the light and looked at it closely. "It's a water rat," he said.

"Ain't you got anything better to do than to catch rats?" asked the jailer.

"It's disgraceful that they should be here at all," was the irritated reply. "Take this one away and kill it. There are dozens more where it came from."

The jailer took the wriggling, squirmy rodent and flung it down on the floor violently. It gave one squeak and lay still. Later he reported the incident to the warden, who only smiled.

Still later that afternoon the outside armed guard on Cell 13 side of the prison looked up again at the window and saw the prisoner looking out. He saw a hand raised to the barred window and then something white fluttered to the ground, directly under the window of Cell 13. It was a little roll of linen, evidently of white shirting material, and tied around it was a five-dollar bill. The guard looked up at the window again, but the face had disappeared.

With a grim smile he took the little linen roll and the five-dollar bill to the warden's office. There together they deciphered something which was written on it with a queer sort of ink, frequently blurred. On the outside was this:

"Finder of this please deliver to Dr. Charles Ransome."

"Ah," said the warden, with a chuckle. "Plan of escape number one has gone wrong." Then, as an afterthought: "But why did he address it to Dr. Ransome?"

"And where did he get the pen and ink to write with?" asked the guard.

The warden looked at the guard and the guard looked at the warden. There was no apparent solution of that mystery. The warden studied the writing carefully, then shook his head.

"Well, let's see what he was going to say to Dr. Ransome," he said at length, still puzzled, and he unrolled the inner piece of linen.

"Well, if that—what—what do you think of that?" he asked, dazed.

The guard took the bit of linen and read this:

"Epa cseot d'net niiy awe htto n'si sih. "T."

III

The warden spent an hour wondering what sort of a cipher it was, and half an hour wondering why his prisoner should attempt to communicate with Dr. Ransome, who was the cause of him being there. After this the warden devoted some thought to the question of where the prisoner got writing materials, and what sort of writing materials he had. With the idea of illuminating this point, he examined the linen again. It was a torn part of a white shirt and had ragged edges.

Now it was possible to account for the linen, but what the prisoner had used to write with was another matter. The warden knew it would have been impossible for him to have either pen or pencil, and, besides, neither pen nor pencil had been used in this writing. What, then? The warden decided to personally investigate. The Thinking Machine was his prisoner; he had orders to hold his prisoners; if this one sought to escape by sending cipher messages to persons outside, he would stop it, as he would have stopped it in the case of any other prisoner.

The warden went back to Cell 13 and found The Thinking Machine on his hands and knees on the floor, engaged in nothing more alarming than catching rats. The prisoner heard the warden's step and turned to him quickly.

"It's disgraceful," he snapped, "these rats. There are scores of them."

"Other men have been able to stand them," said the warden. "Here is another shirt for you—let me have the one you have on."

"Why?" demanded The Thinking Machine, quickly. His tone was hardly natural, his manner suggested actual perturbation.

"You have attempted to communicate with Dr. Ransome," said the warden severely. "As my prisoner, it is my duty to put a stop to it."

The Thinking Machine was silent for a moment.

"All right," he said, finally. "Do your duty."

The warden smiled grimly. The prisoner arose from the floor and removed the white shirt, putting on instead a striped convict shirt the warden had brought. The warden took the white shirt eagerly, and then and there compared the pieces of linen on which was written the cipher with certain torn places in the shirt. The Thinking Machine looked on curiously.

"The guard brought *you* those, then?" he asked.

"He certainly did," replied the warden triumphantly. "And that ends your first attempt to escape."

The Thinking Machine watched the warden as he, by comparison, established to his own satisfaction that only two pieces of linen had been torn from the white shirt.

"What did you write this with?" demanded the warden.

"I should think it a part of your duty to find out," said The Thinking Machine, irritably.

The warden started to say some harsh things, then restrained himself and made a minute search of the cell and of the prisoner instead. He found absolutely nothing; not even a match or toothpick which might have been used for a pen. The same mystery surrounded the fluid with which the cipher had been written. Although the warden left Cell 13 visibly annoyed, he took the torn shirt in triumph.

"Well, writing notes on a shirt won't get him out, that's certain," he told himself with some complacency. He put the linen scraps into his desk to await developments. "If that man escapes from that cell I'll—hang it—I'll resign."

On the third day of his incarceration The Thinking Machine openly attempted to bribe his way out. The jailer had brought his dinner and was leaning against the barred door, waiting, when The Thinking Machine began the conversation.

"The drainage pipes of the prison lead to the river, don't they?" he asked.

"Yes," said the jailer.

"I suppose they are very small?"

"Too small to crawl through, if that's what you're thinking about," was the grinning response.

There was silence until The Thinking Machine finished his meal. Then:

"You know I'm not a criminal, don't you?"

"Yes."

"And that I've a perfect right to be freed if I demand it?"

"Yes."

"Well, I came here believing that I could make my escape," said the prisoner, and his squint eyes studied the face of the jailer. "Would you consider a financial reward for aiding me to escape?"

The jailer, who happened to be an honest man, looked at the slender, weak figure of the prisoner, at the large head with its mass of yellow hair, and was almost sorry.

"I guess prisons like these were not built for the likes of you to get out of," he said, at last.

"But would you consider a proposition to help me get out?" the prisoner insisted, almost beseechingly.

"No," said the jailer, shortly.

"Five hundred dollars," urged The Thinking Machine. "I am not a criminal."

"No," said the jailer.

"A thousand?"

"No," again said the jailer, and he started away hurriedly to escape further temptation. Then he turned back. "If you should give me ten thousand dollars I couldn't get you out. You'd have to pass through seven doors, and I only have the keys to two."

Then he told the warden all about it.

"Plan number two fails," said the warden, smiling grimly. "First a cipher, then bribery."

When the jailer was on his way to Cell 13 at six o'clock, again bearing food to The Thinking Machine, he paused, startled by the unmistakable scrape, scrape of steel against steel. It stopped at the sound of his steps, then craftily the jailer, who was beyond the prisoner's range of vision, resumed his tramping, the sound being apparently that of a man going away from Cell 13. As a matter of fact he was in the same spot.

After a moment there came again the steady scrape, scrape, and the jailer crept cautiously on tiptoes to the door and peered between the bars. The Thinking Machine was standing on the iron bed working at the bars of the little window. He was using a file, judging from the backward and forward swing of his arms.

Cautiously the jailer crept back to the office, summoned the warden in person, and they returned to Cell 13 on tiptoes. The steady scrape was still audible. The warden listened to satisfy himself and then suddenly appeared at the door.

"Well?" he demanded, and there was a smile on his face.

The Thinking Machine glanced back from his perch on the bed and leaped suddenly to the floor, making frantic efforts to hide something. The warden went in, with hand extended.

"Give it up," he said.

"No," said the prisoner sharply.

"Come, give it up," urged the warden. "I don't want to have to search you again."

"No," repeated the prisoner.

"What was it, a file?" asked the warden.

The Thinking Machine was silent and stood squinting at the warden with something very nearly approaching disappointment on his face—nearly, but not quite. The warden was almost sympathetic.

"Plan number three fails, eh?" he asked, good-naturedly. "Too bad, isn't it?"

The prisoner didn't say.

"Search him," instructed the warden.

The jailer searched the prisoner carefully. At last, artfully concealed in the waistband of the trousers, he found a piece of steel about two inches long, with one side curved like a half moon.

"Ah," said the warden, as he received it from the jailer. "From your shoe heel," and he smiled pleasantly.

The jailer continued his search and on the other side of the trousers waistband was another piece of steel identical with the first. The edges showed where they had been worn against the bars of the window.

"You couldn't saw a way through those bars with these," said the warden.

"I could have," said The Thinking Machine firmly.

"In six months, perhaps," said the warden, good-naturedly.

The warden shook his head slowly as he gazed into the slightly flushed face of his prisoner.

"Ready to give it up?" he asked.

"I haven't started yet," was the prompt reply.

Then came another exhaustive search of the cell. Carefully the two men went over it, finally turning out the bed and searching that. Nothing. The warden in person climbed upon the bed and examined the bars of the window where the prisoner had been sawing. When he looked he was amused.

"Just made it a little bright by hard rubbing," he said to the prisoner, who stood looking on with a somewhat crestfallen air. The warden grasped the iron bars in his strong hands and tried to shake them. They were immovable, set firmly in the solid granite. He examined each in turn and found them all satisfactory. Finally he climbed down from the bed.

"Give it up, professor," he advised.

The Thinking Machine shook his head and the warden and jailer passed on again. As they disappeared down the corridor The Thinking Machine sat on the edge of the bed with his head in his hands.

"He's crazy to try to get out of that cell," commented the jailer.

"Of course he can't get out," said the warden. "But he's clever. I would like to know what he wrote that cipher with."

. . . . .

It was four o'clock next morning when an awful, heart-racking shriek of terror resounded through the great prison. It came from a cell, somewhere about the center, and its tone told a tale of horror, agony, terrible fear. The warden heard and with three of his men rushed into the long corridor leading to Cell 13.

IV

As they ran there came again that awful cry. It died away in a sort of wail. The white faces of prisoners appeared at cell doors upstairs and down, staring out wonderingly, frightened.

"It's that fool in Cell 13," grumbled the warden.

He stopped and stared in as one of the jailers flashed a lantern. "That fool in Cell 13" lay comfortably on his cot, flat on his back with his mouth open, snoring. Even as they looked there came again the piercing cry, from somewhere above. The warden's face blanched a little as he started up the stairs. There on the top floor he found a man in Cell 43, directly above Cell 13, but two floors higher, cowering in a corner of his cell.

"What's the matter?" demanded the warden.

"Thank God you've come," exclaimed the prisoner, and he cast himself against the bars of his cell.

"What is it?" demanded the warden again.

He threw open the door and went in. The prisoner dropped on his knees and clasped the warden about the body. His face was white with terror, his eyes were widely distended, and he was shuddering. His hands, icy cold, clutched at the warden's.

"Take me out of this cell, please take me out," he pleaded.

"What's the matter with you, anyhow?" insisted the warden, impatiently.

"I heard something—something," said the prisoner, and his eyes roved nervously around the cell.

"What did you hear?"

"I—I can't tell you," stammered the prisoner. Then, in a sudden burst of terror: "Take me out of this cell—put me anywhere—but take me out of here."

The warden and the three jailers exchanged glances.

"Who is this fellow? What's he accused of?" asked the warden.

"Joseph Ballard," said one of the jailers. "He's accused of throwing acid in a woman's face. She died from it."

"But they can't prove it," gasped the prisoner. "They can't prove it. Please put me in some other cell."

He was still clinging to the warden, and that official threw his arms off roughly. Then for a time he stood looking at the cowering wretch, who seemed possessed of all the wild, unreasoning terror of a child.

"Look here, Ballard," said the warden, finally, "if you heard anything, I want to know what it was. Now tell me."

"I can't, I can't," was the reply. He was sobbing.

"Where did it come from?"

"I don't know. Everywhere—nowhere. I just heard it."

"What was it—a voice?"

"Please don't make me answer," pleaded the prisoner.

"You must answer," said the warden, sharply.

"It was a voice—but—but it wasn't human," was the sobbing reply.

"Voice, but not human?" repeated the warden, puzzled.

"It sounded muffled and—and far away—and ghostly," explained the man.

"Did it come from inside or outside the prison?"

"It didn't seem to come from anywhere—it was just here, here, everywhere. I heard it. I heard it."

For an hour the warden tried to get the story, but Ballard had become suddenly obstinate and would say nothing—only pleaded to be placed in another cell, or to have one of the jailers remain near him until daylight. These requests were gruffly refused.

"And see here," said the warden, in conclusion, "if there's any more of this screaming I'll put you in the padded cell."

Then the warden went his way, a sadly puzzled man. Ballard sat at his cell door until daylight, his face, drawn and white with terror, pressed against the bars, and looked out into the prison with wide, staring eyes.

That day, the fourth since the incarceration of The Thinking Machine, was enlivened considerably by the volunteer prisoner, who spent most of his time at the little window of his cell. He began proceedings by throwing another piece of linen down to the guard, who picked it up dutifully and took it to the warden. On it was written:

"Only three days more."

The warden was in no way surprised at what he read; he understood that The Thinking Machine meant only three days more of his imprisonment, and he regarded the note as a boast. But how was the thing written? Where had The Thinking Machine found this new piece of linen? Where? How? He carefully examined the linen. It was white, of fine texture, shirting material. He took the shirt which he had taken and carefully fitted the two original pieces of the linen to the torn places. This third piece was entirely superfluous; it didn't fit anywhere, and yet it was unmistakably the same goods.

"And where—where does he get anything to write with?" demanded the warden of the world at large.

Still later on the fourth day The Thinking Machine, through the window of his cell, spoke to the armed guard outside.

"What day of the month is it?" he asked.

"The fifteenth," was the answer.

The Thinking Machine made a mental astronomical calculation and satisfied himself that the moon would not rise until after nine o'clock that night. Then he asked another question:

"Who attends to those arc lights?"

"Man from the company."

"You have no electricians in the building?"

"No."

"I should think you could save money if you had your own man."

"None of my business," replied the guard.

The guard noticed The Thinking Machine at the cell window frequently during that day, but always the face seemed listless and there was a certain wistfulness in the squint eyes behind the glasses. After a while he accepted the presence of the leonine head as a matter of course. He had seen other prisoners do the same thing; it was the longing for the outside world.

That afternoon, just before the day guard was relieved, the head appeared at the window again, and The Thinking Machine's hand held something out between the bars. It fluttered to the ground and the guard picked it up. It was a five-dollar bill.

"That's for you," called the prisoner.

As usual, the guard took it to the warden. That gentleman looked at it suspiciously; he looked at everything that came from Cell 13 with suspicion.

"He said it was for me," explained the guard.

"It's a sort of a tip, I suppose," said the warden. "I see no particular reason why you shouldn't accept—"

Suddenly he stopped. He had remembered that The Thinking Machine had gone into Cell 13 with one five-dollar bill and two ten-dollar bills; twenty-five dollars in all. Now a five-dollar bill had been tied around the first pieces of linen that came from the cell. The warden still had it, and to convince himself he took it out and looked at it. It was five dollars; yet here was another five dollars, and The Thinking Machine had only had ten-dollar bills.

"Perhaps somebody changed one of the bills for him," he thought at last, with a sigh of relief.

But then and there he made up his mind. He would search Cell 13 as a cell was never before searched in this world. When a man could write at will, and change money, and do other wholly inexplicable things, there was something radically wrong with his prison. He planned to enter the cell at night—three o'clock would be an excellent time. The Thinking Machine must do all the weird things he did some time. Night seemed the most reasonable.

Thus it happened that the warden stealthily descended upon Cell 13 that night at three o'clock. He paused at the door and listened. There was no sound save the steady, regular breathing of the prisoner. The keys unfastened the double locks with scarcely a clank, and the warden entered, locking the door behind him. Suddenly he flashed his dark-lantern in the face of the recumbent figure.

If the warden had planned to startle The Thinking Machine he was mistaken, for that individual merely opened his eyes quietly, reached for his glasses and inquired, in a most matter-of-fact tone:

"Who is it?"

It would be useless to describe the search that the warden made. It was minute. Not one inch of the cell or the bed was overlooked. He found the round hole in the floor, and with a flash of inspiration thrust his thick fingers into it. After a moment of fumbling there he drew up something and looked at it in the light of his lantern.

"Ugh!" he exclaimed.

The thing he had taken out was a rat—a dead rat. His inspiration fled as a mist before the sun. But he continued the search.

The Thinking Machine, without a word, arose and kicked the rat out of the cell into the corridor.

The warden climbed on the bed and tried the steel bars in the tiny window. They were perfectly rigid; every bar of the door was the same.

Then the warden searched the prisoner's clothing, beginning at the shoes. Nothing hidden in them! Then the trousers waistband. Still nothing! Then the pockets of the trousers. From one side he drew out some paper money and examined it.

"Five one-dollar bills," he gasped.

"That's right," said the prisoner.

"But the—you had two tens and a five—what the—how do you do it?"

"That's my business," said The Thinking Machine.

"Did any of my men change this money for you—on your word of honor?"

The Thinking Machine paused just a fraction of a second.

"No," he said.

"Well, do you make it?" asked the warden. He was prepared to believe anything.

"That's my business," again said the prisoner.

The warden glared at the eminent scientist fiercely. He felt—he knew—that this man was making a fool of him, yet he didn't know how. If he were a real prisoner he would get the truth—but, then, perhaps, those inexplicable things which had happened would not have been brought before him so sharply. Neither of the men spoke for a long time, then suddenly the warden turned fiercely and left the cell, slamming the door behind him. He didn't dare to speak, then.

He glanced at the clock. It was ten minutes to four. He had hardly settled himself in bed when again came that heart-breaking shriek through the prison. With a few muttered words, which, while not elegant, were highly expressive, he relighted his lantern and rushed through the prison again to the cell on the upper floor.

Again Ballard was crushing himself against the steel door, shrieking, shrieking at the top of his voice. He stopped only when the warden flashed his lamp in the cell.

"Take me out, take me out," he screamed. "I did it, I did it, I killed her. Take it away."

"Take what away?" asked the warden.

"I threw the acid in her face—I did it—I confess. Take me out of here."

Ballard's condition was pitiable; it was only an act of mercy to let him out into the corridor. There he crouched in a corner, like an animal at bay, and clasped his hands to his ears. It took half an hour to calm him sufficiently for him to speak. Then he told incoherently what had happened. On the night before at four o'clock he had heard a voice—a sepulchral voice, muffled and wailing in tone.

"What did it say?" asked the warden, curiously.

"Acid—acid—acid!" gasped the prisoner. "It accused me. Acid! I threw the acid, and the woman died. Oh!" It was a long, shuddering wail of terror.

"Acid?" echoed the warden, puzzled. The case was beyond him.

"Acid. That's all I heard—that one word, repeated several times. There were other things, too, but I didn't hear them."

"That was last night, eh?" asked the warden. "What happened to-night—what frightened you just now?"

"It was the same thing," gasped the prisoner. "Acid—acid—acid." He covered his face with his hands and sat shivering. "It was acid I used on her, but I didn't mean to kill her. I just heard the words. It was something accusing me—accusing me." He mumbled, and was silent.

"Did you hear anything else?"

"Yes—but I couldn't understand—only a little bit—just a word or two."

"Well, what was it?"

"I heard 'acid' three times, then I heard a long, moaning sound, then—then—I heard 'No. 8 hat.' I heard that voice."

"No. 8 hat," repeated the warden. "What the devil—No. 8 hat? Accusing voices of conscience have never talked about No. 8 hats, so far as I ever heard."

"He's insane," said one of the jailers, with an air of finality.

"I believe you," said the warden. "He must be. He probably heard something and got frightened. He's trembling now. No. 8 hat! What the—"

V

When the fifth day of The Thinking Machine's imprisonment rolled around the warden was wearing a hunted look. He was anxious for the end of the thing. He could not help but feel that his distinguished prisoner had been amusing himself. And if this were so, The Thinking Machine had lost none of his sense of humor. For on this fifth day he flung down another linen note to the outside guard, bearing the words: "Only two days more." Also he flung down half a dollar.

Now the warden knew—he *knew*—that the man in Cell 13 didn't have any half dollars—he *couldn't* have any half dollars, no more than he could have pen and ink and linen, and yet he did have them. It was a condition, not a theory; that is one reason why the warden was wearing a hunted look.

That ghastly, uncanny thing, too, about "Acid" and "No. 8 hat" clung to him tenaciously. They didn't mean anything, of course, merely the ravings of an insane murderer who had been driven by fear to confess his crime, still there were so many things that "didn't mean anything" happening in the prison now since The Thinking Machine was there.

On the sixth day the warden received a postal stating that Dr. Ransome and Mr. Fielding would be at Chisholm Prison on the following evening, Thursday, and in the event Professor Van Dusen had not yet escaped—and they presumed he had not because they had not heard from him—they would meet him there.

"In the event he had not yet escaped!" The warden smiled grimly. Escaped!

The Thinking Machine enlivened this day for the warden with three notes. They were on the usual linen and bore generally on the appointment at half-past eight o'clock Thursday night, which appointment the scientist had made at the time of his imprisonment.

On the afternoon of the seventh day the warden passed Cell 13 and glanced in. The Thinking Machine was lying on the iron bed, apparently sleeping lightly. The cell appeared precisely as it always did from a casual glance. The warden would swear that no man was going to leave it between that hour—it was then four o'clock—and half-past eight o'clock that evening.

On his way back past the cell the warden heard the steady breathing again, and coming close to the door looked in. He wouldn't have done so if The Thinking Machine had been looking, but now—well, it was different.

A ray of light came through the high window and fell on the face of the sleeping man. It occurred to the warden for the first time that his prisoner appeared haggard and weary. Just then The Thinking Machine stirred slightly and the warden hurried on up the corridor guiltily. That evening after six o'clock he saw the jailer.

"Everything all right in Cell 13?" he asked.

"Yes, sir," replied the jailer. "He didn't eat much, though."

It was with a feeling of having done his duty that the warden received Dr. Ransome and Mr. Fielding shortly after seven o'clock. He intended to show them the linen notes and lay before them the full story of his woes, which was a long one. But before this came to pass the guard from the river side of the prison yard entered the office.

"The arc light in my side of the yard won't light," he informed the warden.

"Confound it, that man's a hoodoo," thundered the official. "Everything has happened since he's been here."

The guard went back to his post in the darkness, and the warden phoned to the electric light company.

"This is Chisholm Prison," he said through the 'phone. "Send three or four men down here quick, to fix an arc light."

The reply was evidently satisfactory, for the warden hung up the receiver and passed out into the yard. While Dr. Ransome and Mr. Fielding sat waiting, the guard at the outer gate came in with a special delivery letter. Dr. Ransome happened to notice the address, and, when the guard went out, looked at the letter more closely.

"By George!" he exclaimed.

"What is it?" asked Mr. Fielding.

Silently the doctor offered the letter. Mr. Fielding examined it closely. "Coincidence," he said. "It must be."

It was nearly eight o'clock when the warden returned to his office. The electricians had arrived in a wagon, and were now at work. The warden pressed the buzz-button communicating with the man at the outer gate in the wall.

"How many electricians came in?" he asked, over the short 'phone. "Four? Three workmen in jumpers and overalls and the manager? Frock coat and silk hat? All right. Be certain that only four go out. That's all."

He turned to Dr. Ransome and Mr. Fielding. "We have to be careful here—particularly," and there was broad sarcasm in his tone, "since we have scientists locked up."

The warden picked up the special delivery letter carelessly, and then began to open it.

"When I read this I want to tell you gentlemen something about how— Great Caesar!" he ended, suddenly, as he glanced at the letter. He sat with mouth open, motionless, from astonishment.

"What is it?" asked Mr. Fielding.

"A special delivery letter from Cell 13," gasped the warden. "An invitation to supper."

"What?" and the two others arose, unanimously.

The warden sat dazed, staring at the letter for a moment, then called sharply to a guard outside in the corridor.

"Run down to Cell 13 and see if that man's in there."

The guard went as directed, while Dr. Ransome and Mr. Fielding examined the letter.

"It's Van Dusen's handwriting; there's no question of that," said Dr. Ransome. "I've seen too much of it."

Just then the buzz on the telephone from the outer gate sounded, and the warden, in a semi-trance, picked up the receiver.

"Hello! Two reporters, eh? Let 'em come in." He turned suddenly to the doctor and Mr. Fielding. "Why, the man *can't* be out. He must be in his cell."

Just at that moment the guard returned.

"He's still in his cell, sir," he reported. "I saw him. He's lying down."

"There, I told you so," said the warden, and he breathed freely again. "But how did he mail that letter?"

There was a rap on the steel door which led from the jail yard into the warden's office.

"It's the reporters," said the warden. "Let them in," he instructed the guard; then to the two other gentlemen: "Don't say anything about this before them, because I'd never hear the last of it."

The door opened, and the two men from the front gate entered.

"Good-evening, gentlemen," said one. That was Hutchinson Hatch; the warden knew him well.

"Well?" demanded the other, irritably. "I'm here."

That was The Thinking Machine.

He squinted belligerently at the warden, who sat with mouth agape. For the moment that official had nothing to say. Dr. Ransome and Mr. Fielding were amazed, but they didn't know what the warden knew. They were only amazed; he was paralyzed. Hutchinson Hatch, the reporter, took in the scene with greedy eyes.

"How—how—how did you do it?" gasped the warden, finally.

"Come back to the cell," said The Thinking Machine, in the irritated voice which his scientific associates knew so well.

The warden, still in a condition bordering on trance, led the way.

"Flash your light in there," directed The Thinking Machine.

The warden did so. There was nothing unusual in the appearance of the cell, and there—there on the bed lay the figure of The Thinking Machine. Certainly! There was the yellow hair! Again the warden looked at the man beside him and wondered at the strangeness of his own dreams.

With trembling hands he unlocked the cell door and The Thinking Machine passed inside.

"See here," he said.

He kicked at the steel bars in the bottom of the cell door and three of them were pushed out of place. A fourth broke off and rolled away in the corridor.

"And here, too," directed the erstwhile prisoner as he stood on the bed to reach the small window. He swept his hand across the opening and every bar came out.

"What's this in the bed?" demanded the warden, who was slowly recovering.

"A wig," was the reply. "Turn down the cover."

The warden did so. Beneath it lay a large coil of strong rope, thirty feet or more, a dagger, three files, ten feet of electric wire, a thin, powerful pair of steel pliers, a small tack hammer with its handle, and—and a Derringer pistol.

"How did you do it?" demanded the warden.

"You gentlemen have an engagement to supper with me at half-past nine o'clock," said The Thinking Machine. "Come on, or we shall be late."

"But how did you do it?" insisted the warden.

"Don't ever think you can hold any man who can use his brain," said The Thinking Machine. "Come on; we shall be late."

VI

It was an impatient supper party in the rooms of Professor Van Dusen and a somewhat silent one. The guests were Dr. Ransome, Albert Fielding, the warden, and Hutchinson Hatch, reporter. The meal was served to the minute, in accordance with Professor Van Dusen's instructions of one week before; Dr. Ransome found the artichokes delicious. At last the supper was finished and The Thinking Machine turned full on Dr. Ransome and squinted at him fiercely.

"Do you believe it now?" he demanded.

"I do," replied Dr. Ransome.

"Do you admit that it was a fair test?"

"I do."

With the others, particularly the warden, he was waiting anxiously for the explanation.

"Suppose you tell us how—" began Mr. Fielding.

"Yes, tell us how," said the warden.

The Thinking Machine readjusted his glasses, took a couple of preparatory squints at his audience, and began the story. He told it from the beginning logically; and no man ever talked to more interested listeners.

"My agreement was," he began, "to go into a cell, carrying nothing except what was necessary to wear, and to leave that cell within a week. I had never seen Chisholm Prison. When I went into the cell I asked for tooth powder, two ten and one five-dollar bills, and also to have my shoes blacked. Even if these requests had been refused it would not have mattered seriously. But you agreed to them.

"I knew there would be nothing in the cell which you thought I might use to advantage. So when the warden locked the door on me I was apparently helpless, unless I could turn three seemingly innocent things to use. They were things which would have been permitted any prisoner under sentence of death, were they not, warden?"

"Tooth powder and polished shoes, yes, but not money," replied the warden.

"Anything is dangerous in the hands of a man who knows how to use it," went on The Thinking Machine. "I did nothing that first night but sleep and chase rats." He glared at the warden. "When the matter was broached I knew I could do nothing that night, so suggested next day. You gentlemen thought I wanted time to arrange an escape with outside assistance, but this was not true. I knew I could communicate with whom I pleased, when I pleased."

The warden stared at him a moment, then went on smoking solemnly.

"I was aroused next morning at six o'clock by the jailer with my breakfast," continued the scientist. "He told me dinner was at twelve and supper at six. Between these times, I gathered, I would be pretty much to myself. So immediately after breakfast I examined my outside surroundings from my cell window. One look told me it would be useless to try to scale the wall, even should I decide to leave my cell by the window, for my purpose was to leave not only the cell, but the prison. Of course, I could have gone over the wall, but it would have taken me longer to lay my plans that way. Therefore, for the moment, I dismissed all idea of that.

"From this first observation I knew the river was on that side of the prison, and that there was also a playground there. Subsequently these surmises were verified by a keeper. I knew then one important thing—that any one might approach the prison wall from that side if necessary without attracting any particular attention. That was well to remember. I remembered it.

"But the outside thing which most attracted my attention was the feed wire to the arc light which ran within a few feet—probably three or four—of my cell window. I knew that would be valuable in the event I found it necessary to cut off that arc light."

"Oh, you shut it off to-night, then?" asked the warden.

"Having learned all I could from that window," resumed The Thinking Machine, without heeding the interruption, "I considered the idea of escaping through the prison proper. I recalled just how I had come into the cell, which I knew would be the only way. Seven doors lay between me and the outside. So, also for the time being, I gave up the idea of escaping that way. And I couldn't go through the solid granite walls of the cell."

The Thinking Machine paused for a moment and Dr. Ransome lighted a new cigar. For several minutes there was silence, then the scientific jail-breaker went on:

"While I was thinking about these things a rat ran across my foot. It suggested a new line of thought. There were at least half a dozen rats in the cell—I could see their beady eyes. Yet I had noticed none come under the cell door. I frightened them purposely and watched the cell door to see if they went out that way. They did not, but they were gone. Obviously they went another way. Another way meant another opening.

"I searched for this opening and found it. It was an old drain pipe, long unused and partly choked with dirt and dust. But this was the way the rats had come. They came from somewhere. Where? Drain pipes usually lead outside prison grounds. This one probably led to the river, or near it. The rats must therefore come from that direction. If they came a part of the way, I reasoned that they came all the way, because it was extremely unlikely that a solid iron or lead pipe would have any hole in it except at the exit.

"When the jailer came with my luncheon he told me two important things, although he didn't know it. One was that a new system of plumbing had been put in the prison seven years before; another that the river was only three hundred feet away. Then I knew positively that the pipe was a part of an old system; I knew, too, that it slanted generally toward the river. But did the pipe end in the water or on land?

"This was the next question to be decided. I decided it by catching several of the rats in the cell. My jailer was surprised to see me engaged in this work. I examined at least a dozen of them. They were perfectly dry; they had come through the pipe, and, most important of all, they were *not house rats, but field rats.* The other end of the pipe was on land, then, outside the prison walls. So far, so good.

"Then, I knew that if I worked freely from this point I must attract the warden's attention in another direction. You see, by telling the warden that I had come there to escape you made the test more severe, because I had to trick him by false scents."

The warden looked up with a sad expression in his eyes.

"The first thing was to make him think I was trying to communicate with you, Dr. Ransome. So I wrote a note on a piece of linen I tore from my shirt, addressed it to Dr. Ransome, tied a five-dollar bill around it and threw it out the window. I knew the guard would take it to the warden, but I rather hoped the warden would send it as addressed. Have you that first linen note, warden?"

The warden produced the cipher.

"What the deuce does it mean, anyhow?" he asked.

"Read it backward, beginning with the 'T' signature and disregard the division into words," instructed The Thinking Machine.

The warden did so.

"T-h-i-s, this," he spelled, studied it a moment, then read it off, grinning: "This is not the way I intend to escape."

"Well, now what do you think o' that?" he demanded, still grinning.

"I knew that would attract your attention, just as it did," said The Thinking Machine, "and if you really found out what it was it would be a sort of gentle rebuke."

"What did you write it with?" asked Dr. Ransome, after he had examined the linen and passed it to Mr. Fielding.

"This," said the erstwhile prisoner, and he extended his foot. On it was the shoe he had worn in prison, though the polish was gone—scraped off clean. "The shoe blacking, moistened with water, was my ink; the metal tip of the shoe lace made a fairly good pen."

The warden looked up and suddenly burst into a laugh, half of relief, half of amusement.

"You're a wonder," he said, admiringly. "Go on."

"That precipitated a search of my cell by the warden, as I had intended," continued The Thinking Machine. "I was anxious to get the warden into the habit of searching my cell, so that finally, constantly finding nothing, he would get disgusted and quit. This at last happened, practically."

The warden blushed.

"He then took my white shirt away and gave me a prison shirt. He was satisfied that those two pieces of the shirt were all that was missing. But while he was searching my cell I had another piece of that same shirt, about nine inches square, rolled into a small ball in my mouth."

"Nine inches of that shirt?" demanded the warden. "Where did it come from?"

"The bosoms of all stiff white shirts are of triple thickness," was the explanation. "I tore out the inside thickness, leaving the bosom only two thicknesses. I knew you wouldn't see it. So much for that."

There was a little pause, and the warden looked from one to another of the men with a sheepish grin.

"Having disposed of the warden for the time being by giving him something else to think about, I took my first serious step toward freedom," said Professor Van Dusen. "I knew, within reason, that the pipe led somewhere to the playground outside; I knew a great many boys played there; I knew that rats came into my cell from out there. Could I communicate with some one outside with these things at hand?

"First was necessary, I saw, a long and fairly reliable thread, so—but here," he pulled up his trousers legs and showed that the tops of both stockings, of fine, strong lisle, were gone. "I unraveled those—after I got them started it wasn't difficult—and I had easily a quarter of a mile of thread that I could depend on.

"Then on half of my remaining linen I wrote, laboriously enough, I assure you, a letter explaining my situation to this gentleman here," and he indicated Hutchinson Hatch. "I knew he would assist me—for the value of the newspaper story. I tied firmly to this linen letter a ten-dollar bill—there is no surer way of attracting the eye of any one—and wrote on the linen:

'Finder of this deliver to Hutchinson Hatch, *Daily American,* who will give another ten dollars for the information.'

"The next thing was to get this note outside on that playground where a boy might find it. There were two ways, but I chose the best. I took one of the rats—I became adept in catching them—tied the linen and money firmly to one leg, fastened my lisle thread to another, and turned him loose in the drain pipe. I reasoned that the natural fright of the rodent would make him run until he was outside the pipe and then out on earth he would probably stop to gnaw off the linen and money.

"From the moment the rat disappeared into that dusty pipe I became anxious. I was taking so many chances. The rat might gnaw the string, of which I held one end; other rats might gnaw it; the rat might run out of the pipe and leave the linen and money where they would never be found; a thousand other things might have happened. So began some nervous hours, but the fact that the rat ran on until only a few feet of the string remained in my cell made me think he was outside the pipe. I had carefully instructed Mr. Hatch what to do in case the note reached him. The question was: Would it reach him?

"This done, I could only wait and make other plans in case this one failed. I openly attempted to bribe my jailer, and learned from him that he held the keys to only two of seven doors between me and freedom. Then I did something else to make the warden nervous. I took the steel supports out of the heels of my shoes and made a pretense of sawing the bars of my cell window. The warden raised a pretty row about that. He developed, too, the habit of shaking the bars of my cell window to see if they were solid. They were—then."

Again the warden grinned. He had ceased being astonished.

"With this one plan I had done all I could and could only wait to see what happened," the scientist went on. "I couldn't know whether my note had been delivered or even found, or whether the rat had gnawed it up. And I didn't dare to draw back through the pipe that one slender thread which connected me with the outside.

"When I went to bed that night I didn't sleep, for fear there would come the slight signal twitch at the thread which was to tell me that Mr. Hatch had received the note. At half-past three o'clock, I judge, I felt this twitch, and no prisoner actually under sentence of death ever welcomed a thing more heartily."

The Thinking Machine stopped and turned to the reporter.

"You'd better explain just what you did," he said.

"The linen note was brought to me by a small boy who had been playing baseball," said Mr. Hatch. "I immediately saw a big story in it, so I gave the boy another ten dollars, and got several spools of silk, some twine, and a roll of light, pliable wire. The professor's note suggested that I have the finder of the note show me just where it was picked up, and told me to make my search from there, beginning at two o'clock in the morning. If I found the other end of the thread I was to twitch it gently three times, then a fourth.

"I began to search with a small bulb electric light. It was an hour and twenty minutes before I found the end of the drain pipe, half hidden in weeds. The pipe was very large there, say twelve inches across. Then I found the end of the lisle thread, twitched it as directed and immediately I got an answering twitch.

"Then I fastened the silk to this and Professor Van Dusen began to pull it into his cell. I nearly had heart disease for fear the string would break. To the end of the silk I fastened the twine, and when that had been pulled in I tied on the wire. Then that was drawn into the pipe and we had a substantial line, which the rats couldn't gnaw, from the mouth of the drain into the cell."

The Thinking Machine raised his hand and Hatch stopped.

"All this was done in absolute silence," said the scientist. "But when the wire reached my hand I could have shouted. Then we tried another experiment, which Mr. Hatch was prepared for. I tested the pipe as a speaking tube. Neither of us could hear very clearly, but I dared not speak loud for fear of attracting attention in the prison. At last I made him understand what I wanted immediately. He seemed to have great difficulty in understanding when I asked for nitric acid, and I repeated the word 'acid' several times.

"Then I heard a shriek from a cell above me. I knew instantly that someone had overheard, and when I heard you coming, Mr. Warden, I feigned sleep. If you had entered my cell at that moment that whole plan of escape would have ended there. But you passed on. That was the nearest I ever came to being caught.

"Having established this improvised trolley it is easy to see how I got things in the cell and made them disappear at will. I merely dropped them back into the pipe. You, Mr. Warden, could not have reached the connecting wire with your fingers; they are too large. My fingers, you see, are longer and more slender. In addition I guarded the top of that pipe with a rat—you remember how."

"I remember," said the warden, with a grimace.

"I thought that if any one were tempted to investigate that hole the rat would dampen his ardor. Mr. Hatch could not send me anything useful through the pipe until next night, although he did send me change for ten dollars as a test, so I proceeded with other parts of my plan. Then I evolved the method of escape, which I finally employed.

"In order to carry this out successfully it was necessary for the guard in the yard to get accustomed to seeing me at the cell window. I arranged this by dropping linen notes to him, boastful in tone, to make the warden believe, if possible, one of his assistants was communicating with the outside for me. I would stand at my window for hours gazing out, so the guard could see, and occasionally I spoke to him. In that way I learned that the prison had no electricians of its own, but was dependent upon the lighting company if anything should go wrong.

"That cleared the way to freedom perfectly. Early in the evening of the last day of my imprisonment, when it was dark, I planned to cut the feed wire which was only a few feet from my window, reaching it with an acid-tipped wire I had. That would make that side of the prison perfectly dark while the electricians were searching for the break. That would also bring Mr. Hatch into the prison yard.

"There was only one more thing to do before I actually began the work of setting myself free. This was to arrange final details with Mr. Hatch through our speaking tube. I did this within half an hour after the warden left my cell on the fourth night of my imprisonment. Mr. Hatch again had serious difficulty in understanding me, and I repeated the word 'acid' to him several times, and later the words: 'Number eight hat'—that's my size—and these were the things which made a prisoner upstairs confess to murder, so one of the jailers told me next day. This prisoner heard our voices, confused of course, through the pipe, which also went to his cell. The cell directly over me was not occupied, hence no one else heard.

"Of course the actual work of cutting the steel bars out of the window and door was comparatively easy with nitric acid, which I got through the pipe in thin bottles, but it took time. Hour after hour on the fifth and sixth and seventh days the guard below was looking at me as I worked on the bars of the window with the acid on a piece of wire. I used the tooth powder to prevent the acid spreading. I looked away abstractedly as I worked and each minute the acid cut deeper into the metal. I noticed that the jailers always tried the door by shaking the upper part, never the lower bars, therefore I cut the lower bars, leaving them hanging in place by thin strips of metal. But that was a bit of dare-deviltry. I could not have gone that way so easily."

The Thinking Machine sat silent for several minutes.

"I think that makes everything clear," he went on. "Whatever points I have not explained were merely to confuse the warden and jailers. These things in my bed I brought in to please Mr. Hatch, who wanted to improve the story. Of course, the wig was necessary in my plan. The special delivery letter I wrote and directed in my cell with Mr. Hatch's fountain pen, then sent it out to him and he mailed it. That's all, I think."

"But your actually leaving the prison grounds and then coming in through the outer gate to my office?" asked the warden.

"Perfectly simple," said the scientist. "I cut the electric light wire with acid, as I said, when the current was off. Therefore when the current was turned on the arc didn't light. I knew it would take some time to find out what was the matter and make repairs. When the guard went to report to you the yard was dark. I crept out the window—it was a tight fit, too—replaced the bars by standing on a narrow ledge and remained in a shadow until the force of electricians arrived. Mr Hatch was one of them.

"When I saw him I spoke and he handed me a cap, a jumper and overalls, which I put on within ten feet of you, Mr. Warden, while you were in the yard. Later Mr. Hatch called me, presumably as a workman, and together we went out the gate to get something out of the wagon. The gate guard let us pass out readily as two workmen who had just passed in. We changed our clothing and reappeared, asking to see you. We saw you. That's all."

There was silence for several minutes. Dr. Ransome was first to speak.

"Wonderful!" he exclaimed. "Perfectly amazing."

"How did Mr. Hatch happen to come with the electricians?" asked Mr. Fielding.

"His father is manager of the company," replied The Thinking Machine.

"But what if there had been no Mr. Hatch outside to help?"

"Every prisoner has one friend outside who would help him escape if he could."

"Suppose—just suppose—there had been no old plumbing system there?" asked the warden, curiously.

"There were two other ways out," said The Thinking Machine, enigmatically.

Ten minutes later the telephone bell rang. It was a request for the warden.

"Light all right, eh?" the warden asked, through the 'phone. "Good. Wire cut beside Cell 13? Yes, I know. One electrician too many? What's that? Two came out?"

The warden turned to the others with a puzzled expression.

"He only let in four electricians, he has let out two and says there are three left."

"I was the odd one," said The Thinking Machine.

"Oh," said the warden. "I see." Then through the 'phone: "Let the fifth man go. He's all right."

ACTIVITIES

1) "Nothing is impossible," declares The Thinking Machine in the story. "The mind is the master of all things. When science fully recognizes that fact a great advance will have been made."

Would you agree with this contention? Or would you say that there are things that the mind can never master? In such a philosophical discussion, it is extremely important to back up generalities with specifics.

2) Memorable characters in literature are endowed by their creators with distinctive physical characteristics and behavioral patterns. Write a paragraph delineating your first impression of Professor Van Dusen and then compare that with Futrelle's actual description of him in the story. Remember that an author characterizes not only by direct word description but also by the actions he has his characters perform. It might be interesting to compare your paragraph with those of your classmates.

3) Was Jacques Futrelle's solution to this "impossible" situation plausible? Could what took place in the story actually occur in real life? Explain.

4) Think back to what was said in a previous chapter about *protagonists* and *antagonists* in literature. Who was the antagonist in the preceding tale? Along this line, how is this story different from previous ones in this book?

G. K. Chesterton—and Father Brown

Edgar Allan Poe and Sir Arthur Conan Doyle had wanted to "escape" from detective fiction. On the other hand, the English writer G. K. Chesterton was the first serious man-of-letters who tried to "escape" *to* the new literary form.

It happened in the year 1911.

Chesterton was thirty-seven and he had already made a name for himself as a poet, essayist, critic, and novelist. He had written important studies of Charles Dickens, Robert Browning, George Bernard Shaw, and others; his contemporaries thought him one of the finest stylists of his day. This author started reading the creations of Poe and Doyle and decided that he had to try this new form of writing himself.

He enjoyed his labors immensely and added to his literary accomplishments by becoming one of the finest of the post-Doyle detective authors. He brought into existence the most novel of fictional sleuths yet—a Catholic priest.

Father Brown was his name.

Like Sherlock Holmes, the new sleuth had a prototype, Father John O'Connor, a close friend of Chesterton's. Later, in his autobiography, Chesterton was to state that he had learned more facts about the criminal nature of man from Father O'Connor than he had picked up from any of his more worldly acquaintances.

"It was a curious experience," he wrote, "to find that this quiet and pleasant celibate had plumbed those abysses far better than I."[2]

Inspired by O'Connor, Chesterton evolved a personality for Father Brown. He was an unassuming priest giving the impression of great innocence, but, in fact, he knew more about crime than the criminals did. In some of the stories, Chesterton even created an original Watson for his sleuth, a criminal by the name of Flambeau. Or, we should say, this Watson started out as a criminal until he encountered Father Brown; after the priest convinced him of the error of his ways, Flambeau reformed and became a private detective. Father Brown was the first of the fictional detectives to make use of the new sciences of psychology and psychiatry then developing through the work of Dr. Sigmund Freud of Vienna.

Because of the writings of the brilliant Chesterton, the detective story gained a dimension and a distinction it had never previously possessed. Father Brown garnered many disciples to whom he taught a new and important lesson, which was: Don't be fooled by appearances.

Which you will learn, too—after you read our next offering . . .

The Invisible Man

In the cool blue twilight of two steep streets in Camden Town, the shop at the corner, a confectioner's, glowed like the butt of a cigar. One should rather say, perhaps, like the butt of a firework, for the light was of many colours and some complexity, broken up by many mirrors and dancing on many gilt and gaily-coloured cakes and sweetmeats. Against this one fiery glass were glued the noses of many gutter-snipes, for the chocolates were all wrapped in those red and gold and green metallic colours which are almost better than chocolate itself; and the huge white wedding-cake in the window was somehow at once remote and satisfying, just as if the whole North Pole were good to eat. Such rainbow provocations could naturally collect the youth of the neighbourhood up to the ages of ten or twelve. But this corner was also attractive to youth at a later stage; and a young man, not less than twenty-four, was staring into the same shop window. To him, also, the shop was of fiery charm, but this attraction was not wholly to be explained by chocolates; which, however, he was far from despising.

He was a tall, burly, red-haired young man, with a resolute face but a listless manner. He carried under his arm a flat, grey portfolio of black-and-white sketches, which he had sold with more or less success to publishers ever since his uncle (who was an admiral) had disinherited him for Socialism, because of a lecture which he had delivered against that economic theory. His name was John Turnbull Angus.

Entering at last, he walked through the confectioner's shop to the back room, which was a sort of pastry-cook restaurant, merely raising his hat to the young lady who was serving there. She was a dark, elegant, alert girl in black, with a high colour and very quick, dark eyes; and after the ordinary interval she followed him into the inner room to take his order.

His order was evidently a usual one. "I want, please," he said with precision, "one halfpenny bun and a small cup of black coffee." An instant before the girl could turn away he added, "Also, I want you to marry me."

The young lady of the shop stiffened suddenly and said, "Those are jokes I don't allow."

The red-haired young man lifted grey eyes of an unexpected gravity.

"Really and truly," he said, "it's as serious—as serious as the half-penny bun. It is expensive, like the bun; one pays for it. It is indigestible, like the bun. It hurts."

The dark young lady had never taken her dark eyes off him, but seemed to be studying him with almost tragic exactitude. At the end of her scrutiny she had something like the shadow of a smile, and she sat down in a chair.

"Don't you think," observed Angus, absently, "that it's rather cruel to eat these halfpenny buns? They might grow up into penny buns. I shall give up these brutal sports when we are married."

The dark young lady rose from her chair and walked to the window, evidently in a state of strong but not unsympathetic cogitation. When at last she swung round again with an air of resolution she was bewildered to observe that the young man was carefully laying out on the table various objects from the shop-window. They included a pyramid of highly coloured sweets, several plates of sandwiches, and the two decanters containing that mysterious port and sherry which are peculiar to pastry-cooks. In the middle of this neat arrangement he had carefully let down the enormous load of white sugared cake which had been the huge ornament of the window.

"What on earth are you doing?" she asked.

"Duty, my dear Laura," he began.

"Oh, for the Lord's sake, stop a minute," she cried, "and don't talk to me in that way. I mean, what is all that?"

"A ceremonial meal, Miss Hope."

"And what is *that?*" she asked impatiently, pointing to the mountain of sugar.

"The wedding-cake, Mrs. Angus," he said.

The girl marched to that article, removed it with some clatter, and put it back in the shop window; she then returned, and, putting her elegant elbows on the table, regarded the young man not unfavourably but with considerable exasperation.

"You don't give me any time to think," she said.

"I'm not such a fool," he answered; "that's my Christian humility."

She was still looking at him; but she had grown considerably graver behind the smile.

"Mr. Angus," she said steadily, "before there is a minute more of this nonsense I must tell you something about myself as shortly as I can."

"Delighted," replied Angus gravely. "You might tell me something about myself, too, while you are about it."

"Oh, do hold your tongue and listen," she said. "It's nothing that I'm ashamed of, and it isn't even anything that I'm specially sorry about. But what would you say if there were something that is no business of mine and yet is my nightmare?"

"In that case," said the man seriously, "I should suggest that you bring back the cake."

"Well, you must listen to the story first," said Laura, persistently. "To begin with, I must tell you that my father owned the inn called the 'Red Fish' at Ludbury, and I used to serve people in the bar."

"I have often wondered," he said, "why there was a kind of a Christian air about this one confectioner's shop."

"Ludbury is a sleepy, grassy little hole in the Eastern Counties, and the only kind of people who ever came to the 'Red Fish' were occasional commercial travellers, and for the rest, the most awful people you can see, only you've never seen them. I mean little, loungy men, who had just enough to live on and had nothing to do but lean about in bar-rooms and bet on horses, in bad clothes that were just too good for them. Even these wretched young rotters were not very common at our house; but there were two of them that were a lot too common—common in every sort of way. They both lived on money of their own, and were wearisomely idle and over-dressed. But yet I was a bit sorry for them, because I half believe they slunk into our little empty bar because each of them had a slight deformity; the sort of thing that some yokels laugh at. It wasn't exactly a deformity either; it was more an oddity. One of them was a surprisingly small man, something like a dwarf, or at least like a jockey. He was not at all jockeyish to look at, though; he had a round black head and a well-trimmed black beard, bright eyes like a bird's; he jingled money in his pockets; he jangled a great gold watch chain; and he never turned up except dressed just too much like a gentleman to be one. He was no fool though, though a futile idler; he was curiously clever at all kinds of things that couldn't be the slightest use; a sort of impromptu conjuring; making fifteen matches set fire to each other like a regular firework; or cutting a banana or some such thing into a dancing doll. His name was Isidore Smythe; and I can see him still, with his little dark face, just coming up to the counter, making a jumping kangaroo out of five cigars.

"The other fellow was more silent and more ordinary; but somehow he alarmed me much more than poor little Smythe. He was very tall and slight, and light-haired; his nose had a high bridge, and he might almost have been handsome in a spectral sort of way; but he had one of the most appalling squints I have ever seen or heard of. When he looked straight at you, you didn't know where you were yourself, let alone what he was looking at. I fancy this sort of disfigurement embittered the poor chap a little; for while Smythe was ready to show off his monkey tricks anywhere, James Welkin (that was the squinting man's name) never did anything except soak in our bar parlour, and go for great walks by himself in the flat, grey country all round. All the same, I think Smythe, too, was a little sensitive about being so small, though he carried it off more smartly. And so it was that I was really puzzled, as well as startled, and very sorry, when they both offered to marry me in the same week.

"Well, I did what I've since thought was perhaps a silly thing. But, after all, these freaks were my friends in a way; and I had a horror of their thinking I refused them for the real reason, which was that they were so impossibly ugly. So I made up some gas of another sort, about never meaning to marry anyone who hadn't carved his way in the world. I said it was a point of principle with me not to live on money that was just inherited like theirs. Two days after I had talked in this well-meaning sort of way, the whole trouble began. The first thing I heard was that both of them had gone off to seek their fortunes, as if they were in some silly fairy tale.

"Well, I've never seen either of them from that day to this. But I've had two letters from the little man called Smythe, and really they were rather exciting."

"Ever heard of the other man?" asked Angus.

"No, he never wrote," said the girl, after an instant's hesitation. "Smythe's first letter was simply to say that he had started out walking with Welkin to London; but Welkin was such a good walker that the little man dropped out of it, and took a rest by the roadside. He happened to be picked up by some travelling show, and, partly because he was nearly a dwarf, and partly because he was really a clever little wretch, he got on quite well in the show business, and was soon sent up to the Aquarium, to do some tricks that I forget. That was his first letter. His second was much more of a startler, and I only got it last week."

The man called Angus emptied his coffee-cup and regarded her with mild and patient eyes. Her own mouth took a slight twist of laughter as she resumed, "I suppose you've seen on the hoardings all about this 'Smythe's Silent Service'? Or you must be the only person that hasn't. Oh, I don't know much about it, it's some clockwork invention for doing all the housework by machinery. You know the sort of thing: 'Press a button—A Butler who Never Drinks.' 'Turn a Handle—Ten Housemaids who Never Flirt.' You must have seen the advertisements. Well, whatever these machines are, they are making pots of money; and they are making it all for that little imp whom I knew down in Ludbury. I can't help feeling pleased the poor little chap has fallen on his feet; but the plain fact is, I'm in terror of his turning up any minute and telling me he's carved his way in the world—as he certainly has."

"And the other man?" repeated Angus with a sort of obstinate quietude.

Laura Hope got to her feet suddenly. "My friend," she said, "I think you are a witch. Yes, you are quite right. I have not seen a line of the other man's writing; and I have no more notion than the dead of what or where he is. But it is of him that I am frightened. It is he who is all about my path. It is he who has half driven me mad. Indeed, I think he has driven me mad; for I have felt him where he could not have been, and I have heard his voice when he could not have spoken."

"Well, my dear," said the young man, cheerfully, "if he were Satan himself, he is done for now you have told somebody. One goes mad all alone, old girl. But when was it you fancied you felt and heard our squinting friend?"

"I heard James Welkin laugh as plainly as I hear you speak," said the girl, steadily. "There was nobody there, for I stood just outside the shop at the corner, and could see down both streets at once. I had forgotten how he laughed, though his laugh was as odd as his squint. I had not thought of him for nearly a year. But it's a solemn truth that a few seconds later the first letter came from his rival."

"Did you ever make the spectre speak or squeak, or anything?" asked Angus, with some interest.

Laura suddenly shuddered, and then said, with an unshaken voice, "Yes. Just when I had finished reading the second letter from Isidore Smythe announcing his success, just then, I heard Welkin say, 'He shan't have you, though.' It was quite plain, as if he were in the room. It is awful; I think I must be mad."

"If you really were mad," said the young man, "you would think you must be sane. But certainly there seems to me to be something a little rum about this unseen gentleman. Two heads are better than one—I spare you allusions to any other organs—and really, if you would allow me, as a sturdy, practical man, to bring back the wedding-cake out of the window—"

Even as he spoke, there was a sort of steely shriek in the street outside, and a small motor, driven at devilish speed, shot up to the door of the shop and stuck there. In the same flash of time a small man in a shiny top hat stood stamping in the outer room.

Angus, who had hitherto maintained hilarious ease from motives of mental hygiene, revealed the strain of his soul by striding abruptly out of the inner room and confronting the new-comer. A glance at him was quite sufficient to confirm the savage guesswork of a man in love. This very dapper but dwarfish figure, with the spike of black beard carried insolently forward, the clever unrestful eyes, the neat but very nervous fingers, could be none other than the man just described to him: Isidore Smythe, who made dolls out of banana skins and match-boxes; Isidore Smythe, who made millions out of undrinking butlers and unflirting housemaids of metal. For a moment the two men, instinctively understanding each other's air of possession, looked at each other with that curious cold generosity which is the soul of rivalry.

Mr. Smythe, however, made no allusion to the ultimate ground of their antagonism, but said simply and explosively: "Has Miss Hope seen that thing on the window?"

"On the window?" repeated the staring Angus.

"There's no time to explain other things," said the small millionaire shortly. "There's some tomfoolery going on here that has to be investigated."

He pointed his polished walking-stick at the window, recently depleted by the bridal preparations of Mr. Angus; and that gentleman was astonished to see along the front of the glass a long strip of paper pasted, which had certainly not been on the window when he had looked through it some time before. Following the energetic Smythe outside into the street, he found that some yard and a half of stamp paper had been carefully gummed along the glass outside, and on this was written in straggly characters, "If you marry Smythe, he will die."

"Laura," said Angus, putting his big red head into the shop, "you're not mad."

"It's the writing of that fellow Welkin," said Smythe gruffly. "I haven't seen him for years, but he's always bothering me. Five times in the last fortnight he's had threatening letters left at my flat, and I can't even find out who leaves them, let alone if it is Welkin himself. The porter of the flats swears that no suspicious characters have been seen, and here he has pasted up a sort of dado on a public shop window, while the people in the shop—"

"Quite so," said Angus modestly, "while the people in the shop were having tea. Well, sir, I can assure you I appreciate your common sense in dealing so directly with the matter. We can talk about other things afterwards. The fellow cannot be very far off yet, for I swear there was no paper there when I went last to the window, ten or fifteen minutes ago. On the other hand, he's too far off to be chased, as we don't even know the direction. If you'll take my advice, Mr. Smythe, you'll put this at once in the hands of some energetic inquiry man, private rather than public. I know an extremely clever fellow, who has set up in business five minutes from here in your car. His name's Flambeau, and though his youth was a bit stormy, he's a strictly honest man now, and his brains are worth money. He lives in Lucknow Mansions, Hampstead."

"That is odd," said the little man, arching his black eyebrows. "I live, myself, in Himylaya Mansions, round the corner. Perhaps you might care to come with me; I can go to my rooms and sort out these queer Welkin documents, while you run round and get your friend the detective."

"You are very good," said Angus politely. "Well, the sooner we act the better."

Both men, with a queer kind of impromptu fairness, took the same sort of formal farewell of the lady, and both jumped into the brisk little car. As Smythe took the handles and they turned the great corner of the street, Angus was amused to see a gigantesque poster of "Smythe's Silent Service," with a picture of a huge headless iron doll, carrying a saucepan with the legend, "A Cook Who is Never Cross."

"I use them in my own flat," said the little black-bearded man, laughing, "partly for advertisements, and partly for real convenience. Honestly, and all above board, those big clockwork dolls of mine do bring you coals or claret or a timetable quicker than any live servants I've ever known, if you know which knob to press. But I'll never deny, between ourselves, that such servants have their disadvantages, too."

"Indeed?" said Angus; "is there something they can't do?"

"Yes," replied Smythe coolly; "they can't tell me who left those threatening letters at my flat."

The man's motor was small and swift like himself; in fact, like his domestic service, it was of his own invention. If he was an advertising quack, he was one who believed in his own wares. The sense of something tiny and flying was accentuated as they swept up long white curves of road in the dead but open daylight of evening. Soon the white curves came sharper and dizzier; they were upon ascending spirals, as they say in the modern religions. For, indeed, they were cresting a corner of London which is almost as precipitous as Edinburgh, if not quite so picturesque. Terrace rose above terrace, and the special tower of flats they sought, rose above them all to almost Egyptian height, gilt by the level sunset. The change, as they turned the corner and entered the crescent known as Himylaya Mansions, was as abrupt as the opening of a window; for they found that pile of flats sitting above London as above a green sea of slate. Opposite to the mansions, on the other side of the gravel crescent, was a bushy enclosure more like a steep hedge or dyke than a garden, and some way below that ran a strip of artificial water, a sort of canal, like the moat of that embowered fortress. As the car swept round the crescent it passed, at one corner, the stray stall of a man selling chestnuts; and right away at the other end of the curve, Angus could see a dim blue policeman walking slowly. These were the only human shapes in that high suburban solitude; but he had an irrational sense that they expressed the speechless poetry of London. He felt as if they were figures in a story.

The little car shot up to the right house like a bullet, and shot out its owner like a bomb shell. He was immediately inquiring of a tall commissionaire in shining braid, and a short porter in shirt sleeves, whether anybody or anything had been seeking his apartments. He was assured that nobody and nothing had passed these officials since his last inquiries; whereupon he and the slightly bewildered Angus were shot up in the lift like a rocket, till they reached the top floor.

"Just come in for a minute," said the breathless Smythe. "I want to show you those Welkin letters. Then you might run round the corner and fetch your friend." He pressed a button concealed in the wall, and the door opened of itself.

It opened on a long, commodious ante-room, of which the only arresting features, ordinarily speaking, were the rows of tall half-human mechanical figures that stood up on both sides like tailors' dummies. Like tailors' dummies they were headless; and like tailors' dummies they had a handsome unnecessary humpiness in the shoulders, and a pigeon-breasted protuberance of chest; but barring this, they were not much more like a human figure than any automatic machine at a station that is about the human height. They had two great hooks like arms, for carrying trays; and they were painted pea-green, or vermillion, or black for convenience of distinction; in every other way they were only automatic machines and nobody would have looked twice at them. On this occasion, at least, nobody did. For between the two rows of these domestic dummies lay something more interesting than most of the mechanics of the world. It was a white, tattered scrap of paper scrawled with red ink; and the agile inventor had snatched it up almost as soon as the door flew open. He handed it to Angus without a word. The red ink on it actually was not dry, and the message ran, "If you have been to see her today, I shall kill you."

There was a short silence, and then Isidore Smythe said quietly, "Would you like a little whiskey? I rather feel as if I should."

"Thank you; I should like a little Flambeau," said Angus, gloomily. "This business seems to me to be getting rather grave. I'm going round at once to fetch him."

"Right you are," said the other, with admirable cheerfulness. "Bring him round here as quick as you can."

But as Angus closed the front door behind him he saw Smythe push back a button, and one of the clockwork images glided from its place and slid along a groove in the floor carrying a tray with syphon and decanter. There did seem something a trifle weird about leaving the little man alone among those dead servants, who were coming to life as the door closed.

Six steps down from Smythe's landing the man in shirt sleeves was doing something with a pail. Angus stopped to extract a promise, fortified with a prospective bribe, that he would remain in that place until the return with the detective, and would keep count of any kind of stranger coming up those stairs. Dashing down to the front hall he then laid similar charges of vigilance on the commissionaire at the front door, from whom he learned the simplifying circumstances that there was no back door. Not content with this, he captured the floating policeman and induced him to stand opposite the entrance and watch it; and finally paused an instant for a pennyworth of chestnuts, and an inquiry as to the probable length of the merchant's stay in the neighbourhood.

The chestnut seller, turning up the collar of his coat, told him he should probably be moving shortly, as he thought it was going to snow. Indeed, the evening was growing grey and bitter, but Angus, with all his eloquence, proceeded to nail the chestnut man to his post.

"Keep yourself warm on your own chestnuts," he said earnestly. "Eat up your whole stock; I'll make it worth your while. I'll give you a sovereign if you'll wait here till I come back, and then tell me whether any man, woman, or child has gone into that house where the commissionaire is standing."

He then walked away smartly, with a last look at the besieged tower.

"I've made a ring round that room, anyhow," he said. "They can't all four of them be Mr. Welkin's accomplices."

Lucknow Mansions were, so to speak, on a lower platform of that hill of houses, of which Himylaya Mansions might be called the peak. Mr. Flambeau's semi-official flat was on the ground floor, and presented in every way a marked contrast to the American machinery and cold hotel-like luxury of the flat of the Silent Service. Flambeau, who was a friend of Angus, received him in a rococo artistic den behind his office, of which the ornaments were sabres, harquebuses,* Eastern curiosities, flasks of Italian wine, savage cooking-pots, a plumy Persian cat, and a small dusty-looking Roman Catholic priest, who looked particularly out of place.

"This is my friend Father Brown," said Flambeau. "I've often wanted you to meet him. Splendid weather, this; a little cold for Southerners like me."

"Yes, I think it will keep clear," said Angus, sitting down on a violet-striped Eastern ottoman.

"No," said the priest quietly, "it has begun to snow."

And, indeed, as he spoke, the first few flakes, foreseen by the man of chestnuts, began to drift across the darkening window-pane.

"Well," said Angus heavily. "I'm afraid I've come on business, and rather jumpy business at that. The fact is, Flambeau, within a stone's throw of your house is a fellow who badly wants your help; he's perpetually being haunted and threatened by an invisible enemy—a scoundrel whom nobody has even seen." As Angus proceeded to tell the whole tale of Smythe and Welkin, beginning with Laura's story, and going on with his own, the supernatural laugh at the corner of two empty streets, the strange distinct words spoken in an empty room, Flambeau grew more and more vividly concerned, and the little priest seemed to be left out of it, like a piece of furniture. When it came to the scribbled stamp-paper pasted on the window, Flambeau rose, seeming to fill the room with his huge shoulders.

"If you don't mind," he said, "I think you had better tell me the rest on the nearest road to this man's house. It strikes me, somehow, that there is no time to be lost."

*An obsolete portable gun

"Delighted," said Angus, rising also, "though he's safe enough for the present, for I've set four men to watch the only hole to his burrow."

They turned out into the street, the small priest trundling after them with the docility of a small dog. He merely said, in a cheerful way, like one making conversation, "How quick the snow gets thick on the ground."

As they threaded the steep side streets already powdered with silver, Angus finished his story; and by the time they reached the crescent with the towering flats, he had leisure to turn his attention to the four sentinels. The chestnut seller, both before and after receiving a sovereign, swore stubbornly that he had watched the door and seen no visitor enter. The policeman was even more emphatic. He said he had had experience of crooks of all kinds, in top hats and in rags; he wasn't so green as to expect suspicious characters to look suspicious; he looked out for anybody, and, so help him, there had been nobody. And when all three men gathered round the gilded commissionaire, who still stood smiling astride of the porch, the verdict was more final still.

"I've got a right to ask any man, duke or dustman, what he wants in these flats," said the genial and gold-laced giant, "and I'll swear there's been nobody to ask since this gentleman went away."

The unimportant Father Brown, who stood back, looking modestly at the pavement, here ventured to say meekly, "Has nobody been up and down stairs, then, since the snow began to fall? It began while we were all round at Flambeau's."

"Nobody's been in here, sir, you can take it from me," said the official, with beaming authority.

"Then I wonder what that is?" said the priest, and stared at the ground blankly like a fish.

The others all looked down also; and Flambeau used a fierce exclamation and a French gesture. For it was unquestionably true that down the middle of the entrance guarded by the man in gold lace, actually between the arrogant, stretched legs of that colossus, ran a stringy pattern of grey footprints stamped upon the white snow.

"God!" cried Angus involuntarily, "the Invisible Man!"

Without another word he turned and dashed up the stairs, with Flambeau following; but Father Brown still stood looking about him in the snowclad street as if he had lost interest in his query.

Flambeau was plainly in a mood to break down the door with his big shoulders; but the Scotchman, with more reason, if less intuition, fumbled about on the frame of the door till he found the invisible button; and the door swung slowly open.

It showed substantially the same serried interior; the hall had grown darker, though it was still struck here and there with the last crimson shafts of sunset, and one or two of the headless machines had been moved from their places for this or that purpose, and stood here and there about the twilit place. The green and red of their coats were all darkened in the dusk; and their likeness to human shapes slightly increased by their very shapelessness. But in the middle of them all, exactly where the paper with the red ink had lain, there lay something that looked like red ink spilt out of its bottle. But it was not red ink.

With a French combination of reason and violence Flambeau simply said "Murder!" and, plunging into the flat, had explored every corner and cupboard of it in five minutes. But if he expected to find a corpse he found none. Isidore Smythe was not in the place, either dead or alive. After the most tearing search the two men met each other in the outer hall, with streaming faces and staring eyes. "My friend," said Flambeau, talking French in his excitement, "not only is your murderer invisible, but he makes invisible also the murdered man."

Angus looked round at the dim room full of dummies, and in some Celtic corner of his Scotch soul a shudder started. One of the life-size dolls stood immediately overshadowing the blood stain, summoned, perhaps, by the slain man an instant before he fell. One of the high-shouldered hooks that served the thing for arms, was a little lifted, and Angus had suddenly the horrid fancy that poor Smythe's own iron child had struck him down. Matter had rebelled, and these machines had killed their master. But even so, what had they done with him?

"Eaten him?" said the nightmare at his ear; and he sickened for an instant at the idea of rent, human remains absorbed and crushed into all that acephalous* clockwork.

He recovered his mental health by an emphatic effort, and said to Flambeau, "Well, there it is. The poor fellow has evaporated like a cloud and left a red streak on the floor. The tale does not belong to this world."

"There is only one thing to be done," said Flambeau, "whether it belongs to this world or the other, I must go down and talk to my friend."

They descended, passing the man with the pail, who again asseverated that he had let no intruder pass, down to the commissionaire and the hovering chestnut man, who rigidly reasserted their own watchfulness. But when Angus looked round for his fourth confirmation he could not see it, and called out with some nervousness, "Where is the policeman?"

"I beg your pardon," said Father Brown; "that is my fault. I just sent him down the road to investigate something—that I just thought worth investigating."

"Well, we want him back pretty soon," said Angus abruptly, "for the wretched man upstairs has not only been murdered, but wiped out."

"How?" asked the priest.

"Father," said Flambeau, after a pause, "upon my soul I believe it is more in your department than mine. No friend or foe has entered the house, but Smythe is gone, as if stolen by the fairies. If that is not supernatural, I—"

As he spoke they were all checked by an unusual sight; the big blue policeman came round the corner of the crescent, running. He came straight up to Brown.

---

*Headless.

"You're right, sir," he panted, "they've just found poor Mr. Smythe's body in the canal down below."

Angus put his hand wildly to his head. "Did he run down and drown himself?" he asked.

"He never came down, I'll swear," said the constable, "and he wasn't drowned either, for he died of a great stab over the heart."

"And yet you saw no one enter?" said Flambeau in a grave voice.

"Let us walk down the road a little," said the priest.

As they reached the other end of the crescent he observed abruptly, "Stupid of me! I forgot to ask the policeman something. I wonder if they found a light brown sack."

"Why a light brown sack?" asked Angus, astonished.

"Because if it was any other coloured sack, the case must begin over again," said Father Brown; "but if it was a light brown sack, why, the case is finished."

"I am pleased to hear it," said Angus with hearty irony. "It hasn't begun, so far as I am concerned."

"You must tell us all about it," said Flambeau with a strange heavy simplicity, like a child.

Unconsciously they were walking with quickening steps down the long sweep of road on the other side of the high crescent, Father Brown leading briskly, though in silence. At last he said with an almost touching vagueness, "Well, I'm afraid you'll think it so prosy. We always begin at the abstract end of things, and you can't begin this story anywhere else.

"Have you ever noticed this—that people never answer what you say? They answer what you mean—or what they think you mean. Suppose one lady says to another in a country house, 'Is anybody staying with you?' the lady doesn't answer 'Yes; the butler, the three footmen, the parlourmaid, and so on,' though the parlourmaid may be in the room, or the butler behind her chair. She says 'There is *nobody* staying with us,' meaning nobody of the sort you mean. But suppose a doctor inquiring into an epidemic asks, 'Who is staying in the house?' then the lady will remember the butler, parlourmaid, and the rest. All language is used like that; you never get a question answered literally, even when you get it answered truly. When those four quite honest men said that no man had gone into the Mansions, they did not really mean that *no man* had gone into them. They meant no man whom they could suspect of being your man. A man did go into the house, and did come out of it, but they never noticed him."

"An invisible man?" inquired Angus, raising his red eyebrows.

"A mentally invisible man," said Father Brown.

A minute or two after he resumed in the same unassuming voice, like a man thinking his way. "Of course you can't think of such a man, until you do think of him. That's where his cleverness comes in. But I came to think of him through two or three little things in the tale Mr. Angus told us. First, there was the fact that this Welkin went for long walks. And then there was the vast lot of stamp paper on the window. And then, most of all, there were the two things the young lady said—things that couldn't be true. Don't get annoyed," he added hastily, noting a sudden movement of the Scotchman's head; "she thought they were true. A person *can't* be quite alone in a street a second before she receives a letter. She can't be quite alone in a street when she starts reading a letter just received. There must be somebody pretty near her; he must be mentally invisible."

"Why must there be somebody near her?" asked Angus.

"Because," said Father Brown, "barring carrier-pigeons, somebody must have brought her the letter."

"Do you really mean to say," asked Flambeau, with energy, "that Welkin carried his rival's letters to his lady?"

"Yes," said the priest. "Welkin carried his rival's letters to his lady. You see, he had to."

"Oh, I can't stand much more of this," exploded Flambeau. "Who is this fellow? What does he look like. What is the usual get-up of a mentally invisible man?"

"He is dressed rather handsomely in red, blue and gold," replied the priest promptly with precision, "and in this striking, and even showy, costume he entered Himylaya Mansions under eight human eyes; he killed Smythe in cold blood, and came down into the street again carrying the dead body in his arms—"

"Reverend sir," cried Angus, standing still, "are you raving mad, or am I?"

"You are not mad," said Brown, "only a little unobservant. You have not noticed such a man as this, for example."

He took three quick strides forward, and put his hand on the shoulder of an ordinary passing postman who had bustled by them unnoticed under the shade of the trees.

"Nobody ever notices postmen somehow," he said thoughtfully; "yet they have passions like other men, and even carry large bags where a small corpse can be stowed quite easily."

The postman, instead of turning naturally, had ducked and tumbled against the garden fence. He was a lean fair-bearded man of very ordinary appearance, but as he turned an alarmed face over his shoulder, all three men were fixed with an almost fiendish squint.

Flambeau went back to his sabres, purple rugs and Persian cat, having many things to attend to. John Turnbull Angus went back to the lady at the shop, with whom that imprudent young man contrives to be extremely comfortable. But Father Brown walked those snow-covered hills under the stars for many hours with a murderer, and what they said to each other will never be known.

ACTIVITIES

1) Chesterton's "The Invisible Man" is an interesting variation of Poe's "The Purloined Letter." Can you point out how this is so?

2) In the story, Father Brown inquires: "Have you ever noticed this—

that people never answer what you say? They answer what you mean—or what they think you mean."

What exactly is he trying to get across to his listeners?

3)   The tale ends: "But Father Brown walked those snow-covered hills under the stars for many hours with a murderer, and what they said to each other will never be known."

You know the kind of person James Welkin is and you know that Father Brown is a man of God. Can you guess at what may have been said? Remember that Flambeau, the private detective, had once been a criminal. How is the ending of this narrative different from the others in this textbook?

4)   Father Brown talks of the postman as a "mentally invisible man." What exactly does he mean here? Can you point out other "mentally invisible people" in our society?

Research Activity

A very intriguing paper could be written on the subject, "Father Brown, Psychologist." You would, of course, have to read more of the Father Brown stories (see page 277) and also some psychology material.

Such an essay could prove useful in that you are likely to learn something about yourself.

Agatha Christie—and Hercule Poirot

Agatha Christie was the first great woman detective story writer. Not, mind you, the first to try her pen in the genre but certainly the first to rank with the male "greats" Poe, Doyle, and Queen.

In one way, she even outranked the men.

According to the masculine stereotype, men are the stronger sex, the more durable. But, if you were to research the question of who is the most prolific detective story writer, lo and behold, you would discover it was a woman—the aforementioned Ms. Christie.

Her first detective story appeared in 1920. Since then she has been writing them at the rate of one novel or one short story anthology per year. And she's continued that pace for more than fifty years. Yes, no other detective writer, male or female, can claim that kind of productivity.

She was born in 1890, on the Devon coast of England, to an American father and an English mother. At the age of six, her father died; she was raised by her mother, who encouraged her to write. Her early stories were of the Gothic variety in which most of the characters ended up dying. Then, in the year 1915, her sister challenged her to write a good detective story.

For the world, it was a fortunate challenge.

Because when she accepted it and produced *The Mysterious Affair at Styles,* the name of a talented woman was added to a predominantly male roster of accomplishment in the field of detective literature. Interestingly enough, her first great series sleuth was a man—Hercule Poirot; later, she produced an equally important woman detective, Miss Marple—but more about that in the next chapter.

In 1914, she married Archibald Christie, a pilot for the Royal Air Force (R.A.F.), World War I had begun and she became a Red Cross volunteer; in this capacity she gleaned a good working knowledge of poisons, a definite asset for her future profession.

In 1926, two critical events occurred. First, she published *The Murder of Roger Ackroyd,* probably the most controversial detective novel ever produced. What was vastly unprecedented in its construction was that the narrator (the "I" of the tale and therefore the least likely suspect) turned out to be the criminal. A violent debate took place in detective story circles—one school deplored her literary device; another thought it the greatest innovation since the invention of the form itself. The controversy continues to this day.

Second, in the same year, Ms. Christie suddenly vanished from her home. The event became a target for an assortment of amateur sleuths who came forth with fantastic deductions galore. Ultimately, the missing writer was found registered under an assumed name at a Yorkshire health resort. Doctors called it a classic case of amnesia but the English press accused Ms. Christie of staging a publicity stunt in order to sell her books.

The press was proven wrong. Pressure from work—plus the strain of a dissolving marriage—had brought about the amnesia. Had the illness never occurred, her little Belgian detective—M. Hercule Poirot—would have obtained for her all the publicity she ever needed.[3]

Like his fictional predecessors, Poirot was memorable; short and stocky, he had an egg-shaped head with waxed mustaches twirled to the finest of points. With his black patent leather shoes, cane, and youthful hair (to which he always applied a certain "tonic, not a dye"), he was the epitome of a "dandy."

Like Holmes and The Thinking Machine, Poirot relied heavily upon his ability to reason—his "little grey cells," as he called them. Unlike Holmes, he scorned getting down on all fours in search of clues. Rather, he enjoyed playing the role of "armchair detective," letting others, notably his frequent companion, Captain Hastings, do his leg-work for him. Though his use of the English language was abominable, Poirot more than made up for it by his superlative deductive abilities—which you will witness yourself when you read the next story.

More about Agatha Christie's life in Chapter V.

The Mystery of Hunter's Lodge

"After all," murmured Poirot, "it is possible that I shall not die this time."

Coming from a convalescent influenza patient, I hailed the remark as showing a beneficial optimism. I myself had been the first sufferer from the disease. Poirot in his turn had gone down. He was now sitting up in bed, propped up with pillows, his head muffled in a woollen shawl, and was slowly sipping a particularly noxious *tisane* which I had prepared according to his directions. His eye rested with pleasure upon a neatly graduated row of medicine bottles which adorned the mantelpiece.

"Yes, yes," my little friend continued. "Once more shall I be myself again, the great Hercule Poirot, the terror of evildoers! Figure to yourself, *mon ami,* that I have a little paragraph to myself in *Society Gossip*. But yes! Here it is: 'Go it—criminals—all out! Hercule Poirot—and believe me, girls, he's some Hercules!—our own pet society detective can't get a grip on you. 'Cause why? 'Cause he's got *la grippe* himself'!"

I laughed.

"Good for you, Poirot. You are becoming quite a public character. And fortunately you haven't missed anything of particular interest during this time."

"That is true. The few cases I have had to decline did not fill me with any regret."

Our landlady stuck her head in at the door.

"There's a gentleman downstairs. Says he must see Monsieur Poirot or you, Captain. Seeing as he was in a great to-do—and with all that quite the gentleman—I brought up 'is card."

She handed me the bit of pasteboard. "Mr. Roger Havering," I read.

Poirot motioned with his head towards the bookcase, and I obediently pulled forth *Who's Who*. Poirot took it from me and scanned the pages rapidly.

"Second son of fifth Baron Windsor. Married 1913 Zoe, fourth daughter of William Crabb."

"H'm!" I said. "I rather fancy that's the girl who used to act at the Frivolity—only she called herself Zoe Carrisbrook. I remember she married some young man about town just before the War."

"Would it interest you, Hastings, to go down and hear what our visitor's particular little trouble is? Make him all my excuses."

Roger Havering was a man of about forty, well set up and of smart appearance. His face, however, was haggard, and he was evidently labouring under great agitation.

"Captain Hastings? You are Monsieur Poirot's partner, I understand. It is imperative that he should come with me to Derbyshire to-day."

"I'm afraid that's impossible," I replied. "Poirot is ill in bed—influenza."

His face fell.

"Dear me, that is a great blow to me."

"The matter on which you want to consult him is serious?"

"My God, yes! My uncle, the best friend I have in the world, was foully murdered last night."

"Here in London?"

"No, in Derbyshire. I was in town and received a telegram from my wife this morning. Immediately upon its receipt I determined to come round and beg Monsieur Poirot to undertake the case."

"If you will excuse me a minute," I said, struck by a sudden idea.

I rushed upstairs, and in a few brief words acquainted Poirot with the situation. He took any further words out of my mouth.

"I see. I see. You want to go yourself, is it not so? Well, why not? You should know my methods by now. All I ask is that you should report to me fully every day, and follow implicitly any instructions I may wire you."

To this I willingly agreed.

. . . . .

An hour later I was sitting opposite Mr. Havering in a first-class carriage on the Midland Railway, speeding rapidly away from London.

"To begin with, Captain Hastings, you must understand that Hunter's Lodge, where we are going, and where the tragedy took place, is only a small shooting-box in the heart of the Derbyshire moors. Our real home is near Newmarket, and we usually rent a flat in town for the season. Hunter's Lodge is looked after by a housekeeper who is quite capable of doing all we need when we run down for an occasional week-end. Of course, during the shooting season, we take down some of our own servants from Newmarket. My uncle, Mr. Harrington Pace (as you may know, my mother was a Miss Pace of New York), has, for the last three years, made his home with us. He never got on well with my father, or my elder brother, and I suspect that my being somewhat of a prodigal son myself rather increased than diminished his affection towards me. Of course I am a poor man, and my uncle was a rich one—in other words, he paid the piper! But, though exacting in many ways, he was not really hard to get on with, and we all three lived very harmoniously together. Two days ago my uncle, rather wearied with some recent gaieties of ours in town, suggested that we should run down to Derbyshire for a day or two. My wife telegraphed to Mrs. Middleton, the housekeeper, and we went down that same afternoon. Yesterday evening I was forced to return to town, but my wife and my uncle remained on. This morning I received this telegram." He handed it over to me:

"Come at once uncle harrington murdered last night bring good detective if you can but do come—Zoe."

"Then, as yet you know no details?"

"No, I suppose it will be in the evening papers. Without doubt the police are in charge."

It was about three o'clock when we arrived at the little station of Elmer's

Dale. From there a five-mile drive brought us to a small grey stone building in the midst of the rugged moors.

"A lonely place," I observed with a shiver.

Havering nodded.

"I shall try and get rid of it. I could never live here again."

We unlatched the gate and were walking up the narrow path to the oak door when a familiar figure emerged and came to meet us.

"Japp!" I ejaculated.

The Scotland Yard inspector grinned at me in a friendly fashion before addressing my companion.

"Mr. Havering, I think? I've been sent down from London to take charge of this case, and I'd like a word with you, if I may, sir."

"My wife—"

"I've seen your good lady, sir—and the housekeeper. I won't keep you a moment, but I'm anxious to get back to the village now that I've seen all there is to see here."

"I know nothing as yet as to what—"

"Ex-actly," said Japp soothingly. "But there are just one or two little points I'd like your opinion about all the same. Captain Hastings here, he knows me, and he'll go on up to the house and tell them you're coming. What have you done with the little man, by the way, Captain Hastings?"

"He's ill in bed with influenza."

"Is he now? I'm sorry to hear that. Rather the case of the cart without the horse, your being here without him, isn't it?"

And on his rather ill-timed jest I went on to the house. I rang the bell, as Japp had closed the door behind him. After some moments it was opened to me by a middle-aged woman in black.

"Mr. Havering will be here in a moment," I explained. "He has been detained by the inspector. I have come down with him from London to look into the case. Perhaps you can tell me briefly what occurred last night."

"Come inside, sir." She closed the door behind me, and we stood in the dimly-lighted hall. "It was after dinner last night, sir, that the man came. He asked to see Mr. Pace, sir, and, seeing that he spoke the same way, I thought it was an American gentleman friend of Mr. Pace's and I showed him into the gun-room, and then went to tell Mr. Pace. He wouldn't give any name, which, of course, was a bit odd, now I come to think of it. I told Mr. Pace, and he seemed puzzled like, but he said to the mistress: 'Excuse me, Zoe, while I just see what this fellow wants.' He went off to the gun-room, and I went back to the kitchen, but after a while I heard loud voices, as if they were quarrelling, and I came out into the hall. At the same time, the mistress she comes out too, and just then there was a shot and then a dreadful silence. We both ran to the gun-room door, but it was locked and we had to go round to the window. It was open, and there inside was Mr. Pace, all shot and bleeding."

"What became of the man?"

"He must have got away through the window, sir, before we got to it."

"And then?"

"Mrs. Havering sent me to fetch the police. Five miles to walk it was.

They came back with me, and the constable he stayed all night, and this morning the police gentleman from London arrived."

"What was this man like who called to see Mr. Pace?"

The housekeeper reflected.

"He had a black beard, sir, and was about middle-aged, and had on a light overcoat. Beyond the fact that he spoke like an American I didn't notice much about him."

"I see. Now I wonder if I can see Mrs. Havering?"

"She's upstairs, sir. Shall I tell her?"

"If you please. Tell her that Mr. Havering is outside with Inspector Japp, and that the gentleman he has brought back with him from London is anxious to speak to her as soon as possible."

"Very good, sir."

I was in a fever of impatience to get at all the facts. Japp had two or three hours' start of me, and his anxiety to be gone made me keen to be close at his heels.

Mrs. Havering did not keep me waiting long. In a few minutes I heard a light step descending the stairs, and looked up to see a very handsome young woman coming towards me. She wore a flame-coloured jumper, that set off the slender boyishness of her figure. On her dark head was a little hat of flame-coloured leather. Even the present tragedy could not dim the vitality of her personality.

I introduced myself, and she nodded in quick comprehension.

"Of course I have often heard of you and your colleague, Monsieur Poirot. You have done some wonderful things together, haven't you? It was very clever of my husband to get you so promptly. Now will you ask me questions? That is the easiest way, isn't it, of getting to know all you want to about this dreadful affair?"

"Thank you, Mrs. Havering. Now what time was it that this man arrived?"

"It must have been just before nine o'clock. We had finished dinner, and were sitting over our coffee and cigarettes."

"Your husband had already left for London?"

"Yes, he went up by the 6.15."

"Did he go by car to the station, or did he walk?"

"Our own car isn't down here. One came out from the garage in Elmer's Dale to fetch him in time for the train."

"Was Mr. Pace quite his usual self?"

"Absolutely. Most normal in every way."

"Now, can you describe this visitor at all?"

"I'm afraid not. I didn't see him. Mrs. Middleton showed him straight into the gun-room and then came to tell my uncle."

"What did your uncle say?"

"He seemed rather annoyed, but went off at once. It was about five minutes later that I heard the sound of raised voices. I ran out into the hall and almost collided with Mrs. Middleton. Then we heard the shot. The gun-room door was locked on the inside, and we had to go right round the house to the window. Of course that took some time, and the murderer had been able to get well away. My poor uncle"—her voice faltered—"had been shot through the head. I saw at once that he was dead. I sent Mrs. Middleton for the police. I was careful to touch nothing in the room but to leave it exactly as I found it."

I nodded approval.

"Now, as to the weapon?"

"Well, I can make a guess at it, Captain Hastings. A pair of revolvers of my husband's were mounted upon the wall. One of them is missing. I pointed this out to the police, and they took the other one away with them. When they have extracted the bullet, I suppose they will know for certain."

"May I go to the gun-room?"

"Certainly. The police have finished with it. But the body has been removed."

She accompanied me to the scene of the crime. At that moment Havering entered the hall, and with a quick apology his wife ran to him. I was left to undertake my investigations alone.

I may as well confess at once that they were rather disappointing. In detective novels clues abound, but here I could find nothing that struck me as out of the ordinary except a large blood-stain on the carpet where I judged the dead man had fallen. I examined everything with painstaking care and took a couple of pictures of the room with my little camera which I had brought with me. I also examined the ground outside the window, but it appeared to have been so heavily trampled underfoot that I judged it was useless to waste time over it. No, I had seen all that Hunter's Lodge had to show me. I must go back to Elmer's Dale and get into touch with Japp. Accordingly I took leave of the Haverings, and was driven off in the car that had brought us up from the station.

I found Japp at the Matlock Arms and he took me forthwith to see the body. Harrington Pace was a small, spare, clean-shaven man, typically American in appearance. He had been shot through the back of the head, and the revolver had been discharged at close quarters.

"Turned away for a moment," remarked Japp, "and the other fellow snatched up a revolver and shot him. The one Mrs. Havering handed over to us was fully loaded and I suppose the other one was also. Curious what darn fool things people do. Fancy keeping two loaded revolvers hanging up on your wall."

"What do you think of the case?" I asked, as we left the gruesome chamber behind us.

"Well, I'd got my eye on Havering to begin with. Oh, yes!"—noting my exclamation of astonishment. "Havering has one or two shady incidents in his past. When he was a boy at Oxford there was some funny business about the signature on one of his father's cheques. All hushed up of course. Then, he's pretty heavily in debt now, and they're the kind of debts he wouldn't like to go to his uncle about, whereas you may be sure the uncle's will would be in his favour. Yes, I'd got my eye on him, and that's why I wanted to speak to him before he saw his wife, but their statements dovetail all right, and I've been to the station and there's no doubt whatever that he left by the 6.15. That gets up to London about 10.30. He went straight to his club, he says, and if that's confirmed all right—why, he couldn't have been shooting his uncle here at nine o'clock in a black beard!"

"Ah, yes, I was going to ask you what you thought about that beard?" Japp winked.

"I think it grew pretty fast—grew in the five miles from Elmer's Dale to Hunter's Lodge. Americans that I've met are mostly clean-shaven. Yes, it's amongst Mr. Pace's American associates that we'll have to look for the murderer. I questioned the housekeeper first, and then her mistress, and their stories agree all right, but I'm sorry Mrs. Havering didn't get a look at the fellow. She's a smart woman, and she might have noticed something that would set us on the track."

I sat down and wrote a minute and lengthy account to Poirot. I was able to add various further items of information before I posted the letter.

The bullet had been extracted and was proved to have been fired from a revolver identical with the one held by the police. Furthermore, Mr. Havering's movements on the night in question had been checked and verified, and it was proved beyond a doubt that he had actually arrived in London by the train in question. And, thirdly, a sensational development had occurred. A city gentleman, living at Ealing, on crossing Haven Green to get to the District Railway Station that morning, had observed a brown-paper parcel stuck between the railings. Opening it, he found that it contained a revolver. He handed the parcel over to the local police station, and before night it was proved to be the one we were in search of, the fellow to that given us by Mrs. Havering. One bullet had been fired from it.

All this I added to my report. A wire from Poirot arrived whilst I was at breakfast the following morning:

"Of course black-bearded man was not Havering only you or Japp would have such an idea wire me description of housekeeper and what clothes she wore this morning same of Mrs. Havering do not waste time taking photographs of interiors they are underexposed and not in the least artistic."

It seemed to me that Poirot's style was unnecessarily facetious. I also fancied he was a shade jealous of my position on the spot with full facilities for handling the case. His request for a description of the clothes worn by the two women appeared to me to be simply ridiculous, but I complied as well as I, a mere man, was able to.

At eleven a reply wire came from Poirot:

"Advise Japp arrest housekeeper before it is too late."

Dumbfounded, I took the wire to Japp. He swore softly under his breath.

"He's the goods, Monsieur Poirot! If he says so, there's something in it. And I hardly noticed the woman. I don't know that I can go so far as arresting her, but I'll have her watched. We'll go up right away, and take another look at her."

But it was too late. Mrs. Middleton, that quiet middle-aged woman, who had appeared so normal and respectable, had vanished into thin air. Her box had been left behind. It contained only ordinary wearing apparel. There was no clue in it to her identity, or as to her whereabouts.

From Mrs. Havering we elicited all the facts we could:

"I engaged her about three weeks ago when Mrs. Emery, our former housekeeper, left. She came to me from Mrs. Selbourne's Agency in Mount Street—a very well-known place. I get all my servants from there. They sent several women to see me, but this Mrs. Middleton seemed much the nicest, and had splendid references. I engaged her on the spot, and notified the Agency of the fact. I can't believe that there was anything wrong with her. She was such a nice quiet woman."

The thing was certainly a mystery. Whilst it was clear that the woman herself could not have committed the crime, since at the moment the shot was fired Mrs. Havering was with her in the hall, nevertheless she must have some connection with the murder, or why should she suddenly take to her heels and bolt?

I wired the latest development to Poirot and suggested returning to London and making inquiries at Selbourne's Agency.

Poirot's reply was prompt:

"Useless to inquire at agency they will never have heard of her find out what vehicle took her up to hunters lodge when she first arrived there."

Though mystified, I was obedient. The means of transport in Elmer's Dale were limited. The local garage had two battered Ford cars, and there were two station flies. None of these had been requisitioned on the date in question. Questioned, Mrs. Havering explained that she had given the woman the money for her fare down to Derbyshire and sufficient to hire a car or fly to take her up to Hunter's Lodge. There was usually one of the Fords at the station on the chance of its being required. Taking into consideration the further fact that nobody at the station had noticed the arrival of a stranger, black-bearded or otherwise, on the fatal evening, everything seemed to point to the conclusion that the murderer had come to the spot in a car, which had been waiting near at hand to aid his escape, and that the same car had brought the mysterious housekeeper to her new post. I may mention that inquiries at the Agency in London bore out Poirot's prognostication. No such woman as "Mrs. Middleton" had ever been on their books. They had received the Hon. Mrs. Havering's application for a housekeeper, and had sent her various applicants for the post. When she sent them the engagement fee, she omitted to mention which woman she had selected.

Somewhat crestfallen, I returned to London. I found Poirot established in an arm-chair by the fire in a garish, silk dressing-gown. He greeted me with much affection.

"*Mon ami* Hastings! But how glad I am to see you. Veritably I have for you a great affection! And you have enjoyed yourself? You have run to and fro with the good Japp? You have interrogated and investigated to your heart's content?"

"Poirot," I cried, "the thing's a dark mystery! It will never be solved."

"It is true that we are not likely to cover ourselves with glory over it."

"No, indeed. It's a hard nut to crack."

"Oh, as far as that goes, I am very good at cracking the nuts! A veritable squirrel! It is not that which embarrasses me. I know well enough who killed Mr. Harrington Pace."

"You know? How did you find out?"

"Your illuminating answers to my wires supplied me with the truth. See here, Hastings, let us examine the facts methodically and in order. Mr. Harrington Pace is a man with a considerable fortune which at his death will doubtless pass to his nephew. Point No. 1. His nephew is known to be desperately hard up. Point No. 2. His nephew is also known to be—shall we say a man of rather loose moral fibre? Point No. 3."

"But Roger Havering is proved to have journeyed straight up to London."

"*Précisément**—and therefore, as Mr. Havering left Elmer's Dale at 6.15, and since Mr. Pace cannot have been killed before he left, or the doctor would have spotted the time of the crime as being given wrongly when he examined the body, we conclude quite rightly, that Mr. Havering did *not* shoot his uncle. But there is a Mrs. Havering, Hastings."

"Impossible! The housekeeper was with her when the shot was fired."

"Ah, yes, the housekeeper. But she has disappeared."

"She will be found."

"I think not. There is something peculiarly elusive about that housekeeper, don't you think so, Hastings? It struck me at once."

"She played her part, I suppose, and then got out in the nick of time."

"And what was her part?"

"Well, presumably to admit her confederate, the black-bearded man."

"Oh, no, that was not her part! Her part was what you have just mentioned, to provide an alibi for Mrs. Havering at the moment the shot was fired. And no one will ever find her, *mon ami,* because she does not exist! 'There's no sech person,' as your so great Shakespeare says."

"It was Dickens," I murmured, unable to suppress a smile. "But what do you mean, Poirot?"

"I mean that Zoe Havering was an actress before her marriage, that you and Japp only saw the housekeeper in a dark hall, a dim middle-aged figure in black with a faint subdued voice, and finally that neither you nor Japp, nor the local police whom the housekeeper fetched, ever saw Mrs. Middleton and her mistress at one and the same time. It was child's play for that clever and daring woman. On the pretext of summoning her mistress, she runs upstairs, slips on a bright jumper and a hat with black curls attached which she jams down over the grey transformation. A few deft touches, and the make-up is removed, a slight dusting of rouge, and the brilliant Zoe

---

*Precisely (French)

Havering comes down with her clear ringing voice. Nobody looks particularly at the housekeeper. Why should they? There is nothing to connect her with the crime. She, too, has an alibi."

"But the revolver that was found at Ealing? Mrs. Havering could not have placed it there?"

"No, that was Roger Havering's job—but it was a mistake on their part. It put me on the right track. A man who has committed murder with a revolver which he found on the spot would fling it away at once, he would not carry it up to London with him. No, the motive was clear, the criminals wished to focus the interest of the police on a spot far removed from Derbyshire, they were anxious to get the police away as soon as possible from the vicinity of Hunter's Lodge. Of course the revolver found at Ealing was not the one with which Mr. Pace was shot. Roger Havering discharged one shot from it, brought it up to London, went straight to his club to establish his alibi, then went quickly out to Ealing by the District, a matter of about twenty minutes only, placed the parcel where it was found and so back to town. That charming creature, his wife, quietly shoots Mr. Pace after dinner—you remember he was shot from behind? Another significant point, that!—reloads the revolver and puts it back in its place, and then starts off with her desperate little comedy."

"It's incredible," I murmured, fascinated, "and yet——"

"And yet it is true. *Bien sûr,** my friend, it is true. But to bring that precious pair to justice, that is another matter. Well, Japp must do what he can—I have written him fully—but I very much fear, Hastings, that we shall be obliged to leave them to Fate, or *le bon Dieu,*† whichever you prefer."

"The wicked flourish like a green bay tree," I reminded him.

"But at a price, Hastings, always at a price, *croyez-moi!*"‡

Poirot's forebodings were confirmed. Japp, though convinced of the truth of his theory, was unable to get together the necessary evidence to ensure a conviction.

Mr. Pace's huge fortune passed into the hands of his murderers. Nevertheless, Nemesis did overtake them, and when I read in the paper that the Hon. Roger and Mrs. Havering were amongst those killed in the crashing of the Air Mail to Paris I knew that Justice was satisfied.

ACTIVITIES

1) Why did Poirot wire Captain Hastings for "... a description of housekeeper and what clothes she wore this morning same of Mrs. Havering ...?" Keeping the final solution in mind, explain why he later wired "Advise Japp to arrest housekeeper before it is too late."

---

*Surely (French)
†The good God (French)
‡Believe me! (French)

2) An eminent scholar of detective literature has labeled Captain Hastings ". . . easily the stupidest of all modern-Watsons."[4] From your first impression of Hastings, would you agree?

3) This story is an example of a classic "armchair detective" plot, in which the sleuth never visits the scene of the crime, eventually solving the case "long distance," so to speak. (Those of you who read "The Mystery of Marie Rogêt" will remember Dupin as the first armchair detective.)

Actually the armchair detective plot has been labeled a locked room story in reverse. Can you explain such a description? (Use Ms. Christie's story for reference.)

RESEARCH ACTIVITIES

1) Bring the controversy that raged over Agatha Christie's *The Murder of Roger Ackroyd* into your own classroom. This can be done by organizing a panel composed of the class's best literary critics, who will, of course, have to read the work. You will discover that some will want to defend the book, others attack it.

Enjoy the debate that will follow but do not expect to do what many others could not—that is, settle the question for all time.

2) Many of Agatha Christie's stories have been filmed. One of the best of these was a colorful 1975 production of *Murder on the Orient Express* in which Albert Finney gave a brilliant performance as M. Hercule Poirot.

You may be able to see this film at movie theaters or on television. If you do, write a review of it in which you compare the rendering of detective fiction on film with what is done in literature. These reviews could instigate a lively discussion of the merits and demerits of the two media.

Dorothy L. Sayers—and Lord Peter Wimsey

The second great female name in detective literature was Dorothy L. Sayers, also of England. One of her novels, *The Nine Tailors,* was labeled by Critic Howard Haycraft as "one of the truly great detective stories of all time."[5] Whether one agrees with Haycraft's judgement or not, one cannot deny that this author's work came close to approaching the standards usually prescribed for "serious" literature.

Born in 1893, Miss Sayers grew up in Britain's East-Anglican fen country. Her father, a clergyman-schoolmaster, sent her to Somerville College, Oxford, where she graduated with high honors in the field of medieval literature. She was one of the first women ever to receive a degree from that ancient and prestigious European university.

Her first job was with a London advertising agency that paid her a very low salary. Anxious to be financially independent, she turned to writing. Because of her frugal economic situation, she found herself admiring those with affluence and position like the members of the British aristocracy, and she filled her early stories with characters like them. Thus it was that when the time came for her to fashion an interesting protagonist-sleuth, she found herself thinking in terms of an English nobleman: Lord Peter Wimsey.

It was a risky choice. Some readers accused her of snobbishness.[6] But Lord Peter turned out to be as democratic as any of his plebeian predecessors. In point of fact, he evolved into a rebel who constantly criticized his family and class and later married a commoner.

Eventually, a whole series, short stories as well as novels, appeared about Lord Peter through which readers became familiar with the entire Wimsey clan as well as two "Watsons": Bunter, a valet, and Parker, a police inspector. By the time Dorothy Sayers stopped writing the Lord Peter stories—a span of thirty-three years—she had presented the public with perhaps the richest characterization of a fictional sleuth that had ever appeared.

Before she died—in the year 1957—Dorothy L. Sayers, like Ellery Queen, had also earned for herself a reputation as a scholar in the field of detective literature. She published several anthologies of other authors' works and wrote many penetrating critical essays about the genre. She also delved into other areas of literature, including religious studies.[7]

And now—on to Lord Peter . . .

The Adventurous Exploit of the Cave of Ali Baba

In the front room of a grim and narrow house in Lambeth a man sat eating kippers and glancing through the *Morning Post*. He was smallish and spare, with brown hair rather too regularly waved and a strong, brown beard, cut to a point. His double-breasted suit of navy-blue and his socks, tie, and handkerchief, all scrupulously matched, were a trifle more point-device than the best taste approves, and his boots were slightly too bright a brown. He did not look a gentleman, not even a gentleman's gentleman, yet there was something about his appearance which suggested that he was accustomed to the manner of life in good families. The breakfast-table, which he had set with his own hands, was arrayed with the attention to detail which is exacted of good-class servants. His action, as he walked over to a little side-table and carved himself a plate of ham, was the action of a superior butler; yet he was not old enough to be a retired butler; a footman, perhaps, who had come into a legacy.

He finished the ham with good appetite, and, as he sipped his coffee, read through attentively a paragraph which he had already noticed and put aside for consideration.

"LORD PETER WIMSEY'S WILL
BEQUEST TO VALET
£10,000 TO CHARITIES

"The will of Lord Peter Wimsey, who was killed last December while shooting big game in Tanganyika, was proved yesterday at £500,000. A sum of £10,000 was left to various charities, including [here followed a list of bequests]. To his valet, Mervyn Bunter, was left an annuity of £500 and the lease of the testator's flat in Piccadilly. [Then followed a number of personal bequests.] The remainder of the estate, including the valuable collection of books and pictures at 110a Piccadilly, was left to the testator's mother, the Dowager Duchess of Denver.

"Lord Peter Wimsey was thirty-seven at the time of his death. He was the younger brother of the present Duke of Denver, who is the wealthiest peer in the United Kingdom. Lord Peter was distinguished as a criminologist and took an active part in the solution of several famous mysteries. He was a well-known book collector and man-about-town."

The man gave a sigh of relief.

"No doubt about that," he said aloud. "People don't give their money away if they're going to come back again. The blighter's dead and buried right enough. I'm free."

He finished his coffee, cleared the table, and washed up the crockery, took his bowler hat from the hall-stand, and went out.

A bus took him to Bermondsey. He alighted, and plunged into a network of gloomy streets, arriving after a quarter of an hour's walk at a seedy-looking public-house in a low quarter. He entered and called for a double whisky.

The house had only just opened, but a number of customers, who had apparently been waiting on the doorstep for this desirable event, were already clustered about the bar. The man who might have been a footman reached for his glass, and in doing so jostled the elbow of a flash person in a check suit and regrettable tie.

"Here!" expostulated the flash person, "What d'yer mean by it? We don't want your sort here. Get out!"

He emphasised his remarks with a few highly coloured words, and a violent push in the chest.

"Bar's free to everybody, isn't it?" said the other, returning the shove with interest.

"Now then!" said the barmaid, "none o' that. The gentleman didn't do it intentional, Mr. Jukes."

"Didn't he?" said Mr. Jukes. "Well, I *did.*"

"And you ought to be ashamed of yourself," retorted the young lady, with a toss of the head. "I'll have no quarrelling in my bar—not this time in the morning."

"It was quite an accident," said the man from Lambeth. "I'm not one to make a disturbance, having always been used to the best houses. But if any gentleman *wants* to make trouble—"

"All right, all right," said Mr. Jukes, more pacifically. "I'm not keen to give you a new face. Not but what any alteration wouldn't be for the better. Mind your manners another time, that's all. What'll you have?"

"No, no," protested the other, "this one must be on me. Sorry I pushed you. I didn't mean it. But I didn't like to be taken up so short."

"Say no more about it," said Mr. Jukes generously. "I'm standing this. Another double whisky, miss, and one of the usual. Come over here where there isn't so much of a crowd, or you'll be getting yourself into trouble again."

He led the way to a small table in the corner of the room.

"That's all right," said Mr. Jukes. "Very nicely done. I don't think there's any danger here, but you can't be too careful. Now, what about it, Rogers. Have you made up your mind to come in with us?

"Yes," said Rogers, with a glance over his shoulder, "yes, I have. That is, mind you, if everything seems all right. I'm not looking for trouble, and I don't want to get let in for any dangerous games. I don't mind giving you information, but it's understood as I take no active part in whatever goes on. Is that straight?"

"You wouldn't be allowed to take an active part if you wanted to," said Mr. Jukes. "Why, you poor fish, Number One wouldn't have anybody but experts on his jobs. All you have to do is let us know where the stuff is and how to get it. The Society does the rest. It's some organisation, I can tell you. You won't even know who's doing it, or how it's done. You won't know anybody, and nobody will know you—except Number One, of course. He knows everybody."

"And you," said Rogers.

"And me, of course. But I shall be transferred to another district. We shan't meet again after to-day, except at the general meetings, and then we shall all be masked."

"Go on!" said Rogers incredulously.

"Fact. You'll be taken to Number One—he'll see you, but you won't see him. Then, if he thinks you're any good, you'll be put on the roll, and after that you'll be told where to make your reports to. There is a divisional meeting called once a fortnight, and every three months there's a general meeting and share-out. Each member is called up by number and has his whack handed over to him. That's all."

"Well, but suppose two members are put on the same job together?"

"If it's a daylight job, they'll be so disguised their mothers wouldn't know 'em. But it's mostly night work."

"I see. But, look here—what's to prevent somebody following me home and giving me away to the police?"

"Nothing, of course. Only I wouldn't advise him to try it, that's all. The

last man who had that bright idea was fished out of the river down Rother-
hithe way, before he had time to get his precious report in. Number One
knows everybody, you see."

"Oh!—and who is this Number One?"

"There's lots of people would give a good bit to know that."

"Does nobody know?"

"Nobody. He's a fair marvel, is Number One. He's a gentleman, I can tell
you that, and a pretty high-up one, from his ways. *And* he's got eyes all
round his head. *And* he's got an arm as long as from here to Australia. *But*
nobody knows anything about him, unless it's Number Two, and I'm not
even sure about her."

"There are women in it, then?"

"You can bet your boots there are. You can't do a job without 'em
nowadays. But that needn't worry you. The women are safe enough. They
don't want to come to a sticky end, no more than you and me."

"But, look here, Jukes—how about the money? It's a big risk to take. Is
it worth it?"

"Worth it?" Jukes leant across the little marble-topped table and whispered.

"Coo!" gasped Rogers. "And how much of that would I get, now?"

"You'd share and share alike with the rest, whether you'd been in that
particular job or not. There's fifty members, and you'd get one-fiftieth, same
as Number One and same as me."

"Really? No kidding?"

"See that wet, see that dry!" Jukes laughed. "Say, can you beat it? There's
never been anything like it. It's the biggest thing ever been known. He's a
great man, is Number One."

"And do you pull off many jobs?"

"Many? Listen. You remember the Carruthers necklace, and the Gorles-
ton Bank robbery? And the Faversham burglary? And the big Rubens that
disappeared from the National Gallery? And the Frensham pearls? All done
by the Society. And never one of them cleared up."

Rogers licked his lips.

"But now, look here," he said cautiously. "Supposing I was a spy, as you
might say, and supposing I was to go straight off and tell the police about
what you've been saying?"

"Ah" said Jukes, "suppose you did, eh? Well, supposing something nasty
didn't happen to you on the way there—which I wouldn't answer for,
mind—"

"Do you mean to say you've got me watched?"

"You can bet your sweet life we have. Yes. Well, *supposing* nothing
happened on the way there, and you was to bring the slops to this pub,
looking for yours truly—"

"Yes?"

"You wouldn't find me, that's all. I should have gone to Number Five."

"Who's Number Five?"

"Ah! I don't know. But he's the man that makes you a new face while you wait. Plastic surgery, they call it. And new finger-prints. New every-thing. We go in for up-to-date methods in our show."

Rogers whistled.

"Well, how about it?" asked Jukes, eyeing his acquaintance over the rim of his tumbler.

"Look here—you've told me a lot of things. Shall I be safe if I say 'no'?"

"Oh yes—if you behave yourself and don't make trouble for us."

"H'm, I see. And if I say 'yes'?"

"Then you'll be a rich man in less than no time, with money in your pocket to live like a gentleman. And nothing to do for it, except to tell us what you know about the houses you've been to when you were in service. It's money for jam if you act straight by the Society."

Rogers was silent, thinking it over.

"I'll do it!" he said at last.

"Good for you. Miss! The same again, please. Here's to it, Rogers! I knew you were one of the right sort the minute I set eyes on you. Here's to money for jam, and take care of Number One! Talking of Number One, you'd better come round and see him to-night. No time like the present."

"Right you are. Where'll I come to? Here?"

"Nix. No more of this little pub for us. It's a pity, because it's nice and comfortable, but it can't be helped. Now, what you've got to do is this. At ten o'clock to-night exactly, you walk north across Lambeth Bridge" (Rogers winced at this intimation that his abode was known), "and you'll see a yellow taxi standing there, with the driver doing something to his engine. You'll say to him, 'Is your bus fit to go?' and he'll say, 'Depends where you want to go to.' And you'll say, 'Take me to Number One, London.' There's a shop called that, by the way, but he won't take you there. You won't know where he *is* taking you, because the taxi-windows will be covered up, but you mustn't mind that. It's the rule for the first visit. Afterwards, when you're regularly one of us, you'll be told the name of the place. And when you get there, do as you're told and speak the truth, because, if you don't, Number One will deal with you. See?"

"I see."

"Are you game? You're not afraid?"

"Of course I'm not afraid."

"Good man! Well, we'd better be moving now. And I'll say good-bye, because we shan't see each other again. Good-bye—and good luck!"

"Good-bye."

They passed through the swing-doors, and out into the mean and dirty street.

The two years subsequent to the enrolment of the ex-footman Rogers in a crook society were marked by a number of startling and successful raids on the houses of distinguished people. There was the theft of the great diamond tiara from the Dowager Duchess of Denver; the burglary at the flat formerly occupied by the late Lord Peter Wimsey, resulting in the disappearance of £7,000 worth of silver and gold plate; the burglary at the country mansion of Theodore Winthrop, the millionaire—which, incidentally, exposed that thriving gentleman as a confirmed Society blackmailer and caused a reverberating scandal in Mayfair; and the snatching of the famous eight-string necklace of pearls from the neck of the Marchioness of Dinglewood during the singing of the Jewel Song in *Faust* at Covent Garden. It is true that the pearls turned out to be imitation, the original string having been pawned by the noble lady under circumstances highly painful to the Marquis, but the coup was nevertheless a sensational one.

On a Saturday afternoon in January, Rogers was sitting in his room in Lambeth, when a slight noise at the front door caught his ear. He sprang up almost before it had ceased, dashed through the small hallway, and flung the door open. The street was deserted. Nevertheless, as he turned back to the sitting-room, he saw an envelope lying on the hat-stand. It was addressed briefly to "Number Twenty-one." Accustomed by this time to the somewhat dramatic methods used by the Society to deliver its correspondence, he merely shrugged his shoulders, and opened the note.

It was written in cipher, and, when transcribed, ran thus:

> "Number Twenty-one,—An Extraordinary General Meeting will be held tonight at the house of Number One at 11:30. You will be absent at your peril. The word is FINALITY."

Rogers stood for a little time considering this. Then he made his way to a room at the back of the house, in which there was a tall safe, built into the wall. He manipulated the combination and walked into the safe, which ran back for some distance, forming, indeed, a small strongroom. He pulled out a drawer marked "Correspondence," and added the paper he had just received to the contents.

After a few moments he emerged, re-set the lock to a new combination, and returned to the sitting-room.

"Finality," he said. "Yes—I think so." He stretched out his hand to the telephone—then appeared to alter his mind.

He went upstairs to an attic, and thence climbed into a loft close under the roof. Crawling among the rafters, he made his way into the farthest corner: then carefully pressed a knot on the timber-work. A concealed trap-door swung open. He crept through it, and found himself in the corresponding loft of the next house. A soft cooing noise greeted him as he entered. Under the skylight stood three cages, each containing a carrier pigeon.

He glanced cautiously out of the skylight, which looked out upon a high blank wall at the back of some factory or other. There was nobody in the dim little courtyard, and no window within sight. He drew his head in again, and, taking a small fragment of thin paper from his pocketbook, wrote a few letters and numbers upon it. Going to the nearest cage, he took out the pigeon and attached the message to its wing. Then he carefully set the bird on the window-ledge. It hesitated a moment, shifted its pink feet a few times, lifted its wings, and was gone. He saw it tower up into the already darkening sky over the factory roof and vanish into the distance.

He glanced at his watch and returned downstairs. An hour later he released the second pigeon, and in another hour the third. Then he sat down to wait.

At half-past nine he went up to the attic again. It was dark, but a few frosty stars were shining, and a cold air blew through the open window. Something pale gleamed faintly on the floor. He picked it up—it was warm and feathery. The answer had come.

He ruffled the soft plumes and found the paper. Before reading it, he fed the pigeon and put it into one of the cages. As he was about to fasten the door, he checked himself.

"If anything happens to me," he said, "there's no need for you to starve to death, my child."

He pushed the window a little wider open and went downstairs again. The paper in his hand bore only the two letters, "O.K." It seemed to have been written hurriedly, for there was a long smear of ink in the upper left-hand corner. He noted this with a smile, put the paper in the fire, and, going out into the kitchen, prepared and ate a hearty meal of eggs and corned beef from a new tin. He ate it without bread, though there was a loaf on the shelf near at hand, and washed it down with water from the tap, which he let run for some time before venturing to drink it. Even then he carefully wiped the tap, both inside and outside, before drinking.

When he had finished, he took a revolver from a locked drawer, inspecting the mechanism with attention to see that it was in working order, and loaded it with new cartridges from an unbroken packet. Then he sat down to wait again.

At a quarter before eleven, he rose and went out into the street. He walked briskly, keeping well away from the wall, till he came out into a well-lighted thoroughfare. Here he took a bus, securing the corner seat next the conductor, from which he could see everybody who got on and off. A succession of buses eventually brought him to a respectable residential quarter of Hampstead. Here he alighted and, still keeping well away from the walls, made his way up to the Heath.

The night was moonless, but not altogether black, and, as he crossed a deserted part of the Heath, he observed one or two other dark forms closing in upon him from various directions. He paused in the shelter of a large tree, and adjusted to his face a black velvet mask, which covered him from brow to chin. At its base the number 21 was clearly embroidered in white thread.

At length a slight dip in the ground disclosed one of those agreeable villas which stand, somewhat isolated, among the rural surroundings of the Heath. One of the windows was lighted. As he made his way to the door, other dark figures, masked like himself, pressed forward and surrounded him. He counted six of them.

The foremost man knocked on the door of the solitary house. After a moment, it was opened slightly. The man advanced his head to the opening; there was a murmur, and the door opened wide. The man stepped in, and the door was shut.

When three of the men had entered, Rogers found himself to be the next in turn. He knocked, three times loudly, then twice faintly. The door opened to the extent of two or three inches, and an ear was presented to the chink. Rogers whispered "Finality." The ear was withdrawn, the door opened, and he passed in.

Without any further word of greeting, Number Twenty-one passed into a small room on the left, which was furnished like an office, with a desk, a safe, and a couple of chairs. At the desk sat a massive man in evening dress, with a ledger before him. The new arrival shut the door carefully after him; it clicked to, on a spring lock. Advancing to the desk, he announced, "Number Twenty-one, sir," and stood respectfully waiting. The big man looked up, showing the number 1 startlingly white on his velvet mask. His eyes, of a curious hard blue, scanned Rogers attentively. At a sign from him, Rogers removed his mask. Having verified his identity with care, the President said, "Very well, Number Twenty-one," and made an entry in the ledger. The voice was hard and metallic, like his eyes. The close scrutiny from behind the immovable black mask seemed to make Rogers uneasy; he shifted his feet, and his eyes fell. Number One made a sign of dismissal, and Rogers, with a faint sigh as though of relief, replaced his mask and left the room. As he came out, the next comer passed in in his place.

The room in which the Society met was a large one, made by knocking the two largest of the first-floor rooms into one. It was furnished in the standardised taste of twentieth-century suburbia and brilliantly lighted. A gramophone in one corner blared out a jazz tune, to which about ten couples of masked men and women were dancing, some in evening dress and others in tweeds and jumpers.

In one corner of the room was an American bar. Rogers went up and asked the masked man in charge for a double whisky. He consumed it slowly, leaning on the bar. The room filled. Presently somebody moved across to the gramophone and stopped it. He looked round. Number One had appeared on the threshold. A tall woman in black stood beside him. The mask, embroidered with a white 2, covered hair and face completely; only her fine bearing and her white arms and bosom and the dark eyes shining through the eye-slits proclaimed her a woman of power and physical attraction.

"Ladies and gentlemen." Number One was standing at the upper end of the room. The woman sat beside him; her eyes were cast down and betrayed nothing, but her hands were clenched on the arms of the chair and her whole figure seemed tensely aware.

"Ladies and gentlemen. Our numbers are two short to-night." The masks moved; eyes were turned, seeking and counting. "I need not inform you of the disastrous failure of our plan for securing the plans of the Court-Windlesham helicopter. Our courageous and devoted comrades, Number Fifteen and Number Forty-eight, were betrayed and taken by the police."

An uneasy murmur arose among the company.

"It may have occurred to some of you that even the well-known steadfastness of these comrades might give way under examination. There is no cause for alarm. The usual orders have been issued, and I have this evening received the report that their tongues have been effectually silenced. You will, I am sure, be glad to know that these two brave men have been spared the ordeal of so great a temptation to dishonour, and that they will not be called upon to face a public trial and the rigours of a long imprisonment."

A hiss of intaken breath moved across the assembled members like the wind over a barley-field.

"Their dependants will be discreetly compensated in the usual manner. I called upon Numbers Twelve and Thirty-four to undertake this agreeable task. They will attend me in my office for their instructions after the meeting. Will the Numbers I have named kindly signify that they are able and willing to perform this duty?"

Two hands were raised in salute. The President continued, looking at his watch:

"Ladies and gentlemen, please take your partners for the next dance."

The gramophone struck up again. Rogers turned to a girl near him in a red dress. She nodded, and they slipped into the movement of a fox-trot. The couples gyrated solemnly and in silence. Their shadows were flung against the blinds as they turned and stepped to and fro.

"What has happened?" breathed the girl in a whisper, scarcely moving her lips. "I'm frightened, aren't you? I feel as if something awful was going to happen."

"It does take one a bit short, the President's way of doing things," agreed Rogers, "but it's safer like that."

"Those poor men—"

A dancer, turning and following on their heels, touched Rogers on the shoulder.

"No talking, please," he said. His eyes gleamed sternly; he twirled his partner into the middle of the crowd and was gone. The girl shuddered.

The gramophone stopped. There was a burst of clapping. The dancers again clustered before the President's seat.

"Ladies and gentlemen. You may wonder why this extraordinary meeting has been called. The reason is a serious one. The failure of our recent attempt was no accident. The police were not on the premises that night by chance. We have a traitor among us."

Partners who had been standing close together fell distrustfully apart. Each member seemed to shrink, as a snail shrinks from the touch of a finger.

"You will remember the disappointing outcome of the Dinglewood affair," went on the President, in his harsh voice. "You may recall other smaller matters which have not turned out satisfactorily. All these troubles have been traced to their origin. I am happy to say that our minds can now be easy. The offender has been discovered and will be removed. There will be no more mistakes. The misguided member who introduced the traitor to our Society will be placed in a position where his lack of caution will have no further ill-effects. There is no cause for alarm."

Every eye roved about the company, searching for the traitor and his unfortunate sponsor. Somewhere beneath the black masks a face must have turned white; somewhere under the stifling velvet there must have been a brow sweating, not with the heat of the dance. But the masks hid everything.

"Ladies and gentlemen, please take your partners for the next dance."

The gramophone struck into an old and half-forgotten tune: "There ain't nobody loves me." The girl in red was claimed by a tall mask in evening dress. A hand laid on Rogers's arm made him start. A small, plump woman in a green jumper slipped a cold hand into his. The dance went on.

When it stopped, amid the usual applause, everyone stood, detached, stiffened in expectation. The President's voice was raised again.

"Ladies and gentlemen, please behave naturally. This is a dance, not a public meeting."

Rogers led his partner to a chair and fetched her an ice. As he stooped over her, he noticed the hurried rise and fall of her bosom.

"Ladies and gentlemen." The endless interval was over. "You will no doubt wish to be immediately relieved from suspense. I will name the persons involved. Number Thirty-seven!"

A man sprang up with a fearful, strangled cry.

"Silence!"

The wretch choked and gasped.

"I never—I swear I never—I'm innocent."

"Silence. You have failed in discretion. You will be dealt with. If you have anything to say in defence of your folly, I will hear it later. Sit down."

Number Thirty-seven sank down upon a chair. He pushed his handkerchief under the mask to wipe his face. Two tall men closed in upon him. The rest fell back, feeling the recoil of humanity from one stricken by mortal disease.

The gramophone struck up.

"Ladies and gentlemen, I will now name the traitor. Number Twenty-one, stand forward."

Rogers stepped forward. The concentrated fear and loathing of forty-eight pairs of eyes burned upon him. The miserable Jukes set up a fresh wail.

"Oh, my God! Oh, my God!"

"Silence! Number Twenty-one, take off your mask." The traitor pulled the thick covering from his face. The intense hatred of the eyes devoured him.

"Number Thirty-seven, this man was introduced here by you, under the name of Joseph Rogers, formerly second footman in the service of the Duke of Denver, dismissed for pilfering. Did you take steps to verify that statement?"

"I did—I did! As God's my witness, it was all straight. I had him identified by two of the servants. I made enquiries. The tale was straight—I'll swear it was."

The President consulted a paper before him, then he looked at his watch again.

"Ladies and gentlemen, please take your partners ..."

Number Twenty-one, his arms twisted behind him and bound, and his wrists handcuffed, stood motionless, while the dance of doom circled about him. The clapping, as it ended, sounded like the clapping of the men and women who sat, thirsty-lipped beneath the guillotine.

"Number Twenty-one, your name has been given as Joseph Rogers, footman, dismissed for theft. Is that your real name?"

"No."

"What is your name?"

"Peter Death Bredon Wimsey."

"We thought you were dead."

"Naturally. You were intended to think so."

"What has become of the genuine Joseph Rogers?"

"He died abroad. I took his place. I may say that no real blame attaches to your people for not having realised who I was. I not only took Rogers's place; I *was* Rogers. Even when I was alone, I walked like Rogers, I sat like Rogers, I read Rogers's books, and wore Rogers's clothes. In the end, I almost thought Rogers's thoughts. The only way to keep up a successful impersonation is never to relax."

"I see. The robbery of your own flat was arranged?"

"Obviously."

"The robbery of the Dowager Duchess, your mother, was connived at by you?"

"It was. It was a very ugly tiara—no real loss to anybody with decent taste. May I smoke, by the way?"

"You may not. Ladies and gentlemen . . ."

The dance was like the mechanical jigging of puppets. Limbs jerked, feet faltered. The prisoner watched with an air of critical detachment.

"Numbers Fifteen, Twenty-two, and Forty-nine. You have watched the prisoner. Has he made any attempts to communicate with anybody?"

"None." Number Twenty-two was the spokesman. "His letters and parcels have been opened, his telephone tapped, and his movements followed. His water-pipes have been under observation for Morse signals."

"You are sure of what you say?"

"Absolutely."

"Prisoner, have you been alone in this adventure? Speak the truth, or things will be made somewhat more unpleasant for you than they might otherwise be."

"I have been alone. I have taken no unnecessary risks."

"It may be so. It will, however, be as well that steps should be taken to silence the man at Scotland Yard—what is his name?—Parker. Also the prisoner's manservant, Mervyn Bunter, and possibly also his mother and sister. The brother is a stupid oaf, and not, I think, likely to have been taken into the prisoner's confidence. A precautionary watch will, I think, meet the necessities of his case."

The prisoner appeared, for the first time, to be moved.

"Sir, I assure you that my mother and sister know nothing which could possibly bring danger on the Society."

"You should have thought of their situation earlier. Ladies and gentlemen, please take——"

"No—no!" Flesh and blood could endure the mockery no longer. "No! Finish with him. Get it over. Break up the meeting. It's dangerous. The police——"

"Silence!"

The President glanced round at the crowd. It had a dangerous look about it. He gave way.

"Very well. Take the prisoner away and silence him. He will receive Number 4 treatment. And be sure you explain it to him carefully first."

"Ah!"

The eyes expressed a wolfish satisfaction. Strong hands gripped Wimsey's arms.

"One moment—for God's sake, let me die decently."

"You should have thought this over earlier. Take him away. Ladies and gentlemen, be satisfied—he will not die quickly."

"Stop! Wait!" cried Wimsey desperately. "I have something to say. I don't ask for life—only for a quick death. I—I have something to sell."

"To sell?"

"Yes."

"We make no bargains with traitors."

"No—but listen! Do you think I have not thought of this? I am not so mad. I have left a letter."

"Ah! now it is coming. A letter. To whom?"

"To the police. If I do not return to-morrow——"

"Well?"

"The letter will be opened."

"Sir," broke in Number Fifteen. "This is bluff. The prisoner has not sent any letter. He has been strictly watched for many months."

"Ah! but listen. I left the letter before I came to Lambeth."

"Then it can contain no information of value."

"Oh, but it does."

"What?"

"The combination of my safe."

"Indeed? Has this man's safe been searched?"

"Yes, sir."

"What did it contain?"

"No information of importance, sir. An outline of our organisation—the name of this house—nothing that cannot be altered and covered before morning."

Wimsey smiled.

"Did you investigate the inner compartment of the safe?"

There was a pause.

"You hear what he says," snapped the President sharply. "Did you find this inner compartment?"

"There was no inner compartment, sir. He is trying to bluff."

"I hate to contradict you," said Wimsey, with an effort at his ordinary pleasant tone, "but I really think you must have overlooked the inner compartment."

"Well," said the President, "and what do you say is in this inner compartment, if it does exist?"

"The names of every member of this Society, with their addresses, photographs, and finger-prints."

"What?"

The eyes round him now were ugly with fear. Wimsey kept his face steadily turned towards the President.

"How do you say you have contrived to get this information?"

"Well, I have been doing a little detective work on my own, you know."

"But you have been watched."

"True. The finger-prints of my watchers adorn the first page of the collection."

"This statement can be proved?"

"Certainly. I will prove it. The name of Number Fifty, for example——"

A fierce muttering arose. The President silenced it with a gesture.

"If you mention names here, you will certainly have no hope of mercy. There is a fifth treatment—kept specially for people who mention names. Bring the prisoner to my office. Keep the dance going."

The President took an automatic from his hip-pocket and faced his tightly fettered prisoner across the desk.

"Now speak!" he said.

"I should put that thing away, if I were you," said Wimsey contemptuously. "It would be a much pleasanter form of death than treatment Number 5, and I might be tempted to ask for it."

"Ingenious," said the President, "but a little too ingenious. Now, be quick; tell me what you know."

"Will you spare me if I tell you?"

"I make no promises. Be quick."

Wimsey shrugged his bound and aching shoulders.

"Certainly. I will tell you what I know. Stop me when you have heard enough."

He leaned forward and spoke low. Overhead the noise of the gramophone and the shuffling of feet bore witness that the dance was going on. Stray passers-by crossing the Heath noted that the people in the lonely house were making a night of it again.

"Well," said Wimsey, "am I to go on?"

From beneath the mask the President's voice sounded as though he were grimly smiling.

"My lord," he said, "your story fills me with regret that you are not, in fact, a member of our Society. Wit, courage, and industry are valuable to an association like ours. I fear I cannot persuade you? No—I supposed not."

He touched a bell on his desk.

"Ask the members kindly to proceed to the supper-room," he said to the mask who entered.

The "supper-room" was on the ground-floor, shuttered and curtained. Down its centre ran a long, bare table, with chairs set about it.

"A Barmecide feast,* I see," said Wimsey pleasantly. It was the first time he had seen this room. At the far end, a trap-door in the floor gaped ominously.

The President took the head of the table.

"Ladies and gentlemen," he began, as usual—and the foolish courtesy had never sounded so sinister—"I will not conceal from you the seriousness of the situation. The prisoner has recited to me more than twenty names and addresses which were thought to be unknown, except to their owners and to me. There has been great carelessness"—his voice rang harshly—"which will have to be looked into. Finger-prints have been obtained—he has shown me the photographs of some of them. How our investigators came to overlook the inner door of this safe is a matter which calls for enquiry."

"Don't blame them," put in Wimsey. "It was meant to be overlooked, you know. I made it like that on purpose."

The President went on, without seeming to notice the interruption.

"The prisoner informs me that the book with the names and addresses is to be found in this inner compartment, together with certain letters and papers stolen from the houses of members, and numerous objects bearing authentic finger-prints. I believe him to be telling the truth. He offers the combination of the safe in exchange for a quick death. I think the offer should be accepted. What is your opinion, ladies and gentlemen?"

"The combination is known already," said Number Twenty-two.

"Imbecile! This man has told us, and has proved to me, that he is Lord Peter Wimsey. Do you think he will have forgotten to alter the combination? And then there is the secret of the inner door. If he disappears to-night and the police enter his house——"

"I say," said a woman's rich voice, "that the promise should be given and the information used—and quickly. Time is getting short."

A murmur of agreement went round the table.

"You hear," said the President, addressing Wimsey. "The Society offers you the privilege of a quick death in return for the combination of the safe and the secret of the inner door."

"I have your word for it?"

"You have."

"Thank you. And my mother and sister?"

"If you in your turn will give us your word—you are a man of honour—that these women know nothing that could harm us, they shall be spared."

"Thank you, sir. You may rest assured, upon my honour, that they know nothing. I should not think of burdening any woman with such dangerous secrets—particularly those who are dear to me."

"Very well. It is agreed—yes?"

The murmur of assent was given, though with less readiness than before.

---

*In *The Arabian Nights*, a Barmecide feast was an imaginary banquet; a table was lavishly set to haunt a hungry man.

"Then I am willing to give you the information you want. The word of the combination is UNRELIABILITY."

"And the inner door?"

"In anticipation of the visit of the police, the inner door—which might have presented difficulties—is open."

"Good! You understand that if the police interfere with our messenger——"

"That would not help me, would it?"

"It is a risk," said the President thoughtfully, "but a risk which I think we must take. Carry the prisoner down to the cellar. He can amuse himself by contemplating apparatus Number 5. In the meantime, Numbers Twelve and Forty-six——"

"No, no!"

A sullen mutter of dissent arose and swelled threateningly.

"No," said a tall man with a voice like treacle. "No—why should any members be put in possession of this evidence? We have found one traitor among us to-night and more than one fool. How are we to know that Numbers Twelve and Forty-six are not fools and traitors also?"

The two men turned savagely upon the speaker, but a girl's voice struck into the discussion, high and agitated.

"Hear, hear! That's right, I say. How about us? We ain't going to have our names read by somebody we don't know nothing about. I've had enough of this. They might sell the 'ole lot of us to the narks."

"I agree," said another member. "Nobody ought to be trusted, nobody at all."

The President shrugged his shoulders.

"Then what, ladies and gentlemen, do you suggest?"

There was a pause. Then the same girl shrilled out again:

"I say Mr. President oughter go himself. He's the only one as knows all the names. It won't be no cop to him. Why should we take all the risk and trouble and him sit at home and collar the money? Let him go himself, that's what I say."

A long rustle of approbation went round the table.

"I second that motion," said a stout man who wore a bunch of gold seals at his fob. Wimsey smiled as he looked at the seals; it was that trifling vanity which had led him directly to the name and address of the stout man, and he felt a certain affection for the trinkets on that account.

The President looked round.

"It is the wish of the meeting, then, that I should go?" he said, in an ominous voice.

Forty-five hands were raised in approbation. Only the woman known as Number Two remained motionless and silent, her strong white hands clenched on the arm of the chair.

The President rolled his eyes slowly round the threatening ring till they rested upon her.

"Am I to take it that this vote is unanimous?" he enquired.

The woman raised her head.

"Don't go," she gasped faintly.

"You hear," said the President, in a faintly derisive tone, "This lady says, don't go."

"I submit that what Number Two says is neither here nor there," said the man with the treacly voice. "Our own ladies might not like us to be going, if they were in madam's privileged position." His voice was an insult.

"Hear, hear!" cried another man. "This is a democratic society, this is. We don't want no privileged classes."

"Very well," said the President. "You hear, Number Two. The feeling of the meeting is against you. Have you any reasons to put forward in favour of your opinion?"

"A hundred. The President is the head and soul of our Society. If anything should happen to him—where should we be? You"—she swept the company magnificently with her eyes—"you have all blundered. We have your carelessness to thank for all this. Do you think we should be safe for five minutes if the President were not here to repair your follies?"

"Something in that," said a man who had not hitherto spoken.

"Pardon my suggesting," said Wimsey maliciously, "that, as the lady appears to be in a position peculiarly favourable for the reception of the President's confidences, the contents of my modest volume will probably be no news to her. Why should not Number Two go herself?"

"Because I say she must not," said the President sternly, checking the quick reply that rose to his companion's lips. "If it is the will of the meeting, I will go. Give me the key of the house."

One of the men extracted it from Wimsey's jacket pocket and handed it over.

"Is the house watched?" he demanded of Wimsey.

"No."

"That is the truth?"

"It is the truth."

The President turned at the door.

"If I have not returned in two hours' time," he said, "act for the best to save yourselves, and do what you like with the prisoner. Number Two will give orders in my absence."

He left the room. Number Two rose from her seat with a gesture of command.

"Ladies and gentlemen. Supper is now considered over. Start the dancing again."

Down in the cellar the time passed slowly, in the contemplation of apparatus Number 5. The miserable Jukes, alternately wailing and raving, at length shrieked himself into exhaustion. The four members guarding the prisoners whispered together from time to time.

"An hour and a half since the President left," said one.

Wimsey glanced up. Then he returned to his examination of the room. There were many curious things in it, which he wanted to memorise.

Presently the trap-door was flung open. "Bring him up!" cried a voice. Wimsey rose immediately, and his face was rather pale.

The members of the gang were again seated round the table. Number Two occupied the President's chair, and her eyes fastened on Wimsey's face with a tigerish fury, but when she spoke it was with a self-control which roused his admiration.

"The President has been two hours gone," she said. "What has happened to him? Traitor twice over—what has happened to him?"

"How should I know?" said Wimsey. "Perhaps he has looked after Number One and gone while the going was good!"

She sprang up with a little cry of rage, and came close to him.

"Beast! liar!" she said, and struck him on the mouth. "You know he would never do that. He is faithful to his friends. What have you done with him? Speak—or I will make you speak. You two, there—bring the irons. He *shall* speak!"

"I can only form a guess, Madame," replied Wimsey, "and I shall not guess any the better for being stimulated with hot irons, like Pantaloon* at the circus. Calm yourself, and I will tell you what I think. I think—indeed, I greatly fear—that Monsieur le President in his hurry to examine the interesting exhibits in my safe may, quite inadvertently, no doubt, have let the door of the inner compartment close behind him. In which case——"

He raised his eyebrows, his shoulders being too sore for shrugging, and gazed at her with a limpid and innocent regret.

"What do you mean?"

Wimsey glanced round the circle.

"I think," he said, "I had better begin from the beginning by explaining to you the mechanism of my safe. It is rather a nice safe," he added plaintively. "I invented the idea myself—not the principle of its working, of course; that is a matter for scientists—but just the idea of the thing.

"The combination I gave you is perfectly correct as far as it goes. It is a three-alphabet thirteen-letter lock by Bunn & Fishett—a very good one of its kind. It opens the outer door, leading into the ordinary strong-room, where I keep my cash and my Froth Blower's cuff-links and all that. But there is an inner compartment with two doors, which open in a quite different manner. The outermost of these two inner doors is merely a thin steel skin, painted to look like the back of the safe and fitting closely, so as not to betray any join. It lies in the same plane as the wall of the room, you understand, so that if you were to measure the outside and the inside of the safe you would discover no discrepancy. It opens outwards with an ordinary key, and, as I truly assured the President, it was left open when I quitted my flat."

"Do you think," said the woman sneeringly, "that the President is so simple as to be caught in a so obvious trap? He will have wedged open that inner door undoubtedly."

---

*Comic but sad figure in old Italian comedy performances.

"Undoubtedly, madame. But the sole purpose of that outer inner door, if I may so express myself, is to appear to be the only inner door. But hidden behind the hinge of that door is another door, a sliding panel, set so closely in the thickness of the wall that you would hardly see it unless you knew it was there. This door was also left open. Our revered Number One had nothing to do but to walk straight through into the inner compartment of the safe, which, by the way, is built into the chimney of the old basement kitchen, which runs up the house at that point. I hope I make myself clear?"

"Yes, yes—get on. Make your story short."

Wimsey bowed, and, speaking with even greater deliberation than ever, resumed:

"Now, this interesting list of the Society's activities, which I have had the honour of compiling, is written in a very large book—bigger, even, than Monsieur le President's ledger which he uses downstairs. (I trust, by the way, madame, that you have borne in mind the necessity of putting that ledger in a safe place. Apart from the risk of investigation by some officious policeman, it would be inadvisable that any junior member of the Society should get hold of it. The feeling of the meeting would, I fancy, be opposed to such an occurrence.)"

"It is secure," she answered hastily. "*Mon dieu!* get on with your story."

"Thank you—you have relieved my mind. Very good. This big book lies on a steel shelf at the back of the inner compartment. Just a moment. I have not described this inner compartment to you. It is six feet high, three feet wide, and three feet deep. One can stand up in it quite comfortably, unless one is very tall. It suits me nicely—as you may see, I am not more than five feet eight and a half. The President has the advantage of me in height; he might be a little cramped, but there would be room for him to squat if he grew tired of standing. By the way, I don't know if you know it, but you have tied me up rather tightly."

"I would have you tied till your bones were locked together. Beat him, you! He is trying to gain time."

"If you beat me," said Wimsey, "I'm damned if I'll speak at all. Control yourself, madame; it does not do to move hastily when your king is in check."

"Get on!" she cried again, stamping with rage.

"Where was I? Ah! the inner compartment. As I say, it is a little snug—the more so that it is not ventilated in any way. Did I mention that the book lay on a steel shelf?"

"You did."

"Yes. The steel shelf is balanced on a very delicate concealed spring. When the weight of the book—a heavy one, as I said—is lifted, the shelf rises almost imperceptibly. In rising it makes an electrical contact. Imagine to yourself, madame; our revered President steps in—propping the false door open behind him—he sees the book—quickly he snatches it up. To make sure that it is the right one, he opens it—he studies the pages. He looks about for the other objects I have mentioned, which bear the marks of fingerprints. And silently, but very, very quickly—you can imagine it, can you not?—the secret panel, released by the rising of the shelf, leaps across like a panther behind him. Rather a trite simile, but apt, don't you think?"

"My God! oh, my God!" Her hand went up as though to tear the choking mask from her face. "You—you devil—devil! What is the word that opens the inner door? Quick! I will have it torn out of you—the word!"

"It is not a hard word to remember, madame—though it has been forgotten before now. Do you recollect, when you were a child, being told the tale of 'Ali Baba and the Forty Thieves'? When I had that door made, my mind reverted, with rather a pretty touch of sentimentality, in my opinion, to the happy hours of my childhood. The words that open the door are—'Open Sesame.' "

"Ah! How long can a man live in this devil's trap of yours?"

"Oh," said Wimsey cheerfully, "I should think he might hold out a few hours if he kept cool and didn't use up the available oxygen by shouting and hammering. If we went there at once, I dare say we should find him fairly all right."

"I shall go myself. Take this man and—do your worst with him. Don't finish him till I come back. I want to see him die!"

"One moment," said Wimsey, unmoved by this amiable wish. "I think you had better take me with you."

"Why—why?"

"Because, you see, I'm the only person who can open the door."

"But you have given me the word. Was that a lie?"

"No—the word's all right. But, you see, it's one of these new-style electric doors. In fact, it's really the very latest thing in doors. I'm rather proud of it. It opens to the words 'Open Sesame' all right—*but to my voice only.*"

"Your voice? I will choke your voice with my own hands. What do you mean—your voice only?"

"Just what I say. Don't clutch my throat like that, or you may alter my voice so that the door won't recognise it. That's better. It's apt to be rather pernickety about voices. It got stuck up for a week once, when I had a cold and could only implore it in a hoarse whisper. Even in the ordinary way, I sometimes have to try several times before I hit on the exact right intonation."

She turned and appealed to a short, thick-set man standing beside her. "Is this true? Is it possible?"

"Perfectly, ma'am, I'm afraid," said the man civilly. From his voice Wimsey took him to be a superior workman of some kind—probably an engineer.

"Is it an electrical device? Do you understand it?"

"Yes, ma'am. It will have a microphone arrangement somewhere, which converts the sound into a series of vibrations controlling an electric needle. When the needle has traced the correct pattern, the circuit is completed and the door opens. The same thing can be done by light vibrations equally easily."

"Couldn't you open it with tools?"

"In time, yes, ma'am. But only by smashing the mechanism, which is probably well protected."

"You may take that for granted," interjected Wimsey reassuringly.

She put her hands to her head.

"I'm afraid we're done in," said the engineer, with a kind of respect in his tone for a good job of work.

"No—wait! Somebody must know—the workmen who made this thing?"

"In Germany," said Wimsey briefly.

"Or—yes, yes, I have it—a gramophone. This—this—*he*—shall be made to say the word for us. Quick—how can it be done?"

"Not possible, ma'am. Where should we get the apparatus at half-past three on a Sunday morning? The poor gentleman would be dead long before——"

There was a silence, during which the sounds of the awakening day came through the shuttered windows. A motor-horn sounded distantly.

"I give in," she said. "We must let him go. Take the ropes off him. You will free him, won't you?" she went on, turning piteously to Wimsey. "Devil as you are, you are not such a devil as that! You will go straight back and save him!"

"Let him go, nothing!" broke in one of the men. "He doesn't go to preach to the police, my lady, don't you think it. The President's done in, that's all, and we'd all better make tracks while we can. It's all up, boys. Chuck this fellow down the cellar and fasten him in, so he can't make a row and wake the place up. I'm going to destroy the ledgers. You can see it done if you don't trust me. And you, Thirty, you know where the switch is. Give us a quarter of an hour to clear, and then you can blow the place to glory."

"No! You can't go—you can't leave him to die—your President—your leader—my—I won't let it happen. Set this devil free. Help me, one of you, with the ropes—"

"None of that, now," said the man who had spoken before. He caught her by the wrists, and she twisted, shrieking, in his arms, biting and struggling to get free.

"Think, think," said the man with the treacly voice. "It's getting on to morning. It'll be light in an hour or two. The police may be here any minute."

"The police!" She seemed to control herself by a violent effort. "Yes, yes, you are right. We must not imperil the safety of all for the sake of one man. *He* himself would not wish it. That is so. We will put this carrion in the cellar where it cannot harm us, and depart, every one to his own place, while there is time."

"And the other prisoner?"

"He? Poor fool—he can do no harm. He knows nothing. Let him go," she answered contemptuously.

In a few minutes' time Wimsey found himself bundled unceremoniously into the depths of the cellar. He was a little puzzled. That they should refuse to let him go, even at the price of Number One's life, he could understand. He had taken the risk with his eyes open. But that they should leave him as a witness against them seemed incredible.

The men who had taken him down strapped his ankles together and departed, switching the lights out as they went.

"Hi! Kamerad!" said Wimsey. "It's a bit lonely sitting here. You might leave the light on."

"It's all right, my friend," was the reply. "You will not be in the dark long. They have set the time-fuse."

The other man laughed with rich enjoyment, and they went out together. So that was it. He was to be blown up with the house. In that case the President would certainly be dead before he was extricated. This worried Wimsey; he would rather have been able to bring the big crook to justice. After all, Scotland Yard had been waiting six years to break up this gang.

He waited, straining his ears. It seemed to him that he heard footsteps over his head. The gang had all crept out by this time. . . .

There was certainly a creak. The trap-door had opened; he felt, rather than heard, somebody creeping into the cellar.

"Hush!" said a voice in his ear. Soft hands passed over his face, and went fumbling about his body. There came the cold touch of steel on his wrists. The ropes slackened and dropped off. A key clicked in the handcuffs. The strap about his ankles was unbuckled.

"Quick! quick! they have set the time-switch. The house is mined. Follow me as fast as you can. I stole back—I said I had left my jewellery. It was true. I left it on purpose. *He* must be saved—only you can do it. Make haste."

Wimsey, staggering with pain, as the blood rushed back into his bound and numbed arms, crawled after her into the room above. A moment, and she had flung back the shutters and thrown the window open.

"Now go! Release him! You promise?"

"I promise. And I warn you, madame, that this house is surrounded. When my safe-door closed it gave a signal which sent my servant to Scotland Yard. Your friends are all taken——"

"Ah! But you go—never mind me—quick! The time is almost up."

"Come away from this!"

He caught her by the arm, and they went running and stumbling across the little garden. An electric torch shone suddenly in the bushes.

"That you, Parker?" cried Wimsey. "Get your fellows away. Quick! the house is going up in a minute."

The garden seemed suddenly full of shouting, hurrying men. Wimsey, floundering in the darkness, was brought up violently against the wall. He made a leap at the coping, caught it, and hoisted himself up. His hands groped for the woman; he swung her up beside him. They jumped; everyone was jumping; the woman caught her foot and fell with a gasping cry. Wimsey tried to stop himself, tripped over a stone, and came down headlong. Then, with a flash and a roar, the night went up in fire.

Wimsey picked himself painfully out from among the débris of the garden wall. A faint moaning near him proclaimed that his companion was still alive. A lantern was turned suddenly upon them.

"Here you are!" said a cheerful voice. "Are you all right, old thing? Good lord! what a hairy monster!"

"All right," said Wimsey. "Only a bit winded. Is the lady safe? H'm—arm broken, apparently—otherwise sound. What's happened?"

"About half a dozen of 'em got blown up; the rest we've bagged." Wimsey became aware of a circle of dark forms in the wintry dawn. "Good Lord, what a day! What a come-back for a public character! You old stinker—to let us go on for two years thinking you were dead! I bought a bit of black for an arm-band. I did, really. Did anybody know, besides Bunter?"

"Only my mother and sister. I put it in a secret trust—you know, the thing you send to executors and people. We shall have an awful time with the lawyers, I'm afraid, proving I'm me. Hullo! Is that friend Sugg?"

"Yes, my lord," said Inspector Sugg, grinning and nearly weeping with excitement. "Damned glad to see your lordship again. Fine piece of work, your lordship. They're all wanting to shake hands with you, sir."

"Oh, Lord! I wish I could get washed and shaved first. Awfully glad to see you all again, after two years' exile in Lambeth. Been a good little show, hasn't it?"

"Is he safe?"

Wimsey started at the agonised cry.

"Good Lord!" he cried. "I forgot the gentleman in the safe. Here, fetch a car, quickly. I've got the great big top Moriarty of the whole bunch quietly asphyxiating at home. Here—hop in, and put the lady in too. I promised we'd get back and save him—though" (he finished the sentence in Parker's ear) "there may be murder charges too, and I wouldn't give much for his chance at the Old Bailey. Whack her up. He can't last much longer shut up there. He's the bloke you've been wanting, the man at the back of the Morrison case and the Hope-Wilmington case, and hundreds of others."

The cold morning had turned the streets grey when they drew up before the door of the house in Lambeth. Wimsey took the woman by the arm and helped her out. The mask was off now, and showed her face, haggard and desperate, and white with fear and pain.

"Russian, eh?" whispered Parker in Wimsey's ear.

"Something of the sort. Damn! the front door's blown shut, and the blighter's got the key with him in the safe. Hop through the window, will you?"

Parker bundled obligingly in, and in a few seconds threw open the door to them. The house seemed very still. Wimsey led the way to the back room, where the strong-room stood. The outer door and the second door stood propped open with chairs. The inner door faced them like a blank green wall.

"Only hope he hasn't upset the adjustment with thumping at it," muttered Wimsey. The anxious hand on his arm clutched feverishly. He pulled himself together, forcing his tone to one of cheerful commonplace.

"Come on, old thing," he said, addressing himself conversationally to the door. "Show us your paces. Open Sesame, confound you. Open Sesame!"

The green door slid suddenly away into the wall. The woman sprang forward and caught in her arms the humped and senseless thing that rolled out from the safe. Its clothes were torn to ribbons, and its battered hands dripped blood.

"It's all right," said Wimsey, "it's all right! He'll live—to stand his trial."

ACTIVITIES

1) Many readers will know Lord Peter Wimsey from Masterpiece Theatre on television. If, however, this is your first meeting with Lord Peter Wimsey, describe your initial impression of him. Is he resourceful? Loyal? Courageous? Does he possess a sense of humor? Is there anything about him that would tend to make you feel his creator was snobbish?

2) Like Father Brown, Lord Peter is a fine student of human behavior. From the text, can you pick out episodes in which he exhibits his psychological abilities?

3) Compare and contrast Dorothy Sayers' "The Adventurous Exploit of the Cave of Ali Baba" with Conan Doyle's "The Final Problem." Which is the better story? Who is the more formidable antagonist—Number One or Professor James Moriarty?

RESEARCH ACTIVITY

If you enjoyed the literate style and British setting of the Sayers' story, you might want to read other authors on your own—especially Margery Allingham, Ngaio Marsh (New Zealand born but living in England), and Josephine Tey. Their French counterpart is Georges Simenon, whose intellectual mysteries involving Inspector Maigret are highly acclaimed for their psychological insights. Compare and contrast the fictional sleuth-protagonist created by any one of these authors with Lord Peter and with Sherlock Holmes.

William Brittain—and Mr. Strang

William Brittain is a contemporary detective story writer.

You may be surprised to learn he is also a junior high school English teacher—and, if you are one of those who believe that teachers lead "boring" lives—wait till you read one of his stories.

As a matter of fact, the tremendous job of characterization that Brittain has done on his fictional sleuth should appeal to all of you. Mr. Strang, the hero of this author's famous detective series, is a science teacher at Aldershot High School who doubles as a detective and solves intriguing cases of misbehavior right within familiar school situations.

William Brittain is one of many writers who boast of their alumni status with *Ellery Queen's Mystery Magazine.* Brittain states: "I began (writing) in 1955 when I read a story in EQMM and thought I could do better. But it took ten years of trying before I made my first sale—to *Alfred Hitchcock's Mystery Magazine*. A year later came my second sale—this time to EQMM."[8]

Brittain pays great tribute to Frederic Dannay's influence upon his career. As stated before, Dannay and Lee (creators of Ellery Queen) turned out to be sensitive writing teachers as well as talented authors. Teacher Brittain "caught the eye" of Teacher Dannay and became one of his students.

"I owe this man a debt I'll never be able to repay," Brittain has written. "He's the one who helped me develop the school teacher-detective who eventually became Mr. Strang."[9]

Mr. Brittain was born in 1931 in Spencertown, New York, a very small town. He is married, has two children, and has been teaching for twenty-three years, twenty-one of them in the Lawrence-Cedarhurst system of Long Island, New York. Despite his teaching job, he has managed to turn out fifty-five short stories, many of which have been anthologized and distributed to the countries of five continents. His Mr. Strang stories have become a regular series item with *Ellery Queen's Mystery Magazine.*

Incidentally, Mr. Brittain teaches a course in the history and development of detective fiction at his junior high school.

We hope that after you meet Mr. Strang—and through him, Mr. Brittain, of course—your "image" of teachers will change greatly.

Mr. Strang Performs an Experiment

Mr. Strang stood behind the demonstration table, a satanic smile on his face, and held aloft the human skull in his hand. "Hugo, here," he said, pointing to the fleshless jaws, "was probably a rather young man. You will note that his teeth are in excellent condition—he undoubtedly brushed after every meal and saw his dentist twice a year."

Although one or two of the girls were turning a bit green, the twenty-eight students in Mr. Strang's biology class laughed dutifully. Mr. Strang smiled appreciatively in return. The thin science teacher had enough of the ham actor in him to play to an audience—even to a captive one—when the occasion presented itself.

The bell rang, ending the period. The students shifted restlessly but did not rise from their seats. They had learned early in the semester that in Mr. Strang's classes there was only one signal for dismissal. Mr. Strang took a long look at the skull and murmured, "Alas, poor Yorick!"—while twenty-eight pairs of eyes stared fixedly at the black-rimmed glasses on the demonstration table.

Mr. Strang picked up his glasses and put them in his jacket pocket.

There was a scraping of chairs and a few minor skirmishes at the rear of the classroom as most of the students tried to get through the doorway at the same time. The man who was standing just outside the room, about to enter, was swept aside by the mass of teen-age humanity.

Finally the doorway cleared, and the man entered Mr. Strang's room. Mr. Strang looked up, smiled, and placed the skull in a plastic bag on the table. "Come in, Russ," he said, "and I'll make you a cup of coffee. I've got a free period now, and my brew is better than that mud they make down in the Faculty Room."

Mr. Strang busied himself heating water over a Bunsen burner and arranging filter paper in a glass funnel. He spooned coffee into the filter-paper cone and poured boiling water over it, watching the brown liquid flow down the stem of the funnel and into the flask below it. Only when each had been provided with a beakerful of steaming coffee did Mr. Strang ask his question.

"What's bothering you, Russ?"

"It's—it's awful, Mr. Strang. I've got to talk to somebody. It just can't be happening to me. But how did you know about it? Did somebody tell you?"

"Coelenterata!" muttered Mr. Strang, making Phylum IV of animal classification sound like a wizard's magic word. "Russell Donato, do you take me for an idiot? You walk in here pale as a ghost, and with your hands shaking as if you had the St. Vitus's dance. And then while you wonder how I know you're worried, you keep gnawing at that thumbnail as if you want to leave nothing but a mashed stump. Now let's not beat around the bush. What's the trouble?"

"I've just come from Mr. Guthrey's office," said the younger man. "I've been suspended."

"Suspended? What do you mean?"

"Mr. Guthrey just handed me a thirty-day suspension. I can't teach here or anywhere else for the next month. Maybe never, for all I know."

Mr. Strang's jaw dropped. Although it was only the beginning of his second year at Aldershot High School, Russell Donato had the makings of an excellent chemistry teacher. He knew his field, he was a hard worker, and he had quickly learned to deal with his students without overstepping the thin line between friendliness and familiarity. The students not only liked him, they respected him, and to Mr. Strang, the second was far more important than the first. For Aldershot High School to lose him would be, in Mr. Strang's eyes, little short of a crime. He ran thin fingers through his rapidly disappearing hair.

"Why, Russ?" he asked.

"Because of Sheila Palinger," answered Donato.

"Who?"

"Sheila Palinger. She's a sophomore in my seventh-period study hall. She told Mr. Guthrey that I—well, she was in my room and—how do you say a thing like that, Mr. Strang?"

"She accused you of molesting her. Is that what you mean, Russ?"

"Yes. And now I've been suspended while the Board of Education makes its investigation."

Mr. Strang toyed for several seconds with a glass rod on the table. "Did you do it, Russ?" he asked finally.

Donato turned suddenly. His face showed hurt and anger. "Of course not," he snapped. "What do you think I am?"

"That's what the Board of Education has thirty days to find out," said Mr. Strang. "Do you want to tell me what happened?"

Donato shrugged. "There's not much to tell," he said. "I was working late in my classroom yesterday, correcting some examination papers I wanted to give back this morning. About four o'clock Sheila Palinger walked in and asked me if I'd help her with some footnotes for an English term paper. I suggested that she see her English teacher, but she said everybody had gone home, and she needed the information right away."

"Does Sheila take chemistry?"

"No, she's majoring in art. Anyway, I wasn't too sure about footnoting myself, but I hauled out an old book I had on forms for written reports and found what she wanted. She wasn't in the room more than five minutes."

"But surely Mr. Guthrey knows that not much could have happened in five minutes."

"Mr. Strang, you ought to hear the story Sheila told. According to her, she spent almost half an hour in my room after school yesterday. And she sounded pretty convincing, believe me. She told things about the way the room looked that even I couldn't remember. But when I checked this morning, she was absolutely perfect—one hundred per cent. What was on my desk, the exact way the seats were arranged—everything."

Mr. Strang looked thoughtfully at the skull in its transparent bag. "Russ," he said finally, "I wouldn't worry too much about this. The principal and the Board aren't completely against you. But after all, an accusation has been made. You can't expect them to ignore it. Let me see what I can find out from Mr. Guthrey."

"But can they do this, Mr. Strang? Can they kick me out just on the word of one kid?"

"I'm afraid if it comes to a showdown, they can, Russ. You haven't got tenure yet, and until you get it, the Board of Education can suspend you or even fire you just because they don't like the style of shoes you wear or the color of your socks. But don't get too excited until I see Mr. Guthrey. Tell me one thing. Is there any reason why Sheila Palinger would make trouble for you?"

Donato shook his head. "None that I can think of," he said. "Oh, she's kind of a pain-in-the-neck in the study hall. Keeps coming up with idiotic questions about her work, hangs around my desk most of the period—things like that. But she's never made any real trouble. I just can't understand it."

"Well, Russ, don't be in too much of a hurry to leave the school. I may want to talk to you again later. But right now, I want to hear what Mr. Guthrey has to say."

As he went down the stairs toward the main office, Mr. Strang found it hard to keep the worried expression from his own face. In the outer office he passed the Lost and Found Box and noticed that a chemistry textbook topped the pile of misplaced articles. He walked through the door marked *Marvin W. Guthrey* without knocking, an action that was not likely to endear him to the principal of Aldershot High School, and sat stiffly in a chair in front of Guthrey's enormous desk.

Behind the desk Guthrey, a small man with a head of wavy, snow-white hair of which he was inordinately proud, was talking on the telephone. His eyebrows shot up in surprise at the sight of the science teacher.

"I'll call you back on this, Fred," he said into the phone, "or maybe we can talk about it just before the Board meeting. In the meantime I'll try to find out what I can at this end." The principal hung up the phone. "Now then, Mr. Strang," he said, turning in his swivel chair, "perhaps you can tell me the meaning of this. I'm not in the habit of having—"

"I'm here about Russ Donato," interrupted Mr. Strang.

"I suppose Donato has told you what the trouble is," said Guthrey, "so there's nothing more for me to add. Fred Landerhoff—he's on the Board of Education, you know—has been on the phone all morning. He just finished his fourth call to me when you walked in. He's the one who ordered me to suspend Donato."

"So what happens now, Mr. Guthrey? How do you go about finding out whether Donato is innocent or guilty?"

Guthrey let out a long breath. "I wish I knew, Mr. Strang," he said. "A situation like this is hard on everybody. As soon as word leaks out, I'm going to get a hundred calls asking why I hired Donato in the first place. Of course, if there's no proof of guilt, we'll keep Donato on—at least, until the end of the year. By that time, the good citizens of Aldershot will probably make it so hot for him that he'll have to leave."

"Shades of *Alice in Wonderland*," muttered Mr. Strang.

"I beg your pardon?"

"I was just thinking of Alice's trial, where the Red Queen says 'Sentence first—verdict afterwards.' The analogy seems to apply."

"Unfortunately, that's true. Words like 'perversion' and 'sex maniac' are going to be tossed around pretty carelessly. Donato will have a rough time finding another teaching job if we have to let him go. Oh, if he leaves, I'll write him a good recommendation, of course."

"Protozoa, Mesozoa, Porifera," growled Mr. Strang. His face turned an angry red. "Make up your mind. If he attacked the girl or did anything at all improper, he's not fit to be in a classroom—*any* classroom. If he didn't, give him a chance to defend himself. But don't hang the man on the unsupported testimony of a child."

Guthrey stuck out his chin belligerently. "Mr. Strang," he rumbled, "you burst in here without permission to question me about Donato. Taking into consideration your friendship with him as well as your years of service to the school, I overlooked this breach of the rules and decided to discuss the matter with you. But I do not intend to—to—"

Guthrey raised his hand dramatically and then let it fall slowly to the desk. "Oh, hell, Leonard," he said, looking sadly at the science teacher. "They've got me over a barrel. You know there isn't a chance in a thousand of getting any evidence. It's just Donato's word against Sheila's. And you won't find a parent in a thousand who thinks his child—his flesh and blood —would lie about a thing like this. The kids know it, and there are some— only a very few, fortunately—who are just waiting for the chance to take advantage of it."

Marvin Guthrey looked forlornly at Mr. Strang and seemed tiny and lost in his huge swivel chair. For the first time in many years the science teacher could find it in his heart to feel sorry for his principal.

There was a thick silence, broken only by the ticking of the clock on the wall. Then Mr. Strang banged his fist loudly on Guthrey's desk.

"No!" he shouted.

"What is it, Mr. Strang?" asked Guthrey.

"Are we going to let a man's reputation—his whole future—be ruined? Are we going to let the good name of this school be dragged through the mud, with every teacher afraid to be pleasant and helpful with his students because of the possible consequences? Are we all going to cringe every time some asinine accusation is made? No! No! No!" He pounded the desk three times to punctuate his last words.

Guthrey looked at the teacher as if he'd lost his senses. "But what can you do, Mr. Strang?" he asked, a worried look on his face.

"There must be some indication somewhere of what really happened yesterday, and we're going to find it. If Russ Donato is guilty, at least we'll have cleaned our own house. And if he's innocent—which I'm sure is the case—we'll serve notice that nobody can make such a bald accusation and get away with it. Mr. Guthrey, can you get somebody to take over my classes for the next couple of periods? Anybody in the department ought to be able to describe that skull as well as I can."

"What are you going to do?"

"We," said Mr. Strang, indicating Guthrey and himself, "are going to have a little talk with Sheila Palinger. She's still in the building, isn't she?"

Guthrey smiled wryly. "You must have passed Sheila and her mother when you came through the outer office," he said. "They were camped at my door when I got here this morning. I spent over an hour listening to them go on and on about Donato, and my secretary says they want to see me again as soon as I'm free. Between those two and Fred Landerhoff, I haven't had time to take a deep breath yet today." He spread his hands helplessly. "I don't know what I can tell them that they haven't already heard."

"You won't have to say a word, Mr. Guthrey," the teacher replied. "But if that girl's as big a liar as I think she is, I'd just as soon have a witness to what's said here during the next few minutes."

Mr. Guthrey called his secretary, and a few minutes later Sheila Palinger entered the office. She was wearing a simple cotton dress and a tragic expression that would have done credit to an actress playing Camille. Behind her came her mother, a look of self-pity on her face.

After the introductions had been made, Mr. Strang turned to the girl. "Sheila," he began, "according to Mr. Guthrey, you've made a rather serious charge against Mr. Donato. I wonder if you'd tell me about it."

"Sheila already told him everything," interrupted Mrs. Palinger, indicating Guthrey with a jerk of her thumb, "and I gave Fred Landerhoff the whole story on the telephone last night. Fred's a good friend of mine. I can't see any sense in repeating it all and disturbing the child. I just want to find out what you're going to do about that—that *teacher.*"

"No, Mother," said Sheila. "I'll tell them. I want to cooperate in any way I can. I feel I owe it to my classmates and to the school."

Mr. Strang had all he could do to keep from shouting, "Academy Award!"

"What is it you want to know?" Sheila asked.

"Just tell us in your own words what happened, Sheila," said Mr. Strang in a kindly voice. "Right from the beginning."

"Well," Sheila began, her voice becoming low and confidential, "it was about five minutes to four yesterday. School had been out for almost an hour, and the halls were completely empty. I had some questions about an English assignment, and Mr. Donato was the only one I could find in the building, so I went to his room. He was there—alone."

"So nobody saw you go into the room?" asked Mr. Strang.

"Nobody," answered Sheila. "When I was inside, Mr. Donato asked me to sit down. He walked over to the windows and pulled down the shades. I didn't know why at the time.

"While I was waiting, I noticed a pile of examination papers on Mr. Donato's desk. He had corrected about half of them. The paper on top had a mark of eighty. He also had a chemistry book propped open to page seventy-three."

Mr. Strang's eyes widened. The girl seemed to have total recall concerning all the details of the meeting. "Did you happen to notice the color of Mr. Donato's necktie?" he asked sarcastically.

"Oh, yes. It was blue, with little red squares on it. Each square had a white dot in the center. I thought it went well with his gray suit."

Mr. Strang couldn't even remember the color of the tie he was wearing today. He looked down to check. Brown, with green acid stains.

"Mr. Donato came over to my desk with a book," Sheila continued. "I remember thinking how dim the room was with the shades down and the lights out. But still I could see that gold college ring Mr. Donato wears, and I thought it was funny that the ring should shine in such a soft light.

"As he leaned over my desk to help me, he pointed to the book with one hand. But he kept brushing my hair very lightly with the fingers of the other hand."

And since he was leaning over the desk, he probably fell flat on his face, thought Mr. Strang, since he couldn't use either hand to prop himself up. But the science teacher remained silent.

"Pretty soon," the girl went on, "he closed the book and just stared into my eyes. I began to get a little frightened. But I didn't dare say anything.

After all, Mr. Donato *was* a teacher. Then he said—he said—"

"What did he say?" Mr. Strang asked gently.

"He began telling me how—how lovely he thought I was—and how it meant so much to him to be alone with me. Then he began to touch me. He—he—Oh!" She buried her face in her hands.

Guthrey cleared his throat loudly. "And what did you do, Sheila?"

"I didn't know what to do, Mr. Guthrey. I remember getting up and backing away from Mr. Donato toward the door. Then I ran out."

"But you did remember to take your books, didn't you?" asked Mr. Strang.

"I must have. That part isn't too clear."

"You seemed to remember every little detail of what went on in the room before—er—anything happened."

Mrs. Palinger burst into the conversation. "That's not too unusual, is it? After all, the child's had a severe emotional upset. And now you two are almost acting as if you don't believe her."

Mr. Strang ignored the interruption. "Sheila," he said, "how long were you in Mr. Donato's room?"

"It must have been at least half an hour."

"Mr. Donato said that you were there no longer than five minutes."

"He's lying!" cried the girl. "Why, he even had time to do his old experiment before he started talking to me."

"Experiment?" said Mr. Strang. "I don't recall Mr. Donato saying anything about an experiment when he talked to me. What experiment was it, Sheila?"

"How should I know? I don't take chemistry. But anyway, he did it while I was there. That ought to prove I was in the room more than five minutes."

"But there was no sign this morning of any experiment having been done," said Guthrey.

"Hummph," snorted Mrs. Palinger. "He probably cleaned it all up before anybody saw it. Just the thing you'd expect of a snake like him."

"Do you remember anything about the experiment, Sheila?" asked Mr. Strang.

"Well, he had an iron stand on the table, and under it was one of those burners—"

"A Bunsen burner?"

"Yes, I guess so. There was this big glass thing like a bottle on the stand, and some tubes and—Oh, I don't know. It's kind of hard to explain. It was like what you see in the mad-scientist movies. But I could draw you a picture of how it looked."

"Splendid," said Mr. Strang. He gave Sheila a pencil and a piece of paper from Guthrey's desk. The girl busied herself with them, and in a few minutes she showed the results to Mr. Strang.

If Sheila Palinger knew nothing about chemistry, she was an excellent artist. The picture showed a ring stand over a Bunsen burner. On the stand was a large flask with a rubber stopper in it. A glass tube and a funnel were stuck through holes in the stopper. At one side of the flask were two bottles. Although the labels on the bottles were visible, their small size in the drawing had made it necessary for Sheila to omit the printing on them. But the extreme realism of the sketch made it certain that Sheila had seen the experiment somewhere. Guthrey looked worriedly at Mr. Strang.

"Sheila," said the teacher, "about those two bottles. What was in them?"

"Let me see. Oh, yes. One of them had 'Hickle' on the label."

"Hickle?"

"Yes. And the other one was full of a black powder called 'Fess.' "

"I never heard of 'Hickle' and 'Fess'," said Guthrey. "Mean anything to you, Mr. Strang?"

Mr. Strang's eyebrows narrowed in a frown. He reached into a pocket and dragged out a battered briar pipe and a pouch of tobacco. Ramming tobacco into the bowl of the pipe, he lit it and sent clouds of smoke billowing into the small office. Guthrey and Mrs. Palinger wrinkled their noses disapprovingly, but Mr. Strang ignored them. He leaned back in his chair and closed his eyes.

Several minutes passed, and Guthrey was just about to inquire if Mr. Strang was feeling all right when a smile spread over the face of the science teacher. He chuckled softly, and then not so softly. Soon he was emitting gales of laughter while his slender body shook with mirth.

"Hickle and Fess!" he gasped when he could catch his breath. "Sounds like a vaudeville team, doesn't it, Mr. Guthrey?"

"Let me in on it, Leonard," replied Guthrey. "What's so funny?"

Instead of answering, Mr. Strang took the drawing and made some rapid marks on the back of it with his pen. "Is this what you saw on the labels, Sheila?" he asked, showing her the paper.

"Yes, that's it."

Mr. Strang turned the paper so that Guthrey and Mrs. Palinger could see it. Printed on the paper in red ink were the two chemical symbols, HCl and FeS.

" 'Hickle'—HCl," explained the teacher, "is the chemical symbol for hydrochloric acid. And FeS is ferrous sulfide. I'm afraid Sheila made words out of the chemical symbols."

"That still doesn't prove anything against her," said Mrs. Palinger. "Sheila couldn't be expected to know—she told you she doesn't take chemistry."

"No, she doesn't," Mr. Strang agreed. "Now then, Sheila, what did Mr. Donato do with the Hickle and Fess?"

"He mixed them together in the big bottle."

"It's called a flask, Sheila. What happened then—to the experiment, I mean?"

"Mr. Donato put it over the flame. But I don't remember anything else about it. That was when he started to—you know."

"I see," said Mr. Strang. "Well, you've been very helpful, Sheila, and I think we have a pretty good idea of what really happened. I wonder, though, if it would be possible for you to come back to school this evening—with your mother, of course—just to tie up a few loose ends. Say, about eight o'clock?"

Mother and daughter looked at one another and shrugged. "Eight o'clock will be all right," said Mrs. Palinger finally. "Just so long as Mr. Donato is dismissed from this school. The very idea of letting a man like that teach our children!"

"I assure you, Mrs. Palinger, that the entire truth of the situation will be brought to light this evening. And you mentioned Mr. Landerhoff on the Board of Education. Would you mind bringing him along? We'll be meeting in Mr. Donato's room."

"If it'll help get rid of that—that monster, I'll see that Fred Landerhoff's there," replied Mrs. Palinger. She stood and patted her daughter's head lovingly.

"Until tonight, then," smiled Mr. Strang, holding the office door open.

When the Palingers had left, Guthrey leaned across his desk and scowled at Mr. Strang. "I hope you know what you're doing," he rumbled. "Parents, kids, a member of the Board—what's on your mind, Leonard?"

"You forgot one other person I'm inviting to the meeting," said the teacher.

"Who's that?"

"My principal. See you tonight at eight, Mr. Guthrey."

The gathering in Mr. Donato's science room that evening resembled a meeting between the legendary Hatfields and McCoys at the height of their feud. In one rear corner of the room sat Russ Donato. He was looking daggers at Sheila Palinger and her mother, who were sitting as far removed from the accused teacher as the walls of the room permitted.

In the center of the room Marvin Guthrey whispered nervously to Board member Landerhoff. From behind the demonstration table Mr. Strang grinned at his strange assortment of "students" like some diabolic gnome while he busily arranged the materials of the experiment Sheila Palinger had described earlier.

When he had completed his preparations, Mr. Strang rapped for order. An uneasy quiet descended on the room. "I believe you all know each other," he said, "so introductions will be unnecessary."

Fred Landerhoff raised his hand. Although he was here representing the Aldershot Board of Education, the sight of the thin science teacher in the front of the room made him feel like a schoolboy who didn't have his lesson prepared.

"This is highly irregular, Mr. Strang," he said. "I'd like to make it quite clear that I'm here at Mrs. Palinger's request. While I'm naturally interested in getting to the bottom of this incident, I'm here to see that—"

"We're all here to see that justice is done, Mr. Landerhoff," interrupted Mr. Strang, "and although the circumstances of this meeting are unusual, it's my opinion that recent events warrant it. I would like it noted, however, that the idea for the meeting was my own. Mr. Guthrey had no part in it."

The nervous principal let out a sigh.

"Today," Mr. Strang continued, "Mr. Donato was accused of—shall we say—making improper advances yesterday toward Miss Palinger, here. The school administration followed the only course of action open to it. Mr. Donato was suspended, pending an investigation."

Mr. Strang removed his glasses and polished them on his necktie. Holding the glasses between the thumb and forefinger of his right hand, he examined them closely. Then he inserted his other hand deep into his left jacket pocket and leaned across the table, shaking the glasses at the group in front of him. He was ready to teach his "class."

"The difficulty in a situation like this," he went on, "is the lack of evidence. Nobody witnessed the alleged incident—for all intents and purposes, the building was empty. And if there is no evidence, Mr. Donato can neither be proved innocent nor guilty.

"But consider the effect of the accusation itself. Should the parents of this community be asked to entrust their children to a man who is guilty of the charge made against Mr. Donato? Absolutely not. On the other hand, if the accusation is false, what of Mr. Donato's reputation? The man is damned without proof.

"No, the whole situation is intolerable. And for that reason I began to look for something that would confirm Mr. Donato's guilt or innocence. I believe I've found it."

Mr. Strang reached into a drawer of the demonstration table and pulled out the sketch of the experiment Sheila had made earlier. "When I saw this drawing, which Sheila made," he went on, "I couldn't help noticing the striking resemblance to a picture in the chemistry textbook used in Mr. Donato's classes. Look."

He took a book titled *Elements of Chemistry* from the drawer and opened it to a previously marked page. The page showed a photograph of an experiment in progress. Holding Sheila's drawing next to the photograph, he continued.

"Notice the position of the bottles in the drawing and in the photograph," he said. "Look at the shadow cast by the ring stand. It goes off at the same angle as the one in Sheila's sketch. There are other points of similarity I might draw to your attention, such as the fact that all the objects in the photograph are in the same relative places as they are in the drawing, but I think you can see my point. It is possible that Sheila drew not from life, but from this photo in the textbook."

"But why on earth would my daughter do a thing like that?" demanded Mrs. Palinger angrily.

"Simply in order to 'prove' that she had spent half an hour in this room, rather than the five minutes claimed by Mr. Donato."

Fred Landerhoff peered closely at the book and the drawing. "It's possible, Mr. Strang," he said, "but hardly conclusive. It could be just coincidence."

"True," said the teacher. "But let's go a step further. According to the description of the experiment in the book, one of the bottles in the photograph contains hydrochloric acid—notice the HCl label—and the other is filled with ferrous sulfide, chemical formula FeS."

"But my daughter told you all that this morning," cried Mrs. Palinger, "so how do you know she didn't see that very experiment being done by Mr. Donato right here in this room?"

"As a matter of fact," replied Mr. Strang, "I'm proceeding on the assumption that she *did* see it here, rather than in the book. And in order to clear up any confusion as to what really happened yesterday, I'd like to re-enact the events just as Sheila described them—including this experiment."

"No!" cried Sheila. "I won't let that man—"

"I will play the part of Mr. Donato," said Mr. Strang gently. "You have nothing to fear from me, Sheila. Now according to the way the experiment is described in the book, we first dump in some—er—fess." He removed the stopper from the flask and poured in a black powder from a bottle labeled FeS.

"Now for the hydrochloric acid." Mr. Strang replaced the stopper and poured a generous amount of liquid from the acid bottle down through the funnel. "And finally the flask goes on the stand over the flame." He lit the Bunsen burner.

"Now what?" asked Landerhoff.

"I pull down the shades," said Mr. Strang. "You did say they were down, didn't you Sheila?"

"Yes, that's right." The flask on the front table bubbled gently. Mr. Guthrey wrinkled his nose and peered furtively at Landerhoff.

"Now, Sheila," smiled Mr. Strang when the shades had been pulled down, "pretend that I'm Mr. Donato. What happens next?" The teacher noticed that Donato was chuckling to himself, while Mrs. Palinger had taken a perfumed handkerchief from her purse and placed it over her nose.

"Why—" Sheila began to shift restlessly in her seat. Her eyes were on the bubbling flask in the front of the room. "Why, Mr. Donato came over to the desk—"

"Like this?" Mr. Strang walked slowly up beside Sheila. Those in the rear of the room started coughing loudly. Fred Landerhoff fanned the air in front of his face with a small notebook.

"Yes, sir," replied Sheila. "Then he touched my hair with his hand."

The chemicals in the flask were bubbling more violently now.

"And then?"

"He put his face down into my hair. He said it smelled like—like—"

"Rotten eggs!" cried a voice.

"What?" said Mr. Strang gently. "I'm afraid you're out of order, Mr. Landerhoff."

"Maybe so, but that kid's out of her mind if she wants me to believe that somebody made love to her in a room where there was a stink like this! It smells like all the rotten eggs in the world! Mr. Strang, I'm willing to agree that Donato's not guilty of anything. Just let me out of this room before I suffocate. What is that stuff, anyway?"

Without waiting for an answer he dashed to the door, flinging the movable desks aside in his hurry to escape the overpowering stench. He was followed in rapid succession by the Palingers, Guthrey, and Donato.

Mr. Strang remained behind only long enough to pour the bubbling mixture from the flask into the small sink and throw open all the windows of the room; then he too dashed into the hallway and took several deep breaths of comparatively fresh air.

Later, in Guthrey's office, Landerhoff repeated his question. "I've asked Sheila and her mother to wait outside," he said. "Now what was that stuff, Mr. Strang?"

"Hydrogen sulfide," said the teacher. "It's a gas formed when hydrochloric acid is combined with ferrous sulfide and heated. As you noticed up in the classroom, it's the same gas that gives rotten eggs their characteristic odor. I admit to using a bit more of the chemicals than is ordinarily used, but I think my point was made. One good whiff of that gas is enough to dispel all thoughts of *l'amour.*"

"When did you first catch on that Sheila was lying?" asked Landerhoff.

"Just as soon as I realized that the experiment she was describing was the manufacture of hydrogen sulfide. She said that Russ began the experiment shortly after she entered the room. But I knew she couldn't have lasted in there for thirty minutes with a smell like that.

"Of course, when I saw that picture she drew, I knew she'd gotten it from the textbook—I've taught enough chemistry to know that book by heart. She'd have been better off if she hadn't been such a good artist. Fortunately for Mr. Donato, she didn't know the devastating effect that hydrogen sulfide has on the olfactory nerves."

"But why didn't Donato recognize the experiment?"

"She never mentioned it to him. It was only after Mr. Guthrey had sent Donato out of the office that Sheila realized time might be an issue. It wouldn't have been hard for her to find the chemistry text in the Lost and Found Box while she and her mother were waiting in the outer office. It was just too bad for her that she happened to turn to that particular experiment."

"But why would Sheila do a thing like this?" asked Donato.

"Maybe it was a way of getting into the limelight among her friends. Or it could be as simple as her coming home late and blaming you so she wouldn't be punished. Also, you're a fairly handsome young man, Russ. Perhaps it was a case of puppy love, and she carried her daydreaming too far. Perhaps Sheila herself doesn't know the real reason."

"What happens now, Fred?" Guthrey asked Landerhoff.

"Well, Mr. Donato will be reinstated with our apologies, of course," replied Landerhoff, "and I think I can convince Mrs. Palinger that Sheila should have a psychiatric examination. But what I'm wondering is what will happen if a similar situation comes up in the future."

"That's up to you, Mr. Landerhoff," said Mr. Strang. "You have a duty as a member of the Board of Education not only to the children of the district but to the men and women who teach them. Given an accusation without proof, who will you believe—the child or the teacher?"

Landerhoff looked from Mr. Strang to Donato and back again. He couldn't give an answer to Mr. Strang's question. He just didn't know.

Mr. Strang smiled. The look of doubt in Landerhoff's eyes was enough for him. Just a reasonable doubt.

That was enough.

ACTIVITIES

1) Would you like to have Mr. Strang as a teacher? Be sure that when you give your preference, for or against, you discuss him as a human being, as well as a science instructor and a detective.

2) In his story, William Brittain deals with an explosive school social issue as well as an intriguing mystery plot. Do you think that he has dealt with the problem fairly and sensitively? In your opinion, how should a school board treat "an accusation without proof"?

3) Sheila Palinger's accusation of Mr. Donato might have succeeded were it not for "a tragic flaw" in her personality. What was it? How did the "flaw" succeed in "undoing" her?

RESEARCH ACTIVITY

Writers are often asked, "Where do you get your ideas?"

Many will reply that ideas come from their everyday lives, from what they experience while undergoing a normal routine of work, play, and travel. Mr. Brittain's ideas obviously came from his working routine within an American secondary school, a source with which you also are very familiar—and which can provide you with ideas for stories, too.

Think of all the things that happen to you in a normal school day and then make a list of those that, in your opinion, might be good springboards for suspenseful narratives like the one you have just read. If you feel that your ideas will not be fruitful, try working with someone else in the collaborative style of Dannay and Lee.

The next step is to try writing your own detective story but—more about that later.

"Reading Maketh a Full Man . . ." (and Woman, too)

"Reading maketh a full man . . ." stated Sir Francis Bacon in the sixteenth century. Undoubtedly he was using the word "man" metaphorically and did not mean to exclude women.

Creating complete human beings is what education is all about. Schools and teachers cannot do the entire job. They need your cooperation and one way in which you can help is to follow Sir Francis' dictum on your own.

If you enjoyed the stories in this chapter, there is no need to wait for further class assignments to try more. There are many other Thinking Machine, Father Brown, Hercule Poirot, Lord Peter Wimsey, and Mr.

Strang tales available. To help you get started on an independent reading program, we are listing some additional titles for you.

More *"Thinking Machine" Adventures* by Jacques Futrelle

"The Crystal Gazer"
"The Scarlet Thread"
"The Flaming Phantom"
"The Problem of the Stolen Rubens"
"The Missing Necklace"
"The Fatal Cipher"

"The Phantom Motor"
"The Brown Coat"
"His Perfect Alibi"
"The Lost Radium"
"Kidnapped Baby Blake, Millionaire"

More *"Father Brown" Adventures* by G. K. Chesterton

"The Absence of Mr. Glass"
"The Hammer of God"
"The Paradise of Thieves"
"The Purple Wig"
"The Sign of the Broken Sword"
"The Three Tools of Death"
"The Eye of Apollo"
"The Queer Feet"
"The Secret Garden"
"The Duel of Dr. Hirsch"

"The Arrow of Heaven"
"The Flying Stars"
"The Honour of Israel Gow"
"The Wrong Shape"
"The Sins of Prince Saradine"
"The Blue Cross"
"The Man in the Passage"
"The Mistake of the Machine"
"The God of the Gongs"
"The Fairy Tale of Father Brown"

And many others ...

More *"Lord Peter Wimsey" Adventures* by Dorothy L. Sayers

Short Stories:
"The Abominable History of the Man with Copper Fingers"
"The Entertaining Episode of the Article in Question"
"The Fascinating Problem of Uncle Meleager's Will"
"The Fantastic Horror of the Cat in the Bag"
"The Unprincipled Affair of the Practical Joker"
"The Vindictive Story of the Footsteps That Ran"
"The Bibulous Business of a Matter of Taste"
"The Learned Adventure of the Dragon's Head"
"The Piscatorial Farce of the Stolen Stomach"
"The Unsolved Puzzle of the Man with No Face"
Novels:
The Nine Tailors

Murder Must Advertise
Strong Poison
Gaudy Night
Whose Body?
Unnatural Death
The Unpleasantness of the Bellona Club
Busman's Honeymoon
        And many others . . .

More *"Mr. Strang" Adventures* by William Brittain

"Mr. Strang Gives a Lecture"   "Mr. Strang Checks a Record"
"Mr. Strang Finds the Answers" "Mr. Strang Finds a Car"
"Mr. Strang Sees a Play"   "Mr. Strang Versus the Snowman"
"Mr. Strang Takes a Field Trip" "Mr. Strang Examines a Legend"
"Mr. Strang Pulls a Switch"   "Mr. Strang Invents a Strange Device"
"Mr. Strang Takes a Hand"   "Mr. Strang Follows Through"
"Mr. Strang Lifts a Glass"   "Mr. Strang Discovers a Bug"
"Mr. Strang Finds an Angle"   "Mr. Strang Under Arrest"
"Mr. Strang Hunts a Bear"   "Mr. Strang and the Cat Lady"
            And others . . .

5.

There Were Female Sleuths Before Women's Liberation

Introduction

Long before the advent of the Women's Liberation Movement with its demands for full female equality, more than a hundred years before, there were women sleuths operating as full-time protagonists in literature. True, the male fictional detective came first—Poe's Dupin in that historic year of 1841—but even in the nineteenth century, women were battling to assert themselves in an era that was even more dominated by men than today's. Twenty years later, their efforts began to bear some results for, in 1861, the first female protagonist made her debut in a detective story.

Her name was Mrs. Paschal and she appeared in the pages of a London novel entitled *The Experiences of a Lady Detective.* The author used the nom de plume "Anonyma," but, unlike Ellery Queen, his or her true identity was never uncovered. Unlike Dupin, Mrs. Paschal never achieved "star" status, but once she appeared on the stage of literary history, other authors realized the vast possibilities inherent in female detective characterizations.

Other such protagonists followed—but, for a long time, these early women investigators proved no match for their male counterparts as far as popularity was concerned. Such feminine appellations as C. L. Pirkis' Loveday Brooke (1894), George R. Sims' Dorcas Dene (1898), M. McDonnell Bodkin's Dora Myrl (1900), Richard Marsh's Judith Lee (1912), and Arthur Reeves' Constance Dunlap (1916) were relative "strangers" to the reading public, compared with the recognition accorded to Dupin, Holmes, The Thinking Machine, and others.

The first woman ever to "practice the (detective) form in any land or language" was America's Anna Katherine Green. She created a male sleuth and a female sleuth as well (Ebenezer Gryce and Violet Strange) but, of the two, Gryce proved the better characterization and became better known.[1]

It was not until the period of World War I (the 1910s and '20s) that the names of some women protagonists became as well known as the men's. Responsible for this new prominence were two remarkable women authors, America's Mary Roberts Rinehart and England's Agatha Christie; their memorable creations, Miss Pinkerton and Miss Jane Marple, made the reading public "sit up and take notice."

That public began asking for more female detective characterizations.

More were produced—from the pens of both male and female authors. Dupin, Holmes, Queen, and company found themselves in the stellar company of distaff colleagues (in addition to Pinkerton and Marple) like Hildegarde Withers, Sally Cardiff, Susan Dare, Sister Ursula, Mom, the Mayvin, and many others. The female sleuth, like women everywhere, was "on the road to liberation."[2]

Which is the way it should be . . .

And now, let's meet some of the women detectives.

Mary Roberts Rinehart—and Miss Pinkerton

In America, the first woman to earn recognition as a mystery and detective writer of importance was Mary Roberts Rinehart. Unlike her male and female colleagues who used appealing protagonists in sustaining series of stories, Mrs. Rinehart—with one notable exception—never repeated a detective characterization, even though she was a prolific author whose career spanned a period of fifty years.

She must have liked that one character, a sleuth whom she nicknamed Miss Pinkerton.

Miss Pinkerton—her given name, Hilda Adams—first appeared in a 1914 short story entitled "The Buckled Bag." She was an unusual protagonist for the time, a nurse doubling as an operative for a private detective agency. Later—when Mrs. Rinehart became well-known and three more Miss Pinkerton tales appeared—the public learned that the model for Hilda Adams had been the author herself.

Born in Pittsburgh in 1876, Mary Roberts, at the age of 17, entered the Pittsburgh Training School to become one of the less than five hundred graduate nurses then practicing in the country. This early experience inspired Hilda Adams and may explain why she repeated the character in further stories.

Mrs. Rinehart became a writer out of financial need. At 19, she married Dr. Stanley Rinehart and later gave birth to three sons. When a stock market crash occurred in 1903, the Rineharts' small savings were wiped out and the family found itself in debt. Wanting to contribute to the family's support, she began writing short stories. The stories sold, confirming the fact that she had writing, as well as nursing, talent.

Because women appeared extensively in her studies—in detective as well as Watson roles—and she was not averse to using romantic sub-plots, she attracted a feminine readership to what had previously been categorized as a masculine genre. That should not give you the wrong impression, however; men enjoyed her stories, too. Today, she is known as the dean of America's women detective story writers.[3]

Before her death in 1958, Mrs. Rinehart was to see Hilda Adams become "America's favorite nurse-detective." Hollywood sustained Miss Pinkerton's popularity by continuing her adventures on the screen with actress Joan Blondell in the role of Hilda.

Let's now present her to you . . .

Locked Doors

Chapter I

"You promised," I reminded Mr. Patton, "to play with cards on the table."

"My dear young lady," he replied, "I have no cards! I suspect a game, that's all."

"Then—do you need me?"

The detective bent forward, his arms on his desk, and looked me over carefully.

"What sort of shape are you in? Tired?"

"No."

"Nervous?"

"Not enough to hurt."

"I want you take another case, following a nurse who has gone to pieces," he said, selecting his words carefully. "I don't want to tell you a lot—I want you to go in with a fresh mind. It promises to be an extraordinary case."

"How long was the other nurse there?"

"Four days."

"She went to pieces in four days!"

"Well, she's pretty much unstrung. The worst is, she hasn't any real reason. A family chooses to live in an unusual manner, because they like it, or perhaps they're afraid of something. The girl was, that's sure. I had never seen her until this morning, a big, healthy-looking young woman; but she came in looking back over her shoulder as if she expected a knife in her back. She said she was a nurse from St. Luke's and that she'd been on a case for four days. She'd left that morning after about three hours' sleep in that entire period, being locked in a room most of the time, and having little but crackers and milk for food. She thought it was a case for the police."

"Who is ill in the house? Who was her patient?"

"There is no illness, I believe. The French governess had gone, and they wished the children competently cared for until they replaced her. That was the reason given her when she went. Afterward she—well, she was puzzled."

"How are you going to get me there?"

He gathered acquiescence from my question and smiled approval.

"Good girl!" he said. "Never mind how I'll get you there. You are the most dependable woman I know."

"The most curious, perhaps?" I retorted. "Four days on the case, three hours' sleep, locked in and yelling 'Police!' Is it out of town?"

"No, in the heart of the city, on Beauregard Square. Can you get some St. Luke's uniforms? They want another St. Luke's nurse."

I said I could get the uniforms, and he wrote the address on a card.

"Better arrive early in the evening," he said.

"But—if they are not expecting me?"

"They will be expecting you," he replied enigmatically.

"The doctor, if he's a St. Luke's man—"

"There is no doctor."

It was six months since I had solved, or helped to solve, the mystery of the buckled bag for Mr. Patton. I had had other cases for him in the interval, cases in which the police could not get close enough. As I said when I began this record of my crusade against crime and the criminal, a trained nurse gets under the very skin of the soul.

Gradually I had come to see that Mr. Patton's point of view was right: that if the criminal uses every means against society, why not society against the criminal? At first I had used this as a flag of truce to my nurse's ethical training; now I flaunted it, a mental and moral banner. The criminal against society, and I against the criminal! And, more than that, against misery, healing pain by augmenting it sometimes, but working like a surgeon, for good.

I had had six cases in six months. Only in one had I failed to land my criminal, and that without any suspicion of my white uniform and rubber-soled shoes. Although I played a double game, no patient of mine had suffered. I was a nurse first and a police agent second. If it was a question between turpentine compresses—stupes, professionally—and seeing what letters came in or went out of the house, the compress went on first, and cracking hot, too. I am not boasting. That is my method, the only way I can work, and it speaks well for it that, as I say, only one man escaped arrest, an arson case in which the factory owner hanged himself in the bathroom needle shower—in the house he had bought with the insurance money—while I was fixing his breakfast tray. And even he might have been saved for justice had the cook not burned the toast and been obliged to make it fresh.

I was no longer staying at a nurses' home. I had taken a bachelor suite of three rooms and bath, comfortably downtown. I cooked my own breakfasts when I was off duty and I dined at a restaurant nearby. Luncheon I did not bother much about. Now and then Mr. Patton telephoned me and we lunched together in remote places where we would not be known. He would tell me of his cases and sometimes he asked my advice.

I bought my uniforms that day and took them home in a taxicab. The dresses were blue, and over them for the street the St. Luke's girls wore long cloaks, English fashion, of navy blue serge, and a blue bonnet with a white ruching and white lawn ties. I felt curious in it, but it was becoming and convenient. Certainly I looked professional.

At three o'clock that afternoon a messenger brought a small box, registered. It contained a St. Luke's badge of gold and blue enamel.

At four o'clock my telephone rang. I was packing my suitcase according to the list I keep pasted in the lid. Under the list, which was of uniforms, aprons, thermometer, instruments, a nurse's simple set of probe, forceps and bandage scissors, was the word "box." This always went in first—a wooden box with a lock, the key of which was round my neck. It contained skeleton keys, a small black revolver of which I was in deadly fear, a pair of handcuffs, a pocket flashlight, and my badge from the chief of police. I was examining the revolver nervously when the telephone rang, and I came within an ace of sending a bullet into the flat below.

Did you ever notice how much you get out of a telephone voice? We can dissemble with our faces, but under stress the vocal cords seem to draw up tight and the voice comes thin and colorless. There's a little woman in the flat beneath—the one I nearly bombarded—who sings like a bird at her piano half the day, scaling vocal heights that make me dizzy. Now and then she has a visitor, a nice young man, and she disgraces herself, flats F, fogs E even, finally takes cowardly refuge in a wretched mezzo-soprano and doubtless cries herself to sleep later on.

The man who called me had the thin-drawn voice of extreme strain—a youngish voice.

"Miss Adams," he said, "this is Francis Reed speaking. I have called St.

Luke's and they referred me to you. Are you free to take a case this afternoon?"

I fenced. I was trying to read the voice.

"This afternoon?"

"Well, before night anyhow; as—as early this evening as possible."

The voice was strained and tired, desperately tired. It was not peevish. It was even rather pleasant.

"What is the case, Mr. Reed?"

He hesitated. "It is not illness. It is merely—the governess has gone and there are two small children. We want someone to give her undivided attention to the children."

"I see."

"Are you a heavy sleeper, Miss Adams?"

"A very light one." I fancied he breathed freer.

"I hope you are not tired from a previous case?" I was beginning to like the voice.

"I'm quite fresh," I replied almost gayly. "Even if I were not, I like children, especially well ones. I shan't find looking after them very wearying, I'm sure."

Again the odd little pause. Then he gave me the address on Beauregard Square, and asked me to be sure not to be late.

"I must warn you," he added, "we are living in a sort of casual way. Our servants left us without warning. Mrs. Reed has been getting along as best she could. Most of our meals are being sent in."

I was thinking fast. No servants! A good many people think a trained nurse is a sort of upper servant. I've been in houses where they were amazed to discover that I was a college woman and, finding the two things irreconcilable, have openly accused me of having been driven to such a desperate course as a hospital training by an unfortunate love affair.

"Of course you understand that I will look after the children to the best of my ability, but that I will not replace the servants."

I fancied he smiled grimly.

"That, of course. Will you ring twice when you come?"

"Ring twice?"

"The doorbell," he replied impatiently,

I said I would ring the doorbell twice.

The young woman below was caroling gayly, ignorant of the six-chambered menace over her head. I knelt again by my suitcase, but packed little and thought a great deal. I was to arrive before dusk at a house where there were no servants and to ring the doorbell twice. I was to be a light sleeper, although I was to look after two healthy children. It was not much in itself, but, in connection with the previous nurse's appeal to the police, it took on new possibilities.

At six I started out to dinner. It was early spring and cold, but quite light. At the first corner I saw Mr. Patton waiting for a street car, and at his quick nod I saw I was to get in also. He did not pay my fare or speak to me. It was a part of the game that we were never seen together except at the remote restaurant I mentioned before. The car thinned out and I could watch him easily. Far downtown he alighted and so did I. The restaurant was near. I went in alone and sat down at a table in a recess, and very soon he joined me. We were in the main dining room but not of it, a sop at once to the conventions and to the necessity, where he was so well known, for caution.

"I got a little information—on—the affair we were talking of," he said as he sat down. "I'm not so sure I want you to take the case after all."

"Certainly I shall take it," I retorted with some sharpness. "I've promised to go."

"Tut! I'm not going to send you into danger unnecessarily."

"I am not afraid."

"Exactly. A lot of generals were lost in the Civil War because they were not afraid and wanted to lead their troops instead of saving themselves and their expensive West Point training by sitting back in a safe spot and directing the fight. Any fool can run into danger. It takes intelligence to keep out."

I felt my color rising indignantly. "Then you brought me here to tell me I am not to go?"

"Will you let me read you two reports?"

"You could have told me that at the corner!"

"Will you let me read you two reports?"

"If you don't mind, I'll first order something to eat. I'm to be there before dark."

"Will you let me—"

"I'm going, and you know I'm going. If you don't want me to represent you, I'll go on my own. They want a nurse, and they're in trouble."

I think he was really angry. I know I was. If there is anything that takes the very soul out of a woman, it is to be kept from doing a thing she has set her heart on, because some man thinks it dangerous. If she has any spirit, that rouses it.

Mr. Patton quietly replaced the reports in his wallet, and his wallet in the inside pocket of his coat, and fell to a judicial survey of the menu. But although he barely glanced at me, he must have seen the determination in my face, for he ordered things that were quickly prepared and told the waiter to hurry.

"I have wondered lately," he said slowly, "whether the mildness of your manner at the hospital was acting, or the chastening effect of three years under an order book."

"A man always likes a woman to be a sheep."

"Not at all. But it is rather disconcerting to have a pet lamb turn round and take a bite out of one."

"Will you read the reports now?"

"I think," he said quietly, "they had better wait until we have eaten. We will probably both feel calmer. Suppose we arrange that nothing said before the oysters counts?"

I agreed, rather sulkily, and the meal went off well enough. I was rather anxious to hurry but he ate deliberately, drank his demi-tasse, paid the waiter, and at last met my impatient eyes and smiled.

"After all," he said, "since you are determined to go anyhow, what's the use of reading the reports? Inside of an hour you'll know all you need to know." But he saw that I did not take his teasing well, and drew out his wallet.

There were two typewritten papers clamped together.

They are on my desk before me now. The first one is endorsed:

Statement by Laura J. Bosworth, nurse, of St. Luke's Home for Graduate Nurses.

Miss Bosworth says:

I do not know just why I came to the police. But I know I'm frightened. That's the fact. I think there is something terribly wrong in the house of Francis M. Reed, 71 Beauregard Square. I think a crime of some sort has been committed. There are four people in the family, Mr. and Mrs. Reed and two children. I was to look after the children.

I was there four days and the children were never allowed out of the room. At night we were locked in. I kept wondering what I would do if there was a fire. The telephone wires are cut so no one can call the house, and I believe the doorbell was disconnected, too. But that's fixed now. Mrs. Reed went round all the time with a face like chalk and her eyes staring. At all hours of the night she'd unlock the bedroom door and come in and look at the children.

Almost all the doors through the house were locked. If I wanted to get to the kitchen to boil eggs for the children's breakfast—for there were no servants, and Mrs. Reed is young and doesn't know anything about cooking—Mr. Reed had to unlock about four doors for me.

If Mrs. Reed looked bad, he was dreadful—sunken-eyed and white and wouldn't eat. I think he has killed someone and is making away with the body.

Last night I said I had to have air, and they let me go out. I called up a friend from a pay station, another nurse. This morning she sent me a special-delivery letter that I was needed on another case, and I got away. That's all; it sounds foolish, but try it and see if it doesn't get on your nerves.

Mr. Patton looked up at me as he finished reading.

"Now you see what I mean," he said. "That woman was there four days, and she is as temperamental as a cow, but in those four days her nervous system went to smash."

"Doors locked!" I reflected. "Servants gone; state of fear—it looks like a siege!"

"But why a trained nurse? Why not a policeman, if there is danger? Why anyone at all, if there is something that the police are not to know?"

"That is what I intend to find out," I replied. He shrugged his shoulders and read the other paper:

Report of Detective Bennett on Francis M. Reed, April 5.

Francis M. Reed is thirty-six years of age, married, a chemist at the Olympic Paint Works. He has two children, both boys. Has a small independent income and owns the house on Beauregard Square, which was built by his grandfather, General F. R. Reed. Is supposed to be living beyond his means.

House is usually full of servants, and grocer in the neighborhood has had to wait for money several times.

On March twenty-ninth he dismissed all servants without warning. No reason given, but a week's wages instead of notice.

On March thirtieth he applied to the owners of the paint factory for two weeks' vacation. Gave as his reason nervousness and insomnia. He said he was "going to lay off and get some sleep." Has not been back at the works since. House under surveillance this afternoon. No visitors.

Mr. Reed telephoned for a nurse at four o'clock from a store on Eleventh Street. Explained that his telephone was out of order.

Mr. Patton folded up the papers and thrust them back into his pocket. Evidently he saw I was determined, for he only said, "Have you got your revolver?"

"Yes."

"Do you know anything about telephones? Could you repair that one in an emergency?"

"In an emergency," I retorted, "there is no time to repair a telephone. But I've got a voice and there are windows. If I really put my mind to it, you will hear me yell at headquarters."

He smiled grimly.

Chapter II

Beauregard Square is a small, exclusive neighborhood; a dozen or more solid citizens built their homes there in the early 70's, occupying large lots, the houses flush with the streets and with gardens behind. Six on one street, six on another, back to back with the gardens in the center, they occupy the whole block. And the gardens are not fenced off, but make a sort of small park, unsuspected from the streets. Here and there bits of flowering shrubbery sketchily outline a property, but the general impression is of lawn and trees, free of access to all the owners. Thus, with the square in front and the gardens in the rear, the Reed house faces in two directions on the early spring green.

In the gardens the old tar walks are still there, and a fountain which no longer plays, but on whose stone coping I believe the young Beauregard Squarites made their first climbing ventures.

The gardens are always alive with birds, and eventually, from my windows, I learned the reason. It seems to have been a custom sanctified by years that the crumbs from the twelve tables should be thrown into the dry basin of the fountain for the birds. It is a common sight to see stately butlers and chic little waitresses in black and white coming out after luncheon or dinner with silver trays of crumbs. Many a scrap of gossip, as well as scrap of food, has been passed along at the old stone fountain, I believe. I know that it was there that I heard of the "basement ghost" of Beauregard Square —a whisper at first, a panic later.

I arrived at eight o'clock and rang the doorbell twice. The door was opened at once by Mr. Reed, a tall, blond young man, carefully dressed. He threw away his cigarette when he saw me and shook hands. The hall was brightly lighted and most cheerful; in fact the whole house was ablaze with light. Certainly nothing could be less mysterious than the house, or than the debonair young man who motioned me into the library.

"I told Mrs. Reed I would talk to you before you go upstairs," he said. "Will you sit down?"

I sat down. The library was even brighter than the hall, and now I saw that, although he smiled as cheerfully as ever, his face was almost colorless, and his eyes, which looked frankly enough into mine for a moment, went wandering off round the room. I had the impression somehow that Mr. Patton had had of the nurse at headquarters that morning—that he looked as if he expected a knife in his back. It seemed to me that he wanted to look over his shoulder and by sheer will power did not.

"You know the rule, Miss Adams," he said. "When there's an emergency, get a trained nurse. I told you our emergency—no servants and two small children."

"This should be a good time to secure servants," I said briskly. "City houses are being deserted for country places, and a percentage of servants won't leave town."

He hesitated. "We've been doing very nicely, although of course it's hardly more than just living. Our meals are sent in from a hotel, and—well, we thought, since we are going away so soon, that perhaps we could manage."

The impulse was too strong for him at that moment. He wheeled and looked behind him, not a hasty glance, but a deliberate inspection that took in every part of that end of the room. It was so unexpected that it left me gasping.

The next moment he was himself again.

"When I say that there is no illness," he said, "I am hardly exact. There is no illness, but there has been an epidemic of children's diseases among the Beauregard Square children and we are keeping the youngsters indoors."

"Don't you think they could be safeguarded without being shut up in the house?"

He responded eagerly. "If I only thought—" He checked himself. "No," he said decidedly; "for a time, at least, I believe it is not wise."

I did not argue with him. There was nothing to be gained by antagonizing him. And as Mrs. Reed came in just then, the subject was dropped. She was hardly more than a girl, almost as blonde as her husband, very pretty, and with the weariest eyes I have ever seen, unless perhaps the eyes of a man who has waited a long time for death.

I liked her at once. She did not attempt to smile. She rather clung to my hand when I held it out.

"I am glad St. Luke's still trusts us," she said. "I was afraid the other nurse ... Frank, will you take Miss Adams's suitcase upstairs?"

She held out a key. He took it, but he turned at the door and said, "I wish you wouldn't wear those things, Anne. You gave me your promise yesterday, you remember."

"I can't work round the children in anything else," she protested.

"Those things" were charming. She wore a rose silk negligee trimmed with soft bands of lace and blue satin flowers, a petticoat to match that garment, and a lace cap.

He hesitated in the doorway and looked at her—a curious glance, I thought, full of tenderness, reproof—and perhaps apprehension.

"I'll take them off, dear," she replied to the glance. "I wanted Miss Adams to know that, even if we haven't a servant in the house, we are at least civilized. I—I haven't taken cold." This last was clearly an afterthought.

He went out then and left us together.

She came over to me swiftly. "What did the other nurse say?" she demanded.

"I do not know her at all. I have not seen her."

"Didn't she report at the hospital that we were—queer?"

I smiled. "That's hardly likely, is it?"

Unexpectedly she went to the door opening into the hall and closed it, coming back swiftly.

"Mr. Reed thinks it is not necessary, but—there are some things that will puzzle you. Perhaps I should have spoken to the other nurse. If—if anything strikes you as unusual, Miss Adams, just please don't see it! It is all right, everything is all right. But something has occurred—not very much, but disturbing—and we are all of us doing the very best we can."

She was quivering with nervousness.

I was not the police agent then, I'm afraid.

"Nurses are accustomed to disturbing things. Perhaps I can help."

"You can, by watching the children. That's the only thing that matters to me—the children. I don't want them left alone. If you have to leave them, call me."

"Don't you think I will be able to watch them more intelligently if I know just what the danger is?"

I think she very nearly told me. She was so tired, evidently so anxious to shift her burden to fresh shoulders.

"Mr. Reed said," I prompted her, "that there was an epidemic of children's diseases. But from what you say—"

But I was not to learn, after all, for her husband opened the hall door.

"Yes, children's diseases," she said vaguely. "So many children are down. Shall we go up, Frank?"

The extraordinary bareness of the house had been dawning on me for some time. It was well lighted and well furnished. But the floors were innocent of rugs, the handsome furniture was without arrangement and, in the library at least, stood huddled in the center of the room. The hall and stairs were also uncarpeted, but there were marks where carpets had recently lain and had been jerked up.

The progress up the staircase was not calculated to soothe my nerves. The thought of my little revolver, locked in my suitcase, was poor comfort. For with every four steps or so Mr. Reed, who led the way, turned automatically and peered into the hallway below; he was listening, too, his head bent slightly forward. And each time that he turned, his wife, behind me, turned also. Cold terror suddenly got me by the spine, and yet the hall was bright with light.

(NOTE: Surely fear is a contagion. Could one isolate the germ of it and find an antitoxin? Or is it merely a form of nervous activity run amuck, like a runaway locomotive, colliding with other nervous activities and causing catastrophe? Take this up with Mr. Patton. But would he know? He, I am almost sure, has never been really afraid.)

I had a vision of my oxlike predecessor making this head-over-shoulder journey up the staircase, and in spite of my nervousness I smiled. But at that moment Mrs. Reed put a hand on my arm, and I screamed. I remember yet the way she dropped back against the wall and turned white.

Mr. Reed whirled on me instantly. "What did you see?" he demanded.

"Nothing at all." I was horribly ashamed. "Your wife touched my arm unexpectedly. I dare say I am nervous."

"It's all right, Anne," he reassured her. And to me, almost irritably, "I thought you nurses had no nerves."

"Under ordinary circumstances I have none."

It was all ridiculous. We were still on the staircase.

"Just what do you mean by that?"

"If you will stop looking down into that hall, I'll be calm enough. You make me jumpy."

He muttered something about being sorry and went on quickly. But at the top he went through an inward struggle, evidently succumbed, and took a final furtive survey of the hallway below. I was so wrought up that had a door slammed anywhere just then, I think I should have dropped where I stood.

The absolute silence of the house added to the strangeness of the situation. Beauregard Square is not close to a trolley line, and quiet is the neighborhood tradition. The first rubber-tired vehicles in the city drew up before Beauregard Square houses. Beauregard Square children speak in low voices and never bang their spoons on their plates. Beauregard Square servants wear felt-soled shoes. And such outside noises as venture to intrude themselves must filter through double brick walls and doors built when lumber was selling by the thousand acres instead of the square foot.

Through this silence our feet echoed along the bare floor of the upper hall, as well lighted as belowstairs and as dismantled, to the door of the day nursery. The door was locked—double locked, in fact. For the key had been turned in the old-fashioned lock, and in addition an ordinary bolt had been newly fastened on the outside of the door. On the outside! Was that to keep me in? It was certainly not to keep anyone or anything out. The feeblest touch moved the bolt.

We were all three outside the door. We seemed to keep our compactness by common consent. No one of us left the group willingly; or, leaving it, we slid back again quickly. That was my impression, at least. But the bolt rather alarmed me.

"This is your room," Mrs. Reed said. "It is generally the day nursery, but we have put a bed and some other things in it. I hope you will be comfortable."

I touched the bolt with my finger and smiled into Mr. Reed's eyes.

"I hope I am not to be fastened in!" I said.

He looked back squarely enough, but somehow I knew he lied.

"Certainly not," he replied, and opened the door.

If there had been mystery outside, and bareness, the nursery was charming—a corner room with many windows, hung with the simplest of nursery papers and full of glass-doored closets filled with orderly rows of toys. In one corner a small single bed had been added without spoiling the room. The window sills were full of flowering plants. There was a bowl of goldfish on a stand, and a tiny dwarf parrot in a cage. A white-tiled bathroom connected with this room and also with the night nursery beyond.

Mr. Reed did not come in. I had an uneasy feeling, however, that he was just beyond the door. The children were not asleep. Mrs. Reed left me so that I could put on my uniform. When she came back, her face was troubled.

"They are not sleeping well," she complained. "I suppose it comes from having no exercise. They are always excited."

"I'll take their temperatures," I said. "Sometimes a tepid bath and a cup of hot milk will make them sleep."

The two little boys were wide awake. They sat up to look at me and both spoke at once.

"Can you tell fairy tales out of your head?"

"Did you see Chang?"

They were small, sleek-headed, fair-skinned youngsters, adorably clean and rumpled.

"Chang is their dog, a Pekingese," explained the mother. "He has been lost for several days."

"But he isn't lost, Mother. I can hear him crying every now and then. You'll look again, Mother, won't you?"

"We heard him through the furnace pipe," shrilled the smaller of the two. "You said you would look."

"I did look, darlings. He isn't there. And you promised not to cry about him, Freddie."

Freddie, thus put on his honor, protested he was not crying for the dog.

"I want to go out and take a walk, that's why I'm crying," he wailed. "And I want Mademoiselle, and my buttons are all off. And my ear aches when I lie on it."

The room was close. I threw up the windows, and turned to find Mrs. Reed at my elbow. She was glancing out apprehensively.

"I suppose the air is necessary," she said, "and these windows are all right. But—I have a reason for asking it—please do not open the others."

She went very soon, and I listened as she went out. I had promised to lock the door behind her, and I did so. The bolt outside was not shot.

After I had quieted the children with my mildest fairy story, I made an inventory of my new quarters. I drew a diagram of the second floor, which I gave to Mr. Patton later. That night, of course, I investigated only the two nurseries. But, so strangely had the fear that hung over the house infected me, I confess that I made my little tour of bathroom and clothes-closet with my revolver in my hand!

I found nothing, of course. The disorder of the house had not extended itself here. The bathroom was spotless with white tile; the large clothes-closet, which opened off the passage between the two rooms, was full of neatly folded clothing for the children. The closet was to play its part later, a darkish little room faintly lighted during the day by a ground-glass transom opening into the center hall, but dependent mostly on electric light.

Outside the windows Mrs. Reed had asked me not to open was a porte-cochère* roof almost level with the sills. Then was it an outside intruder she feared? And in that case, why the bolts on the outside of the two nursery doors? For the night nursery, I found, must have one also. I turned the key, but the door would not open.

I decided not to try to sleep that night, but to keep on watch. So powerfully had the mother's anxiety about her children and their mysterious danger impressed me that I made frequent excursions into the back room. Up to midnight there was nothing whatever to alarm me. I darkened both rooms and sat, waiting for I know not what; for some sound to show that the house stirred, perhaps. At a few minutes after twelve, faint noises penetrated to my room from the hall: Mr. Reed's nervous voice and a piece of furniture scraping over the floor. Then silence again for half an hour or so.

Then—I was quite certain that the bolt on my door had been shot. I do not think I heard it. Perhaps I felt it. Perhaps I only feared it. I unlocked the door; it was fastened outside.

There is a hideous feeling of helplessness about being locked in. I pretended to myself at first that I was only interested and curious. But I was frightened; I know that now. I sat there in the dark and wondered what I would do if the house took fire, or if some hideous tragedy enacted itself outside that locked door and I were helpless.

By two o'clock I had worked myself into a panic. The house was no longer silent. Someone was moving about downstairs, and not stealthily. The sounds came up through the heavy joists and flooring of the old house.

I determined to make at least a struggle to free myself. There was no way to get at the bolts, of course. The porte-cochère roof remained, and the transom in the clothes-closet. True, I might have raised an alarm and been freed at once, but naturally I rejected this method. The roof of the porte-cochère proved impracticable. The tin bent and cracked under my first step. The transom then.

I carried a chair into the closet and found the transom easy to lower. But it threatened to creak. I put liquid soap on the hinges—it was all I had, and it worked very well—and lowered the transom inch by inch. Even then I

---

*Carriage-house. A covered entrance for carriage passengers (French)

could not see over it. I had worked so far without a sound, but in climbing to a shelf my foot slipped and I thought I heard a sharp movement outside. It was five minutes before I stirred. I hung there, every muscle cramped, listening and waiting. Then I lifted myself by sheer force of muscle and looked out. The upper landing of the staircase, brilliantly lighted, was to my right. Across the head of the stairs had been pushed a cotbed, made up for the night, but it was unoccupied.

Mrs. Reed, in a long, dark ulster, was standing beside it, staring with fixed and glassy eyes at something in the lower hall.

Chapter III

Sometime after four o'clock my door was unlocked from without; the bolt slipped as noiselessly as it had been shot. I got a little sleep until seven, when the boys trotted into my room in their bathrobes and slippers and perched on my bed.

"It's a nice day," observed Harry, the elder. "Is that bump your feet?"

I wriggled my toes and assured him he had surmised correctly.

"You're pretty long, aren't you? Do you think we can play in the fountain today?"

"We'll make a try for it, son. It will do us all good to get out into the sunshine."

"We always took Chang for a walk every day, Mademoiselle and Chang and Freddie and I."

Freddie had found my cap on the dressing table and had put it on his yellow head. But now, on hearing the beloved name of his pet, he burst into loud grief-stricken howls.

"Want Mam'selle," he cried. "Want Chang, too. Poor Freddie!"

The children were adorable. I bathed and dressed them and, mindful of my predecessor's story of crackers and milk, prepared for an excursion kitchenward. The nights might be full of mystery, murder might romp from room to room, but I intended to see that the youngsters breakfasted. But before I was ready to go down, breakfast arrived.

Perhaps the other nurse had told the Reeds a few plain truths before she left; perhaps—and this, I think, was the case—the cloud had lifted just a little. Whatever it may have been, two rather flushed and flurried young people tapped at the door that morning and were admitted, Mr. Reed first, with a tray, Mrs. Reed following with a coffeepot and cream.

The little nursery table was small for five, but we made room somehow. What if the eggs were underdone and the toast dry? The children munched blissfully. What if Mr. Reed's face was still drawn and haggard and his wife a limp little huddle on the floor? She sat with her head against his knee and her eyes on the little boys, and drank her pale coffee slowly. She was very tired, poor thing. She dropped asleep sitting there, and he sat for a long time, not liking to disturb her.

It made me feel homesick for the home I didn't have. I've had the same feeling before, of being a rank outsider—a sort of defrauded feeling. I've had it when I've seen the look in a man's eyes when his wife comes to after an operation. And I've had it, for that matter, when I've put a new baby in its mother's arms for the first time. I had it for sure that morning, while she slept there and he stroked her pretty hair.

I put in my plea for the children then.

"It's bright and sunny," I argued. "And if you are nervous, I'll keep them away from other children. But if you want to keep them well, you must give them exercise."

It was the argument about keeping them well that influenced him, I think. He sat silent for a long time. His wife was still asleep, her lips parted.

"Very well," he said finally, "from two to three, Miss Adams. But not in the garden back of the house. Take them on the street."

I agreed to that.

"I shall want a short walk every evening myself," I added. "That is a rule of mine. I am a more useful person and a more agreeable one if I have it."

I think he would have demurred if he dared. But one does not easily deny so sane a request. He yielded grudgingly.

That first day was calm and quiet enough. Had it not been for the strange condition of the house and the necessity for keeping the children locked in, I would have smiled at my terror of the night. Luncheon was sent in; so was dinner. The children and I lunched and supped alone. As far as I could see, Mrs. Reed made no attempt at housework; but the cot at the head of the stairs disappeared in the early morning and the dog did not howl again.

I took the boys out for an hour in the early afternoon. Two incidents occurred, both of them significant. I bought myself a screwdriver—that was one. The other was our meeting with a slender young woman in black who knew the boys and stopped them. She proved to be one of the dismissed servants—the waitress, she said.

"Why, Freddie!" she cried. "And Harry, too! Aren't you going to speak to Nora?"

After a moment or two she turned to me, and I felt she wanted to say something, but hardly dared.

"How is Mrs. Reed?" she asked. "Not sick, I hope?" She glanced at my St. Luke's cloak and bonnet.

"No, she is quite well."

"And Mr. Reed?"

"Quite well also."

"Is Mademoiselle still there?"

"No, there is no one there but the family. There are no maids in the house."

She stared at me curiously. "Mademoiselle has gone? Are you cer—Excuse me, miss. But I thought she would never go. The children were like her own."

"She is not there, Nora."

She stood for a moment, debating, I thought. Then she burst out, "Mr. Reed made a mistake, miss. You can't take a houseful of first-class servants and dismiss them the way he did—not even half an hour to get out bag and baggage—without making talk. And there's talk enough all through the neighborhood."

"What sort of talk?"

"Different people say different things. They say Mademoiselle is still there, locked in her room on the third floor. There's a light there sometimes, but nobody sees her. And other folks say Mr. Reed is crazy. And there is worse being said than that."

But she refused to tell me any more—evidently concluded she had said too much and got away as quickly as she could, looking rather worried.

I was a trifle over my hour getting back, but nothing was said. To leave the clean and tidy street for the disordered house was not pleasant. But once in the children's suite, with the goldfish in the aquarium darting like tongues of flame in the sunlight, with the tulips and hyacinths of the window-boxes glowing and the orderly toys on their white shelves, I felt comforted. After all, disorder and dust did not imply crime.

But one thing I did that afternoon—did it with firmness and no attempt at secrecy, and after asking permission of no one. I took the new screwdriver and unfastened the bolt from the outside of my door.

I was prepared, if necessary, to make a stand on that issue. But although it was noticed, I knew, no mention of it was made to me.

Mrs. Reed pleaded a headache that evening, and I believe her husband ate alone in the dismantled dining room. For every room on the lower floor, I had discovered, was in the same curious disorder.

At seven Mr. Reed relieved me, so that I could go out. The children were in bed. He did not go into the day nursery, but placed a straight chair outside the door of the back room and sat there, bent over, elbows on knees, chin cupped in his palm, staring at the staircase. He roused enough to ask me to bring an evening paper when I returned.

When I am on a department case, I always take my off-duty in the evening by arrangement and walk round the block. Sometime in my walk I am sure to see Mr. Patton himself if the case is big enough, or one of his agents if he cannot come. If I have nothing to communicate, it resolves itself into a bow and nothing more.

I was nervous on this particular jaunt. For one thing, my St. Luke's cloak and bonnet marked me at once, made me conspicuous; for another, I was afraid Mr. Patton would think the Reed house no place for a woman and order me home.

It was a quarter to eight and quite dark before he fell into step beside me.

"Well," I told him rather shakily; "I'm still alive, as you see."

"Then it is pretty bad?"

"It's exceedingly queer," I admitted, and told my story. I had meant to conceal the bolt on the outside of my door, and one or two other things, but I blurted them all out right then and there, and felt a lot better at once.

He listened intently.

"It's fear of the deadliest sort," I finished.

"Fear of the police?"

"I—I think not. It is fear of something in the house. They are always listening and watching at the top of the front stairs. They have lifted all the carpets, so that every footstep echoes through the whole house. Mrs. Reed goes down to the first floor, but never alone. Today I found that the back staircase is locked off at top and bottom. There are doors."

I gave him my rough diagram of the house. It was too dark to see it.

"It is only tentative," I explained. "So much of the house is locked up, and every movement of mine is under surveillance. Without baths there are about twelve large rooms, counting the third floor. I've not been able to get there, but I thought that tonight I'd try to look about."

"You had no sleep last night?"

"Three hours—from about four to seven this morning."

We had crossed into the public square and were walking slowly under the trees. Now he stopped and faced me.

"I don't like the look of it, Miss Adams," he said. "Ordinary panic goes and hides. But here's a fear that knows what it's afraid of and takes methodical steps for protection. I didn't want you to take the case, you know that; but now I'm not going to insult you by asking you to give it up. But I'm going to see that you are protected. There will be someone across the street every night as long as you are in the house."

"Have you any theory?" I asked him. He is not strong for theories generally. He is very practical. "That is, do you think the other nurse was right and there is some sort of crime being concealed?"

"Well, think about it," he prompted me. "If a murder has been committed, what are they afraid of? The police? Then why a trained nurse and all this caution about the children? A ghost? Would they lift the carpets so that they could hear the specter tramping about?"

"If there is no crime, but something—a lunatic perhaps?" I asked.

"Possibly. But then why this secrecy and keeping out the police? It is, of course, possible that your respected employers have both gone off mentally, and the whole thing is a nightmare delusion. On my word, it sounds like it. But it's too much for credulity to believe they've both gone crazy with the same form of delusion."

"Perhaps I'm the lunatic," I said despairingly. "When you reduce it to an absurdity like that, I wonder if I didn't imagine it all, the lights burning everywhere and the carpets up, and Mrs. Reed staring down the staircase, and me locked in a room and hanging on by my nails to peer out through a closet transom."

"Perhaps. But how about the deadly sane young woman who preceded you? She had no imagination. Now about Reed and his wife—how do they strike you? They get along all right and that sort of thing, I suppose?"

"They are nice people," I said emphatically. "He's a gentleman and they're devoted. He just looks like a big boy who's got into an awful mess and doesn't know how to get out. And she's backing him up. She's a dear."

"Humph!" said Mr. Patton. "Don't suppress any evidence because she's a dear and he's a handsome big boy!"

"I didn't say he was handsome," I snapped.

"Did you ever see a ghost or think you saw one?" he inquired suddenly.

"No, but one of my aunts has. Hers always carry their heads. She asked one a question once and the head nodded."

"Then you believe in things of that sort?"

"Not a particle—but I'm afraid of them."

He smiled, and shortly after that I went back to the house. I think he was sorry about the ghost question, for he explained that he had been trying me out, and that I looked well in my cloak and bonnet.

"I'm afraid of your chin generally," he said; "but the white lawn ties have a softening effect. In view of the ties I almost have the courage . . ."

"Yes?"

"I think not, after all," he decided. "The chin is there, ties or no ties. Good night, and—for heaven's sake don't run any unnecessary risks."

The change from his facetious tone to earnestness was so unexpected that I was still standing there on the pavement when he plunged into the darkness of the square and disappeared.

Chapter IV

At ten minutes after eight I was back in the house. Mr. Reed admitted me, going through the tedious process of unlocking outer and inner vestibule doors and fastening them again behind me. He inquired politely if I had had a pleasant walk, and without waiting for my reply, fell to reading the evening paper. He seemed to have forgotten me absolutely. First he scanned the headlines; then he turned feverishly to something farther on and ran his fingers down along a column. His lips were twitching, but evidently he did not find what he expected—or feared—for he threw the paper away and did not glance at it again. I watched him from the angle of the stairs.

Even for that short interval, Mrs. Reed had taken his place at the children's door.

She wore a black dress, long sleeved and high at the throat, instead of the silk negligee of the previous evening, and she held a book. But she was not reading. She smiled rather wistfully when she saw me.

"How fresh you always look!" she said. "And so self-reliant. I wish I had your courage."

"I am perfectly well. I dare say that explains a lot. Kiddies asleep?"

"Freddie isn't. He's been crying for Chang. I hate night, Miss Adams. I'm like Freddie. All my troubles come up about this time. I'm horribly depressed." Her blue eyes filled with tears. "And I haven't been sleeping well," she confessed.

I should think not!

Without taking off my things, I went down to Mr. Reed in the lower hall.

"I'm going to insist on something," I said. "Mrs. Reed is highly nervous. She says she has not been sleeping. I think if I give her a sedative and she gets an entire night's sleep, it may save her a breakdown."

I looked straight in his eyes, and for once he did not evade me.

"I'm afraid I've been very selfish," he said. "Of course she must have sleep. I'll give you a powder, unless you have something you prefer to use."

I remembered then that he was a chemist, and said I would gladly use whatever he gave me.

"There is another thing I wanted to speak about, Mr. Reed," I said. "The children are mourning their dog. Don't you think he may have been accidentally shut up somewhere in the house, on one of the upper floors?"

"Why do you say that?" he demanded sharply.

"They say they have heard him howling."

He hesitated for barely a moment. Then: "Possibly. But they will not hear him again. The little chap has been sick, and he—died today. Of course the boys are not to know."

No one watched the staircase that night. I gave Mrs. Reed the powder and saw her comfortably into bed. When I went back fifteen minutes later, she was resting, but not asleep. Sedatives sometimes make people garrulous for a little while—sheer comfort, perhaps, and relaxed tension. I've had stockbrokers and bankers in the hospital give me tips, after a hypodermic of morphia, that would have made me wealthy had I not been limited to my training allowance of twelve dollars a month.

"I was just wondering," she said as I tucked her up, "where a woman owes the most allegiance—to her husband or to her children?"

"Why not split it up," I said cheerfully, "and try doing what seems best for both?"

"But that's only a compromise!" she complained, and was asleep almost immediately. I lowered the light and closed the door, and shortly after, I heard Mr. Reed locking it from the outside.

With the bolt off my door and Mrs. Reed asleep, my plan for the night was easily carried out. I went to bed for a couple of hours and slept calmly. I awakened once with the feeling that someone was looking at me from the passage into the night nursery but there was no one there. However, so strong had been the feeling that I got up and went into the back room. The children were asleep, and all doors opening into the hall were locked. But the window onto the porte-cochère roof was open and the curtain blowing. There was no one on the roof, however, and I closed and locked the window.

It was not twelve o'clock and I went back to bed for an hour.

At one I prepared to make a thorough search of the house. Looking from one of my windows, I thought I saw the shadowy figure of a man across the street, and I was comforted. Help was always close, I felt. And yet, as I stood inside my door in my rubber-soled shoes, with my ulster over my uniform, my revolver, flashlight and skeleton keys in my pockets, my heart was going very fast. The stupid story of the ghost came back and made me shudder, and the next instant I was remembering Mrs. Reed the night before, staring down into the lower hall with fixed glassy eyes.

My plan was to begin at the top of the house and work down. The thing was the more hazardous, of course, because Mr. Reed was most certainly somewhere about. I had no excuse for being on the third floor. Down below

I could say I wanted tea, or hot water—anything. But I did not expect to find Mr. Reed up above. The terror, whatever it was, seemed to lie below.

Access to the third floor was not easy. The main staircase did not go up. To get there I was obliged to unlock the door at the rear of the hall with my own keys. I was working in bright light, trying my keys one after another, and watching over my shoulder as I did so. When the door finally gave, it was a relief to slip into the darkness beyond, ghosts or no ghosts.

I am always a silent worker. Caution about closing doors and squeaking hinges is second nature to me. One learns to be cautious when one's only chance to sleep is not to rouse a peevish patient and have to give a body massage, as like as not, or listen to domestic troubles—"I said" and "he said"—until one is almost crazy.

So I made no noise. I closed the door behind me and stood blinking in the darkness. I listened. There was no sound above or below. Now houses at night have no terror for me. Every nurse is obliged to do more or less going about in the dark. But I was not easy. Suppose Mr. Reed should call me? True, I had locked my door and had the key in my pocket. But a dozen emergencies flew through my mind as I felt for the stair rail.

There was a curious odor through all the back staircase, a pungent, aromatic scent that, with all my familiarity with drugs, was strange to me. As I slowly climbed the stairs it grew more powerful. The air was heavy with it, as though no windows had been opened in that part of the house. There was no door at the top of this staircase, as there was on the second floor. It opened into an upper hall, and across from the head of the stairs was a door leading into a room. This door was closed. On this staircase, as on all the others, the carpet had been newly lifted. My electric flash showed the white boards and painted borders, the carpet tacks, many of them still in place. One, lying loose, penetrated my rubber sole and went into my foot.

I sat down in the dark and took off the shoe. As I did so my flash, on the step beside me, rolled over and down with a crash. I caught it on the next step, but the noise had been like a pistol shot.

Almost immediately a voice spoke above me sharply. At first I thought it was out in the upper hall. Then I realized that the closed door was between it and me.

"Ees that you, Meester Reed?"

Mademoiselle!

"Meester Reed!" plaintively. "Eet comes up again, Meester Reed! I die! Tomorrow I die!"

She listened. When no reply came, she began to groan rhythmically, to a curious accompaniment of creaking. When I had gathered up my nerves again, I realized that she must be sitting in a rocking chair. The groans were really little plaintive grunts.

By the time I had got my shoe on, she was up again, and I could hear her pacing the room, the heavy step of a woman well fleshed and not young. Now and then she stopped inside the door and listened; once she shook the knob and mumbled querulously to herself.

I recovered the flash, and with infinite caution worked my way to the top of the stairs. Mademoiselle was locked in, doubly bolted in. Two strong bolts, above and below, supplemented the door lock.

Her ears must have been very quick, or else she felt my softly padding feet on the boards outside, for suddenly she flung herself against the door and begged for a priest, begged piteously, in jumbled French and English. She wanted food; she was dying of hunger. She wanted a priest.

And all the while I stood outside the door and wondered what I should do. Should I release the woman? Should I go down to the lower floor and get the detective across the street to come in and open the door? Was this the terror that held the house in thrall—this babbling old Frenchwoman calling for food and a priest in one breath?

Surely not. This was a part of the mystery, but not all. The real terror lay below. It was not Mademoiselle, locked in her room on the upper floor, that the Reeds waited for at the top of the stairs. But why was Mademoiselle locked in her room? Why were the children locked in? What was this thing that had turned a home into a jail, a barracks, that had sent away the servants, imprisoned and probably killed the dog, sapped the joy of life from two young people? What was it that Mademoiselle cried "comes up again"?

I looked toward the staircase. Was it coming up the staircase?

I am not afraid of the thing I can see, but it seemed to me, all at once, that if anything was going to come up the staircase, I might as well get down first. A staircase is no place to meet anything, especially if one doesn't know what it is.

I listened again. Mademoiselle was quiet. I flashed my light down the narrow stairs. They were quite empty. I shut off the flash and went down. I tried to go slowly, to retreat with dignity, and by the time I had reached the landing below, I was heartily ashamed of myself. Was this shivering girl the young woman Mr. Patton called his right hand?

I dare say I should have stopped there, for that night at least. My nerves were frayed. But I forced myself on. The mystery lay below. Well, then, I was going down. It could not be so terrible. At least it was nothing supernatural. There must be a natural explanation. And then that silly story about the headless things must pop into my mind and start me down trembling.

The lower rear staircase was black dark, like the upper, but just at the foot a light came in through a barred window. I could see it plainly, and the shadows of the iron grating on the bare floor. I stood there listening. There was not a sound.

It was not easy to tell exactly what followed. I stood there with my hand on the rail. I'd been very silent; my rubber shoes attended to that. And one moment the staircase was clear, with a patch of light at the bottom. The next, something was there, halfway down—a head, it seemed to be, with a pointed hood like a monk's cowl. There was no body. It seemed to lie at my feet. But it was living. It moved. I could tell the moment when the eyes lifted and saw my feet, the slow back-tilting of the head as they looked up my body. All the air was squeezed out of my lungs; a heavy hand seemed to press on my chest. I remember raising a shaking hand and flinging my flashlight at the head. The flash clattered on the stair tread, harmless. Then the head was gone and something living slid over my foot.

I stumbled back to my room and locked the door. It was two hours before I had strength enough to get my aromatic-ammonia bottle.

Chapter V

It seemed to me that I had hardly dropped asleep before the children were in the room, clamoring.

"The goldfish are dead!" Harry said, standing soberly by the bed. "They are all dead with their stummicks turned up."

I sat up. My head ached violently.

"They can't be dead, old chap." I was feeling about for my kimono, but I remembered that, when I had found my way back to the nursery after my fright on the back stairs, I had lain down in my uniform. I crawled out, hardly able to stand. "We gave them fresh water yesterday, and—"

I had got to the aquarium. Harry was right. The little darting flames of pink and gold were still. They floated about, rolling gently as Freddie prodded them with a forefinger, dull-eyed, pale bellies upturned. In his cage above, the little parrot watched out of a crooked eye.

I ran to the medicine closet in the bathroom. Freddie had a weakness for administering medicine. I had only just rescued the parrot from the result of his curiosity—a headache tablet—the day before.

"What did you give them?" I demanded.

"Bread," said Freddie stoutly.

"Only bread?"

"Dirty bread," Harry put in. "I told him it was dirty."

"Where did you get it?"

"On the roof of the porte-cochère!"

Shades of Montessori! The rascals had been out on that sloping tin roof. It turned me rather sick to think of it.

Accused, they admitted it frankly.

"I unlocked the window," Harry said, "and Freddie got the bread. It was out in the gutter. He slipped once."

"Almost went over and made a squash on the pavement," added Freddie. "We gave the little fishes the bread for breakfast, and now they're gone to God."

The bread had contained poison, of course. Even the two little snails that crawled over the sand in the aquarium were motionless. I sniffed the water. It had a slightly foreign odor. I did not recognize it.

Panic seized me then. I wanted to get away and take the children with me. The situation was too hideous. But it was still early. I could only wait until the family roused. In the meantime, however, I made a nerve-racking excursion out onto the tin roof and down to the gutter. There was no more of the bread there. The porte-cochère was at the side of the house. As I stood balancing myself perilously on the edge, summoning my courage to climb back to the window above, I suddenly remembered the guard Mr. Patton had promised and glanced toward the square.

The guard was still there. More than that, he was running across the street toward me. It was Mr. Patton himself. He brought up between the two houses with absolute fury in his face.

"Go back!" he waved. "What are you doing out there anyhow? That roof's as slippery as the devil!"

I turned meekly and crawled back with as much dignity as I could. I did not say anything. There was nothing I could bawl from the roof. I could only close and lock the window and hope that the people in the next house still slept. Mr. Patton must have gone shortly after, for I did not see him again.

I wondered if he had relieved the night watch, or if he could possibly have been on guard himself all that chilly April night.

Mr. Reed did not breakfast with us. I made a point of being cheerful before the children, and their mother was rested and brighter than I had seen her. But more than once I found her staring at me in a puzzled way. She asked me if I had slept.

"I wakened only once," she said. "I thought I heard a crash of some sort. Did you hear it?"

"What sort of crash?" I evaded.

The children had forgotten the goldfish for a time. Now they remembered and clamored their news to her.

"Dead?" she said, and looked at me.

"Poisoned," I explained. "I shall nail the windows over the porte-cochère shut, Mrs. Reed. The boys got out there early this morning and picked up something—bread, I believe. They fed it to the fish and—they are dead."

All the light went out of her face. She looked tired and harassed as she got up.

"I wanted to nail the window," she said vaguely, "but Mr. Reed ... Suppose they had eaten that bread, Miss Adams, instead of giving it to the fish!"

The same thought had chilled me with horror. We gazed at each other over the unconscious heads of the children and my heart ached for her. I made a sudden resolution.

"When I first came," I said to her, "I told you I wanted to help. That's what I'm here for. But how am I to help either you or the children when I do not know what danger it is that threatens? It isn't fair to you, or to them, or even to me."

She was much shaken by the poison incident. I thought she wavered.

"Are you afraid the children will be stolen?"

"Oh, no."

"Or hurt in any way?" I was thinking of the bread on the roof.

"No."

"But you are afraid of something?"

Harry looked up suddenly. "Mother's never afraid," he said stoutly.

I sent them both in to see if the fish were still dead.

"There is something in the house downstairs that you are afraid of?" I persisted.

She took a step forward and caught my arm.

"I had no idea it would be like this, Miss Adams. I'm dying of fear!"

I had a quick vision of the swathed head on the back staircase, and some of my night's terror came back to me. I believe we stared at each other with dilated pupils for a moment. Then I asked, "Is it a real thing?—surely you can tell me this. Are you afraid of a reality, or—is it something supernatural?" I was ashamed of the question. It sounded so absurd in the broad light of that April morning.

"It is a real danger," she replied. Then I think she decided that she had gone as far as she dared, and I went through the ceremony of letting her out and of locking the door behind her.

The day was warm. I threw up some of the windows and the boys and I played ball, using a rolled handkerchief. My part, being to sit on the floor with a newspaper folded into a bat and to bang at the handkerchief as it flew past me, became automatic after a time.

As I look back, I see a pair of disordered young rascals with Russian blouses and bare round knees doing a great deal of yelling and some very crooked throwing; a nurse sitting tailor fashion on the floor, alternately ducking to save her cap and making vigorous but ineffectual passes at the ball with her newspaper bat. And I see sunshine in the room and the dwarf parrot eating sugar out of his claw. And below, the fish floating in the aquarium, belly up and dull-eyed.

Mr. Reed brought up our luncheon tray. He looked tired and depressed and avoided my eyes. I watched him while I spread the bread and butter for the children. He nailed shut the windows that opened on to the porte-cochère roof, and when he thought I was not looking, he examined the registers in the wall to see if the gratings were closed. The boys put the dead fish in a box and made him promise a decent interment in the garden. They called on me for an epitaph, and I scrawled on top of the box:

> These fish are dead
> Because a boy called Fred
>   Went out on a porch roof when he should
> Have been in bed.

I was much pleased with it. It seemed to me that an epitaph, which can do no good to the departed, should at least convey a moral. But to my horror Freddie broke into loud wails and would not be comforted.

It was three o'clock, therefore, before they were both settled for their afternoon naps and I was free. I had determined to do one thing, and to do it in daylight—to examine the back staircase inch by inch. I knew I would be courting discovery, but the thing had to be done, and no power on earth would have made me essay such an investigation after dark.

It was all well enough for me to say to myself that there was a natural explanation; that this had been a human head, of a certainty; that something living and not spectral had slid over my foot in the darkness. I would not have gone back there again at night for youth, love or money. But I did not investigate the staircase that day, after all.

I made a curious discovery after the boys had settled down in their small white beds. A venturesome fly had sailed in through an open window, and I was immediately in pursuit of it with my paper bat. Driven from the cornice to the chandelier, harried here, swatted there, finally he took refuge inside the furnace register.

Perhaps it is my training—I used to know how many million germs a fly packed about with it, and the generous benevolence with which it distributed them; I've forgotten—but the sight of a single fly maddens me. I said that to Mr. Patton once, and he asked what the sight of a married one would do. So I sat down by the register and waited. It was then that I made the curious discovery that the furnace below stairs was burning, and burning hard. A fierce heat assailed me as I opened the grating. I drove the fly out of cover, but I had no time for him. The furnace going full on a warm spring day! It was strange.

Perhaps I was stupid. Perhaps the whole thing should have been clear to me. But it was not. I sat there bewildered and tried to figure it out. I went over it point by point:

The carpets up all over the house, lights going full all night and doors locked.

The cot at the top of the stairs and Mrs. Reed staring down.

The bolt that had been outside my door to lock me in.

The death of Chang.

Mademoiselle locked in her room upstairs and begging for a priest.

The poison on the porch roof.

The head without a body on the staircase and the thing that slid over my foot.

The furnace going, and the thing I recognized as I sat there beside the register—the unmistakable odor of burning cloth.

Should I have known? I wonder. It looks so clear to me now.

I did not investigate the staircase, for the simple reason that my skeleton key, which, the night before, had unfastened the lock of the door at the rear of the second-floor hall, did not open it now. I did not understand at once and stood stupidly working with the lock. The door was bolted on the other side. I wandered as aimlessly as I could down the main staircase and tried the corresponding door on the lower floor. It, too, was locked. Here was an impasse for sure. As far as I could discover, the only other entrance to the back staircase was through the window with the iron grating.

As I turned to go back, I saw my electric flash, badly broken, lying on a table in the hall. I did not claim it.

The lower floor seemed entirely deserted. The drawing room and library were in their usual disorder, undusted and bare of floor. The air everywhere was close and heavy; there was not a window open. I sauntered through the various rooms, picked up a book in the library as an excuse and tried the door of the room behind. It was locked. I thought at first that something moved behind it, but if anything lived there, it did not stir again. And yet

I had a vivid impression that just on the other side of the door ears as keen as mine were listening. It was broad day, but I backed away from the door and out into the wide hall. My nerves were still raw, no doubt, from the night before.

I was to meet Mr. Patton at half after seven that night, and when Mrs. Reed relieved me at seven, I had half an hour to myself. I spent it in Beauregard Gardens, with the dry fountain in the center. The place itself was charming, the trees still black but lightly fringed with new green, early spring flowers in the borders, neat paths and, surrounding it all, the solid, dignified backs of the Beauregard houses. I sat down on the coping of the fountain and surveyed the Reed house. Those windows above were Mademoiselle's. The shades were drawn, but no light came through or round them. The prisoner—for prisoner she was by every rule of bolt and lock—must be sitting in the dark. Was she still begging for her priest? Had she had any food? Was she still listening inside her door for whatever it was that was "coming up"?

In all the other houses, windows were open; curtains waved gently in the spring air; the cheerful signs of the dinner hour were evident nearby— moving servants, a gleam of stately shirt bosom as a butler mixed a salad, a warm radiance of candlelight from dining-room tables and the reflected glow of flowers. Only the Reed house stood gloomy, unlighted, almost sinister.

Beauregard Square dined early. It was one of the traditions, I believe. It liked to get to the theater or the opera early, and it believed in allowing the servants a little time in the evenings. So, although it was only something after seven, the evening rite of the table crumbs began to be observed. Came a colored butler, bowed to me with a word of apology, and dumped the contents of a silver tray into the basin; came a pretty mulatto, flung her crumbs gracefully and smiled with a flash of teeth at the butler.

Then for five minutes I was alone.

It was Nora, the girl we had met on the street, who came next. She saw me and came round to me with a little air of triumph.

"Well, I'm back in the square again, after all, miss," she said. "And a better place than the Reeds'. I don't have the doilies to do."

"I'm very glad you are settled again, Nora."

She lowered her voice. "I'm just trying it out," she observed. "The girl that left said I wouldn't stay. She was scared off. There have been some queer doings—not that I believe in ghosts or anything like that. But my mother in the old country had the second sight, and if there's anything going on, I'll be right sure to see it."

It took encouragement to get her story, and it was secondhand at that, of course. But it appeared that a state of panic had seized the Beauregard servants. The alarm was all belowstairs and had been started by a cook who, coming in late and going to the basement to prepare herself a cup of tea, had found her kitchen door locked and a light going beyond. Suspecting another maid of violating the tea canister, she had gone soft-footed to the outside of the house and had distinctly seen a gray figure crouching in a corner of the room. She had called the butler, and they had made an examination of the entire basement without result. Nothing was missing from the house.

"And that figure has been seen again and again, miss," Nora finished. "The McKennas' butler, Joseph, saw it in this very spot, walking without a sound and the street light beyond there shining straight through it. Over in the Smythe house the laundress, coming in late and going down to the basement to soak her clothes for the morning, met the thing on the basement staircase and fainted dead away."

I had listened intently. "What do they think it is?" I asked.

She shrugged her shoulders and picked up her tray.

"I'm not trying to say and I guess nobody is. But if there's been a murder, it's pretty well known that the ghost walks about until the service is read and it's properly buried." She glanced at the Reed house. "For instance," she demanded, "where is Mademoiselle?"

"She is alive," I said rather sharply. "And even if what they say were true, what in the world would make her wander about the basements? It seems so silly, Nora, a ghost haunting damp cellars and laundries with stationary tubs and all that."

"Well," she contended, "it seems silly for them to sit on cold tombstones —and yet that's where they generally sit, isn't it?"

Mr. Patton listened gravely to my story that night.

"I don't like it," he said when I had finished. "Of course the head on the staircase is nonsense. Your nerves were ragged and our eyes play tricks on all of us. But as for the Frenchwoman—"

"If you accept her, you must accept the head," I snapped. "It was there— it was a head without a body and it looked up at me."

We were walking through a quiet street, and he bent over and caught my wrist.

"Pulse racing," he commented. "I'm going to take you away, that's certain. I can't afford to lose my best assistant. You're too close, Miss Adams; you've lost your perspective."

"I've lost my temper!" I retorted. "I shall not leave until I know what this thing is, unless you choose to ring the doorbell and tell them I'm a spy."

He gave in when he saw that I was firm, but not without a final protest.

"I'm directly responsible for you to your friends," he said. "There's probably a young man somewhere who will come gunning for me if anything happens to you. And I don't care to be gunned for. I get enough of that in my regular line."

"There is no young man," I said shortly.

"Have you been able to see the cellars?"

"No, everything is locked off."

"Do you think the rear staircase goes all the way down?"

"I haven't the slightest idea."

"You are in the house. Have you any suggestions as to the best method of getting into the house? Is Reed on guard all night?"

"I think he is."

"It may interest you to know," he said finally, "that I sent a reliable man to break in there last night, quietly, and that he—couldn't do it. He got a leg through a cellar window, and came near not getting it out again. Reed was just inside in the dark." He laughed a little, but I guessed that the thing galled him.

"I do not believe that he would have found anything if he had succeeded in getting in. There has been no crime, Mr. Patton, I am sure of that. But there is a menace of some sort in the house."

"Then why does Mrs. Reed stay and keep the children if there is danger?"

"I believe she is afraid to leave him. There are times when I think that he is desperate."

"Does he ever leave the house?"

"I think not, unless—"

"Yes?"

"Unless he is the basement ghost of the other houses."

He stopped in his slow walk and considered it.

"It's possible. In that case I could have him waylaid tonight in the gardens and left there, tied. It would be a holdup, you understand. The police have no excuse for coming in yet. Or, if we found him breaking into one of the other houses, we could get him there. He'd be released, of course, but it would give us time. I want to clean the thing up. I'm not easy while you are in that house."

We agreed that I was to wait inside one of my windows that night, and that on a given signal I should go down and open the front door. The whole thing, of course, was contingent on Mr. Reed's leaving the house sometime that night. It was only a chance.

"The house is barred like a fortress," Mr. Patton said as he left me. "The window with the grating is hopeless. That's the one we tried last night."

Chapter VI

I find that my notes on that last night in the house on Beauregard Square are rather confused, some written at the time, some just before. For instance, on the edge of a newspaper clipping I find this:

"Evidently this is the item. R___ went pale on reading it. Did not allow wife to see paper."

The clipping is an account of the sudden death of an elderly gentleman named Smythe, one of the Beauregard families.

The next note is less hasty and is on a yellow symptom record. It has been much folded—I believe I tucked it in my apron belt:

"If the rear staircase is bolted everywhere from the inside, how did the person who locked it, either Mr. or Mrs. Reed, get back into the body of the house again? Or did Mademoiselle do it? In that case she is no longer a prisoner and the bolts outside her room are not fastened.

"At eleven o'clock tonight Harry wakened with earache. I went to the kitchen to heat some mullein oil and laudanum. Mrs. Reed was with the boy and Mr. Reed was not in sight. I slipped into the library and used my skeleton keys on the locked door to the rear room. It is empty even of furniture, but there is a huge box there, with a lid that fastens down with steel hooks. The lid is full of small airholes. I had no time to examine further.

"It is one o'clock. Harry is asleep and his mother is dozing across the foot of his bed. I have found the way to get to the rear staircase. There are outside steps from the basement to the garden. Evidently the staircase goes all the way down to the cellar. Then the lower door in the cellar must be only locked, not bolted from the inside. I shall try to get to the cellar."

The next is a scrawl:

"Cannot get to the outside basement steps. Mr. Reed is wandering round lower floor. I reported Harry's condition and came up again. I must get to the back staircase."

I wonder if I have been able to convey, even faintly, the situation in that highly respectable old house that night: the fear that hung over it, a fear so great that even I, an outsider and stout of nerve, felt it and grew cold; the unnatural brilliancy of light that bespoke dread of the dark; the hushed voices, the locked doors and staring, peering eyes; the babbling Frenchwoman on an upper floor, the dead fish, the dead dog. And, always in my mind, that vision of dread on the back staircase and the thing that slid over my foot.

At two o'clock I saw Mr. Patton, or whoever was on guard in the park across the street, walk quickly toward the house and disappear round the corner toward the gardens in the rear. There had been no signal, but I felt sure that Mr. Reed had left the house. His wife was still asleep across Harry's bed. As I went out, I locked the door behind me, and I also took the key to the night nursery. I thought that something disagreeable, to say the least, was inevitable, and why let her in for it?

The lower hall was lighted, as usual, and empty. I listened, but there were no restless footsteps. I did not like the lower hall. Only a thin wooden door stood between me and the rear staircase, and anyone who thinks about the matter will realize that a door is no barrier to a head that can move about without a body. I am afraid I looked over my shoulder while I unlocked the front door, and I know I breathed better when I was out in the air.

I wore my dark ulster over my uniform, and I had my revolver and keys. My flash, of course, was useless. I missed it horribly. But to get to the staircase was an obsession by that time in spite of my fear of it—to find what it guarded, to solve its mystery. I worked round the house, keeping close to the wall, until I reached the garden. The night was the city night, never absolutely dark. As I hesitated at the top of the basement steps, it seemed to me that figures were moving about among the trees.

The basement door was unlocked and open. I was not prepared for that, and it made me, if anything, more uneasy. I had a box of matches with me, and I wanted light as a starving man wants food. But I dared not light them. I could only keep a tight grip on my courage and go on. A small passage first, with whitewashed stone walls, cold and scaly under my hand; then a

large room, and still darkness. Worse than darkness, something crawling
and scratching round the floor.

I struck my match then, and it seemed to me that something white flashed
into a corner and disappeared. My hands were shaking, but I managed to
light a gas jet and to see that I was in the laundry. The staircase came down
here, narrower than above, and closed off with a door.

The door was closed and there was a heavy bolt on it but no lock.

And now, with the staircase accessible and a gaslight to keep up my
courage, I grew brave, almost reckless. I would tell Mr. Patton all about this
cellar, which his best men had not been able to enter. I would make a sketch
for him—coalbins, laundry tubs, everything. Foolish, of course, but hold the
gas jet responsible—the reckless bravery of light after hideous darkness.

So I went on, forward. The glow from the laundry followed me. I struck
matches, found potatoes and cases of mineral water, bruised my knees on
a discarded bicycle, stumbled over a box of soap. Twice, out of the corner
of my eye, and never there when I looked, I caught the white flash that had
frightened me before. Then at last I brought up before a door and stopped.
It was a curiously barricaded door, nailed against disturbance by a plank
fastened across, and, as if to make intrusion without discovery impossible,
pasted round every crack and over the keyhole with strips of strong yellow
paper. It was an ominous door. I wanted to run away from it, and I also
wanted desperately to stand and look at it and imagine what might lie
beyond. Here again was the strange, spicy odor that I had noticed on the
back staircase.

I think it is indicative of my state of mind that I backed away from the
door. I did not turn and run. Nothing in the world would have made me
turn my back to it.

Somehow or other I got back into the laundry and jerked myself together.

It was ten minutes after two. I had been less than ten minutes in the
basement!

The staircase daunted me in my shaken condition. I made excuses for
delaying my venture, looked for another box of matches, listened at the end
of the passage, finally slid the bolt and opened the door. The silence was
impressive. In the laundry there were small, familiar sounds—the dripping
of water from a faucet, the muffled measure of a gas meter, the ticking of
a clock on the shelf. To leave it all, to climb into that silence . . .

Lying on the lower step was a curious instrument. It was a sort of tongs
made of steel, about two feet long, and fastened together like a pair of
scissors, the joint about five inches from the flattened ends. I carried it to
the light and examined it. One end was smeared with blood and short,
brownish hairs. It made me shudder, but—from that time on I think I knew.
Not the whole story, of course, but somewhere in the back of my head, as
I climbed in that hideous quiet, the explanation was developing itself. I did
not think it out. It worked itself out as, step after step, match after match,
I climbed the staircase.

Up to the first floor there was nothing. The landing was bare of carpet.

I was on the first floor now. On each side, doors, carefully bolted, led into the house. I opened the one into the hall and listened. I had been gone from the children fifteen minutes and they were on my mind. But everything was quiet.

The sight of the lights and the familiar hall gave me courage. After all, if I was right, what could the head on the staircase have been but an optical illusion? And I was right. The evidence—the tongs—was in my hand. I closed and bolted the door and felt my way back to the stairs. I lighted no matches this time. I had only a few, and on this landing there was a little light from the grated window, although the staircase above was in black shadow.

I had one foot on the lower stair, when suddenly overhead came the thudding of hands on a closed door. It broke the silence like an explosion. It sent chills up and down my spine. I could not move for a moment. It was the Frenchwoman!

I believe I thought of fire. The idea had obsessed me in that house of locked doors. I remember a strangling weight of fright on my chest and my effort to breathe. Then I started up the staircase, running as fast as I could lift my weighted feet—I remember that—and getting up perhaps a third of the way. Then there came a plunging forward into space, my hands out, a shriek frozen on my lips, and—quiet.

I do not think I fainted. I know I was always conscious of my arm doubled under me, a pain and darkness. I could hear myself moaning, but almost as if it were someone else. There were other sounds, but they did not concern me much. I was not even curious about my location. I seemed to be a very small consciousness surrounded by a great deal of pain.

Several centuries later a light came and leaned over me from somewhere above. Then the light said, "Here she is!"

"Alive?" I knew that voice, but I could not think whose it was.

"I'm not—Yes, she's moaning."

They got me out somewhere and I believe I still clung to the tongs. I had fallen on them and had a cut on my chin. I could stand, I found, although I swayed. There was plenty of light now in the back hallway, and a man I had never seen was investigating the staircase.

"Four steps off," he said. "Risers and treads gone and the supports sawed away. It's a trap of some sort."

Mr. Patton was examining my broken arm and paid no attention. The man let himself down into the pit under the staircase. When he straightened, only his head rose above the steps. Although I was white with pain to the very lips, I laughed hysterically. "The head!" I cried.

Mr. Patton swore under his breath.

They half led, half carried me into the library. Mr. Reed was there, with a detective on guard over him. He was sitting in his old position, bent forward, chin in palms. In the blaze of light he was a pitiable figure, smeared with dust, disheveled from what had evidently been a struggle. Mr. Patton put me in a chair and dispatched another man for the nearest doctor.

"This young lady," he said curtly to Mr. Reed, "fell into that damnable trap you made in the rear staircase."

"I locked off the staircase—but I am sorry she is hurt. My—my wife will be shocked. Only I wish you'd tell me what all this is about. You can't arrest me for going into a friend's house."

"If I send for some member of the Smythe family, will they acquit you?"

"Certainly they will," he said. "I—I've been raised with the Smythes. You can send for anyone you like." But his tone lacked conviction.

Mr. Patton made me as comfortable as possible, and then, sending the remaining detective out into the hall, he turned to his prisoner.

"Now, Mr. Reed," he said. "I want you to be sensible. For some days a figure has been seen in the basements of the various Beauregard houses. Your friends, the Smythes, reported it. Tonight we are on watch, and we see you breaking into the basement of the Smythe house. We already know some curious things about you, such as your dismissal of all the servants on half an hour's notice and the disappearance of the French governess."

"Mademoiselle! Why, she—" He checked himself.

"When we bring you here tonight, and you ask to be allowed to go upstairs and prepare your wife, she is locked in. The nurse is missing. We find her at last, also locked away, and badly hurt, lying in a staircase trap, where someone, probably yourself, has removed the steps. I do not want to arrest you, but now I've started, I'm going to get to the bottom of all this."

Mr. Reed was ghastly, but he straightened in his chair.

"The Smythes reported this thing, did they?" he asked. "Well, tell me one thing. What killed the old gentleman—old Smythe?"

"I don't know."

"Well, go a little further." His cunning was boyish, pitiful. "How did he die? Or don't you know that either?"

Up to this point I had been rather a detached part of the scene, but now my eyes fell on the tongs beside me.

"Mr. Reed," I said, "isn't this thing too big for you to handle by yourself?"

"What thing?"

"You know what I mean. You've protected yourself well enough, but even if the—the thing you know of did not kill old Mr. Smythe, you cannot tell what will happen next."

"I've got almost all of them," he muttered sullenly. "Another night or two and I'd have had the lot."

"But even then the mischief may go on. It means a crusade; it means rousing the city. Isn't it the square thing now to spread the alarm?"

Mr. Patton could stand the suspense no longer. "Perhaps, Miss Adams," he said, "you will be good enough to let me know what you are talking about."

Mr. Reed looked up at him with heavy eyes. "Rats," he said. "They got away, twenty of them, and some are loaded with bubonic plague."

I went to the hospital the next morning. Mr. Patton thought it best. There was no one in my little flat to look after me, and although the pain in my arm subsided after the fracture was set, I was still shaken.

He came the next afternoon to see me. I was propped up in bed, with my hair braided down in two pigtails and great hollows under my eyes.

"I'm comfortable enough," I said, in response to his inquiry; "but I'm feeling all of my years. This is my birthday. I am thirty today."

"I wonder," he said reflectively, "if I ever reach the mature age of one hundred, if I will carry in my head as many odds and ends of information as you have at thirty!"

"I? What do you mean?" I said rather weakly.

"You. How in the world did you know, for instance about those tongs?"

"It was quite simple. I'd seen something like them in the laboratory here. Of course I didn't know what animals he'd used, but the grayish brown hair looked like rats. The laboratory must be the cellar room. I knew it had been fumigated—it was sealed with paper, even over the keyhole."

So, sitting there beside me, Mr. Patton told me the story as he had got it from Mr. Reed—a tale of the offer in an English scientific journal of a large reward from some plague-ridden country of the East for an anti-plague serum. Mr. Reed had been working along bacteriological lines in his basement laboratory, mostly with guinea pigs and tuberculosis. He was in debt; the offer loomed large.

"He seems to think he was on the right track," Mr. Patton said. "He had twenty of the creatures in deep zinc cans with perforated lids. He says the disease is spread by fleas that infest the rats. So he had muslin over the lids as well. One can had infected rats, six of them. Then one day the French-woman tried to give the dog a bath in a laundry tub and the dog bolted. The laboratory door was open in some way and he ran between the cans, upsetting them. Every rat was out in an instant. The Frenchwoman was frantic. She shut the door and tried to drive the things back. One bit her on the foot. The dog was not bitten, but there was the question of fleas.

"Well, the rats got away, and Mademoiselle retired to her room to die of plague. She was a loyal old soul; she wouldn't let them call a doctor. It would mean exposure, and after all, what could the doctors do? Reed used his serum and she's alive.

"Reed was frantic. His wife would not leave. There was the Frenchwom-an to look after, and I think Mrs. Reed was afraid he would do something desperate. They did the best they could, under the circumstances, for the children. They burned most of the carpets for fear of fleas, and put poison everywhere. Of course he had traps, too.

"He had brass tags on the necks of the rats, and he got back a few—the uninfected ones. The other ones were probably dead. But he couldn't stop at that. He had to be sure that the trouble had not spread. And to add to their horror, the sewer along the street was being relaid, and they had an influx of rats into the house. They found them everywhere on the lower floor. They even climbed the stairs. He says that the night you came he caught a big fellow on the front staircase. There was always the danger that the fleas that carry the trouble had deserted the dead creatures for new fields. They took up all the rest of the carpets and burned them. To add to the general misery, the dog, Chang, developed unmistakable symptoms and had to be killed."

"But the broken staircase?" I asked. "And what was it that Mademoiselle said was coming up?"

"The steps were up for two reasons: The rats could not climb up, and beneath the steps Reed says he caught two of the tagged ones in a trap. As for Mademoiselle, the thing that was coming up was her temperature—pure fright. The head you saw was poor Reed himself wrapped in gauze against trouble and baiting his traps. He caught a lot in the neighbors' cellars and some in the garden."

"But why," I demanded, "why didn't he make it all known?"

Mr. Patton laughed and shrugged his shoulders.

"A man hardly cares to announce that he has menaced the health of a city."

"But that night when I fell—was it only last night?—someone was pounding above. I thought there was a fire."

"The Frenchwoman had seen us waylay Reed from her window. She was crazy."

"And the trouble is over now?"

"Not at all," he replied cheerfully. "The trouble may be only beginning. We're keeping Reed's name out, but the Board of Health has issued a general warning. Personally I think his six pets died without passing anything along."

"But there was a big box with a lid—"

"Ferrets," he assured me. "Nice white ferrets with pink eyes and a taste for rats." He held out a thumb, carefully bandaged. "Reed had a couple under his coat when we took him in the garden. Probably one ran over your foot that night when you surprised him on the back staircase."

I went pale. "But if they are infected!" I cried, "and you are bitten—"

"The first thing a nurse should learn"—he bent forward, smiling—"is not to alarm her patient."

"But you don't understand the danger," I said despairingly. "Oh, if only men had a little bit of sense!"

"I must do something desperate, then? Have the thumb cut off, perhaps?"

I did not answer. I lay back on my pillows with my eyes shut. I had given him the plague, had seen him die and be buried, before he spoke again.

"The chin," he said, "is not so firm as I had thought. The outlines are savage, but the dimple . . . You poor little thing; are you really frightened?"

"I don't like you," I said furiously. "But I'd hate to see anyone with—with that trouble."

"Then I'll confess. I was trying to take your mind off your troubles. The bite is there, but harmless. Those were new ferrets; they had never been out."

I did not speak to him again. I was seething with indignation. He stood for a time looking down at me; then, unexpectedly, he bent over and touched his lips to my bandaged arm.

"Poor arm!" he said. "Poor, brave little arm!" Then he tiptoed out of the room. His very back was sheepish.

ACTIVITIES

1) This story—and the previous Sherlock Holmes ones—utilize what authors call the first person point of view. In this technique, a narrator or "I" who is a character in the plot reveals what he or she sees and is told by other characters. He also tells you what he feels.

As you remember, Doyle's "I" (Watson) was not the hero, or protagonist, of the stories—Holmes was, of course. Watson concentrated upon Holmes's activities and reported them as best he could to the reader.

This is different from what happens in "Locked Doors"; here, the "I" is Hilda Adams herself. In contrast to Watson, her focus of interest is upon her own adventure, and she is definitely the central character.

What are the advantages—and disadvantages—of each of these variations of *the first person point of view?* Why do you think each author chose the variation he or she did? (More will be said about point of view later.)

2) Compare the relationship between Hilda Adams and Mr. Patton with those of the other detective teams in this book.

3) In terms of the final solution to the Reed house mystery, explain the following unusual happenings:

A) The disappearance of the dog, Chang, and its continuing crying.
B) The death of the goldfish.
C) The imprisonment of the governess, Mademoiselle.
D) The head without a body.
E) The burglar of Beauregard Square.
F) The boarded-up room in the basement.
G) The huge box with its lid full of airholes.
H) The mysterious "flashes of white."

4) Why did Francis Reed refuse to seek help from "the outside world" for the predicament he was in? Was his method of coping a realistic one? How would you have handled it?

RESEARCH ACTIVITY

Mary Roberts Rinehart obtained her nickname for Hilda Adams from Allan Pinkerton, a U.S. secret service agent who founded his own detective agency. Later, this agency's operatives, or "Pinkertons" as they were called, became famous because of the various historical events in which they were involved. A very interesting research paper could be written about the history of the "Pinkertons."

Agatha Christie—and Miss Marple

(For the first part of Ms. Christie's biography, see Chapter 4.)

Her unfortunate 1926 experience with the press caused Agatha Christie to shy away from publicity. During her early career, she came to believe that authors should remain "background, shadowy figures"[4] but as the years went by, she became more understanding of the normal curiosity expressed by her fans and began mellowing in her attitude toward journalists. Eventually she became as interesting a literary personality as any of her male predecessors.

In 1928, she divorced Archibald Christie, and two years later she married Professor Max Mallowan, an eminent British archeologist. For many years, she accompanied Professor Mallowan on his numerous scientific expeditions and began using the settings of these explorations as backgrounds for her stories. *Death on the Nile, Murder in Mesopotamia,* and *Appointment with Death* were written this way.

When World War II broke out, she again exhibited her patriotism by resuming her work as a volunteer nurse. During all her experiences, the good years and the bad, she managed to keep up the remarkable writing pace she had long ago set for herself—at least one book a year.

In addition to being prolific, Ms. Christie is very versatile. Besides novels and short stories, she has written some fine detective plays. One of her dramas, *The Mouse Trap,* has had one of the longest runs of any play presented on the London stage. Another, *Witness for the Prosecution,* after its initial theater success, was made into a highly-acclaimed motion picture.

Agatha Christie's masculine sleuth, M. Hercule Poirot, started her on the road to fame. Her female detective, Miss Jane Marple, kept her there.

Like Father Brown, Miss Marple seemed a most unlikely candidate for the profession of sleuth. Firstly, she was a spinster, albeit a sweet-faced one, who lived in the little town of St. Mary Mead, not far from London. Secondly, she was involved with all the commonplaces of small-town living —marketing, knitting, and gossiping.

But once her first mystery came along in 1928, she proved herself as sharp-witted as those male chauvinists, Holmes, Poirot, and Queen. In fact, we doubt if any of those three could have done as well with the following puzzle as Miss Marple.[5]

See if you can discover why we feel this way . . .

Village Murders

Miss Politt took hold of the knocker and rapped politely on the cottage door. After a discreet interval she knocked again. The parcel under her left arm shifted a little as she did so, and she readjusted it. Inside the parcel was Mrs. Spenlow's new green winter dress, ready for fitting. From Miss Politt's left hand dangled a bag of black silk, containing a tape measure, a pincushion, and a large, practical pair of scissors.

Miss Politt was tall and gaunt, with a sharp nose, pursed lips, and meager iron-grey hair. She hesitated before using the knocker for the third time. Glancing down the street, she saw a figure rapidly approaching. Miss Hartnell, jolly, weather-beaten, fifty-five, shouted out in her usual loud bass voice, "Good afternoon, Miss Politt!"

The dressmaker answered, "Good afternoon, Miss Hartnell." Her voice was excessively thin and genteel in its accents. She had started life as a lady's maid. "Excuse me," she went on, "but do you happen to know if by any chance Mrs. Spenlow isn't at home?"

"Not the least idea," said Miss Hartnell.

"It's rather awkward, you see. I was to fit on Mrs. Spenlow's new dress this afternoon. Three-thirty, she said."

Miss Hartnell consulted her wrist watch. "It's a little past the half-hour now."

"Yes. I have knocked three times, but there doesn't seem to be any answer, so I was wondering if perhaps Mrs. Spenlow might have gone out and forgotten. She doesn't forget appointments as a rule, and she wants the dress to wear the day after tomorrow."

Miss Hartnell entered the gate and walked up the path to join Miss Politt outside the door of Laburnam Cottage.

"Why doesn't Gladys answer the door?" she demanded. "Oh, no, of course, it's Thursday—Gladys's day out. I expect Mrs. Spenlow has fallen asleep. I don't expect you've made enough noise with this thing."

Seizing the knocker, she executed a deafening *rat-a-tat-tat* and, in addition, thumped upon the panels of the door. She also called out in a stentorian voice: "What ho, within there!"

There was no response.

Miss Politt murmured, "Oh, I think Mrs. Spenlow must have forgotten and gone out. I'll call round some other time." She began edging away down the path.

"Nonsense," said Miss Hartnell firmly. "She can't have gone out. I'd have met her. I'll just take a look through the windows and see if I can find any signs of life."

She laughed in her usual hearty manner, to indicate that it was a joke, and applied a perfunctory glance to the nearest windowpane—perfunctory because she knew quite well that the front room was seldom used, Mr. and Mrs. Spenlow preferring the small back sitting room.

Perfunctory as it was, though, it succeeded in its object. Miss Hartnell, it is true, saw no signs of life. On the contrary, she saw, through the window, Mrs. Spenlow lying on the hearthrug—dead.

"Of course," said Miss Hartnell, telling the story afterward, "I managed to keep my head. That Politt creature wouldn't have had the least idea of what to do. 'Got to keep our heads,' I said to her. 'You stay here and I'll go for Constable Palk.' She said something about not wanting to be left, but I paid no attention at all. One has to be firm with that sort of person. I've always found they enjoy making a fuss. So I was just going off when, at that very moment, Mr. Spenlow came round the corner of the house."

Here Miss Hartnell made a significant pause. It enabled her audience to ask breathlessly, "Tell me, how did he look?" Miss Hartnell would then go on: "Frankly, I suspected something at once! He was far too calm. He didn't seem surprised in the least. And you may say what you like, it isn't natural for a man to hear that his wife is dead and display no emotion whatever."

Everybody agreed with this statement.

The police agreed with it too. So suspicious did they consider Mr. Spenlow's detachment that they lost no time in ascertaining how that gentleman was situated as a result of his wife's death. When they discovered that Mrs. Spenlow had been the moneyed partner, and that her money went to her husband under a will made soon after their marriage, they were more suspicious than ever.

Miss Marple, that sweet-faced (and some said vinegar-tongued) elderly spinster who lived in the house next to the rectory, was interviewed very early—within half an hour of the discovery of the crime. She was approached by Police Constable Palk, importantly thumbing a notebook. "If you don't mind, ma'am, I've a few questions to ask you."

Miss Marple said, "In connection with the murder of Mrs. Spenlow?"

Palk was startled. "May I ask, madam, how you got to know of it?"

"The fish," said Miss Marple.

The reply was perfectly intelligible to Constable Palk. He assumed correctly that the fishmonger's boy had brought it, together with Miss Marple's evening meal.

Miss Marple continued gently, "Lying on the floor in the sitting room, strangled—possibly by a very narrow belt. But whatever it was, it was taken away."

Palk's face was wrathful. "How that young Fred gets to know everything—"

Miss Marple cut him short adroitly. She said, "There's a pin in your tunic."

Constable Palk looked down, startled. He said, "They do say: 'See a pin and pick it up, all the day you'll have good luck.'"

"I hope that will come true. Now what is it you want me to tell you?"

Constable Palk cleared his throat, looked important, and consulted his notebook. "Statement was made to me by Mr. Arthur Spenlow, husband of the deceased. Mr. Spenlow says that at two-thirty, as far as he can say, he was rung up by Miss Marple and asked if he would come over at a quarter past three, as she was anxious to consult him about something. Now, ma'am, it that true?"

"Certainly not," said Miss Marple.

"You did not ring up Mr. Spenlow at two-thirty?"

"Neither at two-thirty nor any other time."

"Ah," said Constable Palk, and sucked his moustache with a good deal of satisfaction.

"What else did Mr. Spenlow say?"

"Mr. Spenlow's statement was that he came over here as requested, leaving his own house at ten minutes past three; that on arrival here he was informed by the maidservant that Miss Marple was 'not at 'ome.' "

"That part of it is true," said Miss Marple. "He did come here, but I was at a meeting at the Women's Institute."

"Ah," said Constable Palk again.

Miss Marple exclaimed, "Do tell me, Constable, do you suspect Mr. Spenlow?"

"It's not for me to say at this stage, but it looks to me as though somebody, naming no names, had been trying to be artful."

Miss Marple said thoughtfully, "Mr. Spenlow?"

She liked Mr. Spenlow. He was a small, spare man, stiff and conventional in speech, the acme of respectability. It seemed odd that he should have come to live in the country; he had so clearly lived in towns all his life. To Miss Marple he confided the reason. He said, "I have always intended, ever since I was a small boy, to live in the country someday and have a garden of my own. I have always been very much attached to flowers. My wife, you know, kept a flower shop. That's where I saw her first."

A dry statement, but it opened up a vista of romance. A younger, prettier Mrs. Spenlow, seen against a background of flowers.

Mr. Spenlow, however, really knew nothing about flowers. He had no idea of seeds, of cuttings, of bedding out, of annuals or perennials. He had only a vision—a vision of a small cottage garden thickly planted with sweet-smelling, brightly coloured blossoms. He had asked, almost pathetically, for instruction and had noted down Miss Marple's replies to questions in a little book.

He was a man of quiet method. It was, perhaps, because of this trait that the police were interested in him when his wife was found murdered. With patience and perseverance they learned a good deal about the late Mrs. Spenlow—and soon all St. Mary Mead knew it too.

The late Mrs. Spenlow had begun life as a betweenmaid in a large house. She had left that position to marry the second gardener and with him had started a flower shop in London. The shop had prospered. Not so the gardener, who before long had sickened and died.

His widow had carried on the shop and enlarged it in an ambitious way. She had continued to prosper. Then she had sold the business at a handsome price and embarked upon matrimony for the second time—with Mr. Spenlow, a middle-aged jeweler who had inherited a small and struggling business. Not long afterward they had sold the business and come down to St. Mary Mead.

Mrs. Spenlow was a well-to-do woman. The profits from her florist's establishment she had invested—"under spirit guidance," as she explained to all and sundry. The spirits had advised her with unexpected acumen.

All her investments had prospered, some in quite a sensational fashion. Instead, however, of this increasing her belief in spiritualism, Mrs. Spenlow basely deserted mediums and sittings and made a brief but wholehearted plunge into an obscure religion with Indian affinities which was based on various forms of deep breathing. When, however, she arrived at St. Mary Mead, she had relapsed into a period of orthodox Church-of-England beliefs. She was a good deal at the Vicarage and attended church services with assiduity. She patronized the village shops, took an interest in the local happenings, and played village bridge.

A humdrum, everyday life. And—suddenly—murder.

Colonel Melchett, the chief constable, had summoned Inspector Slack.

Slack was a positive type of man. When he made up his mind, he was sure. He was quite sure now. "Husband did it, sir," he said.

"You think so?"

"Quite sure of it. You've only got to look at him. Never showed a sign of grief or emotion. He came back to the house knowing she was dead."

"Wouldn't he at least have tried to act the part of the distracted husband?"

"Not him, sir. Too pleased with himself. Some gentlemen can't act. Too stiff. As I see it, he was just fed up with his wife. She'd got the money and, I should say, was a trying woman to live with—always taking up some 'ism' or other. He cold-bloodedly decided to do away with her and live comfortably on his own."

"Yes, that could be the case, I suppose."

"Depend upon it, that was it. Made his plans careful. Pretended to get a phone call—"

Melchett interrupted him: "No call been traced?"

"No, sir. That means either that he lied or that the call was put through from a public telephone booth. The only two public phones in the village are at the station and the post office. Post office it certainly wasn't. Mrs. Blade sees everyone who comes in. Station it might be. Train arrives at two twenty-seven and there's a bit of bustle then. But the main thing is he says it was Miss Marple who called him up, and that certainly isn't true. The call didn't come from her house, and she herself was away at the Institute."

"You're not overlooking the possibility that the husband was deliberately got out of the way—by someone who wanted to murder Mrs. Spenlow?"

"You're thinking of young Ted Gerard, aren't you, sir? I've been working on him—what we're up against there is lack of motive. He doesn't stand to gain anything."

"He's an undesirable character, though. Quite a pretty little spot of embezzlement to his credit."

"I'm not saying he isn't a wrong 'un. Still, he did go to his boss and own up to that embezzlement. And his employers weren't wise to it."

"An Oxford Grouper," said Melchett.

"Yes, sir. Became a convert and went off to do the straight thing and own up to having pinched money. I'm not saying, mind you, that it mayn't have been astuteness—he may have thought he was suspected and decided to gamble on honest repentance."

"You have a skeptical mind, Slack," said Colonel Melchett. "By the way, have you talked to Miss Marple at all?"

"What's she got to do with it, sir?"

"Oh, nothing. But she hears things, you know. Why don't you go and have a chat with her She's a very sharp old lady."

Slack changed the subject. "One thing I've been meaning to ask you, sir: That domestic-service job where the deceased started her career—Sir Robert Abercrombie's place. That's where the jewel robbery was—emeralds—worth a packet. Never got them. I've been looking it up—must have happened when the Spenlow woman was there, though she'd have been quite a girl at the time. Don't think she was mixed up in it, do you, sir? Spenlow, you know, was one of those little tuppenny-ha'penny jewelers—just the chap for a fence."

Melchett shook his head. "Don't think there's anything in that. She didn't even know Spenlow at the time. I remember the case. Opinion in police circles was that a son of the house was mixed up in it—Jim Abercrombie—awful young waster. Had a pile of debts, and just after the robbery they were all paid off—some rich woman, so they said, but I don't know—old Abercrombie hedged a bit about the case—tried to call the police off."

"It was just an idea, sir," said Slack.

Miss Marple received Inspector Slack with gratification, especially when she heard that he had been sent by Colonel Melchett.

"Now, really, that is very kind of Colonel Melchett. I didn't know he remembered me."

"He remembers you, all right. Told me that what you didn't know of what goes on in St. Mary Mead isn't worth knowing."

"Too kind of him, but really I don't know anything at all. About this murder, I mean."

"You know what the talk about it is."

"Of course—but it wouldn't do, would it, to repeat just idle talk?"

Slack said, with an attempt at geniality, "This isn't an official conversation, you know. It's in confidence, so to speak."

"You mean you really want to know what people are saying? Whether there's any truth in it or not?"

"That's the idea."

"Well, of course, there's been a great deal of talk and speculation. And there are really two distinct camps, if you understand me. To begin with, there are the people who think that the husband did it. A husband or a wife is, in a way, the natural person to suspect, don't you think so?"

"Maybe," said the inspector cautiously.

"Such close quarters, you know. Then, so often, the money angle. I hear that it was Mrs. Spenlow who had the money and therefore Mr. Spenlow does benefit by her death. In this wicked world I'm afraid the most unchari-table assumptions are often justified."

"He comes into a tidy sum, all right."

"Just so. It would seem quite plausible, wouldn't it, for him to strangle her, leave the house by the back, come across the fields to my house, ask for me and pretend he'd had a telephone call from me, then go back and find his wife murdered in his absence—hoping, of course, that the crime would be put down to some tramp or burglar."

The inspector nodded. "What with the money angle—and if they'd been on bad terms lately—"

But Miss Marple interrupted him: "Oh, but they hadn't."

"You know that for a fact?"

"Everyone would have known if they'd quarrelled! The maid, Gladys Brent—she'd have soon spread it round the village."

The inspector said feebly, "She mightn't have known," and received a pitying smile in reply.

Miss Marple went on: "And then there's the other school of thought. Ted Gerard. A good-looking young man. I'm afraid, you know, that good looks are inclined to influence one more than they should. Our last curate but one—quite a magical effect! All the girls came to church—evening service as well as morning. And many older women became unusually active in parish work—and the slippers and scarves that were made for him! Quite embarrassing for the poor young man.

"But let me see, where was I? Oh yes, this young man, Ted Gerard. Of course, there has been talk about him. He's come down to see her so often. Though Mrs. Spenlow told me herself that he was a member of what I think they call the Oxford Group. A religious movement. They are quite sincere and very earnest, I believe, and Mrs. Spenlow was impressed by it all."

Miss Marple took a breath and went on: "And I'm sure there was no reason to believe that there was anything more in it than that, but you know what people are. Quite a lot of people are convinced that Mrs. Spenlow was infatuated with the young man and that she'd lent him quite a lot of money. And it's perfectly true that he was actually seen at the station that day. In the train—the two twenty-seven down train. But of course it would be quite easy, wouldn't it, to slip out of the other side of the train and go through the cutting and over the fence and round by the hedge and never come out of the station entrance at all? So that he need not have been seen going to the cottage. And of course people do think that what Mrs. Spenlow was wearing was rather peculiar."

"Peculiar?"

"A kimono. Not a dress." Miss Marple blushed. "That sort of thing, you know, is, perhaps, rather suggestive to some people."

"You think it was suggestive?"

"Oh no, I don't think so. I think it was perfectly natural."

"You think it was natural?"

"Under the circumstances, yes." Miss Marple's glance was cool and reflective.

Inspector Slack said, "It might give us another motive for the husband. Jealousy."

"Oh no, Mr. Spenlow would never be jealous. He's not the sort of man who notices things. If his wife had gone away and left a note on the pincushion, it would be the first he'd know of anything of that kind."

Inspector Slack was puzzled by the intent way she was looking at him. He had an idea that all her conversation was intended to hint at something he didn't understand. She said now, with some emphasis, "Didn't you find any clues, Inspector—on the spot?"

"People don't leave fingerprints and cigarette ash nowadays, Miss Marple."

"But this, I think," she suggested, "was an old-fashioned crime—"

Slack said sharply, "Now what do you mean by that?"

Miss Marple remarked slowly, "I think, you know, that Constable Palk could help you. He was the first person on the—on the 'scene of the crime,' as they say."

Mr. Spenlow was sitting in a deck chair. He looked bewildered. He said, in his thin, precise voice, "I may, of course, be imagining what occurred. My hearing is not as good as it was. But I distinctly think I heard a small boy call after me, 'Yah, who's a Crippen?' It—it conveyed the impression to me that he was of the opinion that I had—had killed my dear wife."

Miss Marple, gently snipping off a dead rose head, said, "That was the impression he meant to convey, no doubt."

"But what could possibly have put such an idea into a child's head?"

Miss Marple coughed. "Listening, no doubt, to the opinions of his elders."

"You—you really mean that other people think that also?"

"Quite half the people in St. Mary Mead."

"But, my dear lady, what can possibly have given rise to such an idea? I was sincerely attached to my wife. She did not, alas, take to living in the country as much as I had hoped she would do, but perfect agreement on every subject is an impossible ideal. I assure you I feel her loss very keenly."

"Probably. But if you will excuse my saying so, you don't sound as though you do."

Mr. Spenlow drew his meager frame up to its full height. "My dear lady, many years ago I read of a certain Chinese philosopher who, when his dearly loved wife was taken from him, continued calmly to beat a gong in the street—a customary Chinese pastime, I presume—exactly as usual. The people of the city were much impressed by his fortitude."

"But," said Miss Marple, "the people of St. Mary Mead react rather differently. Chinese philosophy does not appeal to them."

"But you understand?"

Miss Marple nodded. "My uncle Henry," she explained, "was a man of unusual self-control. His motto was 'Never display emotion.' He, too, was very fond of flowers."

"I was thinking," said Mr. Spenlow with something like eagerness, "that I might, perhaps, have a pergola on the west side of the cottage. Pink roses and, perhaps, wisteria. And there is a white starry flower, whose name for the moment escapes me—"

In the tone in which she spoke to her grandnephew, aged three, Miss Marple said, "I have a very nice catalogue here, with pictures. Perhaps you would like to look through it—I have to go up to the village."

Leaving Mr. Spenlow sitting happily in the garden with his catalogue, Miss Marple went up to her room, hastily rolled up a dress in a piece of brown paper, and, leaving the house, walked briskly up to the post office. Miss Politt, the dressmaker, lived in rooms over the post office.

But Miss Marple did not at once go through the door and up the stairs. It was just two-thirty, and, a minute late, the Much Benham bus drew up outside the post-office door. It was one of the events of the day in St. Mary Mead. The postmistress hurried out with parcels, parcels connected with the shop side of her business, for the post office also dealt in sweets, cheap books, and children's toys.

For some four minutes Miss Marple was alone in the post office.

Not till the postmistress returned to her post did Miss Marple go upstairs and explain to Miss Politt that she wanted her own grey crepe altered and made more fashionable if that were possible. Miss Politt promised to see what she could do.

The chief constable was rather astonished when Miss Marple's name was brought to him. She came in with many apologies. "So sorry—so very sorry to disturb you. You are so busy, I know, but then you have always been so very kind, Colonel Melchett, and I felt I would rather come to you instead of to Inspector Slack. For one thing, you know, I should hate Constable Palk to get into any trouble. Strictly speaking, I suppose he shouldn't have touched anything at all."

Colonel Melchett was slightly bewildered. He said, "Palk? That's the St. Mary Mead constable, isn't it? What has he been doing?"

"He picked up a pin, you know. It was in his tunic. And it occurred to me at the time that it was quite probable he had actually picked it up in Mrs. Spenlow's house."

"Quite, quite. But, after all, you know, what's a pin? Matter of fact, he did pick the pin up just by Mrs. Spenlow's body. Came and told Slack about it yesterday—you put him up to that, I gather? Oughtn't to have touched anything, of course, but, as I said, what's a pin? It was only a common pin. Sort of thing any woman might use."

"Oh no, Colonel Melchett, that's where you're wrong. To a man's eye, perhaps, it looked like an ordinary pin, but it wasn't. It was a special pin, a very thin pin, the kind you buy by the box, the kind used mostly by dressmakers."

Melchett stared at her, a faint light of comprehension breaking in on him. Miss Marple nodded her head several times eagerly.

"Yes, of course. It seems to me so obvious. She was in her kimono because she was going to try on her new dress, and she went into the front room, and Miss Politt just said something about measurements and put the tape measure round her neck—and then all she'd have to do was to cross it and pull—quite easy, so I've heard. And then of course she'd go outside and pull the door to and stand there knocking as though she'd just arrived. But the pin shows she'd already been in the house."

"And it was Miss Politt who telephoned to Spenlow?"

"Yes. From the post office at two-thirty—just when the bus comes and the post office would be empty."

Colonel Melchett said, "But, my dear Miss Marple, why? In heaven's name, why? You can't have a murder without a motive."

"Well, I think, you know, Colonel Melchett, from all I've heard, that the crime dates from a long time back. It reminds me, you know, of my two cousins, Antony and Gordon. Whatever Antony did always went right for him, and with poor Gordon it was just the other way about: race horses went lame, and stocks went down, and property depreciated. . . . As I see it, the two women were in it together."

"In what?"

"The robbery. Long ago. Very valuable emeralds, so I've heard. The lady's maid and the tweeny. Because one thing hasn't been explained—how, when the tweeny married the gardener, did they have enough money to set up a flower shop?

"The answer is, it was her share of the—the swag, I think is the right expression. Everything she did turned out well. Money made money. But the other one, the lady's maid, must have been unlucky. She came down to being just a village dressmaker. Then they met again. Quite all right at first, I expect, until Mr. Ted Gerard came on the scene.

"Mrs. Spenlow, you see, was already suffering from conscience and was inclined to be emotionally religious. This young man no doubt urged her to 'face up' and to 'come clean,' and I daresay she was strung up to do so. But Miss Politt didn't see it that way. All she saw was that she might go to prison for a robbery she had committed years ago. So she made up her mind to put a stop to it all. I'm afraid, you know, that she was always rather a wicked woman. I don't believe she'd have turned a hair if that nice, stupid Mr. Spenlow had been hanged."

Colonel Melchett said slowly, "We can—er—verify your theory—up to a point. The identity of the Politt woman with the lady's maid at the Abercrombies,' but—"

Miss Marple reassured him.

"It will be all quite easy. She's the kind of woman who will break down at once when she's taxed with the truth. And then, you see, I've got her tape measure. I—er—abstracted it yesterday when I was trying on. When she misses it and thinks the police have got it—well, she's quite an ignorant woman and she'll think it will prove the case against her in some way."

She smiled at him encouragingly. "You'll have no trouble, I can assure you." It was the tone in which his favourite aunt had once assured him that he could not fail to pass his entrance examination into Sandhurst.

And he had passed.

ACTIVITIES

1) In her unobtrusive way, Miss Jane Marple proves to be a very thorough investigator in this adventure. List several instances of this thoroughness and show how each contributed to the solution of the crime.

2) Another characteristic of Miss Marple is her "gossipy" way of providing analogies relating to family and friends. An example of this is when she discusses her two cousins, Antony and Gordon, with Colonel Melchett:

"Whatever Antony did always went right for him, and with poor Gordon it was just the other way about: race horses went lame, and stocks went down, and property depreciated."

Exactly what analogy was she communicating here?

3) Inadvertently, Ted Gerard's arrival in St. Mary Mead precipitated the crime. How?

Stuart Palmer—and Hildegarde Withers

Agatha Christie became famous through her characterization of a male detective, M. Hercule Poirot.

Stuart Palmer, an American writer and contemporary of Ellery Queen, reversed the process; his notable contribution to literary sleuthdom turned out to be a fabulous female ferret named Hildegarde Withers.

Like Mr. Strang, Hildegarde Withers was a schoolteacher. Like Miss Marple, she was a spinster who dazzled police investigators with brilliant solutions to apparently unsolvable crimes. Hildegarde appeared on the literary scene in 1931; she remained for four decades, managing to delight several generations of readers.

Stuart Palmer was introduced to detective fiction at the age of 12 when he read his first Sherlock Holmes story. This took place in the farming community of Baraboo, Wisconsin; from the moment he encountered Holmes, he became a confirmed detective story fan. As he states, ". . . Within a year, I had memorized most the the *Adventures* and *Exploits* and had become official story-teller for the local troop of the Boy Scouts of America. Around the campfire, on our weekly hikes and yearly camping trips . . . I burbled forth as much of the stories as I had been able to retain."[6]

Later on, he chose the field of detective literature for his life's work. The idea for Hildegarde Withers came to him from ". . . a composite of my memories of the acidulous, sniffing (town) librarian, of a horse-faced English teacher in the local high school, of my own Yankee father's sense of humor, and of an impression of Edna May Oliver whom I had seen one night, as a standee, in the last weeks of the first run of Jerome Kern's *Showboat.*"[7]

His first Withers story was a novel, *The Penguin Pool Mystery.* It was an immediate success and scores of further adventures of the oddly-hatted, horse-faced schoolmarm came from his pen; in fact, Hildegarde was to make him one of the important detective writers of the mid-twentieth century.

Before his death in 1968, Stuart Palmer had expanded his literary activities to include screenplay writing and the publication of a noted nonfiction crime treatise, *A Study of Murder.*[8]

As for Hildegarde, she lives on. And you will probably further her existence by your reactions and comments—after you meet her in the following pages. We trust you will enjoy her meeting with Groucho Marx.

You Bet Your Life

Walter McWalters looked upon the imminent end of Walter McWalters with considerable calm. His voice over the phone showed just the proper blend of hurt surprise and immediate cooperation. He would be glad to come down to the District Attorney's office for the "little talk" they requested so urgently; since he was tied up today would ten o'clock tomorrow morning be all right? He hung up the instrument without the slightest trembling of his well-manicured hand. Half an hour later the prominent clubman and mining investment counselor was out of the big house in exclusive Brentwood which his late wife Claire had bought just after their marriage four years ago, taking with him only such necessities as his clothes, shaving gear, and a brief case containing $200,000, mostly in hundreds. McWalters had always liked the feel of hundred-dollar bills.

He was out of the house—and out of this world. He disappeared with less splash but more finality than a stone dropped into the sea. But even the dropping of a stone starts ripples . . .

Six months later a certain whimsical, eccentric spinster made her debut on television. Just before zero hour Miss Hildegarde Withers felt more than a little nervous, because she was not at all sure of her lines. There was more at stake here than any jackpot prize, and she felt that she should have been better prepared for her ordeal than just the short briefing in the little back-stage dressing-room and the powder the make-up man had dabbed on her weather-beaten face.

The clock ticked away, and then loud and clear came the honeyed voice of the announcer, a Mr. George Fenneman. "And now, Groucho, I have another interesting couple for you to meet—a Mr. Wilton Mulvey and a Miss Hildegarde Withers." A youthful, collar-ad face appeared around the backdrop, and a hand beckoned. "Come in, folks, and meet—*GROUCHO MARX!*"

Miss Withers and her nondescript little partner were jostled gently from behind; they took a few steps forward and then they were *on*. She was vaguely aware of the studio audience, the lights, the cameras, the orchestra —but once on stage she had eyes only for the dapper, graying man in the spectacles, the neat tan suit and bright blue bow tie, who perched behind a high desk where a bowl of asters concealed his microphone. In the flesh, Groucho looked like his filmed self only perhaps more so; his famous mustache was undeniably real, too. She had always wondered about that; Miss Withers had had a secret fondness for the zany Marx Brothers ever since *Animal Crackers* days.

"Welcome, welcome to *You Bet Your Life*," cried Groucho cheerily. "Say the Secret Word and you'll receive an extra hundred dollars." He relighted his cigar. "Miss Withers, do you mind if I call you Hildegarde?" There were more of the usual pleasantries, with the famed comedian going into his usual routine of trying to play matchmaker for the two of them after Mr. Mulvey admitted that he was a bachelor. It also developed that Mulvey spent his life engraving things on the heads of pins, which gave Groucho an opening for some jocose remarks. Then he turned on Miss Withers, with a pixyish cock of his head. "Hildegarde, may I ask where you're from?"

"You may, Mr. Marx. I taught public school in New York City for many years. Now I live in a little white cottage in Santa Monica, by the sea. I've retired."

"How often," sighed Groucho, "I've wished all schoolteachers would retire, back in my early days. But I'll have you know that it isn't true they had to burn down the schoolhouse to get me out of the third grade. It was the *fifth!* But Hildegarde, is that all you do, just retire?"

"Of course not. My avocation is criminology."

"Face cream or dairy cream?"

"*Crim*inology, Mr. Marx."

"Oh," Groucho said. "I don't hear well, my glasses must need adjusting. So you're a criminologist. Does that mean you read murder mysteries and try to guess who-done-it before the author tells you in the last chapter?"

"Certainly not! I'm interested in real crimes, particularly in the offbeat sort. It occurred to me long ago that the police have a tendency to follow beaten paths, which works out well enough only when the criminal runs true to form. But—"

"So you're a sleuth, Miss Withers?" Groucho interrupted, picking an aster from the bowl and delicately sniffing at the stem end. "Have you ever actually solved a real crime?"

She shrugged modestly. "Quite a few, as it happens. Do you remember the Rowan murders in New York City, and the Ina Kell affair that wound up out here in Tijuana, and the capture of Eddie the Actor in Chicago? Those were some of my successes."

"A schoolteacher sleuth, doing the work of the police! And I suppose they're very grateful to you for your help?"

"On the contrary, Mr. Marx. Even though I've always been willing to stay in the background and let them get the credit. But—the official mind, you know!"

"Are you working on anything interesting right now, Hildegarde?" Groucho asked.

The schoolteacher steeled herself, then lunged. "Yes. I've become very interested in the McWalters case, right here in town."

Groucho managed a mammoth surprise-take. "McWalters! Isn't he the socialite who's supposed to have walked off some months ago with a suitcase full of somebody else's money—the one who did a disappearing act more famous than anything since Judge Crater's? Isn't he the man the police are looking for all over the United States, to say nothing of Canada and Mexico?" In an aside, he added, "But who am I to say nothing of Canada and Mexico, good neighbors that they are?" He paused. "And Hildegarde, do you really think you have a chance to solve the McWalters mystery, when the biggest police manhunt in recent history has failed to turn up hide or hair of the man?"

In a hotel room in Las Vegas, Jack Finn, licensed private investigator, came out of the bathroom with a highball in his hand and noticed that Sugar had the TV set on. Something caught his eye. "Migawd!" he cried. "Is this Thursday? Where went Wednesday? Look, baby, get packed—and fast! We got to get back to L.A.!" But the big, pasty-faced man himself stayed beside the set, while the ice cubes melted in his drink ...

Over the air waves Miss Withers was saying, "I don't think, Mr. Marx. I *know*. I have the McWalters case solved."

Groucho's eyebrows went up even higher than before. "What?"

"Yes. By a combination of common sense, feminine intuition, a clinical study of what is known of the man's habits and behavior, plus one lucky break, I know *everything*, including his approximate whereabouts. They all make one mistake, you know."

"And are you going to tell our vast unseen audience—most of whom are probably out at the refrigerator getting a can of beer at the moment—all about your discovery?"

"I'm afraid not, Mr. Marx. It's top-secret."

"Oh, I see. You're just telling the police, then?"

"No, Mr. Marx," Miss Withers replied. "I most certainly am *not* telling the police. They have been too rude to me. I'm writing it all up in an article. Of course, when it's published the police can no doubt arrest McWalters in a matter of minutes. But I mustn't say too much—"

In a little bierstube in New York's Yorkville, Inspector Oscar Piper sat frozen on his stool, his face upturned to the TV set hung above the bar. "Lady, you've said it already!" gasped the grizzled little skipper of Homicide West. Hildegarde, he feared, had lost her marbles. And he was fond of the preposterous old biddy, too. They had been friendly enemies since their first meeting above a corpse and a frightened penguin in the old Aquarium, more years ago than he cared to think. His lager slowly went flat, untasted before him.

On the TV screen Groucho Marx was saying, "So you're a writer, too?" For once in his life, Groucho was playing straightman, but he gave her a conspiratorial wink.

The schoolteacher nodded brightly. "I expect to finish my little exposé article this week, and I'm quite confident that it will be snatched up by the editor of one of the largest Sunday supplements. He used to go to school to me, so I have an *in.*"

"Well, Hildegarde, I'll watch the Sunday newspapers, and I only hope that the missing Mr. McWalters reads them too, so he can learn about his mistakes. Good luck. And it's been a lot of fun talking to you two, but now it's time to play *You Bet Your Life.*"

Miss Withers's phone buzzed like an infuriated rattlesnake just after midnight, while she was in the midst of giving her hair its requisite hundred strokes with the brush. Naturally she was on Cloud Seven at hearing the familiar voice of her old friend and sparring partner; also, and just as naturally, she hardly gave him a chance to put a word in edgewise.

"How thoughtful of you, Oscar, to call me! Didn't the show go well? Wasn't it a shame about my idiot partner doing us out of the grand prize? What did you think—?"

"Shut up and listen! Hildegarde, do you know what you've got yourself into with this insane yak-yak over the air?"

"Certainly! One of my more brilliant inspirations."

"Didn't it occur to you that McWalters might be tuned in?"

"We hoped so. Naturally, Oscar, it was a put-up job, my being a guest on the show and all. But one of the first things I learned about McWalters was that he never missed watching a quiz program and that his favorite was *You Bet Your Life*—so I thought that might be the way to trap him. And with the help of Mr. Marx and Mr. Fenneman and the writers, I baited a hook."

Oscar Piper was almost choking. "Baited with your own gizzard! You bet your *own* life . . ."

"Don't be silly, Oscar. If the man saw the broadcast of the show, or listened to the radio version, he's sure to think that I know his secret and that I'm going to publish it to the world. So naturally he'll have to come out of hiding, try to break into my house, and get a look at my manuscript . . ."

"You think McWalters is just a con-man?"

"But he *is,* Oscar! He skipped with $200,000 and there is a big reward out for him that I can well use, though I may have to split some of it. But that isn't my main interest. It's to nab one of these men who prey on defenseless women!"

"Hildegarde," the inspector said, as to a small child, "McWalters is not *just* a con-man and a thief. The grand jury out there indicted him for that, but there are other indictments pending. He's wanted in several states on suspicion of *murder!*"

"Oscar!"

"So when he comes calling on you it won't be just to sneak a look at your imaginary manuscript. It will be to silence you for keeps!" She gasped, and he continued mercilessly. "The guy's last wife *disappeared* nearly a year ago, didn't you know that?"

"But I thought she was supposed to be in a sanitarium."

"That was just one of McWalters' phony explanations to account for her absence. She's dead, all right—and so are several other ladies who got in Mr. McWalters' way. I hope you've got police protection?"

"N-n-no, Oscar. The police said if I bothered them any more about this case they'd have me locked up for observation."

"Not a bad idea. But don't tell me you're home, *alone?*"

"I have Talleyrand—and a toy pistol that nobody could tell from the real thing."

"Oh, *no!* A silly French poodle who loves everybody in the world, and a squirt gun! Hildegarde, you're absolutely out of your mind, and if I may say so it's not much of a trip at that."

Her sniff was audible three thousand miles away. "I might add that a Mr. Finn, a private detective, is having me guarded . . ."

That did it. Oscar Piper was about to let go with one of his better blasts, but the brittle voice of the long distance operator cut in on him. "But damn it, miss, where am I going to get two dollars in change at this hour of the morning? Operator, do you know who I am?" But she ruthlessly cut him off.

Miss Withers sighed philosophically and went back to her hairbrush, but she had lost count. Oscar's warning had not really made her nervous—but she did find herself putting sunburn oil instead of wrinkle cream on her face just before she turned out the lights. Once in bed, sleep seemed miles away.

Visions flashed through her mind, bits of the incomplete picture puzzle she had been forming for weeks. She knew a little more about Walter McWalters than the police did, but not really enough. The man seemed to have had no past—except for what the Inspector had hinted about previous wives. His life had apparently begun when he drove up to the best hotel at Lake Tahoe in a foreign car, cut a wide swathe with the ladies who were vacationing there, and finally carried off her feet the prettiest, plumpest, and richest of the widows—one Claire Visscher. Everyone had said it was a truly romantic marriage, though she was in her thirties and he was on the shady side of fifty.

They had bought—presumably with her money—a $60,000 home in Brentwood and lived in it for some years, uneventfully. McWalters had joined the Jonathan Club; they had been members of half a dozen exclusive country clubs and beach clubs and bridge clubs. There had been no friction in the household, according to Mrs. Lemmon the housekeeper—who seemed, like most members of her sex, to have a soft spot in her heart for McWalters. He had been away a good deal of the time, investigating mining properties upstate and in Nevada; Claire had missed him very much and had been lonely. She played a lot of solitaire and kept a bottle of brandy in her closet behind her hats. McWalters neither smoked nor drank, was always immaculately dressed, kept himself in tip-top shape by golf and swimming, and liked to go only to the fanciest resort hotels and the finest restaurants. They had many acquaintances, but no close friends.

The housekeeper had said, "The McWalterses seemed to be a very devoted couple and she was always kissing him and fixing his tie. I heard him raise his voice to her only once—when she slipped off her diet. One morning when I came to work she was gone, with some of her clothes. He told me she'd gone away to take a cure for alcoholism and sleeping pills, and not to talk about it to anyone."

Mrs. Lemmon thought that McWalters touched up his sideburns and mustache with a dark tint, and that maybe he even wore a toupee. She had seen a denture brush in his bathroom cabinet. He was of average height and weight—about five-ten and 155 pounds—wore glasses only for reading, was fond of bridge and poker, but would always interrupt the game to watch TV quiz shows.

In fact, he seemed to have been the average well-to-do man—the Man on the Street, or at least the Man on the Boulevard. But when the District Attorney's office listened to the appeals of his wife's distant but hopeful relatives and called him in to ask the whereabouts of Claire and why he had told so many conflicting stories to account for her absence, he finished looting her bank accounts and took off in their second-best car, his gray '53 Ford sedan, down The Street of No Return.

So much for the man supposed to be a multiple murderer of *women*. And Miss Withers realized with a shiver—if he was already wanted for several killings he wouldn't have any reason to hesitate at one more.

The minutes crept by, with the little house silent as a tomb except for Talley's soft snores at the foot of the bed. Everything was too still; there was not even the usual rumble of the Pacific surges against the breakwater, or even the sound of a distant auto horn or siren.

And just then she knew there was something in Oscar Piper's dire predictions—because somebody was moving softly, but not quite softly enough, through the dead eucalyptus leaves that littered the side yard. Miss Withers tried to stop breathing, for now the intruder must be just outside her thin-screened windows. No, he was going stealthily on again, toward the rear of the cottage.

She slipped out of bed, pausing only to take the flashlight and squirt gun from under her pillow. She tip-toed back into the kitchen and saw to her horror that the knob of the back door was slowly turning. Next would be a skeleton key, or celluloid strip . . .

At that moment the poodle came yawning up beside her, "Talley, *bark* or *growl* or something!" she whispered fiercely, but he only looked puzzled. Miss Withers took a deep breath. *"Gr-r-raugh!"* she snarled, in what she hoped was a reasonably accurate facsimile. Then in her own voice: "What is it, Wolf? *Down,* boy!" She spoke louder. "Who's there?"

A man's voice mumbled something that might have been "It's all right."

In a flash of sudden relief she guessed the answer. "Oh, you're from Mr. Finn's Agency?"

"Yes, Miss Withers. Just checking." The voice was discreetly hushed, but it was deep and masculine and very comforting. In another moment she would have asked him in for a cup of coffee, but now she heard the man going down the steps and away.

Weak with relief, Miss Withers went back to bed and was almost immediately asleep. What you don't know won't hurt you, they say—and they never said falser. Jack Finn had only one operative in his hole-in-the-wall agency, and that one was the blonde girl known as Sugar, now dozing by his side as he drove across the wide Mojave desert at ninety miles an hour. He pulled up when they reached the town of Barstow, then nudged the girl awake and led her into the rear booth of an all-night café. "Java time, kid," he told her. "But drink it fast. We've got to get back to L.A. pronto, even if you have to drive, God forbid."

"You really think it will pop that soon, Jackie?" She spiked their coffee generously.

He shrugged. "The cops think McWalters is in Mexico, the D.A.'s office thinks he's in Canada. His car's been seen in half a dozen places, but as that schoolteacher dame says, it could be just a red herring. He could have laid a lot of false trails and then doubled back. And if he *did* see that broadcast—"

"You think he'll try to knock her off?"

"Likely. She did a good job on that TV pitch—almost had me believing it myself. He just might fall for it."

"You've always said that the easiest person to con is a con-man. But you don't care whether he knocks her off or not, do you?"

"Damn little," admitted Mr. Finn. "And I'm not out for a piddling piece of the reward, either. I hate that guy's guts—hiring me to look for his missing wife just to make it look good later! And after I'd wasted a month looking for a dame he'd dumped in the ocean or somewhere, paying me off with a check on an account he knew was impounded. All I want is to get to that monkey a few minutes before the cops do."

"Why the revenge stuff?"

Finn smiled. "Not that at all, Sugar. I want to make a deal, that's all. He tells me where his dough is, so I can get it and let him have half for his defense and maybe a little bribing of witnesses. He'll fall for it—all there's against him, unless they find his wife's body which they won't, is forgery of her name and misappropriation of funds. With dough he can beat that rap."

"Only my Jackie will cross him, huh? You'll lose your license."

"Who needs a license, in South America? Let's roll."

The morrow came, as morrows always seem to do. It was far from a bright day, in more ways than one. A thick, pea-soup fog drifted in from the Pacific; it was what the fly-boys call "bird-walking weather." But not dog-walking weather, as Miss Withers firmly explained to Talley as she turned him out into the little fenced backyard. From then until after dark, the schoolteacher tasted the dubious delights of being an overnight celebrity;

her doorbell and her phone never stopped ringing. By eight o'clock in the evening she was at her wits' end and on her fourth pot of coffee, with the phone off the hook and the doorbell disconnected and almost all the lights turned off. She felt more absolutely alone than she ever had in her life.

She froze when suddenly there came a hammering on her front door. It was repeated, louder. "Open up, it's the law!"

"You don't fool me with that one! Go away!" she cried.

Somebody laughed. Hardly daring to believe her ears, she slipped off the chain—and then Oscar Piper came in, to find himself embraced and soundly kissed.

"Oscar!" she cried, hastily putting aside the water pistol. "You've come to my rescue!"

"Well—it was just that we want this McWalters pretty bad back in New York. And I had some vacation time coming ..."

"You look peaked. Have you eaten? Why didn't you phone me from the airport? How long can you stay? What—?"

He sat down wearily. "Relax, Hildegarde! Yes, I ate on the plane. Yes, I did try to phone, but your line was busy. I can stay—" he looked around. "Hey, something's different. Yeah, where's the pooch?"

"Poisoned, Oscar. Early this morning somebody threw some biscuits loaded with weed killer into the yard. I found him and gave him some mustard water, and the vet says he has a chance. But—"

"But somebody wanted him out of the way—to get to you."

She nodded slowly. Talley, as they both knew, was a poor excuse for a watchdog, but no stranger would know that—especially after her synthetic growls of last night. And she herself had given the intruder his cue by leaping to the conclusion that he was from the detective agency, and blurting it out! She told him about that.

The Inspector accepted a cup of coffee. "So that proves McWalters saw the broadcast and is right here in the area!"

"I've thought that all along. But I also believe the man was right here in this house today!"

He almost dropped his cup. "You mean while you were out?"

"I wasn't out. I didn't have a chance to go out, or even to make my bed and clean the dishes. But let me tell it my way."

It had begun early, with the vet's coming to take Talley away in the pet-ambulance. Everything had come thick and fast after that ... phone calls from cranks and curiosity-seekers, but most of them hadn't bothered to phone, they had just come barging in.

"You should have charged admission," the Inspector said.

"Be quiet!" There had been the free-lance photographer who wanted to take pictures of her, but she had sent him packing. Before he had stepped off the porch there had been a Mr. Karff who claimed to be a TV talent agent and wanted to try to get her on "The $64,000 Question." A Mr. Beale had wanted to collaborate with her on a book, *Murderers I Have Known;* there had even been a swami, turban and all, who offered for a fee to go into a trance and tell her the real whereabouts of McWalters; there had been

umpteen reporters, and even a representative of a confidential-type magazine who wanted to bid for her article . . .

"You mean your imaginary article?" Oscar Piper cut in.

"It isn't *entirely* imaginary, Oscar." The schoolteacher indicated a card
table set up near the window, complete with typewriter and assorted papers.
"I left the bait right out in plain sight, as even you can see. But my callers
were coming so thick and fast—" She shook her head. "I couldn't keep my
eye on all of them. But during the day one of the carbon copies of my
manuscript disappeared!"

"Wow!" gasped the Inspector. "Then—"

"Then somebody lifted fifteen pages of gibberish, because the thing made
sense only on page one. My real article is here." And she touched her
forehead.

He nodded. "Who else was here?"

"Dozens, but all the rest had credentials, or else were too young or too
old or of the wrong sex."

"Yeah, how about that? Couldn't McWalters have come dressed like a
woman?"

"No man could fool me in women's clothes—not if he spoke," said
Hildegarde firmly.

"But which one fits McWalters' description?"

"They *all* do! Remember, he has a phobia against being photographed,
and there's only the police artist's re-creation sketch. Remember, too, he's
such an *average* man, except for superficials. If he took out his upper plate,
removed his wig, shaved his mustache, stooped or started wearing elevator
shoes, quit tinting his hair, got fatter by not exercising or not dieting,
changed his entire manner of dress and his habits and way of life, McWalters could be an entirely different person!"

"Criminals aren't that smart," Piper objected reasonably.

"Not the ones you *catch*, you mean! But you'll admit that police usually
locate missing persons by working on the old theory that a man in flight will
in spite of himself revert to his original tastes and habits—if he's a gambler,
look for him at the racetrack or in Las Vegas, and so on. But suppose a man
were clever enough to make himself into just the *opposite* of his former self,
what then?"

"Impossible. He couldn't keep up the disguise."

"That's what the man from the District Attorney's office said when he
was here today. He accused me of withholding evidence, but I soon made
him see I haven't any evidence—yet."

"They're surely going to give you police protection now?"

"No, Oscar. They're still positive McWalters is out of the country. Besides, I've been trusting to Mr. Finn, the private detective. He was out of
town on business until today, but he's very much in on it now. In fact, he's
in that old abandoned building across the street right now, keeping an eye
on me with a pair of binoculars. He set that up an hour ago . . ."

"Phooey on private detectives. Anyway, to sum it up, it looks like
McWalters tried to sneak in on you last night and was scared off, either by
your watchdog imitation or by news that there might be agency men

around. He came right back this morning to get rid of your dog, then returned later in some disguise to steal your so-called manuscript—"

"More likely in the hopes of doing me in then and there, only there were so many people going and coming that he didn't dare."

"Looks that way. Anyway, he must be pretty close. But you forgot to tell me about the D.A.'s man, and Finn. Who else was here?"

Miss Withers was always nettled when he used the official tone on her. "Why—there was the postman. He delivered my mail in person just to get my autograph. And one of those old bleary men who collect old newspapers for the Welfare League, but they come this time every month. And the vet, of course, to get Talley. I guess that's all. You listening?"

He stood up. "Thinking. You say Finn is on the job right now?"

"Certainly. Behind that second floor window shade . . ."

"Then why didn't he show when he saw me barge in?" Piper snorted. "Answer me that!" But she couldn't. "Then he's either crossing you or he's drunk or asleep! I'm going over there!" He was out of the door in a second, with Miss Withers close on his heels.

By the light of the Inspector's pocket-flash they entered the building across the street—a building the wreckers had already started to demolish. Up the creaking stairs and along the hall to the front apartment they went. The door was closed; the schoolteacher was about to knock when Oscar Piper caught her wrist. Then he turned the knob quickly, and plunged in.

The room was bare as a bone—except for a folding chair set up by the window, a thermos flask half full of coffee, an empty whiskey bottle on the floor, and a pair of binoculars on the window sill. It was Miss Withers who noticed the thermos cup that had rolled into a corner—and that the few drops of coffee in it were still warm!

"He could have just stepped out for a minute," she whispered.

The Inspector was studying the scuff-marks in the dust. "And he could have been dragged out," he said, pointing. "This ties it! I bet you the body is in this building—and probably the killer too!"

"McWalters? But how could he have known—?"

"Ten to one he was already using this building to spy on you himself, and heard Finn come in. It's logical."

"You could be right," she said, shivering.

"I'm going to search this dump from top to bottom. But it's no place for you. Rush over and pack some duds and get in your car and scram to the nearest hotel, fast!"

"But Oscar—!"

"Get going," he whispered fiercely. "You're in the way!"

She went. She rushed across the street and into the cottage, finding that in her haste to leave the cottage before, she had left the door ajar. Everything looked undisturbed, but still she snatched up the toy pistol—the model of a Colt .38 that would fool anybody, the sales clerk had said—and methodically searched every inch of the place. Nobody was there. It took her no more than five minutes to fling some necessities in an overnight bag, and then she was out of the back door and running toward the garage.

"*Me,* running away!" she thought bitterly. And the dear Inspector alone in a dark ruin of a building with probably a corpse and a killer for company. But what must be, must be. She flung open the doors to the alley, swooped behind the wheel of her ancient coupe, and jabbed at the rusty starter.

And then, just as the motor began to cough and snort, it happened—right out of the world of nightmare. A man stepped quickly out of the shadows and slipped into the seat beside her. In the gloom she could only see that he was a medium-sized man, slightly overweight, wearing thick glasses. He also wore the cap and uniform of the Welfare League pickup detail, the trash scavengers who were always coming around for her old rags and newspapers —the hopeful, sobered-up, washed and shaved vagrants who had seen the light and were trying to reform.

"I knew it!" she thought.

"Don't bother to scream," the man said quickly, in a voice that was overpleasant, almost syrupy. But she knew it was the same voice she had heard outside her kitchen door last night, the same voice she had failed to recognize in the whine this morning, when he had come to ask for her discarded rubbish.

She felt something sharp against her side. "Just drive, please," said the man who had once been known as Walter McWalters. "And keep driving."

Something sharp entered her side an eighth of an inch, just as she was about to say "I will not!" So she put the car into gear, and started to drive. There was nothing else to do. But while she drove, being Miss Withers, she talked. She hoped that her voice was calm and normal—they said you had to humor them. "I've been looking forward to meeting you," she said. "So you *were* hiding out down on Skid Row right under the noses of the police! Very clever, Mr. McWalters."

The man beside her flicked a smile, and put one arm almost lovingly across the back of the seat behind her shoulders, close to her throat. They were out on the street now. "Just keep driving," he told her.

There were a few cars passing, and a number of pedestrians. If she could twist the wheel and cause a collision ...

"Don't try it," McWalters advised.

She must try to get him talking. "I suppose you keep your money handy in a baggage locker at Union Station, where it's safe as long as you put in a quarter every day, and where you can dig into it for spending money?"

"Bus station" he corrected. It was the first information he had volunteered, and she felt a faint flicker of hope. She was also looking and praying for the sight of a police car, but now they were going south through lonely streets in the manufacturing and lumberyard area.

"If I'm being taken for the proverbial ride, you might at least satisfy my curiosity," she pointed out reasonably. He did not answer, so she plunged blindly on. "I'd really like to know how you disposed of your wife's body so completely. It's unique in the annals of crime, you know."

"Is it now?" he said easily.

"You took all those trips up into the uranium country, I understand. I've driven through some of that, and I noticed that when anybody stakes a claim they mark one corner with a pyramid of stones, a sort of cairn several feet high. You see them all over the desert. Seems to me that would be an ideal place to hide a body. Like Poe's Purloined Letter, right out in plain sight.

"Talk away, my dear lady," he said, unruffled. But she had felt his body tense at the word "desert" and tense again at the word "cairn." So she was sure now. At least it would be a moral victory, a triumph of her intuition—even if posthumously.

"Turn left here, please," McWalters told her, still in that intimate, oozy voice. They turned, and with the turn went her last chance to sideswipe another car.

They had entered a new subdivision with vast curving, unpaved streets lined with little gimcrack houses still in construction. It was—at least, at night—as desolate a spot as anyone could find. On and on they plowed, through red mud and little pools of water.

"Stop here," McWalters said finally. She braked the car to a shuddering halt. "Last stop," he said. He reached past her and flipped the door latch. "Out," he told her, pushing gently.

"I—I won't!"

"None of that." The thing in his hand pressed hard against her. "I just want to borrow your car for my getaway . . ."

Oh, sure! And he didn't want it all blood-stained. Suddenly she jammed her bony elbow hard into his stomach and flung herself out of the car, only to take a few steps and then bog down to her ankles in hopeless mud. She whirled to face him, as he slowly came closer, with the ice pick in his hand held low and menacing. "He actually enjoys this sort of thing!" she thought frantically. He took another step, and in spite of herself she screamed for the first and last time—a scream that echoed futilely and unheard through the raw lone streets and the gap-windowed houses. The pale moonlight showed no place for her to go, no hole for her to crawl into. And McWalters came closer, closer . . .

"*Please!*" she gasped, and her hand went fluttering to her bosom. Then in a flash her hand reappeared, with the water pistol aimed straight in his face. "You stand back and put up your hands!" she screamed. "Or I'll shoot!"

McWalters hesitated for a moment, a wide grin on his face. He seemed to be savoring the moment. "Miss Withers, you kill me!" he said. "I noticed that silly squirt gun of yours a little while ago, when I looked through your house. But I thought this would be more useful." He waved the ice pick—her own ice pick—in her face.

He reached for her, arms held out almost lovingly. Even a cornered kitten will bare its claws and spit in the face of an enemy. Miss Hildegarde Withers shut her eyes and pulled the trigger. And seconds later it was all over . . .

Meanwhile, Inspector Oscar Piper had been having rather a bad time of it too, back in the condemned apartment house with the corpse of Jack Finn, skull crushed in, which he had finally located stuffed into a broom closet. His trouble however was not with the corpse, but with the Santa Monica police, who took a dim view of his discovering dead bodies in their territory, New York inspector or not.

Visiting police officers are required to check in with the local authorities unless their visit to a municipality is purely social. Nor was the local sergeant, whose usual duties only included such crises as noisy beach parties, drunks, and petty theft, especially fond of being told how to conduct a murder investigation.

"I wouldn't handle that bottle if I were you, Sarge," Oscar Piper had said.

"I think it rather fits the hole in the dead man's skull. Ever hear of fingerprints?" The Inspector was a very tense and worried man, or he might have been more tactful. As it was, they kept him in their little headquarters, making out and signing statements, for the next four hours. Finally they let him go, with grudging apologies, and he made a beeline for the nearest phone and started calling hotels. No Hildegarde, and nobody answering her somewhat unusual description. He tried her home, with no avail. As a last resort he tried the downtown Los Angeles station.

"We were just going to send out an all-points on you," the dispatcher said. "Get down here fast, Inspector." And he told him why.

"Judas priest in a revolving door!" murmured Oscar Piper.

"Naturally I used full-strength ammonia in that squirt gun you were so funny about," Miss Withers told him tartly much much later. "You see, I read somewhere that postmen sometimes used that trick on unfriendly dogs."

They were having a huge and expensive lunch at Perrino's, on Wilshire Boulevard. He swallowed a bite of filet, and shook his head. "You're really one for the books," he confessed.

"Maybe I'll even write it up someday," she said. "With you, of course, as comic relief."

"Well, at least it's over." He sighed. "They say McWalters will be the first blind man to go to the death chamber at San Quentin, and even if they don't find his wife's body he's booked for the Finn job. And I hear there's no question about your getting the reward."

"My chief reward, Oscar, is the news that Talley will be all right and can come home tomorrow," she said firmly.

"Then what?"

"Well, Groucho Marx sent word that they'd all like me to do a follow-up performance on *You Bet Your Life* as soon as possible. But I think I'm more the spectator type. I was just wondering, Oscar, if when I get the reward money Talleyrand and I might not take a little trip back to New York. Somehow, after all this, I feel the need for the peace and quiet of Times Square."

The Inspector grinned. "Well, remember the Sullivan Law—and leave your pistol home."

ACTIVITIES

1) Thoroughness is not one of Hildegarde Withers's strong points—as it was with Miss Jane Marple. Point out the incidents wherein Hildegarde's "blunders" cause problems for her.

2) Authors use many "tricks of the trade" to capture your interest and attention. One such device is to omit certain events deliberately, in order to allow your imagination to "fill in the gaps." Can you provide examples of this technique from Mr. Palmer's story?

3) The author's style of writing is light and breezy; at times, it even borders upon the farcical. How do you feel about the use of such a style for a detective story? Does it detract from the plot?

James Yaffe—and Mom

James Yaffe was fifteen years old when he sold his first short story—to the *Ellery Queen Mystery Magazine.* With a start like that, he was bound to "make a name for himself" in detective story writing, and he did.

He was born in Chicago in 1927, later graduating from Yale University with the highest honors. Shortly afterwards, he demonstrated his versatility with words when he began selling articles as well as short stories to such a broad spectrum of magazines as *EQMM, Atlantic Monthly, Ladies Home Journal, Commentary, The Saturday Review,* and a host of others. He also became a novelist, a stage and television playwright, and an author of nonfiction books. Some of his important works are *Mister Margolies* (a novel), *The Deadly Game* (a play), and *The American Jews* (nonfiction).

Yaffe has been asked where he gets the raw material for his characters. His reply: "From my own experience, of course—mostly from my experience of the world I was born and brought up in, the world of middle-class, second and third generation Jews living in New York, Chicago, and Los Angeles."[9]

From this experience came one of the most imaginative, perceptive, and hilarious female sleuths of today, a Jewish mother affectionately known as Mom, the Mayvin.

"A Jewish mother as a detective. You can't be serious?"

Oh, but we are. Through the deftness of James Yaffe's pen, this female becomes as remarkable a personality as Sherlock Holmes. But Mom does more than that; in her own inimitable way, she even punctures the stereotype of the Jewish mother—"liberates her," you might say.

Mayvin is a Yiddish word meaning *expert.* What is Mom an expert at? Well, her son is a detective with the New York police, and—

But enough already. Why not let James Yaffe[10] and Mom speak for themselves?

Mom and the Haunted Mink

"It's my personal opinion," Mom said, "that mink is overrated. I've been wearing it for years, and believe me—"

"With all respect, Mother," said my wife Shirley, "I've been in this family over seven years, and I can't remember *ever* seeing you in mink. In fact, you don't even own—"

"All right, I wouldn't argue with you," Mom said. "If you say I never wore mink—if you say I'm getting *meshuganer** in my old age—it must be the truth. After all, which one of us graduated from Vassar College?" Then Mom took another sip of noodle soup, and sighed, "It isn't as good as what I make at home."

It was a very unusual Friday night. Mom's kitchen stove was being fixed, so she couldn't give Shirley and me dinner up in the Bronx. Instead we were taking *her* to dinner at Fingerhood's, the fancy kosher restaurant near Times Square.

The crowd here was a mixture of sharp Broadway and elderly middle-class. Mom studied her fellow diners with the same penetrating, positively dissecting gaze that she gave to butchers while they weighed her meat. It was a couple in the corner—a little baldheaded man in his fifties and a tall blonde in her twenties, buried in furs—who caused Mom to make her remark about mink.

And of course Shirley couldn't leave the remark unchallenged. After seven years of challenging Mom, Shirley still won't admit that she's out-classed. And so—though *I* couldn't remember Mom ever wearing mink either—I quickly changed the subject. "Talking about mink," I said, "we got a crazy murder case over the week-end."

Mom's eyes lighted up. Nothing makes her forget small injuries faster than a chance to hear about one of my cases at the Homicide Squad. "So maybe you'll tell me about it?" she said.

I started right in. "This Mrs. Laura McCloskey is the wife of Dr. Alfred McCloskey—he's an old-fashioned G.P., one of the vanishing breed. For years he and his wife have lived on the West Side in a three-story brown-stone which he bought back in the thirties. The top two floors are their home, and the ground floor is his office. The neighborhood isn't what it used to be, but I guess he doesn't want to sell the house and move elsewhere. He makes a fairly comfortable living, but nothing spectacular. That's why he never bought his wife a mink coat until recently."

"She's been wanting one for a long time?" Mom said.

"For twenty-five years, since they got married, according to Dr. McCloskey. She hasn't exactly nagged him about it—he was very careful to explain that—but he could tell how she felt every time they passed a mink coat on

---

*Crazy (Yiddish)

the street or every time she mentioned one of her friends' mink coats. Well, I never knew a woman yet who couldn't get her wishes across without coming right out and expressing them."

"It's strictly self-defense," Mom said. "I never knew a man who wouldn't automatically say no if a woman asked him for something right out."

"Anyway, Mom, a couple of months ago Mrs. McCloskey had a birthday, and the doctor gave her a mink coat. For years he'd been saving for this, and he took out a bank loan for the difference, but he still couldn't have managed it without getting an unexpected break. One of his patients told him about Madame Rosa, a wholesale fur dealer who sometimes has unusual bargains to offer. Dr. McCloskey went down to Madame Rosa's place and bought a mink coat that had just come in. It wasn't cheap—he paid close to $5,000 for it, but it would've cost three times as much at any retail store."

"Strictly a legal transaction, I hope?"

"The coat wasn't hot, if that's what you mean. Dr. McCloskey found out its whole history from the wholesaler."

"That's Madame Rosa?"

"Actually it's a man named Harry Schultz, who lives in Englewood, New Jersey. He uses the trade name Madame Rosa, in honor of a fortune-teller in Atlantic City years ago who advised him to go into the fur business. Well, he explained to Dr. McCloskey that the mink coat was part of the estate of Oscar F. Tannenbaum, a stock broker who died a little while ago. This coat was the last thing Tannenbaum ever gave to his wife, Janet—then his investments failed, he lost all his money, and he jumped off the terrace of his Park Avenue apartment.

"Mrs. Tannenbaum was forced to sell all her possessions to pay off her husband's debts. There was a public auction, and she sat in the back of the room. When the mink coat came up for sale, she lost control of herself and starting bidding on it herself. She didn't have a dime, you understand, but the auctioneer just couldn't make her stop bidding. When the coat was finally bought by Madame Rosa—that is, by Harry Schultz—Mrs. Tannenbaum screamed at him that he had no right to it, it was hers, and she'd never let any other woman wear it. Then she collapsed—some kind of stroke—and the next day she was dead.

"And that's the coat's history, as reported by Harry Schultz. We've checked it out, and it seems to be accurate. The auction house, incidentally, valued the coat at $15,000, though they're not obliged to tell us what Harry Schultz actually paid for it."

"And Mrs. McCloskey was happy with her mink?" Mom said.

"At first the doctor was afraid she wouldn't be, because he had picked it out himself, without consulting her. But he wanted the gift to be a surprise— and luckily she loved it. It made her as happy as a girl. First she hugged him and kissed him, then she burst into tears, then she put on the coat and posed in front of her mirror for an hour. And that night she made him take her out to a restaurant so she could show off the coat—even though it was too warm for furs."

"So much emphasis on material possessions!" Shirley said. "No wonder this story has a tragic ending."

Mom turned to Shirley. "If Davie offered you such a material possession right now, you wouldn't take the risk?"

I broke in quickly, before Shirley could commit herself. "Dr. McCloskey told his wife the coat's history—all about the auction and Mrs. Tannenbaum's outburst—and his wife made a funny remark. 'I do hope the poor woman wasn't serious about her threat,' she said. 'I hope she doesn't decide to come back from the grave—' She laughed, although Dr. McCloskey could see that a tiny part of her wasn't really joking.

"But he didn't think twice about it. His wife was the kind of person who goes to séances, follows her horoscope in the daily paper, believes in mind-reading and crystal balls and so on. After twenty-five years of marriage Dr. McCloskey didn't pay much attention to her superstitions."

The waiter came to take away our soup bowls and bring our main courses, so I had to stop my story. The waiters at Fingerhood's are the most accomplished story-killers in New York.

The waiter went away, and I started in again. "A couple of weeks later a funny incident took place. Mrs. McCloskey and the doctor were about to leave the house for a dinner date. She asked her maid—that's Berenice Webley, a colored girl in her late twenties—to fetch the coat for her. The maid went to the bedroom closet, and a moment later she called out, 'I just can't seem to get this coat off the hanger!'

"Mrs. McCloskey went to the closet too, and tugged at the coat, but it stuck fast. 'It's as if something was *holding* it on there,' she said. Finally Dr. McCloskey gave a hard pull, and the coat came off. 'The hanger must've got caught in one of the sleeves,' he said—though he says now that he wasn't really so sure; when he yanked at that coat, it actually did feel as if some force were yanking back. Then his wife said, 'Well, as long as it isn't that Mrs. Tannenbaum carrying out her threat—' But she was too embarrassed to finish her sentence."

"And well she might be," Shirley said. "A dead woman haunting a mink coat! I've never heard of anything so absurd!"

"Dead women can act very much alive sometimes," Mom said. "My nephew Jonathan is still a bachelor, because his mother don't approve of modern girls—and his mother's been dead for eighteen years."

"A week later," I went on, "there was another funny incident. Mrs. McCloskey belonged to a literary club—a group of middle-aged women who meet every Thursday afternoon at one another's homes and discuss the latest best-selling books. Most of the ladies have more money than Mrs. McCloskey—their husbands are successful businessmen or professional men who aren't quite as idealistic as the doctor. For years Mrs. McCloskey was one of the few members of the club who never wore a mink coat to any of the meetings. So naturally, now that she finally owned one, she had to show it off on Thursday afternoon.

"The meeting was held out in Scarsdale, at the home of Mrs. Alonzo Martineau—her husband is a big surgeon with a Park Avenue office. There was always a kind of feud between Mrs. McCloskey and Mrs. Martineau, probably because both husbands are medical men. The first time she saw the mink, Mrs. Martineau made a remark about how pleased she was that Dr. McCloskey's practice was doing so well these days—and Mrs. McCloskey answered that her husband's practice had always done well, only she didn't believe in boasting about such things the way *some* people do.

"Well, a few hours later the meeting broke up, and the ladies left the house and started down the front walk to their cars. Mrs. McCloskey came a little behind the others, in order to be next to her friend Mrs. Harmon, the banker's wife, who was going to give her a ride home. Mrs. Harmon is an elderly lady, and couldn't move as fast as the others.

"Suddenly, halfway down the walk, Mrs. McCloskey gave a yell and grabbed at her neck. As she described it to her husband that night, her mink coat seemed to jump right off her shoulders of its own accord—it landed on the lawn, and started sliding across the grass."

"What kind of drinks do they serve at these literary meetings?" Shirley said.

"Old Mrs. Harmon never takes anything stronger than tea—and she saw the coat go sailing through the air too, and she saw Mrs. McCloskey run after it and scoop it up from the grass. The other ladies didn't turn around soon enough to see the flying coat, so Mrs. McCloskey laughed and told them she had tripped and the coat had fallen off her back. Mrs. Martineau made a crack about people who are so rich they can afford to throw away their minks, and the incident passed off as a joke.

"But Mrs. McCloskey was terribly upset about it. 'There's something *wrong* with this coat,' she kept saying to her husband that night. 'I can feel the *presence* of something—some kind of evil spirit!' And no matter how hard he tried, Dr. McCloskey couldn't calm her down and convince her she was just imagining things."

"But the incident on the lawn was an obvious hallucination," Shirley said. "Subconsciously Mrs. McCloskey rejected and despised the materialistic side of her nature as symbolized by the mink coat. And so, with no voluntary effort or even conscious awareness, she flung it off her back onto Mrs. Martineau's lawn."

"And the old lady, Mrs. Harmon?" Mom said. "She had a hallucination too?"

"There *is* such a thing as mass hypnosis," Shirley said.

"Maybe so," I said, "but there were half a dozen more incidents in the next two weeks, all of which Mrs. McCloskey reported to her husband. She'd try to throw her coat over her chair in a restaurant, and it would keep slipping to the floor. She'd be walking along the street, and suddenly the coat would seem to be pushing against her, trying to move her in the opposite direction. One afternoon, right after she hung it up in her bedroom closet, she thought she heard it thumping against the inside of the closet door. And finally the most frightening incident of all—"

"How's the pot roast—all right?" said the waiter.

"Personally I like to use more paprika," Mom said, "but otherwise it isn't the worst I ever tasted." The waiter shrugged and moved away, and Mom turned back to me.

"So? The most frightening incident of all?"

"At two o'clock in the morning," I said, "Dr. McCloskey was awakened by his wife. She was scared to death, he says, and on the verge of hysterics. 'It's getting away, it's getting away!' she kept screaming. 'It slid across the floor, it went out to the foyer!'

"Dr. McCloskey saw that the door to the bedroom closet was wide open, and the bedroom door was open too. So he got out of bed and went to the foyer—and believe it or not, he saw the mink coat wrapped around the handle of the front door. The foyer light was dim, and the doctor was still half asleep, but he swears that it looked for one moment as if that mink coat were trying to turn the handle of the door—as if it wanted to get out to the stairs and go down to the ground floor and leave the house!

"Well, he grabbed hold of the coat and pulled it off the door handle—and then he told himself that he was developing as big an imagination as his wife."

"Does he think it was his imagination that got the coat from the bedroom closet to the front door?" Mom said.

"He thinks it never *was* in the bedroom closet. His wife and he came in late from a party that night—she was exhausted, a little groggy, and the house was overheated. He thinks she took off her coat the moment she stepped inside and hung it on the door handle without realizing what she was doing, and then went straight to bed. As for seeing the coat slide across the room—well, he thinks she dreamed that, one of those terribly vivid dreams that seem to be real even after you wake up."

Mom gave a snort. "A woman who's dying to have a mink coat all her life—she hangs it up at night on a door handle?"

"What *other* explanation is there?" I said. "Anyway, Mrs. McCloskey couldn't get to sleep the rest of that night, even though her husband put the coat in the closet and locked the closet door. And the next day she made up her mind to find out the truth once and for all—was the coat haunted by the ghost of Mrs. Tannenbaum, or wasn't it?"

"How on earth *could* she find out such a thing?" Shirley said.

"By asking Mrs. Tannenbaum direct, how else?" Mom said. "Am I right, Davie?"

"Absolutely. Mrs. McCloskey believed in séances, as I told you. She had a favorite spiritualist—a Mrs. Vivian who lives in a small apartment on a rundown genteel street in the Village. She's a widow in her fifties—a wispy, gray-haired little woman. For the last ten years, since her husband died, she's been trying to earn a living as a medium and astrologist. The bunco squad knows all about her, but it's never been worthwhile to pull her in. She only operates in a small way—five or ten bucks per customer—and hardly makes enough to pay her monthly rent. What's more, she seems to believe in her own spiritualistic powers. When the dead speak through her mouth, she's just as impressed as any one of her clients.

"So Mrs. McCloskey took her mink coat down to Mrs. Vivian. And she didn't go by herself—she took her friend old Mrs. Harmon of the literary club along. 'Whatever happens,' she said, 'I want to be sure it isn't only in my imagination.'

"Well, Mrs. Vivian put the mink on the table in front of her, turned out the lights, and went into her trance—clasping her hands, rolling her eyes, moaning and groaning. And pretty soon a voice came out of her, much deeper and more belligerent than her own natural voice. 'This is Juliet Tannenbaum talking,' it said. 'How dare you wear the coat that belongs to me! You'd better get rid of it, or I'll never give you any peace! Do what I say, or I'll drive you into an early grave!'

"That was Mrs. Tannenbaum's message—old Mrs. Harmon remembers it word for word, Mrs. McCloskey repeated it later to her husband, and Mrs. Vivian told us about it when we questioned her."

"Mrs. Vivian can hear what she says in her trances?"

"She's wide-awake at all times, Mom. The voice coming out of her, she says, seems to belong to somebody else. She has no idea what it's going to say—she listens to it just as curiously as her clients do.

"Well, after she left Mrs. Vivian's place, Mrs. McCloskey went straight to her husband's office. She told him she wanted to get rid of the coat. It broke her heart to do it, because it was so beautiful, but she was too frightened to keep it. What's more, the experience had upset her so much that she didn't even want another mink coat in its place.

"When the coat was sold, she said, he could keep the money—she had learned her lesson and she was through with expensive luxuries for good. The doctor tried to talk her out of this, but she wouldn't change her mind. Then she left him and went off to her Wednesday afternoon Philharmonic concert, where the coat appeared in public for the last time."

"And the doctor sold the coat?" Mom said.

"After his wife left, he called up Harry Schultz—that is, Madame Rosa—and asked for the name of the auction house which had auctioned off the coat in the first place. Schultz offered to buy the coat back for what the doctor had paid for it, but the doctor decided to take his chances with an auction. He called the auction house and arranged for them to pick up the coat the next day. But they never did."

Mom leaned forward, holding her fork in the air, completely fogetting to plunge it into her baked potato. The fact is, she smelled blood. Nobody on earth has a kinder heart than Mom—when I was a kid, she could never bring herself to spank me; but she *does* enjoy a good murder story.

"The doctor and his wife stayed home that night and watched television," I said. "But around eleven he got an emergency call from a patient in Brooklyn. So he got in his car and drove away, leaving his wife alone in the house."

"The maid don't sleep in?" Mom said.

"Berenice Webley? She comes in early every morning to make breakfast —she's got her own key—and leaves every night after dinner. Well, when the doctor got to Brooklyn he found it wasn't his patient who had called him—it was some kind of practical joke. He was mad as a wet hen, and he drove home again. He was gone nearly two hours. When he got back to his front door, he found it unlocked. This worried him, because he had distinctly heard his wife snap the bolt behind him.

"The doctor stepped inside and called out to her. No answer. He went upstairs and found her in the bedroom, sprawled on the bed. Her dress was torn, and the bedspread was rumpled. She was dead—she had died thirty to sixty minutes earlier. At first Dr. McCloskey thought she might've had a heart attack, but later the autopsy showed she had been smothered to death. Some large thick soft object had been held tightly over her face—or maybe I should say that it held *itself* over her face."

"Meaning?" Mom pushed her chin forward.

"Small bits of fur were found on her lips and in her nostrils. Mink fur, Mom. As for the mink coat—well, its box, with Madame Rosa's label on it, was lying empty on the floor, as if Mrs. McCloskey had been in the act of packing it up. But the mink coat itself was gone."

I stopped talking. Let's face it, I was kind of pleased with the effect I had made.

Finally Shirley spoke up. "For heaven's sake, David, does the New York Homicide Squad—grown men, living in the Twentieth Century!—actually believe that this woman was smothered by a haunted coat?"

"Officially," I said, "the New York Homicide Squad only believes in flesh-and-blood killers. That's what we're looking for in this case. But so far we can't find anybody, outside of that ghost, who has a motive. Mrs. McCloskey was a harmless little woman without an enemy in the world. Her marriage was happy, and her husband hasn't been playing around on the side—and don't think we haven't dug into his private life! All their financial assets, including the house, are in his name—he doesn't inherit a thing by her death, not even any insurance. They've got one son—he's married, practices medicine in Michigan, and hasn't quarreled with his parents. Anyway, he was home in bed on the night of the murder."

"And how about robbery?" Mom said. "A valuable item *is* missing, no?"

"It had to be a very peculiar robber who took that coat. Mrs. McCloskey had a box full of jewelry on top of her dresser—and not one piece was missing. On the bed table was the doctor's billfold, with almost $200 in small bills inside of it, and the contents were intact."

"$200! What was he doing with so much cash?"

"His hobby is collecting books—first editions and so on. Well, the afternoon of the murder he sold a few of his books to a dealer. He got paid in cash, and he had to take the money home with him because the banks were already closed.

"But there's another reason why it probably wasn't a robber who killed her. As soon as the doctor left the house at eleven that night, his wife bolted the front door. He swears he heard her do it—she always *did* do it when she had to be alone in the house at night. But when he got home nearly two hours later, the door was unlocked and unbolted—and no sign that it had been forced, no sign that any of the windows had been forced.

"So it must have been Mrs. McCloskey herself who opened the door to the killer. But she was a nervous woman. She never would've let in a stranger—only somebody she knew."

"Didn't you say her maid had an extra key to the house?" Shirley said.

"The maid, Berenice Webley, has an airtight alibi. She was at a dance up at 125th Street—in full view of a hundred people until after two o'clock in the morning. Besides, her key couldn't have been any use for opening the bolt. So there you are. The killer wasn't a robber, and nobody who knew the woman has the slightest motive. Who's left? Only Mrs. Tannenbaum's ghost."

"Excuse me," Mom said, "but the ghost didn't have a motive either. The ghost told Mrs. McCloskey she should get rid of that mink coat or else she'd end up in an early grave. So Mrs. McCloskey *listened* to the warning, didn't she? She *was* getting rid of the coat. So why did the ghost have to kill her?"

I suddenly felt very tired. For three days the boys down at Homicide—the ones who *weren't* working on this case—had been making jokes about ghosts. The subject of ghosts was beginning to lose its charm for me.

"I don't know, Mom," I said. "Is there a rule that a ghost has to have a sense of fairplay? Maybe this ghost *enjoys* killing people. Or maybe it didn't believe that Mrs. McCloskey really wanted to get rid of the coat. Or maybe—"

But Mom was frowning—that dark frown which shows she's got an idea percolating. "The ghost didn't believe—she didn't really want—" Mom began to nod her head, and then she looked up at me, and there was a big smile on her face. "It's possible, Davie! It's a definite possibility! Thank you kindly for the suggestion!"

"What suggestion, Mom? If you're on to something—"

"On to something? How could this be? A little *nebbish** like me, who don't even know what kind of a coat she wears? But maybe I *could* be on to something—if I heard the answers to three or four questions."

I shot a warning glance at Shirley, then I said, "I'll tell you whatever I can, Mom."

"First call the waiter and order me some of the apple strudel."

I motioned to the waiter, we ordered our desserts, and then Mom raised her finger. "Question Number One. Was Dr. McCloskey selling a lot of his books lately?"

"As a matter of fact, he was—a dozen or more in the last three weeks. Also he was economizing on cigars and steam baths and so on. He figured he had to, if he ever expected to pay off the money the bank had loaned him to buy that mink coat."

Mom gave one of her nods—carefully not letting me know if she was happy with the answer or not. "Question Number Two. The old lady Mrs. Harmon—the one that went to the séance with the doctor's wife—just exactly how near-sighted is she?"

"I'm sorry, Mom, but that's a bad guess. She isn't near-sighted at all. As a matter of fact, Mrs. Harmon is terribly far-sighted. She has to wear glasses for reading, but not for walking along the street."

"She isn't near-sighted? You're positive of this? All right—so, Question

---

*A person worthy of pity (Yiddish)

Number Three. This woman with the séances, this Mrs. Vivian, has she maybe been a little richer lately than she usually is?"

No doubt of it, this question pulled me up short. "I don't know how you knew that, Mom, but she *has* been. We keep a routine check on people connected with murder cases, and the other day our man reported that Mrs. Vivian went to Macy's and paid a lot of money—in cash—for a new living-room sofa. We asked her where she got the money—since she's usually so strapped—and she told us she'd been saving it for years in a box in her closet. Well, we can't *prove* she's lying—but our guess is she's latched on to some gullible female who has more to spend than most of her other clients."

Mom nodded. "So—Question Number Four. The doctor's wife—was she the type person who had trouble remembering people's names?"

"Mom, what kind of question—"

"Am I asking, or am I answering?"

"Okay, okay. Well, actually Mrs. McCloskey *was* that type—vague and forgetful, that is. Her husband told us how she embarrassed him sometimes by calling their oldest friends by the wrong names. He didn't say it about her reproachfully, though—it seemed to be one of the reasons why he loved her."

"Exactly," Mom said. "He loved her, and she loved him. That's the whole point about this case. That's the explanation for the ghost. Good—here's our strudel."

And Mom wouldn't say another word about the murder until she had tasted the strudel, frowned a little, then announced that it needed more cinnamon.

"You were saying, Mom? The explanation for the ghost?"

Mom gave a little smile. "Did I ever tell you about your Aunt Doris that everybody said was the dumbest woman in the United States of America?"

"I never knew I *had* an Aunt Doris."

"She's dead now, poor thing. She married your Papa's oldest brother, Saul. They moved out to Hollywood, California, and he got to be a big shot in the movie business. Such a brilliant man. He read books—long heavy ones, by Russian writers. And he listened to symphony music—he didn't just go to the concert and fall asleep, he actually listened. Everybody said what a shame it was he married a dope like poor Doris—a girl that used to be a salesgirl in Marshall Field's in Chicago, that never finished high school, that couldn't read a serious book if her life depended on it, and every time she opened her mouth she used the wrong word or she mispronounced the right one.

"And the worst thing about her, everybody said, she couldn't get anywhere on time. For theater dates, for dinner at people's houses, Saul and Doris were always showing up late. And she was always apologizing because she forgot what time they were expected, or because she realized at the last minute that she was wearing the wrong dress, so she had to run back and change it. Poor Saul, everybody said—what an embarrassment for him to have such a dumb wife! And then—"

"Mother," Shirley broke in, "does this *really* have anything to do with that mink—"

"And then," Mom said, not even giving Shirley a glance, "your Aunt Doris died. All of a sudden she got sick, and a month later she was dead. Only fifty-one years old—such a tragedy! Saul was so upset, for a long time he wouldn't go out of the house. But finally he started accepting invitations again—dinner parties, theater dates, and so on. And what a surprise everybody got! Everywhere he went, Saul got there late. Dinners got just as cold waiting for him as if Doris was still alive.

"So pretty soon the truth dawned on people. It was *Saul* who was inconsiderate and never showed up on time for his appointments. All these years it hadn't been Doris' fault at all. She used to pretend *she* was the guilty one, she used to let people blame this bad habit on *her* stupidity—because she loved her husband, she wanted to protect him and keep people from thinking bad things about him."

"But Mom, I don't see the point—"

"The point is, even a stupid person can love somebody and think up schemes to help him. Even a silly vain woman can care more about her husband than she cares about a mink coat. Smart people don't have a monopoly on making sacrifices. Waiter, I'll have some more coffee, please— and this time you'll make it hot?"

The coffee came, Mom sipped it and said it was hot enough, then, she went on, "So now it's obvious, isn't it? Mrs. McCloskey, the doctor's wife, had trouble remembering people's names—even people she knew for years. Naturally she'd have trouble remembering the name of the woman that used to own her mink coat. Mrs. Janet Tannenbaum was the woman's name—but in Mrs. McCloskey's mind it could just as easy turn itself into Mrs. *Juliet* Tannenbaum."

"That séance!" I said. "When the ghost spoke through Mrs. Vivian's mouth—"

"The ghost's first words," Mom said, "if I'm remembering correctly, were 'This is Juliet Tannenbaum talking.' All right, even if you believe in ghosts you might have trouble believing in one that forgets her own first name! Somebody *told* Mrs. Vivian to speak in the ghost's voice, somebody wrote out those words for her to say—and paid her a nice bonus for putting on her act, enough so she could suddenly afford a new sofa at Macy's. And the somebody who did it was so vague and forgetful that she gave that ghost the wrong first name!"

"But Mother," Shirley said, "that doesn't necessarily mean it was Mrs. McCloskey—"

"All right, if you want it, there's another piece of evidence that Mrs. McCloskey didn't really believe in the ghost. What did she do as soon as Mrs. Vivian's séance was over? She went to her husband's office, told him to sell the coat, then went off to her afternoon concert—where she wore the coat in public for the last time. So I'm asking you—if she really believed this coat had a ghost in it, if she really believed that threat which Mrs. Tannenbaum made, why didn't she take off the coat as soon as she could? Why wasn't she scared of wearing it another minute? How could she bring it to the concert and show it off to her friends without a worry in the world? Only one answer—this was a woman who knew that there wasn't any ghost."

"But if she staged that séance," I said, "she must've staged all those other things the ghost did. And I'll be—I mean, I don't see how she could have managed it!"

"It was simple. What *did* the ghost do, when you come right down to it? Most of the incidents—like the ghost pushing against her on the street, thumping at the closet door, falling off chairs in restaurants—happened without any witnesses. And when the coat jumped off her back onto Mrs. Martineau's lawn—isn't it obvious that she *threw* it off her back? She didn't do it subconsciously, like Shirley said, she did it on purpose. She waited till nobody could see her do it except old Mrs. Harmon—who's very far-sighted. Meaning that Mrs. Harmon could see the coat very clear while it was sailing through the air far away from her eyes, but she couldn't see anything except a blur while the coat was on Mrs. McCloskey's shoulders, *close* to her eyes. She couldn't see Mrs. McCloskey pulling off the coat and throwing it, but she *could* see it landing on the grass—so naturally she thought it got there by itself."

"And the night Mrs. McCloskey woke up her husband," I said, "and told him the coat had escaped from the closet and slid out to the front door—you mean she took it from the closet and wrapped it around that doorknob *before* she woke him up!"

"You still haven't explained the very first incident," Shirley said, "when the maid couldn't get the coat off its hanger—"

"That was probably a genuine accident," Mom said. "So a sleeve of the coat got caught on the hanger, just like Dr. McCloskey thought. And Mrs. McCloskey made a remark about Mrs. Tannenbaum's ghost. But later on, when she remembered this incident, it gave her the idea for everything else. It was her inspiration for the rest of the scheme."

"But *why,* Mom? What was her motive?"

"It's your Aunt Doris all over again, Davie. If a woman loves a man, she'll do anything she can to help him—even if it makes *her* look stupid. For years Mrs. McCloskey wanted a mink coat, and finally her husband bought her one, and she was happy with it at first. But pretty soon she began to notice certain things—he was selling his rare books that he loved, he was cutting down on cigars, he was staying away from the steam bath. And maybe, out of curiosity, she accidentally looked through his papers and found out about his loan from the bank.

"And suddenly it came to her: 'These are the sacrifices he made to get me that mink coat!' Right away she hates the sight of that coat. She don't stop thinking it's beautiful—because she's a woman who's only human. But she's ashamed of herself for thinking so—because she's a woman who puts her husband first. All she wants to do now is get rid of the coat and give him back his money."

"But why such an absurd involved way of doing it?" Shirley said.

"How else could she do it? Could she tell him her real reason for getting rid of the coat? Maybe she's a stupid woman, but she knows what a blow this would be to his pride. Like a failure he'd feel, a no-good who couldn't afford to give his wife the things she wanted. So to save his pride she has to convince him she *don't* want that coat any more.

"If she says to him, 'I don't like the looks of it now!' he wouldn't believe her. But if she tells him she's got one of her crazy superstitions about it, if she invents a lot of incidents to account for this superstition, he *will* believe her. There isn't any silly notion he wouldn't think she was capable of—and she knows it.

" 'All right,' she decides, 'I'll make him believe I'm too scared to keep the coat. He'll think I'm acting like an idiot—but after all, he thinks that already. The important thing is, he'll get his books and his money back, and his pride will be saved!' "

Mom stopped, and gave a little sigh. "So that's what was haunting the coat—her love for her husband and her shame over spending his money."

"But Mom, the woman *was* murdered! The coat *has* disappeared!"

"Who's the murderer, is that what you're asking? Believe me, that's the easy part. That I knew right from the start. If you ever had to shop for a family, you'd know it also."

"Shop for a family!"

"You men at the Homicide Squad," Mom said, "you should all be forced to do your family shopping for a few weeks. It's because men don't have experience with such things that they're always such big suckers. Anything the salesgirl tells them they'll believe."

"What salesgirl? I don't see—"

"It's an old rule for shoppers, but it's still a good one—watch your step with a bargain. In this world nobody gives you something for nothing. If a two-dollar bag of oranges is selling for one dollar, you can automatically assume there are some rotten oranges in the bag. And if a $15,000 mink coat is selling for $5,000—"

"You think that coat was a fake, Mom? But the auction house valued Mrs. Tannenbaum's mink at—"

"Who says that Mrs. Tannenbaum's mink was the one Dr. McCloskey got? Who says Madame Rosa or Mr. Schultz or whatever his name is didn't slip a different mink out from his sleeve—or maybe I should say a rabbit? This is a crime, if I'm not mistaken—he could go to jail for it, no?"

"He sure could!"

"So it isn't hard to imagine Mister Rosa's feelings when the doctor called him up and told him he was going to have the coat auctioned off. Nothing gets auctioned at those prices unless it's appraised first. Mr. Rosa *had* to get that coat back before any appraiser could look at it. So he sent the doctor out to Brooklyn on a wild-goose chase, thinking that Mrs. McCloskey would be easier to convince alone. He showed up at the house and rang the bell. She let him in, and he tried to talk her into selling the coat back to him then and there. She wouldn't do it—he was a little too eager maybe—so they got into an argument and he lost his head and he smothered her with the first thing that came to his hand. It happened to be the mink coat."

"If we could prove that, Mom—"

"There was a box on the floor near her body, didn't you say so? A long box with a Madame Rosa label on it. You assumed this was the box that the coat originally came in, that Mrs. McCloskey was about to put the coat back in it for the auction house. But why should she hold onto that box for two months? She intended to keep the coat at the beginning, so naturally she threw its box away.

"The box you found near her body, Davie, was brought there by Mr. Rosa on the night of the murder, because he expected to carry the coat away in it. But after he killed Mrs. McCloskey he maybe panicked and ran away and forgot all about his box. Look it over—maybe it's got his fingerprints on it. Maybe somebody in his shop saw him leaving with it. I'm positive it'll be your proof."

I got to my feet. "I'll have Schultz picked up right now. Then we can start turning his place inside out."

So I left the table and phoned Homicide from the booth in the restaurant lobby. When I got back to the table I was just in time to hear Mom sighing. "It's like I mentioned earlier—mink is overrated. I've been wearing it for years, and believe me—"

And once again Shirley couldn't keep her mouth shut. "When did you ever wear mink, Mother? Just tell me one occasion!"

Mom met Shirley's gaze, and her voice couldn't have been softer. "All my life I've been wearing it. I shut my eyes and run my hands over my shoulders and what do I feel? Mink—thick and soft, all the way down to my knees—the highest quality—"

"Oh, I see!" Shirley cried. "This mink is in your *imagination!*"

Mom spread her hands. "And why not? Isn't that the most beautiful kind?" For a moment there was a sad look on her face. But then the waiter came with the check. Mom took one look at it and let out a yelp. "From now on, stove or no stove, we're eating up in the Bronx!"

ACTIVITIES

1) What is a stereotype? After you have discussed your definition with your teacher and classmates, describe the specific stereotype of the Jewish mother. How does Mom as a detective protagonist help to break down this stereotype?

2) Mom asks four questions relating to Mrs. Tannenbaum's haunted mink. Can you point out the specific incident in Davie's narration that prompted each question?

3) Mr. Yaffe's characterization of Mom and daughter-in-law Shirley is sharp and concise. With an economy of words, he lets you know that Shirley has probably taken a course in psychology but that Mom is the better psychologist. Describe specifically how he does this.

4) Compare Mom with the other female sleuths presented in this chapter. Which one does she resemble most, and why? In what way is Mom's style completely distinct from the others?

Double Your "Double Pleasure"

"It is a double pleasure to deceive the deceiver," stated Jean de la Fontaine in the seventeenth century. He was talking about real villains then, but the statement aptly describes one of the great joys inherent in reading a detective story.

Have our female sleuths provided you with this pleasure in your perusal of their adventures? Have they enabled you to pit your wits against "the deceivers" with the same gusto, imagination, and verve of their male counterparts?

If so, your acquaintance with them does not have to end here. You can double the "double pleasure" as often as you like by prolonging your reading relationship with them. Here are the titles—the rest is up to you:

More "Miss Pinkerton" Adventures by Mary Roberts Rinehart

"The Buckled Bag"
Miss Pinkerton
Haunted Lady

And many others featuring an assortment of detective protagonists . . .

More "Miss Marple" Adventures by Agatha Christie

"Strange Jest"	"The Companion"
"Sanctuary"	"The Four Suspects"
"Greenshaw's Folly"	"Motive v. Opportunity"
"The Case of the Perfect Maid"	"The Thumbmark of St. Peter"
"The Case of the Caretaker"	"The Bloodstained Pavement"
"The Blue Geranium"	"The Herb of Death"

More "Hildegarde Withers" Adventures by Stuart Palmer

The Penguin Pool Mystery	"Tomorrow's Murder"
The Green Ace	"Green Ice"
The Red Stallion	"The Riddle of the Tired Bullet"
"The Riddle of the Black Museum"	"Where Angels Fear to Tread"

And others . . .

More "Mom, the Mayvin" Adventures by James Yaffe

"Mom in the Spring"
"Mom Sings an Aria"
"Mom Remembers"

6.
Variations

Introduction

In the beginning, the function of the detective story was to entertain. This is still true.

Librarians will tell you that the books which circulate most, those which draw readers from all levels of society, are the ones featuring detection and mystery. Two former presidents of the United States, Abraham Lincoln and Franklin Roosevelt, were ardent detective story readers. Physicians and firemen, scholars and secretaries, musicians and mechanics have been and will continue to be attracted to the genre because, for a few hours, they can escape from their real problems to a world of action, romance, and, to use a favorite Poe word, "ratiocination."

Aware of this tremendous appeal and realizing also that "variety is the spice of life," many modern detective authors expanded their stories in various directions, some serious and some entertaining. They began to blend in social commentary, sports, science-fiction, psychology, and even humor.

Thus, an evolutionary process was set into motion that has resulted in the genre developing sub-genres—and the subs, their sub-subs.

Here is how the "variations" came into being . . .

The Detective Story and Social Commentary

Traditionally, it was the "serious" writer who was supposed to deal with socially significant themes.

This kind of literary stereotyping came about because of the habit of labeling or categorizing things as "good" or "bad"—or, in the case of literature, as "serious" or "popular."

Categorizing is an intellectual technique by which we simplify first, in order to later cope with complex problems. Sometimes it is a technique producing beneficial results. At other time, it can lead us into difficulties—which is what happened when it was applied to the detective story.

When the new literary form appeared, the early critics immediately placed it into the "popular" category. In order to ascertain why, let us explore what standards the critics used to set up these classifications.

One was based upon *intent*. It was taken for granted that all literature should entertain, or—to put it another way—tell a good story. But "serious" or important literature was expected to serve another function—to inform. Because it was adjudged that detective fiction did a lot of entertaining and little or no informing, critics refused "to take it seriously."

Another standard was that of *social significance*. A detective story dealing with a local crime, or even a national one, was never considered as important as a great historical episode dealing with slavery or "taxation without representation" or labor history.

Still another was *durability*. "Popular" literature was a "will of the wisp" phenomenon, here today, gone tomorrow. "Serious" literature, on the other hand, was supposed to retain its appeal forever.

Then there was *grandeur of theme*. Many of the great works of literature had dealt with universal themes such as ruthless ambition leads to destruction, great love defies even death, and intolerance results in alienation, while detective literature kept repeating a much less significant refrain, crime does not pay, over and over again.

The early critics also "pointed a finger" at the readers first attracted to the new form. They were mainly factory workers, office boys, mechanics, and farmers, people supposedly devoid of culture or literary taste. Another reason for the "popular" designation.

The early detective story writers accepted this categorization. Remember Poe and Doyle and their elaborate attempts to escape to "something better." Their early successors maintained this apologetic attitude toward detective stories; in a sense, they played out the roles that critics and society had assigned to them, rather than seeking their own and thereby enhancing their field.

It was the detective story itself that began to rebel against this kind of classification. As you know, the form did not disappear; it "hung around" and even began to propagate. Moreover, some highly educated and intellectually respected individuals like H. G. Wells, G. K. Chesterton, and Mark Twain let it be known that they were "consuming" mysteries as avidly as their supposed "inferiors." In addition, C. Auguste Dupin and Sherlock Holmes seemed to grow upon the public consciousness in almost the same manner as had Don Quixote, Hamlet, Hester Prynne, Huckleberry Finn, and other great literary characters.

The critics started having second thoughts.

They took another look and began noticing that Dupin and Holmes, besides detecting, were also suggesting to mankind that perhaps we should respect and cultivate the power of reason. They became aware that Father Brown was telling us that intuition and a knowledge of human motivation were as important as reason and logic.

Detective story authors also had second thoughts. Emboldened by the continued popularity and growth of their genre, they decided to try some experimenting.

Here are just a few of the things that happened:

1) Writer Dorothy L. Sayers, whom you have met, had always wanted to do a novel about "women's colleges and intellectual integrity." She decided to incorporate this socially significant theme into the framework of a detective story. The result: a highly experimental novel entitled *Gaudy Night* in which the "crime does not pay" theme was de-emphasized. This Lord Peter tale proved as successful as its predecessors; readers seemed to appreciate the fact that the scope of the detective story had been expanded.[1]

2) Writer Dashiell Hammett was tired of the perennial "intellectual" protagonists of detective literature. He felt that such protagonists bore little relationship to real detectives. Hammett went to work and created some brilliant "hard-boiled" detectives. Hammett's protagonists, Sam Spade, The Thin Man, The Continental Op, and others were a completely different breed from Dupin, Holmes, Queen, and company. In a way, the Hammett stories were more realistic than the classic tales, but they were also good literature. Raymond Chandler created Phillip Marlowe, another much-loved character of this kind.[2]

3) As you already know, teacher-writer William Brittain had created a teacher-detective as his protagonist. During the '60s, a host of problems began to proliferate within public education. Brittain

thought that he could comment upon what was happening within his working milieu through the vehicle of the short story—and his Mr. Strang.

There were other innovations of this kind, but they are simply too numerous to describe in our limited space.

Partly as a result of this experimentation, the detective story broke out of the "categorization" bind and was being taken very seriously indeed. By the end of the 1960s, departments of English within many American high schools and junior colleges were beginning to include a course in detective literature as part of their curricula. The genre continued to entertain but it had broadened its basic *crime does not pay* theme to include many highly significant topics—such as the one confronting our next hero.

John Ball—and Virgil Tibbs

In the year 1965, the name of Virgil Tibbs was added to the honor roll of fictional detectives. What was unique about Tibbs was that he was black.

Detective fans took the new sleuth to their hearts and came to realize that, up to the end of the '50s, their beloved genre had largely been a literature with which only whites could identify. There had never been a black protagonist, male or female, in detective fiction. A scattering of Negro characters had appeared in the stories, but these characters had been predominantly stereotypes reflecting the bias and ignorance of a hostile white society.

During the '60s, relationships between whites and blacks began to change. Blacks and other minority groups engaged in social action to begin clearing away all barriers to full equality. Minorities started to gain opportunities in areas of our national life such as housing, education, government, and the professions.

Detective literature began to reflect social change. Some short stories appeared with black protagonists—but these early Negro characterizations did not catch on in the manner of their popular white counterparts. And then novelist John Ball created Virgil Tibbs.

Tibbs made his debut in a novel entitled *In the Heat of the Night.* Not only was it a detective story but it contained a socially mature viewpoint that struck a powerful blow against racial discrimination. Tibbs was more than just another detective—albeit black—solving another murder case. Ball's tale was concerned with the core of black-white relationships in the South. Virgil Tibbs's blackness became an essential part of the central conflict in the book. Tibbs had to find a murderer, true, but his very dignity as a human being and a black man were also at stake.

His creator, John Ball, might be termed a modern-day version of a

Renaissance man. Like Leonardo da Vinci, Michaelangelo, and other marvelous artists of the Renaissance, Mr. Ball possesses talents that are many and varied.

Ball was born in Schenectady, New York, in 1911. He became a commercial airline pilot and flew for the U.S. Army Air Transport Command during World War II. Later, he worked in the area of music as an annotator and music editor for the Brooklyn *Daily Eagle* and the New York *World-Telegram*. He also worked in the fields of advertising and public relations, in addition to becoming expert in such diverse areas as Japanese-American culture, model-railroading, sports, astronomy, and sociology. He has written about his many vocations and avocations in newspaper and magazine articles, nonfiction essays and books, and, of course, in short stories and novels. He is also reputed to have a music library containing more than 18,000 recordings.[3]

In The Heat of the Night won an Edgar from The Mystery Writers of America in 1965 for being the best detective novel of that year. Later the book was purchased by Hollywood and made into a powerful motion picture starring Sidney Poitier as Virgil Tibbs.

Following are some excerpts from this famous work, good examples of social commentary in the detective story at its finest.

In The Heat of the Night

Synopsis of Chapter 1

It is a hot and stagnant night in the small Southern town of Wells, Georgia, near Atlanta. At this late hour, the most important man awake and on duty is Officer Sam Wood, cruising the streets in his official police car.

Sam completes his check of the main residential section and then enters Shantyville, the sprawling black area of town. Finished, he heads back toward the main district and stops at an all-night diner. It is hotter inside than out. Ralph, the 19-year-old counterman, serves Sam a King Coke and a slice of cake. As the policeman tries to cool himself, Ralph discourses upon what he considers to be an oddity of boxing, upon the fact that six top divisional champs are Negroes. Sam replies with a nasty stereotype about blacks' strength.

Leaving the diner, Sam enters his car and drives slowly through the small downtown district. His headlights pick out something lying in the road.

Stopping he approaches what turns out to be the lifeless body of a man sprawled on the pavement.

Chapter 2

At four minutes after four in the morning, the phone rang at the bedside of Bill Gillespie, chief of police of the city of Wells. Gillespie took a few seconds to shake himself partially awake before he answered. As he reached for the instrument he already knew that it was trouble, and probably big trouble, otherwise the night desk man would have handled it. The night man was on the line.

"Chief, I hate to wake you, but if Sam Wood is right, we may have a first-class murder on our hands."

Gillespie forced himself to sit up and swing his legs over the side of the bed. "Tourists?"

"No, not exactly. Sam has tentatively identified the body as that of Enrico Mantoli—you know, the fellow who was going to set up a music festival here. Understand, Chief, that we aren't even sure yet that the man is dead, but if he is, and if Sam's identification is correct, then somebody has knocked off our local celebrity and our whole music-festival deal probably has gone to pot."

Bill Gillespie was fully awake now. While he felt automatically for his slippers with his feet, he knew that he was expected to take command. The schooling in his profession he had had back in Texas told him what to say. "All right, listen to me. I'll come right down. Get a doctor and the ambulance there right away, a photographer, and dig up a couple more men. Have Wood stay where he is until I get there. You know the routine?"

The night desk man, who never before had had to deal with a murder, answered that he did. As soon as he hung up, Gillespie rose to his full six feet four and began quickly to climb into his clothes, running over in his mind exactly what he would do when he reached the murder scene. He had been chief of police and a Wells resident for only nine weeks, and now he would have to prove himself. As he bent to tie his shoes, he knew that he could trust himself to do the right thing, but he still wished that the hurdles immediately before him had already been cleared.

Despite the fact that he was only thirty-two, Bill Gillespie had abundant confidence in his own ability to meet whatever challenges were thrown at him. His size made it possible for him to look down literally on most men. His forcefulness, which had cost him the girl he had wanted to marry, swept away many normal obstacles as though they had never existed. If he had a murder on his hands he would solve it, and no one would dare to question him while he was in the process.

Then he remembered that he had not been told where the murder was. He picked up the phone angrily and misdialed in his haste. He slammed the instrument back into its cradle before what he knew would be a wrong number could ring, and then, forcing himself to be calm, tried again.

The night police desk man, who had been expecting the call, answered immediately. "Where is it?" Gillespie demanded.

"On the highway, Chief, just below Piney. The ambulance is there and the doctor has pronounced the victim dead. No positive identification yet."

"All right," the chief acknowledged, and dropped the instrument into position. He didn't like having to admit that he had had to call back to know where to go. He should have been told the body's position the first time.

Bill Gillespie's personal car was equipped with a siren, red lights in the rear window, and a police radio set. He jumped in, kicked the starter, and jerked the car away from the curb and up to speed without any regard whatever for the cold engine. In less than five minutes he saw ahead of him the police car, the ambulance, and a little knot of people gathered in the middle of the highway. Gillespie drove up quickly, set the brake, and was out of the car before it had come to a complete stop.

Without speaking to anyone, he strode rapidly to where the body still lay in the street, then squatted down and began to run his hands quickly over the fallen man. "Where's his wallet?" he demanded.

Sam Wood stepped forward to reply. "It's missing. At least I didn't find it on the body."

"Any positive identification?" Gillespie snapped.

The young doctor who had come with the ambulance answered that. "It's Enrico Mantoli, the conductor. He was the spark plug behind the musical festival we've been planning here."

"I know that," Gillespie retorted curtly, and turned his attention again to the body. He had a strong desire to tell it to sit up, wipe the dirt off its face, and tell him what happened, who did it. But this was one man whom he could not command. All right then, it would have to be done some other way. Gillespie looked up.

"Sam, take your car, check the railroad station and the north end of town to see if anyone is crazy enough to try to hitchhike out of here. Wait a minute." He turned his head quickly toward the doctor. "How long has this man been dead?"

"Less than an hour, I should say, possibly less than forty-five minutes. Whoever did it can't be too far away."

Gillespie allowed an expression of angry annoyance to cross his face. "All I asked you was how long he has been dead; you don't have to tell me my job, I'll tell you. I want photographs of the body from all angles, including some shots long enough to show its position relative to the curb and the buildings on the west side of the street. Then mark the position in chalk outline and barricade the area to keep traffic off this spot. After that you can take the body away." He stood up and saw Sam standing quietly by. "What did I tell you to do?" he demanded.

"You told me to wait a minute," Sam answered evenly.

"All right then, you can get going. Hop to it."

Sam moved quickly to his patrol car, and drove away with enough speed to avoid any possible criticism later. As he headed toward the railroad station, for a brief moment he allowed himself to hope that Gillespie would somehow make a public fool of himself and bungle the case. Then he realized that such a thought was totally unworthy of a sworn peace officer and he resolved that no matter what happened, his part would be done promptly and well.

At the last moment, as he approached the silent railroad station, he slowed his car down to avoid giving any undue warning to a possible murderer lurking inside. Sam pulled up close to the wooden platform and climbed out without hesitation. The station was a small one which dated back at least fifty years; at night it was inadequately lighted by a few dusty bulbs which seemed as ageless as the worn hard benches or the unyielding tile floor. As Sam walked rapidly toward the main waiting-room door, he had a sudden desire to loosen the pressure of his uniform cap. He rejected the idea at once and entered the station every inch a police officer, his right hand on his gun. The waiting room was deserted.

Sam sniffed the air rapidly and detected nothing to suggest that anyone had been there recently. No fresh cigarette smoke, only the habitual aroma of all such railroad stations, the evidence of thousands of nameless people who had passed through and gone on.

The ticket window was closed; the glass panel was down. Posted inside was a square of cardboard with the arrival times of the night trains printed in heavy crayon. Sam looked carefully about the room once more while he thought. If the murderer was here, he probably did not have a gun. He had killed by hitting the dead man on the back of the head with a blunt instrument, and with a blunt instrument Sam was confident he could deal. He bent and checked the small area under the benches. It was clear except for dirt and a few bits of paper.

Striding through the room, Sam pushed open the door to the train platform and looked both ways. The platform, too, was deserted. Walking with firm, authoritative steps, Sam passed the locked baggage-room door, which he tested and found secure, and paused by the dingier door over which a white board sign specified COLORED. With his right hand once more on his sidearm, Sam pushed into the poorly lighted room and then drew a quick gulp of breath. There was someone there.

Sam sized him up at a glance, and knew at once that he did not belong in Wells. He was fairly slender and dressed up in city clothes, including a white shirt and a tie. Sam guessed that he might be about thirty, but it was always hard to tell about blacks. Instead of being stretched out on the bench, he was wide awake and sitting up straight as though he were expecting something to happen. His coat was off and laid neatly beside him. He had been reading a paperback book up to the moment Sam entered; when he looked up, Sam saw that his face lacked the broad nose and thick, heavy lips that characterized so many southern laborers. His nose was almost like a white man's and the line of his mouth was straight and disciplined. If he had been a little lighter, Sam would have seen white blood in him, but his skin was too black for that.

The Negro forgot his book and let his hands fall into his lap while he looked up into Sam's broad face.

Sam took immediate command. "On your feet, black boy," he ordered, and crossed the room in five quick steps.

The Negro reached for his coat. "No you don't!" Sam knocked his arm aside and with a single swift motion spun his man around and clamped his own powerful forearm hard under the Negro's chin. In this position Sam could control him easily and still leave his right hand and arm free. Swiftly Sam searched his captive, an action which the Negro appeared too frightened to resist. When he had finished, Sam released the pressure on the man's windpipe and issued further orders. "Stand against the wall, face to it. Put your hands up, fingers apart, and lean against them. Keep them up where I can see them. Don't move until I tell you to."

The Negro obeyed without a word. When his order had been executed, Sam picked up the Negro's coat and felt inside the breast pocket. There was a wallet and it felt unusually thick.

With a strange prickle of excitement Sam pulled the wallet out and checked its contents. It was well stuffed with money. Sam ran his thumb down the edges of the bills; they were mostly tens and twenties; when he stopped his riffling at the long, narrow oval that marked a fifty, Sam was satisfied. He snapped the wallet shut and put it into his own pocket. The prisoner remained motionless, his feet out from the wall, leaning forward with part of his weight supported by his outstretched hands. Sam looked at him carefully again from the rear. He guessed that the suspect was around a hundred and fifty pounds, maybe a little more, but not much. He was about five feet nine, large enough to have done the job. There was a hint of a crease on the back of his trousers, so his suit had at some time been pressed. He did not have the big butt Sam was accustomed to on many Negroes, but that didn't mean he was frail. When Sam slapped him to see if he had a weapon, the Negro's body was firm and hard under his hand.

Sam folded the man's coat across his own arm. "Go out the door to your left," he ordered. "There's a police car in the drive. Get in the back seat and shut the door. Make one false move and I'll drop you right then with a bullet in your spine. Now move."

The Negro turned as directed, walked out onto the city side of the platform, and obediently climbed into the back seat of Sam's waiting car. The prisoner slammed the door just enough to be sure that it was properly latched and settled back in the seat. He made no move to do anything other than what he was directed.

Sam climbed in behind the wheel. There were no inside door handles in the patrol car and he knew that his prisoner could not escape. For a moment he thought of the way Mantoli had been killed—hit over the head presumably from the rear and probably by the prime suspect who was sitting behind him at that moment. Then Sam reassured himself with the thought that there was nothing in the rear seat which the Negro could use for a weapon, and with a bare-hand attack Sam could easily deal. He would have welcomed one; the prospect of a little action was attractive, particularly with someone as easy to handle as his captive.

Sam picked up the radio microphone and spoke tersely. "Wood from the railroad station. Bringing in a colored suspect." He paused, thought a moment, and decided to add nothing else. The rest of it could wait until he got to the station. The less police business put on the air the better.

The prisoner made no sound as Sam drove, smoothly and expertly, the eleven blocks to the police station. Two men were waiting at the drive-in entrance when he got there; Sam waved them aside, confident of his ability to handle his prisoner without help. He took his time as he climbed out, walked around the car, and swung the rear door open. "Out," he ordered.

The Negro climbed out and submitted without protest when Sam seized his upper arm and piloted him into the police station. Sam walked in properly, exactly as the illustrations in the manuals he had studied told him to do. With his powerful left arm he controlled his prisoner, his right hand resting, instantly ready, on his police automatic. Sam regretted that there was no one to take a picture of that moment, and then realized that once more he had forgotten himself and the dignity of his position.

As Sam turned the corner toward the row of cells, he was intercepted by the night desk man, who pointed silently to the office of Chief Gillespie. Sam nodded, steered his man up to the door, and knocked.

"Come in." Gillespie's strident voice echoed through the door. Sam turned the knob with his right hand, pushed his man through the opening, and waited before Gillespie's desk. The chief was pretending that he was occupied with some papers before him. Then he laid down the pen he had been holding and stared hard at the prisoner for a full twenty seconds. Sam could not see the prisoner's reaction and did not dare to turn his head to look for fear of breaking the psychological spell.

"What's your name!" Gillespie demanded suddenly. The question came out of his lips like a shot.

The Negro astonished Sam by speaking, for the first time, in a calm, unhurried voice. "My name is Tibbs, Virgil Tibbs," he replied, and then stood completely still. Sam relaxed his hold on the man's arm, but the prisoner made no attempt to sit in the empty chair beside him.

"What were you doing in the station?" This time the question was slightly less explosive, more matter-of-fact.

The Negro answered without shifting his weight. "I was waiting for the five-seventeen train for Washington." The scene of complete silence was repeated: Sam did not move, Gillespie sat perfectly still, and the prisoner made no attempt to do anything.

"When and how did you get into town?" This time Gillespie's question was deceptively mild and patient in tone.

"I came in on the twelve-thirty-five. It was three-quarters of an hour late."

"*What* twelve-thirty-five?" Gillespie barked suddenly.

The prisoner's tone in answering was unchanged. "The one from downstate. The local." The idea forced itself on Sam that this was an educated black, one of the sort that hung around the United Nations in New York, according to the newsreels. That might make it a little harder for Gillespie. Sam clamped his teeth together and held the corners of his mouth firm so he could not betray himself by smiling.

"What were you doing downstate?"

"I went to visit my mother."

There was a pause before the next question. Sam guessed that it would be an important one and that Gillespie was waiting deliberately to give it added force.

"Where did you get the money for your train fare?"

Before the prisoner could answer, Sam came to life. He fished the Negro's wallet from his own pocket and handed it to Gillespie. The chief looked quickly in the money compartment and slammed the wallet down hard onto the top of his desk. "Where did you get all *this* dough?" he demanded, and rose just enough from the seat of his chair so that the prisoner could see his size.

"I earned it," the Negro replied.

Gillespie dropped back into his chair, satisfied. Colored couldn't make money like that, or keep it if they did, and he knew it. The verdict was in, and the load was off his shoulders.

"Where do you work?" he demanded in a voice that told Sam the chief was ready to go home and back to bed.

"In Pasadena, California."

Bill Gillespie permitted himself a grim smile. Two thousand miles was a long way to most people, especially to colored. Far enough to make them think that a checkup wouldn't be made. Bill leaned forward across his desk to drive the next question home.

"And what do you do in Pasadena, California, that makes you money like that?"

The prisoner took the barest moment before he replied.

"I'm a police officer," he said.

Chapter 3

As a matter of principle Sam Wood did not like Negroes, at least not on anything that approached a man-to-man basis. It therefore confused him for a moment when he discovered within himself a stab of admiration for the slender man who stood beside him. Sam was a sportsman and therefore he enjoyed seeing someone, anyone, stand up successfully to Wells's new chief of police.

Until Gillespie arrived in town, Sam Wood had been rated a big man, but Gillespie's towering size automatically demoted Sam Wood to near normal stature. The new chief was only three years his senior—too young, Sam thought, for his job, even in a city as small as Wells. Furthermore Gillespie came from Texas, a state for which Sam felt no fraternal affection. But most of all Sam resented, consciously, Gillespie's hard, inconsiderate, and demanding manner. Sam arrived at the conclusion that he felt no liking for the Negro, only rich satisfaction in seeing Gillespie apparently confounded. Before he could think any further, Gillespie was looking at him.

"Did you question this man at all before you brought him in?" Gillespie demanded.

"No, sir," Sam answered. The "sir" stuck in his throat.

"Why not?" Gillespie barked the question in what Sam decided was a deliberately offensive manner. But if the Negro could keep his composure, Sam decided, he could, too. He thought for an instant and then replied as calmly as he could.

"Your orders were to check the railroad station and then to look for possible hitchhikers or anyone else worth checking. When I found this ni—this man in the railroad station, I brought him in immediately so I could carry out the rest of your orders. Shall I go now?"

Sam was proud of himself. He knew he wasn't much with words, but that, he felt sure, had been a good speech.

"I want to finish checking this man out first." Gillespie looked toward Tibbs. "You say you're a cop in California?"

"Yes, I am," Tibbs replied, still standing patiently beside the empty hard chair.

"Prove it."

"There's an ID card in my wallet."

Gillespie picked up the wallet from his desk with the air of handling something distasteful and somewhat unclean. He opened the pass-card section and stared hard at the small white card in the first transparent sleeve, then snapped the wallet shut and tossed it carelessly toward the young Negro. Tibbs caught it and slipped it quietly into his pocket.

"What have you been doing all night?" There was an edge of irritation in Gillespie's voice now. The voice was trying to pick a fight, and daring anyone to defy it.

"After I got off the train, I went in the station and waited. I didn't leave the station platform." There was still no change in Tibb's manner, something which Gillespie apparently found irritating. He changed the topic abruptly.

"You know we wouldn't let the likes of you try to be a cop down here, don't you?"

He waited; the room remained still.

"You knew enough to stay out of the white waiting room. You knew that, didn't you?" Once more Gillespie pressed his huge hands against the desk and positioned himself as if to rise.

"Yes, I knew that."

Gillespie made a decision. "All right, you stick around awhile. I'm going to check up on you. Take care of him, Sam."

Without speaking, Sam Wood turned around and followed Virgil Tibbs out of the room. Ordinarily he would not have permitted a Negro to precede him through a doorway, but this Negro did not wait for him to go first and Sam decided it was a bad moment to raise an issue. As soon as the two men had left, Gillespie raised one massive fist and slammed it down hard on the top of his desk. Then he scooped up the phone and dictated a wire to the police department of Pasadena, California.

Sam Wood showed Virgil Tibbs to a hard bench in the small detention room. Tibbs thanked him, sat down, pulled out the paperback book that he had had in the station, and returned to reading. Sam glanced at the cover.

It was *On Understanding Science* by Conant. Sam sat down and wished that he, too, had a book to read.

When the sky began to gray through the window, and then grew streaked with curiously dirty stripes of high clouds against a lightening background, Sam knew that he would not be driving his patrol car anymore that night—it was too late for that. He began to ache from sitting on the hard bench. He wanted a cup of coffee despite the heat; he wanted to move around. He was debating whether he wanted to stand up and stretch, and make a slight exhibit of himself doing so, when Gillespie abruptly appeared in the doorway. Tibbs looked up with quiet inquiry in his eyes.

"You can go if you want to," Gillespie said, looking at Tibbs. "You've missed your train and there won't be another one until afternoon. If you want to wait here, we'll see you get some breakfast."

"Thank you," Tibbs acknowledged. Sam decided this was his cue, and stood up. As soon as Gillespie cleared the doorway, Sam walked out and down the short hall to the door marked MEN—WHITE. The night desk man was inside, washing his hands. Something about the twist of the man's mouth told Sam there was undisclosed news. "Got anything, Pete?" he asked.

Pete nodded, splashed water over his face, and buried it in a towel. When he came up for air, he replied. "Chief got a wire a few minutes ago." He paused, bent down, and checked that all the toilet compartments were empty. "From Pasadena. Gillespie sent one out that said: 'We have serious homicide here. Request information re Virgil Tibbs, colored, who claims to be member Pasadena Police Department. Holding him as possible suspect.'"

"I don't blame him for checking up," Sam said.

"Wait till you hear what he got back." Pete lowered his voice so that Sam had to take a step closer to hear him. " 'Confirm Virgil Tibbs member Pasadena Police Department past ten years. Present rank investigator. Specialist homicide, other major crimes. Reputation excellent. Advise if his services needed your area. Agree homicide serious.' "

"Wow," Sam said softly.

"Exactly," Pete agreed. "I bet Gillespie doesn't know a damn thing about homicide investigation. If he doesn't clear this one up, and fast, the whole town will be down on his neck. So he has the offer of a specialist who is both chief suspect and a nig—" He paused when Sam shot up his hand as a warning. Footsteps passed down the corridor and disappeared into silence.

"What I want to know," Sam inquired, "is if Gillespie is as stupid as I think he is, how did he get this job in the first place? He was supposed to have been a hotshot in Texas, wasn't he?"

Pete shook his head. "He was never a cop; he's over the height limit. He was a jailor—a strong-arm boy who could handle the drunks. After three years of that, he answered an ad and got this job. He probably figures it will set him up for something bigger after a little while. But if he flubs this one he's done for, and he knows it."

"How did you get all this dope?"

Pete pressed his lips together and grinned. "I've been in this business a long time, and I've made quite a few friends here and there. I think I'll stick around awhile and see what happens. I go on days beginning tomorrow so it will look all right. How about you?"

"I think I will, too," Sam agreed.

Synopsis: Chapter 3 to the Middle of Chapter 8

Reluctantly, Chief Gillespie decides to make use of Virgil's talents. When Maestro Mantoli's body is brought in, Tibbs is invited to the morgue to conduct an inspection of the corpse. In the meantime, a new suspect is brought to the station; he is a young man named Harvey Oberst who was picked up by the police with Mantoli's wallet in his possession. Thinking the murderer has been found, a relieved Gillespie orders his black homicide expert back to Pasadena.

Virgil agrees to leave but he also presents his opinion about Harvey Oberst. Oberst has testified that he encountered the dead Mantoli on the road before Sam found him. Needing money, he searched the body, found the wallet, and ran. Virgil believes this story because he is convinced, after his examination of the corpse, that the maestro was killed by a right-handed man; Oberst, he points out, is left-handed.

Meanwhile Sam Wood drives to the hillside home of City Councilman George Endicott at whose house Mantoli and his daughter, Duena, were guests. Endicott offers to return with Sam in order to identify the body formally.

At the station, Endicott, a former Northerner, meets Virgil Tibbs and is impressed by him. He asks the mayor of the city, Frank Shubert, to have Gillespie keep Virgil in town to help assist him in finding the murderer. At first, Gillespie balks—but when Mayor Shubert points out that Tibbs could be the perfect "patsy" if the chief fails to solve the crime, Gillespie gives in.

Virgil succeeds in obtaining Harvey Oberst's release from jail. As the black detective uncovers additional evidence, he succeeds in obtaining some grudging respect from Officer Sam Wood.

Chapter 8

When Sam Wood reported for work at a quarter of twelve that night, he was surprised to find Virgil Tibbs sitting quietly in the lobby. He was even more surprised when he learned that Virgil was waiting for him.

After Sam had completed his check-in procedure, Tibbs came over and spoke to him. "If you don't mind, I'd like to ride with you tonight."

Sam was puzzled by the request. He could think of several reasons why the Negro detective should and should not ride with him. "You mean all night?" Sam asked.

Tibbs nodded. "All night."

"I don't know what Gillespie would say." Sam hesitated.

"He told me to do what I liked. I'd like to ride with you."

"Come along then." Sam didn't like the idea of eight hours of companionship with Tibbs, but then he reflected that after three years of patrolling his shift alone, it wouldn't hurt too much to have a passenger for one night. In fact it might be a good night to have someone else in the car. He recalled with a stab of conscience his uneasy concern of the previous night. And if he had refused to take Tibbs, Gillespie might have lit into him for that, too. The night man was a witness that Tibbs had asked him and had indicated that Gillespie had given his blessing. Sam decided to make the best of it and led the way to his patrol car.

When Sam slid behind the wheel, Tibbs opened the opposite door with quiet casualness and sat in the front seat beside him. Sam gripped the wheel firmly and wondered what to say about it. Still, they had sat this way on the drive up to the Endicott house; very well, he could stand it again. He started the engine and backed out of the police parking lot.

"What do you want me to do?" he asked as soon as the car was well away from the station.

"If it's not too much trouble," Tibbs replied, "I'd like you, as closely as you can, to do exactly as you did the night Mantoli was killed. Try to follow the same route and at the same speed. Do you think you can do that?"

"I can follow the same route exactly, and I won't miss the time by five minutes when I make out my report."

"That would help a great deal. Do you want me to keep still and just ride?"

"Talk all you like," Sam retorted. "You won't mix me up any."

Nevertheless they rode silently for some time. Sam took a steadily mounting professional pride in being able to guide his car expertly over the very tracks he had taken. He glanced at his watch. "Are you learning anything?" he asked.

"I'm learning how hot it can be in the middle of the night," Tibbs answered.

"I thought you knew that," Sam reminded him.

"Touché," Tibbs replied.

"Exactly what does that word mean?" Sam asked.

"It's a fencing term. When your opponent scores, you acknowledge it by saying 'touché.' Literally it means 'touched.' "

"In what language?"

"French."

"You've got a lot of education, Virgil, I'll grant you that." Sam swung the car silently around a corner and glanced at his watch.

"I can't drive as well as you can," Tibbs replied. "I've never seen a man who was better."

Despite himself Sam was pleased; he knew that if he could do nothing else, he could drive a car with the best. He was glad that someone else was aware of it, too. Despite his training, he was beginning to like Tibbs as a person.

"Maybe you know the answer to something, Virgil. I read a story once about a man that was real scared. He was out walking at night just waiting for somebody to jump out at him and he thought he could smell fear in the air, if that makes sense. Anyhow, the writer used a word for it—I can't remember it, but it began with an *m*. Sort of—oh, cat sounding. I remember I looked it up at the time."

"Hm-m. Let me think. Could it be 'miasma'?" Tibbs said.

"That's it," Sam exclaimed. "That thing has been bothering me. It's a kind of a rare word. How come you know it?"

"I read it in a story, too. More than once, so it was impressed on my mind. Just a coincidence."

"I wish I could have gone to school longer," Sam said, astonishing himself with the burst of confidence. "I went to high school for a while and then I got a job in a garage. I worked there for a while before I got this job."

"Did you go through the FBI school?" Tibbs asked.

"No, I didn't, no chance to. Say, that reminds me, I want to ask you something."

Tibbs waited a moment, then he said, "Go ahead and ask."

"Maybe this isn't any of my business, but I heard that you told something to Gillespie today that seems to have shook him. I'd sure like to know what it was."

Virgil Tibbs stared out of the window for a moment and inspected the pavement over which they were riding. "I told him that Mantoli wasn't killed where you found him, that his body had been brought there and dumped. That was why Gottschalk, the missile engineer, is obviously in the clear. The body undoubtedly wasn't there when he went through. It had to be brought from the scene of the murder to the highway and you found it within minutes."

"Virgil, how the hell do you know all this?"

"You'd know it, too, Sam, if you'd had a chance to examine the body."

Sam winced under the use of his first name. Just when he found himself beginning to like the dark man beside him, he did something to suggest equality and that Sam simply would not allow. But for the moment he decided to let it ride. He asked a question instead; one word was enough: "How?"

"From the palms of the hands."

"Suppose you take it from the top." Still irked, Sam tried to make it sound like a command, but when he formed the words they were in a milder tone.

"All right, Sam, let's go back to the moment that Mantoli was hit on the head. We know now that it was a fatal blow, but it isn't clear whether the man died instantly or was still conscious for at least a few seconds after he was struck."

Sam swung the car up a gentle grade and again glanced at his watch. He was exactly on schedule. And he was listening carefully.

"Now if the man died instantly, or was knocked unconscious at once, exactly what would happen?"

"He would fall down."

"Yes, but *how* would he fall down? Remember now, he's either unconscious or dead."

Sam thought about that one for a moment. "I think he'd go down like a sack of potatoes." He glanced over at Tibbs, who was half turned toward him, his right arm resting on the windowsill.

"That's exactly right; his knees would unlock, his shoulders would sag, his head would fall forward, and down he would go more or less in a heap."

Sam's mind leaped ahead as the light began to dawn. "But Mantoli's body was all spread out. His hands were over his head!"

"That's right," Tibbs agreed. "I saw the pictures of the body just as you found it."

"Wait a minute," Sam interrupted. "Suppose he was still conscious for a few seconds or so after he was hit. . . ."

"Go on," Tibbs invited.

"Then he'd throw out his arms and try to save himself."

"Now you're beginning to sound like a homicide man," Virgil encouraged.

"And that's the way I found him."

"That's right."

"So perhaps he was conscious after he was hit."

Sam was so interested in the conversation that he missed a turning. Looking quickly behind him, he made a U turn a quarter of the way up the block and fed a spurt of gas to make up the time he had lost.

"I don't think so," Tibbs said.

"Maybe I missed a point."

"Suppose Mantoli had been hit where you found him. For his body to be spread out that way, he would have had to try and break his fall with his hands."

"I get it!" Sam exploded. "If he had done that, the pavement would have scratched his hands, probably taken off some skin."

"So?"

"Then if there was no skin off the palms of the hands, or any marks like that, that wasn't where he fell."

"Or if it was," Tibbs finished, "someone was careful to spread the body out afterward."

"Yes; though that isn't likely," Sam added. "Because it was in the middle of the highway and a car could have come along any time. I could have."

"Sam," Tibbs said, "you have the makings of a real professional."

This time Sam didn't even notice that Tibbs had used his first name. His mind was jumping ahead to himself, Sam Wood, professional homicide detective. Then he remembered that the black man seated beside him was just that. "How did you learn your trade, Virgil?" he asked.

"Some of the best training in the world and ten years' experience. Everybody who joins the Pasadena force starts out by going to school. It's amazing how much they teach you in a comparatively short time."

Sam thought carefully for a minute before he asked his next question. "Virgil, I'm going to ask you something you aren't going to like. But I want to know. How did they happen to take you? No, that isn't what I mean. I want to ask you point-blank how come a colored man got all those advantages. Now if you want to get mad, go ahead."

Tibbs countered with a question of his own. "You've always lived in the South, haven't you?"

"I've never been further than Atlanta," Sam acknowledged.

"Then it may be hard for you to believe, but there are places in this country where a colored man, to use your words for it, is simply a human being like everybody else. Not everybody feels that way, but enough do so that at home I can go weeks at a time without anybody reminding me that I'm a Negro. Here I can't go fifteen minutes. If you went somewhere where people despised you because of your southern accent, and all you were doing was speaking naturally and the best way that you could, you might have a very slight idea of what it is to be constantly cursed for something that isn't your fault and shouldn't make any difference anyhow."

Sam shook his head. "Some guys down here would kill you for saying a thing like that," he cautioned.

"You made my point," Tibbs replied.

Sam pondered that one for some time. Then he decided that he had had enough conversation and he remained silent until he at last slid the car up to the curb across from the Simon Pharmacy. When he checked his watch for the last time, he was exactly a minute ahead of schedule. Carefully he picked up the clipboard and slowly filled in the report line. Then he looked at his watch, which now showed him that he had succeeded in filling half of the surplus minute. With a clear conscience, he noted down the time and then, switching on the dome light, handed the board silently to Tibbs.

The Negro detective studied it carefully and then handed it back. Sam knew without asking that he would have noticed that the times this evening and on the fatal night were identical. And he was right. "That's amazing, Sam," Tibbs told him. "I know very few men who could have done that and come out right on the nose the way you did." Tibbs paused for a moment. "The next part is the most critical; you know that, of course."

"Naturally I know it, *Mr.* Tibbs." Sam let a touch of venom drip into his voice.

"Then my confidence in you is justified," Tibbs answered. The answer baffled Sam; he wasn't sure just how it was meant. But there was no clear way he could take exception. "All right, let's go," he said, and put the car into gear.

Still edgy, he bumped across the railroad tracks and into shantyville and the Negro area of the city. When he got there, he leaned up over the wheel and watched as usual for sleeping dogs in the street. There were none. Carefully he retraced his route past the tiny, unpainted frame houses, across the siding, and up the street that led past the Purdy house.

At that moment Sam thought about Delores. What if she were to be up and about again? It had happened twice before. That would give a Negro a look at a pretty white girl with no clothes on. Two blocks short of the Purdy house, Sam swung the car to the right and jogged two blocks down.

A small sense of guilt fought for recognition, but Sam suppressed it. And the slight deviation, he felt, was absolutely undetectable.

At the end of the two blocks, Sam turned again to the left and continued up the dark street exactly as he had driven all evening. When the car jolted suddenly on an unpaved patch of road, Sam was startled, then he remembered that at the next corner there was a cross street that would get him back on his route. And it was the block past the Purdy house. When the corner came he took it smoothly, climbed back onto the pavement, and kept straight ahead until he reached the highway. He made his stop, as he always did, and then turned right toward the diner.

As he picked up speed, he wondered what to do with Virgil while he was at the diner; colored were not allowed inside. No clear answer had come to him by the time he pulled into the parking lot. He looked at his watch. "Still on schedule?" Tibbs asked.

Sam nodded. "I stop here fifteen minutes to eat."

Before he could say more, Tibbs relieved his embarrassment. "Go ahead, and don't hurry," he said. "I'll wait for you here."

Inside the diner, Sam's conscience nibbled at his mood. It had been awakened by the slight detour, unimportant in itself and taken for a good reason, but keeping a man waiting, even a black one, while he refreshed himself in comparative comfort annoyed Sam. He turned to Ralph. "Fix me up a ham sandwich to go, and wrap up a piece of pie. Better add a carton of milk and some straws."

"It ain't for that nigger cop, is it?" Ralph demanded. "If it is, we're all out."

Sam pulled himself up to his full height. "When I tell you what to do," he barked, "you do it. What I want that food for is none of your damn business."

Ralph shrank visibly before his eyes, but he did not give up. "My boss won't like it," he countered.

"Move," Sam ordered.

Ralph moved, and balefully. When Sam laid a dollar on the counter, the night man rang it up and handed out the change as though it were something unclean. And when the policeman had closed the door behind him, the thin, pimply youth let a sneer twist his features. "Nigger lover!" No matter what happened now, he was going to tell his boss. *He* was a councilman and Sam Wood wouldn't push *him* around!

Ralph's displeasure didn't faze Sam a bit; it even helped to mollify his conscience. As he passed the food to Virgil Tibbs he felt proud of himself. He started the car, drove down the highway, checked his watch, and received his reward—he was on time to the minute. Carefully he pulled the car up to the spot where he had found the body, turned on his red warning lights, and stopped.

"How closely on time are you?" Tibbs asked.

"To the minute," Sam answered.

"Thank you very much," Tibbs said. "You've helped me a great deal, more than you may realize. And thank you, too, for getting some lunch for me." He paused to take a bite of his sandwich and a sip from the container of milk.

"Now I want to ask you just one thing: Why did you deliberately change your route when we were across the tracks a little while ago?"

We have tried to show in these summaries and excerpts that a detective story can provide important social commentary as well as good entertainment. If you are interested in how the plot is resolved, we suggest you read the novel in its entirety.

ACTIVITIES

1) Most sociologists have stated that racial segregation is a socially unproductive phenomenon. How do the excerpts from John Ball's novel demonstrate this thesis?

2) You will recall the first person point of view literary technique utilized by Sir Arthur Conan Doyle and Mary Roberts Rinehart in their Sherlock Holmes and Miss Pinkerton stories. The excerpts from *In The Heat of the Night* demonstrate another technique known as *the omniscient point of view.* Here, the narrator is not a character in the story but an outsider, or third person who relates what is happening. In addition, like a superhuman being, he is omniscient or all-knowing; that is, he is able to see into the minds and record the thoughts of the people involved in the events described.

Can you provide specific instances from the preceding excerpts where John Ball utilizes this technique? Then, see if you can show how the omniscient style of writing actually contributes to the social commentary in the story.

The Sport of Murder

In his introduction to *Sporting Blood,* Ellery Queen's anthology of sports-detective stories, the famous sports writer, Grantland Rice, had the following to say:

"A combination of sports and mystery is an extremely interesting hook-up. In sport, one can rarely tell what is going to happen or who is going to win out until the game is over. In any good mystery, this same thing must take place."[4]

What does happen when the suspense of sports is combined with that of a good detective yarn? Does it add up to—*double suspense?*

Long before Grantland Rice explored the combination, Sir Arthur Conan Doyle became intrigued by the possibilities and so he placed Holmes and Watson into the world of horseracing. What resulted was an early sports-detective tale entitled "Silver Blaze."

It was not Doyle's most popular Sherlock Holmes story—but it was not his worst either. He never tried another sports-detective story because he felt he was not knowledgeable about athletics.

Not so Ellery Queen.

In the year 1940, Queen published an anthology of short stories entitled *The New Adventures of Ellery Queen.* Included in the collection were four sports-detective tales dealing with the great American pastimes of baseball, football, boxing, and horseracing. Unlike his great predecessor, Doyle, Queen felt perfectly at ease within the milieu of sports; two years later, he was to edit the first sports-detective anthology ever published.

Other well-known detective authors who have tried the "sports-mystery hookup" are G. K. Chesterton, Agatha Christie, Stuart Palmer, Dashiell Hammett, and Rex Stout.

We have picked Mr. Stout's tale as our next presentation mainly because his hero might be termed the most un-athletic protagonist ever to grace the halls of fictional sleuthdom. Placing such a sedentary figure into the virile sporting world took "a great deal of doing," and we believe that such literary daring should be rewarded . . .

Rex Stout—and Nero Wolfe

At the age of 48, Rex Stout published his first detective novel, *Fer de Lance.* Its singular protagonist, Nero Wolfe, could only be described by such colorful appellations as elephantine, gargantuan, corpulent—or, to put it more bluntly: *fat.* Critics discovered there was little physical resemblance between author and hero. They liked Nero despite his physiognomy and, surprise, they labeled his assistant, Archie Goodwin, one of the most imaginative and likeable Watsons yet.

Indiana-born (1886) and Kansas-raised, Rex Stout joined the Navy at age 18, served a two year hitch, and then opted to become a lawyer. That notion was promptly abandoned when he sold a poem to *Smart Set Magazine* and discovered that he enjoyed seeing his creative efforts in print. While supporting himself by an assortment of jobs and a business career, he wrote short stories and novels, some of which were published. Then the Depression of 1929 came along and, as he says, ". . . took most of my money and caused me to switch to mystery stories."[5]

As more Nero Wolfe and Archie tales flowed from his pen, the critics began to realize that Stout was "liberalizing" the routine detective story by contributing keen wit, deft literary skill, and a superbly unique detective duo. Another example of this liberalization was his attempt to yank Nero Wolfe from his office "armchair" into the world of baseball.

Let's watch Nero *"play ball!"*

The World Series Murder

At the end of the sixth inning the score was Boston 11, New York 1. I would not have believed that the day would ever come when, seated in a lower box between home and first, at the seventh and deciding game of a World Series between New York and Boston, I would find myself glomming a girl. I am by no means above glomming a girl if she is worthy, but not at a ball game, where my mind is otherwise occupied. That awful day, though, I did.

The situation was complex and will have to be explained. It was a mess even before the game started. Pierre Mondor, owner of a famous restaurant in Paris, was visiting New York and was our house guest at Nero Wolfe's old brownstone on West 35th Street. He got the notion, somehow, that Wolfe had to take him to a baseball game, and Wolfe as his host couldn't refuse. Tickets were no problem, since Emil Chisholm, oil millionaire and part owner of the New York team, considered himself deeply in Wolfe's debt on account of a case we had handled for him a few years back.

So that October afternoon, a Wednesday, I got the pair of them—the noted private detective and the noted chef—up to the ball park. It was twenty past 1, only ten minutes to game time, and the stands were jammed. I motioned to Mondor, and he slid in and sat. Wolfe stood and glared down at the wooden slats and metal arms. Then he glared at me.

"Are you out of your senses?" he demanded.

"I warned you," I said coldly. "It was designed for men, not mammoths."

He tightened his lips, moved his bulk, lowered it, and tried to squeeze between the arms. No. He grasped the rail in front with both hands, wriggled loose, and perched on the edge of the seat.

Mondor called to me across the great expanse of Wolfe's back: "I depend with confidence on you, Arshee! You must make clear as it develops! What are the little white things?"

I love baseball, I love the New York team, I had 50 bucks up on that game, but I would have got up and gone but for one thing: It was working hours and Wolfe pays my salary, and there were too many people, some of them alive and loose, who felt strongly that he had already lived too long. He is seldom out in the open, easy to get at, and when he is I like to be nearby. So I gritted my teeth and stuck.

The ground crew finished smoothing off and hauled their drags away; the umpires did a huddle, the home team trotted out on the field to their stations; the throng gave with a lusty, excited roar; we all stood up for *The Star-Spangled Banner,* and then sat down again. After southpaw Ed Romeike, 22-4 for the season, had burned a few over for the range, Lew Baker, the catcher, fired it to Tiny Garth at second. The Boston lead-off man came to the white line, the plate umpire said go, and Romeike looked around at the field, toed the rubber, went into his tricky windup, and shot a fast one over the outside corner for strike one. The crowd let out a short, sharp yell.

My personal nightmare was bad enough. Mondor was our guest, and trying to tell a foreigner what a base on balls is during a World Series game, with two men on, two down, and Oaky Asmussen at bat, is hard on the nerves. As for Wolfe, it wasn't so much the sight of him there in his concentrated misery; it was the certainty that by tomorrow he would have figured out a way to blame it on me, and that would start a feud.

Bad enough, but more was to come, and not for me alone. One fly had plopped into the soup even before the game started, when the line-up was announced and Tiny Garth was named for second base, with no explanation. A buzz of amazement had filled the stands. Why not Nick Ferrone? Ferrone, a lanky, big-eared kid just up from the bush five months back, had fielded and batted himself so far to the front that it was taken for granted he would be voted rookie of the year. He had been spectacular in the first six games of the Series, batting .427. Where was he today? Why Garth?

Then the game. That was no personal nightmare of mine; it was all too public. In the first inning Con Prentiss, New York's shortstop, bobbled an easy grounder, and two minutes later Lew Baker, the catcher, trying to nab a runner at second, threw the ball six feet over Garth's head into the outfield. With luck the visitors scored only one run. In the second inning Nat Neill, center fielder, misjudged a fly he could have walked under, tried to run in three directions at once, and had to chase it to the fence; and soon after that, Prentiss grabbed a hard-hit ball on the hop and hurled it into the dirt three paces to the left of third base. By the time they got three out, Boston had two more runs.

As the New York team came in for their turn at bat in the second, bitter sarcasms from the stands greeted them. Then our section was distracted by an incident. A man in a hurry came plunging down the aisle, bumping my elbow as he passed, and pulled up alongside a front box occupied by six men, among them the Mayor of New York and oilman Emil Chisholm, who had provided our tickets. The man spoke into the ear of Chisholm, who looked anything but happy. Chisholm said something to his boxmates, arose, and beat it up the aisle double-quick, followed by cutting remarks from nearby fans who had recognized him. As my eyes went back to the arena, Con Prentiss, New York shortstop, swung at a floater and missed by a mile.

There is no point in my retailing the agony. As I said, at the end of the sixth the score was 11 to 1. Romeike was hurling all right, but his support would have been pitiful on a sand lot. Joe Eston, the third baseman, and Nat Neill had each made two errors, and Con Prentiss and Lew Baker three apiece. As they came to the dugout in the sixth one wit yelled, "Say it ain't true, Joe!" at Eston, and the crowd, recognizing that classic moan to Shoeless Joe Jackson, let out a howl. They were getting really rough. As for me, I had had plenty of the tragedy out on the diamond and was looking around for something less painful, when I caught sight of the girl, in a box off to my right.

I glommed her, not offensively. There were two of them. One was a redhead who would start to get plump in a couple of years; almost worthy, but not quite. The other one, the glommee, had light-brown hair and dark-brown eyes, and was fully qualified. I had the feeling that she was not a complete stranger, that I had seen her somewhere before, but couldn't place her.

The pleasure it gave me to look at her was not pure, because it was adulterated with resentment. She looked happy. Her eyes sparkled. Apparently she liked the way things were going. There is no law barring enemy fans from a ball park, but I resented it. Nevertheless, I continued the glommation. She was the only object I had seen there that day, on or off the field, that didn't make me want to shut my eyes.

Something came between her and me. A man stopped at my elbow, and asked my ear: "Are you Archie Goodwin?"

I told him yes.

"Is that Nero Wolfe?"

I nodded.

"Mr. Chisholm wants him in the clubhouse, quick."

I reflected for two seconds, decided that this was straight from heaven, and slid forward to tell Wolfe: "Mr. Chisholm invites us to the clubhouse. We'll avoid the crush. There's a chair there. He wants to see you."

He didn't growl, "What about?" He didn't even growl. He muttered something to Mondor, pulled himself erect, and side-stepped past me to the aisle. Mondor came after him. The courier led the way and I brought up the rear. As we went up the concrete steps single file a shout came from somewhere on the left:

"Go get 'em, Nero! Sic 'em!"

Such is fame. . . .

"This is urgent!" Emil Chisholm squeaked. "It's urgent."

There was no chair in the clubroom of the size Wolfe likes and needs, but there was a big leather couch, and he was on it, breathing hard and scowling. Mondor was seated over against the wall, out of it. Chisholm, a hefty, broad-shouldered guy, with a wide, thick mouth and a long, straight nose, was too upset to stand or sit, so he was boiling around. I was standing near an open window. Through it came a sudden swelling roar from the crowd out in the stands.

"Shut that window!" Chisholm barked.

I did so.

"I'm going home," Wolfe stated in his most conclusive tone. "But not until they have left. Perhaps, if you will tell me briefly—"

"We've lost the Series!" Chisholm shouted.

Wolfe closed his eyes, and opened them again. "If you'll keep your voice down," he suggested. "I've had enough noise today. If losing the Series is your problem, I'm afraid I can't help."

"No. Nobody can." Chisholm stood facing him. "I blew up. I'm sorry. I've got to get hold of myself. This is what happened: Out there before the game Art got a suspicion—"

"Art?"

"Art Kinney, our manager. Naturally, he was watching the boys like a hawk, and he got a suspicion something was wrong. That first—"

"Why was he watching them like a hawk?"

"That's his job! He's manager!" Chisholm realized he was shouting again, stopped, clamped his jaw, and clenched his fists. After a second he went on: "Also, Nick Ferrone has disappeared. He was here with them in the club-house, he had got into uniform; then, after they went out to the dugout, he just wasn't there. Art sent Doc Soffer back here to get him, but he couldn't find him. He was simply gone. Art had to put Garth at second base. Natural-ly, he was on edge, and he noticed things—the way some of the boys looked and acted—that made him suspicious. Then—"

A door opened and a guy came running in, yelling, "Fitch hit one and Neill let it get by, and Asmussen scored! Fitch went on to third!"

I recognized him, chiefly by his crooked nose, which had got in the way of a line drive back in the twenties, when he was a star infielder. It was Beaky Durkin, now a New York scout, with a new lease on life because he had dug up Nick Ferrone out in Arkansas.

Chisholm yelled at him, "Get out!" He took a threatening step. "Get out! ... Hey, Doc! Come in here!"

Durkin, backing out, collided with a man in the doorway. This was Doc Soffer, New York's veteran medico, bald, wearing black-rimmed glasses; he had a long torso and short legs. Entering, he looked as if his ten best-paying patients had just died on him.

"I can't sweat it, Doc," Chisholm told him. "I'm going nuts! This is Nero Wolfe. You tell him."

"Who are you?" Wolfe demanded.

Soffer stopped before him. "I'm Dr. Horton Soffer," he said, clipping it. "Four of my men have been drugged. They're out there now, trying to play ball, and they can't." He stopped, looking as if he were about to break down and cry, gulped, and went on:

"They didn't seem right, there in the dugout. I noticed it and so did Kinney. That first inning there was no doubt about it, something was wrong. The second inning it was even worse—and the same four men, Baker, Prentiss, Neill, and Eston. I got an idea, and came here to investigate. You see that cooler?"

He pointed to a big, white-enameled refrigerator standing against a wall. Wolfe nodded. "Well?"

"It contains mostly an assortment of drinks in bottles. I know my men's habits, every little habit they've got and every big one, too. I know that after they get into uniform before a game those four men—the four I named—have the habit of getting a bottle of Beebright out of the cooler."

"What is Beebright?"

"It's a carbonated drink that's supposed to have honey in it instead of sugar. Each of those four men drinks a bottle of it, or part of one, before he goes out to the field, practically without exception. And it was those four that were off—terrible! I never saw anything like it. That's how I got my idea. I told Kinney, and he said to come and see.

"Usually the clubhouse boy cleans up here after the men leave for the field, but this being the deciding game of the World Series, today he didn't. Stuff was scattered around—as you see, it still is—and there was a Beebright bottle there on that table with a little left in it. It didn't smell wrong, and I didn't want to waste any tasting. I had sent for Mr. Chisholm, and when he came we decided what to do. He sent for Beaky Durkin, who had a seat in the grandstand, because he knew Ferrone better than anyone else. We thought he might have some idea that would help explain what had happened to Ferrone and those four other boys. I took the Beebright down the street to a drugstore, and made two tests. The first one, Ranwez's, didn't prove anything, but that was probably because it is limited—"

"Negatives may be skipped," Wolfe muttered.

"I'm telling you what I did," Soffer snapped. "Ranwez's test took over half an hour. The second, Ekkert's, took less. I did it twice, to check. It was conclusive. The Beebright contained sodium phenobarbital. I couldn't get the quantity, in a hurry like that, but on a guess it was two grains, possibly a little more, in the full bottle. Anyone can get hold of it. Certainly that would be no problem for a bigtime gambler who wanted to clean up on a World Series game."

Chisholm swore, audibly.

Doc Soffer nodded. "And somebody put it in the bottles, knowing those four men would drink it just before the game. All he had to do was remove the caps, drop the tablets, in, replace the caps, and shake the bottles a little—not much, because it's very soluble. They must have been placed in the refrigerator not much before noon; otherwise someone else might have drunk them. Besides, if they were fixed very far in advance, the drinks would have gone stale and the men would have noticed it. So it must have been someone—"

Chisholm had marched to the window. He whirled and yelled, "Ferrone did it! He did it and lammed!"

Doc Soffer said, "I don't know about that, but I've got to tell Art—" He almost ran from the room.

Beaky Durkin appeared again. He came through the door and halted, facing Chisholm. He was trembling and his face was white, all but the crooked nose.

"Not Nick," he said hoarsely. "Not that boy. Nick didn't do it!"

"Oh, no?" Chisholm was bitter. "Did I ask you? A fine rookie of the year you brought in from Arkansas! Where is he? Bring him here and let me get my hands on him! Go find him!"

Beaky looked bewildered. "Go where?"

"How do I know? He's your pet, not mine," Chisholm said savagely. "Get him and bring him in and I'll offer him a new contract—that will *be* a contract. Now beat it!"

Durkin lifted helpless hands, but turned and left the room.

Wolfe grunted. "Sit down, please," he told Chisholm. "When I address you I want to look at you, and my neck is not elastic. . . . Thank you, sir. You want to hire me for a job?"

"Yes. I want—"

"Please. Is this correct? Four of your best players, drugged as described by Dr. Soffer, could not perform properly, and as a result a game is lost and a World Series?"

"We're losing it." Chisholm's head swung toward the window and back again. "Art's pulling out the drugged men, but of course it's lost."

"And you assume a gambler or a group of gamblers is responsible. How much could he or they win on a game?"

"On today's game, any amount. Fifty thousand, or double that, easy."

"I see. Then you need the police. At once."

Chisholm shook his head. "I don't want to. Baseball is a wonderful game, the best and cleanest game on earth. This is the dirtiest thing that's happened in baseball in 30 years, and it's got to be handled right and handled fast. You're the best detective in the business, and you're right here. With a swarm of cops trooping in, who knows what'll happen! If we have to have them later, all right, but now you're here. Go to it!"

Wolfe was frowning. "You think this Nick Ferrone did it."

"I don't know!" Chisholm was yelling again. "How do I know what I think? He's a harebrained kid just out of the sticks, and he's disappeared. What does that look like?"

Wolfe nodded. "Very well." He drew a deep sigh. "I can at least make some gestures, and see." He aimed a finger at the door Beaky Durkin and Doc Soffer had used. "Is that an office?"

"It leads to Kinney's office—the manager's."

"Then it has a phone. You will call police headquarters and report the disappearance of Nick Ferrone, and ask them to find him. Such a job, when urgent, is beyond my resources. Tell them nothing more for the present if you want it that way. Where do the players change clothing?"

"Through there." Chisholm indicated another door. "That's the locker room. The shower room is beyond."

Wolfe's eyes came to me: "Archie. You will look around all premises adjoining this room. This room you can leave to me."

"Anything in particular?" I asked.

"No. You have good eyes and a head of sorts. Use them."

"I could wait to phone the police," Chisholm suggested, "until you—"

"No," Wolfe snapped. "In ten minutes you can have every cop in New York looking for Mr. Ferrone, and it will cost you ten cents. Spend it. I charge more for less."

Chisholm went out, through the door at the left. I thought I might as well start in that direction, and followed him across a hall and into another room. It was good-sized, furnished with desk, chairs, and accessories. Beaky Durkin sat in a corner with his ear to a radio tuned low, and Doc Soffer was there with him. Chisholm barked, "Shut that thing off!" and crossed to a desk with a phone.

Under other circumstances I would have enjoyed having a look at the office of Art Kinney, the New York manager, but I was on a mission and there was too big an audience. I about-faced and backtracked to the clubroom. As I crossed to the door in the far wall, Wolfe was standing by the open door of the refrigerator with a bottle of Beebright in his hand, holding it at arm's length, sneering at it, and Mondor was beside him.

I passed through the door and was in a room both long and wide, with two rows of lockers, benches and stools, and a couple of chairs. The locker doors were marked with numbers and names. I tried three; they were locked. Through a doorway at the left was the shower room. I went to the far end, glancing in at each of the shower stalls, was disappointed to see no pillbox that might have contained sodium phenobarbital, and returned to the locker room.

In the middle of the row on the right was the locker marked "Ferrone." Its door was locked. With my portable key collection I could have operated, but I don't take it along to ball games, and nothing on my personal ring was usable. It seemed to me that the inside of that locker was the first place that needed attention, so I returned to the clubroom, made a face at Wolfe as I went by, and entered Kinney's office. Chisholm had finished phoning and was seated at a desk, staring at the floor. Beaky Durkin and Doc Soffer had their ears glued to the radio.

I asked Chisholm, "Have you got a key to Ferrone's locker?"

His head jerked up. "No. I think Kinney has a master key. I don't know where he keeps it."

"Fifteen to two," Durkin informed us, or maybe he was just talking to himself. "New York batting in the ninth, two down. Garth got a home run, bases empty. It's all—"

"Shut up!" Chisholm yelled at him.

Since Kinney would soon be with us, and since Ferrone's locker had first call, I thought I might as well wait there for him. However, with our client sitting there glaring at me it would be well to display some interest and energy, so I moved. I went to the filing cabinets and looked them over. I opened a door, saw a hall leading to stairs going down, and shut the door. I crossed to another door in the opposite wall, and opened that.

Since I hadn't the faintest expectation of finding anything pertinent beyond that door, let alone a corpse, I must have made some sign of surprise, but if so it wasn't noticed. I stood for three seconds, then slipped inside and squatted long enough to get an answer to the main question. I arose, backed out, and addressed Soffer:

"Take a look here, Doc. I think he's dead."

He made a noise, stared, and moved. I marched into the clubroom and crossed to the couch where Wolfe was sitting.

"Found something," I told him. "Nick Ferrone, in uniform, on the floor of a closet, with a baseball bat alongside him and his head smashed in. He's dead, according to me, but Doc Soffer is checking, if you want an expert opinion."

Wolfe grunted. "Call the police."

"Yes, sir. A question: Any minute the ballplayers will be coming in here. The cops won't like it if they mess around. Do we care? It won't be Cramer. This is the Bronx, not Manhattan. Do we—?"

A bellow, Chisholm's, came through: "Wolfe! Come in here!"

Wolfe got up, growling. "We owe the police nothing, but we have a client—I think we have. I'll see. Meanwhile, you stay here. Everyone entering this room remains, under surveillance." He headed for Kinney's office.

Another door opened, the one in the west wall, and Nat Neill, New York's center fielder, entered the clubroom, his jaw set and his eyes blazing. Following him came Lew Baker, the catcher. Behind them on the stairs, was a clatter of footsteps.

The game was over. New York had lost. . . .

Another thing I don't take along to ball games is a gun, but that day there was a moment when I wished I had. After an ordinary game, even a lost one, I suppose the team might have been merely irritated if, on getting to the clubhouse, they found a stranger backed up against the door to the locker room telling them they could not pass. But that day they were ready to plug one another, so why not a stranger?

The first dozen were ganging me, about to start using hands, when Art Kinney, the manager, appeared. He strode, tight-lipped, through to his office and the gang let up to consider; all but Bill Moyse, the second-string catcher, six-feet-two and over 200 pounds. He had come late, after Kinney. He strode up to me, making fists, and announced that his wife was waiting for him, he was going in to change, and either I would move or he would move me.

One of his teammates called: "Show him her picture, Bill! That'll move him!"

Moyse whirled and leaped. Hands grabbed for him but he kept going. Whether he reached his target or not I can't say, because, first, I was staying put and it was quite a mix-up, and, second, I was seeing something that wasn't present. The mention of Moyse's wife and her picture had done it. What I was seeing was a picture of a girl that had appeared in the *Gazette* a couple of months back, with a caption tagging her as the showgirl bride of William Moyse, the ballplayer; and it was the girl I had been glomming in a nearby box when the summons had come from Chisholm. No question about it. That was interesting.

Meanwhile, Moyse was doing me a service by making a diversion. Three or four men had hold of him, and others were gathered around his target, Con Prentiss, the shortstop. They were all jabbering. Prentiss, who was wiry and tough, was showing his teeth in a grin, not an attractive one. Moyse suddenly whirled again and was heading back for me. It was useless to start slugging that mountain of muscle, and I was set to try blocking him, when a loud voice came from the doorway to the manager's office:

"Here! Attention, all of you!"

It was Art Kinney. His face was absolutely white and his neck cords were twitching, as they all turned toward him.

"I'm full up." he said, half hysterical. "This is Nero Wolfe, the detective. He'll tell you something."

Muttering began as Kinney stepped aside and Wolfe took his place in the doorway. The great man's eyes swept over them, and then he spoke:

"You deserve an explanation, gentlemen, but the police are coming and there's not much time. You have just lost a ball game by knavery. Four of you were drugged, in a drink called Beebright, and could not perform properly. You will learn—"

They drowned him out. It was an explosion of astonished rage.

"Gentlemen!" Wolfe thundered. "Will you listen?" He glowered. "You will learn more of that later, but there is something more urgent. The dead body of one of your colleagues, Mr. Nick Ferrone, has been discovered on these premises. He was murdered. It is supposed, naturally, that the two events, the drugging and the murder, are connected. In any case, if you do not know what a murder investigation means to everyone within reach, innocent or not, you are about to learn. For the moment you will not leave this room. When the police arrive they will tell you—"

Heavy feet were clomping in the hall. The door swung open and a uniformed cop stepped in, followed by three others. The one in front, a sergeant, halted and demanded indignantly:

"What's all this? Where is it?"

The team looked at the cops, and hadn't a word to say. . . .

Inspector Hennessy of Bronx Homicide was tall and straight, silver-haired, with a bony face and quick-moving gray eyes. Two years before he had told Nero Wolfe that if he ever again tried poking into a murder in the Bronx he would be escorted to the Harlem River and dunked. But when, at 9 o'clock that evening, Hennessy breezed through the clubroom, passing in front of the leather couch where Wolfe was seated, with a ham sandwich in one hand and a bottle of beer in the other, he didn't even toss him a glance. He was much too busy.

The Police Commissioner was in Manager Kinney's office with Chisholm and others. The Bronx District Attorney and an assistant were in the locker room, along with an assortment of Homicide men, giving various athletes their third or fourth quiz. There were still a couple of dozen city employees in the clubhouse, though the scientists—the photographers and fingerprint hounds—had all finished and gone.

I had standing as the finder of the corpse, but also I was a part of Wolfe. Technically, Wolfe was not poking into a murder; he had been hired by Chisholm, before the corpse had been found, to find out who had doped the ballplayers. However, in gathering facts for relay to Wolfe I had not discriminated. I saw Nick Ferrone's locker opened and the contents examined, with no startling disclosures.

While I was in Kinney's office watching a basket squad load the corpse and carry it out, I heard a lieutenant on the phone giving instructions for a roundup of gamblers throughout the metropolitan area. A little later I picked up a bunch of signed statements from a table, and sat down and read them through, without anyone noticing. By that time the commissioner and the district attorney had arrived, and they had eight or nine quiz posts going in the various rooms, and Hennessy was doing his best to keep it organized.

I collected all I could for Wolfe. The bat that had been used to crack Ferrone's skull was no stock item, but a valued trophy. With it, years back, there had been belted a grand slam home run that had won a pennant, and it had been displayed on a wall rack in the manager's office. The murderer could have simply grabbed it from the rack. It had no usable fingerprints. Of eight bottles of Beebright left in the cooler, the two in front had been doped and the other six had not. No other drinks had been tampered with. Everyone had known of the liking of those four—Baker, Prentiss, Neill, and Eston—for Beebright, and their habit of drinking a bottle of it before a game. No good prints. No sign anywhere of a container of sodium phenobarbital tablets.

There were a thousand other negatives; for instance, the clubhouse boy, Jimmie Burr. The custom was that when he wasn't around, the players would put chits in a little box for what they took; and he hadn't been around. For that game someone had got him a box seat, and he had beat it to the grandstand while most of the players were in the locker room, changing. A sergeant jumped on it: Who had got him out of the way by providing a ticket for a box seat? But it had been Art Kinney himself.

Around 8 o'clock they turned a big batch loose. Twenty men, including coaches and the bat boy, were allowed to go to the locker room to change, under surveillance, and then let out, with instructions to keep available. They were not in the picture as it then looked.

It was established that Ferrone had arrived at the clubhouse shortly after 1 o'clock and had got into uniform; a dozen of the men had been in the locker room with him. He had been present during a pre-game session with Kinney in the clubroom, and no one remembered seeing him leave afterward. When they trooped out and down the stairs and emerged onto the field, Ferrone's absence was not noticed until they had been in the dugout for some minutes.

As the cops figured it, he couldn't have been slammed with a baseball bat in Kinney's office only a few yards away, while the team was in the clubroom, and therefore all who had unquestionably left for the field with the gang, and had stayed there, were in the clear until further notice. With them went Pierre Mondor, who had wanted to see a ball game and had picked a beaut.

As I said, when Inspector Hennessy breezed through the clubroom at 9 o'clock, coming from the locker room and headed for Kinney's office, he didn't even toss a glance at the leather couch where Wolfe and I were seated. He disappeared. But soon he was back again, speaking from the doorway:

"Come in here, will you, Wolfe?"

"No," Wolfe said. "I'm eating."

"The commissioner wants you."

"Is he eating?" Waiting for no reply, Wolfe turned his head and bellowed, "Mr. Skinner! I'm dining!"

It wasn't very polite, I thought, to be sarcastic about the sandwiches and beer Chisholm had provided. Hennessy started a remark which indicated that he agreed with me, but it was interrupted by the appearance of Commissioner Skinner at his elbow. Hennessy stepped in and aside, and Skinner approached the couch, followed by Chisholm.

Skinner kept it friendly: "I've just learned that four men who were told they could go are still here: Baker, Prentiss, Neill, and Eston. When Inspector Hennessy asked them why, they told him that Mr. Chisholm had asked them to stay. Mr. Chisholm says that he did so at your suggestion. He understood that you wanted to speak with them after our men have all left. Is that correct?"

Wolfe nodded. "I made it quite plain, I thought."

"M-m." The commissioner regarded him. "You see, I know you fairly well. You wouldn't dream of hanging on here half the night to speak with those men merely as a routine step in an investigation. And, besides, at Mr. Chisholm's request you have already been permitted to speak with them, and with several others. You're cooking something. Those are the four men who were drugged, but they left the clubhouse for the field with the rest of the team, so the way we figure it, none of them killed Ferrone. How do you figure it?"

Wolfe swallowed the last of a well-chewed bite. "I don't."

Hennessy growled and set his jaw.

Skinner said, "I don't believe it," with his tone friendlier than his words. "You're cooking something," he insisted. "What's the play with those four men?"

Wolfe shook his head. "No, sir."

Hennessy took a step forward. "Look," he said; "this is the Bronx. You don't turn *this* murder into a parlor game."

Wolfe raised brows at him. "Murder? I am not concerned with murder. Mr. Chisholm hired me to investigate the drugging of his employees. The two events may, of course, be connected, but the murder is your job. And they were not necessarily connected. I understand that a man named Moyse is in there now with the district attorney"—Wolfe aimed a thumb at the door to the locker room—"because it has been learned that he has twice within a month assaulted Mr. Ferrone physically through resentment at Ferrone's interest in his wife, injudiciously displayed. And that Moyse did not leave the clubhouse with the others, but arrived at the dugout three or four minutes later, just before Ferrone's absence was noticed. For your murder, Mr. Hennessy, that should be a help; but it doesn't get me on with my job—disclosure of the culprit who drugged the drinks. Have you charged Mr. Moyse?"

"No." Hennessy was curt. "So you're not interested in the murder?"

"Not as a job, since it's not mine. But if you want a comment from a specialist, you're closing your lines too soon."

"We haven't closed any lines."

"You let twenty men walk out of here. You are keeping Moyse for the reasons given. You are keeping Dr. Soffer, I suppose, because when Ferrone was missed in the dugout Soffer came here to look for him, and he could have found him here alive and killed him. You are keeping Mr. Durkin, I suppose again, because he, too, could have been here alone with Ferrone. He says he left the clubhouse shortly before the team did and went to his seat in the grandstand, and stayed there. Has he been either contradicted or corroborated?"

"No."

"Then you regard him as vulnerable on opportunity?"

"Yes."

"Are you holding Mr. Chisholm for the same reason?"

Chisholm made a noise. Skinner and Hennessy stared. Skinner said, "We're not holding Mr. Chisholm."

"You should be, for consistency," Wolfe declared. "This afternoon, when I reached my seat in the stands, at twenty minutes past one, the mayor and others were there in a nearby box, but Mr. Chisholm was not. He arrived a few minutes later. He has told me that when he arrived with his party, about 1 o'clock, he had the others escorted to the stands, that he started for the clubhouse for a word with his employees, that he was delayed by the crowd and decided it was too late, and then proceeded to the box. If the others are vulnerable on opportunity, so is he."

They made remarks, all three of them, not appreciative.

Wolfe put the beer bottle to his lips, tilted it, and swallowed. He put the bottle down empty.

"I was merely," he said mildly, "commenting on the murder as a specialist. As for my job, learning who drugged the drinks, I haven't even made a start. How could I in this confounded hubbub? Trampled by an army. I have been permitted to sit here and talk to people, yes, with a succession of your subordinates standing behind me breathing down my neck. Pfui!"

"Very rude, I'm sure," Hennessy said dryly. "The commissioner has asked you, what's the play with those four men?"

Wolfe shook his head. "Not only those four. I included others in my request to Mr. Chisholm: Dr. Soffer, Mr. Kinney, Mr. Durkin, and of course Mr. Chisholm himself. I am not arranging a parlor game. I make a living as a professional detective, and I need their help on this job I've undertaken. I think I know why—engrossed as you are with the most sensational case you've had in years—you're spending all this time chatting with me: You suspect I'm contriving a finesse. Well, I am."

"You are?"

"Yes." Wolfe suddenly was peevish. "Haven't I sat here for five hours submerged in your pandemonium? Haven't you all the facts that I have, and many more besides? Haven't you thousands of men to command—and I but one? One little fact strikes me, as apparently it has not struck you, and in my forlorn desperation I decide to test my interpretation of it. For that test I need help, and I ask Mr. Chisholm to provide it."

"We'll be glad to help," Skinner offered. "Which fact, and how do you interpret it?"

"No, sir." Wolfe was positive. "It is my one slender chance to earn a fee. I intend—"

"But we may not know this fact."

"Certainly you do. I have stated it explicitly during this conversation, but I won't point at it for you. If I did you'd spoil it for me, and, slender as it is, I intend to test it. I am not beset with the urgency of murder, as you are, but I'm in a fix; I don't need a motive strong enough to incite a man to murder, merely one to persuade him to drug some bottled drinks—mildly, far from lethally. A thousand dollars? Twenty thousand? That would be only a fraction of the possible winnings on a World Series game. As for opportunity, anyone at all could have slipped in here late this morning, before others had arrived, with drugged bottles of that drink and put them in the cooler—and earned a fortune. Those twenty men you let go, Mr. Hennessy —how many of them can you say positively did not drug the drinks?"

The inspector was scowling at him. "I can say that I don't think any of them killed Ferrone."

"Ah, but I'm not after the murderer; that's your job." Wolfe upturned a palm. "You see why I am driven to a forlorn finesse?"

We all turned, as a man came in from the locker room. District Attorney Megalech of the Bronx was as masterful as they come and bald as a doorknob. He strode across and told Skinner and Hennessy he wanted to speak with them, took an elbow of each, and steered them through the door to Kinney's office. Chisholm, uninvited, wheeled and followed them.

Wolfe reached for a sandwich and I arose and stood looking down at him. I asked, "How good is this fact you're saving up?"

"Not very." He chewed and swallowed. "Good enough to try if we get nothing better. Evidently they have nothing at all. You heard them."

"Yeah. You told them they have all the facts you have, but they haven't. The one I gave you about Mrs. Moyse? That's not the one you're interpreting privately?"

"No."

"She might still be around, waiting. I might possibly get something better than the one you're saving. Shall I go try?"

He grunted. I took it for a yes, and moved. Outside the hall door stood a cop. I addressed him: "I'm going down to buy Mr. Wolfe a pickle. Do I need to be passed out or in?"

"You?" He used only the right half of his mouth for talking. "Shoot your way through. Huh?"

"Right. Many thanks." I went. . . .

It was dumb to be so surprised, but I was. I might have known that the news that New York had been doped out of the game and the Series, and that Nick Ferrone, the rookie of the year, had been murdered, would draw a record mob. Downstairs inside the entrance there were sentries, and outside a regiment was stretched into a cordon. I was explaining to a sergeant who I was and telling him I would be returning, when three desperate men, one of whom I recognized, came springing at me. All they wanted was the truth, the whole truth, and nothing but the truth. I had to get really rude. I have been clawed at by newspapermen more than once, but I had never seen them quite as hungry as they were that October night. As they wouldn't shake loose, I dived through the cordon and into the mob.

It looked hopeless. The only parked cars in sight on that side of the street were police cars. I pushed through to the fringe of the throng and made my way two blocks south. Having made inquiries of two members of the team hours before, I knew what I was looking for: a light-blue sedan.

I crossed the street and headed for the parking plaza. Two cops in the cordon gave me a look, but it wasn't the plaza they were guarding and I marched on through. In the dim light I could see three cars over at the north end. Closer up, one was a light-blue sedan. I went up to it. Two females on the front seat were gazing at me through the window, and one of them was my glommee. The radio was on. I opened the door and said hello.

"Who are you?" she demanded.

"My name's Archie Goodwin. I'll show credentials if you are Mrs. William Moyse."

"What if I am?"

She was rapidly erasing the pleasant memory I had of her. Not that she had turned homely in a few hours, but her expression was not only unfriendly but sour, and her voice was not agreeable. I got out my wallet and extracted my license card. "If you are who I think you are," I said, "this will identify me."

"Okay, your name's Goodman." She ignored the card. "So what?"

"Not Goodman." I pronounced it for her: "Archie Goodwin. I work for Nero Wolfe, who is up in the clubhouse. I just came from there. Why not turn off the radio?"

"I'd rather turn you off," she said bitterly.

Her companion, the redhead who had been with her in the box, reached for the knob, and the radio died. "Look, Lila," she said earnestly; "you're acting like a sap. Invite him in. He may be human. Maybe Bill sent him."

"What did Walt tell us?" Lila snapped at her. "Nero Wolfe is there working with the cops." She came back at me: "Did my husband send you? Prove it."

I put a foot on the edge of the frame, not aggressively. "That's one reason," I said, "why Mr. Wolfe can't stand women. The way they flop around, intellectually. I didn't say your husband sent me. He didn't. He couldn't even if he wanted to, because for the past hour he has been kept in the locker room conversing with a gathering of homicide hounds, and still is. Mr. Wolfe sent me. But in a way it's a personal problem I've got, and no one but you can help me."

"*You've* got a personal problem! *You* have! Take it away."

"I will if you say so, but wait till I tell you. Up to now they have only one reason for picking on your husband. The players left the clubhouse for the field in a bunch—all but one of them, who left later and got to the dugout a few minutes after the others. It was Bill Moyse. They all agreed on that, and Bill admits it. The cops figure that he had seen or heard something that made him suspect Nick Ferrone of doping the drinks—you know about that? That the Beebright was doped?"

"Yes. Walt Goidell told me." She gestured toward the redhead. "Helen's husband. He's on the team."

"And that he stayed behind with Ferrone to put it to him, and Nick got tough, and he got tougher, with a baseball bat. That's how the cops figure it, and that's why they're after Bill. But I have a private reason, confided only to Nero Wolfe, to think that the cops have got it twisted. Mr. Wolfe is inclined to agree with me, but he hasn't told the cops, because he has been hired by Chisholm and wants to earn a fat fee. My private slant is that if Bill did kill Ferrone—please note the 'if'—it wasn't because he caught Ferrone doping the drinks, but the other way around. Ferrone caught Bill doping the drinks, and was going to spill it, and Bill killed him."

She was goggling at me. "You have the nerve—!"

"Hold it. I'm telling you. This afternoon at the game I was in a box. By the sixth inning I had had plenty of the game and looked around for something to take my mind off it, and I saw an extremely attractive girl. I looked at her some more. I had a feeling that I had seen her before, but couldn't place her. The score was 11 to 1, the home team were flat on their faces, and that lovely specimen was exactly what my eyes needed—except for one flaw. She was having a swell time. Her whole face and manner showed it. She liked what was happening out on the field."

She was trying to say something, but I raised my voice a little: "Wait till I tell you. Later, after the game, in the clubhouse, Bill Moyse said his wife was waiting for him, and someone made a crack about showing me her picture. Then it clicked. I remembered seeing a picture of his bride in the *Gazette,* and it was the girl I had seen in the stands. Then, later, I had a chance to ask some of the players some questions, and I learned that she usually drove to games in Bill's light-blue sedan and waited for him after the game. It puzzled me that it made the wife of a New York player happy to see his team getting walloped in the deciding game of a World Series, and Mr. Wolfe agreed. Why were you tickled stiff to see them losing?"

"I wasn't."

"It's perfectly ridiculous," the redhead snorted.

I shook my head. "That won't do. Mr. Wolfe accepts my judgment on girls, and I have told him you were happy. If I go back and report that you flatly deny it, I don't see how he can do anything but tell the cops, and that will be bad. They'll figure that you wanted New York to lose because you knew Bill did, and why. Then, of course, they'll refigure the murder and get a new answer—that Ferrone found out that Bill had doped the drinks, and Bill killed him. They'll start on Bill all over again and—"

"Stop it!"

"I was only saying, if they—"

The redhead horned in, then. "How dumb can you get?" she demanded. "You say you know girls! Do you know baseball girls? I'm one! I'm Helen Goidell, Walt's wife. I would have liked to slap Lila this afternoon, sitting there gloating, much as I love her. But I'm not a sap like you! She's not married to the team, she's married to Bill! Lew Baker had batted .132 in the first six games of the Series, and he had made four errors and had nine bases stolen on him, and still they wouldn't give Bill a chance. Lila had sat through those six games praying to see Bill walk out—and not once! What did she care about the Series? She wanted to see Bill in it. And look at Baker this afternoon! If he had been doped, all right, but Lila didn't know it then. All she knew was that Bill was probably going to get his chance. What you know about girls, you nitwit!"

She was blazing.

"I'm still willing to learn," I said agreeably. "Is she right, Mrs. Moyse?"

"Yes."

"Then I am, too, on the main point? You were pleased to see New York losing?"

"I said she was right."

"Yeah. Then I've still got a problem. If I accept your version, and report to Wolfe accordingly, he'll accept it, too. Whether you think I know girls or not, he does. So that's some responsibility for me. What if you're a lot smoother and trickier than I think you are? Your husband is suspected of murder, and they're still working on him. What if he's guilty and they manage to squeeze out of you what they need to hook him? How will I look if they do? Any suggestions?"

Lila had none. She sat with her head lowered, silent.

"You sound almost human," Helen Goidell said.

"That's deceptive," I told her. "I turn it on and off. If I thought she had something Mr. Wolfe could use I'd stop at nothing, even hair-pulling. But at the moment I really don't think she has. I think she's pure and innocent and wholesome. Her husband is another matter. For her sake, I hope he wriggles out of it somehow, but I'm not taking any bets. The cops seem to like him, and I know cops as well as I do girls." I removed my foot from the car frame. "So long and so forth." I turned to go.

"Wait a minute." It was Lila.

I turned back. Her head was up.

"Is this straight?" she asked.

"Is what straight"

"You're going to tell Mr. Wolfe you're satisfied about me?"

"Well. Satisfied is quite a word. I'm going to tell him I have bought your explanation of your happiness at the game—or, rather, Mrs. Goidell's."

"You could be a liar."

"Not only could be, I often am, but not at the moment."

She regarded me. "Maybe you can tell me about Bill," she said. "They don't really think he killed Nick Ferrone, do they?"

"They think maybe he did."

"I know he didn't."

"Good for you. But you weren't there, so you don't have a vote."

She nodded. She was being hard and practical. "Are they going to arrest him? Will they really charge him with murder?"

"I can't say. But Bill is the leading candidate."

"Then I've got to do something. I wish I knew what he's telling them. Do you know?"

"Only that he's denying he knows anything about it. He says he left the clubhouse after the others had gone, because he went back to the locker room to change to other shoes."

She shook her head. "I don't mean that. I mean, whether he told them—" She stopped. "No. I know he didn't. He wouldn't. He knows something and I know it, too, about a man trying to fix that game. Only, he wouldn't tell, on account of me. I have to go and see someone downtown. Will you come along?"

"To see who?"

"I'll tell you on the way."

Helen Goidell blurted, "For heaven's sake, Lila, do you know what you're saying?"

If Lila replied I missed it, for I was on my way around the car. It was a little headstrong to dash off with a damsel, leaving Wolfe up there with mass-production sandwiches, warm beer, and his one measly little fact he was saving up, but this might be really hot.

By the time I got around to the other door Helen had it open and was getting out. Her feet on the ground, she turned to speak: "I don't want any part of this, Lila. I do not! I wish I'd gone with Walt instead of staying with you!"

She turned and trotted off, toward the street. I climbed in and pulled the door shut.

"She'll tell Walt," Lila said.

I nodded. "Yeah. But does she know where we're going?"

"No."

"Then let's go."

She started the engine, levered to reverse, and backed the car.

Under ordinary circumstances she was probably a pretty good driver, but that night wasn't ordinary for her. Swinging right, there was a little click on my side as we grazed the fender of a stopped car. Rolling up the grade, we slipped between two taxis, clearing by an inch, and both hackmen yelled at her. Stopping for a light at the crest, she turned her head and spoke:

"It's my Uncle Dan. His name is Gale. He came last night and asked me—"

She fed gas and we shot forward, but a car heading uptown and squeezing the light was suddenly there smack in our path. With a lightning reflex her foot hit the brake, the other car zipped by with at least a foot to spare, she fed gas again, and the sedan jerked forward.

I asked her, "Taking the Highway?"

"Yes, it's quicker."

"It will be if you make it. Just concentrate on that and let the details wait."

She got to the downtown side of the highway without any actual contact with other vehicles, turned into the left lane and stepped on it. The speedometer said 55 when she spoke again.

"If I go ahead and tell you, I can't change my mind. He wanted me to persuade Bill to fix the game. He said he'd give us $10,000. I didn't even want to tell Bill, but he insisted, so I did. I knew what Bill would say—"

She broke off to do some expert weaving, swerving to the middle lane, then a sprint, then swinging back to the left again in front of a couple of cars that had slowed her down to under 50.

"Look," I told her; "you could gain up to two minutes this way with luck, but getting stopped and getting a ticket would take at least ten. You're driving, okay, but don't try to talk, too."

She didn't argue, but she held the pace. I twisted around to keep an eye on the rear through the window, and stayed that way clear to 57th street. We rolled down the ramp and a block south, turned left on 56th Street, had a green light at Eleventh Avenue, and went through. A little short of Tenth Avenue we turned into the curb and stopped. Lila reached for the hand brake and gave it a yank.

"Let's hear it," I said. "Enough to go on. Is Uncle Dan a gambler?"

"No." Her face turned to me. "I'm afraid of him."

"Then what is he?"

"He runs a drugstore. He owns it. That's where we're going to see him. My father and mother died when I was just a kid, and Uncle Dan has been good to me—as good as he could. If it hadn't been for him I'd have been brought up in an orphans' home. Of course, Bill wanted to tell Art Kinney last night, but he didn't on account of me, and that's why he's not telling the cops."

"Maybe he is telling them, or soon will."

She shook her head. "I know Bill. We decided we wouldn't tell, and that settled it. Uncle Dan made me promise we wouldn't tell before he said what he wanted."

I grunted. "Even so, he was crowding his luck, telling you two about the program before signing you up. If he explained the idea of doping the Beebright—"

"But he didn't! He didn't say how it was to be done. He didn't get that far, because Bill said nothing doing, as I knew he would."

I eyed her. "This was last night?"

"Yes."

"What time?"

"Around 8 o'clock. We had dinner early with Helen and Walt Goidell, and when we got home Uncle Dan was there waiting for us."

"Where's home?"

"Our apartment on Seventy-ninth Street. He spoke to me alone first, and then insisted I had to ask Bill."

"And Bill turned him down flat?"

"Of course he did!"

"Bill didn't see him alone later?"

"Of course not!"

"All right, don't bite. I need to know. Now what?"

"We're going to see him. We're going to tell him that we have to tell the cops, and we're going to try to get him to come along. That's why I wanted you with me, because I'm afraid of him—I mean, I'm afraid he'll talk me out of it. But they've got to know that Bill was asked to fix the game and he wouldn't. If it's hard on Uncle Dan that's too bad, but I can't help it. I'm for Bill, all the way."

I was making myself look at her, for discipline. I was having the normal male impulses at the sight and sound of a good-looking girl in trouble, and they were worse than normal because I was partly responsible. I had given her the impression that the cops were about set to take her Bill on the big one, which was an exaggeration. I hadn't mentioned that one reason they were keeping him was his reaction to the interest Nick Ferrone had shown in her, which of course had no bearing on anyone's attempt to fix a ball game. True, she had been in a mess before I had got to her, but I had shoved her in deeper. What she needed now was understanding and sympathy, and I was all she had. Which was I, a man or a detective?

"Okay," I said, "let's go see Uncle Dan."

The engine was running. She released the hand brake, fed gas, and we rolled. Three minutes got us to Eighth Avenue, where we turned downtown. The car slowed and she pulled in at the curb.

"There it is." She pointed. "Gale's Pharmacy."

It was ten paces down. There were lights in the window, but otherwise it looked drab. I got out and held the door, and she joined me on the sidewalk. She put a hand on my arm.

"You're staying right with me," she stated.

"Absolutely," I assured her. "I'm good with uncles."

As we crossed to the entrance and went inside I was feeling not fully dressed. I have a routine habit of wearing a gun when I'm on a case involving people who may go to extremes, but, as I said, I do not go armed to ball games. However, at first sight of Daniel Gale I did not put him in that category. His drugstore was so narrow that a fat man would have had to squeeze between the soda-fountain stools and the central showcase, and that made it look long, but it wasn't. Five or six customers were on the stools, and the soda jerk was busy.

At the cosmetics counter on the left, a woman was being waited on by a little guy with a pale, tight-skinned face, wearing glasses.

"That's him," Lila whispered to me.

We waited near the door. Uncle Dan, concentrating on the customer, hadn't seen us. Finally the customer made her choice and, as he tore off paper to wrap the purchase, his eyes lifted and he saw Lila. Also, he saw me, beside her. He froze. He held it, rigid, for seconds, then came to, went on with the wrapping job, and was handed a bill by the customer. While he was at the cash register Lila and I crossed to the counter. As he handed the woman her change, Lila spoke:

"Uncle Dan, I've got to tell you—"

She stopped because he was gone. Without speaking, he turned and made for the rear, disappeared behind a partition, and a door closed. I didn't like it, but didn't want to start a commotion by hurdling the counter, so I stepped to the end and circled, went to the door that had closed, and turned the knob. It was locked. There I was, out at first, unless I was prepared to smash the door in.

The soda jerk called, "Hey, Mac, come out of that!"

"It's all right," Lila told him. "I'm his niece—Mr. Gale is my Uncle Dan."

"I never saw you before, lady. . . . You, Mac, come out here where you belong! Whose uncle are you?"

A couple of the fountain customers gave him his laugh. Then the door I was standing by popped open and Uncle Dan was there, beside me.

"Henry!" he called.

"Right here!" the soda jerk called back.

"Take over for a while—I'll be busy. Come here, Lila, will you?"

Lila circled the end of the counter and approached us. There wasn't room enough to be gallant and let her pass, so I followed Gale through the door into the back room ahead of her. It was small, and the stacks of shipping cartons and other objects took most of what space there was. The rows of shelves were crammed with packaged merchandise, except those along the right wall, which held labeled bottles. Gale stopped near the door, and Lila and I went on by.

"We don't want to be disturbed," Gale said, and bolted the door.

"Why not?" I inquired.

He faced me, and from a distance of five arms' lengths, with Lila between us, I had my first good view of the eyes behind the specs. They were cold and deadly.

"Because," he was telling me, "this is a private matter. You see, I recognized you, Mr. Goodwin. Your face is not as well known as your employer's, but it has been in the papers on several occasions, and you were in my mind on account of the news. The radio bulletins have included the detail that Nero Wolfe and his assistant were present and engaged by Mr. Chisholm. So when I saw you with my niece I realized we should talk privately. But you're an impulsive young man, and for fear you may not like what I say, I make conditions. I shall stay here near the door. You will move to that packing case back of you and sit on it, with your hands in sight and making no unnecessary movements. My niece will put the chair here in front of me and sit on it, facing you, between you and me. That way I will feel free to talk."

I thought he was batty. As a setup against one of my impulses, including a gun if I had had one, it made no sense at all. I backed up to the packing case and lowered myself, resting my hands on my knees to humor him. When Lila saw me complying she moved the chair, the only one there, as directed, and sat with her back to her uncle. He, himself, went to a narrow counter, picked up a bottle of colorless liquid, removed the glass stopper, held it to his nose, and sniffed.

"I do not have fainting spells," he said apologetically, "but at the moment I am a little unstrung. Seeing my niece here with you was a real shock for me. I came back here to consider what it might mean, but reached no conclusion. Perhaps you'll explain?"

"Your niece will. Tell him, Lila."

She started to twist around in the chair, but he commanded her: "No, my dear, stay as you were. Face Mr. Goodwin." He took another sniff at the bottle.

She obeyed. "It's Bill," she said. "They're going to arrest him for murder, and they mustn't. They won't, if we tell them how you offered to pay him for fixing the game and he wouldn't do it. He won't tell them, on account of me, so we have to. I know I promised you I wouldn't, but now I've got to. You see how it is, Uncle Dan; I've got to."

"You haven't told the police?"

"No. I thought the best way was to come and get you to go with me. I was afraid to come alone, because I know how bad it will be for you, but it will be worse for Bill if we don't. Don't you see, Uncle—?"

"Keep your back turned, Lila. I insist on it. That's right; stay that way." He had been talking in an even low tone, but now his voice became thin and strained: "I'll tell you why I want your back to me—so I can't see your face.... Remember, Goodwin, don't move! ... This is a bottle of pure sulphuric acid. I was smelling it just to explain why I had it; of course, it has no smell. I suppose you know what it will do. This bottle is nearly full, and I'm holding it carefully, because one drop on your skin will scar you for life. That's why I want your back to me, Lila. I'm very fond of you, and I don't want to see your face if I have to use this acid. If you move, Lila dear, I'll use it. Or you, Goodwin; especially you. I hope you both understand?"

His hand holding the bottle hovered inches above her head. She looked as if she might keel over, and I urged her, "Sit tight, Lila, and don't scream."

"Yes," Uncle Dan said approvingly. "I should have mentioned that. Screaming would be as bad as moving. I had to tell you about the acid before I discussed matters. I'm not surprised at your fantastic suggestion, Lila, because I know how foolish you can be, but I'm surprised at you, Goodwin. How could you expect me to consent to my complete ruin? Did Lila persuade you that I am an utter fool?"

"I guess she must have," I admitted. "What kind of man are you?"

He proceeded to tell me, and I pretended to listen. I also tried to keep my eyes on his pale, tight-skinned face, but that wasn't easy, because they were fascinated by the bottle he was holding. Meanwhile, my brain was buzzing. Unless he was plain loony the only practical purpose of the bottle must be to gain time—and for what?

". . . and I will," he was saying. "This won't kill you, Lila dear, but it will be horrible, and I don't want to do it unless I have to. Only, you mustn't think I won't. You don't really know me very well, because to you I'm just Uncle Dan. You didn't know that I once had a million dollars and I was an important and dangerous man. There were people who knew me and feared me, but I was unlucky. I have gambled and made fortunes, and lost them. That affects a man's nerves. It changes a man's outlook on life. I borrowed enough money to buy this place, and for years I worked hard and did well—well enough to pay it all back. But that was my ruin. I owed nothing and had a little cash and decided to celebrate by losing $100 to some old friends—just $100, but I didn't lose. I won several thousand. After that I went on, and lost what I had won, and I lost this place.

"So I don't own this place; my friends do. They are very old friends, and they gave me a chance to get this place back. I'm telling you about this, Lila dear, because I want you to understand. I came to you and Bill with that offer because I had to, and you promised me, you swore you would tell no one. I have been an unlucky man, and sometimes a weak one, but I am never going to be weak again—Don't move!"

Lila, who had lifted her head a little, stiffened. I sat gazing at Gale. Obviously, he was stalling for time, but what could he expect to happen? It could be only one thing: he expected somebody to come. He expected help.

As soon as he had seen us he had scooted back here to phone somebody. Help was on the way, the kind of help that would deal with Lila and me efficiently and finally; and big-time gamblers who could provide ten grand to fix a game are just the babies to be ready with that kind of help.

Either he was loony or that was it. But then what? They might come any second; they might be entering the drugstore right now. Any second a knock on the door might come . . .

Gale was talking: "I didn't think you'd tell, Lila, after all I've done for you. You promised me you wouldn't. Now, of course, you've told Goodwin and it can't be helped. If I just tip this bottle—"

"Nuts," I said emphatically, but not raising my voice. "You haven't got it staged right." I had my eyes straight on his specs. "Maybe you don't want to see her face, but the way you've got her, with her back to you, it's no good. What if she suddenly ducked, and dived forward? You might get some on her clothes or her feet, but the chair would be in your way. Have you considered that? . . . Better still, what if she suddenly darted sideways in between those cartons? The instant she moved I'd be moving, too, and that would take her out of my path. She'd be taking a chance, but that would be better than sitting there waiting for the next act. Unquestionably, it would be better for her to go sideways—with her head down and her arms out. You see how bum your arrangement is? But if you make her turn and face you—"

She moved. She went sideways, to her left, her head down and her arms out, diving for the cartons.

I lost a tenth of a second because I hadn't dared to pull my feet back ready for the spring, but that was all I lost. I didn't leap, I just went, with all the force my leg muscles could give it. My target was the bottom of the left front leg of the chair, and I went in flat, face down, and had the leg before he could get under way. The impact of the chair knocked him back against the door, and I kept going and grabbed his ankle and jerked.

Of course, the bottle could have landed right on me, but I had to get him off his feet. As I yanked his ankle I kept my face down, and he tumbled. The next thing I knew I was on top of him, pinning him, with a grip on his throat, looking around for the bottle. It had never reached the floor. It had landed on a carton six feet to my right and lay there on its side, the stuff gurgling out. The floor slanted toward the wall, so no flood threatened me.

"Okay, Lila," I said. "I need help."

She was scrambling to her feet. "Did he—did it—?" She giggled.

"No. If you have hysterics I'll tell Bill. Slap yourself; I can't."

"But he—"

"Shut up. Company's coming and we've got to get out of here. I want some adhesive tape quick." She started looking on shelves and in drawers. "Watch your step," I told her. "That stuff's spreading to the floor. . . . When

I said I was good with uncles I didn't mean uncles like him. He's a lulu. He—"

"Here it is."

"Good girl. Tear off a piece six inches long ... that's it. Now across his mouth good and tight, diagonally. Now one the other way.... That ought to do it, thank you, nurse. Now find some nice sterile bandage."

She found that, too, and held his arms while I sat on his knees and tied his ankles. Then I fastened his wrists behind him and anchored the strip of bandage to the handle of a locked drawer. I squatted for a look at the tape on his mouth, gave it a rub, stood up, went to the door, and pushed the bolt.

"Come on," I told her.

I opened the door and she passed through. I followed and pulled the door to. There were customers on the fountain stools, and Henry was selling a man a pack of cigarettes. I paused on my way to the street door to tell him that Mr. Gale would be out soon, then opened the door to Lila. On the sidewalk I told her to wait in the car while I made a phone call.

Up twenty paces was a bar and grill. I went in, found a phone booth, dialed Manhattan Homicide, asked for Sergeant Purley Stebbins, and got him. He wanted to know if I was still up at the ball park.

I told him no. "Where I am," I said, "is top secret. I'm giving you a hot one." I gave him the address of Gale's Pharmacy. "Get a prowl car there fast, and plenty of reinforcements. Gale, the owner, on information received, was the go-between for the gamblers who fixed the ball game. He's in the back room of his store, gagged and tied."

"Is *this* a gag?"

"No. The reason for the hurry is that I think Gale sent for a rescue squad to deal with certain parties who are no longer there, and it would be nice to get there in time to welcome them. So PD cars should not park in front. Be sure to tell them not to step in the stuff on the floor that looks like water, because it's sulphuric acid. That's all. Got the address?"

"Yes. Where are you? And—"

"Sorry, I've got a date. This could make you a lieutenant. Step on it."

I went out and back to the car. Lila was on the driver's side, gripping the steering wheel with both hands.

"Move over," I said. "I'll do the driving this time."

She slid across, and I got in and pulled the door to. I sat. Half a minute went by.

"Where are we going?" she asked. Her voice was so weak I barely got it.

"Uptown. Where Bill is." Maybe he was.

"Why don't we start?"

"I phoned for cops. If others come before the cops do I want to get a look at them. In case I forget it later, I want to mention that that was a beautiful dive you made, and the timing couldn't have been better. I'm for you, only spiritually of course, since you're happily married."

"I want to get away from here. I want to see Bill."

"You will. Relax."

We sat, but not for long. It couldn't have been more than four minutes before a pair of cops swung around the corner, headed for the entrance to Gale's Pharmacy, and entered. I pushed the starter button. . . .

It was only half an hour short of midnight when I stopped the car at the curb across the street from the main entrance to the ball park. The mob had dwindled to a few small knots, and of the long line of police cars only three were left. Two cops were having a tête-à-tête in front of the entrance.

Lila was a quick mover. She had got out and circled the car to my side by the time I hit the pavement. I gave her the ignition key and we were crossing the street when suddenly she let out a squawk and started to run. I took another step, and stopped. Bill Moyse was there, emerging from the entrance, with a dick on either side of him and one behind. Lila ended her run in a flying leap and was on him. The startled dicks grabbed for her, and the two uniformed cops started toward them.

I would have liked to deliver Lila to Wolfe, or at least to Hennessy, but there was a fat chance of tearing her loose from her second-string catcher. Also, I did not care to get hung up explaining to a bunch of underlings how I happened to be chauffering for Mrs. Moyse, so I detoured around the cluster, made it inside the entrance, and headed for the clubhouse stairs. Hearing heavy footsteps above, starting down, and voices, one of them Hennessy's, I slipped quietly behind a pillar.

Surely Stebbins had informed the Bronx of my phone call about the situation at Gale's Pharmacy, and so surely Hennessy would be inquisitive enough to want to take me along wherever he was going. I didn't risk peeking around the pillar, but, judging from the footsteps, there were four or five men. As soon as they had faded out I went on up the stairs. I was not chipper. I did not have Lila. I had been gone more than two hours. Wolfe might have gone home. They might all be gone.

But they weren't. Wolfe was in the clubroom, on the leather couch, and Chisholm was standing. As I entered, their heads turned to me.

"The police are looking for you," Wolfe said coldly.

"Uh-huh." I played it indifferent. "I just dodged a squad."

"Why did you go to that drugstore?"

I raised the brows. "Oh, you've heard about it?"

"Yes. Mr. Hennessy did, and he was kind enough to tell me." He was dripping sarcasm. "It is a novel experience, learning of your movements through the courtesy of a policeman."

"I was too busy to phone." I glanced at Chisholm. "Maybe I should report privately."

"This is getting to be a farce," Chisholm growled. His tie was crooked, his eyes were bloodshot, and he had a smear of mustard at the side of his mouth.

"No," Wolfe said, to me, not to Chisholm. "Go ahead. But be brief."

I obeyed. With the training and experience I have had I can report a day of dialogue practically verbatim, but he had said to be brief, so I condensed it, including all essentials.

"Then you don't know whether Gale was actually involved or not. When he failed with Mr. and Mrs. Moyse he may have quit trying."

"I doubt it."

"You could have resolved the doubt. You were sitting on him. Or you could have brought him here."

I might have made three or four cutting remarks if an outsider hadn't been present. I stayed calm. "Maybe I didn't make it clear," I conceded generously. "It was ten to one he had phoned for help, the kind of help that would leave no doubts to resolve, and it might have come any second. Not that I was scared—I was too busy—but I wanted to see you once more so I could resign. I resign."

"Bosh." Wolfe put his hands on the leather seat for leverage and raised himself to his feet. "Very well. I'll have to try it."

Chisholm put in, "Inspector Hennessy said to notify him immediately if Goodwin showed up."

Wolfe wheeled on him, snarling. "Am I working for you? Yes! Notify Mr. Hennessy? Bah!" He turned and strode through the door that led to Art Kinney's office.

Chisholm and I fell in behind.

They were all in there. The four who were famous athletes didn't look very athletic just at present. Their sap had started draining with the first inning of that awful ball game, and it hadn't stopped for more than ten hours. Lew Baker, catcher, and Con Prentiss, shortstop, were perched on a desk. Joe Eston, third baseman, and Nat Neill, center-fielder, were on chairs.

Art Kinney, the manager, was standing over by a window. Doc Soffer was seated at Kinney's desk, bent over, with his elbows on his knees and his face covered by his hands. Beaky Durkin was propped against a table, saggy and bleary-eyed.

"It had better be good," someone said. I didn't know who, because I was placing a chair for Wolfe where he could see them all without straining his neck. When he was in it, with nothing to spare between the arms, I crossed to a vacant seat over by the radio. Chisholm was there, at my right.

Wolfe's head moved from side to side and back again. "I hope," he said grumpily, "you're not expecting too much."

"I'm through expecting," Kinney muttered.

Wolfe nodded. "I know how you feel, Mr. Kinney. All of you. You are weary and low in spirit. You have been personally and professionally humiliated. You have all been talked at too much. I'm sorry I have to prolong it, but I had to wait until the police were gone. Also, since I have no evidence, I had to let them complete their elaborate and skilled routine in search of some. They got none. Actually, they have nothing but a druggist that Mr. Goodwin got for them."

"They've got Bill Moyse," Con Prentiss rumbled.

"Yes, but on suspicion, not on evidence. Of course I admit, because I must, that I am in the same fix. I, too, have a suspicion but no evidence, only mine is better-grounded. I suspect one of you eight men of drugging the drinks and killing Ferrone. What I—"

They made enough noise to stop him. He held up a palm.

"If you please, gentlemen. I have a question to put. I suspect one of you, but I have no evidence and no way of getting any speedily. That is why I asked Mr. Chisholm to keep you here for consultation with me after the departure of the police. I wanted to ask you: Do you want to help? I would like to tell you the reason for my suspicion and ask you to help me get evidence to support it. I think you can if you will. Well?"

"One of *us?* " Joe Eston demanded.

It was interesting to see them. Naturally, they all had an impulse, all but one, anyway, to look around at faces, but no two of them handled it exactly alike. Chisholm looked straight and full at each in turn. Beaky Durkin sent quick little glances here and there. Doc Soffer, frowning and pursing his lips, turned his head slowly left to right.

"Go ahead!" Kinney blurted. "Have you got something or not?"

"Yes, I have something," Wolfe assured him, "But I don't know how good it is. Without your help it is no good at all."

"We'll help if we can. Let's hear it."

"Well. First the background. Were the two events—the drugging of the drinks and the murder—connected? The reasonable supposition is yes, until and unless it is contradicted. If they were connected, how? Did Ferrone drug the drinks, and did one of his teammates discover it and, enraged, go for him with the bat? It seems unlikely."

Wolfe focused on Beaky Durkin: "Mr. Durkin, you knew Ferrone better than anyone else. You discovered him and got him here. You were his roommate and counselor. You told me that because of his brilliant performance this season his salary for next year would be doubled; that his heart was set on winning today's game and the Series; that winning or losing meant a difference of some two thousand dollars to him personally; that his Series money would pay his debts, with some to spare; and that, knowing him intimately, you are positive that he could not have been bribed to drug the drinks. Is that correct?"

"It sure is." Durkin was hoarse and cleared his throat. "Nick was a swell kid." He looked around as if ready for an argument, but nobody started one.

"Do any of you dispute it?" Wolfe asked.

They didn't.

"Then without evidence it is idiotic to assume that he drugged the drinks. The alternative, suppose that the two events were connected, is the reverse: that someone drugged the drinks and Ferrone knew or suspected it and was going to expose him, and was killed. That is how I see it. Call him X. X could have—"

"Don't beat around the bush," Kinney blurted. "Name him!"

"Presently. X could have put the drugged drinks in the cooler any time during the late morning, as opportunity offered. What led Ferrone to suspect him of skulduggery may not be known, but conjecture offers a wide choice. Ferrone's suspicion may have been only superficial, but to X any suspicion whatever was a mortal menace, knowing, as he did, what was going to happen on the ball field. When Ferrone questioned him he had to act. The two were, of course, in this room together, at the time the rest of you were leaving the clubroom for the field or shortly after. X was, as so many have been, the victim of progressive emergency. At first he needed only money, and to get it he stooped to scoundrelism; but it betrayed him into needing the life of a fellow man."

"Cut the rhetoric," Chisholm snapped. "Name him."

Wolfe nodded. "Naming him is easy. But it is pointless to name him, and expose myself to an action for slander, unless I can enlist your help. As I said, I have no evidence. All I have is a fact about one of you, a fact known to all of you and to the police, which seems to me to point to guilt. But I admit that other interpretations are conceivable. You are better judges of that than I am, and I'm going to present it for your consideration."

He aimed his gaze at Baker and Prentiss, perched on a desk, raised a hand, slowly, and scratched the tip of his nose. His eyes moved to pin Doc Soffer. His head jerked to the left, to focus on Chisholm, and the right, to Beaky Durkin. He spoke:

"I'll illustrate my meaning. Take you, Mr. Durkin. You have accounted for yourself, but you have been neither contradicted nor corroborated. You say you left the clubhouse shortly before the team did and went to your seat in the grandstand."

"That's right." Durkin was still hoarse. "And I didn't kill Nick."

"I didn't say you did. I am merely expounding. You say you remained in your seat, watching the game, until the third inning, when you were sent for by Mr. Chisholm to come to the clubhouse. That, too, is neither contradicted nor corroborated. Certainly you were there when you were sent for, but there is no proof that you had been there continuously since the game started and even before."

"I don't know about proof, but I was. I can probably find the guy that was sitting next to me."

"You didn't leave your seat once during that time?"

"I did not."

Wolfe looked around. "Well, gentlemen. That's the fact I can't explain. Can you?"

They were gawking at him. "Do we have to?" Baker demanded.

"Someone does." Wolfe's voice sharpened: "Consider the situation. Consider the relationship of those two men. The discovery of Ferrone is Durkin's proudest achievement as a baseball scout. He fosters him and treasures him. Today, now yesterday, at the game that was to be the climax of Ferrone's triumphant season, Durkin is in the clubroom and sees Ferrone there in uniform, with the others, young, sound, mighty, valiant. He leaves the clubhouse and goes to a seat in the grandstand. Before long the loudspeaker announces that Garth, not Ferrone, will play second base. Durkin keeps his seat. The players take the field, and the game starts, with no Ferrone. Durkin keeps his seat. They play the first inning badly. Durkin keeps his seat. They play the second inning badly. Durkin keeps—"

"Good lord!" Art Kinney yelled.

"Exactly." Wolfe lifted a hand. "Please, gentlemen, keep your seats. It is clearly fantastic. The announcement that Garth would play second base could have been taken by Durkin merely as a blunder, but when they took the field without Ferrone his consternation would have been insupportable. The one thing he couldn't possibly have done was to stay in his seat. Why did you, Mr. Durkin?"

"I couldn't think—" He tried to clear his throat and almost choked. "What could I do?"

"I don't know. I said I can't explain what you did do, but I can try. Suppose the nonappearance of Ferrone was no surprise to you, because you knew where he was and what had happened to him. Suppose, further, you were in a state of severe systemic shock because you had murdered him. I submit that explanation of your keeping your seat is plausible. Can you offer any other?"

Durkin took two steps. "Look here," he said; "you can't sit there and accuse me of a thing like that. I don't have to stay and take it, and I'm not going to."

He started for the door, but Lew Baker was suddenly there in his path. "Back up, Beaky. I said back up!"

Beaky did so, literally. He backed until his rump hit the edge of the table. He groped for support and braced himself.

Wolfe was grim. "I was supposing, Mr. Durkin, not accusing. But I am now ready to accuse, and I do. I explained, when I was calling you X, how and why you acted." His eyes moved. "Gentlemen, I ask you to look at him. Look at his face, his eyes. Look at his hands, clutching the table in dismay and despair. Yes, I accuse him. I say that that man drugged your drinks, caused you to lose your game, and, threatened with exposure, murdered your teammate."

They were all on their feet, including Art Kinney. They were making threatening sounds.

"Wait!" Wolfe said sharply, and they turned to him. "I must warn you, you approach him at your peril, for I have no proof. It will be gratifying to press a confession out of him, but a confession is not evidence, and we need some. I suggest that you try for it. He did it for money, and surely he was paid something in advance, unless he is a fool. Where is it? Certainly not on his person, since you have all been searched, but it is somewhere, and it would do admirably. Where is it?"

Lew Baker got to Durkin ahead of the others. He told him in a thin, tight voice, so tight it twanged, "I wouldn't want to touch you, Beaky, you dirty rat. Where is it? Where's the jack?"

"Lew, I swear to—"

"Skip it! You fixed us, did you? And Nick—you fixed him. I'd hate to touch you, but if I do—"

The others were there, Kinney and Doc Soffer with them, crowding in on Durkin, who had pulled back onto the table, still gripping the edge. I went to the end of the table and stood. They were all strong and hard, and their nervous systems had had a tough day. Aside from the killing of Nick Ferrone, this was the bird who had made them play ball like half-witted apes in the most important game of their lives, to an audience of fifty million.

"Give me room, fellows," Nat Neill said. "I'm going to plug him."

Durkin didn't flinch. His jaw was quivering and his eyes looked sick, but he didn't flinch.

"This is wrong," Con Prentiss said. "He wants us to hurt him. He'd like to be knocked cold. He's not a coward; he's just a snake."

"It's a moral question," Joe Eston said. "That's the way to handle it."

Art Kinney shouldered between two of them to get his face within ten inches of Durkin's. "Look, Beaky. You've been in baseball 30 years. You know everybody in the majors and we know you. What do you think's going to happen? Where could you light? We've got you here now and we're going to keep you. I'll send for the whole team. How will you like that?"

"I want a lawyer," Durkin said.

Neill roared. "He wants a lawyer! I'm going to clip him!"

"No, Beaky, no lawyers," Kinney said. "I'll send for the boys and we'll lock the doors. Where's the money? Where is it?"

Durkin's head went forward, down. Kinney put a fist under his chin and yanked it up and held it. "No, you don't. Look at me. We've got you, but even if we didn't where could you go? Where are you going to sleep and eat?"

"Let me hold his chin," Neill requested. "I'll fix it for him."

"Shut up," Eston told him. "It's a moral question."

Kinney's fist was still propping Durkin's chin. "I think," he said, "the boys ought to have a look at you. They won't be sleeping anyhow, not tonight. Con, get on the phone and find them. You, too, Lew, the one in the clubroom. Get 'em here—get all of 'em you can. And tell them not to spill it. We don't want any cops yet."

"No!" Durkin squawked.

"No what, Beaky?" Kinney removed his fist.

"I didn't mean to kill Nick." He was slobbering. "I swear I didn't, Art. He suspected. He found out I bet a grand against us and he threw it at me. I brought him here to explain. But he wouldn't believe me and was going to tell you, and he got sore and came at me, and I grabbed the bat just to stop him, and when I saw he was dead—You've got to believe me, Art. I didn't want to kill Nick!"

"You got more than a grand for doping the drinks."

"I'm coming clean, Art. You can check me and I'm coming clean. I got five grand and I've got five more coming. I had to have it, Art, because the bookies had me down and I was sunk. I was listed good if I didn't come through. I had it on me, but with the cops coming I knew we'd be frisked, so I ditched it. You see I'm coming clean, Art. I ditched it there in the radio. I stuffed it in through a slot."

There was a scramble and a race. Prentiss tangled with a chair and went down with it, sprawling. Nat Neill won. He jerked the radio around and started clawing at the back, but the panel was screwed on.

"Here," I said, "I've got a—"

He hauled off and swung with his bare fist; he yanked, and half the panel came off. He looked inside and started to stick his hand in, but I shouldered him, good and hard, and sent him sideways. The others were there, three of them, surrounding me.

"Well?" Wolfe called.

"A good, fat roll," I told him and the world. "The one on the outside is a C."

Beaky Durkin, left to himself on the table, suddenly moved fast. He was on his feet and streaking for the door. Joe Eston, who had claimed it was a moral issue, leaped for him as if he had been a blazing line drive trying to get by, got to him, and landed with his right.

"That will do," Wolfe said, as one who had earned the right to command. "Thank you, gentlemen. Archie, get Mr. Hennessy."

I went to Kinney's desk and reached for the phone. At the instant my fingers touched it, it rang. So instead of dialing I lifted it and, feeling cocky, told it, "Nero Wolfe's Bronx office, Goodwin speaking."

"This is Inspector Hennessy. Is Durkin there?"

I said yes.

"Fine. Hold him, and hold him good. We cracked Gale and he spilled everything. Durkin is it. Gale got to him and bought him. You'll get credit for getting Gale—that'll be all right—but I'll appreciate it if you'll hold off and let it be announced officially. We'll be there for Durkin in five minutes."

"He's stretched out here on the floor. Mr. Wolfe hung it on him. Also, we have found a roll of lettuce he cached in the radio."

I hung up and turned to Wolfe: "That was Hennessy. They broke Gale and he unloaded. He gave them Durkin and they're coming for him.

"The trouble is this: Which of us crossed the plate first, you with your one little fact, or me with my druggist? You can't deny that Hennessy's call came before I started to dial him. How can we settle it?"

We can't. That was months ago, and it's not settled yet.

ACTIVITIES

1) A factor that makes Archie Goodwin such a delightful Watson is his refusal to allow Nero Wolfe's personality to dominate his own. Can you recall some of the scenes that demonstrate this? Do you think Archie could have worked for Sherlock Holmes?

2) Rex Stout always sprinkles his exciting Nero Wolfe tales with dashes of humor, some of it "situational," some of it "gag." Skim the story once more and see if you can find examples of both.

3) The term *jargon* is sometimes used to refer to the language of a special group, profession, or class. You have probably noticed that Mr. Stout seems very familiar with baseball jargon. For those in your class who may not be baseball fans, list some of the specialized words or expressions used in this story and then explain what each means.

4) Think back to the five plot ingredients introduced by Edgar Allan Poe in his "Murders in the Rue Morgue."

In his own inimitable fashion, Rex Stout treats these ingredients very irreverently. Review these ingredients and then demonstrate how Stout subtly changes some of them.

Detectives with Only One Life

A cat has nine lives, a series-detective many more depending, of course, upon the number of stories in which he or she appears.

However, many detective tales have been published in which the hero-sleuth's career spans the fictional period of the one story. He never appears in another.

Why?

Many reasons.

Perhaps he or she lacks charisma and the public does not demand a return appearance. Or maybe the writer does not want to limit his energies to one "star," preferring instead to work with a host of varied protagonists. Writing mysteries is more difficult that way—but also more challenging.

Late in his career, Ellery Queen accepted this challenge; he began to write novels in which he and the fictional Ellery parted company to be replaced by a non-series hero. Thus, Queen showed that he could create appealing temporary protagonists, too.

Other prominent detective story practitioners who "took vacations" from their heroes were Rex Stout, Edgar Allan Poe (remember "The Gold Bug"), Agatha Christie, G. K. Chesterton, Dorothy L. Sayers, and John D. Mac-Donald. Of course, Mary Roberts Rinehart, except for her "repeat" of Miss Pinkerton, never re-used her other detective characterizations.

A story without a series sleuth has to be darn good to keep the reader's interest. Let's focus in on one of these yarns ...

Hugh Pentecost—and an "Unknown"

Hugh Pentecost has probably created more series-sleuths than any detective story author of the modern era. And yet, one of his most memorable tales contained no prominent name or domineering personality. *In fact, it is doubtful if one can even call its sleuth a protagonist.*

Mr. Pentecost was born Judson Pentecost Philips in 1903. In 1939, he won the Dodd, Mead Mystery Competition for his first novel, *A Woman in Red*. Three decades later, 1973 to be exact, he received the Mystery Writers of America Grand Master Award for distinction in the novel and short story. In between those years, he created a myriad of well-known detective personalities such as Lieutenant Pascal, a policeman; Julian Quist, a public relations man; John Jericho, an artist-detective; and Pierre Chambrin, a hotel manager. Also in between, he worked in radio, television, and motion pictures and was associated with the Sharon Playhouse, one of the East's prominent summer theaters.

Mr. Pentecost's Pascal, Quist, Jericho, and Chambrin are all fascinating people, of the caliber of any presented herein. But the "star" of the following story may very well be the story itself. Incidently, among the several mysteries with which you will be grappling is: Who is going to solve the thing anyway?

The Day the Children Vanished

On a bright, clear winter's afternoon the nine children in the town of Clayton who traveled each day to the Regional School in Lakeview disappeared from the face of the earth, along with the bus in which they traveled and its driver, as completely as if they had been sucked up into outer space by some monstrous interplanetary vacuum cleaner.

Actually, in the time of hysteria which followed the disappearance, this theory was put forward by some distraught citizen of Clayton, and not a few people, completely stumped for an explanation, gave consideration to it.

There was, of course, nothing interplanetary or supernatural about the disappearance of nine children, one adult, and a specialbodied station wagon which was used as a school bus. It was the result of callous human villainy. But, because there was no possible explanation for it, it assumed all the aspects of black magic in the minds of tortured parents and a bewildered citizenry.

Clayton is seven miles from Lakeview. Clayton is a rapidly growing quarry town. Lakeview, considerably larger and with a long history of planning for growth, recently built a new school. It was agreed between the boards of education of the two towns that nine children living at the east end of Clayton should be sent to the Lakeview School where there was adequate space and teaching staff. It was to be just a temporary expedient.

Since there were only nine children, they did not send one of the big, forty-eight-passenger school buses to get them. A nine-passenger station wagon was acquired, properly painted and marked as a school bus, and Jerry Mahoney, a mechanic in the East Clayton Garage, was hired to make the two trips each day with the children.

Jerry Mahoney was well liked and respected. He had been a mechanic in the Air Force during his tour of duty in the armed services. He was a wizard with engines. He was engaged to be married to Elizabeth Deering, who worked in the Clayton Bank and was one of Clayton's choice picks. They were both nice people, responsible people.

The disappearance of the station wagon, the nine children and Jerry Mahoney took place on a two-mile stretch of road where disappearance was impossible. It was called the "dugway," and it wound along the side of the lake. Heavy wire guard rails protected the road from the lake for the full two miles. There was not a gap in it anywhere.

The ground on the other side of the road rose abruptly upward into thousands of acres of mountain woodlands, so thickly grown that not even a tractor could have made its way up any part of it except for a few yards of deserted road that led to an abandoned quarry. Even over this old road nothing could have passed without leaving a trail of torn brush and broken saplings.

At the Lakeview end of the dugway was a filling station owned by old Jake Nugent. On the afternoon of the disappearance the bus, with Jerry Mahoney at the wheel and his carload of kids laughing and shouting at each other, stopped at old man Nugent's. Jerry Mahoney had brought the old man a special delivery letter from the post office, thus saving the RFD driver from making a special trip. Jerry and old Jake exchanged greetings, the old man signed the receipt for his letter—which was from his son in Chicago asking for a loan of fifty dollars—and Jerry drove off into the dugway with his cargo of kids.

At the Clayton end of the dugway was Joe Gorman's Diner, and one of the children in Jerry's bus was Peter Gorman, Joe's son. The Diner was Jerry's first stop coming out of the dugway with his cargo of kids.

It was four-thirty in the afternoon when Joe Gorman realized that the bus was nearly three-quarters of an hour late. Worried, he called the school in Lakeview and was told by Miss Bromfield, the principal, that the bus had left on schedule.

"He may have had a flat, or something," Miss Bromfield suggested.

This was one of seven calls Miss Bromfield was to get in the next half hour, all inquiring about the bus. Nine children; seven families.

Joe Gorman was the first to do anything about it seriously. He called Jake Nugent's filling station to ask about the bus, and old Jake told him it had gone through from his place on schedule. So something had happened to Jerry and his busload of kids in the dugway. Joe got out his jeep and headed through the dugway toward Lakeview. He got all the way to Jake Nugent's without seeing the bus or passing anyone coming the other way.

Jake Nugent was a shrewd old gent, in complete possession of all his faculties. He didn't drink. When he said he had seen the bus—that it had stopped to deliver him his letter—and that he had watched it drive off into the dugway, you had to believe it. Cold sweat broke out on Joe Gorman's face as he listened. The dugway had a tendency to be icy. He had noticed coming over that it hadn't been sanded. Joe hadn't been looking for a major tragedy. But if the bus had skidded, gone through the guard rail . . .

He used Jake's phone to call the Dicklers in Clayton. The Dicklers' two children, Dorothy and Donald, were part of Jerry's load and they were the next stop after Joe's Diner. The Dicklers were already alarmed because their children hadn't appeared.

Joe didn't offer any theories. He was scared, though. He called the trooper barracks in Lakeview and told them about the missing bus. They didn't take it too seriously, but said they'd send a man out.

Joe headed back for Clayton. This time his heart was a lump in his throat. He drove slowly, staring at every inch of the wire guard rails. There was not a break anywhere, not a broken or bent post. The bus simply couldn't have skidded over the embankment into the lake without smashing through the wire guard rail.

Joe Gorman felt better when he came out at his diner at the Clayton end. He felt better, but he felt dizzy. Five minutes later Trooper Teliski came whizzing through from Lakeview and stopped his car.

"What's the gag?" he asked Joe.

Joe tried to light a cigarette and his hands were shaking so badly he couldn't make it. Teliski snapped on his lighter and held it out. Joe dragged smoke deep into his lungs.

"Look," he said, "The bus started through the dugway at the regular time." He told about Jerry's stop at Nugent's. "It never came out this end."

A nerve twitched in Teliski's cheek. "The lake," he said.

Joe shook his head. "I—I thought of that, right off. I just came through ahead of you—looking. Not a break in the guard rail anywhere. Not a scratch. Not a bent post. The bus didn't go into the lake. I'll stake my life on that."

"Then what else?" Teliski asked. "It couldn't go up the mountain."

"I know," Joe said, and the two men stared at each other.

"It's some kind of a joke," Teliski said.

"What kind of a joke? It's no joke to me—or the Dicklers. I talked to them."

"Maybe they had permission to go to a special movie or something," Teliski said.

"Without notifying the parents? Miss Bromfield would have told me, anyway. I talked to her. Listen, Teliski. The bus went into the dugway and it didn't come out. It's not in the dugway now, and it didn't go into the lake."

Teliski was silent for a moment, and then he spoke with a solid attempt at common sense. "It didn't come out this end," he said. "We'll check back on that guard rail, but let's say you're right. It didn't skid into the lake. It couldn't go up the mountain. So where does that leave us?"

"Going nuts!" Joe said.

"It leaves us with only one answer. The station wagon never went into the dugway."

Joe Gorman nodded. "That's logic." he said. "But why would Jake Nugent lie? Jerry's an hour and three-quarters late now. If he didn't go in the dugway, where is he? Where *could* he go? Why hasn't he telephoned if everything is okay?"

A car drove up and stopped. A man got out and came running toward them. It was Karl Dickler, father of two of the missing children. "Thank God you're here, Teliski. What's happened?"

"Some kind of a gag," Teliski said. "We can't figure it out. The bus never came through the dugway."

"But it did!" Karl Dickler said.

"It never came out this end," Joe Gorman said. "I was watching for Pete, naturally."

"But it did come through!" Dickler said. "I passed them myself on the way to Lakeview. They were about half a mile this way from Jake Nugent's. I saw them! I waved at my own kids!"

The three men stared at each other.

"It never came out this end." Joe Gorman said, in a choked voice.

Dickler swayed and reached out to the trooper to steady himself. "The lake!" he whispered.

But they were not in the lake. Joe Gorman's survey proved accurate; no broken wire, no bent post, not even a scratch . . .

It was nearly dark when the real search began. Troopers, the families of the children, the selectmen, the sheriff and twenty-five or thirty volunteer deputies, a hundred or more school friends of the missing children.

The lake was definitely out. Not only was the guard rail intact, but the lake was frozen over with about an inch of ice. There wasn't a break in the smooth surface of the ice anywhere along the two miles of shore bordering the dugway.

Men and women and children swarmed through the woods on the other side of the road, knowing all the time it was useless. The road was called the "dugway" because it had been dug out of the side of the mountain. There was a gravel bank about seven feet high running almost unbrokenly along that side of the road. There was the one old abandoned trail leading to the quarry. It was clear, after walking the first ten yards of it, that no car had come that way. It couldn't.

A hundred phone calls were made to surrounding towns and villages. No one had seen the station wagon, the children or Jerry Mahoney. The impossible had to be faced.

The bus had gone into the dugway and it hadn't come out. It hadn't skidded into the lake and it hadn't climbed the impenetrable brush of the mountain. It was just gone! Vanished into thin air! . . .

Everyone was deeply concerned for and sympathetic with the Dicklers, and Joe Gorman, and the Williamses, the Trents, the Ishams, the Nortons, and the Jennings, parents of the missing children. Nobody thought much about Jerry Mahoney's family, or his girl.

It wasn't reasonable, but as the evening wore on and not one speck of evidence was found or one reasonable theory advanced, people began to talk about Jerry Mahoney. He was the driver. The bus had to have been driven somewhere. It couldn't navigate without Jerry Mahoney at the wheel. Jerry was the only adult involved. However it had been worked—this disappearance—Jerry must have had a hand in it.

It didn't matter that, until an hour ago, Jerry had been respected, trusted, liked. Their children were gone and Jerry had taken them somewhere. Why? Ransom. They would all get ransom letters in the morning, they said. A mass kidnaping. Jerry had the kids somewhere. There weren't any rich kids in Clayton so he was going to demand ransom from all seven families.

So Jerry Mahoney became a villain because there was no one else to suspect. Nobody stopped to think that Jerry's father and Jerry's girl might be as anxious about his absence as the others were about the missing children.

At nine-thirty Sergeant Mason and Trooper Teliski of the State Police, George Peabody, the sheriff, and a dozen men of the community including Joe Gorman and Karl Dickler stormed into the living room of Jerry Mahoney's house where an old man with silvery white hair sat in an overstuffed armchair with Elizabeth Deering, Jerry's fiancée, huddled on the floor beside him, her face buried on his knees, weeping.

The old man wore a rather sharply cut gray flannel suit, a bright scarlet vest with brass buttons and a green necktie that must have been designed for a St. Patrick's Day parade. As he stroked the girl's blond hair, the light from the lamp reflected glittering shafts from a square-cut diamond in a heavy gold setting he wore on his little finger. He looked up at Sergeant Mason and his small army of followers, and his blue eyes stopped twinkling as he saw the stern look on the Sergeant's face.

"All right, Pat," Sergeant Mason said. "What's Jerry done with those kids?" Pat Mahoney's pale blue eyes met the Sergeant's stare steadily. Then crinkles of mirth appeared at the corners of his eyes and mouth.

"I'd like to ask you something before I try to answer that," Pat Mahoney said.

"Well?"

"Have you stopped beating you wife, Sergeant?" Pat Mahoney asked. His cackle of laughter was the only sound in the room . . .

There are those who are old enough to remember the days when Mahoney and Faye were listed about fourth on a bill of eight star acts all around the Keith-Orpheum vaudeville circuit. Pat Mahoney was an Irish comic with dancing feet, and Nora Faye—Mrs. Mahoney to you—could match him at dancing and had the soprano voice of an angel.

Like so many people in show business, Pat was a blusterer, a boaster, a name dropper, but with it all a solid professional who would practice for hours a day to perfect a new routine, never missed an entrance in forty years, and up to the day young Jerry was born in a cheap hotel in Grand Rapids, Michigan, had given away half what he earned to deadbeats and hopeless failures.

The diamond ring he wore today had been in and out of a hundred hock shops. It had been the basis of his and Nora's security for more years than he liked to remember.

If you were left alone with Pat for more than five minutes, he went back to the old days—to the people he had idolized, like Sophie Tucker, and Smith and Dale, and Williams and Wolfus, and Joe Jackson. He'd known them all, played on the same bills with them all. "But," he would tell you, and a strange radiance would come into the pale blue eyes, "the greatest of them all was Nora Faye—Mrs. Mahoney to you."

Once he was started on his Nora, there was no way of stopping Pat Mahoney. He told of her talents as a singer and dancer, but in the end it was a saga of endless patience, of kindness and understanding, of love for a fat-headed, vain little Irish comic, of tenderness as a mother, and finally of clear-eyed courage in the face of stark tragedy.

Mahoney and Faye had never played the Palace, the Broadway goal of all vaudevillians. Pat had worked on a dozen acts that would crack the ice and finally he'd made it.

"We'd come out in cowboy suits, all covered with jewels, and jeweled guns, and jeweled boots, and we'd do a little soft shoe routine, and then suddenly all the lights would go out and only the jewels would show—they were made special for that—and we'd go into a fast routine, pulling the guns, and twirling and juggling them, and the roof would fall in! Oh, we tried it out of town, and our agent finally got us the booking at the Palace we'd always dreamed of."

There'd be a long silence then, and Pat would take a gaudy handkerchief from his hip pocket and blow his nose with a kind of angry violence. "I can show you the costumes still. They're packed away in a trunk in the attic. Just the way we wore them—me and Nora—the last time we ever played. Atlantic City it was. And she came off after the act with the cheers still ringing in our ears, and down she went on the floor of the dressing room, writhing in pain.

"Then she told me. It had been getting worse for months. She didn't want me to know. The doctor had told her straight out. She'd only a few months she could count on. She'd never said a word to me—working toward the Palace—knowing I'd dreamed of it. And only three weeks after that—she left us. Me and Jerry—she left us. We were standing by her bed when she left—and the last words she spoke were to Jerry. 'Take care of Pat,' she says to him. 'He'll be helpless without someone to take care of him.' And then she smiled at me, and all the years were in that smile."

And then, wherever he happened to be when he told the story, Pat Mahoney would wipe the back of his hand across his eyes and say: "If you'll excuse me, I think I'll be going home. . . ."

Nobody laughed when Pat pulled the old courtroom wheeze about "have you stopped beating your wife" on Sergeant Mason. Pat looked past the Sergeant at Trooper Teliski, and Joe Gorman, and Karl Dickler, and Mr. and Mrs. Jennings, whose two daughters were in the missing bus, and George Peabody, the fat, wheezing sheriff.

"The question I asked you, Sergeant," he said, "makes just as much sense as the one you asked me. You asked me what Nora's boy has done with those kids. There's no answer to that question. Do I hear you saying, 'I know what you must be feeling, Pat Mahoney, and you, Elizabeth Deering? And is there anything we can do for you in this hour of your terrible anxiety?' I don't hear you saying that, Sergeant."

"I'm sorry, Pat," Mason said. "Those kids are missing. Jerry had to take them somewhere."

"No!" Liz Deering cried. "You all know Jerry better than that!"

They didn't, it seemed, but they could be forgiven. You can't confront people with the inexplicable without frightening them and throwing them off balance. You can't endanger their children and expect a sane reaction. They muttered angrily, and old Pat saw the tortured faces of Joe Gorman and Karl Dickler and the swollen red eyes of Mrs. Jennings.

"Has he talked in any way queerly to you, Pat?" Mason asked. "Has he acted normal of late?"

"Nora's boy is the most normal boy you ever met," Pat Mahoney said. "You know that, Sergeant. Why, you've known him since he was a child."

Mrs. Jennings screamed out: "He'd protect his son. Naturally he'd protect his son. But he's stolen our children!"

"The Pied Piper rides again," Pat Mahoney said.

"Make him talk!" Mrs. Jennings cried, and the crowd around her muttered louder.

"When did you last see Jerry, Pat?"

"Breakfast," Pat said. "He has his lunch at Joe Gorman's Diner." The corner of his mouth twitched. "He should have been home for dinner long ago."

"Did he have a need for money?" Mason asked.

"Money? He was a man respected—until now—wasn't he? He was a man with a fine girl in love with him, wasn't he? What need would he have for money?"

"Make him answer sensibly!" Mrs. Jennings pleaded in a despairing voice.

Joe Gorman stepped forward. "Pat, maybe Jerry got sick all of a sudden. It's happened to men who saw action overseas. Maybe you saw signs of something and wouldn't want to tell of it. But my Pete was on that bus, and Karl's two, and Mrs. Jennings' two. We're nowhere, Pat—so if you can tell us anything! Our kids were on that bus!"

Pat Mahoney's eyes, as he listened to Joe Gorman, filled with pain. "My kid is on that bus, too, Joe," he said.

They all stared at him, some with hatred. And then, in the distance, they heard the wail of a siren. The troopers' car was coming from Lakeview.

"Maybe it's news!" someone shouted.

"News!"

And they all went stumbling out of the house to meet the approaching car—all but Elizabeth Deering, who stayed behind, clinging to the old man.

"I don't understand it," she said, her voice shaken. "They think he's harmed their children, Pat! Why? Why would they think he'd do such a thing? Why?"

Old Pat's eyes had a faraway look in them. "Did I ever tell you about The Great Thurston?" he asked. "Greatest magic act I ever saw."

"Pat!" Elizabeth said, her eyes widening in horror.

"First time I ever caught his act was in Sioux City," Pat said. "He came out in a flowing cape, and a silk hat, and he ..."

Dear God, he's losing his reason, Elizabeth Deering told herself. Let the news be good! Let them be found safe!

Outside the siren drew close.

The police car with its wailing siren carried news, but it was not the sort the people of Clayton were hoping to hear.

It was reassuring to know that within a few hours of the tragedy the entire area was alerted, that the moment daylight came a fleet of army helicopters would cover the area for hundreds of miles around, that a five-state alarm was out for the missing station wagon and its passengers, and that the Attorney General had sent the best man on his staff to direct and coördinate the search.

Top officials, viewing the case coldly and untouched by the hysteria of personal involvement, had a theory. Of course there had to be a rational explanation of the disappearance of the bus, and Clyde Haviland, tall, stoop-shouldered, scholarly looking investigator from the Attorney General's office, was ordered to produce that explanation as soon as possible upon his arrival in Clayton. But beyond that, officials had no doubt as to the reason for the disappearance: this was a mass kidnaping; something novel in the annals of crime.

Since none of the families involved had means, Haviland and his superiors were convinced the next move in this strange charade would be a demand on the whole community to pay ransom for the children. The FBI was alerted to be ready to act the moment there was any indication of involvement across state lines.

While mothers wept and the menfolk grumbled angrily that Jerry Mahoney, the driver, was at the bottom of this, officialdom worked calmly and efficiently. The Air Force turned over its complete data on Technical Sergeant Jerry Mahoney to the FBI. Men who had known Jerry in the service were waked from their sleep or pulled out of restaurants or theaters to be questioned. Had he ever said anything that would indicate he might move into a world of violence? Did his medical history contain any record of mental illness?

Sitting at a desk in the town hall, Clyde Haviland reported on some of this to George Peabody, the sheriff, the town's three selectmen, Sergeant Mason and a couple of other troopers. Haviland, carefully polishing his shell-rimmed glasses, was a quiet, reassuring sort of man. He had a fine reputation in the state. He was not an unfamiliar figure to people in Clayton because he had solved a particularly brutal murder in the neighboring town of Johnsville, and his investigation had brought him in and out of Clayton for several weeks.

"So far," he said, with a faint smile, "the report on Jerry Mahoney is quite extraordinary."

"In what way?" Sergeant Mason asked, eager for the scent of blood.

"Model citizen," Haviland said. "No one has a bad word for him. No bad temper. Never held grudges. Never chiseled. Saves his money. His savings account in the Clayton bank would surprise some of you. On the face of it, this is the last person in the world to suspect."

"There has to be a first time for everything," Karl Dickler said. He was a selectman as well as one of the bereaved parents.

"It's going down toward zero tonight," George Peabody, the sheriff, said, glumly. "If those kids are out anywhere——"

"They're a long way from here by now, if you ask me," Sergeant Mason said.

Haviland looked at him, his eyes unblinking behind the lenses of his glasses. "Except that they never came out of the dugway."

"Nobody saw them," Mason said, "But they're not there so they did come out."

"They didn't come out," Joe Gorman said. "I was watching for them from the window of my diner at this end."

"That was the three seconds you were getting something out of the icebox in your pantry," Mason said.

"And I suppose everyone else along Main Street had his head in a closet at just that time!" Joe Gorman said.

"Or someone reached down out of the heavens and snatched that station wagon up into space," Haviland said. He was looking at Peabody's pudgy face as he spoke, and something he saw there made him add quickly: "I'm kidding, of course."

Peabody laughed nervously. "It's the only good explanation we've had so far."

Karl Dickler put his hand up to his cheek. There was a nerve there that had started to twitch, regularly as the tick of a clock. "I like Jerry. I'd give the same kind of report on him you've been getting, Mr. Haviland. But you can't pass up the facts. I'd have said he'd defend those kids with his life. But did he? And the old man—his father. He won't answer questions directly. There's something queer about him. Mr. Haviland, my kids are—out there, somewhere!" He waved toward the frost-coated window panes.

"Every highway within two hundred miles of here is being patrolled, Mr. Dickler," Haviland said. "If they'd driven straight away from here in daylight—granting Mason is right and everybody was in a closet when the station wagon went through town—they'd have been seen a hundred times after they left Clayton. There isn't one report of anyone having seen the station wagon with the school-bus markings." Haviland paused to light a cigarette. His tapering fingers were nicotine stained.

"If you'd ever investigated a crime, Mr. Dickler, you'd know we usually are swamped with calls from people who think they've seen the wanted man. A bus—a busload of kids. Somebody *had* to see it! But there isn't even a crackpot report. If there was some place he could have stayed under cover—and don't tell me, I know there isn't—and started moving after dark, he might get some distance. But alarms are out everywhere. He couldn't travel five miles now without being trapped."

"We've told ourselves all these things for hours!" Dickler said, pinching savagely at his twitching cheek. "What are you going to *do*, Haviland?"

"Unless we're all wrong," Haviland said, "we're going to hear from the kidnapers soon. Tonight—or maybe in the morning—by mail, or phone or in some unexpected way. But we'll hear. They'll demand money. What other purpose can there be? Once we hear, we'll have to start to play it by ear. That's the way those cases are."

"Meanwhile you just sit here and wait!" Dickler said, a kind of despair rising in his voice. "What am I going to say to my wife?"

"I think all the parents of the children should go home. You may be the one the kidnapers contact. It may be your child they put on the phone to convince you the kids are safe," Haviland said. "As soon as it's day-light——"

"You think the kids *are* safe?" Dickler cried out.

Haviland stared at the distraught father for a minute. Then he spoke, gently. "What kind of assurance could I give you, Mr. Dickler? Even if I tried, you wouldn't believe me. People who play this kind of game are without feelings, not rational. When you fight them, you have to walk quietly. If you scare them, God knows what to expect. That's why I urge you all to go home and wait." He dropped his cigarette on the floor and heeled it out. "And pray," he said ...

Elizabeth Deering, Jerry Mahoney's girl, was sick with anxiety. Jerry was foremost in her mind; Jerry, missing with the children; Jerry, worse than that, suspected by his friends. But on top of that was old Pat Mahoney.

He hadn't made the slightest sense since the angry crowd had left his house. He had talked on endlessly about the old days in vaudeville. He seemed obsessed with the memory of the first time he had seen The Great Thurston in Sioux City. He remembered card tricks, and sawing the lady in half, and his wife Nora's childish delight in being completely bewildered. He seemed to remember everything he had seen the great man do.

Elizabeth tried, but she could not bring Pat back to the present. The tragedy seemed to have tipped him right out of the world of reason. She was partly relieved when she heard firm steps on the front porch. The other part of her, when she saw Sergeant Mason and the tall stranger, was the fear that they had news—bad news about Jerry.

Mason was less aggressive than he had been on his first visit. He introduced Haviland and said they wanted to talk to Pat. Elizabeth took them back into the living room where old Pat still sat in the overstuffed armchair.

Mason introduced Haviland. "Mr. Haviland is a special investigator from the Attorney General's office, Pat."

Pat's eyes brightened. "Say, you're the fellow that solved that murder over in Johnsville, aren't you?" he said. "Smart piece of work."

"Thanks," Haviland said. He looked at Pat, astonished at his gaudy vest and tie and the glittering diamond on his finger. He had been prepared for Pat, but not adequately.

"Sit down," Pat said. "Maybe Liz would make us some coffee if we asked her pretty."

Mason nodded to Liz, who went out into the kitchen. He followed her to tell her there was no news. Haviland sat down on the couch next to Pat, stretched out his long legs and offered Pat a cigarette.

"Don't smoke," Pat said. "Never really liked anything but cigars. Nora hated the smell of 'em. So what was I to do? You go to vaudeville in the old days, Mr. Haviland?"

"When I was a kid," Haviland said, lighting a cigarette. "I never had the pleasure of seeing you, though, Mr. Mahoney."

"Call me Pat," Pat said. "Everyone does. I was nothing, Mr. Haviland. Just a third-rate song-and-dance man. But Nora—well, if you ever saw my Nora . . ."

Haviland waited for him to go on, but Pat seemed lost in his precious memories.

"You must be very worried about your son, Pat," he said.

For a fractional moment the mask of pleasant incompetence seemed to be stripped from Pat's face. "Wouldn't you be?" he asked, harshly. Then, almost instantly, the mask was fitted back into place and old Pat gave his cackling laugh. "You got theories, Mr. Haviland? How're you going to handle this case?"

"I think," Haviland said, conversationally, "the children and your son have been kidnaped. I think we'll hear from the kidnapers soon. I think, in all probability, the whole town will be asked to get up a large ransom."

Pat nodded. "I'll chip in this diamond ring," he said. "It's got Jerry out of trouble more than once."

Haviland's eyes narrowed. "He's been in trouble before?"

"His main trouble was his Pop," Pat said. "Sometimes there wasn't enough to eat. But we could always raise eating money on this ring." He turned his bright, laughing eyes directly on Haviland. "You figured out how the bus disappeared?"

"No," Haviland said.

"Of course it doesn't really matter, does it?" Pat said.

"Well, if we knew——" Haviland said.

"It wouldn't really matter," Pat said. "It's what's going to happen now that matters."

"You mean the demand for money?"

"If that's what's going to happen," Pat said. The cackling laugh suddenly grated on Haviland's nerves. The old joker did know something!

"You have a different theory, Pat?" Haviland asked, keeping his exasperation out of his voice.

"You ever see the Great Thurston on the Keith-Orpheum circuit?" Pat asked.

"I'm afraid not," Haviland said.

"Greatest magic act I ever saw," Pat said. "Better than Houdini. Better than anyone. I first saw him in Sioux City——"

"About the case here, Pat," Haviland interrupted. "You have a theory?"

"I got no theory," Pat said. "But I know what's going to happen."

Haviland leaned forward. "What's going to happen?"

"One of two things," Pat said. "Everybody in this town is going to be looking for that station wagon in the lake, where they know it isn't and they're going to be looking for it in the woods, where they know it isn't. That's one thing that may happen. The other thing is, they buy this theory of yours, Mr. Haviland—and it's a good theory, mind you—and they all stay home and wait to hear something. There's one same result from both things, isn't there?"

"Same result?"

"Sure. Nobody in Clayton goes to work. The quarries don't operate. The small businesses will shut down. People will be looking and people will be waiting . . ."

"So?"

"So what good will that do anyone?" Pat asked.

Haviland ground out his cigarette in an ash tray. "It won't do anyone any good. The quarry owners will lose some money. The small businesses will lose some money."

"Not much point in it, is there?" Pat said, grinning.

Haviland rose. He'd had about enough. Mason and Elizabeth were coming back from the kitchen with coffee. "There isn't much point to anything you're saying, Mr. Mahoney."

Pat's eyes twinkled. "You said you never saw The Great Thurston, didn't you?"

"I never saw him," Haviland said.

"Well, we'll see. If they're supposed to stay home and wait, they'll stay home and wait. If they're supposed to be out searching, they'll be out searching. Ah, coffee! Smells real good. Pull up a chair, Sergeant. By the way, Mr. Haviland, I'll make you a bet," Pat said.

"I'm not a betting man," Haviland said.

"Oh, just a manner-of-speaking bet," Pat said. "I'll make you a bet that tomorrow morning they'll be out searching. I'll make you a bet that even if you order them to stay home and wait, they'll be out searching."

"Look here, Pat, if you know something . . ."

A dreamy look came into Pat's eyes. "Nora was so taken with The Great Thurston that time in Sioux City I went around to see him afterwards. I thought maybe he'd show me how to do a few simple tricks. I pretended it was for Nora, but really I thought we might use 'em in our act. He wouldn't tell me anything—that is, not about any of his tricks. But he told me the whole principle of his business."

"Sugar?" Elizabeth asked Haviland. Poor old man, she thought.

"The principle is," Pat said, "to make your audience think only what you want them to think, and see only what you want them to see." Pat's eyes brightened. "Which reminds me, there's something I'd like to have you see, Mr. Haviland."

Haviland gulped his coffee. Somehow he felt mesmerized by the old man. Pat was at the foot of the stairs, beckoning. Haviland followed.

Elizabeth looked at Mason and there were tears in her eyes. "It's thrown him completely off base," she said. "You know what he's going to show Mr. Haviland?" Sergeant Mason shook his head.

"A cowboy suit!" Elizabeth said, and dropped down on the couch, crying softly. "He's going to show him a cowboy suit."

And she was right. Haviland found himself in the attic, his head bowed to keep from bumping into the sloping beams. Old Pat had opened a wardrobe trunk and, with the gesture of a waiter taking the silver lid off a tomato surprise, revealed two cowboy suits, one hanging neatly on each side of the trunk—Nora's and his. Chaps, shirt, vest, boots, Stetsons, and gun belts—all studded with stage jewelry.

"... and when the lights went out," Pat was saying, "all you could see was these gewgaws, sparkling. And we'd take out the guns ..." And suddenly Pat had the two jeweled six-shooters in his hands, twirling and spinning them. "In the old days I could draw these guns and twirl 'em into position faster than Jesse James!"

The spell was broken for Haviland. The old guy was cuckoo. "I enjoyed seeing them, Mr. Mahoney," he said. "But now, I'm afraid I've got to get back ..."

As soon as dawn broke, Haviland had Sergeant Mason and Sheriff George Peabody take him out to the scene of the disappearance. Everyone else was at home, waiting to hear from the kidnapers. It had been a terrible night for the whole town, a night filled with forebodings and dark imaginings. Haviland covered every inch of the two-mile stretch of the dugway. You couldn't get away from the facts. There was no way for it to have happened—but it had happened.

About eight-thirty he was back in Clayton in Joe's Diner, stamping his feet to warm them and waiting eagerly for eggs and toast to go with his steaming cup of black coffee. All the parents had been checked. There'd been no phone calls, no notes slipped under doors, nothing in the early-morning mail.

Haviland never got his breakfast. Trooper Teliski came charging into the diner just as Joe Gorman was taking the eggs off the grill. Teliski, a healthy young man, was white as parchment, and the words came out of him in a kind of choking sob. "We've found 'em," he said. "Or at least we know where they are. Helicopters spotted 'em. I just finished passing the word in town."

Joe Gorman dropped the plate of eggs on the floor behind the counter. Haviland spun around on his counter stool. Just looking at Teliski made the hair rise on the back of his neck.

"The old quarry off the dugway," Teliski said, and gulped for air. "No sign of the bus. It didn't drive up there. But the kids." Teliski steadied himself on the counter. "Schoolbooks," he said. "A couple of coats—lying on the edge of the quarry. And in the quarry—more of the same. A red beret belonging to one of the kids——"

"Peter!" Joe Gorman cried out.

Haviland headed for the door. The main street of Clayton was frightening to see. People ran out of houses, screaming at one one another, heading crazily toward the dugway. Those who went for their cars scattered the people in front of them. There was no order—only blind panic.

Haviland stood on the curb outside the diner, ice in his veins. He looked down the street to where old Pat Mahoney lived, just in time to see a wildly weeping woman pick up a stone and throw it through the front window of Pat's house.

"Come on—what's the matter with you?" Teliski shouted from behind the wheel of the State Police car.

Haviland stood where he was, frozen, staring at the broken window of Pat Mahoney's house. The abandoned quarry, he knew, was sixty feet deep, full to within six feet of the top with icy water fed in by constantly bubbling springs.

A fire engine roared past. They were going to try to pump out the quarry. It would be like bailing out the Atlantic Ocean with a tea cup.

"Haviland!" Teliski call desperately.

Haviland still stared at Pat Mahoney's house. A cackling old voice rang in his ears. "I'll make you a bet, Mr. Haviland. I'll make you a bet that even if you order them to stay at home and wait, they'll be out searching."

Rage such as he had never known flooded the ice out of Haviland's veins. So Pat had known! The old codger had known *last night!*

Haviland had never witnessed anything like the scene at the quarry.

The old road, since overgrown, which ran about 200 yards in from the dugway to the quarry, had been trampled down as if by a herd of buffalo.

Within three-quarters of an hour of the news reaching town, it seemed as if everyone from Clayton and half the population of Lakeview had arrived at the quarry's edge.

One of the very first army helicopters which had taken to the air at dawn had spotted the clothes and books at the edge of the abandoned stone pit.

The pilot had dropped down close enough to identify the strange objects and radioed immediately to State Police. The stampede had followed.

Haviland was trained to be objective in the face of tragedy, but he found himself torn to pieces by what he saw. Women crowded forward, screaming, trying to examine the articles of clothing and books. Maybe not all the children were in this icy grave. It was only the hope of desperation. No one really believed it. It seemed, as Trooper Teliski had said, to be the work of a maniac.

Haviland collected as many facts about the quarry as he could from a shaken Sheriff Peabody.

"Marble's always been Clayton's business," Peabody said. "Half the big buildings in New York have got their marble out of Clayton quarries. This was one of the first quarries opened up by the Clayton Marble Company nearly sixty years ago. When they started up new ones, this one was abandoned."

In spite of the cold, Peabody was sweating. He wiped the sleeve of his plaid hunting shirt across his face. "Sixty feet down, and sheer walls," he said. "They took the blocks out at ten-foot levels, so there is a little ledge about every ten feet going down. A kid couldn't climb out of it if it was empty."

Haviland glanced over at the fire engine which had started to pump water from the quarry. "Not much use in that," he said.

"The springs are feeding it faster than they can pump it out," Peabody said. "There's no use telling them. They got to feel they're doing something." The fat sheriff's mouth set in a grim slit. "Why would Jerry Mahoney do a thing like this? *Why?* I quess you can only say the old man is a little crazy, and the son has gone off his rocker too."

"There are some things that don't fit," Haviland said. He noticed his own hands weren't steady as he lit a cigarette. The hysterical shrieking of one of the women near the edge of the quarry grated on his nerves. "Where is the station wagon?"

"He must have driven up here and—and done what he did to the kids," Peabody said. "Then waited till after dark to make a getaway."

"But you searched this part of the woods before dark last night," Haviland said.

"We missed it somehow, that's all," Peabody said, stubbornly.

"A nine-passenger station wagon is pretty hard to miss," Haviland said.

"So we missed it," Peabody said "God knows how, but we missed it." He shook his head. "I suppose the only thing that'll work here is grappling hooks. They're sending a crane over from one of the active quarries. Take an hour or more to get it here. Nobody'll leave here till the hooks have scraped the bottom of the place and they've brought up the kids."

Unless, Haviland thought to himself, the lynching spirit gets into them. He was thinking of an old man in a red vest and a green necktie and a diamond twinkling on his little finger. He was thinking of a broken window pane—and of the way he'd seen mobs act before in his time.

Someone gripped the sleeve of Haviland's coat and he looked down into the horror-struck face of Elizabeth Deering, Jerry Mahoney's girl.

"It's true then," she whispered. She swayed on her feet, holding tight to Haviland for support.

"It's true they found some things belonging to the kids," he said. "That's all that's true at the moment, Miss Deering." He was a little astonished by his own words. He realized that, instinctively, he was not believing everything that he saw in front of him. "This whole area was searched last night before dark." he said. "No one found any schoolbooks or coats or berets then. No one saw the station wagon."

"What's the use of talking that way?" Peabody said. His eyes were narrowed, staring at Liz Deering. "I don't want to believe what I see either, Mr. Haviland. But I got to." The next words came out of the fat man with a bitterness that stung like a whiplash. "Maybe you're the only one in Clayton that's lucky, Liz. You found out he was a homicidal maniac in time—before you got married to him."

"Please, George!" the girl cried. "How can you believe——"

"What can anyone believe but that?" Peabody said, and turned away.

Liz Deering clung to Haviland, sobbing. The tall man stared over her head at the hundreds of people grouped around the quarry's edge. He was reminded of a mine disaster he had seen once in Pennsylvania: a whole town waiting at the head of the mine shaft for the dead to be brought to the surface.

"Let's get out of here," he said to Liz Deering, with sudden energy . . .

Clayton was a dead town. Stores were closed. Joe's Diner was closed. The railroad station agent was on the job, handling dozens of telegrams that were coming in from friends and relatives of the parents of the missing children. The two girls in the telephone office, across the street from the bank, were at their posts.

Old Mr. Granger, a teller in the bank, and one of the stenographers were all of the bank staff that had stayed on the job. Old Mr. Granger was preparing the payroll for the Clayton Marble Company. He didn't know whether the truck from the company's offices with the two guards would show up for the money or not.

Nothing else was working on schedule today. Even the hotel down the street had shut up shop. One or two salesmen had driven into town, heard the news, and gone off down the dugway toward the scene of the tragedy. A few very old people tottered in and out the front doors of houses, looking anxiously down Main Street toward the dugway. Even the clinic was closed. The town's doctors and nurses had all gone to the scene of the disaster.

Down the street a piece of newspaper had been taped over the hole in Pat Mahoney's front window. Pat Mahoney sat in the big overstuffed armchair in his living room. He rocked slowly back and forth, staring at an open scrapbook spread across his knees. A big black headline from a show-business paper was pasted across the top.

MAHONEY AND FAYE
BOFFO BUFFALO

Under it were pictures of Pat and Nora in their jeweled cowboy suits, their six-shooters drawn, pointing straight at the camera. There was a description of the act, the dance in the dark with only the jewels showing and the six-shooters spouting flame. "Most original number of its kind seen in years," a Buffalo critic had written. "The ever popular Mahoney and Faye have added something to their familiar routines that should please theater audiences from coast to coast. We are not surprised to hear that they have been booked into the Palace."

Pat closed the scrapbook and put it down on the floor beside him. From the inside pocket of his jacket he took a wallet. It bulged with papers and cards. He was an honorary Elk, honorary police chief of Wichita in 1927, a Friar, a Lamb.

Carefully protected by an isinglass guard were some snapshots. They were faded now, but anyone could see they were pictures of Nora with little Jerry at various stages of his growth. There was Jerry at six months, Jerry at a year, Jerry at four years. And Nora, smiling gently at her son. The love seemed to shine right out of the pictures, Pat thought.

Pat replaced the pictures and put the wallet back in his pocket. He got up from his chair and moved toward the stairway. People who knew him would have been surprised. No one had ever seen Pat when his movements weren't brisk and youthful. He could still go into a tap routine at the drop of a hat, and he always gave the impression that he was on the verge of doing so. Now he moved slowly, almost painfully—a tired old man, with no need to hide it from anyone. There was no one to hide it from; Jerry was missing, Liz was gone.

He climbed to the second floor and turned to the attic door. He opened it, switched on the lights, and climbed up to the area under the eaves. There he opened the wardrobe trunk he'd shown to Haviland. From the left side he took out the cowboy outfit—the chaps, the boots, the vest and shirt and Stetson hat, and the gun belt with the two jeweled six-shooters. Slowly he carried them down to his bedroom on the second floor. There Pat Mahoney proceeded to get into costume.

He stood, at last, in front of the full-length mirror on the back of the bathroom door. The high-heeled boots made him a couple of inches taller than usual. The Stetson was set on his head at a rakish angle. The jeweled chaps and vest glittered in the sunlight from the window. Suddenly old Pat jumped into a flat-footed stance, and the guns were out of the holsters, spinning dizzily and then pointed straight at the mirror.

"Get 'em up, you lily-livered rats!" old Pat shouted. A bejeweled gunman stared back at him fiercely from the mirror.

Then, slowly, he turned away to a silver picture frame on his bureau. Nora, as a very young girl, looked out at him with her gentle smile.

"It'll be all right, honey," Pat said. "You'll see. It'll be another boffo, honey. Don't you worry about your boy. Don't you ever worry about him while I'm around. You'll see."

It was a terrible day for Clayton, but Gertrude Naylor, the chief operator in the telephone office, said afterward that perhaps the worst moment for her was when she spotted old Pat Mahoney walking down the main street— right in the middle of the street—dressed in that crazy cowboy outfit. He walked slowly, looking from right to left, staying right on the white line that divided the street.

"I'd seen it a hundred times before in the movies," Gertrude Naylor said, afterward. "A cowboy, walking down the street of a deserted town, waiting for his enemy to appear—waiting for the moment to draw his guns. Old Pat's hands floated just above those crazy guns in his holster, and he kept rubbing the tips of his fingers against his thumb. I showed him to Millie, and we started to laugh, and then, somehow, it seemed about the most awful thing of all. Jerry Mahoney had murdered those kids and here was his old man, gone nutty as a fruitcake."

Old Mr. Granger, in the bank, had much the same reaction when the aged, bejeweled gun toter walked up to the teller's window.

"Good morning, Mr. Granger," Pat said, cheerfully.

Mr. Granger moistened his pale lips. "Good morning, Pat."

"You're not too busy this morning, I see," Pat said.

"N-no," Mr. Granger said. The killer's father—dressed up like a kid for the circus. He's ready for a padded cell, Mr. Granger thought.

"Since you're not so busy," Pat said, "I'd like to have a look at the detailed statement of my account for the last three months." As he spoke, he turned and leaned against the counter, staring out through the plate-glass bank window at the street. His hands stayed near the guns, and he kept rubbing his fingertips against the ball of his thumb.

"You get a statement each month, Pat," Mr. Granger said.

"Just the same, I'd like to see the detailed statement for the last three months," Pat said.

"I had to humor him, I thought," Mr. Granger said later. "So I went back in the vault to get his records out of the files. Well, I was just inside the vault door when he spoke again, in the most natural way. 'If I were you, Mr. Granger,' he said, 'I'd close that vault door, and I'd stay inside, and I'd set off all the alarms I could lay my hands on. You're about to be stuck up, Mr. Granger.'

"Well, I thought it was part of his craziness," Mr. Granger said, later. "I thought he meant *he* was going to stick up the bank. I thought that was why he'd got all dressed up in that cowboy outfit. Gone back to his childhood, I thought. I was scared, because I figured he was crazy. So I *did* close the vault door. And I *did* set off the alarm, only it didn't work. I didn't know then all the electric wires into the bank had been cut."

Gertrude and Millie, the telephone operators, had a box seat for the rest of it. They saw the black sedan draw up in front of the bank and they saw the four men in dark suits and hats get out of it and start up the steps of the bank. Two of them were carrying small suitcases and two of them were carrying guns.

Then suddenly the bank doors burst open and an ancient cowboy appeared, hands poised over his guns. He did a curious little jig step that brought him out in a solid square stance. The four men were so astonished at the sight of him they seemed to freeze.

"Stick 'em up, you lily-livered rats!" old Pat shouted. The guns were out of the holsters, twirling. Suddenly they belched flame, straight at the bandits.

The four men dived for safety, like men plunging off the deck of a sinking ship. One of them made the corner of the bank building. Two of them got to the safe side of the car. The fourth, trying to scramble back into the car, was caught in the line of fire.

"I shot over your heads that first time!" Pat shouted. "Move another inch and I'll blow you all to kingdom come!" The guns twirled again and then suddenly aimed steadily at the exposed bandit. "All right, come forward and throw your guns down," Pat ordered.

The man in the direct line of fire obeyed at once. His gun bounced on the pavement a few feet from Pat and he raised his arms slowly. Pat inched his way toward the discarded gun.

The other men didn't move. And then Gertrude and Millie saw the one who had gotten around the corner of the bank slowly raise his gun and take deliberate aim at Pat. She and Millie both screamed, and it made old Pat jerk his head around. In that instant there was a roar of gunfire.

Old Pat went down, clutching at his shoulder. But so did the bandit who'd shot him and so did one of the men behind the car. Then Gertrude and Millie saw the tall figure of Mr. Haviland come around the corner of the hotel next door, a smoking gun in his hand. He must have spoken very quietly because Gertrude and Millie couldn't hear him, but whatever he said made the other bandits give up. Then they saw Liz Deering running across the street to where old Pat lay, blood dripping through the fingers that clutched at his shoulder ...

Trooper Teliski's car went racing through the dugway at breakneck speed, siren shrieking. As he came to the turn-in to the old quarry, his tires screamed and he skidded in and up the rugged path, car bounding over stones, ripping through brush. Suddenly just ahead of him on the path loomed the crane from the new quarry, inching up the road on a caterpillar tractor. Trooper Teliski sprang out of his car and ran past the crane, shouting at the tractor driver as he ran.

"Never mind with that!" Teliski shouted. Stumbling and gasping for breath, he raced out into the clearing where hundreds of people waited in a grief-stricken silence for the grappling for bodies to begin.

"Everybody!" Teliski shouted. "Everybody! Listen!" He was half laughing, half strangling for breath. "Your kids aren't there! They're safe. They're all safe—the kids, Jerry Mahoney, everyone! They aren't here. They'll be home before you will! Your kids—" And then he fell forward on his face, sucking in the damp, loam-scented air.

Twenty minutes later Clayton was a mad house. People running, people driving, people hanging onto the running boards of cars and clinging to bumpers. And in the middle of the town, right opposite the bank, was a station wagon with a yellow school bus sign on its roof, and children were spilling out of it, waving and shouting at their parents, who laughed and wept. And a handsome young Irishman with bright blue eyes was locked in a tight embrace with Elizabeth Deering ...

Haviland's fingers shook slightly as he lit a cigarette. Not yet noon and he was on his third pack.

"You can't see him yet," he said to Jerry Mahoney. "The doctor's with him. In a few minutes."

"I still don't get it," Jerry said. "People thought *I* had harmed those kids?"

"You don't know what it's been like here," Liz Deering said, clinging tightly to his arm.

Jerry Mahoney turned and saw the newspaper taped over the broken front window, and his face hardened. "Try and tell me, plain and simple, about Pop," he said.

Haviland shook his head, smiling like a man still dazed. "Your Pop is an amazing man, Mr. Mahoney," he said. "His mind works in its own peculiar ways ... The disappearance of the bus affected him differently from some others. He saw it as a magic trick, and he thought of it as magic trick—or, rather, as *part* of a magic trick. He said it to me and I wouldn't listen. He said it is a magician's job to get you to think what he wants you to think and see what he wants you to see. The disappearance of the children, the ghastly faking of their death in the quarry—it meant one thing to your Pop,

Mr. Mahoney. Someone wanted all the people in Clayton to be out of town. Why?

"There was only one good reason that remarkable Pop of yours could think of. The quarry payroll. Nearly a hundred thousand dollars in cash, and not a soul in town to protect it. Everyone would be looking for the children, and all the bandits had to do was walk in the bank and take the money. No cops, no nothing to interfere with them."

"But why didn't Pop tell you his idea?" Jerry asked.

"You still don't know what it was like here, Mr. Mahoney," Haviland said. "People thought you had done something to those kids; they imagined your Pop knew something about it. If he'd told his story, even to me, I think I'd have thought he was either touched in the head or covering up. So he kept still—although he did throw me a couple of hints. And suddenly, he was, to all intents and purposes, alone in the town. So he went upstairs, got dressed in those cowboy clothes and went, calm as you please, to the bank to meet the bandits he knew must be coming. And they came."

"But why the cowboy suit?" Liz Deering asked.

"A strange and wonderful mind," Haviland said. "He thought the sight of him would be screwy enough to throw the bandits a little off balance. He thought if he started blasting away with his guns they might panic. They almost did."

"What I don't understand," Liz said, "is how, when he fired straight at them, he never hit anybody!"

"Those were stage guns—prop guns," Jerry said. "They only fire blanks."

Haviland nodded. "He thought he could get them to drop their own guns and then he'd have a real weapon and have the drop on them. It almost worked. But the one man who'd ducked around the corner of the building got in a clean shot at him. Fortunately, I arrived at exactly the same minute, and I had them all from behind."

"But how did you happen to turn up?" Jerry asked.

"I couldn't get your father out of my mind," Haviland said. "He seemed to know what was going to happen. He said they'd be searching for the kids, whether I told them to wait at home or not. Suddenly I had to know why he'd said that."

"Thank God," Jerry said. "I gather you got them to tell you where we were?"

Haviland nodded. "I'm still not dead clear how it worked, Jerry."

"It was as simple as pie à la mode," Jerry said. "I was about a half mile into the dugway on the home trip with the kids. We'd just passed Karl Dickler headed the other way when a big trailer truck loomed up ahead of me on the road. It was stopped, and a couple of guys were standing around the tail end of it.

"Broken down, I thought. I pulled up. All of a sudden guns were pointed at me and the kids. They didn't talk much. They just said to do as I was told. They opened the back of the big truck and rolled out a ramp. Then I was ordered to drive the station wagon right up into the body of the truck. I might have tried to make a break for it except for the kids. I drove up into the truck, they closed up the rear end, and that was that. They drove off with us—right through the main street of town here!"

Haviland shook his head. "An old trick used hundreds of times back in bootleg days. And I never thought of it!"

"Not ten minutes later," Jerry went on, "they pulled into that big deserted barn on the Haskell place. We've been shut up there ever since. They were real decent to the kids—hot dogs, ice cream cones, soda.

"So we just waited there, not knowing why, but nobody hurt, and the kids not as scared as you might think," Jerry laughed. "Oh, we came out of the dugway all right—and right by everybody in town. But nobody saw us."

The doctor appeared in the doorway. "You can see him for a minute now, Jerry," he said. "I had to give him a pretty strong sedative. Dug the bullet out of his shoulder and it hurt a bit. He's pretty sleepy—but he'll do better if he sees you, I think. Don't stay too long, though."

Jerry bounded up the stairs and into the bedroom where Pat Mahoney lay, his face very pale, his eyes half closed. Jerry knelt by the bed.

"Pop," he whispered. "You crazy old galoot!"

Pat opened his eyes. "You okay, Jerry?"

"Okay, Pop."

"And the kids?"

"Fine. Not a hair of their heads touched." Jerry reached out and covered Pat's hand with his. "Now look here, Two-Gun Mahoney . . ."

Pat grinned at him. "It was a boffo, Jerry. A real boffo."

"It sure was," Jerry said. He started to speak, but he saw that Pat was looking past him at the silver picture frame on the dresser.

"I told you it'd be all right, honey," Pat whispered. "I told you not to worry about your boy while I was around to take care of him." Then he grinned at Jerry, and his eyes closed and he was asleep.

Jerry tiptoed out of the room to find his own girl.

ACTIVITIES

1) Who is the *protagonist* of "The Day the Children Vanished"? Who is the *antagonist?* Here is a question which may elicit varied responses from your classmates so be sure that you present solid reasoning to back up your choices.

2) Speculation can sometimes be fun, a relaxing break from the continual school routine of having to provide reasoned answers to specific questions. For a change, let's do some speculating—in relation to the question of whether Pat Mahoney or Clyde Haviland would make a good series sleuth. Which kind of detective plot do you prefer, one containing a series sleuth, or one without?

3) Up to now, we have discussed two major point of view literature techniques, the first person and the omniscient. This is a good time to present a third example, one labeled *the third person objective.*

In this point of view, the narrator, like the omniscient story-teller, is an outsider or third person. But whereas the omniscient one has the superhuman ability to enter people's minds, the objective narrator operates more like a newspaper reporter who can only present facts as he sees them.

Mr. Pentecost's choice for this story was a third person objective narrator. Why do you think that he picked this particular point of view?

A CLASS ACTIVITY

After all the reading you have done in this book, you have probably, at times, found yourself fantasizing an interesting fictional sleuth of your own. If you have done this, why not put your imagination to work by writing a one-page biographical sketch of your "dream" detective?

Afterwards, your class could have an interesting session comparing detectives. You may be pleasantly surprised to discover that some of these characterizations are quite good.

The Comic Detective

The comic detective story is largely parody. A famous fictional sleuth is chosen and his style and adventures are irreverently but lovingly burlesqued.

Naturally, the detective most often picked as the target for such parodies is Sherlock Holmes. Thus, the sub-genre of the comic detective tale is yet another tribute to the genius of Sir Arthur Conan Doyle and a continuation of what we have called the glorious "put-on." (See Chapter 2.)

The very name Sherlock Holmes has a tendency for arousing the parodying instinct. Some of the finest authors writing in the English language have attempted pastiches in which the Great Detective's name was ingeniously contorted to Shylock Holmes, Hemlock Jones, Shamrock Jolnes, Thinlock Bones, Shlock Homes, and more. As for Watson, he continued his indispensable assisting in the parodies under such easily recognizable aliases as Whatsup, Potson, Whatsoname, Watney, Potsey, etc. Responsible for these absurd appellations are such illustrious creators as O. Henry, Bret Harte, Agatha Christie, Stephen Leacock, Stuart Palmer, Robert L. Fish, and a slew of others.[6]

And now, an example of the comic detective "on the scent."

Bret Harte—and Mr. Hemlock Jones

Bret Harte, an important figure in American literature, wrote mainly about life in the California mining camps. His short stories are considered classics of the western genre and were the first to describe the picturesque life of the California frontier. Such famous stories of his as "The Luck of Roaring Camp," "The Outcasts of Poker Flat," and "Tennessee's Partner" are a delicate blend of humor and pathos, and he himself believed that his comedic talents derived from both the pre-Civil War humorists and the great English novelist Charles Dickens.

During the latter part of his career, he lived in England, and there he became acquainted with the writings of Sir Arthur Conan Doyle. As a humorist, he was immediately able to visualize the inherent parodying possibilities of the Sherlock Holmes stories. What resulted was the following mis-adventure.

Though a grand spoof, the tale may also be considered one great writer's tribute to another ...

The Stolen Cigar Case

I found Hemlock Jones in the old Brook Street lodgings, musing before the fire. With the freedom of an old friend I at once threw myself in my usual familiar attitude at his feet, and gently caressed his boot. I was induced to do this for two reasons: one, that it enabled me to get a good look at his bent, concentrated face, and the other, that it seemed to indicate my reverence for his superhuman insight. So absorbed was he even then, in tracking some mysterious clue, that he did not seem to notice me. But therein I was wrong—as I always was in my attempt to understand that powerful intellect.

"It is raining," he said, without lifting his head.

"You have been out, then?" I said quickly.

"No. But I see that your umbrella is wet, and that your overcoat has drops of water on it."

I sat aghast at his penetration. After a pause he said carelessly, as if dismissing the subject: "Besides, I hear the rain on the window. Listen."

I listened. I could scarcely credit my ears, but there was the soft pattering of drops on the panes. It was evident there was no deceiving this man!

"Have you been busy lately?" I asked, changing the subject. "What new problem—given up by Scotland Yard as inscrutable—has occupied that gigantic intellect?"

He drew back his foot slightly, and seemed to hesitate ere he returned it to its original position. Then he answered wearily: "Mere trifles—nothing to speak of. The Prince Kupoli has been here to get my advice regarding the disappearance of certain rubies from the Kremlin; the Rajah of Pootibad, after vainly beheading his entire bodyguard, has been obliged to seek my assistance to recover a jeweled sword. The Grand Duchess of Pretzel-Brauntswig is desirous of discovering where her husband was on the night of February 14; and last night"—he lowered his voice slightly—"a lodger in this very house, meeting me on the stairs, wanted to know why they didn't answer his bell."

I could not help smiling—until I saw a frown gathering on his inscrutable forehead.

"Pray remember," he said coldly, "that it was through such an apparently trivial question that I found out Why Paul Ferroll Killed His Wife, and What Happened to Jones!"

I became dumb at once. He paused for a moment, and then suddenly changing back to his usual pitiless, analytical style, he said: "When I say these are trifles, they are so in comparison to an affair that is now before me. A crime has been committed,—and, singularly enough, against myself. You start," he said. "You wonder who would have dared to attempt it. So did I; nevertheless, it has been done. *I* have been *robbed!*"

"*You* robbed! You, Hemlock Jones, the Terror of Peculators!" I gasped in amazement, arising and gripping the table as I faced him.

"Yes! Listen. I would confess it to no other. But *you* who have followed my career, who know my methods; you, for whom I have partly lifted the veil that conceals my plans from ordinary humanity,—you, who have for years rapturously accepted my confidences, passionately admired my inductions and inferences, placed yourself at my beck and call, become my slave, groveled at my feet, given up your practice except those few unremunerative and rapidly decreasing patients to whom, in moments of abstraction over *my* problems, you have administered strychnine for quinine and arsenic for Epsom salts; you, who have sacrificed anything and everybody to me,—*you* I make my confidant!"

I arose and embraced him warmly, yet he was already so engrossed in thought that at the same moment he mechanically placed his hand upon his watch chain as if to consult the time. "Sit down," he said. "Have a cigar?"

"I have given up cigar smoking," I said.

"Why?" he asked.

I hesitated, and perhaps colored. I had really given it up because, with my diminished practice, it was too expensive. I could afford only a pipe. "I prefer a pipe," I said laughingly. "But tell me of this robbery. What have you lost?"

He arose, and planting himself before the fire with his hands under his coat-tails, looked down upon me reflectively for a moment. "Do you remember the cigar case presented to me by the Turkish Ambassador for discovering the missing favorite of the Grand Vizier in the fifth chorus girl at the Hilarity Theater? It was that one. I mean the cigar case. It was incrusted with diamonds."

"And the largest one had been supplanted by paste," I said.

"Ah," he said, with a reflective smile, "you know that?"

"You told me yourself. I remember considering it a proof of your extraordinary perception. But, by Jove, you don't mean to say you have lost it?"

He was silent for a moment. "No; it has been stolen, it is true, but I shall still find it. And by myself alone! In your profession, my dear fellow, when a member is seriously ill, he does not prescribe for himself, but calls in a brother doctor. Therein we differ. I shall take this matter in my own hands."

"And where could you find better?" I said enthusiastically. "I should say the cigar case is as good as recovered already."

"I shall remind you of that again," he said lightly. "And now, to show you my confidence in your judgment, in spite of my determination to pursue this alone, I am willing to listen to any suggestions from you."

He drew a memorandum book from his pocket and, with a grave smile, took up his pencil.

I could scarcely believe my senses. He, the great Hemlock Jones, accepting suggestions from a humble individual like myself! I kissed his hand reverently, and began in a joyous tone:

"First, I should advertise, offering a reward; I should give the same intimation in hand-bills, distributed at the 'pubs' and the pastry-cooks'. I should next visit the different pawnbrokers; I should give notice at the police station. I should examine the servants. I should thoroughly search the house and my own pockets. I speak relatively," I added, with a laugh. "Of course I mean *your* own."

He gravely made an entry of these details.

"Perhaps" I added, "you have already done this?"

"Perhaps," he returned enigmatically. "Now, my dear friend," he continued, putting the notebook in his pocket and rising, "would you excuse me for a few moments? Make yourself perfectly at home until I return; there may be some things," he added with a sweep of his hand toward his heterogeneously filled shelves, "that may interest you and wile away the time. There are pipes and tobacco in that corner."

Then nodding to me with the same inscrutable face he left the room. I was too well accustomed to his methods to think much of his unceremonious withdrawal, and made no doubt he was off to investigate some clue which had suddenly occurred to his active intelligence.

Left to myself I cast a cursory glance over his shelves. There were a number of small glass jars containing earthy substances, labeled "Pavement and Road Sweepings," from the principal thoroughfares and suburbs of London, with the sub-directions "for identifying foot-tracks." There were several other jars, labeled "Fluff from Omnibus and Road Car Seats," "Cocoanut Fibre and Rope Strands from Mattings in Public Places," "Cigarette Stumps and Match Ends from Floor of Palace Theater, Row A, 1 to 50." Everywhere were evidences of this wonderful man's system and perspicacity.

I was thus engaged when I heard the slight creaking of a door, and I looked up as a stranger entered. He was a rough-looking man, with a shabby overcoat and a still more disreputable muffler around his throat and the lower part of his face. Considerably annoyed at his intrusion, I turned upon him rather sharply, when, with a mumbled, growling apology for mistaking the room, he shuffled out again and closed the door. I followed him quickly to the landing and saw that he disappeared down the stairs. With my mind full of the robbery, the incident made a singular impression upon me. I knew my friend's habit of hasty absences from his room in his moments of deep inspiration; it was only too probable that, with his powerful intellect and magnificent perceptive genius concentrated on one subject, he should be careless of his own belongings, and no doubt even forget to take the ordinary precaution of locking up his drawers. I tried one or two and found that I was right, although for some reason I was unable to open one to its fullest extent. The handles were sticky, as if some one had opened them with dirty fingers. Knowing Hemlock's fastidious cleanliness, I resolved to inform him of this circumstance, but I forgot it, alas! until—but I am anticipating my story.

His absence was strangely prolonged. I at last seated myself by the fire, and lulled by warmth and the patter of the rain on the window, I fell asleep. I may have dreamt, for during my sleep I had a vague semi-consciousness as of hands being softly pressed on my pockets—no doubt induced by the story of the robbery. When I came fully to my senses, I found Hemlock Jones sitting on the other side of the hearth, his deeply concentrated gaze fixed on the fire.

"I found you so comfortably asleep that I could not bear to awaken you," he said, with a smile.

I rubbed my eyes. "And what news?" I asked. "How have you succeeded?"

"Better than I expected," he said, "and I think," he added, tapping his note-book. "I owe much to *you*."

Deeply gratified, I awaited more. But in vain. I ought to have remembered that in his moods Hemlock Jones was reticence itself, I told him simply of the strange intrusion, but he only laughed.

Later, when I arose to go, he looked at me playfully.

"If you were a married man," he said, "I would advise you not to go home until you had brushed your sleeve. There are a few short brown sealskin hairs on the inner side of your forearm, just where they would have adhered if your arm had encircled a sealskin coat with some pressure!"

"For once you are at fault," I said triumphantly; "the hair is my own, as you will perceive; I have just had it cut at the hairdresser's, and no doubt this arm projected beyond the apron."

He frowned slightly, yet, nevertheless, on my turning to go he embraced me warmly—a rare exhibition in that man of ice. He even helped me on with my overcoat and pulled out and smoothed down the flaps of my pockets. He was particular, too, in fitting my arm in my overcoat sleeve, shaking the sleeve down from the armhole to the cuff with his deft fingers. "Come again soon!" he said, clapping me on the back.

"At any and all times," I said enthusiastically; "I only ask ten minutes twice a day to eat a crust at my office, and four hours' sleep at night, and the rest of my time is devoted to you always, as you know."

"It is indeed," he said, with his impenetrable smile.

Nevertheless, I did not find him at home when I next called. One afternoon, when nearing my own home, I met him in one of his favorite disguises,—a long blue swallow-tailed coat, striped cotton trousers, large turn-over collar, blacked face, and white hat, carrying a tambourine. Of course to others the disguise was perfect, although it was known to myself, and I passed him—according to an old understanding between us—without the slightest recognition, trusting to a later explanation. At another time, as I was making a professional visit to the wife of a publican at the East End, I saw him, in the disguise of a broken-down artisan, looking into the window of an adjacent pawnshop. I was delighted to see that he was evidently following my suggestions, and in my joy I ventured to tip him a wink; it was abstractedly returned.

Two days later I received a note appointing a meeting at his lodgings that night. That meeting, alas! was the one memorable occurrence of my life, and the last meeting I ever had with Hemlock Jones! I will try to set it down calmly, though my pulses still throb with the recollection of it.

I found him standing before the fire, with that look upon his face which I had seen only once or twice in our acquaintance—a look which I may call an absolute concatenation of inductive and deductive ratiocination—from which all that was human, tender, or sympathetic was absolutely discharged. He was simply an icy algebraic symbol! Indeed, his whole being was concentrated to that extent that his clothes fitted loosely, and his head was absolutely so much reduced in size by his mental compression that his hat tipped back from his forehead and literally hung on his massive ears.

After I had entered he locked the doors, fastened the windows, and even placed a chair before the chimney. As I watched these significant precautions with absorbing interest, he suddenly drew a revolver and, presenting it to my temple, said in low, icy tones:

"Hand over that cigar case!"

Even in my bewilderment my reply was truthful, spontaneous, and involuntary. "I haven't got it," I said.

He smiled bitterly, and threw down his revolver. "I expected that reply! Then let me now confront you with something more awful, more deadly, more relentless and convincing than that mere lethal weapon,—the damning inductive and deductive proofs of your guilt!" He drew from his pocket a roll of paper and a notebook.

"But surely," I gasped, "you are joking! You could not for a moment believe"—

"Silence! Sit down!" I obeyed.

"You have condemned yourself," he went on pitilessly. "Condemned yourself on my processes,—processes familiar to you, applauded by you, accepted by you for years! We will go back to the time when you first saw the cigar case. Your expressions," he said in cold, deliberate tones, consulting his paper, "were, 'How beautiful! I wish it were mine.' This was your first step in crime—and my first indication. From 'I *wish* it were mine' to 'I *will* have it mine,' and the mere detail, '*How can* I make it mine?' the advance was obvious. Silence! But as in my methods it was necessary that there should be an overwhelming inducement to the crime, that unholy admiration of yours for the mere trinket itself was not enough. You are a smoker of cigars."

"But," I burst out passionately, "I told you I had given up smoking cigars."

"Fool!" he said coldly, "that is the *second* time you have committed yourself. Of course you told me! What more natural than for you to blazon forth that prepared and unsolicited statement to *prevent* accusation. Yet, as I said before, even that wretched attempt to cover up your tracks was not enough. I still had to find that overwhelming, impelling motive necessary to affect a man like you. That motive I found in the strongest of all impulses —Love, I suppose you would call it," he added bitterly, "that night you called! You had brought the most conclusive proofs of it on your sleeve."

"But—" I almost screamed.

"Silence!" he thundered. "I know what you would say. You would say that even if you had embraced some Young Person in a sealskin coat, what had that to do with the robbery? Let me tell you, then, that that sealskin coat represented the quality and character of your fatal entanglement! You bartered your honor for it—that stolen cigar case was the purchaser of the sealskin coat!

"Silence! Having thoroughly established your motive, I now proceed to the commission of the crime itself. Ordinary people would have begun with that—with an attempt to discover the whereabouts of the missing object. These are not *my* methods."

So overpowering was his penetration that, although I knew myself innocent, I licked my lips with avidity to hear the further details of this lucid exposition of my crime.

"You committed that theft the night I showed you the cigar case, and after I had carelessly thrown it in that drawer. You were sitting in that chair, and I had arisen to take something from that shelf. In that instant you secured your booty without rising. Silence! Do you remember when I helped you on with your overcoat the other night? I was particular about fitting your arm in. While doing so I measured your arms with a spring tape measure, from the shoulder to the cuff. A later visit to your tailor confirmed that measurement. It proved to be *the exact distance between your chair and that drawer!*"

I sat stunned.

"The rest are mere corroborative details! You were again tampering with the drawer when I discovered you doing so! Do not start! The stranger that blundered into the room with a muffler on—was myself! More, I had placed a little soap on the drawer handles when I purposely left you alone. The soap was on your hand when I shook it at parting. I softly felt your pockets, when you were asleep, for further developments. I embraced you when you left— that I might feel if you had the cigar case or any other articles hidden on your body. This confirmed me in the belief that you had already disposed of it in the manner and for the purpose I have shown you. As I still believed you capable of remorse and confession, I twice allowed you to see I was on your track: once in the garb of an itinerant negro minstrel, and the second time as a workman looking in the window of the pawnshop where you pledged your booty."

"But," I burst out, "if you had asked the pawnbroker, you would have seen how unjust"—

"Fool!" he hissed, "that was one of *your* suggestions—to search the pawnshops! Do you suppose I followed any of your suggestions, the suggestions of the thief? On the contrary, they told me what to avoid."

"And I suppose," I said bitterly, "you have not even searched your drawer?"

"No," he said calmly.

I was for the first time really vexed. I went to the nearest drawer and pulled it out sharply. It stuck as it had before, leaving a part of the drawer unopened. By working it, however, I discovered that it was impeded by some obstacle that had slipped to the upper part of the drawer, and held it firmly fast. Inserting my hand, I pulled out the impeding object. It was the missing cigar case! I turned to him with a cry of joy.

But I was appalled at his expression. A look of contempt was now added to his acute, penetrating gaze. "I have been mistaken," he said slowly; "I had not allowed for your weakness and cowardice! I thought too highly of you even in your guilt! But I see now why you tampered with that drawer the other night. By some inexplicable means—possibly another theft—you took the cigar case out of pawn and, like a whipped hound, restored it to me in this feeble, clumsy fashion. You thought to deceive me, Hemlock Jones! More, you thought to destroy my infallibility. Go! I give you your liberty. I shall not summon the three policemen who wait in the adjoining room—but out of my sight forever!"

As I stood once more dazed and petrified, he took me firmly by the ear and led me into the hall, closing the door behind him. This reopened presently, wide enough to permit him to thrust out my hat, overcoat, umbrella, and overshoes, and then closed against me forever!

I never saw him again. I am bound to say, however, that thereafter my business increased, I recovered much of my old practice, and a few of my patients recovered also. I became rich. I had a brougham and a house in the West End. But I often wondered, pondering on that wonderful man's penetration and insight, if, in some lapse of consciousness, I had not really stolen his cigar case!

ACTIVITIES

1) Parody is a technique involving exaggerations. In order to get an idea as to how a parodist works, make a list of the Sherlock Holmes eccentricities with which you have become familiar. Next to each trait, write the equivalent Hemlock Jones exaggeration.

2) Now the same for Dr. Watson and Bret Harte's "I."

3) How about trying to come up with some interesting parodies for the names, Sherlock Holmes and Dr. Watson? While you are experimenting, attempt some "contortions" of the other prominent detectives' names.

Keeping Up With the "Variations"

We hope that your reading of these "variations" has deepened your appreciation of the pleasurable—*and also the informative*—possibilities of detective literature.

Tastes vary. By now, each of you has probably chosen a favorite from among the myriad of fictional sleuths encountered in this volume. You have also discovered perhaps that you enjoy some types of detective tales more than others. This is as it should be for, as the old saying goes—each to his or her own taste.

But, you will also discover that taste, like everything else, will develop and change only as long as you keep on doing whatever developed the taste in the first place. Which, in this case, means keeping up with your reading of the detective story—and its "variations."

Here are some more titles from within the sub-genres presented to you in this chapter:

More "Virgil Tibbs" Adventures by John Ball

The Cool Cottontail	*Johnny Get Your Gun*
Five Pieces of Jade	*The Eyes of Buddha*

More Sports Detective Stories

"Silver Blaze" by Sir Arthur Conan Doyle (Horseracing)
"Man Bites Dog" by Ellery Queen (Baseball)
"Long Shot" by Ellery Queen (Horseracing)
"Mind Over Matter" by Ellery Queen (Boxing)
"Trojan Horse" by Ellery Queen (Football)
"Tomorrow Murder" by Stuart Palmer (Polo)
"The Fad of the Fisherman" by G. K. Chesterton (Fishing)
"The Loss of Sammy Crockett" by Arthur Morrison (Track and Field)
"His Brother's Keeper" by Dashiell Hammett (Boxing)
And others . . .

More Stories with Non-Series "Sleuths"

"The Grave Grass Quivers" by MacKinlay Kantor
"The Splinter" by Mary Roberts Rinehart
The Suicide Club by Robert Louis Stevenson
"The Man of the Crowd" by Edgar Allan Poe
"Ten Thousand Blunt Instruments" by Philip Wylie

"The Assassin's Club" by Nicholas Blake
And many others . . .

More Sherlock Holmes Parodies

"The Adventures of Shamrock Jolnes" by O. Henry
"A Double-Barrelled Detective Story" by Mark Twain
"The Case of the Missing Lady" by Agatha Christie
"Maddened by Mystery: or, The Defective Detective" by Stephen Leacock
"Holmlock Shears Arrives Too Late" by Maurice Leblanc
"The Adventure of the Remarkable Worm" by Stuart Palmer
"The Adventure of the Marked Man" by Stuart Palmer
The Chronicles of Solar Pons by August Derleth
The Exploits of Shlock Homes by Robert L. Fish

And many, many others . . .

An Epilogue

The Mystery Writers of America, Inc.—What Is It?

We have mentioned The Mystery Writers of America before and you may have wondered about it. Mr. Hillary Waugh, 1975 executive vice-president of the organization and a prominent detective author in his own right, can tell you something about it:

"Mystery Writers of America (MWA) was founded in 1945 and dedicated to the advancement of detective and mystery writers in particular and all writers in general, adopting as its slogan: 'Crime does not pay—enough'. Part of this endeavor is our Annual Awards Dinner, held in late April or early May, at which 'Edgars' (plaster busts of patron saint Edgar Allan Poe) and 'Ravens' are awarded for excellence in various fields of the mystery."[1]

It was predicted many times in the past that the detective genre would decline or die. The Mystery Writers of America is living proof of how wrong the "doomsayers" of yesterday were. Today, MWA is a vital and growing professional organization which has enhanced the detective story immeasurably.

The debate as to whether detective literature is "serious" or "popular" still rages on. In our opinion, the question is unanswerable—as many "either-or" controversies are. As long as categories continue to be used, perhaps the best way of describing a good, classic detective yarn is to view it as a hybrid, a blending of the best features of both "popular" and "serious" literature.

At any rate, we hope that detective literature, with its varied authors, stories, and history, has won your individual respect and consideration.

If it has, you will continue to read detective stories—on your own. Such reading can help guarantee that the detective story and The Mystery Writers of America will have a bright future indeed.

ADDITIONAL CLASS ACTIVITIES

1) Regarding the question of whether detective literature is "popular" or "serious"—what do you think?

You and your class can enjoy a fruitful discussion about this issue; try to formulate your opinions within a framework of firm literary criteria. Your teacher will be able to help you here. Above all, use what you have read in this book as "evidence" to back up what you have to say.

2) In previous class activities, you compiled a list of possible story ideas and also wrote a fictional biography of a "dream" detective. If these activities have not already stirred your creative juices, allow us to do some stirring for you.

Why not try writing an original detective story of your own? It doesn't have to be too long—a short-short will do nicely. Of course, you cannot expect an immediate sale to *EQMM;* becoming a professional takes lots and lots of practice. However, when you finish, perhaps your tale will appeal to your classmates, family, and friends.

In addition, your class can emulate The Mystery Writers of America if desired by holding an Awards Contest of your own, in which "Edgars" and "Ravens" are presented to the worthier stories. And if by now your group has organized a class magazine or journal (in the manner of The Baker Street Irregulars or The Sherlock Holmes Society), then you've really "got it made."

As we have said before, *what better place to see your words in print than your own class journal* . . .

Notes

Chapter 1

1. Quoted in Howard Haycraft, *Murder For Pleasure* (New York, 1941), p. 5

2. *Ibid,* p. 12
3. Quoted in Philip Van Doren Stern, *The Portable Poe* (New York, 1945), p. 331
4. Haycraft, *Murder For Pleasure,* p. 12
5. Quoted in Van Doren Stern, *The Portable Poe* (New York, 1945), p. 331
6. *Ibid,* p. xv
7. *Ibid,* p. xxvii
8. *Ibid,* p. 539
9. *Ibid,* p. 539

Chapter 2

1. Quoted in Sir Arthur Conan Doyle, *Memoirs and Adventures* (Boston, 1924), pp. 20–21
2. Quoted in Mary Hoehling, *The Real Sherlock Holmes* (New York, 1965), p. 32
3. Quoted in Hoehling, *The Real Sherlock Holmes,* p. 101
4. Doyle, *Memoirs and Adventures,* p. 209
5. *Ibid,* p. 210
6. *Ibid,* p. 214
7. *Ibid,* p. 213
8. Sir Arthur Conan Doyle, *Through the Magic Door* (London, 1907), p. 118
9. Quoted in Edgar W. Smith, *Profile by Gaslight* (New York, 1944)
10. *Ibid,* p. 301
11. *The Sherlock Holmes Journal* (London, 1956), pp. 20–21
12. Hoehling, *The Real Sherlock Holmes,* p. 95
13. Quoted in Sir Arthur Conan Doyle, preface to *The Case Book of Sherlock Holmes*

Chapter 3

1. Quoted in publicity blurbs to many Ellery Queen books
2. From introduction to Ellery Queen, *The Roman Hat Mystery* (New York, 1929)
3. More details about the Ellery Queen "hoax" can be obtained from the following: "Messieurs Ellery Queen," *The New Yorker Magazine,* March 16, 1940; *Newsweek Magazine,* June 26, 1939; *Wil-*

son's Library Bulletin, April 1942; *Saturday Review of Literature,* November 22, 1941; and *Life Magazine,* November 22, 1943

4. Quoted in *Coronet Magazine,* February 1956, p. 115
5. More details about the lives and careers of Frederic Dannay and Manfred B. Lee can be obtained from *Life Magazine,* November 22, 1943 and Frances B. Nevins, Jr., *Royal Bloodline: Ellery Queen, Author and Detective,* (Bowling Green, 1974)
6. More details about the career of Frederic Dannay and Manfred B. Lee as editors and teachers can be obtained from the introduction to Anthony Boucher, *The Quintessence of Queen* (New York, 1962)
7. More about Manfred B. Lee's death can be obtained from *The New York Times* of April 5, 1971

Chapter 4

1. More about Jacques Futrelle and The Thinking Machine can be obtained from E. F. Bleiler's introduction to Jacques Futrelle, *Best 'Thinking Machine' Stories* (New York, 1973)
2. G. K. Chesterton, *Autobiography* (New York, 1936), p. 337
3. More about Agatha Christie and Hercule Poirot can be obtained from A. C. Ramsey, *Agatha Christie: Mistress of Mystery* (New York, 1967) and Howard Haycraft, *Murder Without Pleasure,* pp. 129–133
4. Howard Haycraft, *Murder With Pleasure,* p. 132
5. *Ibid,* p. 135
6. Erik Routley, *The Puritan Pleasures of the Detective Story* (London, 1972), p. 139
7. More about Dorothy L. Sayers and Lord Peter Wimsey can be obtained from Howard Haycraft, *Murder With Pleasure* and Erik Routley's *The Puritan Pleasures of the Detective Story.*
8. Letter of April 7, 1975 from William Brittain to Saul Schwartz
9. *Ibid.*

Chapter 5

1. Howard Haycraft, *Murder With Pleasure,* p. 83–85
2. More about the female sleuth can be obtained from the introduction to Ellery Queen, *Female of the Species* (New York, 1943)
3. More about Mary Roberts Rinehart can be obtained from Mary Roberts Rinehart, *My Story* (New York, 1958)

4. Quoted in A. C. Ramsey, *Agatha Christie: Mistress of Mystery,* p. 20

5. More about Agatha Christie and Miss Marple can be obtained from *Ibid,* pp. 129–133

6. Stuart Palmer, "The I.O.U. of Hildegarde Withers," *The Adventure of the Marked Man* (Boulder, 1973), p. 10

7. *Ibid,* p. 11

8. More about Stuart Palmer in Ibid.

9. Quoted in James Vinson, ed., *Contemporary Novelists* (New York and London, 1972), p. 1411

10. More about James Yaffe in Ibid, pp. 1410–1412

Chapter 6

1. More about this in Dorothy L. Sayers, "Gaudy Night," *The Art of the Mystery Story,* ed., Howard Haycraft, (New York, 1947), pp. 208–221

2. More about this in Raymond Chandler, "The Simple Art of Murder," in *Ibid,* pp. 222-237

3. More about John Ball in James Vinson, ed., *Contemporary Novelists* (New York and London, 1972) pp. 61–62

4. Quoted in introduction to Ellery Queen, *Sporting Blood* (Boston, 1942)

5. Quoted in Howard Haycraft and Stanley Kunitz, ed., *Twentieth Century Authors,* (New York, 1942) More about Rex Stout in Ibid, pp. 1354–1355

6. More about the Sherlock Holmes pastiches in Ellery Queen, *The Mis-Adventures of Sherlock Holmes* (New York, 1948)

An Epilogue

1. Letter of April 30, 1975 from Hillary Waugh to Saul Schwartz